HARDSHIP

The Welfare Consequences of Labor Market Problems

A Policy Discussion Paper

Robert Taggart

The W. E. Upjohn Institute for Employment Research

Library of Congress Cataloging in Publication Data

Taggart, Robert, 1945
  Hardship: the welfare consequences of labor market problems.

  Includes bibliographical references and index.
  1. Poor—United States—Statistical methods.
2. Unemployment—United States. 3. Underemployment—United States. 4. Wages—Minimum wage—United States.
I. Title.
HV90.T33   1982   362.5'2'072073   82-16097
ISBN 0-88099-003-1 (pbk.)

Copyright © 1982
by the
W. E. UPJOHN INSTITUTE
FOR EMPLOYMENT RESEARCH

300 South Westnedge Ave.
Kalamazoo, Michigan 49007

This book is dedicated to the memory of Dr. E. Earl Wright. Among his many contributions as director of the W. E. Upjohn Institute, Earl encouraged and guided the preparation of this volume, enriching the process, and hopefully the product, with his unique blend of warmth and wisdom. Fondly remembered and universally respected, he will be sorely missed.

THE AUTHOR

Robert Taggart, who is currently president of the Remediation and Training Institute in Washington, D.C., was formerly director of the Youth Knowledge Development Project, administrator of the Office of Youth Programs, U.S. Department of Labor, and executive director of the National Council on Employment Policy.

Dr. Taggart received his Ph.D. from The George Washington University in 1972.

Among the 26 books he has authored, co-authored, or edited are: *A Fisherman's Guide: An Assessment of Training and Remediation Strategies*; *The Promise of Greatness*; *Still a Dream: The Changing Status of Blacks Since 1960*; *The Labor Market Impacts of the Private Retirement System*; *Jobs for the Disabled*; *The Prison of Unemployment*; and *Low Income Housing: A Critique of Federal Aid*.

Author's Note

The detailed hardship data for 1974 through 1980 which are analyzed in the text are available upon request. These include alternative tabulations for 1979 which use the population estimates from the 1970 Census and the population estimates from the 1980 Census, respectively, to weight the Current Population Survey data. The latter estimates are used in most circumstances. When the 1970 Census-based estimates are utilized because of greater convenience or appropriateness, an asterisk notes this use in the text. The hardship data for 1981, which were only available after this volume was completed, are analyzed in separate publications and can also be provided upon request.

PREFACE

How many really suffer as a result of labor market problems? This is one of the most critical yet contentious social policy questions. In many ways, our social statistics exaggerate the degree of hardship. Unemployment does not have the same dire consequences today as it did in the 1930s when most of the unemployed were primary breadwinners, when income and earnings were usually much closer to the margin of subsistence, and when there was no safety net for those failing in the labor market. Increasing affluence, the rise of multiple earner families, the growing predominance of secondary earners among the unemployed, and improved social welfare protections, have unquestionably mitigated the welfare consequences of joblessness. Earnings and income data also overstate the dimensions of hardship. Among the millions with hourly earnings at or below the minimum wage level, the overwhelming majority are from multiple-earner, relatively affluent families. Most of those counted by the poverty statistics are elderly, handicapped or have family responsibilities which keep them out of the labor force, so the poverty statistics are by no means an accurate indicator of labor market pathologies.

Yet there are also many ways our social statistics underestimate the degree of labor market-related hardship. The unemployment counts exclude the millions of fully employed workers whose wages are so low that their families remain in poverty. Low wages and repeated or prolonged unemployment frequently interact to undermine the capacity for self-support. Since the number experiencing joblessness at some point during the year is several times the number unemployed in any month, those who suffer as a result of forced idleness can equal or exceed average annual unemployment, even though only a minority of the jobless in any month really suffer. For every person counted in the monthly unemployment tallies, there is another working part-time because of the inability to find full-time work, or else outside the labor force but wanting a job. Finally, income transfers in our country have always focused on the elderly, disabled and dependent, neglecting the needs of the working poor, so that the dramatic expansion of cash and in-kind transfers does not necessarily mean that those failing in the labor market are adequately protected.

Mountains of facts, figures and learned treatises have been marshalled to prove that the truly needy are few and far between. An equally imposing volume of contradicting evidence documents uncounted and unmet basic needs. The result is confusion. It is uncertain and bitterly disputed whether those suffering seriously as a result of labor market problems number in the hundreds of thousands or the tens of millions, and, hence, whether high levels of joblessness can be easily tolerated or must be countered by job creation and economic stimulus, whether the safety net needs dismantling or strengthening, and whether the long-term hardship trends justify a "laissez faire" response or demand fundamental restructuring of labor markets and the income distribution system. There is only one area of agreement in this debate—that the existing poverty, employment and earnings statistics are inadequate for one of their primary applications, measuring the welfare consequences of labor market problems.

This book presents a set of new measures developed to determine who really suffers as a result of joblessness, low earnings and involuntary part-time employment. Available employment, earnings and poverty data are structured into an array of core indicators which incorporate alternative need and workforce attachment standards, which assess the severity of problems, as well as the numbers affected, which consider earnings from both an individual and family perspective, as well as considering earnings supplements including in-kind aid. The aggregate measures, in turn, are disaggregated to identify the relative hardship burdens for different population segments and geographic areas.

These measures are, then, used to reassess long-term and cyclical labor market developments, the changing status of minorities, the interrelationships between family patterns and employment problems, the effectiveness of income transfers for the working poor, alternative macroeconomic policies and a host of other issues. The dual aim of these applications is to demonstrate the utility and reliability of the new measures, while providing needed perspective on employment problems and policies.

The aim was not just to develop and gain acceptance for a new statistical indicator, but to design a comprehensive system for measuring and analyzing the welfare consequences of labor market problems. The hardship measures were intended as a "third leg" in our social statistics system, supplementing poverty and unemployment data and providing alternative perspectives on the major issues which have been analyzed using poverty and unemployment as proxies for labor market-related hardship. This ambitious undertaking was based on the assumption that in order to fully address earlier critiques of hardship measures, to cope with the inherently complex issues, to validate the internal consistency of the data and to demonstrate their varied uses, it was necessary to provide detailed information and comprehensive analysis. Tradeoffs were anticipated, though underestimated. The chances for error and its discovery, the difficulties of definitional refinement, tabulation and analysis, as well as the problems of comprehensible presentation, multiplied with each disaggregation and application. In retrospect, the ambitiousness of the effort was naive, somewhat Faustian and probably misplaced. I can only hope that in struggling through the mind-numbing statistics and terminology, or in weighing the inevitable shortcomings and mistakes, the reader will give some credit for my having "dared to fail greatly," as well as for my intellectual persistence, if not perspicacity.

This work is a reflection of fifteen years of collaboration with Sar Levitan. Dr. Levitan was one of the first to recognize the need to integrate income and employment statistics. He was among the initial developers and advocates of hardship measures. As Chairman of the National Commission on Employment and Unemployment Statistics, he worked long and hard to gain consensus for the adoption of hardship indicators. Sar supervised and supported the work on this volume, encouraging greater simplicity and succinctness. He should not be blamed because I ignored this sage advice.

The Bureau of the Census tabulated the hardship measures under contract from Dr. Levitan's Center for Social Policy Studies at The George Washington University and MDC, Incorporated. The Census Bureau is not responsible for any definitional errors, and it does not necessarily endorse nor approve the measurement concepts. However, without the hard work, expertise and good will of its technicians, this book would not have been possible. In particular, I would like to recognize the contributions of Gregory Russell who helped refine and validate the measures, as well as supervising their tabulation.

This study was made possible by grants from the Charles Stewart Mott, Edna McConnell Clark and Ford Foundations. It was only completed because Nancy Kiefer and Cathy Glasgow kept working to the last minute before entering the counts of the unemployed and discouraged, and because Theron remembered what the blind men of Hindustan never learned.

CONTENTS

Page

Chapter 1. MEASURING WHAT MATTERS — 1

- The Consequences of Labor Market Problems — 1
- The Evolution of Hardship Measures — 4
- A Measurement and Assessment System — 16
- Assumptions and Approaches — 20
- Notes — 34

Chapter 2. HARDSHIP IN 1979 — 35

- The Derivation and Dimensions of Hardship — 35
- What Causes Hardship? — 42
- The Burdens of Hardship — 59
- Notes — 83

Chapter 3. HARDSHIP TRENDS OVER THE 1974-1980 PERIOD — 85

- An Overview — 85
- Long-Term Shifts in the Composition and Distribution of Hardship — 97
- The Changing Status of Minorities--A Detailed Assessment — 114
- The Interrelationship of Changing Family Patterns and Labor Market Trends — 131
- Notes — 146

Chapter 4. HARDSHIP OVER THE BUSINESS CYCLE — 147

- Hardship Persists in Good Times and Bad — 147
- The Victims of Recession — 164
- Notes — 179

Chapter 5. APPLYING THE HARDSHIP MEASURES — 181

- Policy Options — 181
- The Safety Net for the Working Poor — 201
- Practical Applications — 217
- Notes — 249

Chapter 6. HARDSHIP--A MATTER OF PERSPECTIVE — 251

- The Feasibility of Hardship Measures — 251
- A Summary of the Findings — 261
- Adding a Third Leg to Social Statistics — 281

Appendix A. Hardship Measures--Technical Details — 283
Appendix B. Detailed Hardship Data for 1979 — 313
Appendix C. Summary Hardship Data for 1974 Through 1980 — 369

CHAPTER 1. MEASURING WHAT MATTERS

The Consequences of Labor Market Problems

The well-being of most individuals and families is determined primarily by their success in the labor market. Since earnings account for three-fourths of total personal income, the unavailability or intermittency of employment, restricted hours of weekly work, or low wages are a major cause of economic hardship. 1/

A substantial share of work force participants encounters such problems. During 1980, for instance, 21.4 million workers aged 16 and over experienced at least a week of joblessness. Another 7.6 million worked part-time involuntarily at least a week. There were an additional 7.3 million full-time and 9.1 million voluntary part-time workers who earned less than the minimum wage equivalent for the cumulative hours they were willing and able to work. Together, these groups with employment and earnings problems accounted for nearly two-fifths of the 118.3 million who participated in the 1980 work force.

Not all of these individuals suffered seriously as a result of their own employment and earnings problems. Some were secondary earners in affluent families or had other sources of income. Others had reduced, but still adequate, earnings. But for all too many, the failures in the labor market resulted in severe distress. Fifteen million work force participants resided in families with earnings below the poverty level and 8.4 million in poor families.

Our present system of labor force concepts and statistics was developed during the 1930s because of, and in order to measure, the suffering which resulted from the massive unemployment of the Great Depression. In the absence of extensive income transfer programs, with the work force composed primarily of breadwinners, and with a large share of the 1930s working population concentrated near the margin of subsistence, unemployment and hardship were synonymous. But the expansion of social welfare protections, the increasing affluence of the population, and the rise of multiple earner families, subsequently reduced the correspondence between joblessness and deprivation.

While extensive information has been gathered for many years on the hourly and weekly wages of American workers, these earnings data have received far less attention than the unemployment counts. It is usually assumed that family heads and primary breadwinners can achieve subsistence earnings if they can find jobs, hence employment has traditionally been considered the key factor affecting well-being. Most of the low-wage workers are new entrants to the labor force and secondary family earners.

Poverty concepts and statistics were developed in the 1960s to measure the dimensions of deprivation. The poverty definition and counts include both persons with labor market-related problems and those unable to work because of age, disability, family responsibilities or other barriers. Poverty is, thus, determined as much, or more, by the adequacy of transfers and private pensions and the demography of the population as by labor market conditions.

Over the years, the unemployment, earnings and poverty statistics have been disaggregated in ever finer detail in order to identify those among the unemployed who really suffer as a result of joblessness, those whose low earnings result in low income, and those whose poverty is caused primarily by labor market problems or could be cured by labor market interventions. But it is extremely difficult to piece together these separate items of detailed information in order to determine how many and who really suffer as a result of labor market problems. In the absence of simple and accepted statistical indicators which link employment and earnings data with measures of well-being, the unemployment and poverty rates tend to predominate in public policy formulation, planning, resource allocation and analysis, as proxies for the hardship resulting from the failings of or failures in the labor market. Unfortunately, these measures do not serve these purposes well.

<u>Unemployment does not always result in deprivation, nor does employment guarantee well-being. Poverty is in many cases unrelated to labor market problems. Low wages are not usually associated with low family income.</u>

- Less than a fifth of the individuals who experienced unemployment during 1980 lived in poor families. On the other hand, over a million persons were employed full-year, full-time--the usual standard of success in the labor market--yet they and their families still lived in poverty.

- Nearly half of the individuals with hourly earnings at or below the minimum wage lived in families with incomes above $15,000 annually, and nearly two-thirds were in families with incomes above $10,000 annually.

- Three-fifths of all poor persons 14 and over did not work at all during 1980 because of illness or disability, school, housekeeping, retirement, or other reasons unrelated to job availability.

<u>Unemployment rates, wage data or aggregate poverty counts alone yield a distorted picture of fluctuations and long-term trends in labor market-related economic hardship.</u>

- The number and proportion of labor force participants with inadequate annual earnings fluctuate less from year to year than the number and proportion who experience unemployment. Hardship is a chronic structural problem, exacerbated by recessions and depressions, alleviated by recoveries, but far less cyclical than joblessness.

- There has been very little improvement in the relative status of blacks as judged by unemployment and poverty rates. In contrast, there has been absolute and relative progress in alleviating labor market-related hardship, largely because of improvements in earnings rates.

● At the beginning of the 1960s, two-thirds of poor family heads worked, and a third worked full-time, full-year. Two decades later, less than half worked at all, and only 16 percent full-time, full-year. In other words, a declining portion of economic hardship (as measured by the poverty counts) is labor market-related.

<u>Policies designed to alleviate labor market-related hardship may be misdirected to the extent they are based on poverty, unemployment, or wage data alone.</u>

● Where unemployment rates are used to distribute employment and training resources, large metropolitan areas and particularly their suburbs receive a far larger share than if hardship measures were used. The volatility of unemployment rates also leads to significant year-to-year fluctuations in local funding, with adverse programmatic consequences, even though the underlying structural problems to which interventions are addressed remain relatively stable. On the other hand, the use of poverty rates for allocation tends to divert resources to areas whose problems may not be labor market-related or amenable to such interventions.

● Local or national employment and training policies which target resources to population subgroups based on their relative unemployment rather than hardship rates divert scare resources to solving temporary problems with less serious consequences; conversely, targeting on the basis of poverty diverts resources to individuals and areas whose problems cannot necessary be solved by employment-oriented interventions.

● Across-the-board increases in the minimum wage have a modest impact on alleviating poverty, and a substantial portion of the benefits are realized by workers in affluent families. Wage data alone suggest only the gains which are realized by minimum wage increases, while hardship measures capture the disemployment effects which may, in part, offset the positive earnings impacts of minimum wage increases.

As these examples suggest, the currently available poverty, employment and earnings statistics are inadequate for one of their primary applications--measuring the welfare consequences of labor market problems. Without a conceptual and measurement framework which links income, employment and earnings information, and without accepted indicators developed specifically to measure labor market-related hardship, it is difficult to determine who needs help most, why, or how it can best be provided. As a result, our understanding is frequently clouded and our policies misdirected.

Because of these shortcomings, there is increasing recognition of the need for a measure or set of measures which considers employment and earnings problems in light of the economic hardship which results. A variety of hardship indicators have, in fact, been developed from available labor market and income statistics, demonstrating the conceptual promise of such measures in providing a better understanding of secular and cyclical trends, income transfer and minimum wage issues, and the relative severity of need for subareas and subgroups in the economy.

However, this analytical work has also suggested the significant definitional, measurement and interpretative problems implicit in hardship measures. There are <u>normative</u> issues inherent in defining any labor market status or income-based needs statistics, such as agreeing on the severity standards and deciding who will and will not be counted relative to these standards. Because hardship measures link poverty, earnings and employment concepts, the issues inherent in each of these separate measurement systems must be addressed. There are <u>conceptual</u> issues which are inherent in seeking to link individual earnings with family or household well-being, since family composition and income other than earnings are affected, but not determined, by labor market factors. There are <u>measurement</u> issues and uncertainties which result from shortcomings in existing data bases. Then, there are <u>interpretative</u> issues related to all of these definitional, conceptual and measurement questions.

Because of these problems, no set of hardship measures or applications has gained wide acceptance. Yet taken together, previous work has provided the foundation for an acceptable and extremely useful hardship measurement system. It is now possible to derive a set of composite measures that strikes an appropriate normative balance, which overcomes many conceptual problems and provides the information for better understanding the unresolvable issues. The composite measures cannot escape the underlying shortcomings in income and labor force statistics, but the needed improvements and their implications can be clearly identified. Based on previous work, it is also possible to dramatically expand the information yield and improve the policy relevance of hardship measures so that they can be institutionalized as a "third leg" in our system of social welfare indicators, supplementing employment and earnings statistics and the poverty measures.

This volume reviews the evolution of hardship measures as well as the underlying normative, conceptual, measurement and interpretative issues. It proposes a modified set of measures and suggests how these will overcome many of the problems in previous hardship indicators. The measures are calculated from existing labor market and income statistics covering 1974 through 1980. The hardship data are presented and analyzed in detail. The policy implications of the measures, the possible improvements, and the remaining issues are, then, discussed.

<u>The Evolution of Hardship Measures</u>

<u>A Summary of Earlier Efforts</u>

The hardship concept was first included in a 1967 <u>Report on Employment and Unemployment in Urban Slums and Ghettos</u> prepared by then Secretary of Labor W. Willard Wirtz. 2/ The measure, which was applied to data from a special survey of ten ghetto areas in eight major cities, included the following:

1. All persons unemployed in the survey week;

2. Individuals employed on a part-time basis but seeking full-time work;

3. Family heads with full-time jobs earning less than $60 weekly (the weekly wage needed to lift a family of four above the poverty threshold) and unrelated individuals under age 65 earning less than $56 weekly in full-time jobs (the minimum wage times 40 hours of weekly work);

4. Half of all males age 20 through 64 who were not in the labor force--an estimate of the number who would be active jobseekers if more and better paying jobs were available; and

5. Half the difference between the measured female and male adult populations--an adjustment for the undercount of males.

Another approach was developed in the 1968 Manpower Report of the President using Current Population Survey annual work experience data gathered each March covering the previous calendar year. 3/ This measure included all persons working full-time, full-year but earning less than $3,000 annually, and all persons unemployed 15 or more weeks during the year.

In 1970, William Spring, Bennett Harrison and Thomas Vietorisz developed an index for the Senate Subcommittee on Employment, Manpower and Poverty based on data collected by the Bureau of the Census for 60 poverty areas in 51 large cities. 4/ The index included the following:

1. Persons unemployed in the survey week;

2. Persons working part-time involuntarily for economic reasons during the survey week;

3. Persons not in the labor force who wanted but were not seeking work because they did not think they could find employment (discouraged workers); and

4. Full-time workers paid less than $80 a week--the amount necessary on an annualized basis to support an urban family of four at the poverty level.

In 1973, Herman P. Miller developed a two-part index also utilizing the same Census Employment Survey data for the 60 poverty areas. 5/ The "subemployment" measure included:

1. Persons unemployed in the survey week;

2. Persons working part-time involuntarily during the week;

3. Persons outside the labor force, wanting jobs but discouraged by the prospects; and

4. Family heads or unrelated individuals employed and earning less than the prevailing minimum wage of $1.60 per hour or working full-time but with annualized weekly earnings below the poverty level for their households.

The Miller subemployment count excluded persons 16 to 21 years of age who were primarily students, as well as persons 65 years and over, on the assumption that their labor force attachment was minimal. The hardship measure was, then, derived by screening from the subemployed all individuals residing in families or households with above average incomes.

The Employment and Earnings Inadequacy Index was developed in 1974 by Sar Levitan and Robert Taggart and was calculated from the Current Population Survey data gathered each March covering current labor market status as well as the previous year's work experience. 6/ It was, like the Miller index, a two-part formulation, with a subemployment measure counting persons with labor market problems and an "Employment and Earnings Inadequacy" (EEI) measure excluding those subemployed residing in families or households with adequate incomes. The subemployment index included:

1. Persons unemployed during the survey week;

2. Persons outside the labor force in the survey week, wanting jobs but discouraged by the prospects;

3. Persons working part-time involuntarily for economic reasons during the survey week; and

4. Family heads and unrelated individuals currently employed full-time whose earnings in the previous 12 months were less than the poverty threshold for their families or households.

Persons age 16 to 21 whose major activity during the survey week was school attendance, as well as persons 65 years of age and over, were excluded from the subemployment count on the assumption that their labor force attachment was limited. The EEI measure, then, screened out all those individuals among the subemployed who resided in families and households with adequate incomes as judged relative to the medians for metropolitan or nonmetropolitan areas for families and unrelated individuals.

In 1975, Thomas Vietorisz, Robert Mier and John Giblin proposed a two-index approach with an "exclusion index" counting persons with individual labor market problems and an "inadequacy index" assessing earnings in light of family needs. 7/ The "exclusion index" counted:

1. Persons unemployed in the survey week;

2. Persons not in the labor force but desiring work;

3. Persons in the labor force full-time but working less than 35 hours in the survey week;

4. Persons currently employed but working less than 50 weeks in the last year for economic reasons; and

5. Full-time, full-year workers earning less than an adequate income defined by a range of annualized wages.

The "inadequacy index" was restricted to individuals counted by the exclusion index who were family heads or unrelated individuals whose incomes were below adequacy standards specified as a range of multiples of the poverty level for each family or household. All heads or unrelated individuals above these income levels were excluded.

Irwin Garfinkel and Robert Haveman in 1977 introduced the concept of "earnings capacity poverty," which was closely related to the hardship notion. 8/ "Earnings capacity" was defined as the annual income that would be produced if the household head and spouse were employed during all weeks of potential work (excluding weeks of illness, disability or unemployment) at the earnings level of other workers matched according to age, schooling, race, sex, region, work pattern and marital status. The earnings capacity poor were defined as the percentage (arbitrarily set at the poverty rate) lowest in the earnings capacity distribution. "Capacity utilization" compared actual earnings over the year to earnings capacity. Earnings capacity utilization, thus, sought to measure the work effort of families and households while earnings capacity poverty identified the household heads and spouses who would be the worst off even if their work effort and earnings were up to potential.

In 1979, Robert Stein of the Bureau of Labor Statistics proposed a simple hardship measure that included all primary earners in the labor force more than half year whose individual earnings were below the poverty line for their families or households, and whose total family or household incomes were less than double the poverty line. 9/

In its 1979 report, Counting the Labor Force, the National Commission on Employment and Unemployment Statistics (NCEUS) developed (although it did not recommend) a hardship index based on work experience and earnings over the previous year. 10/ The measure included full-year, full-time workers whose individual earnings alone were inadequate to lift their households or families out of poverty, excluding those in families or households with a total income more than double the poverty threshold. The full-time, full-year labor force was defined as persons who were in the labor force 40 weeks or more, plus those who did not work at all, sought work at least 15 weeks, but left the labor force because of discouragement over job prospects. Excluded were persons who usually worked part-time voluntarily.

Bruce Klein in 1980 sought to link the Garfinkel/Haveman earnings capacity notion with the hardship concept, assessing the portion of individuals in hardship who would have inadequate income if working and earning up to "capacity." 11/ The "subemployed" were defined as:

1. Persons who did not work during the year but spent at least 13 weeks or more looking for work and did not look in other weeks because they felt they could not find work;

2. Unemployed workers who were looking for work or on layoff 14 weeks or more, worked at some time during the year, and were in the labor force 40 weeks or more;

3. Persons who worked 13 weeks or more part-time during the year but wanted full-time jobs; and

4. Individuals employed full-time for 40 weeks or more whose earnings were below the poverty level for their families.

"Earnings capacity economic hardship" was determined by assigning "potential" earnings to the subemployed and then comparing their augmented income (not including transfers) to an adequacy standard of 150 percent of the poverty threshold for the family or household. Potential earnings were defined as 40 weeks of 40 hours weekly at the minimum wage for discouraged workers; the number of weeks in the labor force times usual weekly earnings for those unemployed during the year; actual earnings times the ratio of 40 hours per week to usual weekly hours for the involuntarily part-time workers; and actual earnings for full-time workers in poverty. In other words, the Klein measure sought to identify those with labor market-related hardship who could not earn an adequate income if fully employed.

The Underlying Issues

There are subtle yet quite significant differences between the assumptions and approaches adopted in these various subemployment, hardship, earnings capacity and earnings adequacy measures. Each had shortcomings, but it is possible to pick and choose the best features in order to develop more useful and acceptable measures:

1. <u>Individual vs. family perspectives</u>. Individuals with similar work force experience may have different family status, income needs and supplements to their own earnings, so that their well-being will differ despite equal earnings. Should income adequacy and hardship be judged in terms of individual needs or in terms of family needs? Three different approaches were advanced to deal with this issue. The Wirtz, <u>1968 Manpower Report</u>, and Spring/Harrison/Vietorisz measures were focused on the individual--assuming that the labor market should provide a basic standard which would lift a family of four out of poverty, whether or not an individual worker had these breadwinning responsibilities.

The Miller, Levitan/Taggart, the NCEUS, Stein and Klein measures used a two-step procedure to determine hardship. The first step defined the subemployed according to individual labor market problems; the second screened out persons whose family or household incomes were adequate. However, none of these measures clearly distinguished individual vs. family problems because the low earners, who constituted a significant portion of the subemployed, were defined in terms of family or household income needs. The Garfinkel/Haveman earnings capacity poor were also defined from a family or household earnings perspective.

The Vietorisz/Mier/Giblin approach derived two indices designed specifically to separate individual earnings problems from aggregate family earnings inadequacy, judging the first relative to wage standards applied to all workers and the second relative to income adequacy standards reflecting each individual's family size and needs. This is conceptually the preferred approach.

2. _Timeframes_. A person employed and with adequate earnings in any given survey week may experience a reduction in hours, hourly earnings or unemployment which generates inadequate earnings over a year. On the other hand, joblessness or reduced hours of employment for a week or two may not create undue hardship if earnings the remaining weeks are adequate. The number who experience labor market problems over a year are several times the number who experience them in any week, while only a small proportion of those with problems in any week will have them recur for a significant duration. The time period for assessing the adequacy of employment, earnings and income is, therefore, critical.

The Wirtz and Spring/Harrison/Vietorisz measures were based on labor force and earnings status in a single survey week. The Miller, Levitan/Taggart and Vietorisz/Mier/Giblin measures based some components on survey week status and other components on experience over the previous year. The 1968 Manpower Report, the NCEUS, Stein, Garfinkel/Haveman and Klein measures all used the work, earnings and income experience over the previous year. This latter approach is conceptually most appropriate for several reasons: First, hardship measures seek to identify individuals with continuing structural problems, rather than those whose labor market difficulties are only short-term and do not have serious consequences for well-being. Second, it is possible to define some weekly status variables in terms of their duration where the necessary information is gathered--for example, including in a definition of hardship only the currently unemployed with 15 or more weeks of unemployment--but this is not possible for most other earnings and employment status variables which are measured only for the survey week and annually. Family or household income data are collected only on an annual basis. Third, the poverty counts, which assess the hardship resulting from both labor market and non-labor market problems, have an annual focus. It makes sense, then, to use this same timeframe in assessing the labor market-related hardship components.

3. _Income and earnings standards_. Assuming an annual timeframe and separate consideration of individual problems and family needs, there are several different standards which could be and have been used to define hardship. The higher the earnings or income standards, the greater the number of individuals and proportion of the population which will be counted in hardship.

The individual earnings standards adopted by the Wirtz, 1968 Manpower Report, Spring/Harrison/Vietorisz and Miller measures were the weekly, hourly or annual earnings needed to lift a family of four out of poverty. Miller and Wirtz also used the minimum wage as the earnings standard for some components. Klein, NCEUS and Levitan/Taggart used the poverty level or its multiple as a minimum earnings standard, thus weighing individual earnings in light of family size. Vietorisz/Mier/Giblin used a parametric approach, defining individual earnings adequacy under a range of hourly earnings standards.

Several different family income standards were utilized. Miller and Levitan/Taggart used the mean and median incomes of families and unrelated individuals as the upper income screens, i.e., parameters which did not consider family size in assessing whether income was more than adequate. NCEUS and Stein used 200 percent of the poverty threshold for each particular family, while Klein used 150 percent. Vietorisz/Mier/Giblin employed a parametric approach with a range of income standards adjusted for family size. The other hardship measures used earnings and income standards synonymously, i.e., low earners were defined in terms of the poverty threshold or the minimum wage, and there was no screening out based on other sources and total levels of family income.

Probably the most defensible standards are the minimum wage for individual earnings and the poverty level for family income. The parametric approach, which calculates hardship under a range of different income and earnings standards, is complex if too many alternatives are utilized, but a few multiples of the basic standards can be extremely helpful in suggesting the sensitivity of hardship counts to alternative standards of need. It is inconsistent to use the minimum wage or family poverty level as an adequacy standard for individual earnings but to use a mid-level income (such as the median, mean, or 200 percent of poverty) as the cutoff point for family income hardship. Consistent income and earnings standards should be used rather than a low-level for screening in individual earnings problems but a mid-level for screening out families judged to have adequate incomes.

4. <u>Nonearned income</u>. Given the overlap between work and welfare, earnings alone may provide a less than adequate income but economic hardship may be alleviated by income transfers or other nonearned income such as private pensions or alimony. The Wirtz, <u>1968 Manpower Report</u>, Spring/Harrison/Vietorisz, Miller, and Vietorisz/Mier/Giblin indices were concerned only with earnings. The Levitan/Taggart, Stein and the NCEUS indices counted all income in assessing adequacy for the families and households of the subemployed. The Garfinkel/Haveman and Klein measures excluded transfer payments but counted other nonearned income.

Three separate but related issues are involved: Whether the labor market is providing minimal earnings for an individual; whether the earnings of family members are adequate to meet minimal family needs; and, when this is not the case, whether nonearned income offsets earnings deficits. Put another way, the focus is, respectively, what an individual needs or should receive as a minimum from work; what he or she needs to earn in light of family status in order to be self-supporting; and what is needed in order to achieve minimal well-being in light of transfer payments or other income. No single measure can address all of these questions.

5. <u>Treatment of secondary earners</u>. One of the reasons for introducing a hardship index is that the increase in multiple earner families has reduced the hardship consequences of unemployment for any single family member. Yet it is clearly more significant if the family member experiencing labor market problems is the primary breadwinner rather than another member who contributes minimally to the family exchequer. Many of the hardship measures, therefore, focused in some way on those assumed to be primary breadwinners. The Vietorisz/Mier/Giblin "exclusion index" meas-

uring individual earnings problems included all workers regardless of family status; however, the "inadequacy" measure assessing well-being included only family heads and unrelated individuals. The Stein measure was restricted to primary earners. The Miller, Levitan/Taggart and Wirtz indices included only family heads or unrelated individuals in the low earners category of the subemployed and hardship measures, although making no distinction on the basis of breadwinner status in the other component categories. The Garfinkel/Haveman measure of earnings capacity poverty considered both family heads and their spouses.

In contrast, the 1968 Manpower Report, Spring/Harrison/Vietorisz, the NCEUS and Klein measures considered all potential earners and did not exclude on the basis of breadwinner status. This is the most consistent and probably the most reasonable approach. If the family or household is considered the appropriate unit for judging income needs and adequacy, then it is inconsistent to count a dollar of actual or potential earnings from one family member differently from that of another. To exclude from the hardship counts those individuals in families with adequate earnings or incomes including the wages and salaries of secondary earners, but to fail to count secondary earners with problems who live in families with below adequate earnings, is also inconsistent. If an inclusive definition is used which counts secondary earners with problems but disaggregates by family status, then hardship due to low earnings of the primary breadwinner can be identified through disaggregation where this is appropriate.

6. <u>Attachment to the labor force</u>. Earnings alone will rarely provide an adequate individual or family income when the weeks and weekly hours of work availability are limited. On the other hand, earnings from even a few additional weeks of work, or from part-time employment by an extra worker, can improve a family's well-being and perhaps lift the family out of poverty. Most of the hardship measures had at least some low earnings components restricted to persons working in full-time, rather than part-time, jobs. Those measures based on annual earnings, income and work experience usually restricted attention to persons with significant labor force attachment, variously defined. The 1968 Manpower Report measure included only low earners employed 50 weeks or more and all other labor force participants who experienced 15 or more weeks of unemployment. The Vietorisz/Mier/Giblin low earnings category also required 50 weeks of attachment. The NCEUS and Klein measures used a 40 week attachment requirement, while Stein required more than half-year participation. The Levitan/Taggart measures restricted the low earners categories to currently employed household heads who were assumed to be attached to the labor force by dint of their current work and breadwinning responsibilities. The remaining indices, which were based only on employment status in the survey week, implicitly required far less continuity of attachment to the labor force.

The degree of labor force attachment is also an issue in defining discouragement. Job search demonstrates availability and desire for work, and one might reasonably doubt the commitment of an individual claiming to want work but saying none is available without having looked. The discouraged in the Vietorisz/Mier/Giblin index included all those outside the labor force claiming to want employment. Spring/Harrison/Vietorisz included persons wanting work who listed inability to find work as either a primary or secondary reason for not looking. The Levitan/Taggart measures restricted the discouraged to those wanting work but not looking primarily because they thought they could not find a job or perceived personal employment barriers (lack of skills or age), while the Miller index was even more restrictive, excluding those who perceived personal employment barriers. The NCEUS and Klein measures included those whose main reason for not working in the last year was the belief that no jobs were available, but added a further requirement of at least 15 weeks of job search in the first case, and 13 in the second. Stein implicitly required 26 weeks of work or unemployment, with no subspecification for those individuals who were discouraged some or all of their weeks outside the labor force.

Attachment was also the basis for exclusion of groups assumed to have alternative income and activities. The Levitan/Taggart and Miller indices excluded persons over age 64 as well as 16- to 21-year-old students. Spring/Harrison/Vietorisz restricted attention to persons age 16 to 65 years. These exclusions, justifiable on average, were unreasonable in many individual cases where younger or older workers had primary breadwinning responsibilities.

There was no agreement, then, on the appropriate length of work force attachment, since the measures based on survey week status required only one week of participation while those with an annual focus had requirements ranging from 13 to 50 weeks. Each approach measured something fundamentally different and reasonable arguments were made for both restrictive and inclusive standards. Clearly, then, it is necessary to incorporate alternative attachment standards within hardship measures. An inclusive approach, i.e., with minimal attachment requirements, can be disaggregated to focus on those with longer attachment, and is preferable to an exclusionary approach defined by a strict attachment standard which, therefore, limits information available on persons with real problems but falling marginally short of the strict standard. As an example, the inclusive approach is used in defining unemployment; the definition encompasses persons seeking just one hour of work a week as well as those seeking 40-hour jobs, or those unemployed one week as well as those jobless a year or more. Attachment is handled by disaggregating part-time and full-time jobseekers and short-term or long-term unemployed.

There are some other reasonable principles which might be applied in order to further simplify the attachment issue:

First, groups of individuals should not be excluded because, on average, they have marginal attachment; inclusion or exclusion should be based, insofar as possible, on individual behavior, experience and needs, treating all individuals by the same rules. In particular, there is no justification for excluding all persons aged 65 years and over, or students, except by the same criteria used for others.

Second, attachment standards should apply consistently. Mixing timeframes so that some persons are included by survey week status but others by annual experience violates this principle. So, too, does inclusion of part-time workers who are unemployed but not part-time workers who receive a subminimum hourly wage, or a low earner who works 35 hours weekly but not one who works 34 hours more weeks which yield more annual hours of work availability.

Third, while the truly discouraged should be included in any hardship count, the definition should include a minimum job search requirement to provide a tangible demonstration of job desire and availability and some proof that the inability to find work is, in fact and not just imagination, a primary reason for nonparticipation.

7. <u>Disaggregations and supplementary statistics</u>. Counts of persons with inadequate income or earnings are one dimensional indicators of need, including persons with no earnings whatsoever as well as those fully employed but with earnings a dollar short of meeting adequacy standards. The Miller, Levitan/Taggart and Klein measures all estimated the average incomes of persons excluded and included in the subemployed and hardship counts, as well as the percentages living in poverty. Combined with the disaggregations by typology of labor market problems, these data provided some indication of the relative severity of different types of problems for individuals included in the counts. Klein introduced the deficit notion, already used in the poverty data system, measuring the dollar shortfall of income or earnings relative to the needs standards.

Hardship may result from low earnings despite full employment, as well as from part-time, intermittent, or no employment, and each of these work experience patterns and problems might be addressed by different policy measures. It is, therefore, necessary to isolate the typology of labor market problems causing hardship. The subemployment measures were usually derived by cumulating separate components defined according to the typology of labor force problem and these separate component totals were usually presented. For instance, the Levitan/Taggart Employment and Earnings Inadequacy count was composited of, and disaggregated for, the unemployed, discouraged workers, fully-employed low earners, the intermittently employed and persons employed part-time involuntarily.

Some of the previous hardship measures were also disaggregated by family status, race, age, sex and other key demographic variables. Geographic breakdowns were also available in a few cases. The Miller, Wirtz and Spring/Harrison/Vietorisz measures were calculated strictly for central city poverty areas, while the NCEUS, Klein and Levitan/Taggart measures included breakdowns for metropolitan and nonmetropolitan areas.

While primary emphasis in previous hardship measurement efforts went to developing acceptable indicators and explaining their meaning rather than utilizing the measurement system for analytical purposes, Levitan/Taggart, NCEUS, and Klein examined cyclical hardship patterns, as well as racial differentials over time. To better identify the causes and cures of hardship, there was some experimentation with simulations in the Garfinkel/Haveman and Klein measures, which estimated hardship after augmentation of individual earnings up to estimated "capacity." These measures also assessed variants with and without income transfers.

Some of the measures also dissaggregated according to different need standards. The Vietorisz/Mier/Giblin measures used a parametric approach in defining need and thus produced several score of alternative indices. The NCEUS and Levitan/Taggart measures were calculated (but not published) with a range of assumptions about attachment and adequacy standards. The hardship measures also, in some cases, calculated exclusion rates--i.e., the proportion in any labor market problem category excluded because of earnings or income above adequacy standards.

The appropriate degree and focus of disaggregation and of derivative measures is suggested not only by the previous work on hardship, which was basically exploratory in nature and focused on developing indicators rather than data systems, but also by the approaches used in presenting and analyzing labor force and poverty statistics. Both annual work experience and poverty data are published with breakdowns by age, marital and family status, number of family earners, income levels and sources, education, occupation, race and region. The poverty data calculate total and average income deficits to measure the severity of poverty. The "near-poor" population is counted using 125 percent of the poverty thresholds. There are supplementary data which identify income sources, measure poverty with and without cash transfers included, and, recently, calculate the incidence of poverty before and after the receipt of in-kind aid. The work experience measures assess severity in terms of frequency and duration of joblessness and the weeks of labor force participation. In other words, the Bureau of Labor Statistics' annual report on work experience, and its monthly report on employment and earnings, as well as the annual Bureau of the Census reports on poverty and income, provide examples of the types of disaggregation which are possible and have proven useful.

The National Commission on Employment and Unemployment Statistics argued for a comparable array of information organizing these data elements from the hardship perspective: 12/

> A single indicator cannot give individual attention to the . . . components of labor market related hardship . . ., deal with multiple classifications of labor force status during a year, or give separate attention to the individual's status and to his or her family's economic status.
>
> The commission therefore recommends that the Bureau of Labor Statistics prepare an annual report containing measures of the different types of labor market related economic hardship resulting from low wages, unemployment and insufficient participation in the labor force. These data, which refer to individuals, would be presented in conjunction with the family relationship and the household income status of the individual . . . .
>
> The purpose of the annual report would be to present employment problems in relation to the most basic economic problem: inadequate income. The Bureau of the Census publishes statistics on the poverty population, with peripheral attention to labor force attachment. The perspective would be reversed in the recommended report from the Bureau of Labor Statistics, which would start with labor force status and labor market conditions and relate them to poverty.

Consensus and Convergence

There is, then, consensus on some hardship measurement issues and convergence on others:

First, the concepts and related indicators linking labor force and income status should differentiate between individual earnings problems disregarding family status, and family earnings shortfalls which consider differing family size and composition.

Second, hardship measures should also differentiate between family <u>earnings</u> shortfalls and family <u>income</u> deficits, while it would be desirable to further differentiate the income deficits before and after cash transfer payments as well as weighing the effects of in-kind aid.

Third, the measures should utilize an annual timeframe, drawing on work experience rather than current work status data, and annual rather than weekly earnings.

Fourth, the minimum wage is the only socially agreed-upon standard for judging the adequacy of individual earnings, while the poverty thresholds are the most frequently used and publicly accepted standards for judging the adequacy of family income. Supplemental calculations assessing hardship relative to multiples of the minimum wage and the poverty level can indicate the sensitivity of the measures to alternate needs standards, can enrich analytical potential and can reduce debate about appropriate needs standards.

Fifth, since a dollar of earnings by any family member has an equal impact on family well-being, the earnings deficits resulting from the labor market problem affecting all family members should be treated consistently. The distinction between "primary" and "secondary" earners should be handled by disaggregation not by exclusion. The severity of an individual's problems should be measured in terms of the dollar decrement which it produces in the income or earnings of the individual and family.

Sixth, various typologies of labor market experience which generate earnings problems should be identified since they result from substantially different causes and require substantially different cures. Along with the numbers affected by each type of problem, the resulting income and earnings shortfalls should also be estimated, since some types of problems usually have more severe consequences than others.

Seventh, the adequacy of earnings and labor force experience should be judged relative to an individual's hours and weeks of availability for work. <u>All</u> work force participants should be included if individual earnings fall short of a minimum adequacy level for their hours of availability and if this shortfall contributes to family earnings and income deficits. Labor force attachment issues should be addressed by disaggregating these more inclusive measures according to the degree of participation in the work force and the size of the individual earnings deficits.

Eighth, the hardship concepts and indicators must have the potential for disaggregation to consider family size and composition, age, race, sex, region, occupation, and education, i.e., paralleling the disaggregations of poverty and work experience data. There should be an annual presentation and analysis of these disaggregated data supporting the composite hardship indicators.

The first step, then, is to define a set of hardship measurement concepts and related indicators that meet these various requirements.

A Measurement and Assessment System

The Primary Indicators

The proposed hardship measurement and assessment system consists of three sets of core indicators which measure the adequacy of individual earnings, the adequacy of family earnings, and the adequacy of family incomes in terms of both the numbers who fall below minimum standards and the dollar shortfalls relative to these standards:

1. The <u>Inadequate Individual Earnings</u> (IIE) measure counts individuals who, because of low wages or limited employment, have earnings less than what would have been provided by employment at the minimum wage (or its multiple) during the annual hours of actual or discouraged labor force participation. The <u>Inadequate Individual Earnings Deficit</u> (IIE Deficit) is the difference between the earnings that would have been generated by minimum wage employment for all hours of availability and actual annual earnings of persons in the IIE.

2. The <u>Inadequate Family Earnings</u> (IFE) measure counts work force participants whose earnings, when added to those of other family members, do not provide a minimally adequate family income as judged by the poverty standard (or its multiple) for the family. An unrelated individual is considered a family of one. The <u>Inadequate Family Earnings Deficit</u> (IFE Deficit) is the difference between the earnings of all workers in the IFE and the poverty levels (or multiples) for their families.

3. The <u>Inadequate Family Income</u> (IFI) measure counts work force participants whose earnings and nonearned incomes, combined with those of other family members, do not provide a minimally adequate family income as judged by the poverty standard (or its multiple). The <u>Inadequate Family Income Deficit</u> (IFI Deficit) is the difference between the incomes of families in the IFI and the poverty levels (or multiples) for these families.

These indices are calculated using three sets of adequacy standards arbitrarily defined as "severe," "intermediate" and "moderate" hardship. The <u>severe hardship standards</u> are the minimum wage for judging the adequacy of individual earnings (IIE) and the poverty thresholds for judging the adequacy of family earnings and family incomes (the IFE and IFI). The <u>intermediate hardship standards</u> compare earnings and incomes to 125 percent of the minimum wage equivalent for the individual and 125 percent of the poverty threshold for the family. The moderate hardship standards use 150 percent of the minimum wage equivalent and 150 percent of the poverty level to define individual and family hardship.

For all those who worked or sought work during the previous year, the adequacy of individual earnings is assessed relative to their total time in the work force. Actual annual earnings are compared to an "individual earnings standard" derived by multiplying the hourly standard (the minimum wage, 125 percent of the minimum or 150 percent of the minimum, depending on whether severe, intermediate or moderate hardship counts are being derived) times each person's weeks in the work force multiplied by the hours they were seeking work or working weekly. Since the legislated minimum wage is changed irregularly, the dollar level equal to the real average minimum wage for the 1967-1980 period is used as the hourly earnings standard for severe hardship.

The adequacy of family earnings and family income are assessed relative to 100, 125, and 150 percent of the poverty standards for each family with at least one member in the work force. The poverty thresholds, of course, vary with family size and farm or nonfarm residence.

Hardship is assessed for all persons participating in the work force over the course of a year, as well as for the subsets of participants in the work force 27 weeks or more, i.e., "half-year," and those in the work force "full-year," defined as 50 weeks or more.

In summary, the system calculates nine basic variants of the IIE, IFE, IFI and their associated IIE, IFE and IFI Deficits: each measure is estimated using severe, intermediate, and moderate hardship standards considering full-year, half-year, and total work force participants.

Supplementary Measures

The hardship measurement system includes several supplementary measures, as well as subclassifications and disaggregations of the primary indicators:

First, all work force participants (whether in the labor force full-year, half-year or less-than-half-year) are classified into mutually exclusive categories based on their work experience patterns over their weeks of participation in the previous year:

1. Employed full-time (35 hours or more weekly) during all weeks of work force participation.

2. Employed part-time some or all weeks for persons employed throughout their period of participation. Subcategories include persons involuntarily employed part-time at least one week and the remainder employed part-time voluntarily.

3. Intermittently employed, combining weeks of employment and weeks of unemployment. Subcategories include those "mostly unemployed" (two-

thirds or more of their weeks in the work force), "mostly employed" (working two-thirds or more of their weeks of participation), and the remainder with a "mixed" pattern.

    4. Nonemployed during weeks of availability for work. Subcategories include persons "unemployed" throughout all weeks in the work force and those searching for work at least four weeks but "discouraged" the remainder of the year.

Second, incidence rates are derived for the IIE, IFE, and IFI, by dividing the number with inadequate individual earnings, family earnings, and family incomes, respectively, by the number in the work force. The IIE index measures the probability that a work force participant will have earnings less than the minimum wage (or a multiple of the minimum) for the hours and weeks of work that individual is an active or discouraged work force participant. The IFE index measures the proportion of the work force whose earnings, combined with those of other family members, would result in some degree of hardship in the absence of other income sources. The IFI index measures the incidence of hardship among work force participants after nonearned income is added to family earnings.

Third, aggregate and average IIE, IFE and IFI Deficits are calculated for individuals in different work force experience categories. The IIE Deficits of persons in any given work experience category are straightforwardly added and averaged. Family earnings and income deficits are allocated among family work force participants in proportion to their shares of the combined individual earnings deficits of family members. Where the combined IIE Deficits of family members are less than the family's earnings or income deficit, the difference is distributed according to family members' shares of family earnings if each received at least minimally adequate individual earnings. This procedure for allocating family deficits among members suggests the relative impact of each member's employment and earnings problem on family hardship. The distribution of the total deficits among persons in each work experience category are also calculated, suggesting the relative severity of different labor force pathologies.

Fourth, all these measures--the IIE, IFE, and IFI counts, their incidence rates and distributions, plus the IIE, IFE, and IFI Deficits, average deficits and deficit distributions as calculated for individuals based on their category of work force experience--are further disaggregated according to age, race, sex, family size and number of earners, individual family status, educational attainment, individual earnings, individual earnings deficit, family income, region and area of residence, and occupation. These calculations parallel the standard disaggregations of the poverty and work experience data.

Interpretative Indices

Individual earnings may be inadequate because of low wages, periods of nonemployment or less than desired hours of weekly employment. A person with Inadequate Individual Earnings may be in a family with adequate family earnings, as exemplified by the teenager in a family with a fully employed and well-paid head. Likewise, a person with adequate individual earnings may reside in a family which, because of large size or few work force participants, may have Inadequate Family Earnings even though no members have Inadequate Individual Earnings. Family income inadequacy, which is assessed only for persons in the adjusted work force, results when family earnings are low and are not adequately supplemented by transfers and other sources of nonearned income.

To help sort out the causes, consequences and cures for hardship, there are a range of interpretative indices in addition to the primary indicators and supplementary measures. To better assess the underlying labor market pathologies and the effectiveness of various labor market interventions, the earnings and incomes of individuals in hardship are augmented in several different ways to simulate certain "what if" conditions. For instance, the IFE and IFE Deficit are calculated after augmenting the earnings of all unemployed and involuntarily part-time workers by providing minimum wage (or multiple) earnings for all hours of idleness. Under a closely related augmentation scheme, these same individuals are ascribed "capacity employment" defined as their usual hourly earnings rate for all hours of forced idleness. The impact of increased hourly wages or earnings supplements is simulated by the "enhanced earnings augmentation" which raises the actual earnings of all workers in the IFE by 10 percent. The attainment of minimally "adequate employment" for all work force participants is simulated by augmenting each worker's annual earnings up to the level of the minimum wage multiplied by the annual hours of availability for work. The impacts of more comprehensive solutions for labor market problems are simulated by an "enhanced capacity" augmentation which first provides workers in the IFE their usual wage for any hours of forced idleness, then increases everyone's annual earnings by 10 percent.

To better assess the interaction between family size and composition and the family's earnings patterns and problems, a variant of the IFE is calculated which considers only persons who also have Inadequate Individual Earnings. The difference between this smaller total and the regular IFE suggests the number whose family hardship results from large families and limited work effort rather than the failure of family members to earn minimum wages during their hours of availability.

To determine the marginal effect of solving the problems of significant segments of the population in hardship, the IFE and IFE Deficit are calculated by augmenting the earnings of particular family member subgroups (such as heads, wives or other family members) and age subgroups, and then determining how many families would remain with earnings below the poverty level (or its multiple), as well as the size of their deficit. The augmentations include providing minimum wage and usual earnings for all hours of forced idleness, and increasing earnings up to the individual earnings standard for all hours of availability.

To better understand the effectiveness of cash and in-kind aid in alleviating the consequences of labor market problems, the IFI and IFI Deficit are calculated with cash transfers excluded from family income. Differencing the Net-of-Transfers IFI and the regular IFI suggests the number of work force participants lifted out of poverty by cash transfer payments. An Earnings Supplementation Rate-Total is also calculated indicating the proportion of persons with Inadequate Family Earnings who are lifted out of hardship by other income sources, and an Earnings Supplementation Rate-Nontransfers indicates the proportion of the IFE escaping poverty (or its multiple) by the receipt of nontransfer earnings supplements alone. Finally, the IFI and IFI Deficit are calculated after adding the estimated value of food stamps to cash income; they are also calculated after adding the estimated values of food stamps, housing subsidies and school lunches.

Thus, the hardship measurement system consists of an array of thirty measures which are calculated separately for individuals in the labor force full-year, half-year, and at any point during the year, using, in each case, the severe, intermediate, and moderate hardship standards (Table 1.1). For each of these nine variants of the data matrix, there are disaggregations of the measures according to work experience patterns, and then these complete data sets are further disaggregated by age, race, sex, family status, occupation, family income, individual earnings and area of residence of the work force participants.

Assumptions and Approaches

All measures involve normative judgments and assumptions translated into a set of decision rules and definitions which are used in considering the information gathered about the status and experience of each individual. The detailed definitions used in the calculation of the hardship measures from the March Current Population Survey responses are presented in Appendix A, but the general assumptions and approaches which are implicit must first be understood.

Inclusiveness

The proposed set of hardship measures is inclusive rather than exclusive, encompassing diverse labor market problems, work force attachment levels, as well as family earnings and income patterns. The adequacy of individual earnings is judged by the standard that each work force participant should earn at least the minimum wage for the hours and weeks he or she is willing and able to work, and that each family with work force participants should be able to at least earn enough to escape poverty. All earnings and earnings shortfalls are considered from an individual as well as family perspective, considering each individual's work experience and his or her family needs. The disaggregation of individuals in the hardship counts according to work experience patterns and duration of work force participation, and the disaggregations by family status and individual characteristics, are used to identify the portion of hardship accounted for by persons with continuous work force attachment, primary breadwinning responsibilities or particular patterns of work experience which may be of concern.

Table 1.1 HARDSHIP MEASURES

Primary Indicators

1. IIE--Number of work force participants failing to earn the minimum wage (or its multiple) for their annual hours in the work force.

2. IIE Deficit--Shortfall of individual annual earnings relative to the minimum wage equivalent.

3. IFE--Number of work force participants in families with earnings below the poverty level (or its multiple).

4. IFE Deficit--Shortfall of family earnings relative to the poverty level (or its multiple) for families with at least one work force participant.

5. IFI--Number of work force participants in families with incomes below the poverty level (or its multiple).

6. IFI Deficit--Poverty deficit for families with at least one work force participant.

Supplementary Measures

7. IIE Incidence--Percent of work force with Inadequate Individual Earnings.

8. IFE Incidence--Percent of work force with Inadequate Family Earnings.

9. IFI Incidence--Percent of work force with Inadequate Family Income.

10. IIE Average Deficit--IIE Deficit divided by IIE count.

11. IFE Average Deficit--IFE Deficit divided by IFE count.

12. IFI Average Deficit--IFI Deficit divided by IFI count.

Interpretative Indices

13. Full Employment IFE--IFE if every individual were employed at minimum wage (or its multiple) for all hours of involuntary idleness.

14. Full Employment IFE Deficit--IFE Deficit if every individual were employed at minimum wage (or its multiple) for all hours of involuntary idleness.

Table 1.1 (Continued)

15. Capacity Employment IFE--IFE if every individual were employed at his or her usual hourly wage for all hours of involuntary idleness.

16. Capacity Employment IFE Deficit--IFE Deficit if every individual were employed at his or her usual hourly wage for all hours of involuntary idleness.

17. Enhanced Earnings IFE--IFE if annual earnings of all workers were raised by 10 percent.

18. Enhanced Earnings IFE Deficit--IFE Deficit if annual earnings were raised by 10 percent.

19. Adequate Employment IFE--IFE if all persons earned at least the minimum wage equivalent (or its multiple) for all hours in the work force.

20. Adequate Employment IFE Deficit--IFE if all persons earned at least the minimum wage equivalent (or its multiple) for all hours in the work force.

21. Enhanced Capacity IFE--IFE if all persons were provided employment at the usual wage for all hours of forced idleness, and earnings of all persons were increased by 10 percent.

22. Enhanced Capacity IFE Deficit--IFE Deficit if all persons were provided employment at the usual wage for all hours of forced idleness, and earnings of all persons were then increased by 10 percent.

23. Earnings Supplementation Rate-Total--Proportion of persons in IFE who escape poverty as a result of nonearned income.

24. Earnings Supplementation Rate-Nontransfers--Proportion of persons in IFE who escape poverty as a result of nontransfer earnings supplements.

25. IFI Net-of-Transfers--Work force participants in families with cash incomes, excluding transfers, which are below the poverty level (or its multiple).

26. IFI Net-of-Transfers Deficit--IFI Deficit when cash transfers are subtracted from family income.

27. IFI Including Food Stamps--IFI when estimated value of food stamps is added to cash income.

28. IFI Deficit Including Food Stamps--IFI Deficit when estimated value of food stamps is added to cash income.

29. IFI Including In-Kind Aid--IFI when estimated value of food stamps, school lunches and housing subsidies are added to cash income.

30. IFI Including In-Kind Aid Deficit--IFI Deficit when estimated value of food stamps, school lunches and housing subsidies are added to cash income.

As noted previously, this inclusive approach was adopted because the exclusion rules used in previous measures to focus on breadwinners and individuals with a serious commitment to work, treated certain situations and individuals inconsistently. For instance, the restriction of hardship counts to "full-year" labor force participants using a 40-week attachment standard excluded an individual unemployed 39 weeks but too ill to work the remainder of the year despite the fact that this individual's labor market experience would have been just as much a source of economic hardship as that of a low earner unemployed for 8 weeks during the year. Likewise, the restriction of previous hardship measures to primary earners and their problems implicitly and incorrectly assumed that an extra dollar of earnings to the primary earner would alleviate hardship while an extra dollar to a secondary earner would not, or that problems of primary earners could be cured more easily (which may or may not be true) or should have higher priority than those of others in the family.

By measuring hardship relative to individually derived standards based on annual hours of work availability, by treating all earners equally in considering family earnings and income adequacy, and by providing disaggregations to get at the issues usually handled by exclusion, these anomalies were reduced. Inclusive measures can be disaggregated to the exclusive measures but the inverse is not true. For instance, if 40 weeks of participation were the standard for counting hardship, data would not be available to assess the problems of those with, say, 35 to 39 weeks of participation. Clearly, then, the information yield is enriched by the inclusive approach adopted in the proposed hardship measures.

How Much Not Just How Many

The use of the earnings and income deficit approach to supplement the hardship counts provides an indicator of the severity of individual and family problems. Previous hardship measures were usually one-dimensional--once included, each individual counted the same as another regardless of the degree of hardship, making it necessary to exclude by definition all those considered to have less serious problems, such as voluntary part-time workers. They are included in the proposed measures if earning less than the minimum wage or living in families with inadequate earnings or income. They might contribute only a small amount to the budget of their families, and the increment from raising their wages to the minimum might be small, but this is revealed by the average earnings and income deficits for such workers. With such information and the weighting which is implicit, there is no reason for arbitrary exclusion.

There is some inherent arbitrariness in allocating family earnings and income shortfalls among family members. While the decision rule is complex, the principle is not. To the extent that family members earn less than the minimum wage equivalent for their hours in the work force, and that these individual shortfalls cause the family earnings or income deficits, these family deficits can reasonably be distributed according to the relative severity of members' individual problems. If all members had at least minimally adequate earnings, any remaining family deficit would require greater earnings from all family members in proportion to their relative contribution to total family earnings.

The hardship counts can be straightforwardly disaggregated to focus on the subsets of all work force participants who are available for work full-year or half-year. However, assumptions are required in order to allocate family income and earnings shortfalls among family members where some may be participating full-year or half-year but others less-than-full-year or less-than-half-year. Where the hardship measures are restricted to full-year or half-year participants, the adopted approach allocates the family deficit by the same two-step procedure outlined above, except that only the individual earnings deficits of the full-year or half-year participants are considered in the first step. In other words, to the extent the individual earnings problems of the full-year or half-year participants lead to a family's earnings or income shortfall, the full-year or half-year participants are assigned this share of the family shortfall. The relative contributions of all family earners are considered in allocating any remaining family earnings or income deficit. This means that the share of the family IFE and IFI Deficits allocated to full-year and half-year participants under the full-year and half-year disaggregations of the hardship measures are not the same as the shares allocated to them under the hardship calculations for the total work force.

Hardship Standards

The choice of the minimum wage to assess the adequacy of individual earnings and the poverty level to measure the adequacy of family earnings and income are based on the fact that the minimum wage and the poverty levels are unquestionably the most accepted and understood needs indicators. Yet there are some implications which must be recognized and some adaptations which must be made.

Because the legislated minimum is adjusted sporadically, sometimes lagging behind the cost of living and then suddenly catching up in a single step, its use would produce irregular fluctuations in the individual earnings adequacy measures reflecting the irregular changes in the law rather than changes in well-being. In years when the legislated minimum was eroded by inflation, the individual hardship count would go down even though real purchasing power of low wage earners would probably be declining. Conversely, there would appear to be an increase in individual hardship in years when the legislated minimum was raised because wage adjustments would not be instantaneous. To avoid this anomaly, the proposed hardship measurement system does not use the legislated minimum wage as the basis for the individual earnings standard, but rather an average of the real value of the legislated minimum, with adjustments to maintain purchasing power from year to year.

Since an indexed minimum rather than the legislated minimum wage is used as the individual earnings standard, its acceptability depends on the base level and the cost index which are used. The Minimum Wage Study Commission suggested indexing the legislated minimum relative to nonfarm earnings because of problems with the Consumer Price Index, particularly the weight given to fluctuating housing mortgage interest costs. However, the poverty level used to assess the adequacy of family earnings and incomes is an absolute rather than relative standard, i.e., it is adjusted each year for the CPI. Thus, the CPI index minus housing interest costs is used to calculate the minimum wage standard for each year, thereby overcoming many of the problems with the regular CPI, while achieving consistency in the use of absolute adequacy standards for both family and individual earnings.

There is no reason to assume that the real value of the legislated minimum wage in any specific year is a better base than another, which is why the adopted approach was to average the real value (adjusted for the CPI minus housing interest costs) of the legislated minimum wage from 1967 through 1980 (using the minimum legislated for pre-1966 covered workers). This relatively long period included minimum wage increases legislated in 1966, 1974, and 1977, as well as the erosion periods of 1969 through 1973 when the minimum was stable despite inflation, and 1980, when it rose but not enough in light of unexpectedly high rates of inflation. The 1966 Fair Labor Standards Act amendments completed most of the extensions in coverage. 13/ In other words, the average for the 1967-1980 period reasonably represents the real standard selected by society over the years when coverage was relatively comprehensive and stable, over periods of minimum wage activism and neglect, as well as during economic growth and recession and changing political cycles.

Another base period would yield different individual earnings standards for each year. For instance, if the average for the 1974-1980 period had been used as the baseline rather than the average for the 1967-1980 period, the standard for each year would have been 1.2 percent lower. Likewise, the use of the total CPI, rather than the CPI minus housing mortgage costs, would have yielded different standards, particularly in 1980 when interest rates rose so much faster than other CPI components.

	Minimum wage standards using 1967-1980 as base and adjusting for CPI minus mortgage interest costs	Minimum wage standards using 1974-1980 as base and adjusting for CPI minus mortgage interest costs	Minimum wage standard using 1967-1980 as base and adjusting for CPI	Legislated minimum wage
1974	$1.99	$1.96	$1.98	$2.00
1975	2.16	2.14	2.16	2.10
1976	2.29	2.26	2.29	2.30
1977	2.44	2.41	2.44	2.30
1978	2.61	2.58	2.62	2.65
1979	2.87	2.84	2.92	2.90
1980	3.21	3.17	3.31	3.10

There is no adjustment for the student learners differential since it is impossible to determine which of the students in the labor force are covered by certificates. Likewise, there is no way to identify workers in jobs not covered by the Fair Labor Standards Act. The disaggregations in the hardship tallies permit adjustments where these are considered appropriate. For instance, teenage students or agricultural workers can be subtracted from the totals.

The use of severe, intermediate and moderate hardship standards not only accommodates varying judgments about what constitutes hardship, but it also increases analytical potential. For instance, one policy might reduce the number in severe hardship more than another, but alter the intermediate hardship count by less. Likewise, some subgroups in the work force may be more concentrated above the severe hardship line but below the intermediate hardship cutoff, while others are concentrated among those with severe hardship. The different data sets can be used like scissors to cut through many critical issues concerning the relative severity of problems, thus supplementing the dimension added by the deficit measures.

The severe, intermediate and moderate income and earnings standards are arbitrary. Rather than 100, 125 and 150 percent of the minimum wage and poverty thresholds, any other multiples could have been used. The choice was dictated largely by the conventions in previous hardship studies and by value judgments based upon examination of the income and earnings distributions in the population. In 1979 the poverty threshold for a nonfarm family of four was $7,412 and for an unrelated individual, $3,800. The minimum wage standard of $2.87 would have produced annual earnings of $5,800 assuming 2,020 annual hours of employment. The median income for households with four members was $22,576. For all unrelated individuals, the median was $7,542, but, perhaps more appropriately, it was $13,321 for unrelated individuals in the labor force full-year. The severe, intermediate and moderate income and earnings standards, thus, represented the following percentages of the medians:

	Severe hardship standards (100 percent of minimum wage or poverty thresholds)	Intermediate hardship standards (125 percent of minimum wage or poverty thresholds)	Moderate hardship standards (150 percent of minimum wage or poverty thresholds)
Family earnings and income standards as percent of median income of--			
Nonfarm family of four	.33	.41	.49
Unrelated individuals	.50	.63	.76
Unrelated individuals in labor force full-year	.28	.36	.43
Individual earnings standards for full-time, full-year worker as percent of median income of--			
Nonfarm family of four	.25	.32	.39
Unrelated individuals	.77	.96	1.15
Unrelated individuals in labor force full-year	.44	.54	.65

Obviously, minimum wage level earnings and multiples provide better for the needs of unrelated individuals than for families, and for small families than for large ones. In 1980, for instance, the Minimum Wage

Commission estimated the hourly earnings needed for an individual full-time worker to provide poverty level annual earnings for households of different sizes:

Hourly wage equivalent for an individual worker employed
full-time and earning at OMB poverty level, 1980

Family members:	1	2	3	4	5	6
Hourly wage required:	$1.82	$2.41	$3.00	$3.58	$4.17	$4.76

Conversely, the poverty threshold is based on family size so that a sole worker in a large family must earn more than a sole worker with fewer breadwinning responsibilities. The divergence between what society considers adequate earnings for an individual and the self-support needs of families is the reason why there are separate measures and standards for individual earnings adequacy and family earnings adequacy.

The minimum wage standards do not vary with residence while the poverty thresholds are lower in farm areas. The income needs of farm residents were estimated to be 25 percent less than those of nonfarm residents when poverty was first defined; the accepted differential was reduced to 15 percent in the poverty counts covering the 1974-1980 period for which the hardship measures are calculated. The minimum wage is uniform for the entire nation and, therefore, does not account at all for cost-of-living differentials. Thus, for rural compared to urban areas, the IIE measures will be relatively larger than the IFE and IFI measures because of the cost adjustment in the poverty standard but not in the minimum wage standard.

It might make sense to utilize cost-of-living adjustments for all earnings and income standards. For instance, the BLS lower living standards which vary for metropolitan areas based on cost survey data, might be utilized rather than the poverty levels. This option would be important if the hardship measures were to be utilized in resource allocation (although the poverty measures which do not utilize such adjustments are used currently without much debate).

Typologies of Work Experience

The categorization of the work force according to their work experience pattern during their weeks of participation is critical in order to understand the nature of the underlying labor market problems and hence the appropriate solutions. This classification is relatively straightforward. The work experience categories include full-time employment during the full-period of work force participation at one extreme, no employment whatsoever at the other extreme, with intermittent employment and unemployment, as well as part-time employment falling between these extremes. The intermittently employed are subcategorized by the proportion of their weeks in the labor force they are employed and unemployed, just as work experience measures subclassify participants according to weeks of joblessness. The intermittently employed include workers whose usual employment is part-time voluntary, part-time involuntary, full-time, or a mixture. The nonemployed and intermittently employed may include individuals seeking part-time work for some or all weeks not working. Workers employed full-period but with some weeks of part-time employment are subcategorized into those who worked part-time voluntarily and those who worked part-time because full-time work was not available. The involuntarily part-time employed include some who worked full-time most of the period, while the voluntarily part-time employed include individuals wanting full-time work some weeks but restricted by reasons other than the lack of full-time work. The important point is that any individual can be classified in one and only one work experience pattern category.

Because the Current Population Survey questions used in calculating the hardship measures are limited, assumptions must be made about the hours of work for individuals who mix full-time and voluntary part-time employment in order to calculate the individual earnings standard. Where an individual works predominantly part-time, 40 hours of availability are assumed during weeks this individual indicates he or she wants more than 35 hours of employment. Where work is predominantly full-time, hours worked when employed part-time are assumed to be 20 hours per week.

Finally, the nonemployed are subcategorized into those who are discouraged vs. those unemployed. The discouraged workers include persons who did not work in the last year, who claimed that the inability to find work was the primary reason, and who looked for a job at least a month. This job search requirement is used in order to weed out individuals who claimed they wanted to work and could not find jobs, but might not have been really eager for employment, or might not have known about available opportunities because of the absence of job search. A more rigorous job search requirement would alter some but not all of the hardship measures. For instance, an individual with five weeks of unemployment, counted as discouraged according to the above definitions, would appear among the totally unemployed in the hardship measures for the total work force even if two months of job search were required to classify an individual as discouraged; on the other hand, this individual with five weeks of unemployment would be excluded from the full-year tallies if a two-month search period were used in the discouraged worker classification. The deficits and interpretative measures which augment earnings are also affected by the stringency of the job search requirement, since those counted as discouraged are ascribed 50 weeks of work force participation in calculating individual earnings standards and deficits, whereas they would only be ascribed their weeks searching for work if included among the totally unemployed. The intermittently employed who were outside the labor force for some weeks might also have been discouraged, but this cannot be determined from the CPS questionnaire since inability to find work is not included as one of the possible reasons for nonparticipation unless it occurs throughout the year. Because earnings adequacy is judged relative to weeks in the labor force for the intermittently employed, the inability to estimate their weeks of discouragement leads to a slight understatement of the number with Inadequate Individual Earnings.

"What If" Measures

The Full Employment, Capacity Employment, Enhanced Earnings, Adequate Employment and Enhanced Capacity IFE and IFE Deficit measures augment the earnings of work force participants in different ways, and then determine how many would remain with family earnings below the poverty level (or its multiple). The aim of these interpretative indices is to help in assessing the impacts and implications of policy alternatives. For instance, the Full Employment IFE yields a general sense of the costs and consequences of a large-scale job creation approach, while the Enhanced Earnings IFE yields some notion of what would occur if minimum wages were raised. This does not mean that guaranteeing minimum wage jobs or increasing the legislated minimum would have these exact effects on hardship. For instance, if minimum wage jobs were guaranteed, there is no doubt that most workers fully employed at less than the minimum would leave their existing jobs for the new positions. Many persons would be attracted from outside the labor force. Likewise, minimum increases would have disemployment effects as well as attracting more workers into the labor force. The augmented measures, thus, provide indicators of relative magnitudes and directions of change associated with alternative policies, but are hardly the last word on their relative impacts.

The augmented measures are disaggregated by the same work force attachment, work experience pattern and demographic categories as are used for the other hardship indicators. In the disaggregations for full-year and half-year workers, only the earnings of the full-year or half-year participants are augmented in the prescribed ways. The "what if" question addressed by these measures is "how many full-year or half-year participants would remain in families with earnings below the poverty level (or multiple) if the earnings of the full-year or half-year participants in the family were augmented in the prescribed ways?"

The work experience and demographic disaggregations for any of the nine hardship severity/work force attachment combinations for the augmented measures include persons in the disaggregated group who are in families with inadequate earnings after all work force participants with the required attachment have their earnings augmented. For instance, in the Full Employment IFE for the total work force, the earnings of the voluntary part-time workers are not augmented because they have no hours of forced idleness; nevertheless, the number of voluntary part-time workers in the Full Employment IFE will be lower than in the regular IFE because some have other family members whose earnings are augmented, raising their families out of poverty.

To shed light on secondary earner issues, the Full Employment, Adequate Employment and Capacity Employment IFE measures are also calculated by augmenting only the earnings of specified subgroups while leaving constant the earnings of all other individuals in the work force. The combined earnings of family members are, then, compared to the poverty standard or multiple, and all family members in the work force are included in the marginally augmented tallies if they fall below the standards or multiples. Because marginal augmentation involves extensive computer time and cost, it is only undertaken for the age/student status and family relationship disaggregations. The disaggregations of the marginally augmented measures for age/student and family status subgroups count <u>all</u> work force participants in families which remain with inadequate earnings after augmentation of the earnings of the specified age/student or family status subgroups. In contrast, the age/student and family relationship disaggregations for the regularly augmented IFE measures include just the subgroup members who remain in families with inadequate earnings after every family member has their earnings augmented in the specified manner.

Valuing In-Kind Aid

The IFI Including Food Stamps and the IFI Including In-Kind Aid estimate how many work force participants remain with a below-poverty living standard after receipt of in-kind aid. These measures are derived from responses to the supplemental questions on noncash benefits which were added to the March 1980 Current Population Survey questionnaire and continued in March 1981. The valuation of food stamps is relatively straightforward, since food stamps are very similar to cash income and since individuals are queried concerning the dollar amount of food stamps received. The IFI Including Food Stamps as income simply adds cash and food stamps received for each family with at least one work force participant and compares this with the poverty level (or its multiple).

The IFI Including In-Kind Aid adds the estimated value of school lunches and housing subsidies to food stamps and cash income. These estimates are much more problematic because the CPS questions concerning lunches and housing are not as specific, and a range of plausible assumptions yields quite different valuations. 14/ The CPS asks how many children in the household received free or reduced price lunches. According to federal program statistics, about 9.9 million children from poor and near-poor families received free meals in 1979, at an average federal subsidy of 93¢ per meal, while 1.7 million received reduced-price lunches, at an average subsidy of 73¢. Another 13 million received lunches at prices modestly below cost because of the provision of federal commodities. It is assumed that families in the latter category will not perceive that they are getting a free or reduced-price meal. This squares with the aggregate counts from the March 1980 in-kind questionnaire, where 11.3 million youth age 5 to 18 lived in households reporting that their children usually received free or reduced price lunches in 1979. The poverty threshold in 1979 for an urban family of four was based on a $1.71 daily feeding cost for each family member. Since six out of seven of the persons receiving free or reduced price lunches got free lunches, and since the subsidy for the reduced price lunch exceeded the amount budgeted for each poverty meal, it is reasonable to assume that all families who reported receipt of a free or reduced price meal, in fact, had their food needs reduced by one-third per person each day a lunch was received. Assuming that meals were available for 182 school days, with a twenty percent absentee rate, that the lunches reduced food costs of each recipient by one-third (i.e., covering one of three meals), and that food costs represented a third of the poverty level (which is the basis of the poverty definition), then each recipient in a family would have augmented family cash income by .044 of its poverty threshold per household member (one-half year times 80 percent attendance times one-third reduction in daily food costs times the one-third of a poverty income which presumably is allocated for food). The estimated value of free lunches for a family of four with two children receiving lunches was $164 in 1979, whereas the supply price to the government was estimated to be $271. Though the subsidized lunch might have supplied more calories and nutrients than the poverty budgeted diet, and certainly cost more to deliver, it hardly eliminated the need for breakfast and dinner for the student.

Valuation of housing benefits is even more conjectural. If benefits were valued at government subsidy cost and added to cash incomes, many of the residents of subsidized housing would be considered nonpoor simply because the units are more costly and presumably more adequate than the alternatives which would have been secured in the absence of housing subsidies. Yet the income remaining after rent might still be less than what is necessary to purchase other needed goods and services. For instance, a family of three with a cash income of $4800 living in a new public housing unit might pay only $100 monthly in rent even though an equivalent unsubsidized unit would rent for $500 monthly. The annual subsidy would cost the government $4800 and the sum of cash and housing valued at this subsidy would be above the poverty threshold for this family. But can a family of three survive on $3600 net of housing costs? Not if housing costs equal just a fourth of the poverty threshold, with three-fourths required for other needs, as the poverty index assumes. Therefore, the crude valuation procedure adopted in the hardship calculations caps the housing subsidy at the estimated housing expenditure share for unsubsidized low income families. In 1979, according to the annual housing survey, occupants of subsidized units paid a median of 24 percent of cash income for gross rent (the public housing formula, for instance, allowed for a rent of 30 percent of adjusted income). Among all households (subsidized and unsubsidized) with less than $3000 cash income, the median percent of cash income going for gross rent was in excess of 60 percent. For renter households with $3000 to $7000 cash incomes, the median was 44 percent; for those with $7000 to $10,000, the median was 31 percent; and for the $10,000 to $15,000 income group, it was 24 percent. Adjusting for the estimated proportions below the median who were in subsidized units, the medians for each income class are estimated to be roughly 65, 50, 35 and 30 percent, respectively, for residents of unsubsidized units with each level of family cash income. Subtracting the 24 percent of cash income that is usually paid as rent in subsidized units means that housing expenditures were reduced by approximately 40, 25, 10, and 5 percent, respectively, of the cash incomes for households in the different cash income classes. This is, admittedly, a very crude estimation procedure. For instance, large and small families with the same cash incomes are estimated to spend the same proportions of income on housing, which is unlikely. Regression analysis from the annual housing survey data could derive a predicted housing cost percentage for each household, and rent subsidy formulae could be used to predict subsidized housing rents. However, such detailed calculations were not justified for the present purposes. Further, since two-thirds of the 2.3 million households in public and leased housing had <u>no</u> reported earners, only a small proportion of all persons in hardship were affected by in-kind housing aid, and in most of the cases where the low-income families with work force participants resided in subsidized units, the estimation procedures should have yielded a reasonable "best guess" of the impacts of housing subsidies on well-being. It is important to stress, however, that the in-kind valuations for housing, like the valuations for school lunches, are below the subsidy costs. The principle which is applied in both cases is to determine whether the cash income, which remains after the specific need is met by in-kind aid, will provide for a poverty level "market basket" after subtracting the price which this "market basket" assumes for each element provided in-kind.

A Comprehensive System

The thrust of this effort is not just to develop an acceptable hardship indicator, but to design a comprehensive system of measurement and analysis to supplement the poverty and labor force statistics systems, as well as the massive body of analytical work covering labor market problems and appropriate public policies which has been based on the poverty and unemployment measures. In particular, the disaggregations and the interpretative measures were designed to provide data usable with minimum adaptation or manipulation to address a range of important theoretical and policy issues. For instance, previous hardship indicators have suggested that the number of persons in hardship fluctuates less than the number unemployed over the business cycle because those who already have structural problems are the ones who suffer most in recessions, i.e., their hardship simply becomes more severe. The proposed measures permit a much better assessment of the shifting severity of need over the business cycle. Because the labor force categories are mutually exclusive and descriptive of all possible work experience patterns, recession or recovery-induced shifts from one category to another can be identified; for instance, shifts from the mostly employed category to the mostly unemployed category as economic conditions worsen. The comparison between the severe, intermediate, and moderate adequacy counts enriches the analysis of the severity issues. The family responses to changing economic conditions such as increased labor force participation and earnings of added family members can be assessed by analysis of the disaggregations. The augmented earnings IFE measures provide varied perspectives on the changes in the composition and causes of hardship over the business cycle. The effectiveness of income transfer programs in protecting against cyclical fluctuations can be determined from relative movements in the IFI and the IFI Net-of-Transfers. In other words, the tabulated data can be added, subtracted and multiplied to address most analytical issues concerning the hardship consequences of macroeconomic changes. The tabulated data are equally useful in assessing secular trends, the problems of minorities, the impacts of changing family size, composition and work patterns, allocation and targeting issues, transfer program impacts, as well as the potentials of policy tools, such as minimum wage increases and full-employment job creation. Such applications are demonstrated in the following analyses using the annual hardship data calculated for the 1974-1980 period.

There are tradeoffs, however, in seeking to develop a hardship measurement system rather than a single indicator, and in trying to accommodate the criticisms of previous hardship measures. The departures from previous approaches overcome most of the criticisms but increase the complexity. There are three primary sets of hardship measures rather than one or two in other hardship systems, and these sets include deficit measures of hardship severity as well as body counts of those who fall below specified standards. Because the measurement system is inclusive, disaggregation is necessary for acceptability in certain contexts, since the aggregated measures include some individuals who may have only minimal attachment to the work force and thus only a small potential contribution to the well-being of their families. The use of severe, intermediate, and moderate income and earnings standards further complicates the picture. Finally, the incorporation of interpretative indices as an integral part of the measurement system increases potential understanding of causes and interactions, but generates even more numbers for consideration.

The critical issue is whether the added complexity of the hardship approach adds to understanding of the interface between work and well-being, whether it leads to increased attention to the structural employment problems which have the most severe consequences, and whether it provides an improved framework for assessing policy alternatives. The subsequent analysis seeks to document the meaningfulness and reasonability of the measures and their utility in analysis of the causes and cures for the critical labor market problems which undermine the well-being of our nation's citizens.

Notes

1. Proprietors' income is included along with wages and salaries as earnings in the hardship calculations.

2. *1967 Manpower Report of the President* (Washington, D.C.: U.S. Government Printing Office, April 1967), pp. 74-76.

3. *1968 Manpower Report of the President* (Washington, D.C.: U.S. Government Printing Office, April 1968), pp. 34, 36.

4. William Spring, Bennett Harrison and Thomas Vietorisz, "Crisis of the Underemployed," *The New York Times Magazine*, November 5, 1972.

5. Herman P. Miller, "Subemployment in Poverty Areas of Large U.S. Cities," *Monthly Labor Review*, October 1973, pp. 10-17.

6. Sar A. Levitan and Robert Taggart, *Employment and Earnings Inadequacy: A New Social Indicator* (Baltimore, Md.: The Johns Hopkins University Press, 1974); and Sar A. Levitan and Robert Taggart, "Do Our Statistics Measure the Real Labor Market Hardships?" American Statistical Association Annual Meeting, Boston, Massachusetts, August 23, 1976.

7. Thomas Vietorisz, Robert Mier and John Giblin, "Subemployment: Exclusion and Inadequacy Indexes," *Monthly Labor Review*, May 1975, pp. 3-12.

8. Irwin Garfinkel and Robert H. Haveman, *Earnings Capacity, Poverty, and Inequality* (New York: Academic Press, 1977).

9. Robert Stein, unpublished Bureau of Labor Statistics paper.

10. National Commission on Employment and Unemployment Statistics, *Counting the Labor Force* (Washington, D.C.: U.S. Government Printing Office, 1979), pp. 57-81.

11. Bruce W. Klein, "The Adequacy of the Earnings Capacity of the Subemployed and Its Policy Implications," unpublished Ph.D dissertation, The George Washington University, August 1981.

12. National Commission on Employment and Unemployment Statistics, *op. cit.*, pp. 60-63.

13. The majority of the additional workers covered in 1974 were government employees and the coverage of these state and local workers was subsequently reversed by a Supreme Court decision.

14. Bureau of the Census, U.S. Department of Commerce, *Technical Paper 50: Alternative Methods for Valuing Selected In-Kind Transfer Benefits and Measuring Their Effect on Poverty* (Washington, D.C.: U.S. Government Printing Office, April 1982).

CHAPTER 2. HARDSHIP IN 1979

The Derivation and Dimensions of Hardship

The Basic Indicators

While the complete array of hardship statistics tabulated for a single year is imposing, including over a half million numbers, and though the unfamiliar terminology can be unwieldy, the underlying notions are quite simple. The core indicators which serve as the building blocks of the hardship measurement system are derived straightforwardly from available work experience, income and earnings statistics. They are designed to address six basic questions:

-- <u>Inadequate Individual Earnings (IIE)</u> - How many of the persons who participate in the work force during the year are unable to earn at least the minimum wage multiplied by their total hours of work availability?

-- <u>IIE Deficit</u> - What additional earnings are needed to raise the wages and salaries of these individuals with inadequate earnings to the minimum wage level?

-- <u>Inadequate Family Earnings (IFE)</u> - How many work force participants are in families whose total wages and salaries are below the poverty level?

-- <u>IFE Deficit</u> - Among work force participants with Inadequate Family Earnings, what is the shortfall between family earnings and poverty threshholds?

-- <u>Inadequate Family Income (IFI)</u> - How many work force participants have earnings and other family income below the poverty level?

-- <u>IFI Deficit</u> - How many dollars of added earnings or other income are needed to raise the families of work force participants in the IFI out of poverty?

Based on the work experience, income, earnings and other information collected in the Current Population Survey each March covering the preceding calendar year, these questions can be answered for each year from 1974 through 1980. However, the derivation and dimensions of hardship are best illustrated using 1979 as a baseline. This last year of the 1970s was also the last in which there was a reasonably healthy economy. The national unemployment rate averaged 5.8 percent--0.4 percentage points below the 1970s average and 1.6 percentage points below the unemployment rate for

1980 and 1981. The annual employment growth in 1979 was a robust 2.5 percent, equalling the employment growth rate averaged over the 1970s and in contrast to a slight decline in total employment during 1980 and 1981. The real value of the legislated minimum wage which prevailed in 1979 very nearly equalled the real value of the legislated minimum averaged over the 1967 to 1980 period. The poverty rate was 11.6 percent, just a shade below the average for the 1970s but significantly below the 13.0 percent rate in 1980. While the cost-of-living (and the poverty thresholds) rose by 13.3 percent in 1979, noticeably above the 7.4 percent annual increase of the 1970s, inflation was more in line with the 11.0 percent annual increase averaged in 1980 and 1981. In other words, 1979 was not the best of years for our nation's economy, but it was generally characteristic of the 1970s and a reasonable baseline for assessing the rather dramatic changes which have occurred in the 1980s.

For this baseline year, the six primary severe hardship measures are estimated as follows:

1. <u>Inadequate Individual Earnings (IIE)</u>. During 1979, seven of every ten persons age 16 or over worked or looked for work in the civilian labor market (Chart 2.1). Among these 117.0 million participants, one of every four, or 28.3 million, had annual earnings less than the amount each would have earned if paid the minimum wage for all hours they were willing and able to work during the year. <u>1/</u>

2. <u>IIE Deficit</u>. To raise the earnings of these individuals up to the minimum wage equivalent for their hours of availability would have required $52.0 billion in additional earnings, which represented 4.0 percent of the nation's total wages and salaries. The average worker in the IIE needed $1,839 more to achieve minimally adequate individual earnings.

3. <u>Inadequate Family Earnings (IFE)</u>. Not all these individuals suffered seriously as a result of their earnings shortfalls; while others, who earned at least the minimum wage equivalent, nevertheless lacked the annual family earnings required to escape poverty either because of their own limited hours of work availability, their large families, or the lack of supplementary family earners. Two-thirds of the 28.3 million persons with Inadequate Individual Earnings lived in families with combined earnings <u>above</u> the poverty level, leaving only 9.1 million in families <u>unable</u> to achieve minimal self-support by the work of family members. On the other hand, there were 4.2 million work force participants with <u>adequate</u> individual earnings relative to their hours of availability who were in families with below-poverty earnings. These 13.3 million work force participants with Inadequate Family Earnings represented 11.4 percent of the total work force.

4. <u>IFE Deficit</u>. Work force participants in the IFE needed an additional $31.7 billion in wages and salaries to raise their families' earnings to the poverty level. This IFE Deficit represented 2.4 percent of the nation's total wages and salaries and

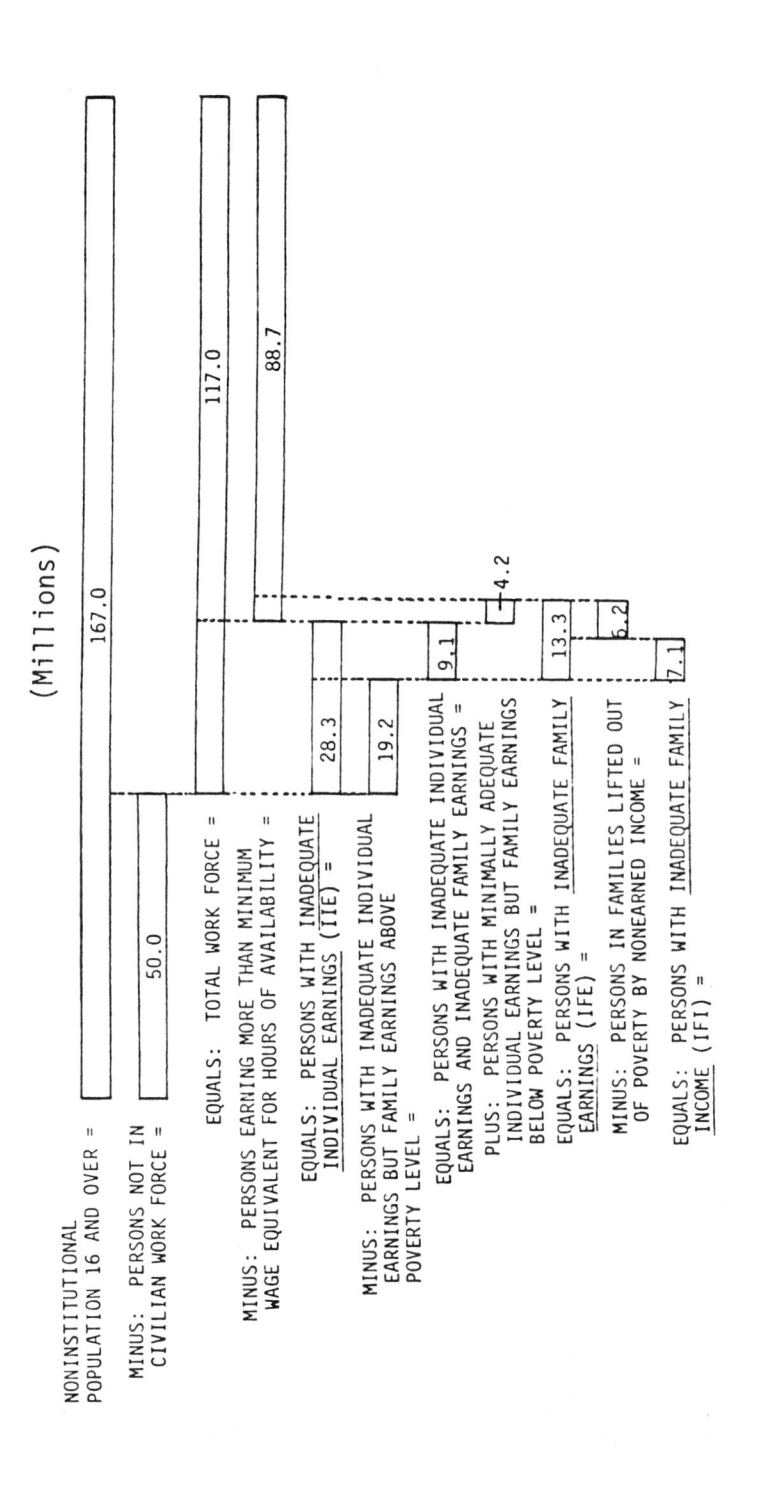

Chart 2.1. PERSONS IN SEVERE HARDSHIP, 1979

(Millions)

NONINSTITUTIONAL
POPULATION 16 AND OVER = 167.0

MINUS: PERSONS NOT IN
CIVILIAN WORK FORCE = 50.0

EQUALS: TOTAL WORK FORCE = 117.0

MINUS: PERSONS EARNING MORE THAN MINIMUM
WAGE EQUIVALENT FOR HOURS OF AVAILABILITY = 88.7

EQUALS: PERSONS WITH INADEQUATE
INDIVIDUAL EARNINGS (IIE) = 28.3

MINUS: PERSONS WITH INADEQUATE INDIVIDUAL
EARNINGS BUT FAMILY EARNINGS ABOVE
POVERTY LEVEL = 19.2

EQUALS: PERSONS WITH INADEQUATE INDIVIDUAL
EARNINGS AND INADEQUATE FAMILY EARNINGS = 9.1

PLUS: PERSONS WITH MINIMALLY ADEQUATE
INDIVIDUAL EARNINGS BUT FAMILY EARNINGS
BELOW POVERTY LEVEL = 4.2

EQUALS: PERSONS WITH INADEQUATE FAMILY
EARNINGS (IFE) = 13.3

MINUS: PERSONS IN FAMILIES LIFTED OUT
OF POVERTY BY NONEARNED INCOME = 6.2

EQUALS: PERSONS WITH INADEQUATE FAMILY
INCOME (IFI) = 7.1

averaged $2,384 for each work force member with Inadequate Family Earnings.

5. <u>Inadequate Family Income (IFI)</u>. Of the 13.3 million in the IFE, 2.8 million were in families lifted out of poverty by the receipt of private pensions, alimony, interest and other nontransfer income. Cash transfers such as welfare and social security, raised an additional 3.4 million above the poverty threshold. Thus, only half of the individuals with Inadequate Family Earnings were in households with Inadequate Family Incomes. This 7.1 million in the IFI represented 6.0 percent of the work force and two-fifths of the poor age 16 and over.

6. <u>IFI Deficit</u>. Transfers and other sources of income reduced the $31.7 billion IFE Deficit by almost three-fifths. The remaining $12.8 billion IFI Deficit for families with members in the work force represented 56 percent of the nation's total poverty deficit. To alleviate poverty among the working poor would have required $1,818 in earnings supplements for each work force participant.

Hardship and Work Force Attachment

These measures of severe hardship count all individuals participating in the work force during 1979, including some working or looking for part-time work totalling just a few hours of availability over the year, but others in the labor force full-time, full-year. The incidence, nature and consequences of employment and earnings problems vary with the annual hours of availability.

In order to understand these interrelationships, the basic hardship indicators are calculated for only those participants in the work force at least half-year, i.e., 27 weeks or more, as well as for those participating full-year, i.e., 50 weeks or more. The half-year hardship counts are a subset of the total hardship counts, while the full-year counts are a subset of the half-year counts. Hardship incidence rates are calculated for these subsets; in other words, the IIE incidence among full-year workers equals persons in the work force for 50 weeks or more who have earnings below the minimum wage level, divided by the total number of full-year participants. The hardship deficits for full-year and half-year participants focus on the individual earnings shortfalls of these individuals and the share of the family earnings and income shortfalls that can be attributed to their labor market problems.

Increased work force attachment reduces the probability of suffering hardship (Chart 2.2). Among those participating less than half-year during 1979, the proportions with Inadequate Family Earnings and Inadequate Family Income were more than four times those among full-year work force participants. Obviously, families with full-year participants had more hours of potential employment and were, therefore, more likely to have family earnings above the poverty level. Yet the IIE incidence among less than half-year participants was also greater than among full year participants, even

Chart 2.2. INCIDENCE OF HARDSHIP BY WORK FORCE ATTACHMENT, 1979

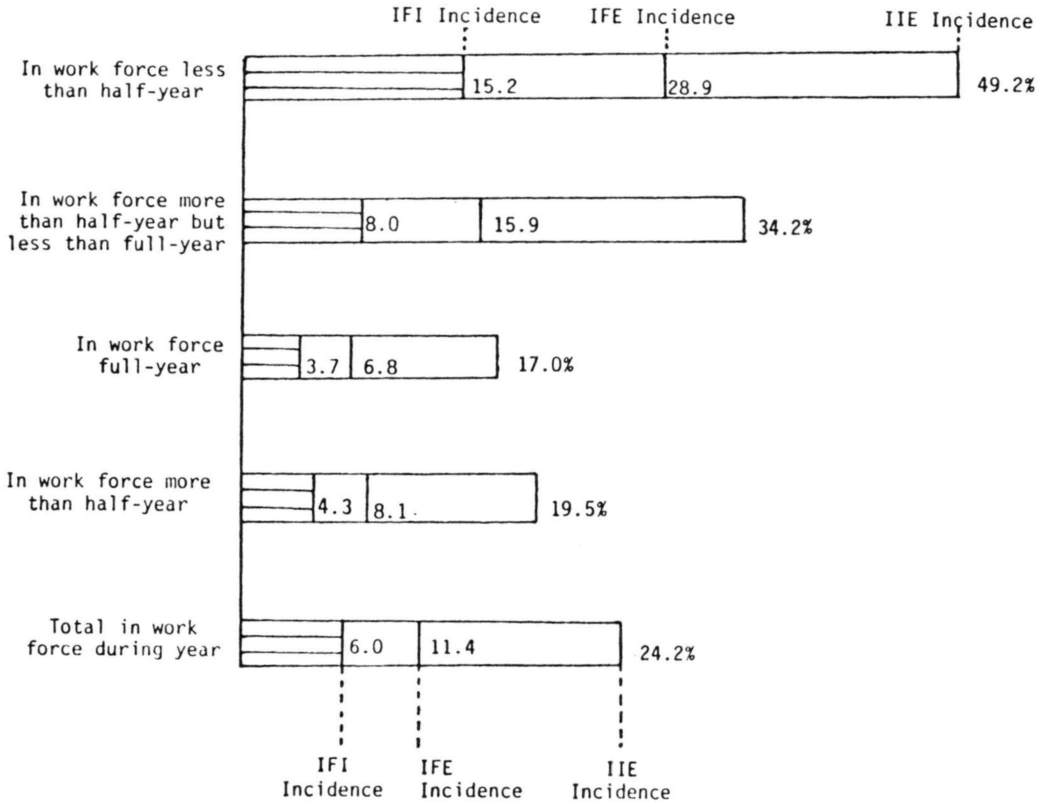

Work Force Attachment	IFI Incidence	IFE Incidence	IIE Incidence
In work force less than half-year	15.2	28.9	49.2%
In work force more than half-year but less than full-year	8.0	15.9	34.2%
In work force full-year	3.7	6.8	17.0%
In work force more than half-year	4.3	8.1	19.5%
Total in work force during year	6.0	11.4	24.2%

though each individual's annual earnings were judged relative to his or her weeks and weekly hours in the work force.

Although seven of every ten work force participants in 1979 worked or looked for work at least 50 weeks, only half of the persons with Inadequate Individual Earnings were full-year participants (Chart 2.3). Among all work force participants with Inadequate Family Earnings and Inadequate Family Income, only three-fifths participated for half a year or more and just two-fifths were full-year participants.

If two individuals averaged the same earnings deficits each week in the work force, the one with more weeks of attachment would have a larger individual earnings deficit and would account for a larger share of the total IIE Deficit. Thus, the work force participants with less than half-year in the labor force accounted for only a ninth of the total IIE Deficit, even though they represented a third of persons in the IIE. Conversely, the half of persons in the total IIE who were in the work force full-year accounted for three-fourths of the aggregate IIE Deficit. If the family earnings and income deficits are allocated among all family work force participants according to each participant's share of the combined individual earnings deficits for all family members where this total exceeds the family's IFE and IFI Deficits, and the remainder of the family's IFE and IFI Deficits, if any, according to each participant's share of family earnings assuming all family workers achieved at least minimally adequate individual earnings, the deficit attributed to each individual represents the relative importance of his or her earnings problem in contributing to the family earnings or income shortfall. Using this procedure for allocating family deficits among family work force participants, the full-year and half-year workers accounted for roughly the same shares of the 1979 IFE and IFI Deficits as they did of the IFE and IFI counts. 2/ This is because the family deficits were less for families with full-year workers, so that even though the average IIE Deficit of full-year workers was substantially larger than that of less-than-full-year workers, the difference in their average IFE and IFI Deficits was less:

SEVERE HARDSHIP DEFICITS BY WORK FORCE ATTACHMENT

	Deficit (millions)			Percent of Total Deficit			Average Deficit		
	IIE	IFE	IFI	IIE	IFE	IFI	IIE	IFE	IFI
Total	$51,998	$31,656	$12,824	100.0%	100.0%	100.0%	$1,839	$2,384	$1,818
Half-Year	46,403	17,891	8,064	89.2	56.5	62.9	2,404	2,232	1,885
Full-Year	38,446	13,306	6,308	73.9	42.0	49.2	2,698	2,345	2,036

Alternative Adequacy Standards

The attainment of minimum wage earnings for individuals and poverty-level earnings for families is hardly a cause for rejoicing. For an urban family of four, the lowest-level food menu of the Department of Agriculture, dinner out at an inexpensive restaurant once every two months, minimally adequate rental housing, no out-of-town trips, auto ownership by

Chart 2.3. SEVERE HARDSHIP COUNTS BY WORK FORCE ATTACHMENT DURING 1979

(Numbers in Thousands)

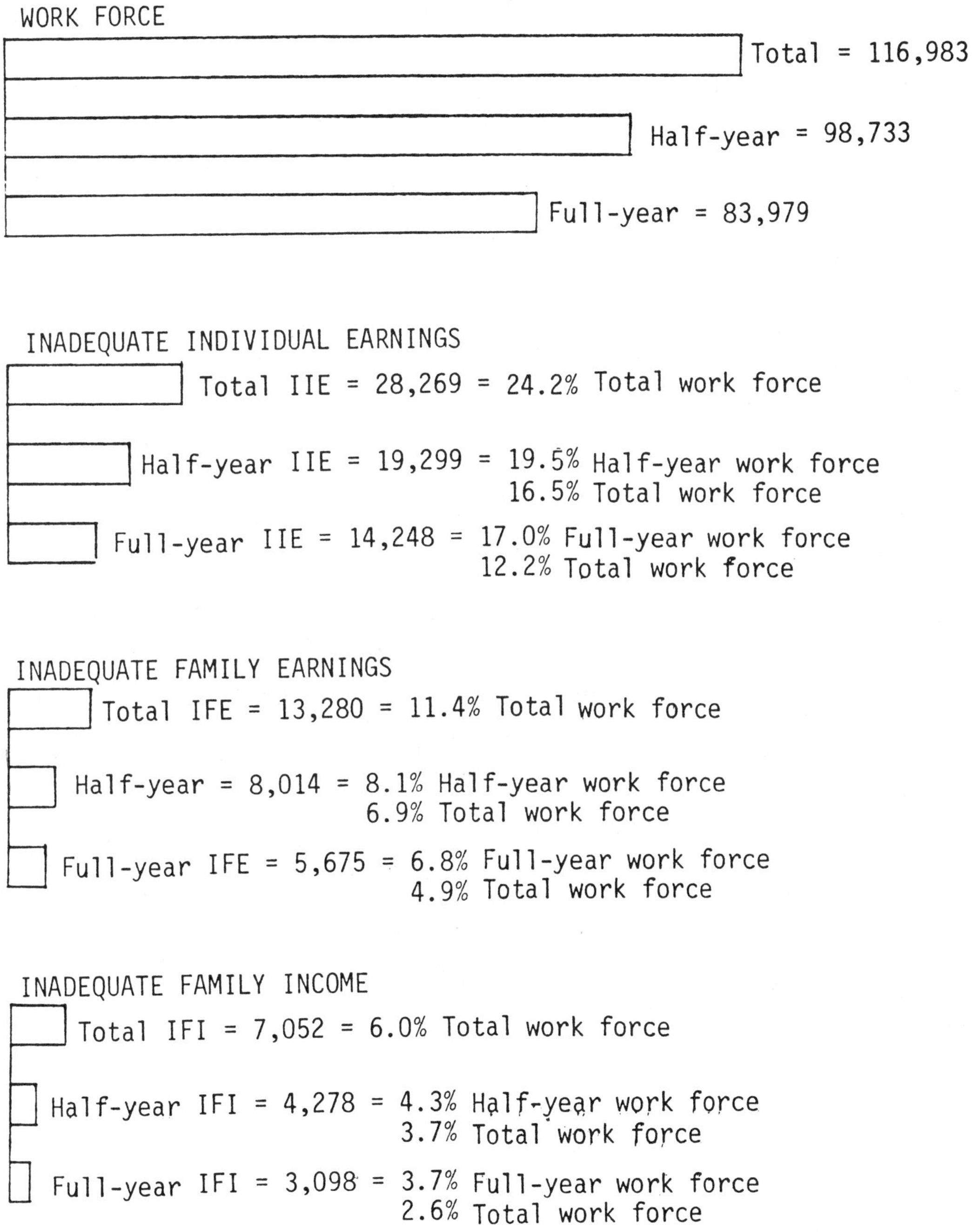

WORK FORCE
- Total = 116,983
- Half-year = 98,733
- Full-year = 83,979

INADEQUATE INDIVIDUAL EARNINGS
- Total IIE = 28,269 = 24.2% Total work force
- Half-year IIE = 19,299 = 19.5% Half-year work force
  16.5% Total work force
- Full-year IIE = 14,248 = 17.0% Full-year work force
  12.2% Total work force

INADEQUATE FAMILY EARNINGS
- Total IFE = 13,280 = 11.4% Total work force
- Half-year = 8,014 = 8.1% Half-year work force
  6.9% Total work force
- Full-year IFE = 5,675 = 6.8% Full-year work force
  4.9% Total work force

INADEQUATE FAMILY INCOME
- Total IFI = 7,052 = 6.0% Total work force
- Half-year IFI = 4,278 = 4.3% Half-year work force
  3.7% Total work force
- Full-year IFI = 3,098 = 3.7% Full-year work force
  2.6% Total work force

just half of families, a movie for the children once a month, no cigarettes, and a six pack of beer three times a month for the family, would have cost an estimated $12,585 in Autumn 1979. 3/ If one family member worked full-time at the minimum wage in 1979, his or her $5,900 in earnings would have provided for less than half of this Bureau of Labor Statistics-defined lower living standard. If a second family member also worked half-time all year, the combined family earnings would be less than three-fourths of the standard, and even full-time, full-year minimum wage earnings by two family members would fall slightly short. Put another way, a family of four with one fully employed full-time worker, and one fully-employed part-time worker, both earning 150 percent of the minimum wage, would just exceed the BLS lower living standard, and a few weeks of unemployment would drop the family below this modest level of sufficiency. A family with income or earnings 150 percent above the poverty level would also fall short. After cutting the three six packs of beer a month and the once-a-month movie, there is little that could be labelled frivolous in the market basket which could be afforded by a family with workers earning 150 percent of the minimum wage or with earnings or income 150 percent above the poverty level. Such workers and families may not be living in absolute deprivation, but they certainly cannot be considered more than marginally self-sufficient.

The use of less severe earnings and income standards increases the hardship counts and related deficits (Chart 2.4). Calculating the IIE by comparing earnings to 125 percent, rather than 100 percent, of the minimum wage for all hours of availability, raises the IIE tally for all work force participants by 45 percent; while comparing family earnings and incomes to 125 percent rather than 100 percent of the poverty level raises the IFE by 30 percent and the IFI by nearly half. Under these "intermediate" hardship standards, the IIE, IFE, and IFI Deficits are two-thirds, one-half, and four-fifths above the severe hardship deficits (Table 2.1). There were 51.4 million work force participants in 1979 who earned less than $4.50 per hour of availability, the moderate hardship standard; while 21.6 million had family earnings less than 150 percent of the poverty level and 14.4 million had family incomes below this level. To provide all work force participants with 150 percent of the minimum wage for their hours of availability would have required $136.4 billion in additional earnings, representing 10.5 percent of the nation's total wages and salaries. To provide earnings and income 150 percent of the poverty level for all families with work force participants would have required $69.7 and $37.2 billion, respectively.

What Causes Hardship?

Labor Market Pathologies

The unemployment rate is our nation's most carefully scrutinized and widely quoted social indicator, to a large extent because of the presumed association between joblessness and suffering. Each week of forced idleness reduces annual earnings and increases the chances that, over the

Chart 2.4. HARDSHIP AMONG 1979 WORK FORCE PARTICIPANTS UNDER ALTERNATIVE ADEQUACY STANDARDS

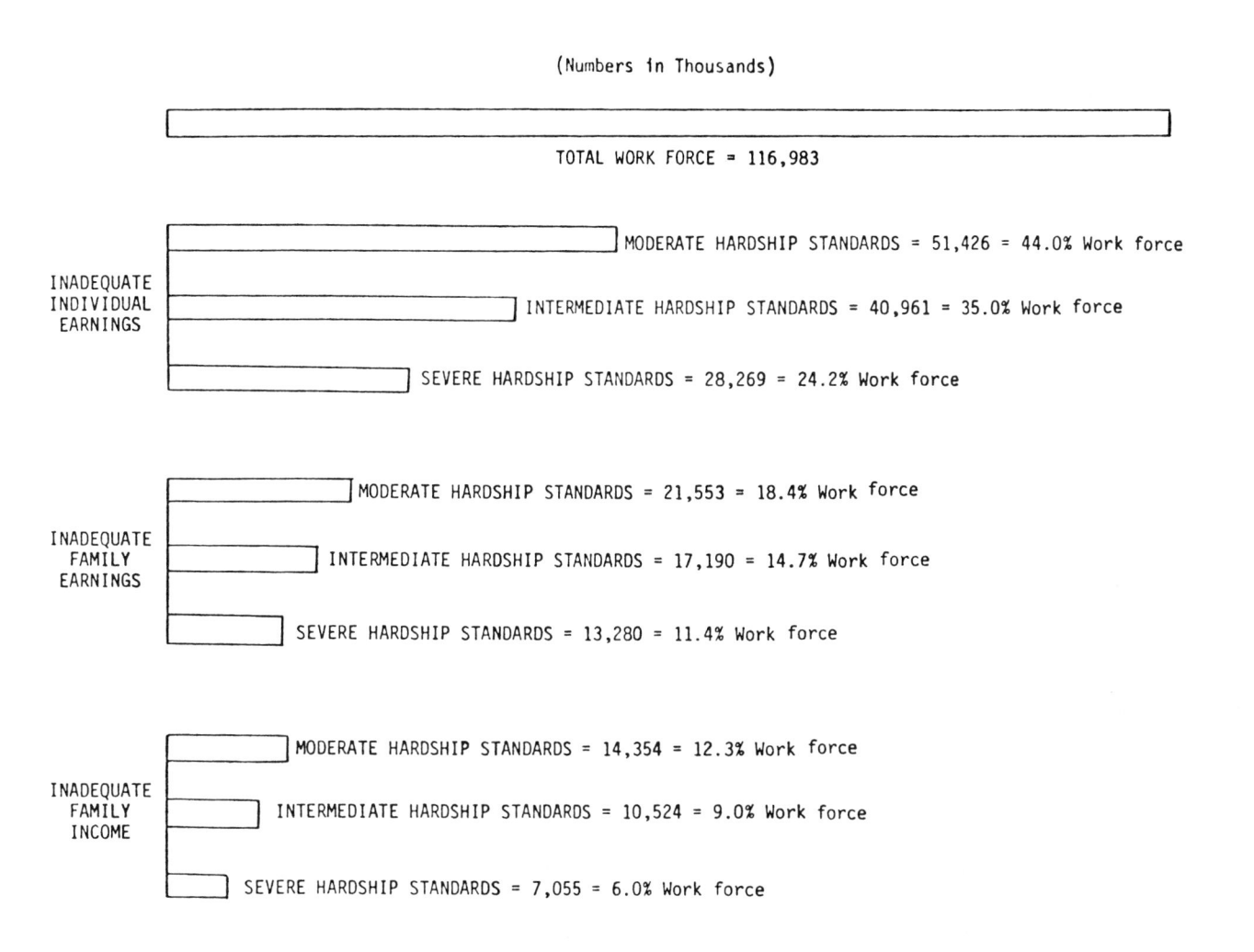

(Numbers in Thousands)

TOTAL WORK FORCE = 116,983

INADEQUATE INDIVIDUAL EARNINGS
- MODERATE HARDSHIP STANDARDS = 51,426 = 44.0% Work force
- INTERMEDIATE HARDSHIP STANDARDS = 40,961 = 35.0% Work force
- SEVERE HARDSHIP STANDARDS = 28,269 = 24.2% Work force

INADEQUATE FAMILY EARNINGS
- MODERATE HARDSHIP STANDARDS = 21,553 = 18.4% Work force
- INTERMEDIATE HARDSHIP STANDARDS = 17,190 = 14.7% Work force
- SEVERE HARDSHIP STANDARDS = 13,280 = 11.4% Work force

INADEQUATE FAMILY INCOME
- MODERATE HARDSHIP STANDARDS = 14,354 = 12.3% Work force
- INTERMEDIATE HARDSHIP STANDARDS = 10,524 = 9.0% Work force
- SEVERE HARDSHIP STANDARDS = 7,055 = 6.0% Work force

Severe Hardship Standard: IIE earnings standard 100 percent of minimum wage and IFE family earnings and IFI family income standard 100 percent of poverty

Intermediate Hardship Standard: IIE earnings standard 125 percent of minimum wage and IFE family earnings and IFI family income standard 125 percent of poverty

Moderate Hardship Standard: IIE earnings standard 150 percent of minimum wage and IFE family earnings and IFI family income standard 150 percent of poverty

Table 2.1. HARDSHIP COUNTS AND DEFICITS UNDER ALTERNATIVE HARDSHIP STANDARDS

	Severe Hardship Standards	Intermediate Hardship Standards	Moderate Hardship Standards
		Total Work Force	
Persons in Hardship (000)			
Inadequate Individual Earnings	28,269	40,961	51,426
Inadequate Family Earnings	13,280	17,190	21,553
Inadequate Family Income	7,055	10,524	14,354
Hardship Deficits (millions)			
Inadequate Individual Earnings Deficit	$51,998	$87,442	$136,402
Inadequate Family Earnings Deficit	31,656	48,556	69,668
Inadequate Family Income Deficit	12,824	23,015	37,173
		Half-Year Work Force	
Persons in Hardship (000)			
Inadequate Individual Earnings	19,299	29,232	28,130
Inadequate Family Earnings	8,014	11,128	14,699
Inadequate Family Income	4,278	6,804	9,776
Hardship Deficits (millions)			
Inadequate Individual Earnings Deficit	$46,403	$78,659	$123,804
Inadequate Family Earnings Deficit	17,891	30,053	46,195
Inadequate Family Income Deficit	8,064	15,391	26,227
		Full-Year Work Force	
Persons in Hardship (000)			
Inadequate Individual Earnings	14,248	22,047	29,442
Inadequate Family Earnings	5,675	8,088	10,981
Inadequate Family Income	3,098	5,075	7,383
Hardship Deficits (millions)			
Inadequate Individual Earnings Deficit	$38,446	$65,053	$102,809
Inadequate Family Earnings Deficit	13,306	22,665	35,456
Inadequate Family Income Deficit	6,308	12,077	20,808

course of the year, earnings will be inadequate (Chart 2.5). Almost all of the 1979 work force participants who were unemployed or discouraged for two-thirds or more of their weeks of participation had annual earnings below the minimum wage level for their yearly hours of availability. Yet among those unemployed less than a third of their weeks in the labor force, only a third had Inadequate Individual Earnings. Since this group with shorter duration unemployment represented three of every five work force participants who experienced unemployment in 1979, only half of all the unemployed were in the IIE. Moreover, among the unemployed with Inadequate Individual Earnings, only two in five resided in families with combined earnings below the poverty level, and only one in four resided in poor families after the receipt of transfers and other nonearned income:

	Experienced unemployment (000)	18,468
−	Unemployed with adequate individual earnings	−8,591
=	Unemployed in IIE	9,877
−	Unemployed with Inadequate Individual Earnings but adequate family earnings	−6,169
+	Unemployed with adequate individual earnings but Inadequate Family Earnings	+502
=	Unemployed in IFE	4,210
−	Unemployed in IFE lifted out of poverty by nontransfer income	−548
−	Unemployed in IFE lifted out of poverty by transfer income	−1,044
=	Unemployed in IFI	2,618

Thus, only half of the unemployed were in the IIE, less than a fourth in the IFE and only one in seven in the IFI. Conversely, over half of the unemployed resided in families with incomes above $15,000 annually, compared with just 6 percent of labor force participants included in the IFE count, and virtually none of those included in the IFI count (Chart 2.6). Without question, the IIE, the IFE, and particularly the IFI rates, are much better indicators of economic hardship than the unemployment rate.

Low hourly earnings and limited hours of employment, rather than unemployment, were the most frequent causes of hardship. Two-thirds of the 28.3 million work force participants with Inadequate Individual Earnings, and a similar proportion of the 13.3 million with Inadequate Family Earnings, suffered no weeks of unemployment during the year. There were 6.4 million low-paid workers who were employed full-time during their participation in the labor force but did not earn the minimum wage equiva-

Chart 2.5. SEVERE HARDSHIP INCIDENCE RATES AMONG INDIVIDUALS WITH DIFFERING PATTERNS OF WORK EXPERIENCE DURING 1979*

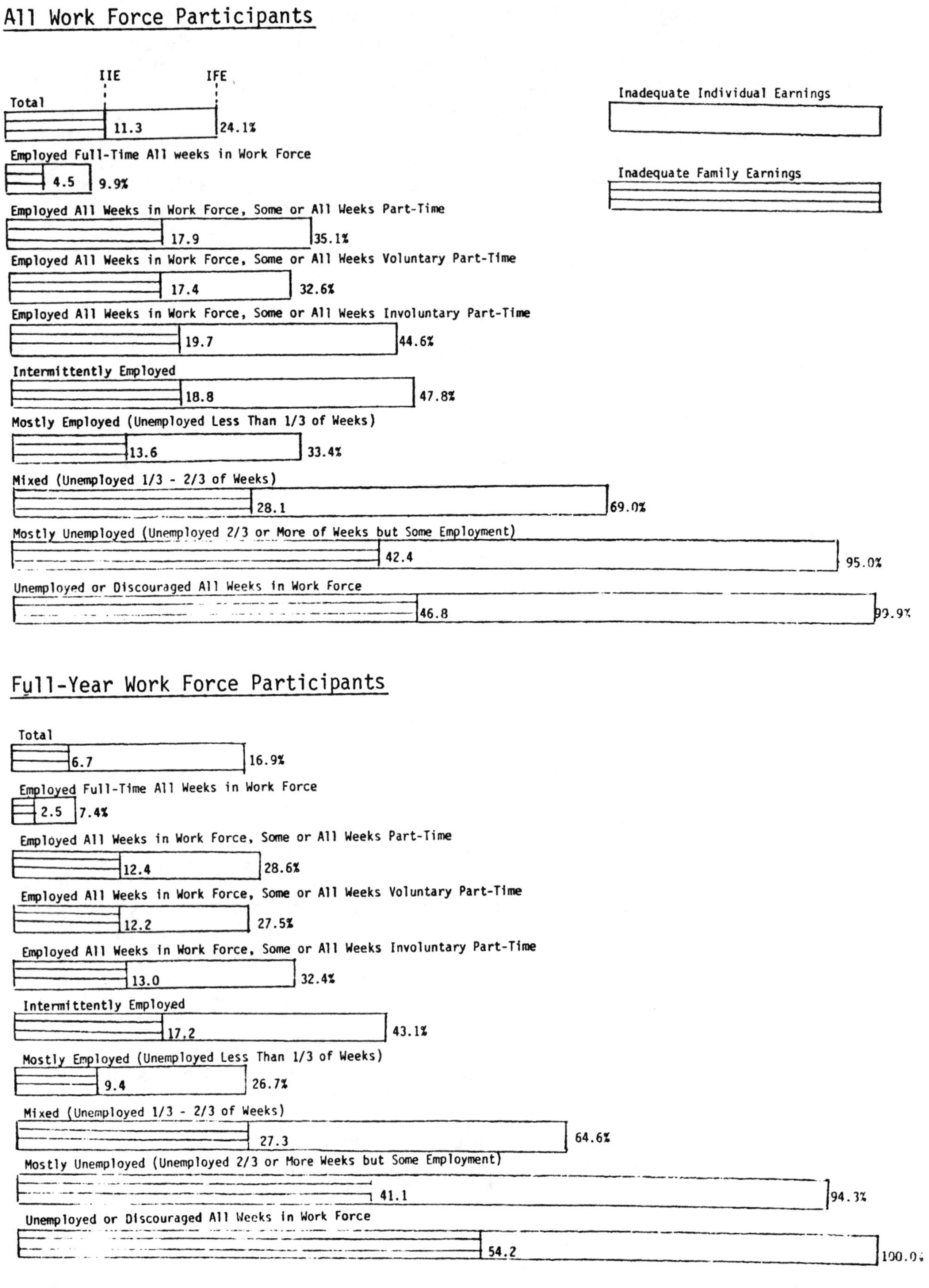

All Work Force Participants

Legend: IIE = Inadequate Individual Earnings; IFE = Inadequate Family Earnings

Category	IIE	IFE
Total	11.3	24.1%
Employed Full-Time All Weeks in Work Force	4.5	9.9%
Employed All Weeks in Work Force, Some or All Weeks Part-Time	17.9	35.1%
Employed All Weeks in Work Force, Some or All Weeks Voluntary Part-Time	17.4	32.6%
Employed All Weeks in Work Force, Some or All Weeks Involuntary Part-Time	19.7	44.6%
Intermittently Employed	18.8	47.8%
Mostly Employed (Unemployed Less Than 1/3 of Weeks)	13.6	33.4%
Mixed (Unemployed 1/3 - 2/3 of Weeks)	28.1	69.0%
Mostly Unemployed (Unemployed 2/3 or More of Weeks but Some Employment)	42.4	95.0%
Unemployed or Discouraged All Weeks in Work Force	46.8	99.9%

Full-Year Work Force Participants

Category	IIE	IFE
Total	6.7	16.9%
Employed Full-Time All Weeks in Work Force	2.5	7.4%
Employed All Weeks in Work Force, Some or All Weeks Part-Time	12.4	28.6%
Employed All Weeks in Work Force, Some or All Weeks Voluntary Part-Time	12.2	27.5%
Employed All Weeks in Work Force, Some or All Weeks Involuntary Part-Time	13.0	32.4%
Intermittently Employed	17.2	43.1%
Mostly Employed (Unemployed Less Than 1/3 of Weeks)	9.4	26.7%
Mixed (Unemployed 1/3 - 2/3 of Weeks)	27.3	64.6%
Mostly Unemployed (Unemployed 2/3 or More Weeks but Some Employment)	41.1	94.3%
Unemployed or Discouraged All Weeks in Work Force	54.2	100.0%

Chart 2.6. DISTRIBUTION OF TOTAL WORK FORCE, UNEMPLOYED AND WORK FORCE MEMBERS IN HARDSHIP BY FAMILY INCOME*

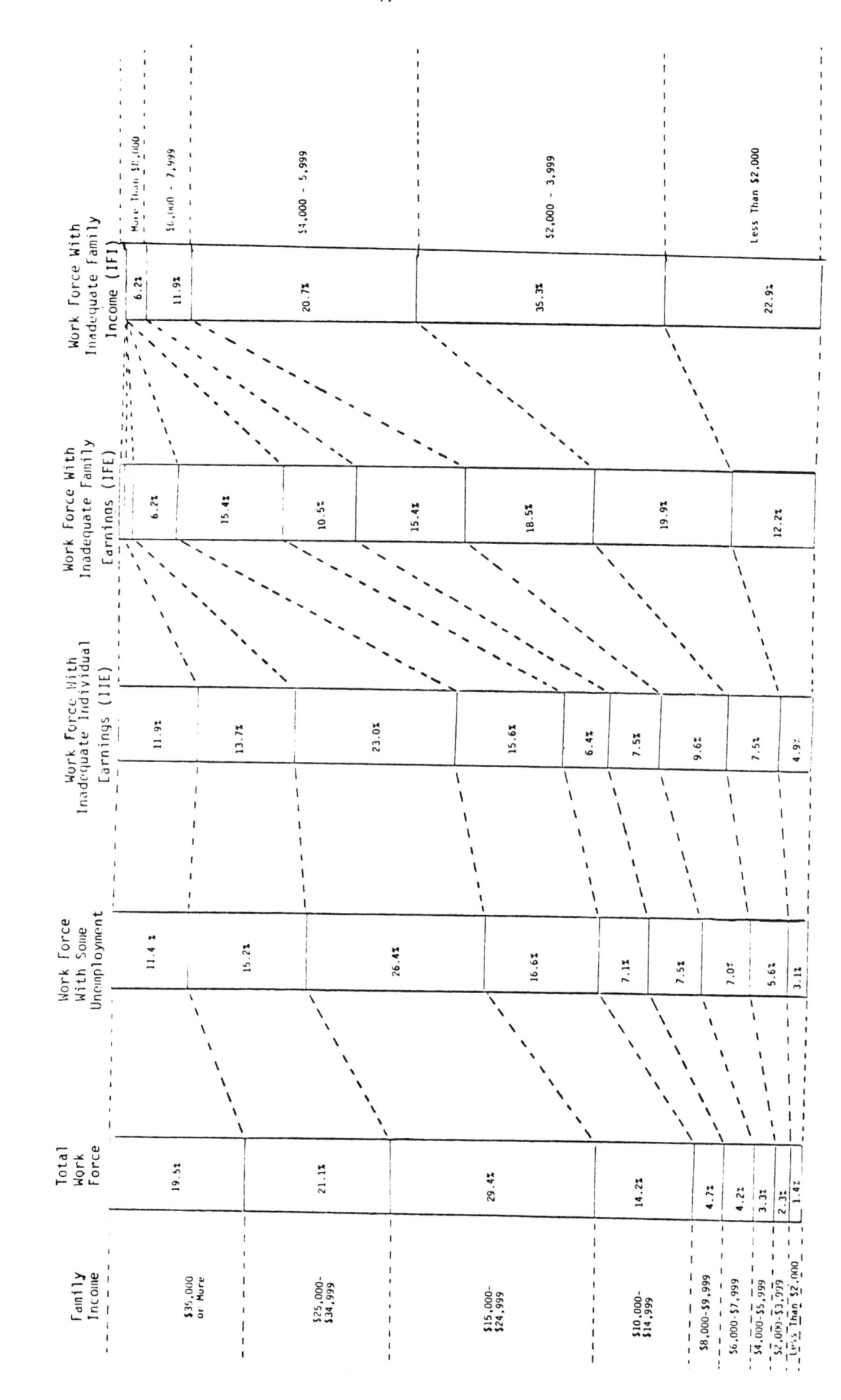

Family Income	Total Work Force	Work Force With Some Unemployment	Work Force With Inadequate Individual Earnings (IIE)	Work Force With Inadequate Family Earnings (IFE)	Work Force With Inadequate Family Income (IFI)
$35,000 or More	19.5%	11.4%	11.9%	6.2%	6.2% (More Than $8,000)
$25,000-$34,999	21.1%	15.2%	13.7%	15.4%	11.9% ($6,000 - 7,999)
$15,000-$24,999	29.4%	26.4%	23.0%	10.5%	20.7% ($4,000 - 5,999)
				15.4%	
$10,000-$14,999	14.2%	16.6%	15.6%	18.5%	35.3% ($2,000 - 3,999)
$8,000-$9,999	4.7%	7.1%	6.4%	19.9%	
$6,000-$7,999	4.2%	7.5%	7.5%		
$4,000-$5,999	3.3%	7.0%	9.6%	12.2%	22.9% (Less Than $2,000)
$2,000-$3,999	2.3%	5.6%	7.5%		
Less Than $2,000	1.4%	3.1%	4.9%		

lent for their hours of availability. Likewise, over a fifth of persons with Inadequate Family Earnings, and a fourth of those with Inadequate Family Incomes, had full-time jobs during all their weeks in the labor force. Thirty-five percent of part-time workers employed all weeks in the labor force did not earn the equivalent of the minimum wage for their hours of availability, and they accounted for over two-fifths of the IIE. Part-time workers also accounted for 46 percent of the IFE and 38 percent of the IFI.

	Work experience pattern distribution of persons in severe hardship counts for total work force			
	Work force	IIE	IFE	IFI
Employed full-time, all weeks	55.0%	22.7%	22.0%	24.8%
Employed part-time voluntarily some or all weeks	23.1	31.1	35.6	26.6
Employed part-time involuntarily some or all weeks	6.1	11.3	10.7	11.6
Unemployed one-third or fewer of weeks in work force	9.4	13.0	11.3	13.3
Unemployed one-third to two-thirds of weeks in work force	3.3	9.5	8.3	8.9
Unemployed over two-thirds of weeks in work force but with some employment	1.4	5.4	5.1	6.0
Not employed	1.7	7.0	7.0	8.9
Total	100.0	100.0	100.0	100.0

Another perspective is provided by the hardship deficit measures. The average hardship deficits for part-time workers were much lower than those for fully-employed, full-time workers:

	Average deficits total work force			Average deficits full-year work force		
	IIE	IFE	IFI	IIE	IFE	IFI
Not employed	$1,974	$4,176	$2,591	$5,960	$5,069	$3,253
Intermittently employed	2,157	2,314	1,747	2,720	2,411	1,956
Part-time involuntary	1,830	2,506	1,954	2,825	2,409	2,120
Part-time voluntary	1,060	2,159	1,553	1,648	1,940	1,670
Employed full-time	2,480	2,196	1,840	3,309	2,334	2,176
Total	$1,839	$2,384	$1,118	$2,698	$2,345	$2,036

In the aggregate, persons in the severe hardship IIE were $52.0 billion short of the minimum wage equivalent for their annual hours in the work force. Those who were employed full-time during their weeks in the work force accounted for 31 percent of this deficit, while those who were employed part-time some or all weeks and experienced no unemployment accounted for 29 percent. Thus, individuals unemployed some or all weeks accounted for only two-fifths of the IIE Deficit. The individuals in the IFE with full-time employment all weeks in the work force accounted for a fifth of the $31.7 billion IFE Deficit and workers employed some weeks part-time and experiencing no unemployment accounted for over two-fifths. In other words, the low earnings of part-time workers in hardship were a major factor in the economic hardship faced by their families.

	Share of severe hardship deficits for total work force by work experience pattern		
	IIE Deficit	IFE Deficit	IFI Deficit
Employed full-time all weeks	30.6%	20.3%	25.1%
Employed part-time voluntarily	17.9	32.3	22.7
Employed part-time involuntarily	11.2	11.2	12.4
Unemployed one-third or fewer of weeks in work force	10.5	8.9	10.9
Unemployed one-third to two-thirds of weeks in work force	11.4	7.9	8.5
Unemployed more than two-thirds of weeks but with some employment	10.9	7.1	7.7
Not employed	7.5	12.3	12.5
Total	100.0	100.0	100.0

The relative importance of unemployment, involuntary part-time work, and low wages received for full-time or voluntary part-time work, varied with the hardship and work force attachment standards. Part-time workers with no unemployment accounted for 31 percent of all work force participants with Inadequate Individual Earnings in 1979, but only 26 percent of the full-year IIE (Table 2.2). Conversely, full-time workers with no unemployment accounted for 23 percent of the total IIE but 29 percent of the full-year IIE. The explanation for this difference is that a lesser proportion of full-year participants were part-time workers (29 percent vs. 21 percent), while the IIE incidence among full-year part-time workers was less than among all part-time workers (29 percent vs. 35 percent).

Fully-employed, full-time workers with no unemployment represented a larger share of the hardship counts and deficits when the income and earnings standards were less stringent. They accounted for 23 percent of the 1979 severe hardship IIE for the total work force but 34 percent of the moderate hardship IIE; their shares of the severe and moderate hardship IFE counts were 22 and 28 percent, respectively. Conversely, the unemployed accounted for 35 percent of the severe hardship IIE for the total work force but only 26 percent of the moderate hardship IIE, while representing

Table 2.2. SHARE OF HARDSHIP BY WORK EXPERIENCE PATTERN*

	TOTAL	Employed Full-Time	Employed Part-Time	(Employed Part-Time Voluntarily)	(Employed Part-Time Involuntarily)	Inter-mittently Employed	(Mostly Employed)	(Mixed)	(Mostly Unemployed)	Not Employed
Inadequate Individual Earnings										
Severe Hardship Standard-										
Total Work Force	100.0	22.7	42.5	(31.2)	(11.4)	27.8	(13.0)	(9.5)	(5.3)	6.9
Half-Year Work Force	100.0	24.7	39.5	(29.4)	(10.1)	33.6	(15.2)	(11.3)	(7.0)	2.2
Full-Year Work Force	100.0	28.6	35.7	(26.2)	(9.5)	33.3	(13.4)	(11.9)	(8.0)	2.4
Intermediate Hardship Standard-										
Total Work Force	100.0	29.1	42.1	(32.1)	(10.0)	23.9	(12.6)	(7.5)	(3.8)	4.8
Moderate Hardship Standard-										
Total Work Force	100.0	34.0	40.4	(31.2)	(9.2)	21.7	(12.3)	(6.4)	(3.0)	3.8
IIE Deficit										
Severe Hardship Standard-										
Total Work Force	100.0	30.8	29.3	(17.9)	(11.3)	32.5	(10.4)	(11.4)	(10.7)	7.4
Half-Year Work Force	100.0	32.3	28.4	(17.6)	(10.8)	34.1	(10.7)	(11.8)	(11.7)	5.2
Full-Year Work Force	100.0	35.2	25.9	(16.0)	(10.0)	33.5	(9.3)	(11.8)	(12.4)	5.4
Intermediate Hardship Standard-										
Total Work Force	100.0	33.1	30.1	(19.0)	(11.1)	31.3	(12.0)	(10.8)	(9.6)	5.5
Moderate Hardship Standard-										
Total Work Force	100.0	36.5	30.0	(19.4)	(10.6)	29.2	(12.6)	(9.7)	(7.0)	2.9
Inadequate Family Earnings										
Severe Hardship Standard-										
Total Work Force	100.0	22.0	46.4	(35.7)	(10.7)	24.6	(11.3)	(8.3)	(5.1)	7.0
Half-Year Work Force	100.0	21.6	42.6	(32.5)	(10.1)	32.7	(14.2)	(11.0)	(7.5)	2.3
Full-Year Work Force	100.0	24.8	38.7	(29.1)	(9.6)	33.2	(11.9)	(12.6)	(9.7)	3.3
Intermediate Hardship Standard-										
Total Work Force	100.0	25.2	44.6	(34.1)	(10.4)	24.4	(18.0)	(7.9)	(4.4)	5.9
Moderate Hardship Standard-										
Total Work Force	100.0	28.4	42.5	(32.3)	(10.2)	24.0	(12.6)	(7.5)	(3.9)	5.1
IFE Deficit										
Severe Hardship Standard-										
Total Work Force	100.0	20.3	43.6	(32.3)	(11.3)	23.9	(8.9)	(7.9)	(7.1)	12.2
Half-Year Work Force	100.0	21.8	37.5	(27.3)	(10.2)	33.9	(11.6)	(10.8)	(11.5)	6.8
Full-Year Work Force	100.0	24.8	33.9	(24.1)	(9.9)	34.2	(9.9)	(12.0)	(12.3)	7.1
Intermediate Hardship Standard-										
Total Work Force	100.0	22.2	42.7	(31.5)	(11.2)	25.0	(10.2)	(8.3)	(6.5)	10.2
Moderate Hardship Standard-										
Total Work Force	100.0	24.4	41.6	(30.5)	(11.1)	25.4	(11.1)	(8.3)	(5.9)	8.7

32 percent of severe hardship IFE but only 29 percent of the moderate hardship IFE.

Alleviating Hardship By Solving Labor Market Problems

The relative importance of different labor force pathologies is suggested by the changes in the hardship counts and deficits which occur when earnings are augmented in various ways. Suppose, for instance, that all labor force participants experiencing unemployment or involuntary part-time employment were ascribed minimum wages for all hours of forced idleness. The combination of these augmented earnings with the wages and salaries of other family members would, in many cases, lift family earnings above the hardship threshhold. The Full Employment IFE--calculated just like the regular IFE but after augmenting the earnings of the unemployed and involuntary part-time workers--was a fourth below the regular IFE in 1979, as was the Full Employment IFE Deficit (Table 2.3).

If the unemployed and involuntary part-time workers in the IFE were ascribed the same wage as they averaged during their hours of employment-- or up to the earnings capacity they demonstrated in the labor market--the Capacity Employment IFE would have been just a sixth below the regular IFE and the Capacity Employment IFE Deficit a fifth below the regular IFE Deficit. Because the impact of augmentation was less when unemployed and involuntary part-time workers were ascribed their usual wage, rather than the minimum wage, for their hours of idleness, it is clear that many in the IFE experiencing forced idleness also received low wages when they worked.

Eliminating Inadequate Individual Earnings would not eliminate Inadequate Family Earnings. If all persons in both the IIE and IFE counts were ascribed the minimum wage equivalent for all hours of availability, and their then adequate individual earnings were added to those of other family members, this Adequate Employment IFE would have been 36 percent below the regular IFE in 1979, but would still have included 8.5 million persons. While the regular IFE Deficit would have been reduced by two-fifths, an Adequate Employment IFE Deficit of $18.8 billion would have remained.

If the annual earnings of the persons in the IFE were enhanced by 10 percent, whether through increased hours of employment or raised hourly wages, the Enhanced Earnings IFE would have been only a tenth below the regular IFE. Even if the unemployed and involuntary part-time workers were first provided employment for all hours of idleness, with wages at their usual hourly rate, and then the earnings of all persons in the IFE were enhanced by 10 percent, this Enhanced Capacity IFE would still have been 55 percent of the regular IFE, and 7.4 million work force participants would have remained in families with earnings below the poverty level.

The family earnings shortfalls of half-year and full-year, as opposed to total, work force participants were much more clearly the result of labor market problems rather than limited work force availability, as suggested by the greater impacts of earnings augmentation for half-year and full-year workers. For instance, if full-year participants with Inade-

Table 2.3. REDUCTIONS IN INADEQUATE FAMILY EARNINGS RESULTING FROM AUGMENTED INDIVIDUAL EARNINGS

	Severe Hardship Standards			Intermediate Hardship Standards			Moderate Hardship Standards		
	Total Work Force	Half-Year Work Force	Full-Year Work Force	Total Work Force	Half-Year Work Force	Full-Year Work Force	Total Work Force	Half-Year Work Force	Full-Year Work Force
Hardship									
IFE	13,280	8,014	5,675	17,190	11,128	8,088	21,553	14,699	10,981
Full Employment IFE[1]	10,078	5,434	3,667	12,802	7,647	5,393	15,660	9,991	7,318
Adequate Employment IFE[2]	8,513	3,959	2,408	10,006	5,110	3,235	11,275	6,079	4,018
Capacity Employment IFE[3]	11,093	6,193	4,278	14,610	9,022	6,397	18,480	12,232	9,014
Enhanced Earnings IFE[4]	11,998	7,000	4,935	15,422	9,728	7,010	19,078	12,663	9,323
Enhanced Capacity IFE[5]	7,379	3,122	1,882	8,623	4,054	2,550	9,602	4,827	3,316
Hardship Deficits									
IFE Deficit	31,656	17,891	13,306	48,556	30,053	22,665	69,668	46,195	35,456
Full Employment IFE Deficit[1]	22,115	10,957	8,142	33,203	18,447	14,111	46,871	28,572	22,682
Adequate Employment IFE Deficit[2]	18,769	7,261	4,766	26,570	11,628	7,990	34,926	16,574	11,886
Capacity Employment IFE Deficit[3]	25,451	13,503	10,231	39,600	23,505	16,213	57,747	37,559	29,908
Enhanced Earnings IFE Deficit[4]	29,231	16,597	12,854	44,605	27,671	21,640	63,820	42,306	33,590
Enhanced Capacity IFE Deficit[5]	16,690	5,631	3,578	23,373	8,972	5,955	30,471	12,769	8,750
Percent Reduction in Regular IFE									
Full Employment IFE[1]	-24	-32	-35	-26	-31	-32	-27	-32	-33
Adequate Employment IFE[2]	-36	-51	-58	-42	-54	-60	-48	-59	-63
Capacity Employment IFE[3]	-16	-23	-24	-15	-19	-21	-14	-17	-18
Enhanced Earnings IFE Deficit[4]	-10	-13	-13	-10	-12	-13	-11	-14	-15
Enhanced Capacity IFE[5]	-45	-61	-67	-50	-64	-69	-56	-67	-07
Percent Reduction in Regular IFE Deficit									
Full Employment IFE Deficit[1]	-30	-39	-39	-32	-39	-38	-33	-38	-36
Adequate Employment IFE Deficit[2]	-41	-59	-64	-45	-61	-65	-50	-64	-66
Capacity Employment IFE Deficit[3]	-20	-25	-23	-18	-22	-20	-17	-19	-16
Enhanced Earnings IFE Deficit[4]	-08	-07	-03	-08	-08	-05	-08	-08	-05
Enhanced Capacity IFE Deficit[5]	-47	-69	-73	-52	-70	-74	-56	-72	-75

[1] In calculating the Full Employment IFE and Deficit, earnings are augmented by providing all unemployed and involuntarily part-time employed persons in the IFE the minimum wage (or 125 and 150 percent of the minimum wage for intermediate and moderate hardship standards) for all hours of forced idleness.

[2] In calculating the Adequate Employment IFE and Deficit, earnings are augmented for all persons in the IFE with Inadequate Individual Earnings. Their earnings are raised to the individual adequacy standard, i.e., the minimum wage or its multiple times their hours of availability.

[3] In calculating the Capacity Employment IFE and Deficit, the unemployed and involuntary part-time workers in the IFE are provided their usual wage (when working) for all hours of forced idleness.

[4] In calculating the Enhanced Earnings IFE and Deficit, the earnings of each person in the IFE are augmented by 10 percent.

[5] In calculating the Enhanced Capacity IFE and Deficit, unemployed and involuntary part-time workers in the IFE are first provided their usual wage (when working) for all hours of forced idleness, then their capacity level earnings, as well as the earnings of all other persons in the IFE, are raised by 10 percent.

quate Family Earnings in 1979 were provided the minimum wage equivalent for all hours of availability, or their actual earnings if higher than this level, the regular full-year IFE would have been reduced by three-fifths. The Enhanced Capacity IFE for full-year participants was only a third of the regular IFE for full-year participants.

Full Employment augmentation had a greater effect on reducing moderate and intermediate hardship than severe hardship; while Capacity Employment augmentation had a lesser effect. Multiples of the minimum wage exceeded the usual earnings of the unemployed, so that when their earnings were augmented by providing 125 or 150 percent of the minimum for each hour of unemployment or involuntary part-time work, this represented a substantially greater increment than when usual earnings were ascribed for all idle hours. Adequate Employment augmentation had a greater effect in reducing moderate than severe hardship because persons with Inadequate Individual Earnings represented a larger share of the moderate hardship IFE than the severe hardship IFE (69 percent of persons in the severe hardship IFE for the total work force had Inadequate Individual Earnings compared to 83 percent of the persons in the moderate hardship IFE).

Breadwinners and Breadwinning Responsibilities

By definition, Inadequate Individual Earnings may result only from low hourly earnings, unemployment, involuntary part-time employment, or some combination. Inadequate Family Earnings often results from these individual labor market problems, but can be compounded by limited work force participation of family members as well as by large families. Among the 13.3 million total work force participants with Inadequate Family Earnings, and the 5.7 million in the full-year IFE, 4.2 million and 1.2 million, respectively, had _adequate_ individual earnings. On the other hand, _individual_ earnings problems were not always, or not even usually, associated with _family_ earnings problems. Among the 28.7 million total work force participants and 14.2 million full-year work force participants with Inadequate Individual Earnings in 1979, only 9.1 and 4.5 million, respectively, were in families with below-poverty earnings.

Overall, the IFE incidence was higher among unrelated individuals and workers who were members of two-person families than among those living in families with three to five members. The IFE incidence was also significant among families with six or more members:

	IFE rate for total work force by family size
One member	20.5%
Two members	12.0
Three members	8.0
Four-five members	7.8
Six or more members	13.9

However, controlling for the number of work force participants, hardship increased with family size. Reflecting the higher IIE rates among part-time and secondary earners, the work force participants from larger families with more than one earner were most likely to have Inadequate Individual Earnings (Table 2.4). Workers with Inadequate Individual Earnings were more likely to have Inadequate Family Earnings if their families were larger. The more family members to support, the greater were the chances that a person with adequate individual earnings would nevertheless have below-poverty family earnings.

Conversely, the likelihood of Inadequate Family Earnings was much lower when there were more breadwinners in the family and when these breadwinners had greater labor force attachment. Families with four to five members had the following probabilities of having annual earnings below the poverty level:

	Probability of below-poverty family earnings
Three or more full-year work force participants	1.6%
Three or more half-year work force participants	2.0
Three or more in work force during year	3.0
Two full-year work force participants	5.5
Two half-year work force participants	6.2
Two in work force during year	8.6
One full-year work force participant	12.3
One half-year work force participant	14.6
One in work force during year	20.5

Supplements to Family Earnings

The economic hardship which would have resulted from Inadequate Family Earnings was significantly mitigated by transfer payments and other nonearned income. Nearly half of all 1979 work force participants with _family earnings_ below the poverty level had at least minimally adequate _family incomes_. Nontransfer earnings supplements accounted for 45 percent of those rising out of poverty, while the addition of transfers accounted for the remainder. The IFE Deficit of $31.7 billion for 1979 was reduced to $24.0 billion by nontransfer income, and reduced further to $12.8 billion (or the IFI Deficit) by cash transfers. This $11.2 billion deficit reduction caused by transfers was _not_ the amount of transfers received by the families of workers in the IFE, since the benefits they received may have exceeded the IFE Deficit in many cases. Nevertheless, the deficit reduction provides an important indicator of the degree to which labor market-related hardship was alleviated by transfers and other income.

The "Earnings Supplementation Rate"--i.e., the probability that a worker with Inadequate Family Earnings will have adequate family income because of transfers and other nonearned income--was, understandably, much

Table 2.4. INCIDENCE OF HARDSHIP BY FAMILY SIZE AND NUMBER OF PARTICIPANTS IN TOTAL WORK FORCE*

	Percent with Inadequate Individual Earnings	Percent with Inadequate Individual Earnings who had Inadequate Family Earnings	Percent with adequate individual earnings who had Inadequate Family Earnings	Percent with Inadequate Family Earnings
One person in work force				
1 in family	20.5	76.8	7.8	23.6
2 in family	21.8	67.9	5.7	20.5
3 in family	21.3	83.1	10.8	28.5
4-5 in family	21.4	88.0	7.6	26.4
4-5 in family	14.6	87.4	7.8	20.5
6 or more in family	21.2	96.8	20.9	41.5
Two persons in work force				
2 in family	21.8	23.3	2.0	7.0
3 in family	19.2	18.9	1.4	5.0
3 in family	21.4	17.9	1.2	5.1
4-5 in family	23.5	26.7	2.3	8.6
6 or more in family	33.2	46.9	9.3	24.8
Three or more persons in work force	32.0	8.9	1.0	3.9
3 in family	27.3	6.0	0.5	2.1
4-5 in family	31.2	7.0	0.8	3.0
6 or more in family	37.7	14.0	2.1	7.4

lower when he or she had a more severe labor market problem or more mouths to feed, and, therefore, a greater deficit to make up by earnings supplements. The Earnings Supplementation Rate for the total work force was 46.9 percent, with a 21.3 percent reduction in the IFE due to nontransfer income (Chart 2.7). Among voluntary part-time workers--who had lower average IFE Deficits--the Earnings Supplementation Rate was 60.4 percent, compared to only 32.8 percent for persons in the IFE who had no employment during their weeks in the work force. Those in the IFE with adequate individual earnings or an individual earnings deficit of less than $250 had a 57.8 percent chance of rising out of poverty as a result of earnings supplements, compared to a 31.7 percent Earnings Supplementation Rate among IFE workers with individual earnings deficits of $4,000 or more. Families with more members were less likely to be lifted out of the IFE, reflecting their larger family earnings deficits. As the number of family earners increased, so did the likelihood of earnings supplementation, again because the extra earnings brought the families closer to the poverty threshold.

Because most cash transfers are income targeted and are reduced as earnings increase, the proportions of 1979 work force participants who were moved out of intermediate and moderate hardship by the receipt of transfers were lower than the proportion moved out of severe hardship, even though the numbers affected were nearly the same. The <u>percentage</u> reduction in the severe hardship IFI Net-of-Transfers Deficit which resulted from cash benefits exceeded the percentage reductions in either the intermediate and moderate IFI Net-of-Transfer Deficits, even though the <u>dollar</u> reductions were much smaller simply because there were more persons and hence more recipients in moderate and intermediate, compared to severe, hardship. Again, the deficit represented only the difference between income net of transfer and the poverty level; the transfers received by persons lifted out of hardship by their receipt may have exceeded this deficit reduction to the degree the cash benefits raised incomes above the poverty level. Since most of the persons in severe hardship who received transfers remained below the moderate hardship standards, most of the transfers received by the poor in the work force were included in the deficit reductions measured using moderate hardship standards:

	Severe hardship standards	Intermediate hardship standards	Moderate hardship standards
IFI Net-of-Transfers (000)	10,457	14,145	18,205
minus IFI	- 7,055	-10,524	-14,354
Transfer effect	- 3,402	- 3,621	- 3,851
Percentage transfer effect	-33%	-26%	-21%
IFI Net-of-Transfers Deficit (millions)	$24,006	$37,970	$55,982
minus IFI Deficit	-12,825	-23,015	-37,173
Transfer effect	-11,181	-14,945	-18,809
Percentage transfer effect	-47%	-39%	-34%

Chart 2.7. PERCENT OF PERSONS IN SEVERE HARDSHIP IFE BUT NOT IN IFI BECAUSE OF EARNINGS SUPPLEMENTS*

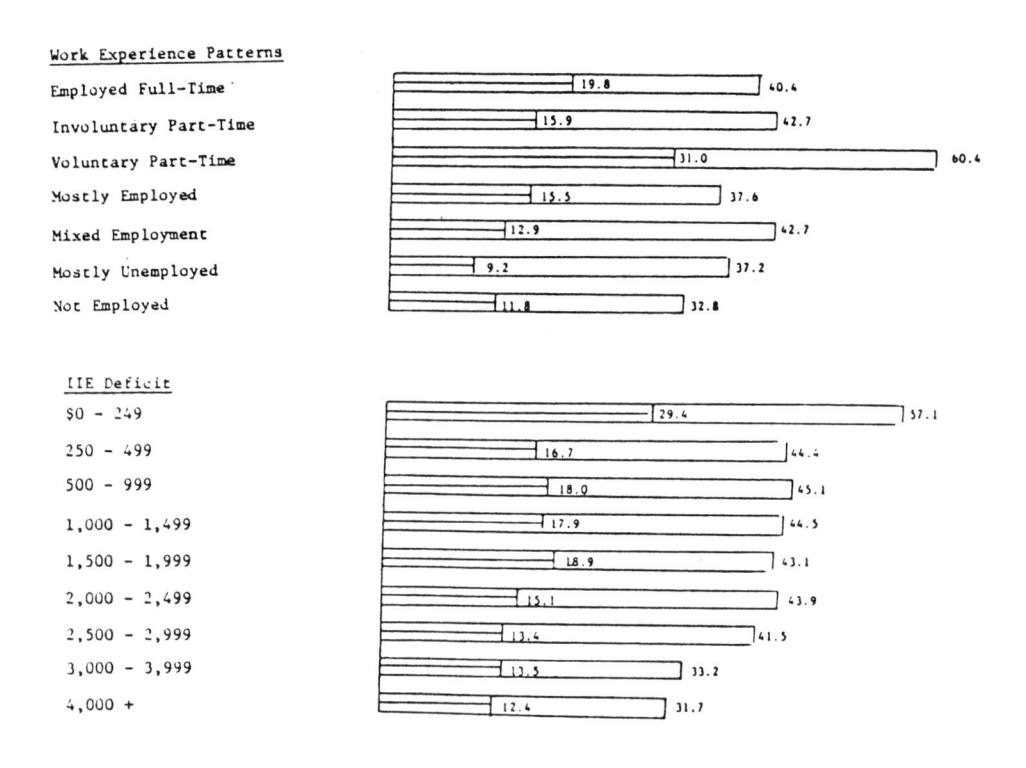

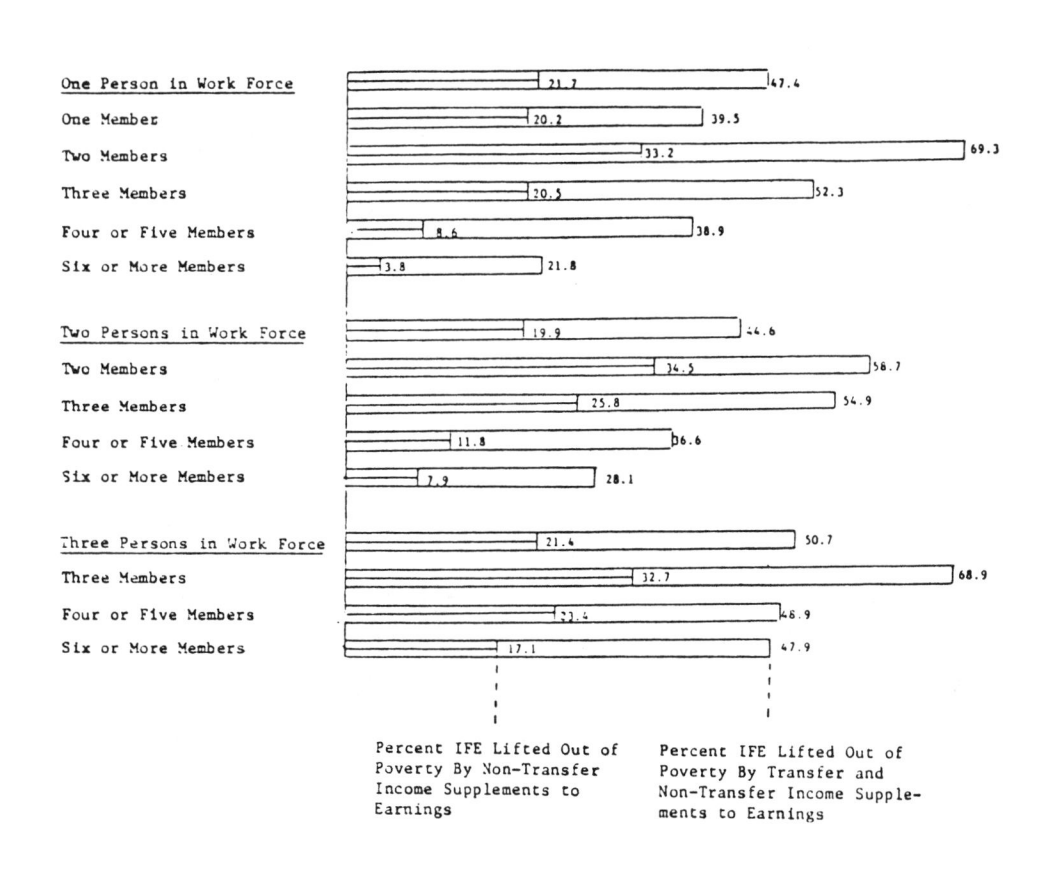

Work Experience Patterns

	Percent IFE Lifted Out of Poverty By Non-Transfer Income Supplements to Earnings	Percent IFE Lifted Out of Poverty By Transfer and Non-Transfer Income Supplements to Earnings
Employed Full-Time	19.8	40.4
Involuntary Part-Time	15.9	42.7
Voluntary Part-Time	31.0	60.4
Mostly Employed	15.5	37.6
Mixed Employment	12.9	42.7
Mostly Unemployed	9.2	37.2
Not Employed	11.8	32.8

IIE Deficit

$0 - 249	29.4	57.1
250 - 499	16.7	44.4
500 - 999	18.0	45.1
1,000 - 1,499	17.9	44.5
1,500 - 1,999	18.9	43.1
2,000 - 2,499	15.1	43.9
2,500 - 2,999	13.4	41.5
3,000 - 3,999	13.5	33.2
4,000 +	12.4	31.7

One Person in Work Force

One Member	21.7	47.4
One Member	20.2	39.5
Two Members	33.2	69.3
Three Members	20.5	52.3
Four or Five Members	8.6	38.9
Six or More Members	3.8	21.8

Two Persons in Work Force

	19.9	44.6
Two Members	34.5	58.7
Three Members	25.8	54.9
Four or Five Members	11.8	36.6
Six or More Members	7.9	28.1

Three Persons in Work Force

	21.4	50.7
Three Members	32.7	68.9
Four or Five Members	22.4	46.9
Six or More Members	17.1	47.9

The IFI considers only cash transfers, but in-kind aid such as subsidized housing and free school lunches may reduce cash needs, while food stamps may actually be used as currency in some communities. Adding the value of food stamps received by a family to its cash income in 1979 reduces the number of work force participants with Inadequate Family Income by half a million and the IFI Deficit from $12.8 to $10.9 billion. Valuing school lunches at the poverty budget expenditure for each meal, and subsidized housing at the estimated percentage reduction in housing expenditure which resulted from subsidies, and adding these amounts to cash and food stamp income for recipient families, reduces the IFI and its Deficit even more. Where there were 7.1 million persons in the severe hardship IFI considering only cash income, and 6.5 million counting the value of food stamps as income, the number drops to 6.2 million when subsidized housing and school lunches are counted as income, reducing the IFI Deficit to $10.4 billion. As in the case of cash transfers, the percentage reductions in hardship counts and deficits resulting from in-kind aid are greater for the severe hardship measures than the intermediate or moderate hardship measures, even though the absolute reductions in the deficits are far less:

	Severe hardship standards	Intermediate hardship standards	Moderate hardship standards
IFI Net of Cash Transfers (000)	10,457	14,145	18,205
minus IFI Including Food Stamps	- 6,522	-10,189	-14,103
Cash and food stamps transfer effect	3,935	3,956	4,102
Percentage cash and food stamps transfer effect	-38%	-28%	-23%
IFI Deficit Net of Cash Transfers (millions)	$24,006	$37,970	$55,982
minus IFI Deficit Including Food Stamps	-10,909	-20,599	-34,429
Cash and food stamps transfer effect	13,097	17,371	21,553
Percentage cash and food stamps transfer effect	-55%	-46%	-39%
IFI Net of Cash Transfers (000)	10,457	14,145	18,205
minus IFI Including Food Stamps, School Lunches and Housing	- 6,241	- 9,909	-13,858
Cash and in-kind transfer effect	4,216	4,236	4,347
Percentage cash and in-kind transfer effect	-40%	-30%	-24%
IFI Deficit Net of Cash Transfers (millions)	$24,006	$37,970	$55,982
minus IFI Deficit Including Food Stamps, School Lunches and Housing	-10,379	-19,646	-33,093
Cash and in-kind transfer effect	13,627	18,324	22,889
Percentage cash and in-kind transfer effect	-57%	-48%	-41%

The Burdens of Hardship

Hardship is concentrated among women, minorities, younger and older work force participants, persons with limited education, workers in blue collar and service jobs, residents of nonmetropolitan, particularly rural, areas as well as large central cities. As a general rule, the concentration of hardship among these subgroups and areas is even greater than the concentration of joblessness, so that the relative severity of the problems of the less advantaged is greater from the hardship perspective.

Sex and Family Status

Only 16.0 percent of females in the work force during 1979 experienced unemployment, very near the 15.4 percent incidence among males. Yet because of lower wages, one of every three female participants had earnings below the minimum wage equivalent for their hours of availability, compared to just one of every six males. One reason was that the males were more likely to be full-year participants (81 percent vs. 61 percent for females), and the IIE among full-year workers tends to be lower than among part-year workers. Yet 23 percent of the women in the work force full-year had earnings below the minimum wage equivalent compared to just 13 percent of male full-year participants:

	Male	Female	Female in proportion to male
Severe hardship--total work force			
Unemployment incidence	15.5%	16.1%	104%
IIE incidence	17.5	32.4	186
IFE incidence	9.7	13.4	137
IFI incidence	5.2	7.1	135
IIE Average Deficit	$2,219	$1,585	71
IFE Average Deficit	2,405	2,365	98
IFI Average Deficit	1,922	1,723	89
Severe hardship--full-year work force			
Unemployment incidence	13.7%	12.9%	94%
IIE incidence	13.0	23.2	178
IFE incidence	6.1	7.7	126
IFI incidence	3.6	3.8	106
IIE Average Deficit	$2,992	$2,441	82
IFE Average Deficit	2,520	2,130	85
IFI Average Deficit	2,238	1,750	78

Females with Inadequate Individual Earnings were less likely than males to live in families with Inadequate Family Earnings, while among individuals with Inadequate Family Earnings, females were more likely than males to escape poverty through the receipt of nonearned income:

	Total work force		Full-year work force	
	Males	Females	Males	Females
Proportion of persons with Inadequate Individual Earnings who were in families with Inadequate Family Earnings	37.1%	29.1%	37.9%	26.2%
Proportion of work force participants in families with Inadequate Family Earnings whose families exited from poverty as a result of nonearned income	46.6	47.2	41.7	50.2

As a result, the sex differentials in IFE and IFI incidence were less than the differential in IIE incidence. Females accounted for three-fifths of the IIE, but only half of the IFE and IFI:

	Female share	
	Total work force	Full-year work force
Work force	44.7%	37.9%
Unemployment	45.6	36.6
Persons with Inadequate Individual Earnings	59.8	52.2
Persons with Inadequate Family Earnings	52.5	43.5
Persons with Inadequate Family Income	52.3	39.7

The labor market problems of women are often downplayed because females are more likely than males to live in families with other earners. Nearly a fourth of all male participants in 1979 were family heads whose wives were either not present or not in the work force compared to only 12 percent of females in the work force who were family heads (Table 2.5). Yet comparing hardship among males and females with similar breadwinning status, women were clearly worse off, increasingly so if they were parents or primary earners:

Table 2.5. DISTRIBUTION OF MALES AND FEMALES IN THE WORK FORCE AND IN SEVERE HARDSHIP BY FAMILY RELATIONSHIP

	Share Work Force	Share Unemployment	Incidence Unemployment	Share IIE	Incidence IIE	Share IFE	Incidence IFE	Share IFI	Incidence IFI
Male	100.0%	100.0%	15.5%	100.0%	17.5%	100.0%	9.7%	100.0%	5.2%
Male Family Householder, No Wife in Work Force	23.9	15.2	9.8	14.0	9.7	34.2	13.8	28.8	6.2
Male Family Householder, Wife in Work Force	41.2	29.8	11.2	21.1	8.9	17.5	4.1	20.0	2.5
Male Other	20.6	35.3	26.4	49.9	42.3	22.9	10.8	19.2	4.8
Male Unrelated Individual	14.4	19.6	20.9	15.6	18.9	25.4	17.1	31.9	11.4
Female	100.0%	100.0%	16.1%	100.0%	32.4%	100.0%	13.4%	100.0%	7.1%
Female Family Householder	11.5	11.5	20.4	10.6	29.8	28.9	33.4	36.0	22.0
Wife	55.3	45.6	13.2	50.7	29.6	27.0	6.5	22.3	2.8
Female Other	18.4	25.1	21.9	27.2	47.7	16.7	12.0	13.1	5.0
Female Unrelated Individual	14.8	14.7	15.9	11.5	25.2	27.4	24.6	28.7	13.6

	Female divided by male unemployment incidence	Female divided by male IIE incidence	Female divided by male IFE incidence	Female divided by male IFI incidence
Family heads, no husbands or wives in work force	208	307	242	355
Male family heads with wives in work force vs. working wives	118	333	159	112
Other family members	83	113	111	104
Unrelated individuals	76	133	144	119

The hardship deficits suggest that the labor market problems of women have serious consequences for themselves and their families. Females account for half of the severe hardship deficits for the total work force despite the lower average deficits of women:

	Female deficit share	
	Total work force	Full-year work force
IIE Deficit	51.6	47.1
IFE Deficit	52.1	39.1
IFI Deficit	49.6	33.9

The Problems of Minorities

Minorities bear a disproportionate share of hardship burdens. Blacks, who represented 10 percent of the total work force in 1979, and 16 percent of those experiencing unemployment, accounted for 15 percent of the severe hardship IIE, 22 percent of the IFE, and 28 percent of the IFI (Table 2.6). The black shares of the severe hardship deficits were 15, 26, and 30 percent, respectively. While the black shares of moderate hardship were somewhat lower, the majority of black work force participants had individual earnings below the moderate hardship standard, or 150 percent of the minimum wage for their hours of availability.

The chances of experiencing unemployment during the year were 165 percent higher for blacks than whites; and the chances of having individual earnings below the minimum wage equivalent were 151 percent higher (Table 2.7). But only a third of the whites with Inadequate Individual Earnings were in families with Inadequate Family Earnings, compared to almost two-thirds of the blacks in the IIE. Thus, the IFE incidence among black

Table 2.6. WHITE, BLACK AND HISPANIC SHARES OF HARDSHIP AND HARDSHIP DEFICITS, 1979

	Work Force	Unemployed	Predominantly[1] Unemployed	Individuals With Inadequate Earnings	IIE Deficit	Individuals With Inadequate Family Earnings	IFE Deficit	Individuals With Inadequate Family Income	IFI Deficit
Whites									
Severe--Total	87.8%	82.1%	74.9%	83.4%	83.0%	76.1%	72.1%	69.5%	67.4%
Half-Year	88.1	83.5	76.8	83.6	83.3	76.2	72.9	71.0	70.9
Full-Year	88.1	82.5	76.2	82.9	83.2	75.1	72.6	70.4	71.1
Intermediate--Total	87.8	82.7	74.9	84.2	83.3	76.9	72.9	71.4	67.7
Moderate--Total	87.8	82.1	74.9	84.9	83.7	77.7	73.6	73.2	68.7
Blacks									
Severe--Total	9.9	15.6	22.7	14.5	14.9	21.5	25.7	27.5	29.7
Half-Year	9.7	14.5	21.3	14.4	14.6	21.7	25.2	16.4	26.6
Full-Year	9.8	15.3	21.6	15.0	14.8	22.8	25.4	27.0	26.5
Intermediate--Total	9.9	15.6	22.7	13.6	14.5	20.6	24.8	25.7	29.4
Moderate--Total	9.9	15.6	22.7	12.9	14.1	19.7	24.0	23.9	28.4
Hispanics									
Severe--Total	5.0	7.1	7.7	6.1	6.1	7.2	7.3	9.7	9.7
Half-Year	5.1	7.1	8.0	6.3	6.1	7.8	8.4	10.2	10.7
Full-Year	5.0	7.4	8.4	6.6	6.2	8.0	8.7	10.3	10.6
Intermediate--Total	5.0	7.1	7.7	6.4	6.4	7.6	7.8	10.0	10.3
Moderate--Total	5.0	7.1	7.7	6.3	6.6	8.0	8.0	10.0	10.6

[1] Individuals unemployed over one-third of their weeks in the work force.

Table 2.7. INCIDENCE AND SEVERITY OF LABOR MARKET PROBLEMS AND HARDSHIP AMONG WHITES, BLACKS AND HISPANICS

UNEMPLOYMENT AND HARDSHIP INDICATORS

	Unemployed	Predominantly Unemployed[1]	Inadequate Individual Earnings	Average IIE Deficit	Inadequate Family Earnings	Average IFE Deficit	Inadequate Family Income	Average IFI Deficit	Earnings Supplementation Rate ($\frac{IFE-IFI}{IFE}$)	Persons with Inadequate Individual and Family Earnings as Proportion of IIE
Whites										
Severe--Total	14.7%	5.4%	22.9%	$1,836	9.8%	$2,265	4.8%	$1,770	51.4%	32.1%
Half-Year	14.2	4.5	18.5	2,405	7.0	2,147	3.5	1,891	50.1	28.8
Full-Year	12.6	4.3	15.9	2,716	5.7	2,278	2.9	2,065	48.7	28.2
Intermediate--Total	14.7	5.4	33.5	2,116	12.8	2,684	7.3	2,079	43.1	30.4
Moderate--Total	14.7	5.4	42.3	2,620	16.2	3,070	10.2	2,438	37.2	31.4
Blacks										
Severe--Total	24.2	14.3	34.6	1,885	24.1	2,836	16.4	1,963	32.0	64.1
Half-Year	22.0	11.2	28.4	2,444	17.9	2,570	11.6	1,904	35.3	57.4
Full-Year	20.8	10.8	25.7	2,638	15.7	2,600	10.1	2,002	35.7	55.9
Intermediate--Total	24.2	14.3	47.9	2,279	29.9	2,294	22.8	2,507	23.9	59.4
Moderate--Total	24.2	14.3	56.2	2,884	35.9	3,928	29.1	3,066	19.1	60.3
Hispanics										
Severe--Total	22.0	9.7	28.5	1,860	16.0	2,447	11.5	1,856	28.4	50.7
Half-Year	21.1	8.2	24.4	2,322	12.4	2,418	8.7	1,972	29.7	46.4
Full-Year	19.6	8.2	22.0	2,570	10.8	2,541	7.5	2,135	30.0	45.0
Intermediate--Total	22.0	9.7	43.8	2,143	21.8	2,987	17.3	2,319	20.3	46.6
Moderate--Total	22.0	9.7	53.9	2,780	28.8	3,274	23.9	2,744	17.0	50.2

UNEMPLOYMENT AND HARDSHIP INDICATORS
FOR BLACKS AND HISPANICS
DIVIDED BY INDICATORS FOR WHITES

Blacks Divided by Whites										
Severe--Total	165%	265%	151%	103%	246%	125%	342%	111%	62%	200%
Half-Year	155	249	154	102	256	120	331	101	70	200
Full-Year	165	251	162	97	275	114	348	97	73	198
Intermediate--Total	165	265	140	108	234	126	312	121	55	195
Moderate--Total	165	265	133	110	222	128	285	126	51	192
Hispanics Divided by Whites										
Severe--Total	150	180	124	101	163	108	240	105	55	158
Half-Year	149	182	132	87	177	113	249	104	59	161
Full-Year	156	182	138	95	189	112	259	103	62	160
Intermediate--Total	150	180	131	101	170	108	237	112	47	153
Moderate--Total	150	180	127	106	178	107	234	114	46	160

[1] Individuals unemployed over one-third of their weeks in the work force.

work force participants was 246 percent the incidence among whites. Furthermore, half of the whites with Inadequate Family Earnings were lifted out of poverty by other family income, compared to less than a third of blacks. As a result, black workers were nearly three and a half times as likely as whites to have Inadequate Family Income.

Hispanics (self-identified according to origin and including both whites and blacks) were better off than blacks in 1979, but lagged far behind whites:

	Hispanic incidence divided by white incidence	Hispanic incidence divided by black incidence
Unemployment incidence	150%	91%
Likelihood predominantly unemployed	180	68
IIE incidence	124	82
IFE incidence	163	66
IFI incidence	240	70

While Hispanics with Inadequate Individual Earnings were less likely than blacks to have Inadequate Family Earnings (51 percent of Hispanics in the severe hardship IIE were also in the IFE compared to 64 percent of blacks), those with Inadequate Family Earnings were more likely to have Inadequate Family Income (the Hispanic IFI was 72 percent of the IFE compared to 68 percent for blacks) largely because they were less protected by transfers. Nonearned income raised 10 percent of the Hispanic IFE out of poverty, and cash transfers 19 percent, compared to Earnings Supplementation Rates of 8 percent and 24 percent, respectively, for blacks in the IFE.

Age and Hardship

The 1979 IIE incidence among work force participants age 65 and over was twice that among workers age 25 to 44 (Chart 2.8). Many older workers remained in the work force because of economic necessity, but those with low family earnings were likely to have other sources of income, particularly transfers, so that while their IFE rate was over five times that among 25- to 44-year-olds, their IFI rate was actually lower.

The IIE incidence among teenagers was three and a half times that among prime age workers. But the younger work force participants with Inadequate Individual Earnings were more likely than prime age workers in the IIE to reside in families with other earners and other income sources which lifted them out of hardship (Table 2.8). This was particularly true of students, who represented three-fifths of all teenage work force participants and a fifth of participants age 20 through 24. 4/ Where 35

Chart 2.8. SEVERE HARDSHIP INCIDENCE RATES BY AGE

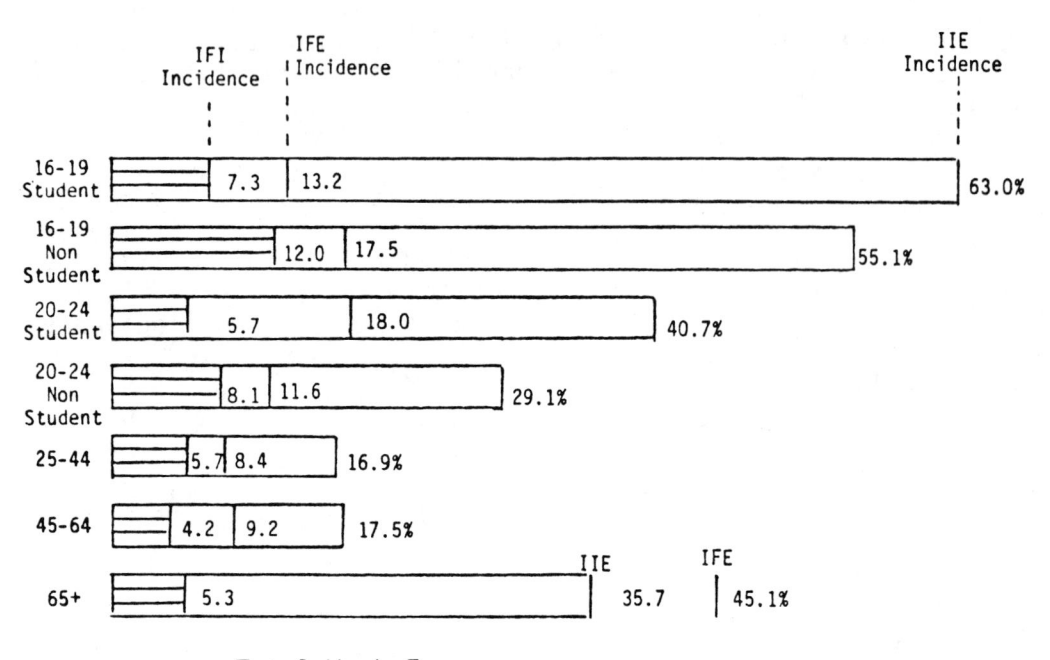

Total Work Force

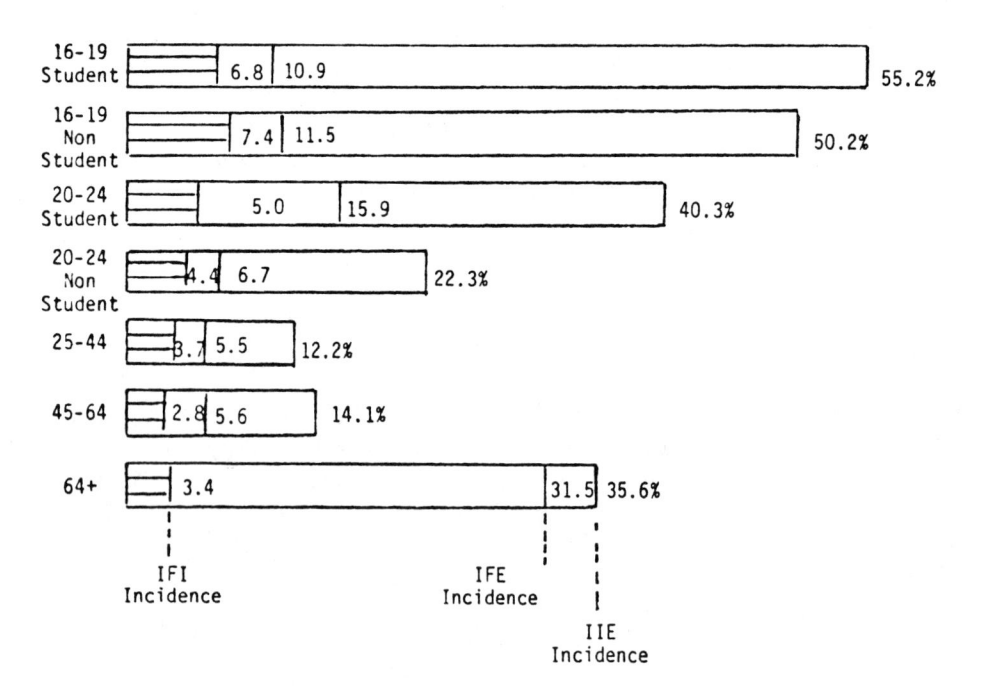

Age	IFI Incidence	IFE Incidence	IIE Incidence
16-19 Student	7.3	13.2	63.0%
16-19 Non Student	12.0	17.5	55.1%
20-24 Student	5.7	18.0	40.7%
20-24 Non Student	8.1	11.6	29.1%
25-44	5.7	8.4	16.9%
45-64	4.2	9.2	17.5%
65+	5.3	35.7 (IIE)	45.1% (IFE)

Full-Year Work Force

Age	IFI Incidence	IFE Incidence	IIE Incidence
16-19 Student	6.8	10.9	55.2%
16-19 Non Student	7.4	11.5	50.2%
20-24 Student	5.0	15.9	40.3%
20-24 Non Student	4.4	6.7	22.3%
25-44	3.7	5.5	12.2%
45-64	2.8	5.6	14.1%
64+	3.4	31.5	35.6%

Table 2.8. INCIDENCE OF SEVERE HARDSHIP BY AGE FOR FULL-YEAR AND TOTAL WORK FORCE PARTICIPANTS*

	IIE Rate	Percent IIE in IFE	Percent not IIE in IFE	IFE Rate	Earnings Supplementation Rate	Earnings Supplementation Rate - Nontransfers	Earnings Supplementation Rate - Transfers	IFI Incidence
Total								
16-19	59.4%	19.2%	9.2%	15.2%	37.9%	15.6%	22.3%	9.2%
16-19 Student	63.0	14.9	10.4	13.2	45.2	19.5	25.7	7.3
20-24	30.8	29.4	5.2	12.7	37.0	19.3	17.7	8.0
20-24 Student	40.7	26.9	11.8	18.0	57.7	42.1	15.6	7.6
25-44	16.9	34.7	3.0	8.4	32.1	12.4	19.7	5.7
45-64	17.5	37.1	3.3	9.2	54.8	28.1	36.7	4.2
65+	35.7	68.7	32.0	45.1	88.2	38.0	50.2	5.3
Full-Year								
16-19	55.2%	16.9%	3.4%	10.9%	37.7%	14.1%	33.6%	6.8%
16-19 Student	64.1	11.8	5.7	9.6	41.8	20.0	21.9	5.6
20-24	23.5	25.5	1.7	7.3	38.8	15.9	22.9	4.4
20-24 Student	40.3	29.2	7.0	15.9	68.7	51.3	17.4	5.0
25-44	12.2	35.2	1.3	5.5	32.2	10.4	21.8	3.7
45-64	14.1	33.4	1.0	5.6	49.5	24.7	24.8	2.8
65+	35.6	61.5	14.9	31.5	89.2	36.5	52.7	3.4

percent of all prime age (25-44) work force participants with Inadequate Individual Earnings also had Inadequate Family Earnings, only 15 percent of teenage students in the IIE, and 27 percent of 20-24 year-old students, resided in families with below-poverty earnings.

These hardship patterns reflect underlying age-related work participation and family patterns. Four-fifths of prime age work force participants in 1979 were in the labor force year-round and 55 percent were employed full-time, full-year (Table 2.9). In contrast, only 55 percent of workers age 65 and older were full-year participants, and less than one in seven worked full-year. Only a third of teenage work force participants in 1979 participated full-year and just 6 percent were employed full-time, full-year. Teenagers represented a quarter of the total work force but only a ninth of the full-time, full-year work force.

Younger and older persons in hardship were more likely than prime age individuals to have been in the work force less than full-year and to have experienced unemployment or part-time employment. For instance, although half of those with Inadequate Individual Earnings were under age 25 or over age 64, younger and older full-year participants accounted for only a fifth of the total IIE, while those working full-time, full-year accounted for only 4 percent.

Because younger and older work force participants had fewer hours of availability, their average hardship deficits were lower than those of prime age workers (Table 2.10). Moreover, the younger and older workers with Inadequate Family Earnings were more likely than prime age participants in the IFE to have had their hardship mitigated by nonearned and particularly transfer income, as suggested by their Earnings Supplementation Rates:

	Percent in IFE lifted out of poverty by all nonearned income	Percent in IFE lifted out of poverty by transfer income
16-19	37.9	22.3
20-24	37.0	17.7
25-44	32.1	19.7
45-64	54.8	26.7
65+	88.2	50.0

As a result, younger and older workers represented a smaller share of hardship deficits than of hardship counts. Prime age participants accounted for 31 percent of the IIE but 35 percent of the IIE Deficit, 33 percent of the IFE but 37 percent of the IFE Deficit, and 42 percent of the IFI but 48 percent of the IFI Deficit.

Table 2.9. AGE, WORK FORCE ATTACHMENT, WORK EXPERIENCE PATTERNS AND HARDSHIP, 1979*

Shares of All Work Force Participants

	Total	Full-Year Work Force Employed Full-Time	Less Than Full-Year Work Force Employed Full-Time During Weeks in Work Force	Full-Year Work Force Employed Part-Time Some or All Weeks in Work Force	Less Than Full-Year Work Force Employed Part-Time Some or All Weeks in Work Force	Full-Year Work Force Unemployed At Least One Week	Less Than Full-Year Work Force Unemployed At Least One Week
16-19 Nonstudent	4.5	.6	.5	.8	1.2	.6	.9
16-19 Student	5.4	--	.7	.8	2.7	.3	.8
20-24 Nonstudent	12.8	4.7	1.2	2.1	1.5	2.2	1.2
20-24 Student	2.2	.1	.5	.4	.8	.1	.3
25-44	44.5	24.3	3.0	6.3	4.3	4.5	2.1
45-64	27.0	16.5	1.9	3.7	2.4	1.8	.7
65+	3.7	.9	.4	1.0	1.2	.1	.1
Total	100.0	47.2	8.0	15.1	14.1	9.7	6.0

Shares of IIE for All Work Force Participants

	Total	Full-Year Work Force Employed Full-Time	Less Than Full-Year Work Force Employed Full-Time During Weeks in Work Force	Full-Year Work Force Employed Part-Time Some or All Weeks in Work Force	Less Than Full-Year Work Force Employed Part-Time Some or All Weeks in Work Force	Full-Year Work Force Unemployed At Least One Week	Less Than Full-Year Work Force Unemployed At Least One Week
16-19 Nonstudent	10.3	.6	.8	1.6	2.8	2.0	2.6
16-19 Student	14.1	.1	1.5	2.1	6.4	.9	3.0
20-24 Nonstudent	15.5	1.9	1.3	2.0	2.6	4.3	3.4
20-24 Student	3.7	.1	.6	.6	1.4	.3	.7
25-44	31.2	5.5	2.3	5.4	6.0	7.0	5.0
45-64	19.6	5.3	1.4	4.5	3.6	3.1	1.7
65+	5.4	.8	.5	1.8	1.7	.4	.3
Total	100.0	14.4	8.3	18.0	24.5	18.0	16.7

Shares of IFE for All Work Force Participants

	Total	Full-Year Work Force Employed Full-Time	Less Than Full-Year Work Force Employed Full-Time During Weeks in Work Force	Full-Year Work Force Employed Part-Time Some or All Weeks in Work Force	Less Than Full-Year Work Force Employed Part-Time Some or All Weeks in Work Force	Full-Year Work Force Unemployed At Least One Week	Less Than Full-Year Work Force Unemployed At Least One Week
16-19 Nonstudent	7.0	.2	.7	.7	2.2	1.3	1.9
16-19 Student	6.3	--	.9	.6	3.2	.3	1.3
20-24 Nonstudent	13.3	1.0	1.7	1.5	2.8	2.8	3.5
20-24 Student	3.6	--	.6	.7	1.5	.2	.6
25-44	33.0	4.8	3.6	4.5	6.5	7.7	6.0
45-64	22.1	3.8	2.7	4.3	6.3	2.9	2.0
65+	14.6	.8	1.2	4.0	7.5	.6	.5
Total	100.0	10.6	11.4	16.6	29.8	15.7	15.8

Shares of IFI for All Work Force Participants

	Total	Full-Year Work Force Employed Full-Time	Less Than Full-Year Work Force Employed Full-Time During Weeks in Work Force	Full-Year Work Force Employed Part-Time Some or All Weeks in Work Force	Less Than Full-Year Work Force Employed Part-Time Some or All Weeks in Work Force	Full-Year Work Force Unemployed At Least One Week	Less Than Full-Year Work Force Unemployed At Least One Week
16-19 Nonstudent	9.1	.3	1.1	.7	2.8	1.5	2.7
16-19 Student	6.5	--	.8	.7	3.2	.4	1.4
20-24 Nonstudent	17.3	1.2	2.6	2.0	3.6	3.4	4.5
20-24 Student	2.8	.1	.5	.3	1.2	.1	.6
25-44	42.2	6.8	4.6	5.8	7.6	9.2	8.1
45-64	18.8	4.4	1.9	3.5	4.2	2.7	2.0
65+	3.3	.4	.1	.7	1.6	.2	.2
Total	100.0	13.3	11.6	13.7	24.2	17.5	19.5

Table 2.10. SHARES AND SEVERITY OF SEVERE HARDSHIP IN 1979, BY AGE*

Total Work Force

	IIE Average Deficit	Share IIE	Share IIE Deficit	IFE Average Deficit	Share IFE	Share IFE Deficit	IFI Average Deficit	Share IFI	Share IFI Deficit
16-19	$1,202	24.4%	15.9%	$2,284	13.3%	12.8%	$1,562	15.6%	13.4%
16-19 Student	914	14.1	7.0	2,140	6.3	5.7	1,351	6.5	4.8
20-24	1,688	19.3	17.6	2,186	16.9	15.5	1,636	20.1	18.0
20-24 Student	1,011	3.8	2.1	1,966	3.6	2.9	1,211	2.8	1.9
25-44	2,049	31.2	34.7	2,685	33.0	37.2	2,063	42.2	47.8
45-64	2,456	19.6	26.2	2,244	22.1	20.8	1,814	18.8	18.7
65+	1,886	5.4	5.6	2,244	14.6	13.8	1,196	3.3	2.1

Full-Year Work Force

16-19	2,252	14.5	12.1	2,594	7.2	7.9	1,662	8.2	6.7
16-19 Student	1,979	6.1	4.4	2,246	2.3	2.2	1,231	2.4	1.5
20-24	2,422	18.4	16.5	2,100	14.3	12.8	1,751	16.0	13.7
20-24 Student	1,722	2.0	1.3	1,794	2.0	1.5	1,213	1.2	0.7
25-44	2,770	35.4	36.3	2,616	39.8	44.2	2,250	49.4	54.4
45-64	3,085	25.7	21.7	2,262	25.6	24.7	2,037	23.7	23.6
65+	2,645	3.0	4.3	1,865	1.3	1.0	1,245	2.6	1.6

The Payoffs of Education

Limited education increases the likelihood of inadequate earnings and income. Over a third of high school dropouts in the 1979 work force had Inadequate Individual Earnings, and one in eight had Inadequate Family Income--incidence rates that were, respectively, 3.7 and 5.5 times those of college graduates (Chart 2.9). In comparison, the incidence of unemployment among dropouts was only 2.6 times the incidence among college graduates. Thus, dropouts accounted for 21 percent of the work force and 29 percent of the unemployed, but 46 percent of the IIE count, and 43 percent of both the IFE and IFI counts (Table 2.11).

The less educated were far less likely to achieve stable, full-time employment during their weeks in the work force, and this, in part, explained the large differentials in hardship incidence rates. During 1979, only two of five dropouts were in the work force full-year and employed full-time, all weeks, compared to half of high school graduates with no further education and nearly two-thirds of college graduates (Table 2.12). Not only did 22 percent of dropouts experience some weeks of joblessness, but 9 percent experienced some weeks of involuntary part-time employment (or three times the incidence of involuntary part-time work among participants with some post-secondary education).

Yet whatever their pattern of work force experience, persons with less education were more likely to suffer individual and family hardship (Table 2.13). For instance, among the less than full-year participants with some weeks of unemployment, the IIE rate for dropouts was half again that of college graduates, the IFE rate was double, and the IFI rate was triple. The college educated with Inadequate Individual Earnings were less likely to reside in families with inadequate earnings, while those in families with inadequate earnings were more likely to have other sources of income lifting them out of poverty:

	Percent IIE in IFE	Percent IFE not in IFI
High school dropouts	44.6%	43.4%
High school graduates	28.7	46.9
1-3 years post-secondary education	30.4	50.2
College degree	32.4	56.2

Good Jobs, Bad Jobs

Not surprisingly, hardship was concentrated among workers in those occupations with low average wages and higher unemployment. The IFE rate among individuals employed primarily as laborers was three times the rate among those employed primarily in technical, professional or managerial jobs (Chart 2.10). Service workers were over four times more likely to have Inadequate Family Income than professional, technical, and managerial workers.

Chart 2.9. SEVERE HARDSHIP INCIDENCE RATES OF TOTAL WORK FORCE BY EDUCATIONAL ATTAINMENT AND STATUS

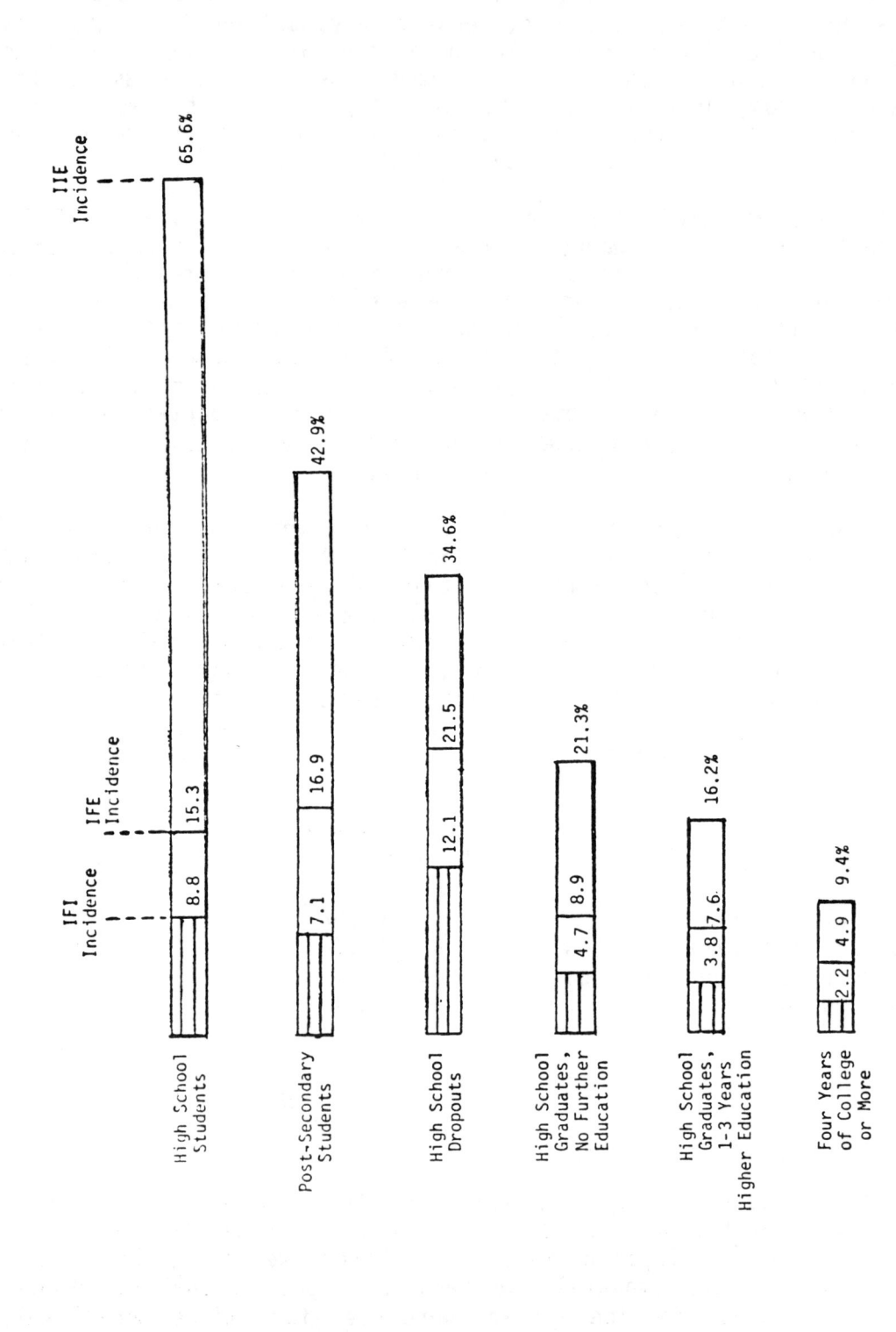

Category	IFI Incidence	IFE Incidence	IIE Incidence
High School Students	8.8	15.3	65.6%
Post-Secondary Students	7.1	16.9	42.9%
High School Dropouts	12.1	21.5	34.6%
High School Graduates, No Further Education	4.7	8.9	21.3%
High School Graduates, 1-3 Years Higher Education	3.8	7.6	16.2%
Four Years of College or More	2.2	4.9	9.4%

Table 2.11. DISTRIBUTION OF WORK FORCE, UNEMPLOYED AND HARDSHIP BY EDUCATIONAL STATUS

Total Work Force

	Work Force	Experienced Unemployment	IIE	IFE	IFI	IIE Deficit	IFE Deficit	IFI Deficit
High School Student	4.3%	6.0%	11.8%	5.9%	6.4%	6.2%	5.7%	5.1%
Post-Secondary Student	4.0	4.7	7.0	6.0	4.7	3.8	5.3	3.5
High School Dropout	20.9	28.8	30.2	39.9	42.7	34.1	42.6	44.8
High School Graduate, No Further Education	38.1	38.4	33.8	30.2	30.2	36.4	28.9	30.6
1-3 Years of Higher Education	15.8	13.0	10.7	10.7	10.0	11.4	10.5	10.2
4 Years or More of Higher Education	16.9	9.0	6.6	7.4	6.1	8.1	7.0	5.9
Total	100.0	100.0	100.0	100.0	100.0	100.0	100.0	100.0

Full-Year Work Force

	Work Force	Experienced Unemployment	IIE	IFE	IFI	IIE Deficit	IFE Deficit	IFI Deficit
High School Student	1.3%	2.5%	5.3%	2.4%	2.6%	4.1%	2.5%	1.8%
Post-Secondary Student	1.4	2.0	3.3	2.8	1.6	2.2	2.2	1.1
High School Dropout	20.2	31.1	33.8	43.5	45.8	35.8	46.3	47.2
High School Graduate, No Further Education	40.8	41.8	38.5	33.2	32.9	37.7	31.1	33.0
1-3 Years of Higher Education	17.1	13.8	11.7	10.6	10.5	11.7	10.7	10.3
4 Years or More of Higher Education	19.1	8.9	7.3	7.4	6.6	8.5	7.1	6.6
Total	100.0	100.0	100.0	100.0	100.0	100.0	100.0	100.0

Table 2.12. WORK EXPERIENCE PATTERN AND WORK FORCE ATTACHMENT BY EDUCATIONAL ATTAINMENT AND STATUS*

	High School Students	Post-Secondary Students	High School Dropouts	High School Graduates, No Further Education	High School Graduates with 1-3 years College	College Graduates
Employed full-time full-year	1.3	3.3	38.3	50.6	54.6	65.3
Employed full-time less than full-year	10.6	23.2	8.5	7.1	6.4	6.8
Employed part-time voluntarily some weeks, in work force full-year	14.8	16.1	11.5	11.6	12.3	8.9
Employed part-time voluntarily some weeks, in work force less than full-year	42.7	32.6	10.9	8.7	9.5	7.5
Employed part-time involuntarily some weeks, in work force full-year	.6	1.0	5.4	4.1	2.8	2.1
Employed part-time involuntarily some weeks, in work force less than full-year	8.3	5.0	3.8	2.1	1.5	1.0
Unemployed some weeks, in work force full-year	5.6	4.9	14.3	10.6	8.5	5.1
Unemployed some weeks, in work force less than full-year	16.1	14.0	7.3	5.2	4.4	3.4
Total	100.0	100.0	100.0	100.0	100.0	100.0

Table 2.13. SEVERE HARDSHIP INCIDENCE BY EDUCATIONAL STATUS AND WORK FORCE EXPERIENCE PATTERN*

	IIE Incidence						IFE Incidence						IFI Incidence					
	High School Students	Post-Secondary Students	High School Dropouts	High School Graduates	One to Three Years Higher Education	College Graduate	High School Students	Post-Secondary Students	High School Dropouts	High School Graduates	One to Three Years Higher Education	College Graduate	High School Students	Post-Secondary Students	High School Dropouts	High School Graduates	One to Three Years Higher Education	College Graduate
Total	65.6	40.8	34.6	21.3	16.2	9.4	15.3	13.4	21.5	8.9	7.6	4.9	8.8	4.3	12.1	4.7	3.8	2.2
Employed full-time, full-year	51.5	15.3	14.8	7.4	5.3	3.1	15.4	3.4	6.5	2.2	1.6	1.0	2.7	2.4	4.4	1.4	1.0	0.6
Employed full-time, less than full-year	60.1	30.2	30.6	21.9	10.2	9.8	16.2	11.6	22.6	15.1	15.3	8.0	9.4	5.4	14.9	8.5	6.5	4.5
Employed part-time, some weeks; in work force full-year	61.6	40.2	37.1	25.8	20.6	16.1	9.7	12.7	22.6	9.8	8.0	7.7	6.3	3.5	9.7	4.5	3.8	2.9
Employed part-time, some weeks; in work force less than full-year	59.9	42.0	46.6	38.7	33.4	24.1	14.9	19.7	40.4	21.3	20.4	17.7	8.1	8.1	18.2	8.8	9.0	5.7
Unemployed some weeks; in work force full-year	84.4	60.3	53.1	41.9	35.4	30.1	18.8	22.4	26.1	14.9	13.8	12.6	10.9	8.7	17.1	8.3	7.6	6.3
Unemployed some weeks; in work force less than half-year	85.3	70.6	76.9	63.8	52.0	41.2	20.0	24.9	45.5	25.8	25.9	22.5	12.2	2.5	33.4	17.5	14.5	10.2

Chart 2.10. SEVERE HARDSHIP INCIDENCE RATES IN 1979 BY OCCUPATION OF LONGEST JOB

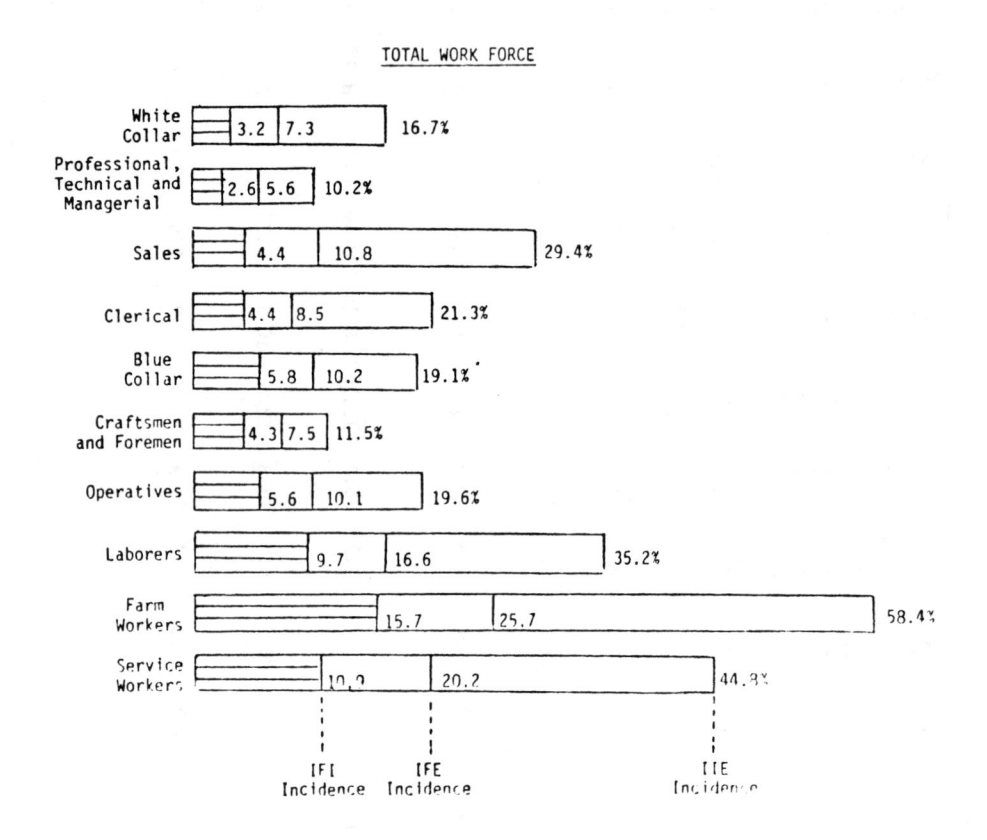

TOTAL WORK FORCE

Occupation	IFI Incidence	IFE Incidence	IIE Incidence
White Collar	3.2	7.3	16.7%
Professional, Technical and Managerial	2.6	5.6	10.2%
Sales	4.4	10.8	29.4%
Clerical	4.4	8.5	21.3%
Blue Collar	5.8	10.2	19.1%
Craftsmen and Foremen	4.3	7.5	11.5%
Operatives	5.6	10.1	19.6%
Laborers	9.7	16.6	35.2%
Farm Workers	15.7	25.7	58.4%
Service Workers	10.2	20.2	44.8%

FULL-YEAR WORK FORCE

Occupation	IFI Incidence	IFE Incidence	IIE Incidence
White Collar	1.8	3.9	11.5%
Professional, Technical and Managerial	1.6	3.0	7.5%
Sales	2.7	7.0	20.8%
Clerical	1.7	4.4	15.0%
Blue Collar	3.9	6.4	14.4%
Craftsmen and Foremen	3.2	4.9	10.5%
Operatives	3.5	6.3	15.1%
Laborers	7.6	11.9	27.4%
Farm Workers	14.4	23.3	57.4%
Service Workers	7.8	14.7	35.9%

	IIE incidence	Percent IIE in IFE	IFE incidence	Earnings Supplementation Rate	IFI incidence
White collar	16.7%	27.0%	7.3%	55.8%	3.2%
Blue collar	19.1	34.3	10.2	43.1	5.8
Service	44.8	31.8	20.2	46.1	10.9

As a result of these disparate hardship rates, white collar workers accounted for half of the work force but only a fourth of the severe hardship IFI and IFI Deficit, and a third of the IFE and IFE Deficit. Conversely, service workers represented a seventh of the work force but a fourth of the IFE, IFI and associated deficits (Table 2.14).

Major differences in the work experience patterns by occupation were reflected in the hardship patterns (Table 2.15). Less than three-fifths of laborers and service workers were full-year work force participants during 1979 compared to over four-fifths of professional, technical and managerial workers. Likewise, less than half of laborers and service workers with Inadequate Individual Earnings were full-year work force participants compared to three-fifths of professional, technical, and managerial workers in the IIE. Blue collar workers in the IFE and IIE were more likely than other workers to have experienced some unemployment during the previous year. Over half of service workers in the IIE and IFE were part-timers employed all weeks in the work force.

The Geography of Hardship

Hardship was concentrated in central cities and nonmetropolitan areas. Central city workers, who represented 28 percent of the work force, accounted for a similar proportion of the IIE and IIE Deficit, but 32 percent of the IFE and 35 percent of the IFE Deficit, as well as 35 percent of the IFI and 37 percent of the IFI Deficit (Table 2.16). The suburban areas surrounding these central cities accounted for 41 percent of the labor force but only 35 percent of the unemployed, 34 percent of the IIE, 31 percent of the IFE and 27 percent of the IFI. Suburban work force participants with Inadequate Individual Earnings were much less likely than their central city counterparts to have Inadequate Family Earnings (26 percent vs. 39 percent). In addition, 52 percent of the suburbanites in the IFE were lifted out of poverty by nonearned income compared to only 42 percent of central city residents with Inadequate Family Earnings (Table 2.17).

Nonmetropolitan areas accounted for 31 percent of the labor force but 39 percent of the IIE, 38 percent of the IFE, and 37 percent of the IFI. While the incidence of unemployment was roughly the same as in metropolitan areas, the rates of family earnings and income inadequacy were two-fifths higher. Hardship was particularly acute in farm areas. Over two-fifths of workers residing in farm areas had Inadequate Individual Earnings, while the IFE incidence was half again that of metropolitan areas.

Table 2.14. DISTRIBUTION OF TOTAL WORK FORCE, UNEMPLOYED AND HARDSHIP COUNTS AND DEFICITS, BY OCCUPATION

	Work force	Unemployed	Predominantly unemployed	IIE	IIE Deficit	IFE	IFE Deficit	IFI	IFI Deficit
White collar	49.3%	29.5%	22.9%	34.2%	33.6%	32.0%	29.6%	26.6%	25.3%
Professional, technical and managerial	25.0	11.3	7.6	10.5	14.6	12.3	12.2	10.8	11.8
Sales	6.1	4.2	3.8	7.4	6.1	5.9	5.3	4.5	3.9
Clerical	18.3	14.1	11.6	16.2	12.9	13.8	12.1	11.4	9.6
Blue collar	31.8	42.4	34.1	25.2	25.0	28.7	27.3	30.8	29.9
Craftsmen and foremen	12.3	13.5	10.2	5.9	7.1	8.1	7.5	8.9	8.8
Operatives	14.2	19.8	14.6	11.6	10.9	12.8	11.8	13.4	12.4
Laborers	5.3	9.2	9.4	7.7	7.0	7.8	8.0	8.5	8.7
Farm workers	2.8	1.9	2.3	6.7	11.8	6.3	6.4	7.3	8.1
Service workers	14.5	15.4	14.2	27.0	22.2	26.0	24.6	26.4	24.1
No work	4.4	12.7	28.8	13.6	19.2	13.3	18.5	16.2	20.7
Total	100.0	100.0	100.0	100.0	100.0	100.0	100.0	100.0	100.0

Table 2.15. WORK EXPERIENCE PATTERN FOR TOTAL WORK FORCE BY OCCUPATION OF LONGEST JOB

	Percent in Work Force Full-Year	Total	Employed Full-Time	Employed Part-Time Voluntarily	Employed Part-Time Involuntarily	Mostly Employed	Mixed	Mostly Unemployed
Work Force	75.7	100.0	63.8	23.0	3.8	6.4	2.1	0.8
White Collar	82.0	100.0	73.1	16.9	2.9	5.1	1.4	0.5
Professional/Technical/Managerial	68.0	100.0	45.5	37.6	6.0	6.9	2.6	1.3
Sales	69.7	100.0	57.3	26.4	4.2	8.1	3.0	1.1
Clerical	76.2	100.0	53.6	17.1	8.3	14.1	5.0	1.8
Blue Collar	83.6	100.0	61.8	14.1	7.0	12.0	3.9	1.3
Craft and Kindred	75.5	100.0	52.8	16.3	9.1	15.3	4.8	1.7
Operatives	60.6	100.0	37.0	26.5	9.2	16.0	8.0	3.3
Laborers	70.8	100.0	44.4	30.2	14.6	5.4	3.3	2.0
Farm Workers	56.2	100.0	37.5	37.4	8.5	10.5	4.1	2.1
IIE	52.4	100.0	26.0	38.0	10.0	12.5	8.9	4.7
White Collar	60.7	100.0	37.7	31.8	8.8	10.5	6.8	4.4
Professional/Technical/Managerial	48.1	100.0	18.3	47.8	11.0	11.4	7.1	4.4
Sales	48.9	100.0	21.8	37.5	10.3	14.3	11.2	4.9
Clerical	57.6	100.0	22.7	22.1	12.5	17.9	15.8	9.0
Blue Collar	69.7	100.0	26.9	18.5	10.7	17.1	16.7	10.1
Craft and Kindred	58.3	100.0	24.4	19.1	13.5	18.8	15.7	8.6
Operatives	47.1	100.0	16.9	29.5	12.3	17.1	15.4	8.7
Laborers	69.7	100.0	39.3	30.9	14.8	6.3	5.2	3.4
Farm Workers	45.0	100.0	20.4	39.1	14.1	13.9	7.8	4.6
IFE	40.8	100.0	24.9	45.2	7.8	11.0	6.6	4.4
White Collar	44.8	100.0	32.1	43.8	6.4	10.6	4.1	3.1
Professional/Technical/Managerial	43.9	100.0	19.1	51.2	9.9	8.9	6.5	4.4
Sales	36.0	100.0	21.0	43.8	8.3	12.3	8.9	5.7
Clerical	48.1	100.0	23.3	27.2	13.4	14.1	14.0	8.0
Blue Collar	54.8	100.0	24.1	26.8	11.1	15.0	14.6	8.3
Craft and Kindred	46.6	100.0	25.3	24.5	14.8	15.0	13.1	7.1
Operatives	43.6	100.0	19.1	32.1	13.2	11.6	14.8	9.2
Laborers	64.3	100.0	35.8	33.5	15.7	6.7	4.9	3.3
Farm Workers	40.8	100.0	19.6	43.4	13.0	12.6	7.1	4.4

Share of Total Work Force in Each Occupation by Employment Pattern

Table 2.16. DISTRIBUTION OF POPULATION, WORK FORCE, UNEMPLOYMENT AND HARDSHIP BY REGION AND METROPOLITAN AREA

	Population	Work Force	Experienced Unemployment	Predominantly Unemployed	IIE	IIE Deficit	IFE	IFE Deficit	IFI	IFI Deficit
Inside SMSA	67.8%	69.0%	68.9%	68.0%	61.5%	56.7%	61.7%	62.7%	62.2%	62.9%
SMSA 1 Million or More	38.4	39.4	38.7	39.5	32.3	29.7	32.8	34.7	33.6	34.0
Central City	(14.4)	(14.2)	(16.2)	(18.8)	(13.0)	(13.0)	(16.6)	(18.7)	(18.7)	(18.9)
Balance	(24.0)	(25.2)	(22.6)	(20.7)	(19.3)	(16.7)	(16.3)	(16.0)	(14.9)	(15.1)
SMSA Less Than 1 Million	29.4	29.6	30.2	28.5	29.2	27.0	28.9	28.1	28.6	29.0
Central City	(13.4)	(13.6)	(15.1)	(15.2)	(14.1)	(12.8)	(15.6)	(15.9)	(16.7)	(18.0)
Balance	(16.0)	(16.0)	(15.1)	(13.4)	(15.1)	(14.3)	(13.3)	(12.1)	(11.9)	(11.0)
Outside SMSA	32.2	31.0	31.1	32.0	38.5	43.3	38.2	37.3	37.8	37.1
Farm	(2.7)	(2.9)	(1.3)	(1.2)	(5.1)	(9.3)	(3.9)	(3.3)	(3.8)	(4.4)
New England	5.4%	5.9%	5.5%	5.1%	5.6%	5.0%	4.9%	4.7%	4.2%	3.6%
Middle Atlantic	16.4	15.7	15.8	18.8	14.0	13.8	13.6	14.6	12.6	12.6
East North Central	18.5	18.6	20.2	20.0	17.6	17.3	15.3	16.2	14.3	14.9
West North Central	7.5	8.1	6.9	5.5	9.1	10.2	8.3	7.5	7.5	6.7
South Atlantic	16.4	16.0	15.2	15.8	17.1	17.1	18.5	17.8	19.1	18.8
East South Central	6.4	6.0	6.1	6.4	7.2	7.2	8.1	8.4	8.5	9.5
West South Central	10.4	10.1	9.0	9.0	11.2	11.3	12.5	12.5	14.3	15.5
Mountain	5.0	5.1	5.1	4.2	5.6	5.9	5.2	4.8	5.4	5.5
Pacific	14.0	14.4	16.1	15.1	12.7	12.2	13.6	13.4	14.7	13.0

Table 2.17. INCIDENCE AND SEVERITY OF UNEMPLOYMENT AND HARDSHIP IN 1979 BY REGION AND METROPOLITAN AREA*

	Percent Unemployed	Percent Predominantly unemployed	IIE incidence	IFE incidence	Percent IIE in IFE	Percent with adequate individual earnings in IFE	IFI incidence	Earnings Supplementation Rate - Total	Earnings Supplementation Rate - Nontransfers	IIE Average Deficit	IFE Average Deficit	IFI Average Deficit
Inside SMSA	15.7%	6.3%	21.4%	10.1%	31.3%	4.3%	5.4%	46.5%	22.8%	$1,699	$2,425	$1,852
SMSA 1 Million or More	15.4	6.3	19.7	9.4	31.2	4.0	5.1	45.7	22.7	1,689	2,515	1,839
Central City	17.9	8.4	22.0	13.1	40.9	5.3	7.9	40.2	17.8	1,831	2,673	1,833
Balance	14.0	5.2	18.4	7.3	24.6	3.4	3.5	51.3	27.7	1,594	2,356	1,847
SMSA Less Than 1 Million	16.0	6.2	23.9	11.1	31.4	4.7	5.8	47.4	22.8	1,709	2,323	1,866
Central City	17.4	7.1	25.0	13.0	36.1	5.4	7.4	43.2	19.3	1,679	2,439	1,985
Balance	14.9	5.3	22.9	9.4	27.1	4.1	4.5	52.3	27.0	1,737	2,185	1,700
Outside SMSA	15.7	6.8	29.8	13.9	33.7	5.4	7.3	47.7	18.7	2,074	2,321	1,778
Farm	7.1	2.6	42.9	15.2	29.4	4.5	7.9	47.7	22.5	3,344	2,040	2,127
New England	14.7%	5.5%	22.8%	9.4%	27.7%	3.9%	4.3%	54.4%	25.8%	$1,646	$2,292	$1,595
Middle Atlantic	15.8	7.6	21.3	9.8	30.7	4.1	4.8	51.0	19.5	1,823	2,551	1,811
East North Central	17.0	6.8	22.7	9.2	29.2	3.4	4.6	50.6	21.8	1,809	2,517	1,897
West North Central	13.3	4.3	27.0	11.5	30.0	4.7	5.6	51.8	25.7	2,056	2,157	1,617
South Atlantic	14.8	6.3	25.8	13.0	35.6	5.2	7.1	45.2	21.5	1,839	2,285	1,797
East South Atlantic	16.0	6.7	28.8	15.2	36.9	6.5	8.4	44.6	16.0	1,837	2,477	2,024
West South Atlantic	14.0	5.7	26.7	14.1	37.0	5.7	8.6	39.0	17.8	1,877	2,407	1,978
Mountain	15.6	5.2	26.2	11.5	30.0	4.9	6.5	43.9	24.1	1,952	2,231	1,849
Pacific	17.5	6.7	21.2	10.6	31.6	5.0	5.9	44.9	22.4	1,778	2,357	1,695

Hardship was concentrated in the South. The South Atlantic region (Delaware, the District of Columbia, Florida, Georgia, Maryland, North and South Carolina, Virginia and West Virginia) accounted for a sixth of the labor force, the unemployed and the predominantly unemployed, but nearly a fifth of the IFE and the IFI. The East South Central area (Alabama, Kentucky, Mississippi and Tennessee) accounted for 6 percent of the labor force and the unemployed, but 7 percent of the IIE, 8 percent of the IFE and 9 percent of the IFI. Finally, the West South Central area (Arkansas, Louisiana, Oklahoma and Texas), with 10 percent of the work force, contained 11 percent of the IIE, 13 percent of the IFE and 14 percent of the IFI. In contrast, the New England (Connecticut, Maine, Massachusetts, New Hampshire, Rhode Island and Vermont), Middle Atlantic (New Jersey, New York and Pennsylvania), and East North Central (Illinois, Indiana, Michigan, Ohio and Wisconsin) areas together contained 40 percent of the labor force and 42 percent of persons experiencing unemployment, but only 37 percent of the IIE, 34 percent of the IFE and 31 percent of the IFI. The West North Central (Iowa, Kansas, Minnesota, Missouri, Nebraska, North and South Dakota) and Mountain (Arizona, Colorado, Idaho, Montana, Nevada, New Mexico, Utah and Wyoming) areas had hardship shares roughly proportional to their labor force shares; while the hardship shares of the Pacific states (Alaska, California, Hawaii, Oregon and Washington) were slightly lower than their labor force and unemployment shares.

The explanations are varied. The New England, Middle Atlantic, and East North Central areas all had below average IIE rates in 1979. For these three areas, the proportions of individuals with inadequate earnings who were in families with inadequate earnings were below the 32.2 percent average for the nation, while the Earnings Supplementation Rates for individuals in the IFE were above the 46.9 percent national average and transfers lifted larger proportions of workers in the IFE above the poverty threshold than the 25.5 percent averaged nationwide.

Notes

1. Unless otherwise indicated, the 1979 data used in this chapter are the 1979 estimates adjusted for 1980 Census weights. The choice of 1970 or 1980 Census weights makes very little or no difference when incidence rates are involved but is usually more of a factor in the levels and distributions of hardship. The 1979 data adjusted for the 1980 Census were not available until most of this chapter and its charts and tables had been completed, so that adjustments were made only in charts and tables where the 1980-weighted figures differed noticeably from the 1970-weighted figures. The use of 1970 weights is noted by an asterisk.

2. In allocating the family IFE and IFI Deficits among family work force participants when the total work force is considered, the IIE Deficits of all family members are first summed, and if this exceeds the IFE and IFI Deficits for the family, the IFE and IFI Deficits are allocated according to shares of the combined IIE Deficits. If the combined IIE Deficits of all family members are less than the IFE and/or IFI Deficits, the difference is allocated according to shares of family earnings which would be contributed by each member if those with IIE had minimally adequate earnings. In the case of the full-year and half-year hardship deficits, the IIE Deficits of only the full-year or half-year participating members are first summed, and the allocations then proceed as indicated above. The IFE or IFI Deficits for the total work force, minus the IFE or IFI Deficits for the full-year or half-year work force, do not equal the IFE or IFI Deficits allocated to the less than full-year or less than half-year workers in the total work force deficit allocations.

3. "Family Budgets," *Monthly Labor Review*, August 1980, pp. 29-30.

4. In determining the adequacy of family income and earnings, college students were counted as members of their regular families unless they had a permanent, independent residence.

CHAPTER 3. HARDSHIP TRENDS OVER THE 1974-1980 PERIOD

An Overview

Seven Lean Years

Is hardship increasing or decreasing? Are the differentials in hardship incidence narrowing or widening? Have changes in the composition of the work force exacerbated hardship? Has the safety net for the working poor been substantially improved? These and other important questions about labor market developments and related hardship trends can be tentatively addressed using the hardship data tabulated for the 1974-1980 period.

These seven years may be remembered fondly, but only in contrast to the depression conditions of the 1980s. Unemployment reached and remained at levels which had previously been considered untenable. The annual unemployment rate averaged 6.8 percent from 1974 through 1980, compared to the 4.7 percent average for 1947 through 1973. The 1974-1980 period witnessed slowed productivity growth and minimal improvements in real wages. Output per hour increased only 7 percent between 1974 and 1980, half the increase over the preceding six years. The purchasing power of average hourly earnings in private nonfarm employment, which had risen by 16 percent between 1964 and 1973, fell by 5 percent between 1974 and 1980. Likewise, progress slowed in the War on Poverty. The poverty rate dropped from 14.2 percent of the population in 1967 to 11.2 percent in 1973, but then rose to 13.0 percent in 1980, largely as a result of the slack labor market conditions.

High unemployment, slowed productivity growth, and increased poverty were, in part, the result of changes in the composition of the working population. Teenagers (16-19) accounted for 7.2 percent of the work force in 1947, but 8.8 percent in 1980; and the 16- to 24-year-old share rose from 19.7 to 23.5 percent. However, by the late 1970s, these trends were reversing, as the teenage share dropped from 9.7 percent between 1974 and 1980, while the 16- to 24-year-old share dropped from 24.1 to 23.5 percent. Other compositional shifts during the 1974-1980 period were more consistent with secular trends. From 1947 to 1973, the female share of the labor force had increased from 28.1 to 38.9 percent. By 1980, it had reached 42.7 percent. Married males with a spouse present declined from 52.3 percent of the work force in 1947 to 44.8 percent in 1973, then further declined to 37.9 percent in 1980. White collar workers had increased from 43.4 percent of the experienced labor force in 1960 to 47.8 percent in 1973, and their share continued to increase to 52.2 percent in 1980. The percent of the labor force who were high school graduates rose from 53.8 percent in 1962 to 67.7 percent in 1973, and continued rising to 76.2

percent in 1980; the proportion with a college degree increased from 11.0 to 14.1 percent, and then 18.2 percent. The long-term population shifts to suburban areas, and to the Southern and Western states, accelerated between 1974 and 1980. 1/

Slowing Progress

With high unemployment, slowed real wage gains, and shifts in the composition of the work force, there was very limited progress in reducing labor market-related hardship. The hardship measure defined by the National Commission on Employment and Unemployment Statistics, (which included persons in the work force 40 weeks or more, plus those discouraged but seeking work at least 15 weeks, whose individual earnings were less than double the poverty level for their families) declined from 11.2 percent in 1967 to 7.9 percent in 1973, but then rose to 8.3 percent in 1979. The Levitan/Taggart Employment and Earnings Inadequacy Index (which included those currently unemployed, discouraged, or working part-time as well as those working full-time but earning less than a poverty income over the previous year, minus all those in families with above average incomes) remained constant between 1968 and 1974, but then rose from 10.5 percent in 1974 to 11.8 percent in 1979. 2/

The hardship measures proposed in this volume reveal a similar picture. Over the 1974-1980 period, for which these measures were tabulated, there was a significant decline in the incidence of Inadequate Individual Earnings, a lesser decline in the incidence of Inadequate Family Earnings, but no improvement in the incidence of Inadequate Family Income. This is suggested by comparisons between the low unemployment years, 1974 and 1979, and the high unemployment years, 1975 and 1980. 3/ The severe hardship IIE rate dropped by 1.6 percentage points between 1974 and 1979, and 1.4 percentage points between 1975 and 1980. The IFE rate fell by 0.2 percentage points in the first period and 0.4 percentage points in the second. The IFI rate rose by 0.5 percentage points between 1975 and 1980:

Changes in severe hardship incidence
for total work force

	1974	1979	1979-1974	1975	1980	1980-1975
IIE	25.8%	24.2%	-1.6%	29.1%	27.7%	-1.4%
IFE	11.6	11.4	-0.2	13.2	12.8	-0.4
IFI	6.1	6.0	-0.1	6.9	7.2	+0.3

Put another way, the number of persons with Inadequate Family Income increased both relative to the number with Inadequate Family Earnings and the number with Inadequate Individual Earnings, while the IFE rose in relation to the IIE:

Relative changes in IIE, IFE and IFI
severe hardship counts

Ratios	1974	1979	1979-1974	1975	1980	1980-1975
IFI ÷ IFE	52.8%	53.1%	+0.3%	52.7%	56.0%	+3.3%
IFI ÷ IIE	23.7	25.0	+1.3	23.9	25.8	+1.9
IFE ÷ IIE	44.9	47.0	+2.1	45.4	46.1	+0.7

Similarly, the average IIE and IFE Deficits, measured in 1980 dollars, declined between 1974 with 1979, as well as between 1975 and 1980, but the average IFI Deficit rose. The IFI Deficit, thus, increased relative to the total IFE and IIE Deficits, while the IFE Deficit increased relative to the IIE Deficit:

Changes in severe hardship deficits

Average deficits ($1980)

	1974	1979	1979-1974	1975	1980	1980-1975
IIE	$2126	$2087	-$39	$2326	$2157	-$169
IFE	2742	2706	- 36	2771	2713	- 58
IFI	2030	2063	+ 33	2013	2062	+ 49

Total deficits ($1980 in millions)

	1974	1979	1979-1974	1975	1980	1980-1975
IIE	$56,862	$59,018	$2156	$70,568	$70,648	$ 80
IFE	32,919	35,929	3010	38,160	41,000	2840
IFI	12,889	14,556	1667	14,603	17,452	2849

Total deficit ratios

	1974	1979	1979-1974	1975	1980	1980-1975
IFI ÷ IFE	39.2%	40.5%	+1.3%	38.3%	42.6%	+4.3%
IFI ÷ IIE	22.7	24.7	+2.0	20.7	24.7	+4.0
IFE ÷ IIE	57.9	60.9	+3.0	54.1	58.0	+3.9

The improvements in the IIE and IFE between 1974 and 1979, as well as between 1975 and 1980, reflected the reductions in unemployment over these same periods (Table 3.1). Yet the numbers in hardship increased relative both to the numbers experiencing unemployment and the numbers predominantly unemployed (i.e., more than one-third of their weeks in the work force). There was an increase in the IFE and IFI rates among persons experiencing unemployment, but declines in all three hardship incidence rates among those who were employed full-time or part-time all weeks in the work force. The proportion of persons with Inadequate Individual Earnings who were in families with Inadequate Family Earnings increased slightly. More critically, however, the proportion of those with Inadequate Family Earnings lifted out of poverty by earnings supplements declined, totally as

Table 3.1. LONG-TERM SHIFTS IN KEY SEVERE HARDSHIP AND UNEMPLOYMENT INDICATORS

	1974	1979	1979-1974	1975	1980	1980-1975
IIE	25.8%	24.2%	-1.6%	29.1%	27.7%	-1.4%
IFE	11.6	11.4	-0.2	13.2	12.8	-0.4
IFI	6.1	6.0	-0.1	6.9	7.2	+0.3
Experienced Unemployment	17.9	15.8	-2.1	20.2	18.1	-2.1
Predominantly Unemployed	7.5	6.4	-1.1	10.4	8.7	-1.7
IIE ÷ Experienced Unemployment	1.44	1.53	+0.09	1.44	1.53	+0.09
IFE ÷ Experienced Unemployment	0.65	0.72	+0.07	0.65	0.77	+0.12
IFI ÷ Experienced Unemployment	0.34	0.38	+0.04	0.34	0.40	+0.06
IIE ÷ Predominantly Unemployed	3.46	3.77	+0.31	2.77	3.16	+0.39
IFE ÷ Predominantly Unemployed	1.55	1.77	+0.22	1.26	1.46	+0.20
IFI ÷ Predominantly Unemployed	0.82	0.94	+0.12	0.66	0.82	+0.12
Percent Unemployed in IIE	54.2	53.5	-0.7	59.9	59.6	-0.3
Percent Unemployed in IFE	21.9	22.8	+0.9	25.6	26.6	+1.0
Percent Unemployed in IFI	13.7	14.2	+0.5	14.4	17.4	+3.0
Unemployed As Percent IIE	37.6	34.9	-2.7	41.6	39.0	-2.6
Unemployed As Percent IFE	33.8	31.7	-2.1	39.3	37.6	-1.7
Unemployed As Percent IFI	39.9	37.1	-2.8	41.8	43.9	+2.1
Percent of Persons Employed All Weeks But in IIE	19.6	18.7	-0.9	21.2	20.6	-0.6
Percent of Persons Employed All Weeks But in IFI	9.3	9.2	-0.1	10.0	9.7	-0.3
Percent of Persons Employed All Weeks But in IFE	4.5	4.5	0	5.1	4.9	-0.2
Percent IIE in IFE	0.31	0.32	+0.01	0.34	0.35	+0.01
Earnings Supplementation Rate-Total	47.1	46.9	-0.2	47.3	44.0	-3.3
Earnings Supplementation Rate-Nontransfers	18.3	21.3	+3.0	16.2	19.5	+3.3
Earnings Supplementation Rate-Transfers	28.8	25.6	-3.2	31.1	24.5	-6.6

a result of the declining impacts of transfers in alleviating severe hardship. If transfers had the same proportional impacts in 1979 as in 1974, and in 1980 as in 1975, the IFI would have declined by more than the IFE, since the impacts of earnings supplements other than transfers increased significantly.

The patterns of change in intermediate and moderate hardship were somewhat more complex. The 1974-1979 and 1975-1980 declines in the severe hardship IIE were not matched by improvements in the intermediate and moderate hardship IIE rates:

	1974	1979	1979-1974	1975	1980	1980-1975	1980-1974
Severe Hardship							
IIE	25.8%	24.2%	-1.6%	29.1%	27.7%	-1.4%	+1.9%
IFE	11.6	11.4	-0.2	13.2	12.8	-0.4	+1.2
IFI	6.1	6.0	-0.1	6.9	7.2	+0.3	+1.1
Intermediate Hardship							
IIE	35.3	35.0	-0.3	38.4	37.9	-0.5	+2.6
IFE	14.9	14.7	-0.2	16.8	16.4	-0.4	+1.5
IFI	9.2	9.0	-0.2	10.3	10.4	+0.1	+1.2
Moderate Hardship							
IIE	44.3	44.0	-0.3	46.6	47.3	+0.7	+3.0
IFE	18.5	18.4	-0.1	20.9	20.5	-0.4	+2.0
IFI	12.8	12.3	-0.5	14.3	14.1	-0.3	+1.3

Consequently, the moderate hardship IIE _increased_ from 1.72 times the severe hardship IIE in 1974 to 1.82 times the IIE in 1979 (Table 3.2). The ratio of the moderate and severe hardship IFEs stayed the same from 1974 to 1979, but the ratio of the moderate and the severe hardship IFIs _declined_ from 2.08 to 2.04.

Changes in Work Force Attachment and Work Experience Patterns

Over the 1974-1980 period, the average work force attachment of all participants increased. In 1974, 70.2 percent of the total work force participated fifty weeks or more compared to 71.8 percent in 1979. The proportion of the total work force with at least half a year of participation rose from 83.0 to 84.4. Since increased weeks in the work force reduce the likelihood of experiencing hardship, this trend toward increased attachment had a positive impact on hardship rates. Weighting hardship incidence among full-year and less than full-year participants in 1979 by their 1974 shares of the total work force, and the 1980 rates by their 1975 shares, and comparing these weighted rates to actual hardship incidence for the total work force in 1979 and 1980, respectvely, suggests that increased attachment was associated with a 0.3 to 0.4 percentage point reduction in the IIE rate and with lesser effects on the IFE and IFI rates:

Table 3.2. CHANGE IN RELATIONSHIP BETWEEN SEVERE, INTERMEDIATE AND MODERATE HARDSHIP FOR TOTAL WORK FORCE

	1974	1979	1979-1974	1975	1980	1980-1975
IIE						
Intermediate + Severe	136.7%	144.9%	8.2%	132.0%	136.8%	4.8%
Moderate + Severe	171.6	181.9	10.3	160.5	170.8	10.3
Intermediate−Severe / Severe	36.6	44.9	8.3	32.0	36.8	4.8
Moderate−Intermediate / Severe	35.0	37.0	2.0	28.4	34.0	5.6
IIE Deficit						
Intermediate + Severe	163.8	168.2	4.4	159.4	163.9	4.5
Moderate + Severe	250.5	262.3	11.7	236.7	249.1	12.4
Intermediate−Severe / Severe	63.8	68.2	4.4	59.4	63.9	4.5
Moderate−Intermediate / Severe	86.7	94.2	7.5	77.3	85.2	7.9
IFE						
Intermediate + Severe	128.5	129.4	1.9	127.2	128.8	1.6
Moderate + Severe	159.3	162.3	3.0	158.7	160.8	1.8
Intermediate−Severe / Severe	28.5	29.4	0.9	27.2	28.8	1.6
Moderate−Intermediate / Severe	30.9	32.9	2.0	31.5	31.7	0.2
IFE Deficit						
Intermediate + Severe	152.8	153.4	0.6	151.9	152.2	0.3
Moderate + Severe	218.9	220.1	1.2	216.6	217.4	0.8
Intermediate−Severe / Severe	52.8	53.4	0.6	51.9	52.2	0.3
Moderate−Intermediate / Severe	66.1	66.7	0.6	64.7	66.7	3.0
IFI						
Intermediate + Severe	150.6	149.2	-1.4	148.3	145.0	-3.3
Moderate + Severe	208.3	203.5	-4.8	206.2	197.3	-8.9
Intermediate−Severe / Severe	50.6	49.2	-1.4	48.3	45.0	-3.3
Moderate−Intermediate / Severe	57.7	54.3	-3.4	57.9	52.4	-6.5
IFI Deficit						
Intermediate + Severe	181.8	179.5	-2.3	181.5	176.6	-4.9
Moderate + Severe	297.5	289.8	-7.7	297.1	282.2	-14.9
Intermediate−Severe / Severe	81.8	79.5	-2.3	81.5	76.6	-4.9
Moderate−Intermediate / Severe	115.7	109.5	-6.2	115.5	105.6	-9.9

	IIE	IFE	IFI
1979 actual severe hardship rate for total work force	24.2%	11.4%	6.0%
1979 if had 1974 proportion full-year participants	24.6	11.6	6.2
1974-1979 improvement from increased attachment	0.4	0.2	0.2
1980 actual severe hardship rates for total work force	27.7	12.8	7.2
1980 if had 1975 proportion full-year participants	28.0	13.0	7.3
1975-1980 improvement from increased attachment	0.3	0.2	0.1
1980 if had 1974 proportion full-year participants	28.7	13.4	7.5
1974-1980 improvement from increased attachment	1.0	0.6	0.3

The incidence of Inadequate Individual Earnings fell among both full-year and less than full-year participants, but more so among the latter than the former (Table 3.3). In contrast, the IFE rate improved more for full-year participants. There was also a decline in the ratio of the average hardship deficits of full-year participants compared to those for the total work force. As a result, the full-year IFE and IFI Deficits declined relative to the total IFE and IFI Deficits despite the relative growth of the full-year work force.

There were two significant and offsetting changes in work experience patterns over the two comparison periods. First, the incidence and severity of unemployment declined. The proportion of the population experiencing unemployment was 2.1 percentage points lower in 1979 than in 1974, and 2.2 percentage points lower in 1980 than 1975 (Table 3.4). Since hardship is more prevalent among the unemployed than the employed, the unemployment incidence declines should have lowered hardship rates. Weighting the 1979 hardship rates among work force participants experiencing unemployment and those not experiencing unemployment by their 1974 shares of the total work force suggests that the reduction in unemployment should have contributed a 0.7 to 0.8 percentage point improvement in the severe hardship IIE for the total work force, a 0.2 to 0.3 percentage point improvement in the IFE rate, and a 0.2 to 0.4 percentage point improvement in the IFI rate:

Table 3.3. RELATIVE CHANGES IN SEVERE HARDSHIP FOR FULL-YEAR, HALF-YEAR AND TOTAL WORK FORCE

	1974	1979	1979-1974	1975	1980	1980-1975
Work Force Ratio						
Full-Year ÷ Total	70.2%	71.8%	1.6%	72.7%	73.9%	1.2%
Half-Year ÷ Total	83.0	84.4	1.4	84.3	85.4	1.1
IIE Incidence						
Total	25.8	24.2	-1.6	29.1	27.7	-1.4
Half-Year	20.8	19.5	-1.3	23.9	23.0	-0.9
Full-Year	18.0	17.0	-1.0	21.3	20.5	-0.8
IIE Ratio						
Full-Year ÷ Total	49.0	50.4	1.4	53.3	54.7	1.4
Half-Year ÷ Total	66.7	68.3	1.6	69.4	71.0	1.6
IIE Deficit Ratio						
Full-Year ÷ Total	73.2	73.9	0.7	76.3	76.4	0.1
Half-Year ÷ Total	88.4	89.2	0.8	89.8	90.4	0.6
IIE Average Deficit Ratio						
Full-Year ÷ Total	1.49	1.47	-0.02	1.43	1.40	-0.03
Half-Year ÷ Total	1.33	1.31	-0.02	1.29	1.27	-0.02
IFE Incidence						
Total	11.6	11.4	-0.2	13.2	12.8	-0.4
Half-Year	8.4	8.1	-0.3	10.1	9.7	-0.4
Full-Year	7.1	6.8	-0.3	8.9	8.3	-0.6
IFE Ratio						
Full-Year ÷ Total	43.0	42.7	-0.3	48.8	48.1	-0.6
Half-Year ÷ Total	60.1	60.3	+0.2	64.5	64.6	+0.1
IFE Deficit Ratio						
Full-Year ÷ Total	43.0	42.0	-1.0	50.1	48.7	-1.4
Half-Year ÷ Total	58.8	56.5	-1.3	64.4	62.8	-1.6
IFE Average Deficit Ratio						
Full-Year ÷ Total	1.00	0.98	-0.02	1.03	1.01	-0.02
Half-Year ÷ Total	0.98	0.94	-0.04	1.00	0.97	-0.03
IFI Incidence						
Total	6.1	6.0	-0.1	6.9	7.2	+0.3
Half-Year	4.4	4.3	-0.1	5.2	5.4	+0.2
Full-Year	3.8	3.7	-0.1	4.6	4.8	+0.2
IFI Ratio						
Full-Year ÷ Total	43.7	43.9	+0.2	48.1	49.8	+1.7
Half-Year ÷ Total	59.7	60.6	+0.9	63.1	65.0	+1.9
IFI Deficit Ratio						
Full-Year ÷ Total	50.0	49.2	-0.8	54.9	54.4	-0.5
Half-Year ÷ Total	65.3	62.9	-2.4	69.2	67.5	-1.7
IFI Average Deficit Ratio						
Full-Year ÷ Total	1.15	1.12	-0.03	1.15	1.09	-0.06
Half-Year ÷ Total	1.09	1.04	-0.05	1.10	1.04	-0.06

Table 3.4. CHANGES IN WORK EXPERIENCE PATTERNS AND WORK FORCE ATTACHMENT, 1974-1980

	1974	1979	1979-1974	1975	1980	1980-1975
<u>Less Than Full-Year Participants</u>	<u>29.8%</u>	<u>28.2%</u>	<u>-1.7%</u>	<u>27.3%</u>	<u>16.1%</u>	<u>-1.2%</u>
Unemployed Some Weeks	<u>7.5</u>	<u>6.1</u>	<u>-1.4</u>	<u>7.2</u>	<u>6.3</u>	<u>-0.9</u>
Not Employed	1.7	1.4	-0.3	2.2	1.6	-0.6
Mostly Unemployed	0.4	0.3	-0.1	0.5	0.5	-0.6
Mixed	1.4	1.1	-0.3	1.3	1.3	0
Mostly Employed	4.0	3.3	-0.7	3.2	2.9	-0.3
Employed All Weeks	<u>22.3</u>	<u>22.1</u>	<u>-0.2</u>	<u>20.1</u>	<u>19.8</u>	<u>-0.3</u>
Part-Time Involuntary	1.7	2.6	+0.9	2.4	2.5	+0.1
Part-Time Voluntary	10.7	11.5	+0.8	9.9	10.2	+0.3
Full-Time	9.8	8.0	+1.8	7.9	7.2	-0.7
<u>Full-Year Participants</u>	<u>70.2</u>	<u>71.8</u>	<u>+1.6</u>	<u>72.7</u>	<u>73.9</u>	<u>+1.2</u>
Unemployed Some Weeks	<u>10.4</u>	<u>9.7</u>	<u>-0.7</u>	<u>13.1</u>	<u>11.8</u>	<u>-1.3</u>
Not Employed	0.4	0.3	-0.1	0.9	0.6	-0.3
Mostly Unemployed	1.1	1.0	-0.1	2.0	1.7	-0.3
Mixed	2.5	2.2	-0.3	3.6	3.1	-0.5
Mostly Employed	6.4	6.1	-0.3	6.6	6.5	-0.1
Employed All Weeks	<u>59.8</u>	<u>62.1</u>	<u>+2.3</u>	<u>59.6</u>	<u>62.1</u>	<u>+2.5</u>
Part-Time Involuntary	2.1	3.6	+1.5	3.5	4.0	+0.5
Part-Time Voluntary	7.9	11.5	+3.6	9.4	10.9	+1.5
Full-Time	49.8	47.0	-2.8	46.7	47.2	+0.5
Total	100.0	100.0	100.0	100.0	100.0	100.0

	1979 actual	1979 if had 1974 proportion unemployed and employed	1974-1979 improvement associated with declining unemployment	1980 actual	1980 if had 1975 proportion unemployed and employed	1975-1980 improvement associated with declining unemployment
IIE	24.2%	24.9%	0.7%	27.7%	28.5%	0.8%
IFE	11.4	11.6	0.2	12.8	13.1	0.3
IFI	6.0	6.4	0.4	7.2	7.4	0.2

The proportion of the unemployed who did not work at all or were out of work over one-third of their weeks in the work force declined from 41.8 percent in 1974 to 40.6 percent in 1979, or from 51.8 percent in 1975 to 48.3 percent in 1980. Since the short-duration unemployed had lower hardship rates, this shift within the unemployed should have been a further positive factor.

The percent of the labor force employed part-time some or all weeks in the work force and experiencing no weeks of unemployment, rose from 22.5 percent in 1974 to 29.2 percent in 1979, or from 25.2 to 27.5 percent between 1975 and 1980. The 1979 severe hardship IIE incidence among part-time workers was 35.1 percent compared to 19.7 percent among all other work force participants; the IFE rates were 13.7 and 8.6 percent, respectively; while the IFI rates were 7.9 and 5.2 percent, respectively. Thus, the increase in part-time work contributed to increased hardship:

	1979 actual	1979 if had 1974 proportion part-time workers	1974-1979 increase in hardship associated with increase in part-time work	1980 actual	1980 if had 1975 proportion part-time workers	1975-1980 increase in hardship associated with increase in part-time work
IIE	24.2%	23.2%	1.0%	27.7%	27.2%	0.5%
IFE	11.4	9.8	1.6	12.8	11.3	1.5
IFI	6.0	5.9	0.1	7.2	7.1	0.1

But the incidence of hardship also changed within the various attachment and work experience pattern subgroups (Table 3.5). The severe hardship IIE incidence increased among both full-year and total work force participants who experienced unemployment, including those not employed at all, mostly unemployed, those mixing employment and unemployment, and even those mostly employed. Because the share of the unemployed who were mostly employed increased, the IIE rate among the unemployed as a whole fell despite the rising incidence in each subgroup. In 1979, 53.5 percent of persons experiencing unemployment had Inadequate Individual Earnings compared to 54.2 percent in 1974. From 1975 to 1980, the severe hardship IIE rate fell from 59.9 to 59.6 percent.

Table 3.5. SHIFTS IN HARDSHIP INCIDENCE RATES AMONG WORK EXPERIENCE PATTERN AND ATTACHMENT SUBGROUPS

	Total					Full-Year				
	1974	1979	1979-1974	1975	1980	1980-1975	1974	1979	1979-1974	1975	1980	1980-1975

IIE rate

Not employed	97.9%	99.4%	+1.5%	98.3%	99.6	+1.3	100.0%	100.0%	0	100.0%	100.0%	0
Mostly unemployed	94.3	95.1	+0.8	93.9	95.3	+1.4	94.3	94.5	+0.2	93.7	95.1	+1.4
Mixed	69.1	69.1	0	67.8	70.9	+3.1	63.0	64.8	+1.8	63.4	67.1	+3.7
Mostly employed	34.1	33.5	-0.6	35.2	36.7	+1.5	24.2	26.9	+2.7	27.1	30.1	+3.0
Part-time involuntary	53.0	44.6	-8.4	48.6	47.8	-0.8	40.8	32.3	-8.5	36.5	37.9	+1.4
Part-time voluntary	38.1	32.6	-5.5	39.7	36.4	-3.3	37.0	27.5	-9.5	35.6	31.6	-4.0
Employed full-time	11.7	10.0	-1.7	11.8	11.3	-0.5	8.7	7.4	-0.7	8.7	8.5	-0.2

IFE rate

Not employed	45.6	46.8	+1.2	47.4	51.7	+4.3	62.2	54.4	-7.8	57.7	60.8	+3.1
Mostly unemployed	44.1	42.4	-1.7	42.5	47.4	+4.9	44.9	41.0	-3.9	43.1	48.5	+5.4
Mixed	25.4	28.1	+2.7	28.2	29.6	+1.4	23.6	27.2	+3.6	27.4	27.5	+0.1
Mostly employed	12.6	13.7	+1.1	13.2	14.4	+1.2	8.4	9.5	+1.1	9.9	10.9	+1.0
Part-time involuntary	22.3	19.8	-2.5	20.0	20.2	+0.2	16.5	13.0	-3.5	14.7	15.4	+0.7
Part-time voluntary	20.1	17.5	-2.6	20.2	19.2	-1.0	16.5	12.2	-4.3	16.2	14.0	-2.2
Employed full-time	5.1	4.5	-0.6	5.4	4.8	-0.6	2.9	2.5	-0.4	3.0	2.7	-0.3

IFI rate

Not employed	30.0	31.6	+1.6	27.6	38.4	+10.8	34.7	37.7	+3.0	29.2	43.8	+14.6
Mostly unemployed	26.9	26.3	-0.6	22.6	30.7	+8.1	26.4	25.0	-1.4	22.0	31.4	+9.4
Mixed	15.5	16.0	+1.5	14.4	17.6	+3.2	13.5	14.6	+1.1	12.9	15.4	+2.5
Mostly employed	7.8	8.6	+0.8	8.1	9.3	+1.2	5.2	5.7	+0.5	5.6	5.9	+0.3
Part-time involuntary	13.6	11.4	-2.2	12.3	12.1	-0.2	10.4	8.1	-2.3	9.3	9.5	+0.2
Part-time voluntary	7.7	6.9	-0.8	8.4	7.8	-0.6	5.6	4.6	-1.0	6.5	5.6	-0.9
Employed full-time	2.9	2.7	-0.2	3.1	2.8	-0.3	1.8	1.7	-0.1	1.9	1.9	0

In contrast, the severe hardship IIE incidence fell among participants employed part-time some or all weeks in the work force, as well as among those employed full-time all weeks of participation. Because part-time workers increased relative to full-time workers, the improvement in IIE incidence for those employed all weeks of participation was slight, declining 0.9 percentage points between 1974 and 1979.

The changes in the severe hardship IFE and IFI rates among the various work experience and work force attachment subgroups were similar, but in these cases, the increased hardship incidence among the unemployed subgroups was not offset by the reduced predominance of unemployment among the intermittently employed. The IFE rate among work force participants experiencing unemployment rose from 21.9 in 1974 to 22.8 percent in 1979, and from 25.6 to 26.6 percent between 1975 and 1980. The IFI rate among the unemployed rose from 13.7 to 14.2 percent in the first period and from 14.4 to 17.4 percent in the second. Even though the IIE incidence among the unemployed had declined over both periods, the proportion of the unemployed with Inadequate Individual Earnings who also had Inadequate Family Earnings increased. In addition, the IFI incidence among the unemployed increased dramatically between 1975 and 1980, primarily as a result of declining transfers:

	Percent of unemployed with Inadequate Individual Earnings	Percent of unemployed in IIE who were also in IFE	Earnings Supplementation Rate among unemployed in IFE	Earnings Supplementation Rate-Transfers among unemployed in IFE	Percent of unemployed with Inadequate Family Income
1974	54.2	35.4	37.6	26.4	13.7
1979	53.5	37.5	37.8	24.8	14.2
1979-1974	-0.7	+2.1	+0.2	-1.6	+0.5
1975	59.9	38.6	43.9	31.7	14.4
1980	59.6	40.8	34.6	23.6	17.4
1980-1975	-0.3	+2.2	-9.3	-8.1	+3.0

The balance of these changes in work force attachment, work experience patterns, and hardship incidence among work attachment/experience subgroups can be assessed by weighting the 1979 incidence rates for each subgroup (i.e., disaggregating the total work force into full-year participants not employed, mostly unemployed, mixing employment and unemployment, mostly employed, employed part-time involuntarily, employed part-time voluntarily and those employed full-time, plus less than full-year participants in these same work experience categories) by their 1974 shares of the total work force. Comparison of the weighted with the actual 1979 hardship rates, then, suggests the effect of changing attachment/experience patterns, while comparison with the actual 1974 hardship rates suggests the effect of incidence rate changes for the subgroups. The same comparisons can be made between 1975 and 1980. Declining IIE incidence within the various work experience/attachment subcategories was responsible for all of the 1974-1979 drop in the severe hardship IIE rate and a third of the 1975-1980 drop. The IFE incidence declines within the various work experience/attachment subcategories were responsible for the slight improvement in the overall severe hardship IFE, but slight increases in incidence from 1975 to 1980 offset the effects of favorable work experience/attachment shifts over this period. The increases in IFI incidence within the various work experience/attachment subcategories were responsible for the rise of the severe hardship IFI, which otherwise would have declined because of the favorable work experience/attachment changes:

IIE

Actual 1979 IIE rate	24.17	Actual 1980 IIE rate	27.67
Weighted rate	23.86	Weighted rate	28.65
Effect of changing distribution 1974-1979	+0.31	Effect of changing distribution 1975-1980	-0.98
Actual 1974 IIE rate	25.83	Actual 1975 IIE rate	29.05
Effect of changing incidence 1974-1979	-1.97	Effect of changing incidence 1975-1980	-0.40

IFE

Actual 1979 IFE rate	11.35	Actual 1980 IFE rate	12.77
Weighted rate	11.24	Weighted rate	13.35
Effect of changing distribution 1974-1979	+0.11	Effect of changing distribution 1975-1980	-0.58
Actual 1974 IFE rate	11.59	Actual 1975 IFE rate	13.18
Effect of changing incidence 1974-1979	-0.35	Effect of changing incidence 1975-1980	+0.17

IFI

Actual 1979 IFI rate	6.03	Actual 1980 IFI rate	7.15
Weighted rate	6.12	Weighted rate	7.61
Effect of changing distribution 1974-1979	-0.09	Effect of changing distribution 1975-1980	-0.46
Actual 1974 IFI rate	6.13	Actual 1980 IFI rate	6.94
Effect of changing incidence 1974-1979	-0.01	Effect of changing incidence 1975-1980	-0.65

Long-Term Shifts in the Composition and Distribution of Hardship

Changes in the demographic, geographic and occupational distributions of the work force were generally favorable over the 1974-1980 period and should have reduced hardship incidence. The favorable factors included the aging of the post-war babies into the prime working years and the exit of older workers, the increased educational attainment of the work force, and increased employment in occupations characterized by lower hardship rates. The shift of population to areas characterized by lower wages and lower transfers was a marginally negative factor, but was balanced by a relative improvement in hardship incidence in the previously worst off areas as well as the suburbanization of metropolitan area populations.

Aging Postwar Babies and Exiting Oldsters

The proportion of the work force who were individuals in their "prime" working and earning years increased noticeably over the late 1970s:

	\multicolumn{7}{c	}{Share of total work force}
	1974	1979	1979-1974	1975	1980	1980-1975	1980-1974
16-19 (Student)	11.0% (6.3)	10.0% (5.4)	-1.0% (-0.9)	10.6% (5.8)	9.3% (5.3)	-1.3% (-0.5)	-1.7% (-1.0)
20-24 (Student)	15.0 (2.4)	15.2 (2.3)	+0.2 (-0.1)	15.0 (2.3)	15.3 (2.2)	+0.3 (-0.1)	+0.3 (-0.2)
25-44	40.2	44.5	+4.3	41.2	45.5	+4.3	+5.3
45-64	29.7	26.6	-3.1	29.2	26.4	-2.8	-3.3
65+	4.1	3.7	-0.4	4.0	3.6	-0.4	-0.5

Weighting the 1979 severe hardship rate for each age group (and counting younger students and nonstudents separately) by its 1974 work force share, suggests that the IIE and IFE rates were reduced noticeably by these changes in age composition. Since older workers have low IFI incidence despite high IFE incidence, their declining share offsets the IFI improvement expected from increased numbers of prime age workers:

	IIE incidence	IFE incidence	IFI incidence
Incidence in 1979 if had 1974 age distribution	24.73%	11.59%	6.01%
Actual 1979 incidence	24.17	11.35	6.07
Changes in hardship incidence rates associated with age shifts	-0.56	-0.24	+0.02

Yet the incidence of hardship among the different age groups also changed with the changes in work force shares, combining to alter the age composition of persons in hardship.

First, the participation rates of 16- to 19-year-olds, and of persons 45 and over, declined, while rising significantly among prime age workers (Table 3.6). This reduced the proportion of the younger and older segments of the work force who were marginal participants likely to be in hardship, thus reducing the relative hardship rates for these age groups.

Second, full-year work force participation rose more among 16- to 24-year-olds than among 25- to 44-year-olds, while full-year participation declined among older workers. This reduced the relative hardship incidence among younger participants, but increased the relative incidence among older participants.

Third, the incidence of unemployment declined more among younger and older workers than among those of prime age, which should have reduced the disparity in hardship incidence.

Fourth, the incidence of Inadequate Individual Earnings declined among unemployed teenagers, while rising more for prime age workers than other age groups.

Fifth, the probability of Inadequate Family Earnings among persons with Inadequate Individual Earnings rose noticeably among prime age workers, with lesser increases or actual declines for younger and older participants in the IIE.

Sixth, the Earnings Supplementation Rate declined substantially among prime age workers in the IFE, while increasing among younger and older workers, with most of this the reflection of more rapidly expanding non-transfer supplements received by the families of younger and older participants in the IFE, as well as a less severe decline in transfer supplements for older participants.

The end result of these various factors was a substantial change in the relative incidence of Inadequate Family Earnings and Income among the different age groups. The IFE rates declined for 16- to 19-year-olds and for work force participants age 45 and over, while increasing for prime age work force participants. The IFI rate rose by 0.9 percentage points for prime age workers between 1975 and 1980, while declining 2.3 percentage points for teenage work force participants and 1.0 percentage points for participants age 65 and over.

The teenager and older-worker shares of hardship declined substantially as a result of their reduced work force shares and their falling hardship rates:

Table 3.6. CHANGES IN WORK FORCE PARTICIPATION, UNEMPLOYMENT AND HARDSHIP BY AGE

Proportion In Work Force

	1974	1979	1979-1974	1975	1980	1980-1975
16-19	70.4%	69.7%	-.7%	67.5%	67.0%	-.5%
16-19 Student	62.5	61.4	-1.1	58.7	59.1	+.4
20-24	86.2	86.8	+.6	84.6	86.9	+2.3
20-24 Student	81.5	77.5	-4.0	76.3	76.6	+.3
25-44	80.1	83.5	+3.4	80.7	84.8	+4.1
45-64	71.5	70.6	-.9	70.6	70.8	+.2
65 +	19.9	17.7	-2.2	19.1	17.1	-2.0

Share of Work Force Participants Experiencing Unemployment

	1974	1979	1979-1974	1975	1980	1980-1975
16-19	31.6%	26.5%	-5.1%	32.5%	29.5%	-3.0
16-19 Student	26.8	21.2	-5.6	26.6	24.3	-2.3
20-24	29.2	25.5	-3.7	32.5	28.8	-3.7
20-24 Student	24.4	17.5	-6.9	26.9	21.0	-5.9
25-44	15.9	14.9	-1.0	18.6	17.5	-1.1
45-64	10.7	9.1	-1.6	13.0	10.6	-2.4
65 +	8.3	5.8	-2.5	10.0	5.6	-4.4

Proportion in Work Force Full-Year

	1974	1979	1979-1974	1975	1980	1980-1975
16-19	30.4%	32.3%	+1.9%	33.4%	34.9%	+1.5%
16-19 Student	20.5	21.5	+1.0	22.1	24.5	+2.4
20-24	59.2	63.2	+4.0	63.3	64.9	+1.6
20-24 Student	22.6	27.2	+4.6	27.7	31.1	+3.4
25-44	78.2	78.9	+.7	79.8	81.0	+1.2
45-64	81.5	81.8	+.3	83.6	83.1	-.5
65 +	57.7	55.1	-2.6	58.3	55.2	-3.1

IIE

	1974	1979	1979-1974	1975	1980	1980-1975
16-19	61.3%	59.4%	-1.7%	69.3%	67.2%	-2.1%
16-19 Student	64.4	63.0	-1.4	72.5	70.0	-2.3
20-24	13.9	30.9	-1.0	37.7	37.2	-.5
20-24 Student	40.7	40.6	-.1	49.3	48.3	-1.0
25-44	17.9	17.0	-.9	20.2	20.4	+.2
45-64	18.6	17.6	-1.0	20.8	19.4	-1.4
65 +	38.4	35.7	-2.7	41.6	38.0	-3.6

IFE

	1974	1979	1979-1974	1975	1980	1980-1975
16-19	15.7%	15.3%	-.4	18.4%	17.7%	-.7
16-19 Student	14.6	13.3	-1.3	16.0	15.3	-.7
20-24	11.9	12.8	+.9	14.5	14.8	+.3
20-24 Student	16.5	18.0	+1.5	19.4	19.6	+.1
25-44	8.4	8.5	+.1	9.9	10.0	+.1
45-64	9.5	9.2	-.3	10.5	10.1	-.4
65 +	46.5	45.1	-1.4	48.4	45.9	-2.5

IFI

	1974	1979	1979-1974	1975	1980	1980-1975
16-19	9.8%	9.5%	-.3%	12.2%	10.9%	-2.3%
16-19 Student	8.4	7.3	-1.1	10.0	8.5	-1.5
20-24	7.7	8.1	+.4	9.4	10.0	+.6
20-24 Student	8.1	8.1	0	10.3	9.8	-.5
25-44	5.6	5.8	+.2	6.1	7.0	+.9
45-64	4.5	4.1	-.4	4.9	4.7	-.2
65 +	7.1	5.3	-1.8	7.2	6.2	-1.0

IIE Incidence Among Those Experiencing Unemployment

	1974	1979	1979-1974	1975	1980	1980-1975
16-19	79.4%	78.3%	-1.1%	85.3%	84.5%	-.8%
16-19 Student	83.5	83.9	+.4	88.6	86.7	-1.9
20-24	55.3	55.0	-.3	63.6	64.3	+.7
20-24 Student	63.1	63.2	+.1	74.5	73.3	-1.2
25-44	43.0	44.4	+1.4	48.9	50.9	+1.1
45-64	46.2	47.2	+1.0	52.6	52.0	-.6
65 +	69.3	74.5	+5.2	76.3	72.3	-4.0

Proportion of IIE in IFE

	1974	1979	1979-1974	1975	1980	1980-1975
16-19	19.3%	19.4%	+.1%	22.1%	21.9%	-.2%
16-19 Student	16.9	15.0	-1.9	18.0	17.3	-.7
20-24	26.8	29.5	+.4	29.1	31.9	+2.8
20-24 Student	21.6	27.0	+.4	24.8	27.7	+1.9
25-44	32.9	34.9	+2.0	36.1	37.4	+1.3
45-64	36.9	36.8	-.1	39.4	38.9	-.5
65 +	70.6	68.7	-1.9	71.6	73.2	+1.6

Proportion Not in IIE But In IFE

	1974	1979	1979-1974	1975	1980	1980-1975
16-19	10.0%	9.3%	-.7%	10.0%	9.3%	-.7
16-19 Student	10.4	10.5	+.1	10.8	10.6	-.2
20-24	5.0	5.3	+.3	5.7	4.7	-1.0
20-24 Student	13.0	11.8	-1.2	14.2	12.0	-2.2
25-44	3.1	3.1	0	3.2	3.0	-.2
45-64	3.2	3.4	+.2	3.0	3.2	+.2
65 +	31.5	32.1	+.6	31.8	29.1	-2.7

Earnings Supplementation Rate-Total

	1974	1979	1979-1974	1975	1980	1980-1975
16-19	37.9	37.8%	-.1%	33.8%	38.4%	+2.6%
16-19 Student	42.2	45.2	+3.0	37.7	44.6	+6.9
20-24	35.1	36.9	+1.8	35.4	36.9	+1.5
20-24 Student	51.0	57.7	+6.7	47.0	49.7	+2.7
25-44	33.3	32.2	-1.1	38.0	30.4	-7.6
45-64	51.9	55.2	+3.3	53.2	54.1	+.9
65 +	84.7	88.2	+3.5	85.0	86.5	+1.5

Earnings Supplementation Rate-Transfers

	1974	1979	1979-1974	1975	1980	1980-1975
16-19	24.9%	22.4%	-2.5%	23.7%	23.7%	0
16-19 Student	26.3	25.8	-.5	26.8	26.5	-.3
20-24	20.6	17.7	-2.9	23.5	17.7	-5.8
20-24 Student	21.3	15.5	-5.8	21.0	13.9	-7.1
25-44	21.8	19.7	-2.1	27.5	18.2	-9.3
45-64	29.5	26.6	-2.9	32.6	27.3	-5.3
65 +	51.7	50.1	-1.7	52.4	47.3	-5.1

Earnings Supplementation Rate-Nontransfers

	1974	1979	1979-1974	1975	1980	1980-1975
16-19	13.0	15.4%	+2.4%	10.1%	14.7%	+14.6%
16-19 Student	15.9	19.4	+3.5	10.9	18.1	+7.2
20-24	14.5	19.2	+4.7	11.9	19.2	+7.3
20-24 Student	29.7	42.2	+12.5	26.0	35.8	+9.8
25-44	11.5	12.5	+1.0	10.5	12.2	+1.7
45-64	24.4	28.6	+6.4	20.6	26.8	+6.2
65 +	33.0	39.1	+5.1	32.6	39.2	+6.6

Shares of severe hardship for total work force

	1974	1979	1979-1974	1975	1980	1980-1975
16-19						
IIE	26.1%	24.5%	-1.6%	25.3%	22.5%	-2.8%
IIE Deficit	17.0	16.1	-0.9	16.8	14.8	-2.0
IFE	14.9	13.4	-1.5	14.8	12.9	-1.9
IFE Deficit	14.3	12.8	-1.5	13.9	11.8	-2.1
IFI	17.5	15.7	-1.8	18.6	14.1	-4.5
IFI Deficit	14.8	13.5	-1.3	15.5	11.8	-3.7
45 and over						
IIE	27.4	24.8	-2.6	26.6	23.5	-3.1
IIE Deficit	35.7	33.2	-2.5	33.9	27.9	-6.0
IFE	40.5	36.2	-4.3	37.8	33.8	-4.0
IFE Deficit	38.2	34.1	-4.1	35.7	31.3	-4.4
IFI	26.7	21.5	-5.2	24.9	20.3	-4.6
IFI Deficit	23.8	20.3	-3.5	19.3	17.9	-1.4

The corollary is that employment problems of teenage and older workers have become less costly to solve, but their alleviation would also have less effect on aggregate hardship. If all 45- to 64-year-olds with Inadequate Individual Earnings in 1974 had, instead, received the minimum wage equivalent for their hours and weeks in the work force, the total IFE would have been 13.1 percent lower (Table 3.7). Similar augmentation of this age subgroup's earnings in 1979 would have reduced the total IFE by only 10.8 percent. Likewise, the provision of minimum wage earnings for all hours of joblessness or involuntary part-time idleness among 45- to 64-year-olds would have reduced the IFE by 0.7 percentage points more in 1974 than in 1979.

Increasing Human Resource Endowments

The educational attainment of the work force improved dramatically over the 1974-1980 period. In 1974, 33.6 percent of total participants did not have a high school degree, outnumbering the 32.4 percent with some post-secondary education. By 1980, the situation was reversed. Dropouts and high school students represented only 24.1 percent of the work force and were far outnumbered by those with some post-secondary education, who represented 37.0 percent:

Table 3.7. PERCENTAGE REDUCTION IN THE TOTAL IFE RESULTING FROM AUGMENTATION OF THE EARNINGS OF SEPARATE AGE SUBGROUPS ONLY

Reduction in IFE resulting from Full Employment augmentation[1]

	1974	1979	1979-1974	1975	1980	1980-1975
16-19	3.91%	3.22%	-0.69%	4.58%	3.79%	-0.79%
20-24	4.70	4.77	+0.07	6.58	6.28	-0.30
25-44	7.59	8.53	+0.94	9.81	11.10	+1.29
45-64	6.97	6.04	-0.93	8.73	7.09	-1.64
65+	2.71	2.29	-0.42	2.68	2.08	-0.60

Reduction in IFE resulting from Adequate Employment augmentation[2]

	1974	1979	1979-1974	1975	1980	1980-1975
16-19	4.89	4.04	-0.85	5.64	4.50	-1.14
20-24	6.30	6.45	+0.15	7.77	8.52	+0.75
25-44	12.79	12.81	+1.02	13.54	17.24	+3.70
45-64	13.14	10.84	-4.40	13.75	11.88	-1.87
65+	4.64	3.48	-1.16	4.26	3.31	-0.95

Reduction in IFE resulting from Capacity Employment augmentation[3]

	1974	1979	1979-1974	1975	1980	1980-1975
16-19	2.31	2.05	-0.26	3.29	2.63	-0.66
20-24	4.05	3.13	-0.92	5.08	5.34	+0.26
25-44	6.57	7.06	+0.49	9.20	10.30	+1.10
45-64	4.78	3.84	-0.94	6.09	5.12	-0.97
65+	0.97	0.96	-0.01	0.96	0.60	-0.36

---

[1] Full Employment augmentation--All unemployed and involuntarily part-time employed in the IFE who are in the specific age cohort are ascribed the minimum wage for all hours of forced idleness, and the effect on the total IFE is calculated.

[2] Adequate Employment augmentation--All persons in the specific age cohort who are in the IFE who have Inadequate Individual Earnings are augmented to a minimally adequate level and the effect on the total IFE is calculated.

[3] Capacity Employment augmentation--All unemployed and involuntarily part-time workers in the IFE are ascribed their usual wage for their hours of forced idleness, and the effect of this augmentation on the total IFE is calculated.

	Share of total work force						
	1974	1979	1979-1974	1975	1980	1980-1975	1980-1974
High school student	4.9%	4.3%	-0.6%	4.5%	4.1%	-0.4%	-0.8%
Post-secondary student	4.3	4.0	-0.3	4.1	4.0	-0.1	-0.3
High school dropout	28.7	20.9	-7.8	24.8	20.0	-4.8	-8.7
High school graduate only	37.3	38.1	+0.8	37.5	38.8	+1.3	+1.5
Post-secondary 1-3 years	14.0	15.8	+1.8	14.0	16.0	+2.0	+2.0
College graduate	14.1	16.9	+2.8	15.0	17.0	+2.0	+2.9

Since hardship incidence declines with increased education, the educational upgrading of the work force was a favorable development. Weighting the 1979 hardship levels for each of the six educational categories by its 1974 share of the total work force, and comparing the weighted hardship rates with the 1979 actuals, suggests that a 2.6 percentage point decline in the IIE rate, 1.5 percentage points in the IFE rate and 0.9 percentage points in the IFI rate, might have been expected as a result of improved education, if all else remained the same. All else clearly did not stay the same, since these decrements exceeded the 1.7, 0.2 and 0.1 percentage point drops in the three hardship rates, but the educational shifts were clearly a highly favorable factor:

IIE rate if 1979 incidence rates among education groups but 1974 shares	26.66%
Actual 1979 IIE incidence	24.17
Reduction in IIE associated with educational improvement	-2.59
IFE rate if 1979 incidence rates among educational groups but 1974 shares	12.82
Actual 1979 IFE incidence	11.35
Reduction in IFE incidence associated with educational improvement	-1.47
IFI rate if 1979 incidence rates among educational groups but 1979 shares	6.91
Actual 1979 IFI incidence	6.03
Reduction in IFI incidence associated with educational improvement	-0.88

Hardship incidence declined more, or rose less, for persons who had completed some post-secondary education than for high school dropouts or high school graduates with no further education (Table 3.8). For instance, the gap between the severe hardship IIE rates for dropouts and college graduates increased 3.8 percentage points between 1974 and 1980; the IFE gap increased by 2.8 percentage points, and the IFI gap by 2.9 percentage points. Interestingly, the differential between the IFE and IFI rates of dropouts and high school graduates with no further education did not increase between 1974 and 1979 or between 1975 and 1980, even though the differentials in unemployment and IIE rates widened over both periods.

The relative decline in hardship incidence among completers of post-secondary education offset, to some degree, their increasing work force share. Yet the persons in hardship in 1979 and 1980 had significantly more education than the persons in hardship in 1974 and 1975. Persons with some post-secondary education accounted for a 3.8 percentage point larger share of the severe hardship IIE in 1980 than in 1974, while their IFE and IFI shares rose 3.5 and 3.3 percentage points, respectively (Table 3.9).

The Impacts of Occupational Upgrading

Hardship is most prevalent among farm workers, laborers and service workers; it is least prevalent among white collar workers. The share of the total work force in the high incidence occupations declined by 1.4 percentage points between 1974 and 1979, while the white collar share increased by 3.1 percentage points (Table 3.10). Weighting the 1979 hardship and unemployment incidence rates in each of the nine occupational subclassifications (professional and managerial, sales, clerical, craft and kindred workers, operatives, laborers, farm and service workers, plus those not employed during the year) by their 1974 work force shares suggests that the occupational shifts were a positive factor in reducing both unemployment and hardship:

Table 3.8. HARDSHIP AND UNEMPLOYMENT RATES AND DIFFERENTIALS BY EDUCATION LEVEL

Percent Experiencing Unemployment / IIE Incidence

	1974	1979	1979-1974	1975	1980	1980-1975	1974	1979	1979-1974	1975	1980	1980-1975
High School Student	28.4%	21.9%	-6.5%	28.4%	27.1%	-1.3%	68.7%	65.5%	-3.1%	76.1%	74.0%	-2.1%
Post-Secondary Student	23.9	18.7	-5.2	25.3	20.5	-4.8	41.6	42.7	+1.1	51.2	49.1	-2.1
High School Dropout	22.0	22.0	0	25.9	25.2	-0.4	34.2	34.9	+0.6	38.7	39.5	+0.8
High School Graduate, No Further Education	17.5	15.9	-1.6	20.1	18.7	-1.4	21.9	21.4	-0.5	25.3	25.7	+0.4
1-3 Years Post-Secondary Education	13.7	13.0	-0.7	16.7	13.9	-2.8	16.7	16.3	-0.4	19.8	18.6	-1.2
College Four Years or More	9.7	8.5	-1.2	10.5	9.0	-1.5	9.2	9.4	+0.2	11.0	10.6	-0.4
High School Dropout- High School Graduate	4.5	6.1	+1.6	5.8	6.8	+1.0	12.4	13.5	+1.1	13.4	13.8	+0.4
High School Dropout- 1-3 Years Post-Secondary Education	8.3	9.0	+0.7	9.2	11.6	+2.4	17.6	18.6	+1.0	18.9	20.9	+2.0
High School Dropout- College	12.3	13.5	+1.2	15.4	16.5	+1.1	25.1	25.5	+0.4	27.7	28.9	+1.2
High School Graduate- 1-3 Years Post-Secondary Education	3.8	2.9	-0.9	3.4	4.8	+1.4	5.2	5.1	-0.1	5.5	7.1	+1.6
High School Graduate- College	7.8	7.4	-0.4	9.6	9.7	+0.1	12.7	12.0	-0.7	14.3	15.1	+0.8
1-3 Years Post-Secondary- College	4.0	4.5	+1.5	6.2	4.9	-1.3	7.5	6.9	-0.6	8.8	8.0	-0.8

IFE Incidence / IFI Incidence

	1974	1979	1979-1974	1975	1980	1980-1975	1974	1979	1979-1974	1975	1980	1980-1975
High School Student	15.9%	15.4%	-0.5%	17.9%	17.6%	-0.3%	9.7%	8.9%	-0.8%	11.3%	10.7%	-0.6%
Post-Secondary Student	15.4	17.1	+1.7	17.3	18.4	+1.1	7.2	7.1	-0.1	9.1	8.8	-0.3
High School Dropout	21.1	21.6	+0.5	24.0	24.5	+0.5	11.7	12.3	+0.6	13.1	14.8	+1.7
High School Graduate, No Further Education	8.1	9.0	+0.9	9.9	10.8	+0.9	4.2	4.8	+0.6	4.2	5.9	+1.7
1-3 Years Post-Secondary Education	7.3	7.6	+0.3	8.8	8.5	-0.3	3.5	3.8	+0.3	4.2	4.3	+0.1
College Four Years or More	4.5	5.0	+0.5	5.2	5.1	-0.1	1.8	2.2	+0.4	2.4	2.4	0
High School Dropout- High School Graduate	13.0	12.6	-0.4	14.1	13.7	-0.4	7.5	7.5	0	8.9	8.9	0
High School Dropout- 1-3 Years Post-Secondary Education	13.8	14.0	+0.2	15.2	16.0	+0.8	8.2	8.5	+0.3	8.9	10.5	+1.6
High School Dropout- College	16.6	16.6	0	18.8	19.4	+0.6	9.9	10.1	+0.2	10.7	12.8	+2.1
High School Graduate- 1-3 Years Post-Secondary Education	0.8	1.4	+0.6	1.1	2.3	+1.2	0.7	1.0	+0.3	0	1.6	+1.6
High School Graduate- College	3.6	4.0	+0.4	4.7	5.7	+1.0	2.4	2.6	+0.2	1.8	3.5	+1.7
1-3 Years Post-Secondary- College	2.8	2.6	-0.2	3.6	3.4	-0.2	0.7	1.6	+0.9	1.8	1.9	+0.1

Table 3.9. INCREASED EDUCATIONAL ATTAINMENT AMONG TOTAL WORK FORCE PARTICIPANTS IN SEVERE HARDSHIP

IIE Share

	1974	1979	1979-1974	1975	1980	1980-1975	1980-1974
High School Student	13.2%	11.8%	-1.4%	11.8%	11.1%	-0.7%	-2.1%
Post-Secondary Student	6.9	7.0	+0.1	7.3	7.1	-0.2	+0.2
High School Dropout	34.6	30.2	-4.4	33.0	28.6	-4.4	-6.0
High School Graduate, No Further Education	31.7	33.8	+2.1	32.7	36.0	+3.3	+4.3
1-3 Years Post-Secondary Education	8.6	10.7	+2.1	9.5	10.7	+1.2	+2.1
College Graduate	5.6	6.6	+1.6	5.7	6.5	+0.8	+1.5

IFE Share

	1974	1979	1979-1974	1975	1980	1980-1975	1980-1974
High School Student	6.8%	5.9%	-0.9%	6.1%	5.7%	-0.4%	-1.1%
Post-Secondary Student	5.9	6.0	+0.1	5.5	5.8	+0.3	-0.1
High School Dropout	47.5	39.9	-7.6	45.1	38.4	-6.7	-9.1
High School Graduate, No Further Education	26.2	30.2	+4.0	28.1	32.7	+4.6	+6.5
1-3 Years Post-Secondary Education	8.3	10.7	+2.4	9.3	10.6	+1.3	+2.3
College Graduate	5.5	7.4	+1.9	5.9	6.8	+0.9	+1.3

IFI Share

	1974	1979	1979-1974	1975	1980	1980-1975	1980-1974
High School Student	7.8%	6.4%	-1.4%	7.3%	6.2%	-1.1%	-1.6%
Post-Secondary Student	5.0	4.7	-0.3	5.4	4.9	-0.5	-0.1
High School Dropout	49.7	42.7	-7.0	46.9	41.3	-5.6	-8.4
High School Graduate, No Further Education	25.6	30.2	+4.6	26.6	32.3	+5.7	+6.7
1-3 Years Post-Secondary Education	7.6	10.0	+2.4	8.5	9.5	+1.0	+1.9
College Graduate	4.3	6.1	+1.8	5.2	5.8	+0.6	+1.5

Table 3.10. OCCUPATIONAL SHIFTS AND CHANGING WORK FORCE ATTACHMENT OVER 1974-1979 PERIOD

	Share Total Work Force 1974	Share Total Work Force 1979	Share Total Work Force 1979-1974	Percent Total Work Force in Each Occupation Participating Full-Year 1974	Percent Total Work Force in Each Occupation Participating Full-Year 1979	Percent Total Work Force in Each Occupation Participating Full-Year 1979-1974	Share Full-Year Work Force 1974	Share Full-Year Work Force 1979	Share Full-Year Work Force 1979-1974
White Collar	46.2%	49.3%	+3.1%	74.9%	75.6%	+0.5%	49.3%	51.9%	+2.6%
Professional, Technical, Managerial and Administrative	22.6	24.9	+2.3	82.6	81.8	-0.8	26.6	28.5	+1.9
Sales	6.2	6.1	-0.1	66.6	68.0	+1.4	5.9	5.8	-0.1
Clerical	17.4	18.3	+0.9	67.9	69.6	+1.7	16.8	17.7	+1.9
Blue Collar	33.6	31.7	-1.9	74.3	76.0	+1.7	35.5	33.6	-1.9
Craft and Kindred	12.7	12.2	-0.5	83.3	83.5	+0.2	14.4	14.2	-0.2
Operatives	15.8	14.2	-1.7	72.4	75.4	+3.0	16.3	14.9	-1.4
Laborers	5.7	5.3	-0.4	60.1	60.5	+0.4	4.9	4.5	-0.4
Farm Workers	3.6	2.7	-0.9	68.4	70.4	+2.0	3.5	2.7	-0.8
Service Workers	14.6	14.5	-0.1	54.0	56.1	+2.1	11.2	11.3	+0.1
No Employment	2.1	1.8	-0.3	17.8	17.8	0	0.5	0.5	0

1979 total unemployment incidence if 1974 occupational distribution but 1979 unemployment rates in each occupation	16.54%
1979 unemployment incidence	15.79
Reduction in unemployment incidence between 1974 and 1979 related to occupational shift	-0.75
1979 IIE if 1974 occupational distribution but 1979 IIE rates for each occupation	25.08
1979 IIE incidence	24.17
Reduction in IIE incidence between 1974 and 1979 related to occupational shift	-0.91
1979 IFE if 1974 occupational distribution but 1979 IFE rates for each occupation	11.87
1979 IFE incidence	11.35
Reduction in IFE incidence between 1974 and 1979 related to occupational shift	-0.52
1979 IFI if 1974 occupational distribution but 1979 IFI rates for each occupation	6.36
1979 IFI incidence	6.03
Reduction in IFI incidence between 1974 and 1979 related to occupational shift	-0.33

For the high incidence occupations, increases in work force attachment reduced the severe hardship rates. For instance, the proportion of farm workers who participated full-year rose by 2.0 percentage points between 1974 and 1979, and the proportion of service workers participating full-year rose by 2.1 percentage points, compared to an increase of only 0.5 percentage points among white collar workers. Reflecting this change, the IFE rate among farm workers declined 9.5 percentage points, and that among service workers fell 2.9 percentage points, while the IFE incidence remained almost stable for white collar workers (Table 3.11). While the variance in unemployment incidence rates within the nine broad occupational categories declined slightly, the variance in hardship rates declined substantially:

Table 3.11. INCIDENCE OF UNEMPLOYMENT AND HARDSHIP IN 1974 AND 1979 BY OCCUPATION

TOTAL WORK FORCE

	Unemployment Incidence 1974	1979	1979-1974	IIE Incidence 1974	1979	1979-1974	IFE Incidence 1974	1979	1979-1974	IFI Incidence 1974	1979	1979-1974
White Collar	10.7%	9.4%	-1.3%	16.9%	16.7%	-0.2%	6.4%	7.4%	+1.0%	2.7%	3.3%	+0.6%
Professional, Technical Managerial and Administrative	7.2	7.1	-0.1	10.2	10.2	0	4.8	5.6	+0.8	2.0	2.6	+0.6
Sales	12.8	10.8	-2.0	29.9	29.5	-0.4	10.3	10.9	+0.6	3.7	4.4	+0.7
Clerical	14.5	12.1	-2.4	20.9	21.3	+0.4	7.1	8.6	+1.5	3.3	3.8	+0.5
Blue Collar	23.9	21.1	-2.8	20.2	19.3	-0.9	10.3	10.3	0	5.7	5.8	+0.1
Craft and Kindred	18.8	17.3	-1.5	20.5	11.6	+1.1	7.1	7.5	+0.4	3.8	4.3	+0.5
Operatives	25.8	22.0	-3.8	23.0	19.9	-3.1	10.3	10.3	0	5.7	5.7	0
Laborers	29.6	27.3	-2.3	32.8	35.3	+2.5	17.2	16.6	-0.6	9.7	9.6	-0.1
Farm Workers	9.4	11.0	+1.6	63.9	54.4	-9.5	31.8	25.8	-6.0	19.7	15.5	-3.9
Service Employment	17.2	16.8	-0.4	47.8	44.9	-2.9	21.2	20.4	-0.8	11.2	11.0	-0.2
No Employment	100.0	100.0	0	97.9	99.4	+1.5	45.6	46.8	+1.2	30.0	31.6	+1.6

FULL-YEAR WORK FORCE

	1974	1979	1979-1974	1974	1979	1979-1974	1974	1979	1979-1974	1974	1979	1979-1974
White Collar	8.0	7.4	-0.6	11.5	11.6	+0.1	3.5	4.0	+0.5	1.5	1.8	+0.3
Professional, Technical Managerial and Administrative	5.8	5.7	-0.1	7.6	7.6	0	2.8	3.1	+0.3	1.4	1.6	+0.2
Sales	9.4	8.6	-0.8	20.9	20.8	-0.1	6.0	7.0	+1.0	1.9	2.7	+0.8
Clerical	11.1	9.7	-1.4	14.4	15.0	+0.6	3.7	4.4	+0.7	1.6	1.8	+0.2
Blue Collar	23.6	21.2	-2.5	14.9	14.6	-0.3	6.3	6.5	+0.2	3.7	3.9	+0.2
Craft and Kindred	18.7	16.9	-1.8	8.5	9.7	+1.2	4.2	4.9	+0.7	2.8	3.2	+0.4
Operatives	25.7	22.0	-3.7	17.0	15.4	-1.6	6.2	6.4	+0.2	3.6	3.6	0
Laborers	30.8	31.2	+1.4	27.2	27.5	+0.3	12.4	11.8	-0.6	7.1	7.5	+0.4
Farm Workers	7.6	10.1	+2.5	63.1	57.4	-5.7	28.8	23.2	-5.6	17.3	14.4	-2.9
Service Workers	15.5	16.6	+1.1	38.5	36.1	-2.4	16.2	14.8	-1.4	8.5	7.8	-0.7
No Employment	100.0	100.0	0	100.0	100.0	0	62.2	54.4	-7.8	34.7	37.7	+3.0

Variance between nine occupational subclassifications in
hardship and unemployment incidence

	Unemployment incidence			IIE incidence			IFE incidence			IFI incidence		
	1974	1979	1979-1974	1974	1979	1979-1974	1974	1979	1979-1974	1974	1979	1979-1974
Total work force												
Standard deviation	7.7%	6.7%	-1.0%	18.4%	15.7%	-2.7%	9.1%	7.0%	-2.1%	5.9%	4.6%	-1.3%
Coefficient of variation (standard deviation ÷ mean)	45.6	42.9	-2.7	61.7	55.4	-6.3	66.6	53.1	-13.5	80.3	63.7	-16.6
Full-year work force												
Standard deviation	9.0	8.4	-0.6	18.5	16.5	-2.0	8.9	8.3	-0.6	5.4	5.2	-0.4
Coefficient of variation (standard deviation ÷ mean)	57.5	55.8	-1.7	75.2	70.0	-5.2	88.6	72.1	-6.5	98.4	82.1	-16.3

The Changing Geography of Hardship

There were significant shifts in the geographic distribution of the work force over the 1974-1980 period. The share residing in the New England, Middle Atlantic, East North Central and East South Central states declined, while the share in the South Atlantic, West South Central, Mountain and Pacific states increased:

	Total work force share		
	1974	1980	1980-1974
New England	6.1%	5.7%	-0.4%
Middle Atlantic	16.6	15.6	-2.0
East North Central	19.8	18.5	-0.7
West North Central	7.9	7.0	0
South Atlantic	15.3	16.2	+0.8
East South Central	6.4	6.1	-0.3
West South Central	9.6	10.4	+0.8
Mountain	4.5	5.1	+0.6
Pacific	13.8	14.4	+0.6

On balance, the regions where hardship was more prevalent grew faster. Weighting the 1979 severe hardship rates for each region by its 1974 work force share suggests that the work force redistribution was a modestly negative factor:

Total IIE rate if 1979 incidence in each region but 1974 share	24.08%
Actual 1979 IIE incidence	24.17
1974-1979 increment in total IIE rate associated with shift to high incidence regions	+0.09
Total IFE rate if 1979 incidence in each region but 1974 share	11.28
Actual 1979 IIE incidence	11.35
1974-1979 increment in total IFE rate associated with shift to high incidence regions	+0.07
Total IFI rate if 1979 incidence in each region but 1974 share	5.98
Actual 1979 IFI incidence	6.03
1974-1979 increment in total IFI rate associated with shift to high incidence regions	+0.05

But the fast growth regions also experienced relative declines in hardship incidence. In the South Atlantic, West South Central, Mountain and Pacific states, the IIE, IFE and IFI rates all declined over both the 1974-1979 and 1975-1980 periods (Table 3.12). These improvements reduced the regional disparity in hardship rates. Even though the standard deviation in unemployment incidence for the nine regions, expressed as a percentage of the mean, actually rose between 1974 and 1980, the variance in regional hardship rates declined. It should be noted, however, that the impacts of the 1980 recession were concentrated in a few regions and increased the variation in hardship over 1975 levels:

Coefficients of variation for unemployment
and hardship rates of nine regions

	1974	1979	1979-1974	1975	1980	1980-1975	1980-1974
Incidence unemployment	10.4%	8.8%	-1.6%	10.3%	11.1%	+0.8%	+0.7%
Incidence predominantly unemployed	17.4	16.3	-1.1	21.4	20.7	-0.7	+3.3
IIE incidence	16.6	11.0	-4.4	10.4	12.9	+2.5	-3.7
IFE incidence	25.5	18.3	-7.2	18.0	18.6	+0.6	-6.9
IFI incidence	37.8	25.9	-11.9	28.1	28.8	+0.7	-9.0

The distribution of the population between metropolitan and nonmetropolitan areas remained fairly stable, but central cities lost ground, particularly those in large SMSAs, as the suburbs grew:

Table 3.12. TRENDS IN REGIONAL SEVERE HARDSHIP INCIDENCE[1]

	IIE							IFE							IFI				
	1974	1979	1979-1974	1975	1980	1980-1975	1980-1974	1974	1979	1979-1974	1975	1980	1980-1975	1980-1974	1974	1979	1979-1974	1975	1980	1980-1975	1980-1974
New England	22.4%	22.9%	+0.5%	30.0%	23.9%	-6.1%	+1.5%	8.7%	9.4%	+0.7%	12.0%	10.6%	-1.4%	+1.9%	3.8%	4.3%	+0.5%	5.5%	5.1%	-0.4%	+1.3
Middle Atlantic	20.4	21.4	+1.0	25.0	24.5	-0.5	+4.1	8.4	9.8	+1.4	10.1	10.7	+0.6	+2.3	4.0	4.8	+0.8	4.8	5.2	+0.4	+1.2
East North Central	23.0	22.8	-0.2	27.1	27.7	+0.6	+4.7	8.7	9.3	+0.6	11.0	11.5	+0.5	+2.8	4.3	4.6	+0.4	5.2	6.3	+1.1	+2.0
West North Central	29.9	27.0	-2.9	31.6	31.7	+0.1	+1.8	12.8	11.6	-1.2	12.6	13.3	+0.7	+0.5	5.8	5.6	-0.2	6.0	7.0	+1.0	+1.2
South Atlantic	27.9	25.9	-2.0	30.8	29.5	-1.3	+1.6	13.2	13.1	-0.1	15.3	14.3	-1.0	+2.1	7.8	7.2	-0.6	9.1	8.6	-0.5	+0.8
East South Central	33.2	28.9	-4.3	34.4	34.4	0	+1.2	16.9	15.3	-1.6	17.2	18.2	+1.0	+1.3	10.3	8.6	-1.7	10.0	11.6	+1.6	+1.3
West South Central	31.8	26.7	-5.1	33.0	29.7	-3.3	-2.1	16.0	14.0	-2.0	16.5	14.8	-1.7	-1.2	10.1	8.5	-1.6	9.7	9.1	-0.6	-1.0
Mountain	28.8	26.7	-2.1	31.2	27.8	-3.4	-1.0	12.6	11.5	-1.1	14.9	13.5	-1.4	+0.9	6.6	6.4	-0.2	8.5	7.8	-0.7	+2.2
Pacific	24.7	21.4	-3.3	26.7	24.0	-2.7	-0.7	12.4	10.7	-1.7	13.5	11.5	-2.0	-0.9	5.9	5.9	0	6.8	6.2	-0.6	+0.3

[1] New England: Connecticut, Maine, Massachusetts, New Hampshire, Rhode Island, Vermont
North Atlantic: New Jersey, New York, Pennsylvania
East North Central: Illinois, Indiana, Michigan, Ohio, Wisconsin
West North Central: Iowa, Kansas, Minnesota, Missouri, Nebraska, North and South Dakota
South Atlantic: Delaware, District of Columbia, Florida, Georgia, Maryland, North and South Carolina, Virginia, West Virginia
East South Central: Alabama, Kentucky, Mississippi, Tennessee
West South Central: Arkansas, Louisiana, Oklahoma, Texas
Mountain: Arizona, Colorado, Idaho, Montana, Nevada, New Mexico, Utah, Wyoming
Pacific: Alaska, California, Hawaii, Oregon, Washington

	\multicolumn{7}{c}{Share of total work force}
	1974	1979	1979-1974	1975	1980	1980-1975	1980-1974
Inside SMSA	68.9%	69.0%	+0.1%	68.8%	68.6%	-0.2%	-0.3%
Outside SMSA	31.1	31.0	-0.1	31.2	31.4	+0.2	+0.3
SMSA central city	29.1	27.8	-1.3	28.7	27.3	-1.4	-1.8
SMSA balance	39.7	41.2	+1.5	40.1	41.2	+1.1	+1.5
SMSA 1 million or more	39.4	39.4	0	39.3	39.4	+0.1	0
SMSA less than 1 million	29.5	29.6	+0.1	29.5	29.2	-0.3	-0.3
SMSA 1 million or more							
Central city	15.4	14.2	-1.2	14.8	14.1	-0.7	-1.3
Balance	23.9	25.2	+1.3	24.5	25.3	+0.8	+1.4
SMSA less than 1 million							
Central city	13.7	13.6	-0.1	13.9	13.2	-0.7	-0.5
Balance	15.8	16.0	+0.2	15.6	15.9	+0.3	+0.1

This suburbanization should have alleviated hardship somewhat, as suggested by weighting the 1979 hardship incidence in central cities in larger and smaller metropolitan areas, suburbs in larger and smaller metropolitan areas, and nonmetropolitan areas, by the 1974 shares of the total work force residing in each type of area:

Total IIE rate if 1979 incidence for each type of area but 1974 distribution	24.21%
Actual 1979 IIE incidence	24.17
IIE incidence reduction associated with suburban shift	-0.04
Total IFE rate if 1979 incidence for each type of area but 1974 distribution	11.41
Actual 1979 IFE incidence	11.35
IFE incidence reduction associated with suburban shift	-0.06
Total IFI rate if 1979 incidence for each type of area but 1974 distribution	6.11
Actual 1979 IFI incidence	6.03
IFI incidence reduction associated with suburban shift	-0.08

The hardship picture improved more in nonmetropolitan than metropolitan areas. Between 1974 and 1979, the IFE and IFI rates in metropolitan areas both rose by 0.3 percentage points, compared to drops of 1.3 and 0.9 percentage points, respectively, in nonmetropolitan areas (Table 3.13). Larger metropolitan areas improved relative to those with under one million population. This occurred despite a relative deterioration of conditions in the large SMSA central cities, where the IFI rate increased by 1.4 percentage points between 1974 and 1979, compared to an increase of only 0.2 percentage points in the surrounding suburbs.

There was a narrowing of the metropolitan/nonmetropolitan and central city/suburban differentials in hardship incidence. Considering five discrete types of areas (central cities and suburban areas in SMSAs with over 1 million population, central cities and suburban areas in smaller SMSAs, and nonmetropolitan areas), the standard deviation in hardship incidence, expressed as the proportion of the mean for the five areas, declined even though the variance in unemployment incidence increased:

Coefficients of variation in hardship and unemployment rates of large and small SMSA central cities, large and small SMSA suburbs and nonmetropolitan area incidence rates

	1974	1979	1979-1974	1975	1980	1980-1975	1980-1974
Incidence unemployment	9.2%	10.5%	+1.3%	7.9%	9.3%	+1.4%	+0.1%
Incidence predominantly unemployed	14.6	20.5	+3.9	11.5	16.7	+5.2	+2.1
IIE incidence	19.2	17.9	-1.3	17.1	18.0	+0.9	-1.2
IFE incidence	29.4	25.5	-3.9	27.6	29.0	+1.4	-0.4
IFI incidence	33.4	33.1	-0.3	31.0	32.1	+1.1	-1.3

The Changing Status of Minorities--A Detailed Assessment

Slow Gains For Blacks

The well-being of black workers and their families improved substantially over the 1960s and early 1970s, both in absolute and relative terms. According to the hardship measure developed by the National Commission on Employment and Unemployment Statistics, the incidence of hardship among nonwhites fell from 3.9 times than that among whites in 1967, to 3.0 times the white rate in 1979, despite the fact that there was no relative improvement in nonwhite unemployment rates (Table 3.14). The incidence of

Table 3.13. LONGER-TERM SHIFTS IN SEVERE HARDSHIP INCIDENCE FOR TOTAL WORK FORCE IN METROPOLITAN AND NONMETROPOLITAN AREAS

	IIE Incidence					
	1974	1979	1979-1974	1975	1980	1980-1975	1980-1974
Inside SMSA	22.7%	21.5%	-1.2%	25.8%	24.6%	-1.2%	+1.9%
SMSA Over 1 Million	20.9	19.8	-1.1	24.2	22.5	-1.7	+1.6
Central City	22.8	22.2	-0.6	25.6	25.2	-0.4	+2.4
Balance	19.7	18.4	-1.3	23.3	21.1	-1.2	+0.4
SMSA Less Than 1 Million	25.0	23.9	-1.1	28.2	27.3	-0.9	+2.3
Central City	25.5	25.0	-0.5	29.3	28.0	-1.3	+2.5
Balance	24.6	23.0	-1.6	27.2	26.7	-0.5	+2.1
Outside SMSA	32.7	30.0	-2.7	36.0	34.5	-1.5	+1.8

	IFE Incidence					
Inside SMSA	9.9	10.2	+0.3	11.3	11.0	-0.3	+1.1
SMSA Over 1 Million	9.3	9.5	+0.2	10.8	9.9	-0.9	+0.6
Central City	12.8	13.3	+0.5	14.3	14.1	-0.2	+1.3
Balance	7.0	7.3	+0.3	8.7	7.6	-1.1	+0.6
SMSA Less Than 1 Million	10.7	11.1	+0.4	11.9	12.4	+0.5	+1.7
Central City	12.7	13.0	+0.3	14.4	14.9	+0.5	+2.2
Balance	8.9	9.4	+0.5	9.8	10.3	+0.5	+1.4
Outside SMSA	15.3	14.0	-1.3	17.3	14.0	-3.3	-1.3

	IFI Incidence					
Inside SMSA	5.1	5.4	+0.3	5.8	6.2	+0.4	+1.1
SMSA Over 1 Million	4.7	5.1	+0.4	5.5	5.7	+0.2	+0.4
Central City	6.6	8.0	+1.4	7.4	8.6	+1.2	+2.0
Balance	3.4	3.6	+0.2	4.3	4.1	-0.2	+0.7
SMSA Less Than 1 Million	5.8	5.8	0	6.3	6.9	+0.6	+1.1
Central City	7.2	7.4	+0.4	7.8	9.0	+1.2	+1.8
Balance	4.5	4.5	0	5.0	5.2	+0.2	+0.7
Outside SMSA	8.3	7.4	-0.9	9.4	9.2	-0.2	+0.9

Table 3.14. CHANGES IN THE RELATIVE INCIDENCE OF UNEMPLOYMENT AND HARDSHIP AMONG WHITES AND NONWHITES BASED ON PREVIOUS SYSTEMS OF HARDSHIP MEASUREMENT

	Nonwhite Unemployment Rate	White Unemployment Rate	Ratio Unemployment Rates	Unemployment Rate Differential	Nonwhite Hardship Incidence	White Hardship Incidence	Ratio Hardship Rates	Differential Between Whites and Nonwhites
NCEUS Measure[1]								
1967	7.4%	3.4%	2.2	4.0%	34.0%	8.7%	3.9	25.3%
1971	9.9	5.4	1.8	4.5	26.2	8.2	3.2	18.0
1979	11.3	5.1	2.2	6.2	20.7	6.8	3.0	13.9
Employment and Earnings Inadequacy Index[2]								
1968	6.7	3.2	2.1	3.5	27.2	8.4	3.2	18.8
1972	10.0	5.0	2.0	5.0	25.2	10.0	2.5	15.2
1978	11.9	5.2	2.3	6.7	26.0	10.1	2.6	15.9

[1] Persons in work force 40 weeks or more, no more than half weeks voluntary part-time; if discouraged, then looked for a job at least 15 weeks; earned less than poverty level for family; family income less than twice poverty level.

[2] Currently unemployed, discouraged, employed full-time but earned less than poverty income in previous years or employed involuntarily part-time; family earned less than median income in previous year.

inadequate employment and earnings among nonwhites, as measured by the Levitan/Taggart hardship index, fell from 3.2 times the incidence among whites in 1968 to 2.6 times the incidence in 1972, even though the nonwhite unemployment rate increased from 2.1 to 2.3 times that of whites. Yet, most of this improvement was realized in the late 1960s and early 1970s. According to the Levitan/Taggart indicator, nonwhites actually lost ground between 1971 and 1979.

The hardship measures as defined in this volume confirm that there was very modest relative improvement in the well-being of black workers and their families over the last half of the 1970s (Table 3.15). The incidence of Inadequate Individual Earnings among black workers declined slightly from 1.55 to 1.53 times the incidence among whites, while the black IFE incidence fell from 2.60 to 2.49 times the rate among whites, and the black IFI incidence from 3.60 to 3.46 times the white IFI rate. Though limited, these gains occurred in spite of a deterioration in relative unemployment, as the annual unemployment rate of blacks increased from 2.08 to 2.39 times the rate for whites.

When judged in terms of intermediate and moderate, rather than severe, hardship, the absolute and relative gains of blacks were more substantial. For instance, the gap between the intermediate hardship IFE rates for blacks and whites narrowed by 2.1 percentage points between 1974 and 1979, even though the gap in their severe hardship IFE rates narrowed by only 0.8 percentage points:

	Black - white incidence 1974	1979	1979-1974	Black ÷ white incidence 1974	1979	1979-1974
IIE incidence						
Severe	13.5%	12.1%	-1.4%	1.55	1.53	-0.02
Intermediate	14.9	13.9	-1.0	1.44	1.41	-0.03
Moderate	15.5	14.3	-1.2	1.36	1.34	-0.02
IFE incidence						
Severe	15.8	14.6	-0.8	2.60	2.49	-0.11
Intermediate	19.5	17.4	-2.1	2.51	2.35	-0.16
Moderate	22.5	20.0	-2.5	2.40	2.23	-0.17
IFI incidence						
Severe	12.5	11.8	-0.7	3.60	3.46	-0.14
Intermediate	17.5	15.8	-1.7	3.36	3.16	-0.20
Moderate	21.7	19.2	-2.8	3.07	2.88	-0.19

As a result, the intermediate hardship IFE declined for blacks relative to their severe hardship IFE; while for whites, intermediate hardship increased relative to severe hardship. Likewise, the ratio of the inter-

Table 3.15. ABSOLUTE AND RELATIVE CHANGES IN UNEMPLOYMENT AND HARDSHIP INCIDENCE FOR BLACKS, HISPANICS AND WHITES

	Average Annual Unemployment						IIE					
	1974	1979	1979-1974	1975	1980	1980-1975	1974	1979	1979-1974	1975	1980	1980-1975
Incidence Rates												
Whites	5.0%	5.1%	+0.1%	7.8%	6.3%	-1.5%	24.4%	22.9%	-1.5%	27.6%	26.2%	-1.4%
Blacks	10.4	12.2	+1.8	14.7	14.1	-0.6	37.9	35.0	-2.9	41.5	39.8	-1.7
Hispanics	8.1	8.3	+0.2	12.2	10.1	-2.1	32.3	29.3	-3.0	34.5	33.7	-0.8
Incidence Ratio												
Blacks ÷ Whites	2.08	2.39	+0.31	1.88	2.23	+0.35	1.55	1.53	-0.02	1.50	1.52	+0.02
Hispanics ÷ Whites	1.62	1.63	+0.01	1.56	1.60	+0.04	1.32	1.28	-0.04	1.25	1.29	+0.04
Blacks ÷ Hispanics	1.28	1.47	+0.19	1.20	1.40	+0.20	1.17	1.19	+0.20	1.20	1.18	-0.02
Differential In Incidence Rates												
Blacks - Whites	6.4	7.1	+0.7	6.9	7.8	+0.9	13.5	12.1	-1.4	13.9	13.6	-0.3
Hispanics - Whites	3.1	3.2	+0.1	4.4	3.7	-0.7	7.9	6.4	-1.5	6.9	7.5	+0.6
Blacks - Hispanics	2.3	3.9	+1.6	2.5	4.0	+1.5	5.6	5.7	+0.1	7.0	6.1	-0.9

	IFE						IFI					
	1974	1979	1979-1974	1975	1980	1980-1975	1974	1979	1979-1974	1975	1980	1980-1975
Incidence Rates												
Whites	9.9	9.8	-0.1	11.6	11.2	-0.4	4.8	4.8	0	5.7	5.8	+0.1
Blacks	25.7	24.4	-1.3	26.5	26.3	-0.2	17.3	16.6	-0.7	17.3	18.7	+1.4
Hispanics	18.0	16.3	-1.7	20.8	18.7	-1.1	13.1	11.6	-1.5	15.4	13.6	-1.8
Incidence Ratio												
Blacks ÷ Whites	2.60	2.49	-0.11	2.28	2.35	+0.07	3.60	3.46	-0.14	3.04	3.25	+0.21
Hispanics ÷ Whites	1.82	1.66	+0.16	1.79	1.67	-0.12	2.73	2.42	-0.31	2.70	2.34	-0.36
Blacks ÷ Hispanics	1.43	1.50	+0.07	1.27	1.41	+0.14	1.32	1.43	+0.11	1.12	1.38	+0.26
Differential In Incidence Rates												
Blacks - Whites	15.8	14.0	-1.2	14.9	15.1	+0.2	12.5	11.8	-0.7	11.6	13.9	+1.3
Hispanics - Whites	8.1	6.5	-1.6	9.2	7.5	-1.7	8.3	6.8	-1.5	9.7	7.8	-1.9
Blacks - Hispanics	7.7	8.1	+0.4	5.7	7.6	+1.9	4.2	5.0	+0.8	1.9	5.1	+3.2

mediate and severe hardship IFI rates declined more for blacks than whites. Thus, the modest relative improvements in severe hardship between 1974 and 1979 were not accomplished by simply moving a few additional black workers above minimum wage earnings levels or family incomes and earnings modestly above poverty levels. A more realistic interpretation is that the gains of those slightly above the severe hardship level created a vacuum which may have pulled up those below:

	1974	1979	1979-1974
IIE incidence			
Whites			
Intermediate + severe	1.38	1.46	+.08
Moderate + severe	1.75	1.85	+.10
Blacks			
Intermediate + severe	1.29	1.36	+.07
Moderate + severe	1.54	1.62	+.08
IFE incidence			
Whites			
Intermediate + severe	1.29	1.31	+.02
Moderate + severe	1.62	1.66	+.04
Blacks			
Intermediate + severe	1.26	1.24	-.02
Moderate + severe	1.50	1.49	-.01
IFI incidence			
Whites			
Intermediate + severe	1.54	1.53	-.01
Moderate + severe	2.19	2.14	-.05
Blacks			
Intermediate + severe	1.44	1.39	-.05
Moderate + severe	1.87	1.77	-.10

Contributing Factors

Several factors contributed to the modest gains of blacks, offsetting the deterioration in their relative unemployment status. The participation rates among blacks age 16 and over declined by 1.3 percentage points between 1974 and 1979, while increasing 1.5 percentage points for whites.

To the extent that the marginal entrants and leavers were those most likely to be in hardship, the at-risk group increased among whites while declining among blacks. Increased attachment of black workers was a positive factor to the extent the chances of inadequate earnings are lower among those participating more weeks. The proportion of blacks in the work force fifty weeks or more rose by 3.3 percentage points compared to a 1.4 percentage point increase among whites (Table 3.16). Likewise, part-time workers more often suffer hardship than full-time workers; and the percent of the total black work force employed full-time during all weeks of participation declined by only 3.4 percentage points, while dropping 4.8 percentage points for whites between 1974 and 1979. The full-time, full-year share of the total black work force declined by 0.5 percentage points compared to a 3.0 percentage point drop among whites.

The earnings of black workers improved, as suggested by the fact that the IIE incidence among persons with no weeks of joblessness declined more for blacks than whites (Table 3.17). In contrast, the IIE incidence among workers with some unemployment rose among blacks while falling among whites. The share of the work force experiencing unemployment dropped 2.3 percentage points for blacks, or slightly more than the 2.1 percent decline among whites, but the share of the unemployed who were jobless for two-thirds or more of their weeks in the work force increased more for blacks than whites:

	IIE incidence		
	1974	1979	1979-1974
Blacks			
Employed full-time	16.1%	13.8%	-2.3%
Employed part-time	53.1	41.8	-7.3
Experienced unemployment	68.8	70.3	+1.5
Whites			
Employed full-time	11.2	9.6	-1.6
Employed part-time	39.4	34.5	-4.9
Experienced unemployment	51.5	50.2	-1.3

The balance of all these changes is suggested by weighting the 1979 IIE rates for full-year and less than full-year participants with each of the seven different work experience patterns by the share of the 1974 total work force in each category, as well as by weighting the 1974 rates by the 1979 patterns. All else remaining the same, the IIE incidence changes between 1974 and 1979 would have reduced the gap between black and white IIE rates by 0.5 percentage points, while the work experience/attachment shifts would have also reduced the differential roughly the same amount. In other words, these two factors contributed about equally to the relative improvement for blacks:

Table 3.16. CHANGES IN LABOR FORCE ATTACHMENT AND WORK EXPERIENCE PATTERNS FOR WHITES, BLACKS AND HISPANICS 1974-1979

PERCENT TOTAL WORK FORCE

	Blacks 1974	Blacks 1979	Blacks 1979-1974	Whites 1974	Whites 1979	Whites 1979-1974	Hispanics 1974	Hispanics 1979	Hispanics 1979-1974
TOTAL									
Employed Full-Time	52.6%	49.2%	-3.4%	60.4%	55.6%	-4.8%	58.4%	52.3%	-6.1%
Employed Part-Time Voluntarily	13.5	18.7	+5.2	19.2	23.6	+4.4	12.5	18.3	+6.8
Employed Part-Time Involuntarily	7.1	7.6	+0.5	3.5	6.0	+2.5	4.6	7.1	+2.5
Mostly Employed	11.6	10.1	-1.5	10.3	9.3	-1.0	13.1	12.5	-0.6
Mixed	6.4	6.2	-0.2	3.6	3.0	-0.6	5.5	5.5	0
Mostly Unemployed	3.2	3.4	+0.2	1.4	1.1	-0.3	2.5	2.0	-0.5
Not Employed	5.7	5.0	-0.7	1.7	1.3	-0.4	3.4	2.4	-1.0
Total	100.0	100.0	0	100.0	100.0	0	100.0	100.0	0
FULL-YEAR									
Employed Full-Time	42.8	41.4	-1.4	50.6	47.6	-3.0	46.3	43.1	-3.4
Employed Part-Time Voluntarily	5.9	9.9	+4.0	8.1	11.8	+3.7	5.3	9.1	+3.8
Employed Part-Time Involuntarily	3.6	4.1	+0.5	2.0	3.5	+1.5	2.5	4.3	+1.8
Mostly Employed	7.5	7.1	-0.4	6.4	6.0	-0.4	8.6	8.2	-0.4
Mixed	4.0	4.1	+0.1	2.3	2.0	-0.3	3.6	4.0	+0.4
Mostly Unemployed	2.3	2.7	+0.4	1.0	0.9	-0.1	2.0	1.6	-0.4
Not Employed	0.9	0.9	0	0.3	0.2	-0.1	0.5	0.5	0
Total	66.9	70.2	+3.3	70.6	72.0	+1.4	68.8	70.8	+2.0

Table 3.17. CHANGES IN THE INCIDENCE OF INADEQUATE INDIVIDUAL EARNINGS BY RACE, LABOR FORCE ATTACHMENT AND WORK EXPERIENCE PATTERN, 1974-1979

IIE INCIDENCE

	Blacks 1974	Blacks 1979	Blacks 1979-1974	Whites 1974	Whites 1979	Whites 1979-1974	Hispanics 1974	Hispanics 1979	Hispanics 1979-1974
TOTAL WORK FORCE									
Employed Full-Time	16.1%	13.8%	-2.3%	11.2%	9.6%	-1.6%	16.8%	14.0%	-2.8%
Employed Part-Time Voluntarily	45.6	34.3	-11.3	37.6	32.6	-5.0	41.9	30.9	-11.0
Employed Part-Time Involuntarily	67.4	60.4	-7.0	49.4	42.2	-7.2	53.8	38.0	-15.8
Mostly Employed	42.3	43.6	+1.3	33.0	32.2	-0.8	34.5	44.6	+10.1
Mixed	76.1	75.9	-0.2	67.8	67.6	-0.2	80.6	69.5	-10.6
Mostly Unemployed	95.8	96.2	+0.4	93.8	94.6	+0.8	99.3	92.6	-6.7
Not Employed	99.3	99.7	+0.4	97.4	99.3	+1.9	100.0	99.8	-0.2
FULL-YEAR WORK FORCE									
Employed Full-Time	12.1	10.0	-2.1	8.3	7.1	-1.2	12.4	11.7	-0.7
Employed Part-Time Voluntarily	41.9	30.3	-11.6	36.7	27.3	-9.4	42.4	24.8	-17.6
Employed Part-Time Involuntarily	61.8	48.9	-12.9	36.2	29.9	-6.3	39.2	28.7	-10.5
Mostly Employed	33.1	38.0	+4.9	22.9	25.3	+2.4	29.0	38.3	+9.3
Mixed	69.8	72.9	+3.1	61.7	63.2	+1.5	76.7	63.7	-13.0
Mostly Unemployed	94.5	95.3	-0.8	94.1	94.0	-0.1	99.2	90.5	-8.7
Not Employed	100.0	100.0	0	100.0	100.0	0	100.0	100.0	0

	Whites	Blacks	Blacks-whites
1979 IIE rate if each work experience/ attachment category had 1979 IIE incidence but 1974 share	23.25%	35.80%	12.55%
Actual 1979 IIE incidence	22.95	35.05	12.10
Reduction in IIE rate associated with changing work force patterns	-0.30	-0.75	-0.45
1979 IIE rate if each work experience/ attachment category had 1974 IIE incidence but 1979 share	24.77	37.39	12.62
Actual 1979 IIE incidence	22.95	35.05	12.10
Reduction in IIE rate associated with declining incidence in each work experience/attachment category	-1.82	-2.34	-0.52

Not only did the IIE incidence decline more for blacks than for whites between 1974 and 1979, the percent of workers with Inadequate Individual Earnings who were in families with Inadequate Family Earnings increased more for whites than for blacks:

	Percent IIE in IFE	
	Whites	Blacks
1974	27.6%	51.9%
1979	28.7	52.6
1979-1974	+1.1	+0.7
1975	30.7	52.5
1980	31.5	53.6
1980-1975	+0.8	+1.1
1980-1974	+3.9	+1.7

The increased incidence of family earnings inadequacy among persons with Inadequate Individual Earnings occurred despite a declining number of dependents per worker in the families of workers in the IIE. The changes in these dependency rates were about the same for blacks as for whites:

| | Other family members per worker in families of persons in IIE ||
	Whites	Blacks
1974	1.04	1.34
1979	0.92	1.27
1979-1974	-0.12	-0.07
1975	1.00	1.31
1980	0.88	1.16
1980-1975	-0.12	-0.15
1980-1974	-0.16	-0.18

The proportion of the blacks with adequate individual earnings who had Inadequate Family Earnings declined slightly between 1974 and 1979, and significantly between 1974 and 1980. In both cases, these declines were more than those experienced by whites:

| | Percent not in IIE who were in IFE ||
	Whites	Blacks
1974	4.70%	9.67%
1979	4.21	9.14
1979-1974	-0.49	-0.53
1975	4.36	8.12
1980	3.91	8.35
1980-1975	-0.45	+0.23
1980-1974	-0.79	-1.32

The ratio of the IFE to the IIE changed very little, with roughly equal shifts among black and white workers:

| | IFE divided by IIE ||
	Whites	Blacks
1974	.41	.68
1979	.43	.70
1979-1974	+.02	+.02
1975	.42	.64
1980	.43	.66
1980-1975	+.01	+.02
1980-1974	+.02	-.02

The IFE rates for black workers who experienced unemployment, as well as those employed full-time or part-time all weeks in the work force, all improved relative to those of whites. Only among the short-term unemployed were the changes more favorable for whites than blacks (Table 3.18):

	IFE incidence		
	1974	1979	1979-1974
Blacks			
Employed full-time	11.0%	9.3%	-1.7%
Employed part-time	42.8	36.0	-6.8
Experience unemployment	44.2	42.4	-1.8
Whites			
Employed full-time	4.5	4.0	-0.5
Employed part-time	18.1	16.2	-1.9
Experienced unemployment	18.3	19.0	+0.7

On balance, the work experience pattern shifts were more favorable for whites than blacks between 1974 and 1979, adding 0.5 percentage points to the black-white IFE differential. In contrast, the IFE incidence rate declines for each work experience category were more favorable for blacks than whites, reducing the differential by 1.5 percentage points:

	Whites	Blacks	Blacks-whites
IFE if 1974 IFE rates among work experience groups but 1979 share	10.75	26.95	16.20
Actual 1974 IFE incidence	9.94	25.67	15.73
Increase in IFE rate between 1974 and 1979 associated with changes in work experience patterns	+0.81	+1.28	+0.47
IFE if 1979 IFE rates among work experence groups but 1974 share	9.41	23.61	14.20
Actual if 1974 IFE incidence	9.94	25.67	15.73
Decline in IFE rate between 1974 and 1979 associated with changes in IFE incidence within each work experience category	-0.53	-2.06	-1.53

The Earnings Supplementation Rate, i.e., the percent of the IFE lifted out of poverty by the receipt of cash transfers and other nonearned income, declined for both blacks and whites over the 1974-1980 period, but more so for blacks than whites. The impact of nontransfer income supplements increased less for blacks than for whites, but the impact of cash transfers declined less for the black working poor than for whites (Table 3.19).

Table 3.18. CHANGES IN THE INCIDENCE OF INADEQUATE FAMILY EARNINGS BY RACE, LABOR FORCE ATTACHMENT AND WORK EXPERIENCE PATTERN, 1974-1979

IFE INCIDENCE

	Blacks 1974	Blacks 1979	Blacks 1979-1974	Whites 1974	Whites 1979	Whites 1979-1974	Hispanics 1974	Hispanics 1979	Hispanics 1979-1974
TOTAL									
Employed Full-Time	11.0%	9.3%	-1.7%	4.5%	4.0%	-0.5%	10.1%	9.6%	-0.5%
Employed Part-Time Voluntarily	42.4	34.2	-8.2	18.3	16.0	-2.3	26.0	20.0	-6.0
Employed Part-Time Involuntarily	43.6	40.7	-2.9	17.0	16.9	-0.1	28.6	22.4	-6.2
Mostly Employed	23.7	28.1	+4.4	11.0	11.8	+0.8	18.3	18.8	+0.5
Mixed	43.0	39.6	-3.4	21.8	25.4	+3.6	39.9	30.4	-9.5
Mostly Unemployed	56.9	56.3	-0.6	40.8	37.8	-3.0	47.3	43.2	-3.9
Not Employed	66.2	63.5	-2.7	37.9	39.3	+1.4	53.1	48.9	-4.2
FULL-YEAR									
Employed Full-Time	6.5	5.8	-0.6	2.6	2.2	-0.4	6.2	6.2	0
Employed Part-Time Voluntarily	35.5	23.8	-11.7	15.0	11.1	-3.9	21.6	11.9	-9.7
Employed Part-Time Involuntarily	36.1	30.5	-5.6	12.1	10.7	-1.4	21.4	18.8	-2.6
Mostly Employed	17.1	20.7	+3.6	7.2	8.0	+0.8	13.0	14.2	+1.2
Mixed	37.7	37.3	-0.4	20.9	24.7	+3.8	35.5	29.0	-6.5
Mostly Unemployed	53.4	53.8	+0.4	42.7	36.6	-6.1	49.4	41.7	-7.7
Not Employed	76.2	61.8	-14.4	58.3	50.5	-7.8	65.6	65.1	-0.5

Table 3.19. CHANGE IN EARNINGS SUPPLEMENTATION RATES BY WORK EXPERIENCE PATTERN FOR BLACKS

	Total Earnings Supplementation Rate					Earnings Supplementation Rate - Nontransfers					Earnings Supplementation Rate - Transfers					Change in Total Earnings Supplementation Rate				Change in Earnings Supplementation Rate - Nontransfers				Change in Earnings Supplementation Rate - Transfers		
	1974	1975	1979	1980		1974	1975	1979	1980		1974	1975	1979	1980		1979-1974	1980-1975	1980-1974		1979-1974	1980-1975	1980-1974		1979-1974	1980-1975	1980-1974
Employed Full-Time																										
Whites	45.9%	43.9%	42.5%	41.7%		20.9%	19.8%	22.9%	22.7%		25.0%	24.1%	19.6%	19.0%		-3.4%	-2.2%	-4.2%		+2.9%	+2.9%	+1.8%		-5.4%	-5.1%	-5.0%
Blacks	33.2	36.1	32.2	30.8		6.8	8.2	8.2	6.4		26.4	27.9	24.0	24.4		-1.0	-5.3	-2.4		+1.4	-1.8	-0.4		-2.4	-3.5	-2.0
Employed Part-Time Voluntarily																										
Whites	66.1	62.3	64.3	62.7		30.9	28.3	34.9	34.3		35.2	34.0	29.4	28.4		-1.8	+0.4	-3.4		+4.0	+6.0	+3.4		-5.8	-5.6	-6.8
Blacks	43.2	42.1	42.6	41.4		9.9	7.1	12.4	10.4		33.3	35.0	30.2	30.0		-0.6	-0.7	-1.8		+2.5	+3.3	+0.5		-3.1	-5.0	-3.3
Employed Part-Time Involuntarily																										
Whites	47.5	42.8	37.4	45.7		19.1	14.2	19.9	19.6		28.4	28.6	27.5	26.1		-0.1	+2.9	-1.8		+0.8	+5.4	+0.5		-0.9	-3.5	-2.3
Blacks	25.5	28.9	30.1	25.0		2.1	8.8	5.2	5.8		23.4	26.1	24.9	19.2		+4.6	-3.9	-0.5		+3.1	+3.0	+3.7		+1.5	-6.9	-4.2
Experienced Some Unemployment																										
Whites	41.3	48.0	42.9	39.0		13.3	12.6	15.8	13.5		28.0	35.4	27.1	25.5		+1.6	-9.0	-2.3		+2.5	+0.9	+0.2		-0.9	-9.9	-2.5
Blacks	28.9	32.5	25.6	24.0		4.7	3.2	6.4	4.7		24.2	29.3	19.2	19.3		-3.3	-8.5	-4.9		+1.7	+1.5	0		-5.0	-10.0	-4.9
TOTAL																										
Whites	51.7	51.2	51.5	48.4		22.0	19.3	25.2	23.2		29.7	31.9	26.3	25.2		-0.2	-2.8	-3.3		+3.2	+3.9	+1.2		-3.4	-6.7	-4.5
Blacks	32.7	34.8	31.8	29.1		6.0	5.0	8.1	6.4		26.7	29.8	23.7	22.7		-0.9	-5.7	-3.6		+2.1	+1.4	+0.4		-3.0	-7.1	-4.0

Among persons employed full-time and voluntarily part-time, the declines in overall Earnings Supplementation Rates between 1974 and 1980, but particularly in transfer supplementation, were relatively greater for whites than blacks. On the other hand, earnings supplements for unemployed blacks, and particularly transfer supplements, declined more than for the white unemployed.

Significant Improvements for Hispanics

Hardship declined substantially for Hispanic workers, much more than for white workers, even though unemployment rate differentials did not narrow. In 1974, the Hispanic average annual unemployment rate was 1.62 times that of whites and remained 1.63 times as high in 1979. Nevertheless, the Hispanic IIE incidence declined from 1.32 to 1.28 times that of whites, while family earnings and income inadequacy declined even more. The Hispanic/white IFE incidence ratio dropped from 1.82 to 1.66, while the IFI incidence ratio fell from 2.73 to 2.42. The absolute differences also declined:

Changes in Hispanic-white severe hardship incidence differentials

	1979-1974	1980-1975	1980-1974
IIE incidence	-1.5%	+0.6%	-0.4%
IFE incidence	-1.6	-1.7	-0.6
IFI incidence	-1.5	-1.9	-0.5

The reductions in severe hardship among Hispanics were apparently achieved by the movement of many individuals and families only slightly above the severe hardship adequacy standards. In contrast to the patterns for blacks, severe hardship gains of Hispanics were not matched or exceeded by declines in moderate and intermediate hardship. The intermediate hardship IIE incidence among Hispanic workers actually rose by 1.0 percentage points between 1974 and 1979 despite a decline of 3.0 percentage points in the severe hardship rate. While the differential in severe hardship IIE rates for Hispanics and whites declined by 1.5 percentage points, the differential in intermediate hardship rates rose by 1.2 percentage points. Likewise, the Hispanic-white severe hardship IFI differential fell by 1.5 percentage points, but the intermediate hardship differential declined by only 1.1 percentage points:

	Hispanics			Whites		
	1974	1979	1979-1974	1974	1979	1979-1974
IIE incidence						
Severe	32.3%	29.3%	-3.0	24.4%	22.9%	-1.5
Intermediate	43.9	44.9	+1.0	33.8	33.6	-0.2
Moderate	55.0	55.2	+0.2	42.8	42.5	-0.3
IIE ratio						
Intermediate ÷ Severe	1.36	1.54	+0.18	1.36	1.46	+0.12
Moderate ÷ Severe	1.70	1.89	+0.19	1.75	1.85	+0.10
IFE incidence						
Severe	18.0	16.3	-2.7	9.9	9.8	-0.1
Intermediate	24.0	26.2	-1.8	12.9	12.9	0
Moderate	30.4	29.3	-1.1	16.1	16.3	+0.2
IFE ratio						
Intermediate ÷ Severe	1.33	1.36	+0.03	1.29	1.31	+0.02
Moderate ÷ Severe	1.69	1.80	+0.11	1.63	1.66	+0.03
IFI incidence						
Severe	13.1	11.6	-1.5	4.8	4.8	0
Intermediate	18.9	17.7	-1.2	7.4	7.3	-0.1
Moderate	26.1	24.4	-1.7	10.5	10.2	-0.3
IFI ratio						
Intermediate ÷ Severe	1.44	1.52	+0.07	1.54	1.53	-0.01
Moderate ÷ Severe	1.99	2.10	+0.11	2.19	2.14	-0.05

The declining hardship experienced by Hispanic workers was not the result of relative improvements in their work experience patterns. Between 1974 and 1980, the Hispanic labor force participation rate increased 2.3 percentage points compared to the 1.5 percentage point increase for whites; thus, more high risk, marginal work force participants were added to the Hispanic work force. While the proportion of all Hispanic workers who participated full-year rose by 1.9 percentage points compared to 1.4 percentage points for whites, the proportion employed full-time, full-year declined by 3.4 percentage points compared to the 3.0 percentage point decline for whites. Part-time work increased significantly. In 1974, 12.5 percent of the total Hispanic work force was employed part-time voluntarily all weeks of participation. By 1979, this share had risen to 18.3 percent, a 6.8 percentage point increase among Hispanics, compared to the 4.4 percentage point increase among whites. Weighting the 1974 IIE rates for each work experience pattern category by its 1979 share suggests that these shifting work patterns were associated with a 0.2 percentage point decline in the Hispanic/white IIE differential. On the other hand, the declining incidence rates within various work experience categories were associated with a 0.9 percentage point reduction in the differential:

	Hispanics	Whites	Hispanics-whites
IIE rate if had 1974 IIE incidence for each work experience category but 1979 share	32.85%	25.19%	7.66%
Actual 1974 IIE incidence	32.32	24.44	7.88
Increment in IIE incidence associated with 1974-1979 changes in work experience patterns	+0.53	+0.75	-0.22
IIE incidence if had 1979 IIE rates for each category but 1974 share	20.19	27.44	7.25
Actual 1979 IIE incidence	22.95	29.26	6.31
Decrement in IIE associated with incidence changes with work experience categories	-2.76	-1.82	-0.94

The absolute and relative declines in family earnings inadequacy among Hispanic workers were even greater than the individual earnings improvements, largely because of favorable changes in family work force participation. For Hispanic families with at least one individual in the IIE, the number of other family members per work force participant declined from 1.59 to 1.28 between 1974 and 1980 compared to the decline from 1.04 to 0.88 for whites:

Other family members per worker in families of persons in IIE

		Whites	Hispanics
1974		1.04	1.59
1979		0.92	1.42
	1979-1974	-0.12	-0.17
1975		1.00	1.50
1980		0.88	1.28
	1980-1975	-0.12	-0.22
	1980-1974	-0.16	-0.31

Thus, the percent of persons with Inadequate Individual Earnings who also had Inadequate Family Earnings declined more (or increased less) for Hispanics than for whites:

	Percent IIE in IFE	
	Whites	Hispanics
1974	27.6%	39.8%
1979	28.7	36.6
1979-1974	+1.1	-3.2
1975	30.7	42.7
1980	31.5	41.4
1980-1975	+0.8	-1.3
1980-1974	+3.9	+0.6

The narrowing of the Hispanic-white IFI differential resulted not only from the relative improvements in the IFE, but also from relative increases in Earnings Supplementation Rates of Hispanics. Between 1974 to 1979, the proportion of the IFE raised out of poverty by nontransfer earnings supplements increased by 3.6 percentage points for Hispanics compared to 3.2 percentage points for whites; while the proportion lifted out of poverty by the addition of transfers declined 3.4 percentage points for whites but only 2.0 percentage points among Hispanics:

	Earnings Supplementation Rate-Total		Earnings Supplementation Rate-Nontransfers		Earnings Supplementation Rate-Transfers	
	Hispanics	Whites	Hispanics	Whites	Hispanics	Whites
1974	27.2%	51.7%	6.9%	22.0%	21.3%	29.7%
1979	28.8	51.5	9.5	25.2	19.3	26.3
1979-1974	+1.6	-0.2	+3.6	+3.2	-2.0	-3.4
1975	25.8	51.2	6.1	19.3	19.7	31.9
1980	27.9	48.4	8.7	23.2	19.2	25.2
1980-1975	+2.1	-2.8	+2.6	+3.9	-0.5	-6.7
1980-1974	+0.7	-3.3	-12.8	+1.2	-2.1	-4.5

The Interrelationship of Changing Family Patterns and Labor Market Trends

The Hardship Consequences of Shifting Family Patterns

With declining family size, the aging of the post-war babies, and increased work force participation of wives and other family members, the number of dependents per breadwinner declined significantly. There were 2.01 persons in the civilian population for each work force participant in 1974 but only 1.90 in 1979. The number of dependents per work force participant in families with at least one worker declined from 0.79 to 0.66:

	Breadwinners and breadwinning responsibilities						
	1974	1979	1979-1974	1975	1980	1980-1975	1980-1974
Participation rate of persons age 16 and over	68.9%	70.1%	+1.2%	68.8%	69.8%	+1.6%	+0.9%
Percent 16 and over in work force full-year	48.4%	50.3%	+1.9%	49.5%	51.6%	+2.1%	+3.0%
Civilian population per person in work force	2.01	1.90	-0.11	2.01	1.90	-0.11	-0.11
Number persons in families with a work force participant per work force participant	1.79	1.66	-0.13	1.78	1.66	-0.12	-0.13
Civilian population per full-year work force participant	2.87	2.65	-0.22	2.77	2.57	-0.02	-0.30
Number persons in families with a member in work force full-year per full-year work force participant	2.55	2.32	-0.23	2.45	2.25	-0.20	-0.30
Persons in families with a member in IIE ÷ total with IIE	2.09	1.98	-0.11	2.05	1.93	-0.12	-0.08

There was a rather dramatic decline in average family size. In 1974, 12.0 percent of the civilian population age 16 and over lived in families with six or more members, while 12.5 percent were in single person families. By 1979, the proportion in large families had declined to 9.3 percent, while the proportion in one-person units had risen to 15.6 percent:

	Distribution of civilian population age 16 and over		
Family members	1974	1979	1979-1974
One	12.5%	15.6%	+3.1%
Two	26.9	27.3	+0.4
Three	18.8	18.9	+0.1
Four or five	29.8	29.0	-0.8
Six or more	12.0	9.3	-2.7

The participation rates for persons age 16 and over living in two-person families, as well as for those living in families with six or more members actually declined, but increased for unrelated individuals and adults in families with three to five members:

	Participation rate for persons 16 and over by family size		
Family members	1974	1979	1979-1974
One	62.0%	65.6%	+3.6%
Two	61.9	60.9	-1.0
Three	73.5	76.3	+2.8
Four or five	74.0	77.1	+3.1
Six or more	71.6	70.7	-0.9

The proportion of the work force who were responsible only for their own support rose from 11.2 percent in 1974 to 14.6 percent in 1979. On the other hand, the proportion who were the sole breadwinners in families with two or more members declined from 18.5 to 15.8 percent. Put another way, 79.2 percent of the workers living in families with two or more members in 1974 were in multiple worker families compared to 81.4 percent in 1979:

Share of total work force by number of work force participants and family size

	1974			1979		
	One participant	Two participants	Three or more participants	One participant	Two participants	Three or more participants
Family size						
One member	11.23	--	--	14.55	--	--
Two members	7.41	16.80	--	7.07	16.58	--
Three members	4.08	10.93	5.06	3.58	11.40	5.57
Four or five members	5.66	13.35	13.04	4.45	13.63	13.77
Six or more members	1.34	3.33	7.76	0.78	1.98	6.62
Total	29.72	44.41	25.86	30.43	43.59	25.96

Reduced family size and increased earners helped to alleviate family earnings and income inadequacy. Weighting the 1979 hardship rates in each of the 15 family size/number of earners categories in the text table above by the 1974 work force share in each of these categories suggests the magnitude of these effects:

IIE incidence if had 1979 IIE rates for each earners/ family size category but 1974 share	24.31%
Actual 1979 IIE incidence	<u>24.17</u>
Improvement associated with changes in family size and earners	-0.14
IFE incidence if had 1979 IFE rates for each earners/ family size category but 1974 share	11.74
Actual 1979 IFE incidence	<u>11.35</u>
Improvement associated with changes in family size and earners	-0.39
IFI incidence if had 1979 IIE rates for each earners/ family size category but 1974 share	6.33
Actual 1979 IFI incidence	<u>6.03</u>
Improvement associated with changes in family size and earners	-0.30

Changes in the sex and family relationship patterns of the work force increased hardship probabilities. Unrelated individuals, who have high IFE and IFI rates, increased from 11.3 to 14.9 percent of the work force between 1974 and 1980 (Table 3.20). Male family heads with no wives in the labor market or no wives present declined from 17.0 to 13.0 percent over this period, while the female share of the work force rose by 2.0 percentage points and the female family head share by 0.7 percentage points. Since males, and particularly male family heads, are less likely to face labor market-related hardship, their declining work force shares offset the positive effects of smaller families and increased breadwinners. Weighting the 1979 severe hardship rate for each of the nine sex/family relationship subgroups (male family heads with and without wives in the work force and without wives present, female family heads, wives, male and female others, plus male and female unrelated individuals) by its 1974 work force share yields weighted hardship rates below the actual 1979 levels:

Table 3.20. CHANGES IN THE SEX AND FAMILY RELATIONSHIPS OF THE WORK FORCE

Share of Total Work Force

	1974	1979	1979-1974	1975	1980	1980-1975	1980-1974
Male Family Head	39.5%	35.9%	-3.6%	39.2%	35.6%	-3.6%	-3.9%
Wife in Work Force	(22.5)	(22.7)	(+0.2)	(22.5)	(22.6)	(+0.1)	(+0.1)
Wife Not in Work Force	(15.9)	(12.1)	(-3.8)	(15.7)	(11.7)	(-4.0)	(-4.2)
Wife Not Present	(1.1)	(1.2)	(+0.1)	(1.0)	(1.3)	(+0.3)	(+0.2)
Male Unrelated Individual	5.9	7.9	+2.0	6.1	8.1	+2.0	+2.2
Other Male	12.1	11.5	-1.4	11.8	11.8	0	-0.3
Total Male	57.4	55.3	-2.1	57.1	55.2	-1.9	-2.2
Female Family Head	4.4	5.1	+0.7	4.4	5.3	+0.9	+0.9
Wife	24.4	24.6	+0.2	24.4	24.5	+0.1	+0.1
Female Unrelated Individual	5.4	6.6	+1.2	5.8	6.8	+1.0	+1.4
Other Female	8.5	8.3	-0.2	8.3	8.2	-0.1	-0.3
Total Female	42.7	44.7	+2.0	42.9	44.8	+1.9	+2.1

IIE rate if had 1979 IIE incidence for each sex/family relationship category but 1974 share	23.87%
Actual 1979 IIE incidence	<u>24.17</u>
IIE rate increment associated with changing sex/family relationship patterns	+0.30
IFE rate if had 1979 IFE incidence for each sex/family relationship category but 1974 share	11.04
Actual 1979 IFE incidence	<u>11.35</u>
IFE rate increment associated with changing sex/family relationship patterns	+0.31
IFI rate if had 1979 IFI incidence for each sex/family relationship category but 1974 share	5.74
Actual 1979 IFI incidence	<u>6.03</u>
IFI rate increment associated with changing sex/family relationship patterns	+0.29

Shifting the Burdens

The incidence of hardship declined among families with three or more workers, as well as among single-person families with a worker (Table 3.21). Hardship incidence increased in families with three or more members but only one person in the work force.

Fortuitously, an increased percentage of the large families had multiple earners and the multiple earners increased their work force attachment. For instance, the percent of workers living in families with four or more members and having at least two full-year participants rose from 52.5 percent of workers in such families in 1974 to 56.6 percent in 1980 (Table 3.22). In other words, more of the "secondary" earners had come to share "primary" breadwinning responsibilities with the family head.

The incidence of hardship declined modestly among all male family heads in the work force, and actually increased for those whose wives did not participate, but the hardship rates dropped significantly among female family heads, as well as among male and female unrelated individuals (Table 3.23). The IIE incidence among female workers dropped significantly, compared to very modest improvements for males. However, this produced no relative improvement in women's chances of attaining adequate family earnings or income because an increasing proportion of females in the work force were family heads or unrelated individuals, both characterized by high IFE and IFI rates.

The changing hardship rates for the various sex/relationship subgroups reflected quite disparate labor market developments. Work force attachment increased significantly among females. It rose among wives and "secondary" family earners. All else being equal, this should have reduced the relative incidence of hardship among these groups:

Table 3.21. HARDSHIP INCIDENCE IN 1974 AND 1979 BY FAMILY SIZE AND NUMBER OF EARNERS

IIE Incidence

	One in Work Force			Two in Work Force			Three or More in Work Force		
	1974	1979	1979-1974	1974	1979	1979-1974	1974	1979	1979-1974
One Member	25.1%	21.8%	-3.3%	--	--	--	--	--	--
Two Members	22.1	21.3	-0.8	21.4	19.2	-2.2	--	--	--
Three Members	20.1	21.4	+1.3	24.7	21.4	-3.3	29.5	27.3	-2.2
Four or Five Members	12.2	14.6	+2.4	25.0	23.5	-1.5	33.0	31.2	-1.8
Six or More Members	17.3	21.2	+3.9	33.0	33.2	+0.2	39.2	37.7	-1.5

IFE Incidence

One Member	23.9	20.5	-3.4	--	--	--	--	--	--
Two Members	27.6	28.5	+0.9	5.2	5.0	-0.2	--	--	--
Three Members	23.1	26.4	+3.3	5.8	5.1	-0.7	2.8	2.1	-0.7
Four or Five Members	15.8	20.5	+4.7	7.3	8.6	+1.3	3.8	3.0	-0.8
Six or More Members	32.6	41.5	+8.9	21.1	24.8	+3.7	9.8	7.4	-2.4

IFI Incidence

One Member	14.3	12.4	-1.9	--	--	--	--	--	--
Two Members	8.1	8.8	+0.7	1.9	2.1	+0.2	--	--	--
Three Members	11.2	12.6	+1.4	2.6	2.3	-0.3	0.7	0.7	0
Four or Five Members	10.7	14.6	+3.9	4.4	5.5	+1.1	2.0	1.5	-0.5
Six or More Members	20.6	32.4	+11.8	15.5	17.9	+2.4	6.6	3.8	-2.8

Table 3.22. INCREASING WORK FORCE ATTACHMENT AND ADDED BREADWINNERS

Share of total work force participants by family size, number of earners and duration of participation

1974

	At Least One Of Family Work Force Participants Participating Half-Year	At Least One Of Family Work Force Participants Participating Full-Year	At Least Two Family Work Force Participants Participating Half-Year	At Least Two Family Work Force Participants Participating Full-Year
One Member	88.9%	77.7%	--	--
Two Members	87.1	74.5	60.4%	51.8%
Three Members	83.0	70.6	64.7	54.5
Four or Five Members	80.3	68.1	63.5	52.5
Six or More Members	74.6	60.5	64.6	51.4

1979

One Member	88.2	74.6	--	--
Two Members	87.8	76.0	61.5	53.3
Three Members	84.3	71.7	68.3	57.9
Four or Five Members	81.4	69.0	68.0	56.6
Six or More Members	74.7	61.8	66.7	54.6

1979-1974

One Member	-0.7	-3.1	--	--
Two Members	+0.7	+1.5	+1.1	+1.5
Three Members	+1.3	+1.1	+3.6	+3.4
Four or Five Members	+1.1	+0.9	+4.5	+4.1
Six or More Members	+0.1	+1.3	+2.1	+3.2

Table 3.23. HARDSHIP RATES IN 1974 AND 1979 FOR SEX/FAMILY RELATIONSHIP SUBGROUPS

	IIE Incidence					IFE Incidence					IFI Incidence				
	1974	1979	1979-1974	1975	1980	1980-1975	1974	1979	1979-1974	1975	1980	1980-1975	1974	1979	1979-1974	1975	1980	1980-1975
Male Family Heads	9.7%	9.3%	-0.4%	11.9%	11.6%	-0.3%	7.9%	7.7%	-0.2%	9.6%	8.9%	-0.7%	4.0%	3.9%	-0.1%	4.8%	4.8%	0%
Wife in Work Force (Male Householder)	9.9	9.0	-0.9	12.3	11.2	-1.1	4.7	4.1	-0.6	6.0	5.1	-0.9	2.7	2.5	-0.2	3.3	3.1	-0.2
Without Wife In Work Force	9.0	9.1	+0.1	11.0	11.3	+0.3	12.1	13.9	+1.8	14.5	15.5	+1.0	5.8	6.1	+0.3	6.8	7.6	+0.8
Male Unrelated Individuals	21.7	18.8	-2.9	24.7	21.2	-3.5	21.2	17.2	-4.0	22.2	17.7	-4.5	13.6	11.4	-2.2	14.1	12.2	-1.9
Other Males	42.9	42.5	-0.5	50.3	49.5	-0.8	11.7	10.9	-0.8	13.3	13.3	0	5.3	5.2	-0.1	6.3	6.4	+0.1
TOTAL MALES	17.9	17.5	-0.4	21.2	20.8	-0.4	10.1	9.7	-0.4	11.7	11.1	-0.6	5.3	5.2	-0.1	6.1	6.2	+0.1
Female Family Heads	34.7	30.0	-4.7	37.1	34.9	-2.2	38.7	33.7	-5.0	37.7	35.1	-2.6	24.1	22.3	-1.8	23.6	12.3	-1.3
Wives	33.2	29.6	-3.6	35.3	32.2	-3.1	6.9	6.5	-0.4	8.1	7.5	-0.6	3.0	2.8	-0.2	3.6	3.4	-0.2
Female Unrelated Individuals	29.0	25.2	-3.8	31.8	28.8	-3.0	26.9	24.6	-2.3	30.0	26.1	-3.9	15.1	13.6	-1.5	17.4	15.2	-2.2
Other Females	51.6	47.8	-3.8	58.5	54.6	-3.9	11.9	12.1	+0.2	13.3	14.1	+0.8	5.8	5.1	-0.7	6.4	6.7	+0.3
TOTAL FEMALES	36.5	32.4	-4.1	39.5	36.1	-3.4	13.7	13.4	-0.4	15.1	14.8	-0.3	7.3	7.1	-0.2	8.1	8.3	+0.2

	Percent participnts in work force at least half-year			Percent participants in work force full-year		
	1974	1979	1979-1974	1974	1979	1979-1974
Male family heads	95.9%	95.9%	0%	88.9%	89.4%	+0.5%
Male unrelated individuals	89.0	91.3	+1.3	76.1	78.4	+1.3
Other males	67.0	68.5	+1.5	51.5	53.8	+2.3
Total males	89.1	89.6	+0.5	79.7	80.4	+0.7
Female family heads	82.4	84.3	+1.9	68.3	71.4	+3.1
Wives	76.2	79.3	+3.1	57.5	61.1	+3.6
Female unrelated individuals	86.5	87.9	+3.1	73.0	72.8	-0.2
Other females	59.5	61.9	+2.4	41.9	45.3	+3.4
Total females	74.7	78.0	+3.3	57.4	61.0	+3.6

The incidence of unemployment declined significantly for wives and other family members, and since hardship is more prevalent among the unemployed than among those working all weeks of participation, this was also a positive development for these subgroups:

	Percent experienced unemployment					
	1974	1979	1979-1974	1975	1980	1980-1975
Male family heads	12.6%	10.7%	-1.9%	15.4%	13.5%	-1.9%
Male heads with wife in labor force	(13.8)	(11.2)	(-2.6)	(16.5)	(14.0)	(-1.5)
Male unrelated individuals	22.5	21.0	-1.5	25.7	22.4	-2.3
Other males	29.9	26.9	-3.0	32.3	31.2	-1.1
Total males	17.3	15.5	-1.8	20.0	18.5	-1.5
Female family heads	22.1	20.5	-1.6	23.6	22.4	-1.2
Wives	16.0	13.3	-2.7	18.0	14.6	-3.4
Female unrelated individuals	16.5	15.9	-0.6	18.4	16.9	-1.5
Other females	26.1	22.0	-4.1	27.6	24.2	-3.4
Total females	18.7	16.1	-2.6	20.5	17.6	-2.9

These changing unemployment probabilities, combined with the changes in the sex/family relationship of the work force, altered the composition of the unemployed, increasing the proportion of the jobless who had primary breadwinning responsibility. Male family heads with no wife in the work force, female family heads, wives with no husband in the work force, and unrelated individuals accounted for 32.8 percent of workers experiencing unemployment in 1974 but 36.7 percent of those experiencing unemployment in 1979:

	Share of persons experiencing unemployment		
	1974	1979	1979-1974
Male family head	27.9	24.3	-3.6
With wife in work force	(17.3)	(16.1)	(-1.2)
Without wife in work force	(10.6)	(8.2)	(-2.4)
Female family head	5.4	6.6	+1.2
Wives	21.8	20.8	-1.0
Other family members	32.6	31.1	-1.7
Unrelated individuals	12.3	17.2	+4.9

As a result, the family earnings and income inadequacy associated with unemployment increased despite a decline in the IIE incidence among the unemployed:

	Hardship incidence among persons who experienced unemployment		
	1974	1979	1979-1974
IIE incidence	54.2%	53.5%	-0.7%
IFE incidence	21.9	22.8	+0.9
IFI incidence	13.7	14.2	+0.5

The Changing Composition of the Hardship Population

These shifts in work force composition and changes in hardship incidence altered the sex/family relationship and family size/earner distribution of the hardship population. Work force participants in families with six or more members accounted for 16.4 percent of the IFE in 1974 but only 11.8 percent in 1979 (Table 3.24). Workers supporting only themselves increased from 23.2 percent of the IFE in 1974 to 26.4 percent in 1979, while participants from families with three or more breadwinners declined from 12.1 percent to 9.0 percent. Female family heads accounted for an increasing share of the hardship population (Table 3.25). Conversely, male family heads, wives and other family earners constituted a declining share. While the female IIE share declined, the female IFE and IFI shares increased.

As a result, the employment and earnings problems of male family heads decreased in relative importance. This is true even when attention is restricted to families with two or more members (i.e., excluding the growing number of unrelated individuals). Male family heads in multiple member families accounted for 36.1 percent of the 1974 IFE Deficits of such

Table 3.24. CHANGES IN THE FAMILY SIZE/EARNERS COMPOSITION OF SEVERE HARDSHIP

IIE SHARE

	1974	1979	1979-1974	1975	1980	1980-1975
One in Work Force	24.0%	26.0%	+2.0%	24.9%	26.6%	+1.7%
One Member	10.9	13.1	+3.2	11.6	13.4	+1.8
Two Members	6.3	6.3	0	6.4	6.4	0
Three Members	3.2	3.2	0	3.0	3.3	+0.3
Four or Five Members	2.7	2.7	0	2.8	2.9	+0.1
Six or More Members	0.9	0.7	-0.2	1.1	0.7	-0.4
Two in Work Force	41.6	39.5	-2.1	40.3	39.7	-0.6
Two Members	13.9	13.3	-0.6	13.7	13.5	-0.2
Three Members	10.4	10.2	-0.2	10.0	10.4	+0.4
Four or Five Members	12.9	13.3	+0.4	12.5	13.3	+0.8
Six or More Members	4.3	2.8	-1.5	4.0	2.6	-1.4
Three or More in Work Force	34.4	34.5	+0.1	34.9	33.6	-1.3
Three Members	5.8	6.3	+0.5	5.8	6.2	+0.4
Four or Five Members	16.8	17.8	+1.0	17.2	17.7	+0.5
Six or More Members	11.8	10.4	-1.4	11.9	9.7	-2.2

IFE SHARE

	1974	1979	1979-1974	1975	1980	1980-1975
One in Work Force	60.4%	63.7%	+3.3%	59.3%	61.2%	+1.9%
One Member	23.2	26.4	+3.2	23.5	25.2	+1.7
Two Members	17.6	17.9	+0.3	16.2	16.6	+0.4
Three Members	8.1	8.4	+0.3	7.6	8.4	+0.8
Four or Five Members	7.7	8.1	+0.4	8.1	8.4	+0.3
Six or More Members	3.8	2.9	-0.9	3.9	2.6	-1.3
Two in Work Force	27.5	27.3	-0.2	28.7	27.6	-1.1
Two Members	7.6	7.3	-0.3	7.4	7.5	+0.1
Three Members	5.5	5.1	-0.4	5.9	5.9	0
Four or Five Members	8.4	10.4	+2.0	9.4	10.3	+0.7
Six or More Members	6.1	4.5	-1.6	6.0	3.9	-2.1
Three or More in Work Force	12.1	9.0	-3.1	12.0	11.3	-0.7
Three Members	1.2	1.0	-0.2	1.2	0.9	-0.3
Four or Five Members	4.3	3.6	-0.7	4.5	5.0	+0.5
Six or More Members	6.5	4.4	-2.1	6.2	5.4	-0.8

IFI SHARE

	1974	1979	1979-1974	1975	1980	1980-1975
One in Work Force	59.1%	63.1%	+4.0%	58.2%	60.9%	+2.1%
One Member	26.3	30.0	+3.7	26.9	28.4	+1.5
Two Members	9.8	10.4	+0.6	9.1	10.3	+1.2
Three Members	7.5	7.6	+0.1	7.0	7.8	+0.8
Four or Five Members	9.9	10.9	+1.0	9.6	10.4	+0.6
Six or More Members	5.6	4.3	-1.3	5.5	3.9	-1.6
Two in Work Force	27.8	28.5	+0.7	28.0	27.7	-0.3
Two Members	5.1	5.7	+0.6	5.3	5.4	+0.1
Three Members	4.7	4.3	-0.4	4.8	5.0	+0.2
Four or Five Members	9.5	12.4	+2.9	10.3	12.1	+1.8
Six or More Members	8.4	6.1	-1.3	7.6	5.3	-2.3
Three or More in Work Force	13.1	8.4	-4.7	13.8	11.4	-2.4
Three Members	0.6	0.6	0	1.0	0.6	-0.4
Four or Five Members	4.2	3.5	-0.7	4.8	4.7	-0.1
Six or More Members	8.3	4.3	-4.0	8.0	6.1	-1.9

IIE DEFICIT SHARE

	1974	1979	1979-1974	1975	1980	1980-1975
One in Work Force	27.9%	29.2%	+1.3%	28.6%	29.9%	+1.3%
One Member	12.8	14.8	+2.0	13.8	15.3	+1.5
Two Members	7.1	6.9	-0.2	7.0	6.8	-0.2
Three Members	3.5	3.6	+0.1	3.3	3.5	+0.2
Four or Five Members	3.3	3.1	-0.2	3.2	3.5	+0.3
Six or More Members	1.2	0.8	-0.4	1.3	0.8	-0.5
Two in Work Force	42.1	40.3	-1.8	40.8	40.5	-0.3
Two Members	16.3	15.0	-1.3	15.4	15.1	-0.3
Three Members	10.5	10.0	-0.5	10.0	10.1	+0.1
Four or Five Members	11.7	12.7	+1.0	11.8	12.9	+1.1
Six or More Members	3.6	2.6	-1.0	3.7	2.5	-0.8
Three or More in Work Force	30.1	30.5	+0.4	30.6	29.6	-1.0
Three Members	5.9	6.0	+0.1	5.9	6.0	+0.1
Four or Five Members	13.9	15.1	+1.2	14.9	14.9	0
Six or More Members	10.1	9.3	-0.8	9.8	8.7	-1.1

IFE DEFICIT SHARE

	1974	1979	1979-1974	1975	1980	1980-1975
One in Work Force	75.6%	77.3%	+1.7%	74.3%	76.0%	+1.7%
One Member	19.9	22.1	+2.2	20.7	21.6	+0.9
Two Members	19.6	20.7	+1.1	18.3	19.3	+1.0
Three Members	11.6	11.8	+0.2	10.8	11.8	+1.0
Four or Five Members	14.6	15.2	+0.6	14.5	16.1	+1.6
Six or More Members	9.9	7.5	-2.4	9.9	7.3	-2.6
Two in Work Force	18.9	18.7	-0.2	19.7	18.9	-0.8
Two Members	3.4	3.4	0	3.2	3.4	+0.2
Three Members	3.0	2.7	-0.3	2.9	3.2	+0.3
Four or Five Members	6.0	7.6	+1.6	7.3	8.1	+0.8
Six or More Members	6.5	5.0	-1.5	6.3	4.2	-2.1
Three or More in Work Force	5.4	4.0	-1.4	6.0	5.1	-0.9
Three Members	0.3	0.3	0	0.4	0.3	-0.1
Four or Five Members	1.7	1.5	-0.2	2.0	2.0	0
Six or More Members	3.4	2.2	-1.2	3.6	2.8	-0.8

IFI DEFICIT SHARE

	1974	1979	1979-1974	1975	1980	1980-1975
One in Work Force	72.2%	75.0%	+2.8%	70.9%	73.4%	+2.5%
One Member	23.4	27.4	+4.0	25.8	26.3	+0.5
Two Members	9.9	11.4	+1.5	8.6	10.6	+2.0
Three Members	9.4	9.2	-0.2	8.4	9.7	+1.3
Four or Five Members	16.5	18.0	+2.5	15.8	17.6	+1.8
Six or More Members	13.0	9.0	-4.0	12.3	9.2	-3.1
Two in Work Force	21.0	21.0	0	21.5	21.1	-0.4
Two Members	2.7	2.8	+0.1	2.8	2.6	-0.2
Three Members	3.0	2.2	-0.8	2.6	3.0	+0.4
Four or Five Members	7.2	9.0	+1.8	8.1	9.9	+1.8
Six or More Members	8.2	7.0	-1.2	8.0	5.5	-2.5
Three or More in Work Force	6.8	4.0	-2.8	7.6	5.5	-2.1
Three Members	0.3	0.3	0	0.3	0.2	-0.1
Four or Five Members	1.7	1.4	-0.3	2.5	1.8	-0.7
Six or More Members	4.8	2.4	-2.4	4.8	3.5	-1.3

Table 3.25. CHANGES IN THE SEX/FAMILY RELATIONSHIP COMPOSITION OF SEVERE HARDSHIP

IIE SHARE

	1974	1979	1979-1974	1975	1980	1980-1975
Male Family Heads	14.9%	13.8%	-0.9%	16.1%	14.9%	-1.2%
Wives in Work Force	8.7	8.5	-0.2	9.5	9.2	-0.3
Wives Not in Work Force	5.6	4.5	-1.1	5.9	4.8	-1.1
Wives Not Present	0.7	0.8	+0.1	0.7	1.0	+0.3
Male Unrelated Individuals	4.9	6.2	+1.3	5.2	6.2	+1.0
Other Males	20.1	20.2	+0.1	20.4	20.4	0
Total Males	39.9	40.2	+0.3	41.7	41.5	-0.2
Female Family Heads	5.9	6.3	+0.4	5.7	6.7	+1.0
Wives	31.3	30.2	-1.1	29.6	28.5	-1.1
Female Unrelated Individuals	6.0	6.9	+0.9	6.3	7.1	+0.8
Other Females	16.9	16.4	-0.5	16.7	16.1	-0.6
Total Females	60.1	59.8	-0.3	58.3	58.5	+0.2

IFE SHARE

	1974	1979	1979-1974	1975	1980	1980-1975
Male Family Heads	26.9%	24.5%	-2.4%	28.6%	24.9%	-3.7%
Wives in Work Force	9.1	8.3	-0.8	10.2	9.1	-1.1
Wives Not in Work Force	16.7	14.8	-1.9	17.3	14.2	-3.1
Wives Not Present	1.2	1.4	+0.2	1.0	1.6	+0.6
Male Unrelated Individuals	10.7	12.0	+1.3	10.3	11.3	+1.0
Other Males	12.2	11.0	-1.2	11.9	11.8	-0.1
Total Males	49.8	47.5	-2.3	50.7	48.0	-2.7
Female Family Heads	14.6	15.2	+0.6	12.7	14.6	+1.9
Wives	14.5	14.1	-0.4	15.0	14.4	-0.6
Female Unrelated Individuals	12.4	14.4	+2.0	13.2	13.9	+0.7
Other Females	8.7	8.8	+0.1	8.4	9.0	+0.6
Total Females	50.2	52.5	+2.3	49.3	52.0	+2.7

IFI SHARE

	1974	1979	1979-1974	1975	1980	1980-1975
Male Family Heads	25.9%	23.2%	-2.7%	27.0%	23.9%	-3.1%
Wives in Work Force	9.9	9.5	-0.4	10.8	9.9	-0.9
Wives Not in Work Force	15.0	12.2	+0.2	15.4	12.4	-3.0
Wives Not Present	1.0	1.5	+0.5	0.7	1.7	+1.0
Male Unrelated Individuals	13.1	15.0	+1.9	12.5	13.9	+1.4
Other Males	10.5	9.5	-1.0	10.8	10.2	-0.6
Total Males	49.5	47.7	-1.8	50.2	48.0	-2.2
Female Family Heads	17.2	18.9	+1.7	15.1	18.3	+3.2
Wives	12.1	11.6	-0.5	12.7	11.6	-1.1
Female Unrelated Individuals	13.2	15.0	+1.8	14.5	14.5	0
Other Females	8.1	7.0	-1.1	7.6	7.6	0
Total Females	50.5	52.3	+1.8	49.8	52.0	+2.2

IIE DEFICIT SHARE

	1974	1979	1979-1974	1975	1980	1980-1975
Male Family Heads	24.1%	21.7%	-2.4%	24.2%	23.0%	-1.2%
Wives in Work Force	14.4	13.6	-0.8	14.8	14.9	+0.1
Wives Not in Work Force	8.8	6.9	-1.9	8.5	6.7	-1.8
Wives Not Present	1.0	1.1	+0.1	0.9	1.4	+0.5
Male Unrelated Individuals	6.8	8.2	+1.4	6.9	8.1	+1.2
Other Males	18.3	18.6	+0.3	18.6	19.1	+0.5
Total Males	49.3	48.4	-0.7	49.7	50.3	+0.5
Female Family Heads	5.7	5.7	0	5.3	6.8	+1.5
Wives	28.0	28.1	+0.1	26.8	25.2	-1.6
Female Unrelated Individuals	6.0	6.6	+0.6	6.9	7.1	+0.2
Other Females	11.1	11.2	+0.1	11.2	10.6	-0.6
Total Females	50.7	51.6	+0.9	50.3	49.7	-0.6

IFE DEFICIT SHARE

	1974	1979	1979-1974	1975	1980	1980-1975
Male Family Heads	28.9%	26.2%	-2.7%	31.2%	27.4%	-3.8%
Wives in Work Force	6.8	6.2	-0.6	7.6	7.2	-0.4
Wives Not in Work Force	20.9	18.6	-2.3	22.6	18.6	-4.0
Wives Not Present	1.2	1.4	+0.2	1.0	1.7	+0.7
Male Unrelated Individuals	9.1	10.3	+1.2	9.2	10.1	+0.9
Other Males	11.3	11.5	+0.2	12.6	11.8	-0.8
Total Males	49.3	47.9	-1.4	53.0	49.3	-3.7
Female Family Heads	21.2	21.0	-0.2	18.2	20.8	+2.6
Wives	10.3	10.2	-0.1	9.8	9.9	+0.1
Female Unrelated Individuals	10.8	11.9	+1.1	11.5	11.5	0
Other Females	9.9	9.0	-0.9	7.5	8.5	+1.0
Total Females	50.7	52.1	+1.4	47.0	50.7	+3.7

IFI DEFICIT SHARE

	1974	1979	1979-1974	1975	1980	1980-1975
Male Family Heads	33.5%	29.0%	-4.5%	33.1%	29.8%	-3.3%
Wives in Work Force	9.6	9.4	-0.2	10.5	9.9	-1.6
Wives Not in Work Force	22.8	17.9	-4.9	21.8	18.1	-3.7
Wives Not Present	1.1	1.7	+0.6	0.8	1.7	+0.9
Male Unrelated Individuals	12.5	14.6	+2.1	12.3	13.8	+1.5
Other Males	7.7	6.8	-0.9	8.4	7.9	-0.5
Total Males	52.6	50.4	-2.2	53.7	51.5	-2.2
Female Family Heads	23.6	24.5	+0.9	20.2	24.1	+3.9
Wives	6.4	6.6	+0.2	7.0	6.3	-0.7
Female Unrelated Individuals	10.9	12.8	+1.8	13.6	12.4	-1.2
Other Females	5.5	5.7	+0.2	5.5	5.6	+0.1
Total Females	47.4	49.6	+2.2	46.3	48.5	+2.2

families but only 33.6 percent of their 1979 IFE Deficits. There was a decline of 4.4 percentage points in their IFE Deficit share between 1975 and 1980:

	Share of severe hardship deficits for families with two or more members					
	1974	1979	1979-1974	1975	1980	1980-1975
IIE Deficit share						
Male family heads	27.7%	25.4%	-2.3%	28.0%	27.2%	-0.8
Female family heads	6.5	6.6	+0.1	6.2	8.0	+1.8
Wives	32.1	33.0	+0.9	31.1	19.7	-0.4
Other	33.7	34.9	+1.2	34.6	35.1	+0.5
IFE Deficit share						
Male family heads	36.1	33.6	-2.5	39.4	35.0	-4.4
Female family heads	26.4	27.0	+0.6	22.9	26.6	+3.7
Wives	12.9	13.1	+0.2	12.3	12.6	+0.3
Other	24.6	26.3	+1.7	25.4	25.9	+0.5
IFI Deficit share						
Male family heads	43.7	39.9	-3.8	44.6	40.4	-4.2
Female family heads	30.8	33.8	+3.0	27.2	32.7	+5.5
Wives	8.3	9.1	+0.8	9.5	8.6	-0.9
Other	17.2	17.2	0	18.7	18.3	-0.4

If all unrelated individuals with Inadequate Individual Earnings and with Inadequate Family Earnings had their earnings augmented to the adequacy level (i.e., the minimum wage standard multiplied by their annual hours of availability for work), two-fifths of unrelated individuals in the IFE would have had augmented earnings above the poverty level, and the aggregate IFE would have been reduced by 9.3 percent in 1974. Augmenation of their earnings to the adequacy level in 1979 would have reduced the IFE by 10.1 percent. In contrast, augmentation of the earnings of male family heads to the adequacy level would have reduced the IFE count by 14.7 percent in 1974, but only 12.4 percent in 1979:

Percent reduction in IFE if earnings
of subgroup members in IFE
were increased to minimally adequate level

	1974	1979	1979-1974	1975	1980	1980-1975
Male family heads	14.71	12.40	-2.31	15.77	14.45	-1.32
Female family heads	3.56	3.51	-0.05	3.73	4.67	+0.94
Wives	7.39	6.02	-1.37	8.15	6.95	-1.20
Other males	5.35	3.99	-1.36	6.15	6.34	+0.19
Other females	3.46	2.98	-0.48	3.30	3.89	+0.59
Male unrelated individuals	4.66	5.45	+0.79	5.20	5.74	+0.54
Female unrelated individuals	3.96	4.68	+0.72	4.87	5.43	+0.56

Notes

1. *Employment and Training Report of the President, 1981* (Washington: U.S. Government Printing Office, 1981), pp. 105-307; and *Money Income and Poverty Status of Families and Persons in the United States: 1980*, Current Population Report P-60, No. 27 (Washington: U.S. Government Printing Office, 1982).

2. Unpublished tabulations from the National Commission on Employment and Unemployment Statistics.

3. To determine the multi-year trends over the 1974-1980 period, it is necessary to sort out the influence of cyclical patterns. Macroeconomic conditions in 1980, when a recession was just taking hold, differed from those in 1974, the last year of a slow recovery from the 1970-71 recession, so that 1974-1980 comparisons reflect both cyclical and secular effects. The 1979 calendar year, when unemployment averaged 5.8 percent, is more comparable with 1974, when the rate was 5.6 percent. Likewise, 1980 and 1975 were both recession years, although the earlier decline was more severe, with an 8.5 percent unemployment rate compared to the 7.1 percent rate in 1979. By comparing 1974 with 1979 hardship levels and patterns, and 1975 with 1980, it is possible, in at least a general way, to separate changes which reflected multi-year trends, from those which reflected business cycles. The 1979 data used in this chapter are normally derived based on 1980 Census weights. An asterisk notes where 1970 Census weights are used.

CHAPTER 4. HARDSHIP OVER THE BUSINESS CYCLE

Hardship Persists in Good Times and Bad

The Cyclicality of Hardship

Hardship rises and falls with the business cycle. When the unemployment rate goes up, more individuals experience weeks without earnings, the duration of unemployment increases and more of the unemployed encounter recurrent bouts of joblessness. This obviously increases the incidence of Inadequate Individual Earnings. Because of the reduced contributions of primary as well as secondary family work force participants, more families experience earnings below the poverty level. Countercyclical income transfers, particularly unemployment insurance, rescue some but not all of these recession victims from severe hardship, so that the number with Inadequate Family Income rises along with the IFE.

In general, however, the cyclicality of hardship is less extreme than the cyclicality of unemployment. During recessions, the number with Inadequate Individual Earnings rises more than the number of unemployed but the IFE count increases by substantially less, while the IFI increment is smaller still. The percentage fluctuations in hardship are less than the percentage fluctuations in joblessness.

There were two periods of rising unemployment within the 1974-1980 period for which the hardship measures were calculated. The national unemployment rate rose from 5.6 percent in 1974 to 8.5 percent in 1975, declining subsequently through 1979. It then rose from 5.8 percent in 1979 to 7.1 percent in 1980. The number of annual average unemployed rose by 54 percent in the 1974-1975 recession, and by 25 percent in the 1979-1980 recession (Table 4.1).

The severe hardship IIE count rose by 3.6 million during the first recession and 4.5 million during the second, compared to increases of 2.8 and 1.5 million, respectively, in average annual unemployment, and 2.6 and 2.9 million, respectively, in the number of work force participants experiencing unemployment during the year. But the IFE counts rose only 1.8 million in each of the two recessions, while the IFI counts increased by only 0.9 and 1.4 million, respectively. 1/

The plots of hardship and unemployment incidence rates and levels for 1974 through 1980 illustrate the similarity in unemployment and IIE changes, but the lesser cyclicality of the IFE, and the even more dampened cyclicality of the IFI (Chart 4.1). Likewise, the constant dollar IIE Deficit was much more cyclically sensitive than the IFE Deficit, while the IFI Deficit was relatively stable (Chart 4.2).

Table 4.1. CHANGES IN SEVERE HARDSHIP AND UNEMPLOYMENT DURING THE 1970s DOWNTURNS

	1974	1975	Increase 1974-1975	Percentage Increase 1974-1975	1979	1980	Increase 1979-1980	Percentage Increase 1979-1980
Average Annual Unemployed	5,076	7,830	2,754	54%	5,963	7,448	1,485	25%
Average Annual Long-Term Unemployed (15 Weeks or More)	937	2,483	1,546	165	1,202	1,829	627	52
Persons Experiencing Unemployment During Year	18,537	21,105	2,568	14	18,468	21,410	2,942	16
Persons Unemployed More Than One-Third of Weeks in Work Force	7,740	10,941	3,201	41	7,492	10,348	2,856	38
IIE	26,756	30,345	3,589	13	28,269	32,747	4,478	16
IFE	12,008	13,768	1,760	15	13,280	15,111	1,831	14
IFI	6,346	7,252	906	14	7,055	8,465	1,410	20
IIE Deficit (1980 $)	56,862	70,568	13,706	24	59,018	70,648	11,630	20
IFE Deficit (1980 $)	32,929	38,160	5,241	16	35,930	41,000	5,070	14
IFI Deficit (1980 $)	12,889	14,603	1,714	13	14,556	17,452	2,896	20
IIE Average Deficit (1980 $)	2,126	2,326	200	9	2,087	2,157	70	3
IFE Average Deficit (1980 $)	2,742	2,771	29	1	2,706	2,713	7	0
IFI Average Deficit (1980 $)	2,030	2,013	-17	-1	2,063	2,062	-1	9

Chart 4.1. SEVERE HARDSHIP AND UNEMPLOYMENT LEVELS AND INCIDENCE, 1974-1980*

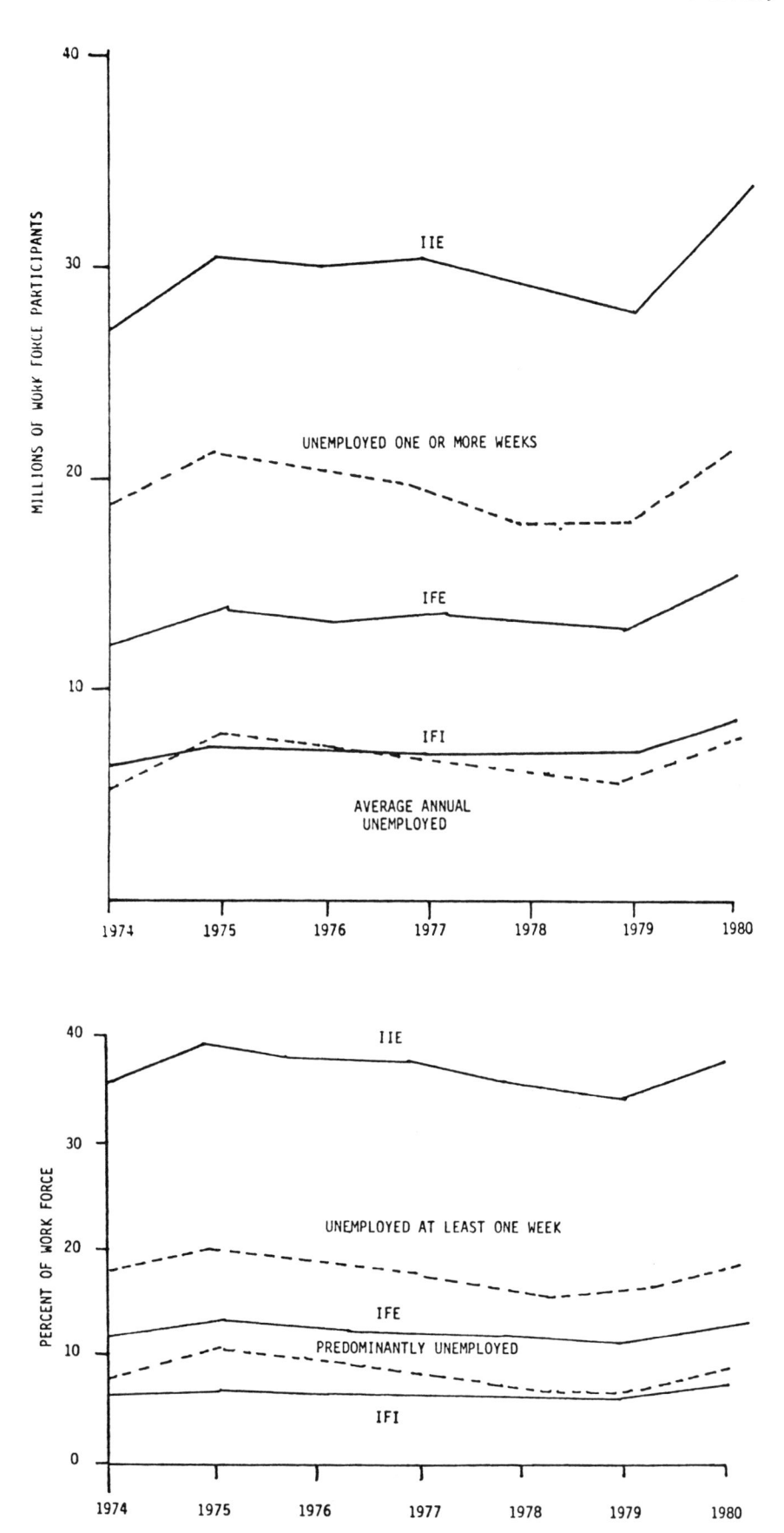

Chart 4.2. SEVERE HARDSHIP DEFICITS IN CONSTANT (1980) DOLLARS, 1974-1980

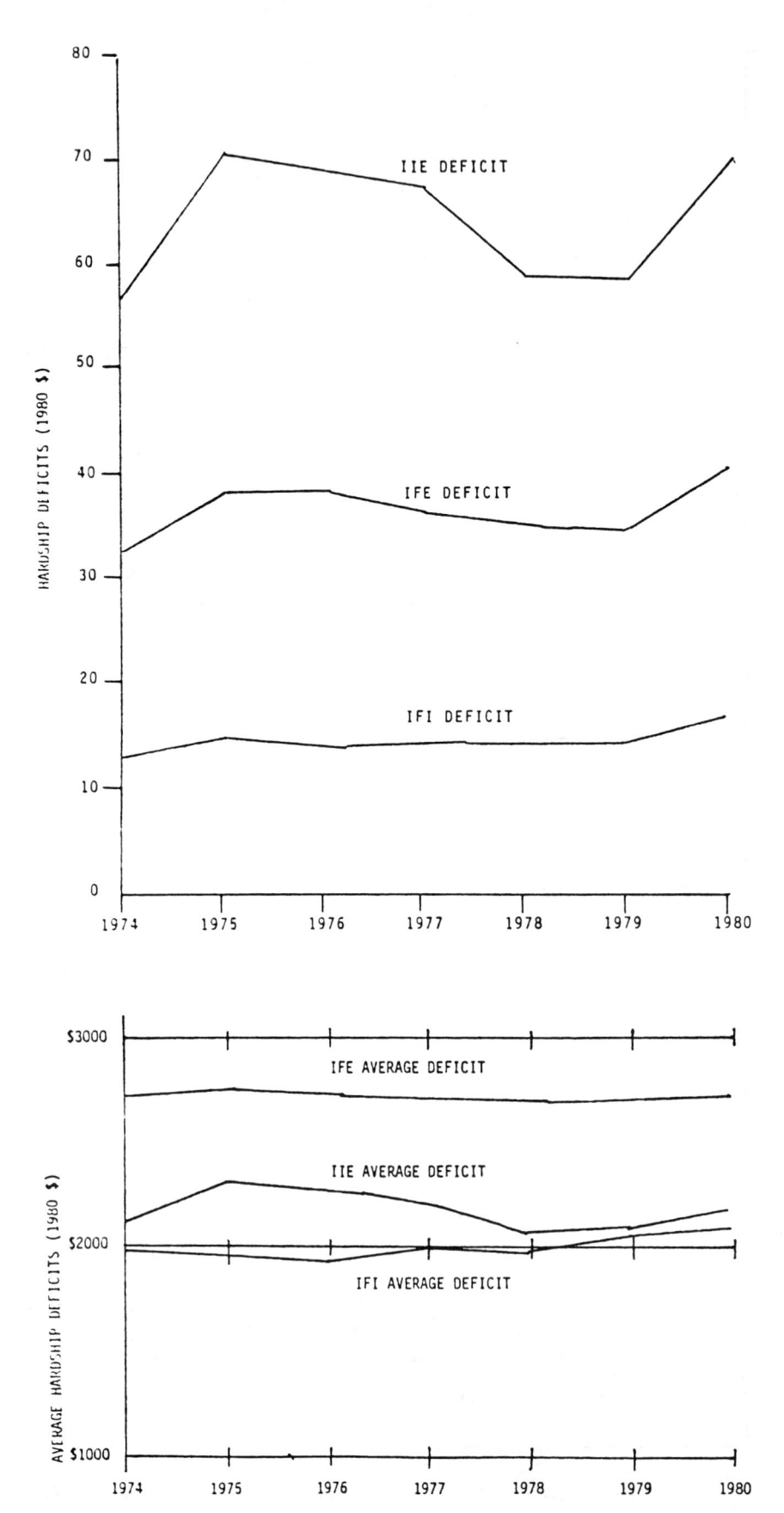

Hardship and unemployment were highly correlated (Table 4.2). The coefficient of correlation between the average annual unemployment and IIE rates was a high 0.92, and the correlation with the IFE rate was 0.94. The relationship between the IFI and unemployment rates was less exact, with a correlation coefficient of 0.78 In fact, the constant dollar average IFI Deficit was _negatively_ related to unemployment, declining during recessions.

The standard deviation in the number of average annual unemployed over the 1974-1980 period was slightly higher than the standard deviation in the IFE total and half again the IFI standard deviation (Table 4.3). Proportionately, however, the fluctuations in unemployment were much greater than the fluctuations in hardship. The standard deviation in average annual unemployment represented 15 percent of its mean, while the standard deviations in the severe hardship IIE, IFE and IFI counts represented 7, 7 and 9 percent of their respective means. Put another way, if resources or concern were allocated in proportion to the levels of need, the cyclical fluctuations in resources and concern would have been much less if the nation focused on the yearly IFE and IFI tallies rather than the annual unemployment counts.

Severe hardship fluctuated relatively more than moderate or intermediate hardship (Table 4.4). The intermediate and moderate IIE increased when unemployment rose, but the increments in the severe hardship components accounted for all of these increases. The differential between the intermediate and severe hardship IIE totals, and the moderate minus intermediate IIE counts, were negatively correlated with the annual average unemployed. In other words, the intermediate and moderate IIE counts declined modestly relative to the severe hardship counts during recessions (Table 4.5). The intermediate and moderate hardship IFI counts, on the other hand, were somewhat _more_ cyclical than the severe hardship IFI counts. Apparently the victims of recession were lifted out of poverty by countercyclical transfers and other income, but were not lifted above the intermediate or moderate hardship adequacy standards.

How Rising Unemployment Causes Hardship

The business cycle impacts are reflected in the changing work experience patterns of persons in the IIE, IFE and IFI. When unemployment rises in a recession, many of the victims are those who were in hardship even in good times. As an example, the IIE cohort employed full-time during all weeks in the work force dropped by half a million between 1974 and 1975, as the fully-employed suffered bouts of joblessness (Table 4.6). By the same token, the incidence of hardship increased among those who experienced unemployment. Three-fifths of the 1975 and 1980 unemployed had Inadequate Individual Earnings compared to 54 and 53 percent, respectively, of the individuals who experienced unemployment during 1974 and 1979:

Table 4.2. CORRELATION COEFFICIENT MATRIX FOR 1974-1980*

	Average Annual Unemployment Rate	Percentage Unemployed During Year	Percentage Predominantly Unemployed During Year	IIE Incidence	IFE Incidence	IFI Incidence	IIE Deficit (1980 $)	IFE Deficit (1980 $)	IFI Deficit (1980 $)	IIE Average Deficit (1980 $)	IFE Average Deficit (1980 $)	IFI Average Deficit (1980 $)
Average Annual Unemployment Rate	1.00	.85	.96	.92	.94	.78	.92	.69	.34	.92	.65	-.34
Percent Unemployed During Year	.85	1.00	.96	.91	.87	.69	.76	.45	.14	.92	.89	-.30
Percent Predominantly Unemployed During Year	.96	.96	1.00	.96	.95	.79	.88	.61	.27	.94	.78	-.37
IIE Incidence	.92	.91	.96	1.00	.97	.82	.91	.66	.33	.87	.64	-.38
IFE Incidence	.94	.87	.95	.97	1.00	.92	.96	.80	.52	.83	.60	-.20
IFI Incidence	.78	.69	.79	.82	.92	1.00	.89	.92	.78	.57	.37	.01
IIE Deficit (1980 $)	.92	.76	.88	.91	.96	.89	1.00	.88	.61	.79	.43	-.18
IFE Deficit (1980 $)	.69	.45	.61	.66	.80	.92	.88	1.00	.91	.43	.10	.16
IFI Deficit (1980 $)	.34	.14	.27	.33	.52	.78	.61	.91	1.00	.05	-.19	.46
IIE Average Deficit (1980 $)	.92	.92	.94	.87	.83	.57	.79	.43	.05	1.00	.83	-.39
IFE Average Deficit (1980 $)	.65	.89	.78	.64	.60	.37	.43	.10	-.19	.83	1.00	-.28
IFI Average Deficit (1980 $)	-.34	-.30	-.37	-.38	-.20	.01	-.18	.16	.46	-.39	-.28	1.00

Table 4.3. STATISTICAL MEASURES OF THE VARIABILITY AND INTERRELATEDNESS OF UNEMPLOYMENT AND HARDSHIP OVER THE 1974-1980 PERIOD*

	Mean[1]	Standard deviation[1]	Coefficient of variation[1]
Average annual unemployment rate	6.8	1.0	15.8
Average annual unemployed (000)	6,644	982	14.8
Percent experiencing unemployment	17.8	1.6	9.2
Persons experiencing unemployment	19,532	1,498	7.7
Percent predominantly unemployed	8.3	1.5	15.8
Persons predominantly unemployed (000)	9,063	1,487	16.4
IIE incidence	26.8	1.7	6.5
IIE (000)	29,471	2,001	6.8
IFE incidence	12.2	0.7	5.8
IFE (000)	13,388	948	7.1
IFI incidence	6.5	0.4	6.6
IFI (000)	7,137	649	9.1
IIE Deficit (Millions 1980 $)	64,346	6,256	9.7
IFE Deficit (Millions 1980 $)	36,508	2,594	7.1
IFI Deficit (Millions 1980 $)	14,429	1,431	9.9
IIE Average Deficit (1980 $)	2,181	103	4.7
IFE Average Deficit (1980 $)	2,727	28	1.0
IFI Average Deficit (1980 $)	2,021	36	1.8

[1] The "standard deviation" is a measure of the absolute variability of a statistic (i.e., two-thirds of the numbers are predicted to be within ± one standard deviation of the mean); the "coefficient of variation," which is the standard deviation divided by the mean, is a measure of the proportionate variability of a statistic (i.e., the variability of numbers with different scales can be compared since the coefficients of variation are all in the same percentage terms); and the "correlation coefficient" is a measure of the proportionate changes in one statistic which occurs with equal proportionate changes in another statistic (i.e., it is close to ±1.0 when the statistics change the same proportionate amounts and it is close to 0 if the changes are not related).

Table 4.4. FLUCTUATIONS IN SEVERE, INTERMEDIATE AND MODERATE HARDSHIP IN RELATIONSHIP TO AVERAGE ANNUAL UNEMPLOYMENT OVER 1974-1980 PERIOD*

IIE

	Severe	Intermediate	Intermediate Minus Severe	Moderate	Moderate Minus Intermediate
Mean (000)	29,471	40,256	10,784	50,062	9,806
Standard Deviation (000)	2,001	2,406	1,106	3,001	862
Coefficient of Variation	6.8	6.0	10.3	6.0	8.8
Correlation With Average Annual Unemployment	.86	.68	-.10	.50	-.12

IFE

	Severe	Intermediate	Intermediate Minus Severe	Moderate	Moderate Minus Intermediate
Mean (000)	13,388	17,186	3,799	21,407	4,220
Standard Deviation (000)	948	1,217	281	1,536	330
Coefficient of Variation	7.1	7.1	7.4	7.2	7.8
Correlation With Average Annual Unemployment	.82	.79	.66	.79	.78

IFI

	Severe	Intermediate	Intermediate Minus Severe	Moderate	Moderate Minus Intermediate
Mean (000)	7,137	10,568	3,433	14,560	3,992
Standard Deviation (000)	649	838	206	1,099	292
Coefficient of Variation	9.1	7.9	6.0	7.6	7.3
Correlation With Average Annual Unemployment	.68	.71	.72	.78	.91

Table 4.5. RELATIVE LEVELS OF SEVERE, INTERMEDIATE AND MODERATE HARDSHIP, 1974-1980*

	IIE		IIE DEFICIT		IFE		IFE DEFICIT		IFI		IFI DEFICIT	
	Intermediate + Severe	Moderate + Severe	Intermediate + Severe	Moderate + Severe	Intermediate + Severe	Moderate + Severe	Intermediate + Severe	Moderate + Severe	Intermediate + Severe	Moderate + Severe	Intermediate + Severe	Moderate + Severe
1974	137	172	164	251	128	159	153	219	151	208	182	297
1975	132	160	159	237	127	159	152	217	148	206	182	297
1976	134	166	160	240	129	161	152	217	148	207	182	298
1977	134	164	162	244	128	158	152	217	151	207	181	295
1978	139	176	167	259	128	159	153	219	146	200	180	292
1979	145	182	168	262	129	162	153	220	149	203	179	289
1980	137	171	164	249	129	161	152	217	145	197	177	282

Table 4.6. CHANGES IN WORK EXPERIENCE PATTERNS OF TOTAL WORK FORCE AND PERSONS IN HARDSHIP, 1974-1975 AND 1979-1980

	Work Force				Year-to-Year Change in Work Force		Work Force Shares				Year-to-Year Change in Work Force Shares	
	1974	1975	1979	1980	1974-1975	1979-1980	1974	1975	1979	1980	1974-1975	1979-1980
Not Employed	2,129	3,202	1,990	2,597	+1,073	+607	2.1%	3.1%	1.7%	2.2%	+1.0%	+0.5%
Mostly Unemployed	1,616	2,568	1,607	2,568	+952	+961	1.6	2.5	1.4	2.2	+0.9	+0.8
Mixed	3,995	5,171	3,898	5,183	+1,176	+1,288	3.9	5.0	3.3	4.4	+1.1	+1.1
Mostly Employed	10,797	10,164	10,976	11,063	-633	+87	10.4	9.7	9.4	9.3	-0.7	-0.1
Employed Part-Time Involuntarily	3,986	6,160	7,172	7,644	+2,174	+472	3.8	5.9	6.1	6.5	+2.1	+0.4
Employed Part-Time Voluntarily	19,325	20,162	26,985	24,948	+837	-2,037	18.5	19.3	23.1	21.1	+0.8	-1.0
Employed Full-Time	61,753	57,016	64,359	64,347	-4,737	-12	59.6	54.6	55.0	54.4	-5.0	-0.6
Total	103,601	104,442	116,983	118,348	+841	+1,365	100.0	100.0	100.0	100.0	0	0

Table 4.6. (Continued)

	IIE 1974	IIE 1975	IIE 1979	IIE 1980	Year-to-Year Change in IIE 1974-1975	Year-to-Year Change in IIE 1979-1980	IIE Shares 1974	IIE Shares 1975	IIE Shares 1979	IIE Shares 1980	Year-to-Year Change in IIE Shares 1974-1975	Year-to-Year Change in IIE Shares 1979-1980
Not Employed	2,084	3,146	1,979	2,536	+1,062	+607	7.8%	10.4%	7.0%	7.9%	+2.6%	+0.9%
Mostly Unemployed	1,524	2,410	1,529	2,447	+886	+918	5.7	7.9	5.4	7.5	+2.2	+2.1
Mixed	2,760	3,508	2,691	3,673	+748	+982	10.3	11.6	9.5	11.2	+1.3	+1.7
Mostly Employed	3,687	3,573	3,679	4,057	-114	+378	13.8	11.8	13.0	12.4	-2.0	-0.6
Employed Part-Time Involuntarily	2,113	2,994	3,196	3,656	+881	+465	7.9	9.6	11.3	11.2	+2.0	-0.1
Employed Part-Time Voluntarily	7,368	7,996	8,788	9,070	+628	+282	27.5	26.4	31.1	27.7	-0.9	-3.4
Employed Full-Time	7,220	6,717	6,408	7,258	-503	+850	27.0	22.1	22.7	22.2	-4.9	-0.5
Total	26,756	30,345	28,269	32,747	+3,589	+4,478	100.0	100.0	100.0	100.0	0	0

Table 4.6. (Continued)

	IFE				Year-to-Year Change in IFE		IFE Shares			Year-to-Year Change in IFE Shares	
	1974	1975	1979	1980	1974-1975	1979-1980	1974	1975	1979	1980	1974-1975	1979-1980
Not Employed	972	1,517	931	1,343	+545	+412	10.1%	11.0%	7.0%	8.9%	+0.9%	+1.9%
Mostly Unemployed	713	1,090	681	1,217	+377	+536	5.9	7.9	5.1	8.1	+2.0	+3.0
Mixed	1,015	1,457	1,096	1,533	+442	+437	8.5	10.6	8.3	10.1	+2.1	+1.8
Mostly Employed	1,358	1,341	1,502	1,593	-17	+91	11.3	9.7	11.3	10.5	-1.6	-0.8
Employed Part-Time Involuntarily	888	1,233	1,419	1,546	+345	+127	7.4	9.0	10.7	10.2	+1.6	-0.5
Employed Part-Time Voluntarily	3,883	4,072	4,732	4,783	+189	+51	32.3	29.6	35.6	31.7	-2.7	-3.9
Employed Full-Time	3,179	3,060	2,919	3,095	-119	+176	26.5	22.2	22.0	20.5	-4.3	-1.5
Total	12,008	13,768	13,280	15,111	+1,760	+1,831	100.0	100.0	100.0	100.0	0	0

Table 4.6. (Continued)

	IFI 1974	IFI 1975	IFI 1979	IFI 1980	Year-to-Year Change in IFI 1974-1975	Year-to-Year Change in IFI 1979-1980	IFI Shares 1974	IFI Shares 1975	IFI Shares 1979	IFI Shares 1980	Year-to-Year Change in IFI Shares 1974-1975	Year-to-Year Change in IFI Shares 1979-1980
Not Employed	638	885	629	996	+247	+367	10.1%	12.2%	8.9%	11.8%	+2.1%	+2.9%
Mostly Unemployed	435	579	423	789	+144	+366	6.9	8.0	6.0	9.3	+1.1	+3.3
Mixed	618	745	625	911	+127	+286	9.7	10.3	8.9	10.8	+0.6	+1.9
Mostly Employed	842	820	941	1,025	-22	+84	13.3	11.3	13.3	12.1	-2.0	-2.2
Employed Part-Time Involuntarily	541	756	815	925	+215	+110	8.5	10.4	11.6	10.9	+1.9	-0.7
Employed Part-Time Voluntarily	1,480	1,687	1,875	1,951	+207	+76	23.3	23.3	26.6	23.0	0	-3.6
Employed Full-Time	1,793	1,780	1,748	1,869	-13	+121	28.3	24.5	24.8	22.1	-3.8	-2.7
Total	6,346	7,252	7,055	8,465	+906	+1,410	100.0	100.0	100.0	100.0	0	0

	Percent with unemployment who had Inadequate Individual Earnings	Percent with unemployment who had Inadequate Family Earnings	Percent with unemployment who had Inadequate Family Income
1974	54.2	21.9	13.7
1975	59.9	25.6	14.4
1976	59.7	24.6	14.3
1977	59.3	23.4	14.7
1978	56.7	24.6	15.6
1979	53.3	22.7	14.1
1979R	53.5	22.8	14.2
1980	59.6	26.6	17.4

The result is that the proportions of the hardship counts who had experienced unemployment during the previous year and who were jobless for more than one-third of their weeks in the work force both rose during recessions (Chart 4.3).

There were significant cyclical changes in work force attachment which were reflected in the full-year and less-than-full-year hardship counts. Over the 1974-1980 period, full-year participants averaged 72 percent of the work force, rising from 70 percent in 1974 to 74 percent in 1980. Among those experiencing unemployment, and among the IIE, IFE and IFI counts, 61, 52, 45, and 46 percent, respectively, were full-year participants on average over the entire period. But the fluctuations around those means varied significantly (Chart 4.4). From 1974 to 1975, the number of full-year work force participants rose by 3.1 million while the less than full-year participants declined by 2.3 million. From 1979 to 1980 (using 1980 Census weights in both cases), the full-year work force grew by 3.5 million while the less than half-year work force declined by 2.1 million. Apparently, more participants stayed in the work force full-year to bolster family earnings in the face of adversity, while many of those with limited attachment were discouraged and did not participate in the work force. Reflecting these patterns, the full-year participant components of the IIE, the IFE, and the IFI rose dramatically in recession years while the less than full-year participants in hardship rose much more modestly.

Transfers helped to mitigate the impacts of recession, but the effects were much greater in the 1974-1975 recession than in the 1979-1980 recession. From 1974 to 1975, 47 percent of those added to the IFI Net-of-Transfers were raised out of poverty by cash benefits compared to just 18 percent of those added to the IFI Net-of-Transfers between 1979 and 1980. The total reduction of the Net-of-Transfers IFI was 37 percent in 1975 but only 30 percent in 1980:

Chart 4.3. THE CHANGING WORK EXPERIENCE PATTERN AND DISTRIBUTION OF PERSONS IN HARDSHIP, 1974-1980

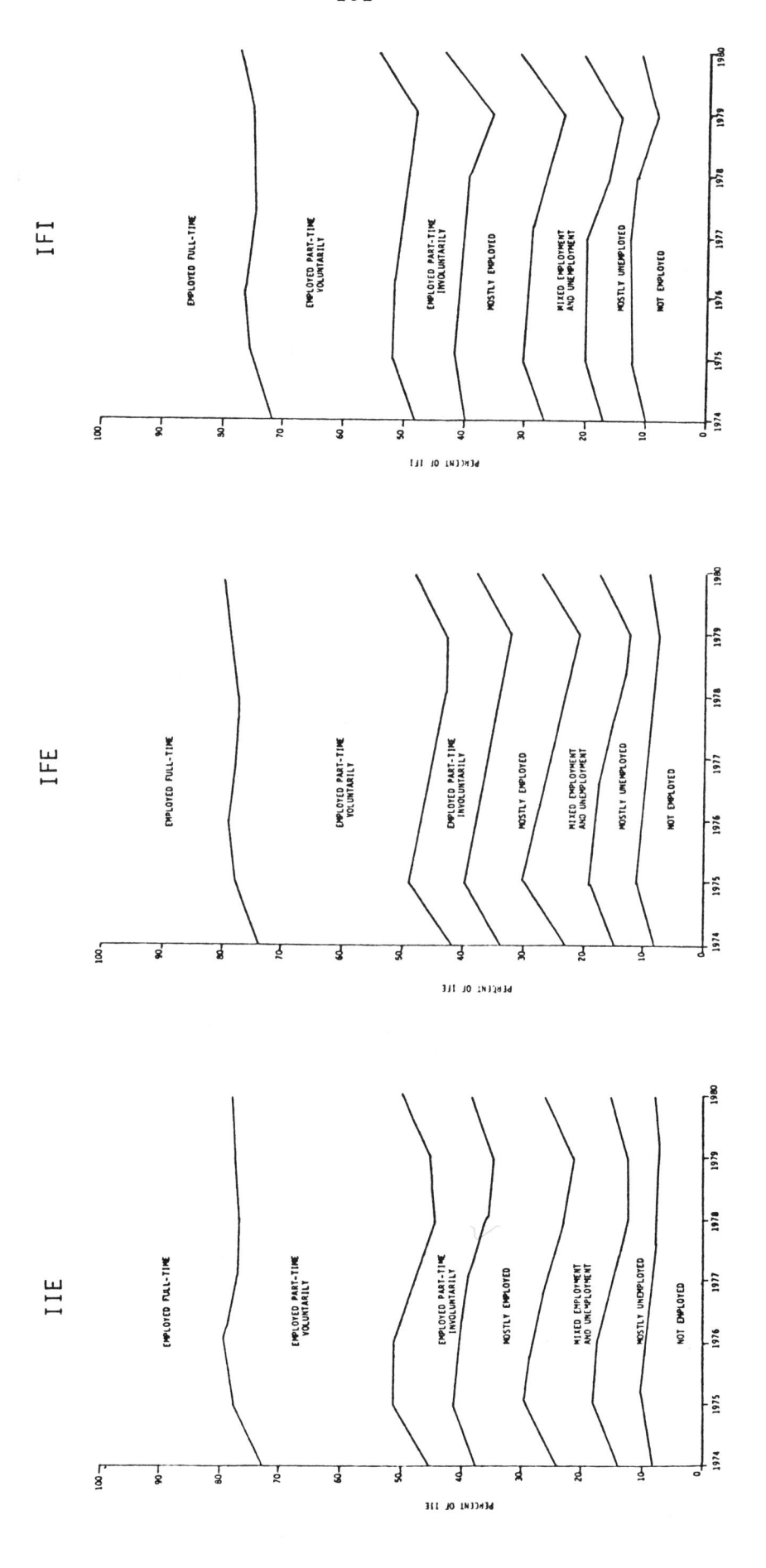

Chart 4.4. YEAR-TO-YEAR CHANGES IN FULL-YEAR AND LESS THAN FULL-YEAR PARTICIPATION IN WORK FORCE AND AMONG UNEMPLOYED AND PERSONS IN HARDSHIP

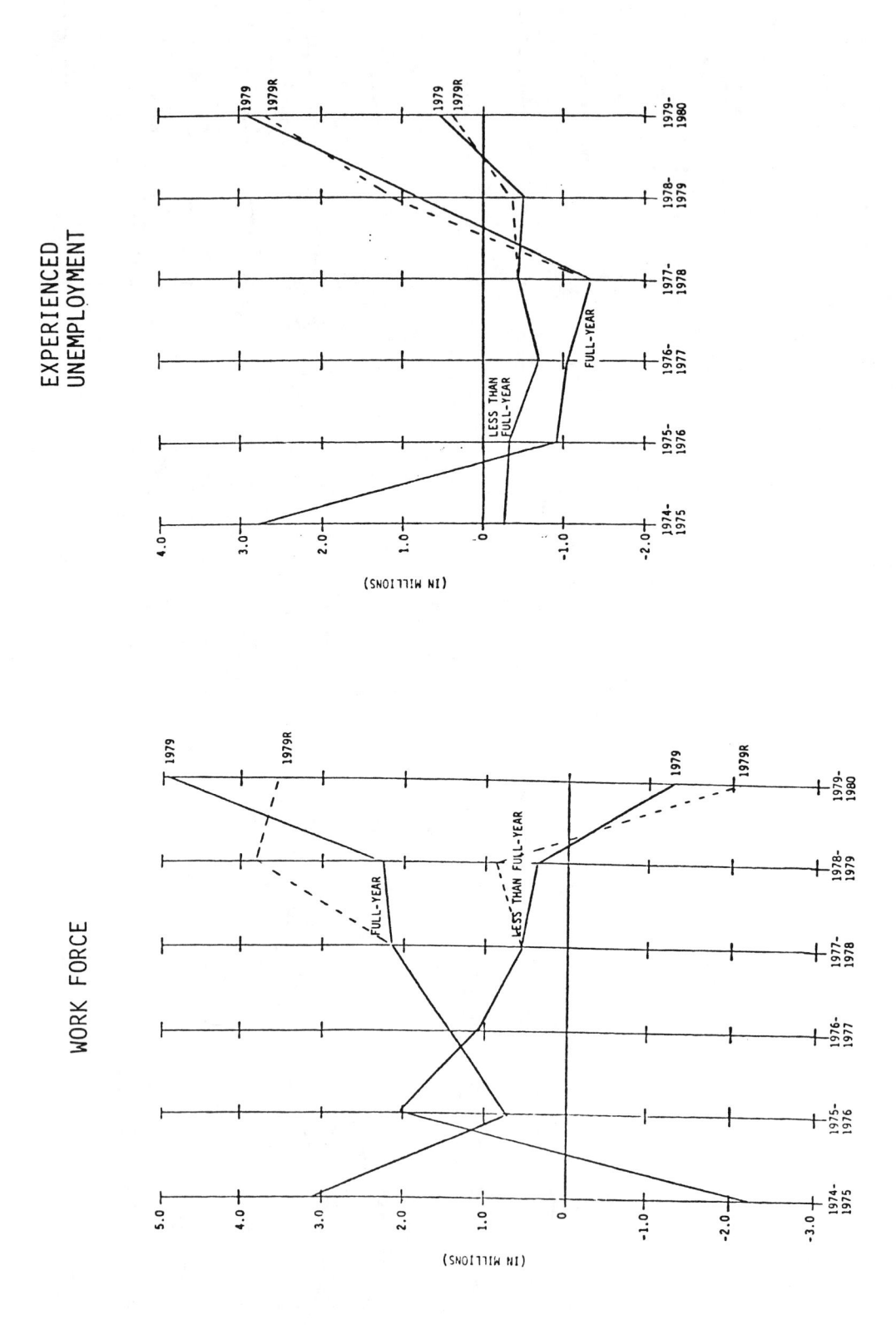

Chart 4.4. (Continued)

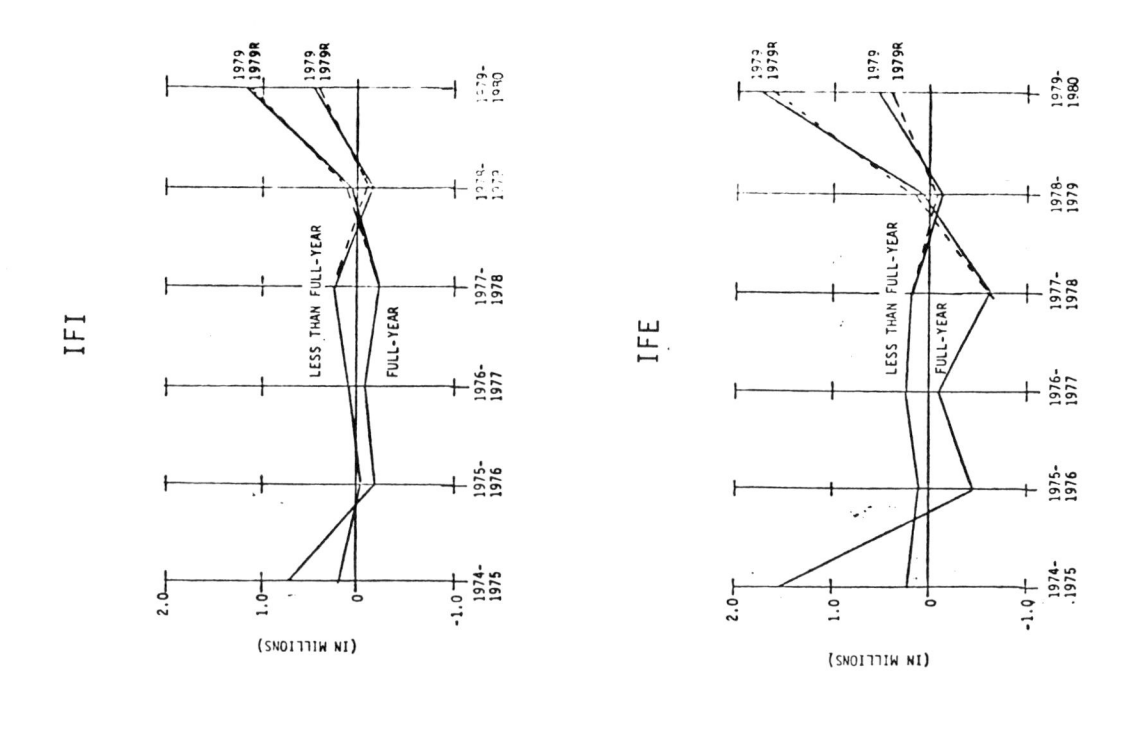

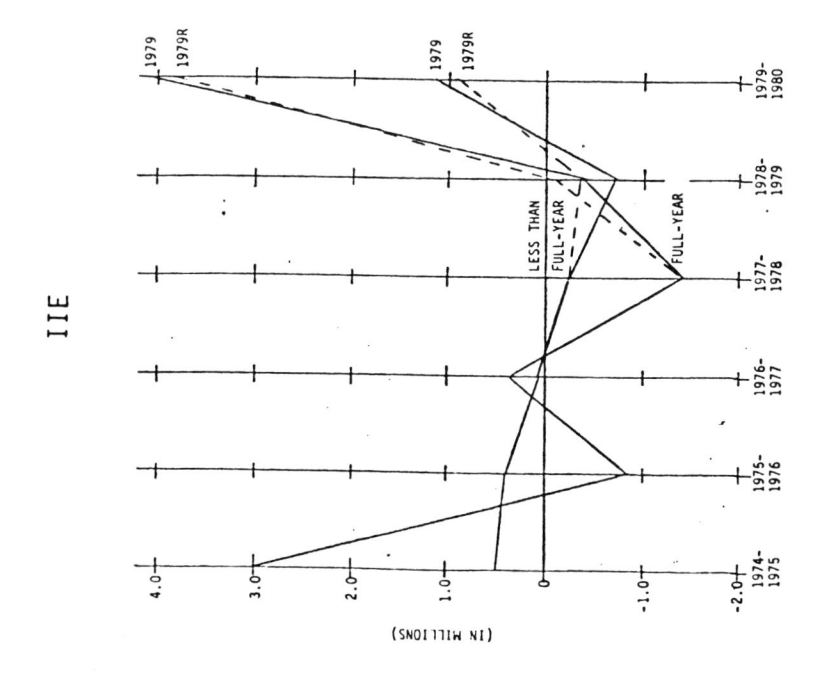

	(1) IFI Excluding Transfers	(2) IFI	(3) Percent difference (1) - (2) (1)	(4) IFI Deficit Excluding Transfers	(5) IFI Deficit	(6) Percent difference (4) - (5) (4)
1974	9,806	6,346	-35	15,562	7,713	-50
1975	11,531	7,252	-37	20,060	9,538	-52
1976	11,059	7,033	-36	20,250	9,573	-53
1977	11,038	6,998	-37	21,380	10,357	-52
1978	10,418	7,012	-33	21,500	11,027	-49
1979	10,177	6,853	-33	23,378	12,499	-47
1979R	10,457	7,055	-33	24,006	12,825	-47
1980	12,158	8,465	-30	31,723	17,452	-45

The Victims of Recession

The victims of recession include prime age workers, males and more skilled workers who rarely suffer hardship in good times. The political responsiveness to recessionary cycles of unemployment in contrast to the the benign neglect of persistent structural problems is explained by these compositional shifts, as the politically leveraged segments only begin to suffer during severe recessions.

The Impacts on Prime Age Workers

In both the 1974-1975 and 1979-1980 recessions, the proportionate increases in unemployment and individual earnings inadequacy were greater among 25-to-44-year-old workers than among older or younger participants (Table 4.7). Inadequate Family Earnings also rose most substantially among 25-to-44-year-olds, although 20-to-24-year-olds were also adversely affected. In the 1974-1975 recession, the IFE rise among prime age workers was mitigated by increased transfer payments; 27.5 percent of the 25-to-44-year-olds with Inadequate Family Earnings were lifted out of poverty by the receipt of transfers in 1975, up from 21.1 percent in 1974. This was not true in the 1979-1980 recession, where the percent of 25-to-44-year-olds in the IFE who were lifted out of poverty by the receipt of transfers actually fell from 19.7 to 18.2 percent between 1979 and 1980. As a result, the prime age workers' share of the IFI rose much more in the second period (Table 4.8).

Some of the recession's impacts on younger and older workers were "disguised" by their withdrawal from the work force (and hence from the hardship tallies) in the face of adversity. The percentage point increases in hardship rates during recessions were greater among teenagers than prime age workers, and if the net reduction in the number of work force participants were added to the measured increases in hardship counts, then the estimated impacts on older and younger workers were substantial.

Table 4.7. ABSOLUTE AND PERCENTAGE CHANGES IN WORK FORCE PARTICIPATION, UNEMPLOYMENT AND HARDSHIP DURING THE 1974-1975 AND 1979-1980 RECESSIONS, BY AGE OF WORKERS

	Change 1974-1975		Change 1979-1980	
	(000)	(%)	(000)	(%)
Work Force				
16-19	-339	-3.0	-693	-5.9
16-19 Student	-400	-6.2	-96	-1.5
20-24	+145	+1.6	+264	+1.5
20-24 Student	-66	-2.7	-64	-2.4
25-44	+1,376	+3.3	+1,740	+3.3
45-64	-274	-0.9	-109	-0.3
65+	-66	-1.6	-54	-1.3
Experienced Unemployment				
16-19	-9	-0.2	+150	+4.9
16-19 Student	-121	-7.0	+168	+12.5
20-24	+452	+9.7	+664	+14.7
20-24 Student	+43	+7.2	+77	+16.7
25-44	+1,376	+20.7	+1,627	+20.9
45-64	+685	+20.8	+500	+17.7
65+	+66	+19.0	-9	-3.8
IIE				
16-19	+680	+9.7	+637	+6.3
16-19 Student	+249	+6.0	+376	+9.5
20-24	+959	+19.3	+1,221	+22.2
20-24 Student	+177	+17.7	+171	+16.0
25-44	+1,236	+16.6	+2,132	+24.1
45-64	+604	+10.5	+610	+11.1
65+	+109	+6.8	+77	+5.0
IFE				
16-19	+244	+13.6	+162	+9.1
16-19 Student	+30	+3.2	+112	+13.3
20-24	+418	+22.5	+408	+18.0
20-24 Student	+59	+14.6	+29	+6.2
25-44	+747	+21.3	+963	+21.4
45-64	+306	+10.5	+292	+9.2
65+	+46	+2.4	+6	+0.3
IFI				
16-19	+234	+21.0	+89	+8.0
16-19 Student	+62	+11.3	+68	+14.8
20-24	+266	+22.1	+371	+25.9
20-24 Student	+48	+24.2	+52	+25.1
25-44	+299	+12.8	+751	+25.1
45-64	+107	+7.6	+164	+12.7
65+	0	0	+34	+15.0

Table 4.8. CHANGES IN THE DISTRIBUTION AND INCIDENCE OF WORK FORCE PARTICIPATION, UNEMPLOYMENT AND HARDSHIP DURING THE 1974-1975 AND 1979-1980 RECESSIONS BY AGE OF WORKERS

SHARE

	1974	1975	Change 1974-1975	1979	1980	Change 1979-1980
Work Force						
16-19	11.0%	10.6%	-0.4%	10.0%	9.3%	-0.7%
20-44	55.2	56.2	+1.0	59.7	60.8	+1.1
45+	33.8	33.2	-0.6	30.3	30.0	-0.3
Experienced Unemployment						
16-19	19.4	17.0	-2.4	16.7	15.1	-1.6
20-44	60.9	62.2	+1.3	66.7	68.3	+2.5
45+	19.7	20.7	+1.0	16.6	16.6	0
IIE						
16-19	26.1	25.3	-0.8	24.5	22.5	-2.0
20-44	46.5	48.2	+1.7	50.7	54.1	+3.4
45+	27.4	26.6	-1.2	24.8	23.5	-1.3
IFE						
16-19	14.9	14.8	-0.1	13.4	12.9	-0.5
20-44	44.6	47.3	+2.7	50.4	53.3	+2.9
45+	40.5	37.8	-2.7	36.2	33.8	-2.4
IFI						
16-19	17.5	18.6	+0.9	15.7	14.1	-1.6
20-44	55.8	56.5	+0.7	62.8	65.6	+2.8
45+	26.7	25.9	-0.8	21.5	20.3	-1.2

INCIDENCE

	1974	1975	Change 1974-1975	1979	1980	Change 1979-1980
Work Force						
16-19	70.1%	67.3%	-2.4%	69.6%	66.9%	-2.7%
20-44	80.6	81.5	+0.9	84.5	84.6	+0.1
45+	54.4	53.3	-1.1	51.9	51.5	-0.4
Experienced Unemployment						
16-19	31.6	32.5	+0.9	26.5	29.5	+3.0
20-44	19.7	22.3	+2.6	17.6	20.3	+2.7
45+	10.4	12.7	+3.1	8.7	10.0	+2.3
IIE						
16-19	61.3	69.3	+8.0	59.4	67.2	+3.0
20-44	21.7	24.9	+3.2	20.5	24.6	+2.7
45+	21.0	23.3	+2.3	19.7	21.7	+1.3
IFE						
16-19	15.7	18.4	+2.7	15.3	17.7	+2.4
20-44	9.4	11.1	+1.7	9.6	11.2	+1.6
45+	13.9	15.1	+1.2	13.6	14.4	+0.8
IFI						
16-19	9.8	12.2	+2.4	9.5	10.9	+1.4
20-44	6.2	7.0	+0.8	6.3	7.7	+1.4
45+	4.9	5.2	+0.3	4.3	4.8	+0.5

Cyclical Patterns for Sex and Family Relationship Subgroups

Males were disproportionately affected by recessions. They represented 56 percent of those experiencing unemployment during 1974, but 65 percent of the 1974-1975 increment in unemployment. By 1979, the male share among the unemployed had fallen to 54 percent, but males were even more adversely affected by the recessions, accounting for 69 percent of the 1979-1980 rise in unemployment. The male shares of the unemployed and of those unemployed over one-third of their weeks in the work force rose by 1.0 and 4.2 percentage points, respectively, from 1974 to 1975, and by 2.0 and 4.0 percentage points, respectively, from 1979 to 1980, while the female shares declined by the same amounts (Table 4.9).

Males were relatively more likely to suffer hardship during recessions, and the male shares of the IIE, IFE and IFI all rose from 1974 to 1975 and from 1979 to 1980. However, the shifts were less pronounced in the hardship shares than in the unemployment shares. For instance, where the male share of persons experiencing unemployment rose by 2.0 percentage points between 1979 and 1980, the male share of the IIE rose by 1.3 percentage points, their share of the IFE by only 0.5 percentage points, and their IFI share by only 0.3 percentage points.

The explanation is apparent when the male and female totals are disaggregated by family relationship. The percentage of the work force who were wives did not change in response to recessions, and the wives' shares of the unemployed and the IIE counts actually declined. Yet their shares of the IFE and the IFI rose. In other words, hardship among families with wives in the work force reflected the problems of both the wives and their working husbands. Wives more frequently had husbands who worked and the husbands, on average, accounted for a larger share of earnings than vice versa. Thus, the individual problems of male heads were reflected more in the tallies for females than the problems of female earners were reflected in the male tallies.

Other males and females, who usually represented secondary or tertiary family earners, withdrew from the work force in the face of economic adversity. Their shares of the unemployed, thus, declined. However, their shares of the severe hardship IFI count rose slightly because the proportion of the IFE who were lifted out of poverty by nonearned income declined during recessions, particularly so in the 1979-1980 recession when their share of the IFE declined by 0.6 percentage points, while their share of the IFI rose by 1.3 percentage points.

Unrelated individuals, both male and female, were particularly affected by the 1974-1975 recession, but less so in the 1979-1980 decline. Their share of the severe hardship IFI count rose by 0.7 percentage points between 1974 and 1975, but dropped by 1.6 percentage points between 1979 and 1980. The changes in the IFE shares were +0.4 and -0.2 percentage points, respectively.

Table 4.9. SEX AND FAMILY RELATIONSHIP DISTRIBUTION OF WORK FORCE, UNEMPLOYED AND WORKERS SUFFERING HARDSHIP DURING 1974-1975 AND 1979-1980 DOWNTURNS

	1974	1975	Percentage Point Change 1974-1975	1979	1980	Percentage Point Change 1979-1980
Total Male						
Work Force	57.4%	57.1%	-0.3	55.3%	55.2%	-0.1
Unemployed	55.5	56.6	+1.0	54.4	56.4	+2.0
Predominantly Unemployed	50.5	54.7	+4.2	50.5	54.5	+4.0
IIE	39.9	41.7	+1.8	40.2	41.5	+1.3
IFE	49.8	50.7	+0.9	47.5	48.0	+0.5
IFI	49.5	50.2	+0.7	47.7	48.0	+0.3
Male Family Head						
Work Force	39.5	39.2	-0.3	35.9	35.6	-0.3
Unemployed	27.9	29.9	+2.0	24.3	26.7	+2.4
Predominantly Unemployed	20.8	25.1	+4.3	18.0	21.8	+3.8
IIE	14.9	16.1	+1.2	13.8	14.9	+1.1
IFE	26.9	28.6	+1.7	24.5	24.9	+0.4
IFI	25.9	27.0	+1.1	23.2	23.9	+0.7
Male Family Head-Wife in Work Force						
Work Force	22.5	22.5	0	22.6	22.7	+0.1
Unemployed	17.3	18.3	+1.0	16.1	17.5	+1.4
Predominantly Unemployed	11.9	15.2	+3.3	11.3	13.9	+2.6
IIE	8.7	9.5	+0.8	8.5	9.2	+0.7
IFE	9.1	10.2	+1.1	8.3	9.1	+0.7
IFI	9.9	10.8	+0.9	9.5	9.9	+0.4
Male Family Head-Wife Not in Work Force						
Work Force	17.0	16.7	-0.3	12.1	11.7	-0.4
Unemployed	10.6	11.6	+1.0	8.2	9.2	+1.0
Predominantly Unemployed	8.9	10.0	+1.1	6.8	7.8	+1.0
IIE	6.1	6.6	+0.5	5.2	5.8	+0.6
IFE	17.9	18.3	+0.4	16.2	15.8	-0.4
IFI	16.0	16.1	+0.1	13.7	14.1	+0.4
Male Unrelated Individual						
Work Force	5.9	6.1	+0.2	7.9	8.1	+0.2
Unemployed	7.4	7.8	+0.4	10.5	10.1	-0.4
Predominantly Unemployed	6.7	7.1	+0.4	9.2	9.8	+0.6
IIE	4.9	5.2	+0.3	6.2	6.2	0
IFE	10.7	10.3	-0.4	12.0	11.3	-0.7
IFI	13.1	12.5	-0.6	15.0	13.9	-1.1
Other Male						
Work Force	12.1	11.8	-0.3	11.5	11.4	-0.1
Unemployed	20.2	18.9	-1.3	19.5	19.6	+0.1
Predominantly Unemployed	23.0	22.4	-0.6	23.3	23.0	-0.3
IIE	20.1	20.4	+0.3	20.2	20.4	+0.2
IFE	12.2	11.9	-0.3	11.8	11.0	-0.8
IFI	10.5	10.8	+0.3	9.5	10.2	+0.7

Table 4.9. (Continued)

	1974	1975	Percentage Point Change 1974-1975	1979	1980	Percentage Point Change 1979-1980
Total Female						
Work Force	42.7%	42.9%	+0.2	44.7%	44.8%	+0.1
Unemployed	44.5	43.4	-1.1	45.6	43.6	-2.0
Predominantly Unemployed	49.5	45.3	-4.2	49.5	45.5	-4.0
IIE	60.1	58.3	-1.7	59.8	58.5	-1.3
IFE	50.2	49.3	-0.9	52.5	52.0	-0.5
IFI	50.5	49.8	-0.7	52.3	52.0	-0.3
Female Family Head						
Work Force	4.4	4.4	0	5.1	5.3	+0.2
Unemployed	5.4	5.2	-0.3	6.6	6.6	0
Predominantly Unemployed	6.7	6.2	-0.5	8.4	8.0	-0.4
IIE	5.9	5.7	-0.2	6.3	6.7	+0.4
IFE	14.6	13.7	-0.9	15.2	14.6	-0.6
IFI	17.2	15.1	-2.1	18.9	18.3	-0.6
Wife						
Work Force	24.4	24.4	0	24.6	24.5	-0.1
Unemployed	21.8	21.6	-0.2	20.8	19.7	-0.9
Predominantly Unemployed	23.9	22.2	-1.7	22.0	20.0	-2.0
IIE	31.3	29.6	-1.7	30.2	28.5	-1.7
IFE	14.5	15.0	+0.5	14.1	14.4	+0.3
IFI	12.1	12.7	+0.6	11.6	11.6	0
Female Unrelated Individual						
Work Force	5.4	5.8	+0.4	6.6	6.8	+0.2
Unemployed	4.9	5.3	+0.4	6.7	6.4	-0.3
Predominantly Unemployed	4.6	4.7	+0.1	5.4	5.2	-0.2
IIE	6.0	6.3	+0.3	6.9	7.1	+0.2
IFE	12.4	13.2	+0.8	13.9	14.4	+0.5
IFI	13.2	14.5	+1.3	15.0	14.5	-0.5
Other Females						
Work Force	8.5	8.3	-0.2	8.3	8.2	-0.1
Unemployed	12.4	11.3	-1.1	11.5	10.9	-0.6
Predominantly Unemployed	14.3	12.2	-2.1	13.8	12.3	-1.5
IIE	16.9	16.7	-0.2	16.4	16.1	-0.3
IFE	8.7	8.4	-0.3	8.8	9.0	+0.2
IFI	8.1	7.6	-0.5	7.0	7.6	+0.6

Education is Less of a Protection in Recessions

In good times and bad, education provides protection from hardship. However, the increments in the hardship counts which result from recessions include a larger share of the better educated. In 1974, for instance, high school dropouts represented 32.0 percent of persons experiencing unemployment, 34.6 percent of the IIE, 47.5 percent of the IFE, and 49.7 percent of the IFI. In contrast, dropouts accounted for only 30.0, 20.7, 28.6 and 27.3 percent, respectively, of the 1974-1975 increases in these unemployment and hardship measures (Table 4.10). Thus, the dropout share of the severe hardship IIE, IFE and IFI counts fell, respectively, by 1.6, 2.4 and 2.8 percentage points between 1974 and 1975. The pattern was similar in the 1979-1980 recession, with the IIE, IFE and IFI shares of dropouts falling by 1.6, 1.5 and 1.4 percentage points, respectively.

One reason was that the less educated withdrew from the work force in the face of economic adversity. During the 1974-1975 recession, the number of dropouts in the work force declined by 1.1 million, or more than double the average annual decline over the 1974-1979 period. Between 1979 and 1980, 0.8 million withdrew from the work force. The number of work force participants with some college education increased by 1.9 million in the first period, only slightly below the 1974-1979 trend increase of 2.0 million per year.

The better educated were far less affected, both in absolute and relative terms, by the 1979-1980 recession than by the 1974-1975 recession. The percent increases in the IIE, IFE and IFI counts for college graduates were 3.5, 2.5 and 5.1 times the percent increases for dropouts in the 1974-1975 recession, but 1.5, 0.4 and 0.9 times the increases for dropouts in the 1979-1980 recession. The hardship share of persons with just a high school education rose by more in the second recession than the first, and for dropouts the share declined by less. Students were much more likely to withdraw from the work force in the earlier recession, so that the declines in their hardship shares were noticeably greater between 1974 and 1975 than between 1979 and 1980.

Race and Recessions

Minorities accounted for a larger share of persons with continuing structural employment problems than of persons with only cyclical employment problems. The number of white workers experiencing unemployment rose by 14.0 percent between 1974 and 1975, and the number who were unemployed for more than one-third of their weeks in the work force rose 44.5 percent, compared to increases of 11.8 and 28.9 percent, respectively, among black workers (Table 4.11). The severe hardship IFE count increased 17.7 percent for whites, compared to only 5.2 percent for blacks. These patterns prevailed despite the fact that white work force participation declined more in response to the recessions than did black participation. The white work force grew 2.2 million annually between 1974 and 1979, but only 547,000 between 1974 and 1975, and 847,000 between 1979 and 1980. In contrast, the black work force growth of 190,000 and 278,000, respectively in the two recession periods, was much closer to the trend line of 279,000 annual growth.

Table 4.10. CHANGES IN WORK FORCE PARTICIPATION, UNEMPLOYMENT AND SEVERE HARDSHIP IN THE 1974-1975 AND 1979-1980 RECESSIONS, BY EDUCATIONAL ATTAINMENT

	Number				Share				
	Change 1974-1975 (000)	(%)	Average Annual Change from 1974-1979 Period (000)	Change 1979-1980 (000)	(%)	1974 (%)	1975 (%)	Change 1974-1975 (Percentage Points)	1979 (%)	1980 (%)	Change 1975-1980 (Percentage Points)

Work Force
	1974-1975 (000)	(%)	Avg Annual 1974-1979 (000)	1979-1980 (000)	(%)	1974 (%)	1975 (%)	Change 1974-1975	1979 (%)	1980 (%)	Change 1975-1980
High School Student	-402	-7.8	-11	-160	-3.2	4.9	4.4	-.5	4.3	4.1	-.2
Post-Secondary Student	-93	-2.1	+39	+87	+1.9	4.3	4.1	-.2	4.0	4.0	0
High School Dropout	-1108	-4.1	-504	-775	-3.2	28.7	24.8	-3.9	20.9	20.9	-.9
High School Graduate	+569	+1.5	+1183	+1398	+3.1	37.3	37.5	+.2	38.1	38.8	+.7
Post-Secondary 1 to 3 years	+783	+5.7	+946	+338	+1.8	14.0	14.0	0	15.8	16.0	+.2
College Graduate	+1092	+7.5	+1018	+461	+2.3	14.1	15.0	+.9	16.9	17.0	+.1

Unemployed
High School Student	-112	-7.7	-69	+219	+19.7	7.8	6.4	-1.4	6.0	6.2	+.2
Post-Secondary Student	+37	+3.5	-38	+102	+11.7	5.2	5.2	0	4.7	4.5	-.2
High School Dropout	+771	+13.0	-124	+738	+13.9	32.0	31.8	-.2	28.8	28.3	-.5
High School Graduate	+1103	+16.3	+64	+1516	+21.4	36.5	37.3	+.8	38.4	40.2	+1.8
Post-Secondary 1 to 3 years	+544	+28.7	+103	+217	+9.0	10.2	11.5	+1.3	13.0	12.3	-.7
College Graduate	+225	+15.8	-50	+151	+9.0	7.7	7.8	+.1	9.0	8.5	-.5

Table 4.10. (Continued)

	1974-1975 (000)	(%)	Number Average Annual Change from 1974-1979R Period (000)	1979-1980 (000)	(%)	Share 1974 (%)	1975 (%)	Change 1974-1975 (Percentage Points)	(%)	1980 (%)	Change 1979-1980 (Percentage Points)
Predominantly Unemployed											
High School Student	+48	+5.6	-29	+194	+29.0	10.5	7.9	-2.6	8.9	8.3	-.6
Post-Secondary Student	194	+50.9	-6	+129	+36.6	4.9	5.3	+.4	4.7	4.6	-.1
High School Dropout	1019	+36.8	-49	+784	+31.1	35.8	34.6	-1.2	33.7	32.0	-1.7
High School Graduate	1320	+50.4	+18	+1281	+32.1	33.9	36.0	+2.1	36.2	38.6	+2.4
Post-Secondary 1 to 3 years	+379	+53.2	+9	+304	+40.3	9.2	10.0	+.8	10.1	10.2	+.1
College Graduate	+238	+53.6	+8	+163	+33.6	5.7	6.2	+.5	6.5	6.3	-.2
IIE											
High School Student	+71	+2.0	-39	+309	+9.3	13.2	11.8	-1.4	11.8	11.1	-.7
Post-Secondary Student	+375	+20.4	+28	+337	+17.0	6.9	7.3	+.4	7.0	7.1	+.1
High School Dropout	+742	+8.0	-146	+831	+9.7	34.6	33.0	-1.6	30.2	28.6	-1.6
High School Graduate	1443	+17.0	+214	+2242	+23.5	31.7	32.7	+1.0	33.8	36.0	+2.2
Post-Secondary 1 to 3 years	+583	+25.3	+144	+482	+16.0	8.6	9.5	+.9	10.7	10.7	0
College Graduate	+375	+27.8	+101	+277	+14.9	5.0	5.7	+.7	6.6	6.5	-.1

Table 4.10. (Continued)

	Number					Share				
	1974-1975 (000)	(%)	Average Annual Change from 1974-1979 Period (000)	1979 (000)	1980 (%)	1974 (%)	1975 (%)	Change 1974-1975 (Percentage Points)	1979 (%)	1980 (%)	Change 1979-1980 (Percentage Points)
IFE											
High School Student	+32	+3.9	−7	+83	+9.6	6.8	6.1	−.7	5.9	5.7	−.2
Post-Secondary Student	+67	+9.8	+22	+76	+9.6	5.9	5.5	−.4	6.0	5.8	−.2
High School Dropout	+504	+8.8	−82	+505	+9.5	47.5	45.1	−2.4	39.9	38.4	−1.5
High School Graduate	+724	+23.0	+174	+933	+23.2	26.2	28.1	+1.3	30.2	32.7	+2.5
Post-Secondary 1 to 3 years	+287	+28.7	+83	+192	+13.6	8.3	9.3	+1.0	10.7	10.6	−.1
College Graduate	+147	+22.2	+64	+41	+4.0	5.5	5.9	+.4	7.4	6.8	−.6
IFI											
High School Student	+34	+6.8	−10	+75	+16.7	7.8	7.3	−.5	6.4	6.2	−.2
Post-Secondary Student	+77	+24.2	+3	+85	+25.7	5.0	5.4	+.4	4.7	4.9	+.2
High School Dropout	+247	+7.8	−28	+489	+16.2	49.7	46.9	−2.8	42.7	41.3	−1.4
High School Graduate	+305	+18.7	+101	+598	+28.0	25.6	26.6	+1.0	30.2	32.3	+2.1
Post-Secondary 1 to 3 years	+135	+28.1	+44	+103	+14.7	7.6	8.5	+.9	10.0	9.5	−.5
College Graduate	+107	+39.6	+32	+60	+13.9	4.3	5.2	+.9	6.1	5.8	−.3

Table 4.11. IMPACTS OF 1974-1975 AND 1979-1980 RECESSIONS ON WHITES, BLACKS AND HISPANICS

	CHANGE IN LEVELS					SHARES					
	1974-1975 (000)	1974-1975 (%)	Average Annual Increase, 1974-1979 (000)	1979 (000)	1980 (%)	1974 (%)	1975 (%)	1975-1974 (%)	1979 (%)	1980 (%)	1980-1979 (%)
Work Force											
White	547	0.6	2,216	847	0.8	88.5	88.3	-0.2	87.8	87.5	-0.3
Black	190	1.8	279	278	2.4	9.9	10.0	+1.0	10.0	10.1	+0.1
Hispanic	-123	-2.7	269	197	3.4	4.4	4.2	-0.2	5.0	5.1	+0.1
Unemployed											
White	2,171	14.0	-64	2,337	15.4	83.6	83.7	+0.1	82.1	81.8	-0.3
Black	326	11.8	21	472	16.4	15.0	14.7	-0.3	15.6	15.7	+0.1
Hispanic	44	4.0	41	82	6.2	6.0	5.5	-0.5	7.1	6.5	-0.6
Predominantly Unemployed											
White	2,687	44.5	-86	2,319	41.3	78.1	79.8	+1.7	74.9	76.7	+1.8
Black	455	28.9	25	441	25.9	20.4	18.6	-1.8	22.7	20.7	-2.0
Hispanic	110	21.4	13	125	21.6	16.6	15.7	-0.9	7.7	6.8	-0.9
IIE											
White	3,077	13.7	235	3,562	15.1	83.8	84.0	+0.2	83.4	82.9	-0.5
Black	488	11.5	40	661	16.1	14.6	14.3	-0.3	14.4	14.5	+0.1
Hispanic	57	3.9	51	328	19.1	5.5	5.0	-0.5	6.1	6.2	+0.1
IIE Deficit											
White	11,462	24.1	307	8,739	17.8	83.5	83.5	0	83.0	81.7	-1.3
Black	2,431	29.6	113	2,306	26.3	14.4	15.1	+0.7	14.9	15.7	+0.8
Hispanic	409	13.4	110	253	7.0	5.4	4.9	-0.5	6.1	5.5	-0.6
IFE											
White	1,618	17.7	199	1,443	14.3	75.9	78.0	+2.1	76.1	76.5	+0.4
Black	137	5.2	41	303	10.6	22.0	20.2	-1.8	21.5	20.9	-0.6
Hispanic	101	12.4	28	179	18.7	6.8	6.7	-0.1	7.2	7.5	+0.3
IFE Deficit											
White	4,457	18.7	410	3,842	14.8	72.5	74.2	+1.7	72.1	72.6	+0.5
Black	754	9.0	162	874	9.5	25.6	24.0	-1.6	25.7	24.6	-1.1
Hispanic	231	9.7	48	564	21.5	7.2	6.8	-0.4	7.3	7.8	+0.5
IFI											
White	835	19.0	99	1,060	21.6	69.4	72.3	+2.9	69.5	70.4	+0.9
Black	34	1.9	32	292	15.0	28.1	25.0	-3.1	27.5	26.4	-1.1
Hispanic	85	14.3	18	145	21.3	9.4	9.4	0	9.7	9.8	+0.1
IFI Deficit											
White	1,338	15.2	197	2,115	21.6	68.4	69.6	+1.2	67.4	68.3	+0.9
Black	312	8.3	110	624	14.4	29.3	28.0	-1.3	29.7	28.3	-1.4
Hispanic	133	10.4	28	440	31.1	9.9	9.6	-0.3	9.7	10.6	+0.9

Blacks represented 15.0 percent of the unemployed in 1974 but only 12.8 percent of the 1974-1975 increment in unemployment. More strikingly, blacks represented 22.0 percent of the 1974 severe hardship IFE count but only 7.4 percent of the 1974-1975 increase:

	Relative shares of structural and cyclical hardship and unemployment by race			
	1974	1974-1975 Increment	1979	1979-1980 Increment
Whites				
Unemployed	83.6%	84.5%	82.1%	79.4%
Predominantly unemployed	78.1	83.9	74.9	80.4
IIE	83.8	85.7	83.4	79.5
IFE	75.9	91.9	76.1	78.8
IFI	69.4	92.2	69.5	75.2
Blacks				
Unemployed	15.0	12.7	15.6	16.0
Predominantly unemployed	20.4	14.2	22.7	15.4
IIE	14.6	12.5	14.5	14.8
IFE	22.0	7.8	21.5	17.2
IFI	28.1	3.8	27.5	20.7
Hispanics[2]				
Unemployed	6.0	1.7	7.1	2.8
Predominantly unemployed	6.6	3.4	7.7	4.4
IIE	5.5	1.6	6.1	7.3
IFE	6.8	5.7	7.2	9.8
IFI	9.4	9.4	9.7	10.3

Blacks and Hispanics suffered more, both relatively and absolutely, during the 1979-1980 downturn than during the more severe 1974-1975 recession. Comparing the recession-induced increments in unemployment and hardship, the 1979-1980 rises for blacks and Hispanics far exceeded those in the 1974-1975 recession. In this earlier recession, the increases in hardship incidence rates for Hispanics were substantially lower than those of whites, while in the second recession they equalled or exceeded those of whites. In part, this occurred because the Hispanic population withdrew from the work force in very substantial numbers in the earlier recession (a measured decline of 123,000, compared to the trend line growth of 269,000 for the 1974-1979 period) but this apparently did not occur in the second recession.

The Geographic Impacts of Recessions

Both the 1974-1975 and 1979-1980 declines had disproportionately large impacts on the East North Central states but limited effects on the Pacific states (Table 4.12). In many other cases, however, the regions that fared comparatively well in the earlier recession were victims of the latter decline and vice versa. For instance, the New England states had increasing shares of hardship in the first recession but declining shares in the second, while the hardship shares of the East Southern Central states declined from 1974 to 1975 but rose from 1979 to 1980.

Surprisingly, the largest central cities within metropolitan areas had declining shares of hardship in both recessions (Table 4.13). The impacts of the 1979-1980 recession were comparatively much more concentrated in nonmetropolitan areas than were the impacts of the 1974-1975 recession.

Table 4.12. CHANGES IN REGIONAL SHARES OF WORK FORCE, UNEMPLOYMENT AND HARDSHIP RESULTING FROM RECESSIONS

	Work Force		Unemployed		Predominantly Unemployed		IIE		IFE		IFI	
	1974-1975	1979-1980	1974-1975	1979-1980	1974-1975	1979-1980	1974-1975	1979-1980	1974-1975	1979-1980	1974-1975	1979-1980
New England	-0.3	-0.2	+0.1	-0.7	+0.7	-0.7	+0.8	-0.7	+0.8	-0.1	+1.0	-0.1
Middle Atlantic	-0.1	-0.1	+1.1	-0.5	+0.8	-1.2	+1.1	-0.1	0	+0.5	+0.4	+1.3
East North Central	-0.4	-0.1	0	+1.4	+0.9	+4.6	+0.5	+0.9	+1.4	+1.4	+0.9	+2.0
West North Central	-0.1	-0.2	0	+0.1	-0.7	+1.1	-0.4	-0.1	-1.1	-0.1	-0.6	+0.3
South Atlantic	+0.2	+0.2	+0.7	+0.1	+2.1	-1.3	-0.1	+0.1	+0.5	-0.4	+0.7	+0.3
East South Central	0	+0.1	-0.5	+0.6	-0.2	+0.7	-0.7	+0.4	-1.1	+0.5	-1.7	+1.3
West South Central	+0.4	+0.3	+0.2	+0.2	-0.1	+1.1	-0.5	0	-0.8	-0.4	-1.9	-1.0
Mountain	+0.1	0	+0.1	0	-0.5	0	0	-0.4	+0.4	+0.2	+0.9	+0.2
Pacific	-0.1	0	-1.8	-1.3	-3.2	-1.1	-0.6	-0.2	-0.6	-0.6	+0.2	-1.6

Table 4.13. CHANGE IN METROPOLITAN AND NONMETROPOLITAN SHARES OF WORK FORCE, UNEMPLOYMENT AND HARDSHIP RESULTING FROM RECESSIONS

YEAR-TO-YEAR PERCENTAGE POINT CHANGE IN SHARES

	Work Force 1974-1975	Work Force 1979-1980	Unemployed 1974-1975	Unemployed 1979-1980	Predominantly Unemployed 1974-1975	Predominantly Unemployed 1979-1980	IIE 1974-1975	IIE 1979-1980	IFE 1974-1975	IFE 1979-1980	IFI 1974-1975	IFI 1979-1980
Inside SMSA	-0.1	-0.4	-1.0	-2.1	-0.3	-1.5	+0.9	-0.6	+0.2	-2.7	0	-2.6
SMSA More Than 1 Million	-0.1	0	-1.5	-1.3	-1.2	-1.9	+0.8	-0.2	+0.7	-2.1	+1.0	-2.2
Central City	-0.6	-0.1	-1.7	-0.8	-1.9	-1.5	-0.5	-0.2	-1.0	-1.0	-0.7	-1.8
Balance	+0.6	+0.1	+0.2	-0.4	+0.6	-0.4	+1.3	0	+1.7	-1.2	+1.6	-0.5
SMSA Less Than 1 Million	0	-0.4	+0.5	-0.8	+0.9	+0.4	0	-0.4	-0.5	-0.6	-0.9	-0.4
Central City	+0.2	-0.4	+0.9	-1.0	+0.7	-0.5	+0.5	-0.7	+0.1	-0.2	-0.5	0
Balance	-0.2	-0.1	-0.3	+0.2	+0.2	+0.7	-0.4	+0.1	-0.6	-0.4	-0.4	-0.4
Outside SMSA	+0.1	+0.4	+1.0	+2.1	+0.3	+1.5	-0.9	+0.6	-0.2	+2.7	0	+2.6

Notes

1. The 1979-1980 comparisons in this chapter utilize the 1980 Census weights for the 1979 survey responses. The time series presentations for the 1974-1980 period present the 1979 data utilizing both the 1970 and 1980 Census weights. Cases where the 1970 Census weights are utilized in calculations are noted by an asterisk.

2. There have been several changes in the survey questions which identify Hispanics, as well as in the Census survey techniques which affect the weights for CPS survey responses. The 1979-1980 data for Hispanics are much more dependable than the 1974-1975 data.

CHAPTER 5. APPLYING THE HARDSHIP MEASURES

Policy Options

A primary aim of economic and social policy is to alleviate the economic hardship which results from labor market problems. The basic tools are macroeconomic policies to stimulate employment and reduce unemployment, minimum wage changes to alter the payoff from employment, transfer programs to offset insufficient earnings, and targeted job creation and training programs to help those in need who are at the end of the labor queue.

The hardship measures provide a useful perspective for assessing these policy options. They demonstrate quite clearly that macroeconomic policies are not likely to significantly alleviate labor market-related hardship, that an array of employment and training interventions are needed to supplement macroeconomic policies, that hardship is not so much an individual problem as a family problem, so that solutions to individual earnings difficulties will not necessarily eliminate family earnings shortfalls, and that welfare and workfare must overlap if hardship is to be eliminated for those in the work force and their dependents.

The Limitations of Macroeconomic Policies

Hardship declines when unemployment falls, and rises during recessions; but it requires an enormous drop in the unemployment rate to achieve a modest percentage decline in hardship. Hardship will continue at significant levels under any foreseeable degree of recovery from the current recession.

As noted previously, only half of those experiencing unemployment during 1979 had Inadequate Individual Earnings, less than a fourth were in families with Inadequate Family Earnings, and only one in seven remained with Inadequate Family Incomes after the receipt of cash transfers and other earnings supplements. In addition, only a minority of persons in hardship experienced any weeks of unemployment: the unemployed constituted 35 percent of the severe hardship IIE count in 1979, 42 percent of the IFE and 37 percent of the IFI. Finally, many who suffered from unemployment and hardship had such limited participation or large breadwinning responsibilities that they would not have escaped poverty even if they found jobs which paid minimally adequate wages. Nearly three-fifths of workers with Inadequate Family Earnings who, themselves, experienced at least a week of joblessness would have remained in the IFE even if all workers were provided minimum wage employment for periods of forced idleness. Thus, any reduction in the aggregate number of unemployed yields a proportionately smaller direct reduction in the severe hardship counts. Indirect impacts are difficult to estimate. As unemployment falls, average wages tend to rise faster, second jobs become readily available, involuntary part-time employment declines, and more second or third family members enter the work force. Yet the percentage decline in hardship is less than the percentage decline in unemployment which occurs during recovery, and vice versa during recessions. The standard deviation in the unemployment rate over the 1974-1980 period was 16 percent of the mean, while the coefficients of variation in the severe hardship IIE, IFE and IFI rates were 7, 7 and 9 percent respectively.

While hardship is the result of limited hourly wages, as well as limited hours of employment, increases in the minimum wage--like reductions in unemployment--have a muted effect on hardship. Only a minority of workers who earn at or below the minimum hourly wage come from low-income families. The Minimum Wage Study Commission found that over two-fifths of all low-wage workers in 1978 were from families with incomes above $15,000 and three-fifths had family incomes over $10,000. 1/ Only 11 percent of minimum wage workers lived in poor families, 17 percent in near poor families, and less than a fourth in families with incomes less than 150 percent of the poverty threshold. Thus, the persons in hardship would benefit from only a small portion of the wage bill generated by any increase in the minimum wage. The Minimum Wage Study Commission concluded that minimum wage increases were associated with higher unemployment among minorities and teenagers and perhaps slightly higher unemployment among disadvantaged adults. Disemployment, thus, would offset some of the benefits resulting from increased hourly wage levels, particularly affecting those in the hardship counts. Moreover, many in hardship would remain there even if their hourly wages were increased. A ten percent increase in wages for persons with Inadequate Family Earnings in 1979 would have lowered the severe hardship IFE by just a tenth in 1979.

On balance, however, hardship does decline when the legislated minimum wage is raised, and increases when the real value of the minimum wage is eroded by inflation. This is almost a tautology in the case of the IIE count, since the severe hardship adequacy standard is the average real value of the legislated minimum for the 1967-1980 period, adjusted for the CPI less home ownership costs, so that workers earning the legislated minimum wage will be counted in the IIE when the legislated minimum falls below this adjusted average real value. But the IFE and IFI counts are also affected, since when the real purchasing power of minimum wages falls, low-wage workers are less likely to be able to raise their families above the cost of living adjusted poverty levels.

The plot of year-to-year changes in hardship and unemployment demonstrates these relationships (Chart 5.1). While hardship generally rose and fell in the same pattern as unemployment during the 1974-1980 period, there was a noticeable increase in the severe hardship IIE between 1976 and 1977 despite declining unemployment. The IFE also rose, and the IFI held constant, even though falling unemployment should have resulted in declines. In 1976 the legislated minimum and the adjusted average real minimum wage were equivalent, but because the legislated minimum was not raised in 1977, it fell below the adjusted real minimum standard. Put

Chart 5.1. YEAR-TO-YEAR CHANGES IN UNEMPLOYMENT AND HARDSHIP, 1974-1980

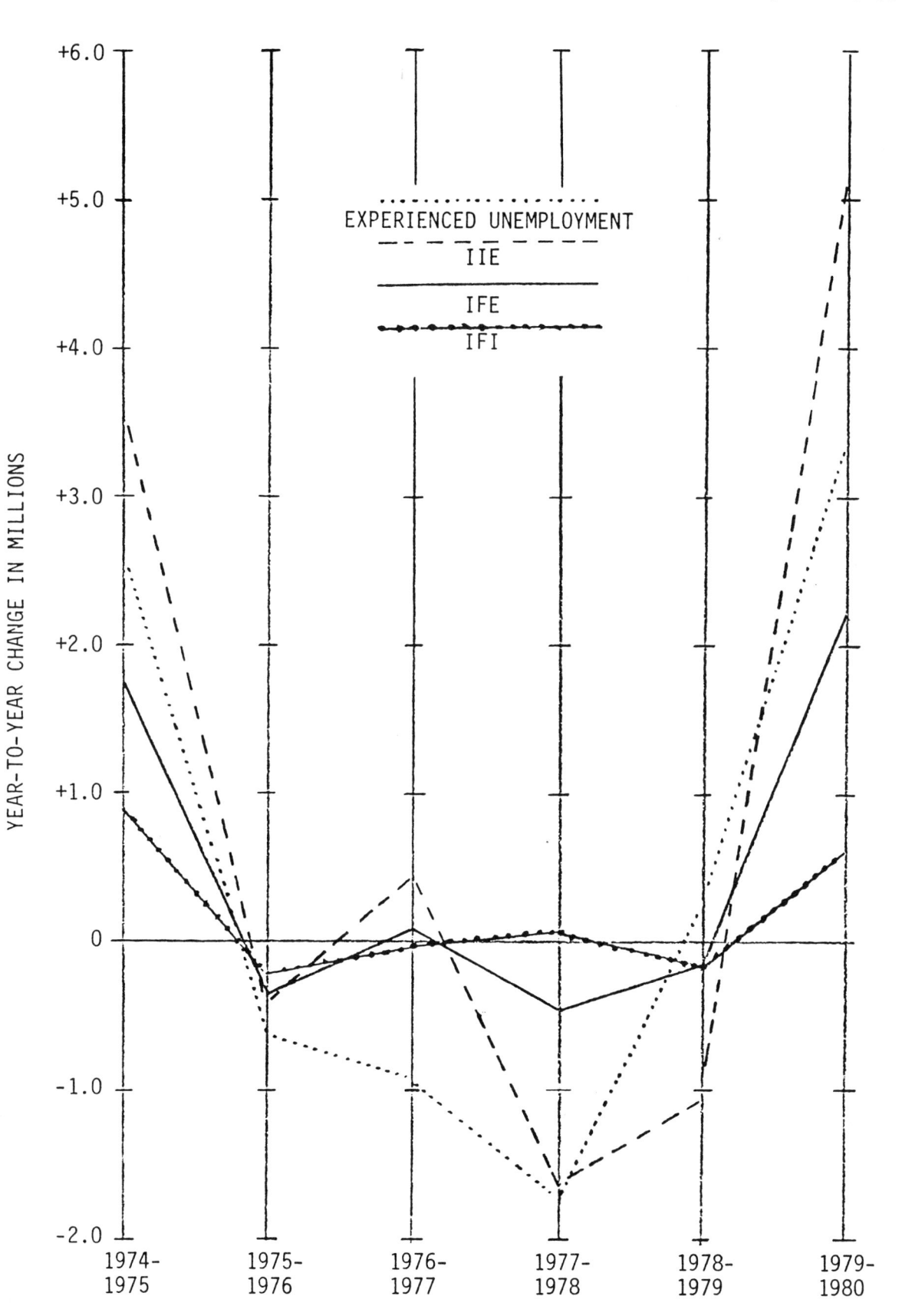

EXPERIENCED UNEMPLOYMENT
IIE
IFE
IFI

another way, workers earning just the legislated minimum in 1976 for their annual hours of availability would have had adequate individual earnings according to the definitions used in the hardship measures, but those earning just the legislated minimum in 1977 would have fallen below the IIE adequacy standard:

	Legislated minimum wage	Adjusted real value of minimum wage 1967-1980	Legislated minimum ÷ real minimum
1974	$2.00	$1.99	$1.01
1975	2.10	2.16	.97
1976	2.30	2.29	1.00
1977	2.30	2.44	.94
1978	2.65	2.61	1.02
1979	2.90	2.87	1.01
1980	3.10	3.21	.97

Since the hardship measures could only be calculated for the 1974-1980 period, it is impossible to derive very precise statistical estimates of the relationship between changes in aggregate unemployment, the legislated minimum wage and hardship levels. However, there were fairly significant fluctuations in the unemployment rate during these seven years, when it ranged from 5.6 to 8.5 percent, and the legislated minimum wage ranged from 94 to 102 percent of the average real minimum wage for the 1967-1980 period. Regression analysis suggests that the severe hardship, unemployment and legislated minimum wage levels were interrelated:

Equation 1: IIE incidence = a + b (annual average unemployment rate) + c (100 X $\frac{\text{average real minimum wage}}{\text{legislated minimum wage}}$)

r^2 = 0.90
a = 1.756
b = 1.25
c = 0.163

Interpretation: An increase in the unemployment rate of 1.0 percentage points was associated with an increase in the severe hardship IIE rate of 1.25 percentage points. An increase in the ratio of the adjusted average real minimum wage to the legislated minimum wage from 100 percent to 110 percent would have increased the IIE incidence by 1.63 percentage points.

Equation 2: IIE incidence = a + b (annual average unemployment rate) + c (100 X $\frac{\text{average real minimum wage}}{\text{legislated minimum wage}}$)
+ d (year = 1 in 1974 to 7 in 1980)

r^2 = 0.93
a = 0.672
b = 1.170
c = 0.185
d = -0.144

Interpretation: An increase in the unemployment rate of 1.0 percentage points was associated with an increase of 1.17 percentage points in the severe hardship IIE rate. An increase in the adjusted average real minimum wage from 100 percent to 110 percent of the legislated minimum wage would have increased the IIE incidence by 1.85 percentage points. There was a downward trend in the incidence of individual earnings inadequacy which lowered the IIE rate for the total work force by an estimated 0.86 percentage points over the 1974-1980 period.

Equation 3: IFE incidence = a + b (annual average unemployment rate) + c (100 X $\frac{\text{average real minimum wage}}{\text{legislated minimum wage}}$)

r^2 = 0.92
a = 2.857
b = 0.540
c = 0.056

Interpretation: An increase in the unemployment rate of 1.0 percentage points was associated with an increase in the severe hardship IFE rate of 0.54 percentage points; thus, IFE incidence was less sensitive to unemployment changes than was IIE incidence. An increase in the ratio of the adjusted average real minimum wage from 100 to 110 percent of the legislated minimum wage would have increased the IFE by 0.56 percentage points; thus, the severe hardship IFE rate was less responsive to the minimum wage level than was the IIE rate.

Equation 4: IFE incidence = a + b (annual average unemployment rate) + c (100 X $\frac{\text{average real minimum wage}}{\text{legislated minimum wage}}$)
+ d (year = 1 in 1974 to 7 in 1980)

r^2 = 0.92
a = 2.900
b = 0.540
c = 0.055
d = 0.007

Interpretation: While the IIE rate trended down over the 1974-1980 period, there was no significant shift in the IFE rate.

Equation 5:   IFI incidence = a + b (annual average unemployment rate + c (100 X $\frac{\text{average real minimum wage}}{\text{legislated minimum wage}}$)

r^2 = 0.634
a = 0.659
b = 0.260
c = 0.040

Interpretation: An increase in the unemployment rate of 1.0 percentage points was associated with an increase in the IFI incidence of 0.26 percentage points; thus, the severe hardship IFI rate was less sensitive to unemployment changes than was the IFE rate. An increase in the ratio of the adjusted average real minimum wage from 100 to 110 percent of the legislated minimum wage would have increased the severe hardship IFI rate by 0.40 percentage points; thus, IFI incidence was less responsive to the minimum wage level changes than was the IFE rate.

Equation 6:   IFI incidence = a + b (annual average unemployment rate) + c (100 X $\frac{\text{average real minimum wage}}{\text{legislated minimum wage}}$)
+ c (year = 1 in 1974 to 7 in 1980)

r^2 = 0.730
a = 1.146
b = 0.300
c = 0.030
d = 0.065

Interpretation: There was apparently an upward trend in the severe hardship IFI rate, adding 0.4 percentage points over the 1974-1980 period. The addition of the trend variable increases the explanative power (r^2) of the equation.

The hardship rates among full-year workers were slightly _less_ responsive to unemployment changes and slightly _more_ responsive to minimum wage changes (Table 5.1). The intermediate and moderate hardship IFE and IFI rates for the total work force were slightly _more_ responsive to aggregate unemployment changes than the severe hardship IFE and IFI rates.

These equations can be used to predict hardship levels for 1981 based on the actual unemployment rate and the ratio of adjusted average real minimum wage to the legislated minimum wage. Estimates for 1982 can be derived by using alternative inflation and unemployment assumptions:

Table 5.1. HARDSHIP INCIDENCE CORRELATIONS OVER TIME WITH UNEMPLOYMENT AND THE MINIMUM WAGE LEVEL

	r^2	a	b (annual average unemployment)	c ($100 \times \frac{\text{average real minimum wage}}{\text{legislated minimum wage}}$)	d (year = 1 in 1974 to 7 in 1980)
Full-year hardship ÷ full-year work force					
IIE	0.94	-9.55	+1.09	+.212	-.039
IFE	0.95	-3.21	+0.63	+.066	-.021
IFI	0.77	-1.36	+0.30	+.033	-.050
Full-year hardship ÷ total work force					
IIE	0.93	-8.04	+0.94	+.151	+.044
IFE	0.92	-3.05	+0.48	+.052	+.012
IFI	0.70	-1.56	+0.24	+.027	+.052
Intermediate hardship					
IIE	0.94	+17.07	+1.05	+.120	+.053
IFE	0.92	+5.56	+0.68	+.053	+.020
IFI	0.78	+0.62	+0.37	+.062	+.037
Moderate hardship					
IIE	0.75	+33.29	+0.95	+.050	+.159
IFE	0.92	+7.54	+0.86	+.058	+.048
IFI	0.82	+3.03	+0.57	+.063	-.002

	Severe hardship for total work force		
	IIE incidence	IFE incidence	IFI incidence
1980 actual	27.7%	12.8%	7.2%
1981 predicted on basis of unemployment and inflation rates	28.3	13.1	7.4
1982 predicted on assumption of--			
9% unemployment; 5.0% inflation	30.7	14.2	8.0
9% unemployment; 7.5% inflation	31.3	14.3	8.1
9.5% unemployment; 5.0% inflation	31.3	14.4	8.2
9.5% unemployment; 7.5% inflation	31.9	14.6	8.3
10% unemployment; 5.0% inflation	32.0	14.7	8.3
10% unemployment; 7.5% inflation	32.4	14.9	8.4

Recognizing the imprecision of forecasts based on only seven years of data, it is clear that hardship is currently a major problem which will not ease significantly under any foreseeable economic scenario. Even if unemployment miraculously fell to 7.0 percent in 1982, with inflation a low 5.0 percent, the severe hardship IFE rate would be 13.2 percent and the IFI rate 7.4 percent. The dramatic changes which have taken place in transfer programs are likely to raise the IFI above even these high levels. Thus, even assuming heathy recovery, both the IFE and IFI rates would be as bad or worse than the highest rate in the 1974-1980 period.

What if Employment Problems Were Solved

The limited relationship between macroeconomic changes and hardship is not just because the benefits of higher wages and increased employment must trickle down to those most in need; it is also a reflection of the inherent limitations of labor market remedies. Inadequate Family Earnings and Inadequate Family Incomes are not just the result of involuntary idleness or low wages, but also result from restricted work force participation relative to breadwinning responsibilities:

● If the annual earnings of all workers in the 1979 severe hardship IFE were increased by ten percent, nine of ten would still have Inadequate Family Earnings.

● If all persons in the severe hardship IFE who were involuntarily idle in 1979 were provided employment at their usual wage for all hours of idleness, more than four of five would still have had Inadequate Family Earnings, and three-fourths would have remained in the IFE if they were provided minimum wage employment for all hours of forced idleness.

● If every person in the severe hardship IFE were provided minimally adequate individual earnings, 64 percent would still have had Inadequate Family Earnings.

- Even if every worker in the IFE were provided employment at their usual wage for all hours of idleness, and earnings were, then, increased by 10 percent, 56 percent would have remained with Inadequate Family Earnings.

The corollary is that transfers are essential if labor market-related hardship is to be eliminated. The IFE Deficit in 1979 was $31.7 billion. Nontransfer earnings supplements reduced this by $7.7 billion, cash transfers by $11.2, and in-kind aid by another $2.2 billion. If the earnings of everyone in the IFE were raised at least to the minimal individual adequacy level, the IFE Deficit would have still been $18.8 billion. Even Enhanced Capacity augmentation, providing the usual wage for all hours of forced idleness, and then increasing the earnings of all individuals by ten percent, would have left a deficit of $16.7 billion. In other words, if nontransfer earnings supplements remained at the same level, transfers could be reduced if earnings were augmented, but they would still be needed to fill the substantial gaps remaining for the working poor.

Moreover, the need for transfers has modestly increased rather than decreased over the 1974-1980 period, as suggested by the decline in the importance of labor market problems as a cause of labor market-related hardship, and in the effectiveness of labor market cures in mitigating hardship. For instance, the Enhanced Capacity IFE was 53.9 percent of the severe hardship IFE in 1974 but 55.6 percent in 1979:

	1974	1979	1979-1974	1975	1980	1980-1975
Full Employment IFE as percent IFE[1]	75.2%	75.9%	+0.7%	69.3%	69.9%	+0.6%
Full Employment IFE Deficit as percent IFE Deficit[1]	70.2	69.9	-0.3	61.4	62.9	+1.5
Adequate Employment IFE as percent IFE[2]	61.2	64.1	+2.9	57.2	57.9	+0.7
Adequate Employment IFE Deficit as percent IFE Deficit[2]	57.9	59.3	+0.4	51.8	53.0	+1.2
Capacity Employment IFE as percent IFE[3]	82.1	83.5	+1.4	76.6	77.1	+0.5
Capacity Employment IFE Deficit as percent IFE Deficit[3]	79.5	80.4	+0.9	71.6	73.4	+1.8
Enhanced Earnings IFE as percent IFE[4]	90.8	90.3	-0.5	90.3	90.3	0
Enhanced Earnings IFE Deficit as percent IFE Deficit[4]	92.7	92.4	-0.3	92.8	92.7	-0.1
Enhanced Capacity IFE as percent IFE[5]	53.9	55.6	+1.7	49.7	50.7	+1.0
Enhanced Capacity IFE Deficit as percent IFE Deficit[5]	51.6	53.8	+2.2	45.6	46.9	+1.3

[1] In calculating the Full Employment IFE and Deficit, earnings are augmented by providing all unemployed and involuntarily part-time employed persons in the IFE the minimum wage for all hours of forced idleness.

[2] In calculating the Adequate Employment IFE and Deficit, earnings are augmented for all persons in the IFE with Inadequate Individual Earnings. Their earnings are raised to the individual adequacy standard, i.e., the minimum wage or its multiple times their hours of availability.

[3] In calculating the Capacity Employment IFE and Deficit, the unemployed and involuntary part-time workers in the IFE are provided their usual wage (when working) for all hours of forced idleness.

[4] In calculating the Enhanced Earnings IFE and Deficit, the earnings of each person in the IFE are augmented by 10 percent.

[5] In calculating the Enhanced Capacity IFE and Deficit, unemployed and involuntary part-time workers in the IFE are first provided their usual wage (when working) for all hours of forced idleness, then their capacity level earnings, as well as the earnings of all other persons in the IFE, are raised by 10 percent.

Different Strokes

The five augmentation alternatives address different labor market problems and provide varying degrees of mitigation. For instance, the

Enhanced Earnings IFE augmentation simulates a 10 percent wage rate increase, assuming no changes in hours of work. The Capacity IFE augmentation eliminates measured forced idleness while the Full Employment IFE goes further in assuring that at least the minimum wage will be paid for hours of forced idleness even if the individuals usually receive less than the minimum. Adequate Employment augmentation affects low-wage, fully-employed workers, as well as those with involuntary idleness, while the Enhanced Capacity IFE augmentation simulates the elimination of forced idleness combined with a 10 percent increase in hourly earnings. In real life, any augmentation of wages or hours of work would likely affect work force participation, attachment and job choice, so that the augmentations provide only very crude indicators of the effects of changes in the employment and earnings variables; nevertheless, they do help in indicating who will benefit from alternative interventions and to what degree.

A worker may escape the IFE as a result of augmentation even if his or her individual earnings are increased little or none, since another family member's earnings may be significantly augmented. For instance, a teenager with no employment in a family with a head working full-time, full-year, but earning 10 percent below the poverty level, will exit the IFE with Enhanced Earnings augmentation even though the teenager's earnings would remain zero. In general, however, the impacts of augmentation on the IFE levels for most segments of the work force suggest the nature of their employment problems and the potential solutions.

Enhanced Earnings augmentation, for instance, had almost no impact on the IFE count among persons without any employment during 1979 and very little on persons unemployed two-thirds or more of their weeks in the work force (Table 5.2). The most significant impacts from this augmentation were experienced by the full-year IFE who were mostly employed. In contrast, Full Employment augmentation reduced the IFE by two-fifths among those who experienced some unemployment but only a sixth among those employed all weeks in the work force.

Reflecting differences in work force problems and their severity, as well as in family status, the augmentation alternatives had quite different impacts on significant segments among workers with Inadequate Family Earnings:

● Females benefited less under all forms of augmentation, and this was particularly true for female family heads (Chart 5.2). Enhanced Capacity augmentation reduced the IFE of female family heads by three-tenths, while reducing the number of male family heads in the IFE by nearly half. In contrast, augmentation significantly reduced the number of wives in the IFE, since frequently both their own and their husbands' earnings were affected by the augmentation.

● The impacts of augmentation were less for work force participants residing in larger families with fewer earners (Table 5.3). The IFE reduction which resulted from Capacity Earnings augmentation was only a little greater when there were more workers in a family; for instance, among participants from three-member families, 14 percent of those from families with one participant were lifted out of the IFE by Capacity Earnings augmentation, 28 percent of those from families with two participants, but 24

Table 5.2. IMPACTS OF ALTERNATIVE EARNINGS AUGMENTATION APPROACHES FOR WORK EXPERIENCE PATTERN/WORK FORCE ATTACHMENT SUBGROUPS OF THE IFE IN 1979[1]

	IFE REDUCTION					IFE DEFICIT REDUCTION					AVERAGE IFE DEFICIT
	Enhanced Earnings Augmentation	Capacity Earnings Augmentation	Full Employment Augmentation	Adequate Employment Augmentation	Enhanced Capacity Augmentation	Enhanced Earnings Augmentation	Capacity Earnings Augmentation	Full Employment Augmentation	Adequate Employment Augmentation	Enhanced Capacity Augmentation	
Total Work Force											
Not Employed	2.0%	23.8%	38.8%	25.9%	29.1%	--	42.3%	55.7%	42.3%	45.2%	$4,176
Mostly Unemployed	4.3	61.7	58.3	61.5	67.8	4.6	71.0	71.2	74.9	78.8	3,314
Mixed	8.0	53.0	52.7	54.7	63.4	10.3	57.7	61.2	61.0	67.5	2,280
Mostly Employed	15.0	25.3	27.8	40.0	51.9	13.2	24.5	24.5	45.2	55.7	1,884
Employed Part-Time Involuntarily	9.7	19.2	26.1	44.0	51.9	8.0	20.8	29.2	45.0	51.0	2,506
Employed Part-Time Voluntarily	8.8	3.4	17.7	21.1	22.9	9.1	2.0	21.4	21.0	9.3	2,159
Employed Full-Time	12.5	5.2	8.2	44.0	52.8	10.5	9.2	2.5	46.8	54.6	2,196
Full-Year Work Force											
Not Employed	1.6	72.4	68.8	73.4	75.5	--	84.8	83.7	84.8	88.3	5,069
Mostly Unemployed	5.6	69.7	68.1	72.5	76.8	--	75.7	76.0	80.5	84.5	3,350
Mixed	9.2	64.9	64.2	67.0	75.8	1.3	62.6	70.5	71.9	80.7	2,216
Mostly Employed	18.8	36.1	38.7	54.1	64.4	76.3	23.2	31.1	53.0	65.9	1,957
Employed Part-Time Involuntarily	10.9	22.9	39.7	72.0	77.3	37.5	18.5	38.0	72.0	79.6	2,409
Employed Part-Time Voluntarily	12.5	2.1	31.3	35.3	47.4	4.6	+8.0	39.9	40.0	51.4	1,940
Employed Full-Time	17.9	3.0	5.9	67.7	77.6	5.5	+8.7	+6.5	71.3	80.8	2,334

[1] In calculating the Full Employment IFE and Deficit, earnings are augmented by providing all unemployed and involuntarily part-time employed persons in the IFE the minimum wage for all hours of forced idleness. In calculating the Adequate Employment IFE and Deficit, earnings are augmented for all persons in the IFE with Inadequate Individual Earnings. Their earnings are raised to the individual adequacy standard, i.e., the minimum wage or its multiple times their hours of availability. In calculating the Capacity Employment IFE and Deficit, the unemployed and involuntary part-time workers in the IFE are provided their usual wage (when working) for all hours of forced idleness. In calculating the Enhanced Earnings IFE and Deficit, the earnings of each person in the IFE are augmented by 10 percent. In calculating the Enhanced Capacity IFE and Deficit, unemployed and involuntary part-time workers in the IFE are first provided their usual wage (when working) for all hours of forced idleness, then their capacity level earnings, as well as the earnings of all other persons in the IFE, are raised by 10 percent.

Chart 5.2. IMPACTS OF EARNINGS AUGMENTATION ON SEX/FAMILY RELATIONSHIP SUBGROUPS

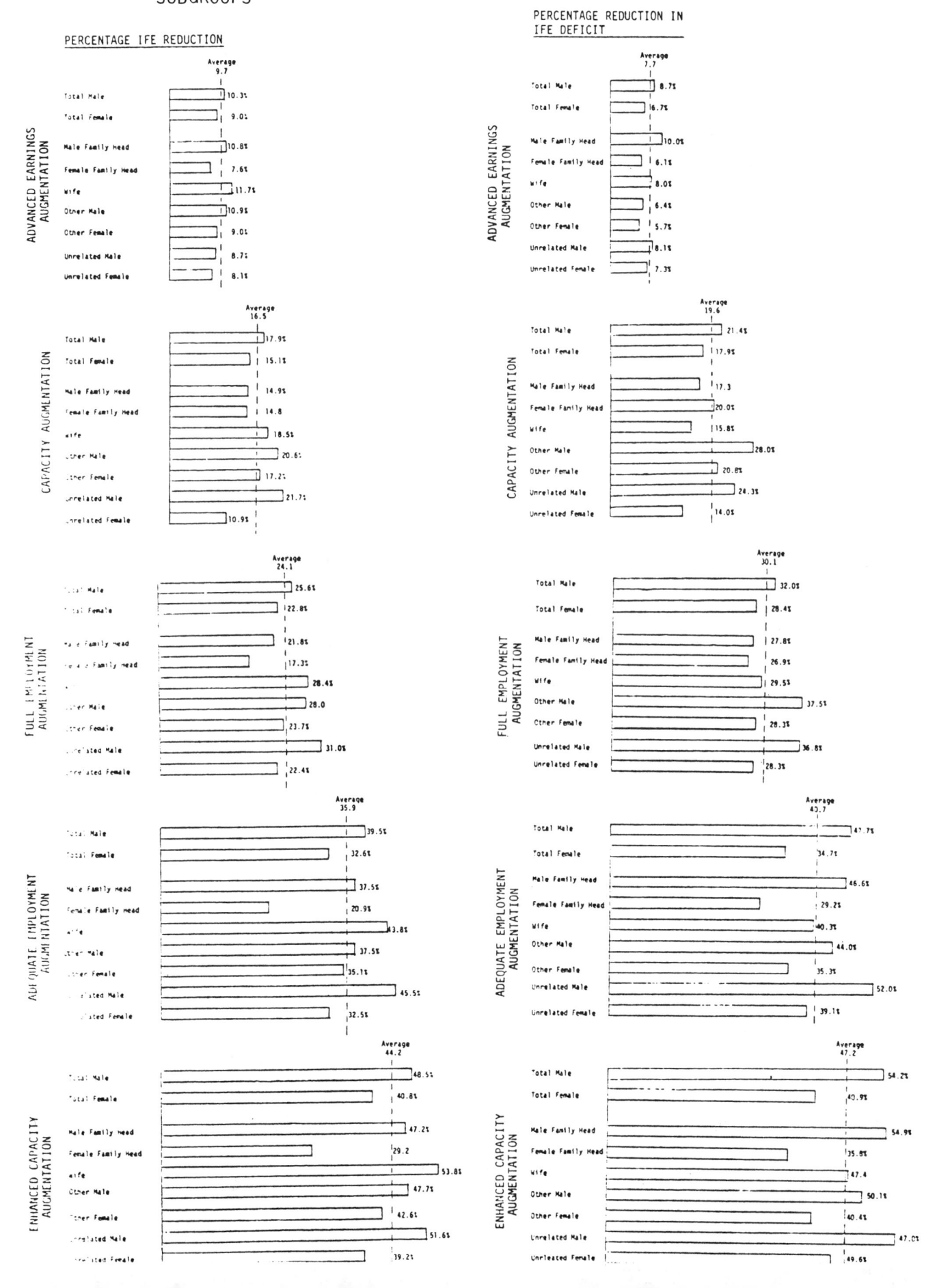

PERCENTAGE IFE REDUCTION

ADVANCED EARNINGS AUGMENTATION (Average 9.7)
- Total Male: 10.3%
- Total Female: 9.0%
- Male Family Head: 10.8%
- Female Family Head: 7.6%
- Wife: 11.7%
- Other Male: 10.9%
- Other Female: 9.0%
- Unrelated Male: 8.7%
- Unrelated Female: 8.1%

CAPACITY AUGMENTATION (Average 16.5)
- Total Male: 17.9%
- Total Female: 15.1%
- Male Family Head: 14.9%
- Female Family Head: 14.8
- Wife: 18.5%
- Other Male: 20.6%
- Other Female: 17.2%
- Unrelated Male: 21.7%
- Unrelated Female: 10.9%

FULL EMPLOYMENT AUGMENTATION (Average 24.1)
- Total Male: 25.6%
- Total Female: 22.8%
- Male Family Head: 21.8%
- Female Family Head: 17.3%
- Wife: 28.4%
- Other Male: 28.0
- Other Female: 23.7%
- Unrelated Male: 31.0%
- Unrelated Female: 22.4%

ADEQUATE EMPLOYMENT AUGMENTATION (Average 35.9)
- Total Male: 39.5%
- Total Female: 32.6%
- Male Family Head: 37.5%
- Female Family Head: 20.9%
- Wife: 43.8%
- Other Male: 37.5%
- Other Female: 35.1%
- Unrelated Male: 45.5%
- Unrelated Female: 32.5%

ENHANCED CAPACITY AUGMENTATION (Average 44.2)
- Total Male: 48.5%
- Total Female: 40.8%
- Male Family Head: 47.2%
- Female Family Head: 29.2
- Wife: 53.8%
- Other Male: 47.7%
- Other Female: 42.6%
- Unrelated Male: 51.6%
- Unrelated Female: 39.2%

PERCENTAGE REDUCTION IN IFE DEFICIT

ADVANCED EARNINGS AUGMENTATION (Average 7.7)
- Total Male: 8.7%
- Total Female: 6.7%
- Male Family Head: 10.0%
- Female Family Head: 6.1%
- Wife: 8.0%
- Other Male: 6.4%
- Other Female: 5.7%
- Unrelated Male: 8.1%
- Unrelated Female: 7.3%

CAPACITY AUGMENTATION (Average 19.6)
- Total Male: 21.4%
- Total Female: 17.9%
- Male Family Head: 17.3
- Female Family Head: 20.0%
- Wife: 15.8%
- Other Male: 28.0%
- Other Female: 20.8%
- Unrelated Male: 24.3%
- Unrelated Female: 14.0%

FULL EMPLOYMENT AUGMENTATION (Average 30.1)
- Total Male: 32.0%
- Total Female: 28.4%
- Male Family Head: 27.8%
- Female Family Head: 26.9%
- Wife: 29.5%
- Other Male: 37.5%
- Other Female: 28.3%
- Unrelated Male: 36.8%
- Unrelated Female: 28.3%

ADEQUATE EMPLOYMENT AUGMENTATION (Average 40.7)
- Total Male: 42.7%
- Total Female: 34.7%
- Male Family Head: 46.6%
- Female Family Head: 29.2%
- Wife: 40.3%
- Other Male: 44.0%
- Other Female: 35.3%
- Unrelated Male: 52.0%
- Unrelated Female: 39.1%

ENHANCED CAPACITY AUGMENTATION (Average 47.2)
- Total Male: 54.2%
- Total Female: 40.9%
- Male Family Head: 54.9%
- Female Family Head: 35.8%
- Wife: 47.4
- Other Male: 50.1%
- Other Female: 40.4%
- Unrelated Male: 47.0%
- Unrelated Female: 49.6%

Table 5.3. IMPACTS OF ALTERNATIVE EARNINGS AUGMENTATION APPROACHES IN 1979 DEPENDING ON FAMILY SIZE AND NUMBER OF EARNERS[1]

	IFE REDUCTION					AVERAGE IFE DEFICIT	IFE DEFICIT REDUCTION				
	Enhanced Earnings Augmentation	Capacity Earnings Augmentation	Full Employment Augmentation	Adequate Employment Augmentation	Enhanced Capacity Augmentation		Enhanced Earnings Augmentation	Capacity Earnings Augmentation	Full Employment Augmentation	Adequate Employment Augmentation	Enhanced Capacity Augmentation
One In Work Force	7.5%	12.8%	18.1%	27.3%	34.7%	$2,893	6.6%	16.5%	25.8%	34.8%	41.2%
1 Member	8.4	15.8	26.3	38.4	44.9	2,000	7.7	18.8	33.2	45.1	50.4
2 Members	6.3	12.6	17.6	25.7	32.5	2,760	6.3	15.6	26.4	33.9	39.3
3 Members	6.8	14.3	13.5	26.3	35.1	3,334	6.1	19.7	28.2	37.8	43.5
4-5 Members	7.9	5.7	3.2	4.7	14.1	4,452	6.0	15.3	19.2	27.2	36.5
6 or More Members	9.2	2.1	0.5	1.6	11.3	6,223	6.1	10.5	12.1	17.5	25.7
Two In Work Force	11.6	20.9	30.7	46.3	56.9	1,633	10.6	29.4	42.7	58.8	66.1
2 Members	9.6	21.2	38.8	57.9	63.1	1,110	10.1	24.9	45.3	64.7	69.5
3 Members	9.6	27.8	40.7	60.5	67.2	1,271	11.4	34.2	53.0	68.8	73.8
4-5 Members	14.3	20.3	26.5	41.3	55.2	1,744	10.9	31.5	44.3	61.6	69.7
6 or More Members	10.7	14.3	15.6	22.9	38.5	2,644	10.1	26.4	32.6	44.9	54.1
Three or More In Work Force	18.7	28.8	46.9	65.3	75.6	1,059	14.3	32.5	55.1	70.4	75.6
3 Members	8.8	24.1	57.7	73.0	85.4	705	14.6	26.0	66.7	84.4	88.5
4-5 Members	23.6	27.3	44.9	66.2	73.7	1,001	12.3	29.0	53.5	67.7	72.1
6 or More Members	17.1	31.1	46.3	62.7	74.8	1,190	15.7	36.0	54.7	70.4	7.6

[1] In calculating the Full Employment IFE and Deficit, earnings are augmented by providing all unemployed and involuntarily part-time employed persons in the IFE the minimum wage for all hours of forced idleness. In calculating the Adequate Employment IFE and Deficit, earnings are augmented for all persons in the IFE with Inadequate Individual Earnings. Their earnings are raised to the individual adequacy standard, i.e., the minimum wage or its multiple times their hours of availability. In calculating the Capacity Employment IFE and Deficit, the unemployed and involuntary part-time workers in the IFE are provided their usual wage (when working) for all hours of forced idleness. In calculating the Enhanced Earnings IFE and Deficit, the earnings of each person in the IFE are augmented by 10 percent. In calculating the Enhanced Capacity IFE and Deficit, unemployed and involuntary part-time workers in the IFE are first provided their usual wage (when working) for all hours of forced idleness, then their capacity level earnings, as well as the earnings of all other persons in the IFE, are raised by 10 percent.

percent of those from families with three participants. The IFE reductions resulting from Full Employment augmentation increased much more significantly with each additional family worker; there was a 14 percent reduction for workers from three-member families with one work force participant, but 58 percent among families with three participants. Obviously, the second and third family earners were usually low paid when they worked compared to unemployed first workers in families.

- Prime age workers in the IFE were relatively more affected by Capacity Earnings and Enhanced Earnings augmentation than Full Employment and Adequate Employment augmentation, suggesting that their earnings rates and totals were relatively higher so that minimum wage employment was not the answer for their needs (Chart 5.3). The 45-to-64-year-olds in the IFE benefited most by Adequate Employment augmentation and Enhanced Capacity augmentation. Not unexpectedly, few teenagers were lifted out of poverty by Capacity Earnings augmentation, while older workers experienced below average reductions under all the different forms of augmentation.

- All of the employment and earnings augmentations helped high school graduates with no further education more than those with greater and lesser education (Chart 5.4). Dropouts benefited relatively more from the Capacity Earnings and Full Employment augmentations which simulated increased hours of employment for periods of forced idleness. In contrast, college graduates did relatively best under the Adequate Employment and Enhanced Capacity augmentations, suggesting that their problems were more frequently limited hours of availability or large family support responsibilities. High school and post-secondary students--those with the fewest hours of availability--benefited least from all of the augmentations.

- Blacks gained relatively more from the Capacity Earnings and Full Employment augmentations simulating reductions in forced idleness (Chart 5.5). In contrast, whites experienced above average IFE reductions from the Enhanced Earnings, Adequate Employment and Enhanced Capacity augmentations which increased earnings for workers with low pay or limited hours of availability relative to support responsibilities. Hispanics benefited more than whites or blacks from Enhanced Earnings augmentation, suggesting that low wages relative to breadwinning responsibilities were a particularly serious problem for them.

- Blue-collar workers benefited relatively more from the Full Employment and Capacity Earnings augmentations compensating for forced idleness (Chart 5.6). White-collar workers, particularly professional, managerial, technical and administrative workers, benefited relatively more from Enhanced Earnings augmentation. The problems of service workers were least likely to be mitigated by any of the labor market-oriented initiatives. Farm workers benefited most from the Adequate Employment and Enhanced Capacity augmentations since they were more likely to be underemployed and with quite low wages.

- Reflecting higher wage levels, the Enhanced Earnings and Capacity Employment augmentations had greater impacts in metropolitan than nonmetropolitan areas. Likewise, reflecting more frequent part-time employment, metropolitan areas benefited relatively more from the Adequate Employment and Enhanced Capacity augmentations (Chart 5.7). Central cities

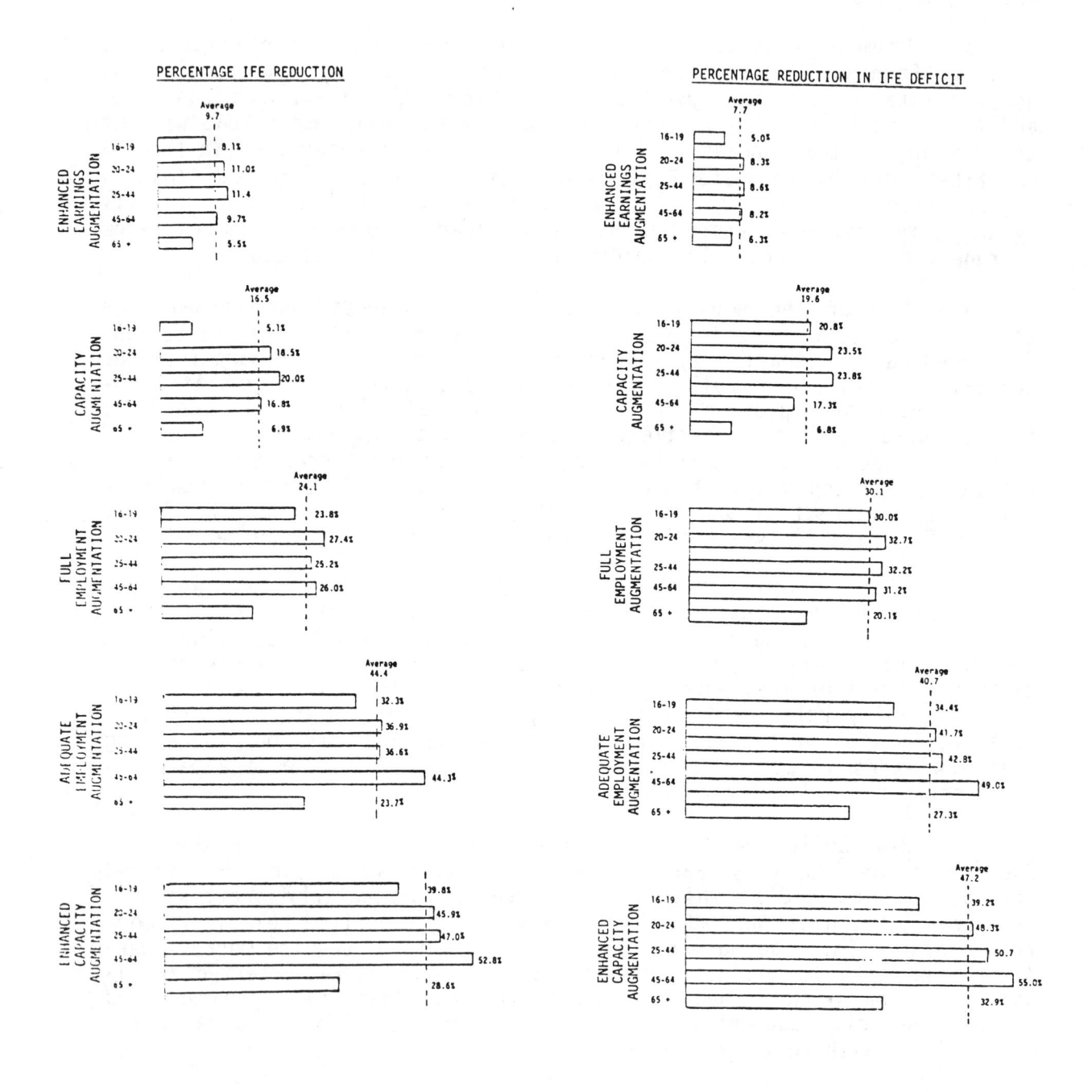

Chart 5.3. IMPACTS OF EARNINGS AUGMENTATION ON AGE GROUPS

PERCENTAGE IFE REDUCTION

ENHANCED EARNINGS AUGMENTATION (Average 9.7)
- 16-19: 8.1%
- 20-24: 11.0%
- 25-44: 11.4%
- 45-64: 9.7%
- 65+: 5.5%

CAPACITY AUGMENTATION (Average 16.5)
- 16-19: 5.1%
- 20-24: 18.5%
- 25-44: 20.0%
- 45-64: 16.8%
- 65+: 6.9%

FULL EMPLOYMENT AUGMENTATION (Average 24.1)
- 16-19: 23.8%
- 20-24: 27.4%
- 25-44: 25.2%
- 45-64: 26.0%
- 65+: —

ADEQUATE EMPLOYMENT AUGMENTATION (Average 44.4)
- 16-19: 32.3%
- 20-24: 36.9%
- 25-44: 36.6%
- 45-64: 44.3%
- 65+: 23.7%

ENHANCED CAPACITY AUGMENTATION
- 16-19: 39.8%
- 20-24: 45.9%
- 25-44: 47.0%
- 45-64: 52.8%
- 65+: 28.6%

PERCENTAGE REDUCTION IN IFE DEFICIT

ENHANCED EARNINGS AUGMENTATION (Average 7.7)
- 16-19: 5.0%
- 20-24: 8.3%
- 25-44: 8.6%
- 45-64: 8.2%
- 65+: 6.3%

CAPACITY AUGMENTATION (Average 19.6)
- 16-19: 20.8%
- 20-24: 23.5%
- 25-44: 23.8%
- 45-64: 17.3%
- 65+: 6.8%

FULL EMPLOYMENT AUGMENTATION (Average 30.1)
- 16-19: 30.0%
- 20-24: 32.7%
- 25-44: 32.2%
- 45-64: 31.2%
- 65+: 20.1%

ADEQUATE EMPLOYMENT AUGMENTATION (Average 40.7)
- 16-19: 34.4%
- 20-24: 41.7%
- 25-44: 42.8%
- 45-64: 49.0%
- 65+: 27.3%

ENHANCED CAPACITY AUGMENTATION (Average 47.2)
- 16-19: 39.2%
- 20-24: 48.3%
- 25-44: 50.7%
- 45-64: 55.0%
- 65+: 32.9%

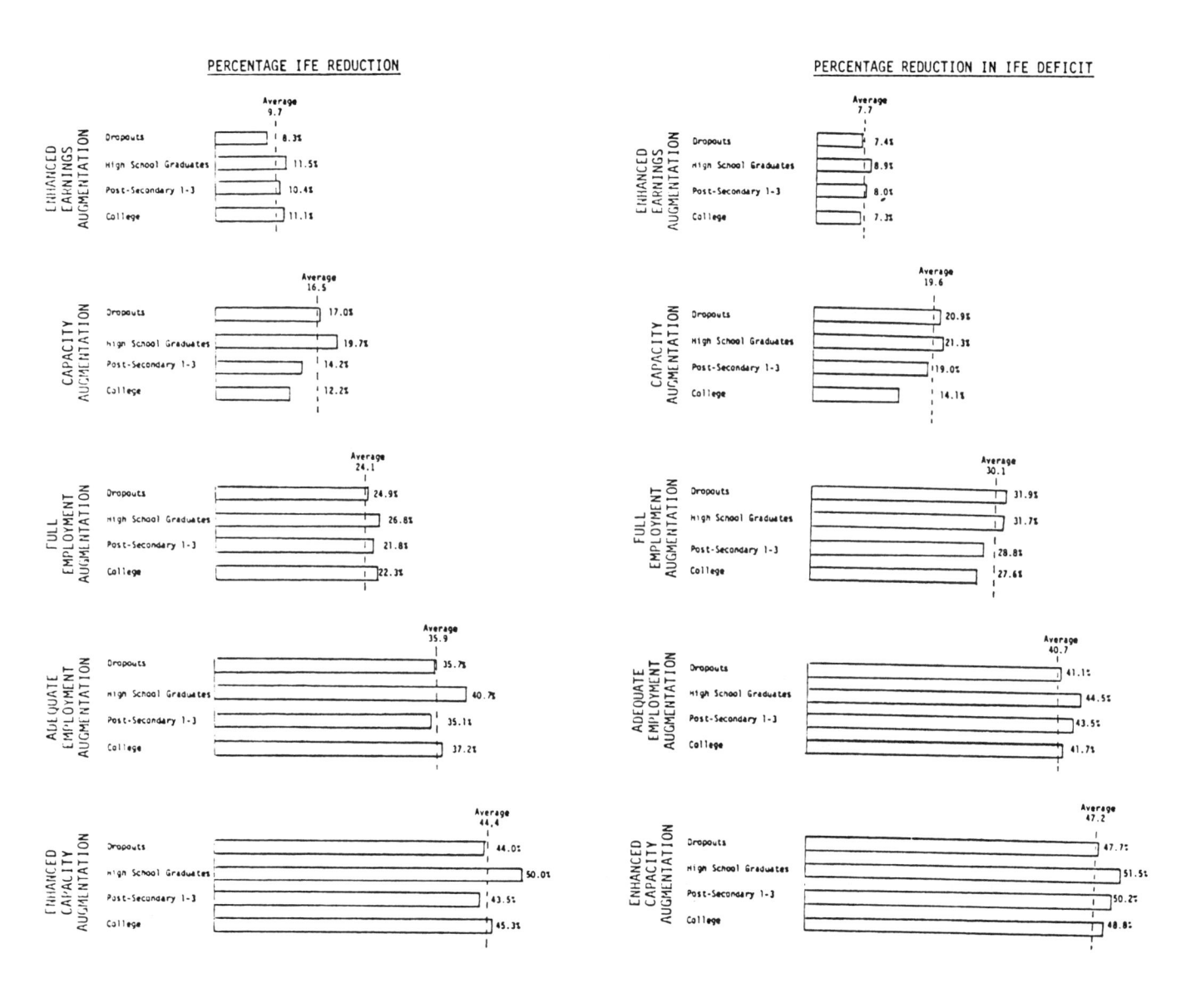

Chart 5.4. IMPACTS OF EARNINGS AUGMENTATION ON EDUCATIONAL GROUPS

PERCENTAGE IFE REDUCTION

ENHANCED EARNINGS AUGMENTATION (Average 9.7)
- Dropouts: 8.3%
- High School Graduates: 11.5%
- Post-Secondary 1-3: 10.4%
- College: 11.1%

CAPACITY AUGMENTATION (Average 16.5)
- Dropouts: 17.0%
- High School Graduates: 19.7%
- Post-Secondary 1-3: 14.2%
- College: 12.2%

FULL EMPLOYMENT AUGMENTATION (Average 24.1)
- Dropouts: 24.9%
- High School Graduates: 26.8%
- Post-Secondary 1-3: 21.8%
- College: 22.3%

ADEQUATE EMPLOYMENT AUGMENTATION (Average 35.9)
- Dropouts: 35.7%
- High School Graduates: 40.7%
- Post-Secondary 1-3: 35.1%
- College: 37.2%

ENHANCED CAPACITY AUGMENTATION (Average 44.4)
- Dropouts: 44.0%
- High School Graduates: 50.0%
- Post-Secondary 1-3: 43.5%
- College: 45.3%

PERCENTAGE REDUCTION IN IFE DEFICIT

ENHANCED EARNINGS AUGMENTATION (Average 7.7)
- Dropouts: 7.4%
- High School Graduates: 8.9%
- Post-Secondary 1-3: 8.0%
- College: 7.3%

CAPACITY AUGMENTATION (Average 19.6)
- Dropouts: 20.9%
- High School Graduates: 21.3%
- Post-Secondary 1-3: 19.0%
- College: 14.1%

FULL EMPLOYMENT AUGMENTATION (Average 30.1)
- Dropouts: 31.9%
- High School Graduates: 31.7%
- Post-Secondary 1-3: 28.8%
- College: 27.6%

ADEQUATE EMPLOYMENT AUGMENTATION (Average 40.7)
- Dropouts: 41.1%
- High School Graduates: 44.5%
- Post-Secondary 1-3: 43.5%
- College: 41.7%

ENHANCED CAPACITY AUGMENTATION (Average 47.2)
- Dropouts: 47.7%
- High School Graduates: 51.5%
- Post-Secondary 1-3: 50.2%
- College: 48.8%

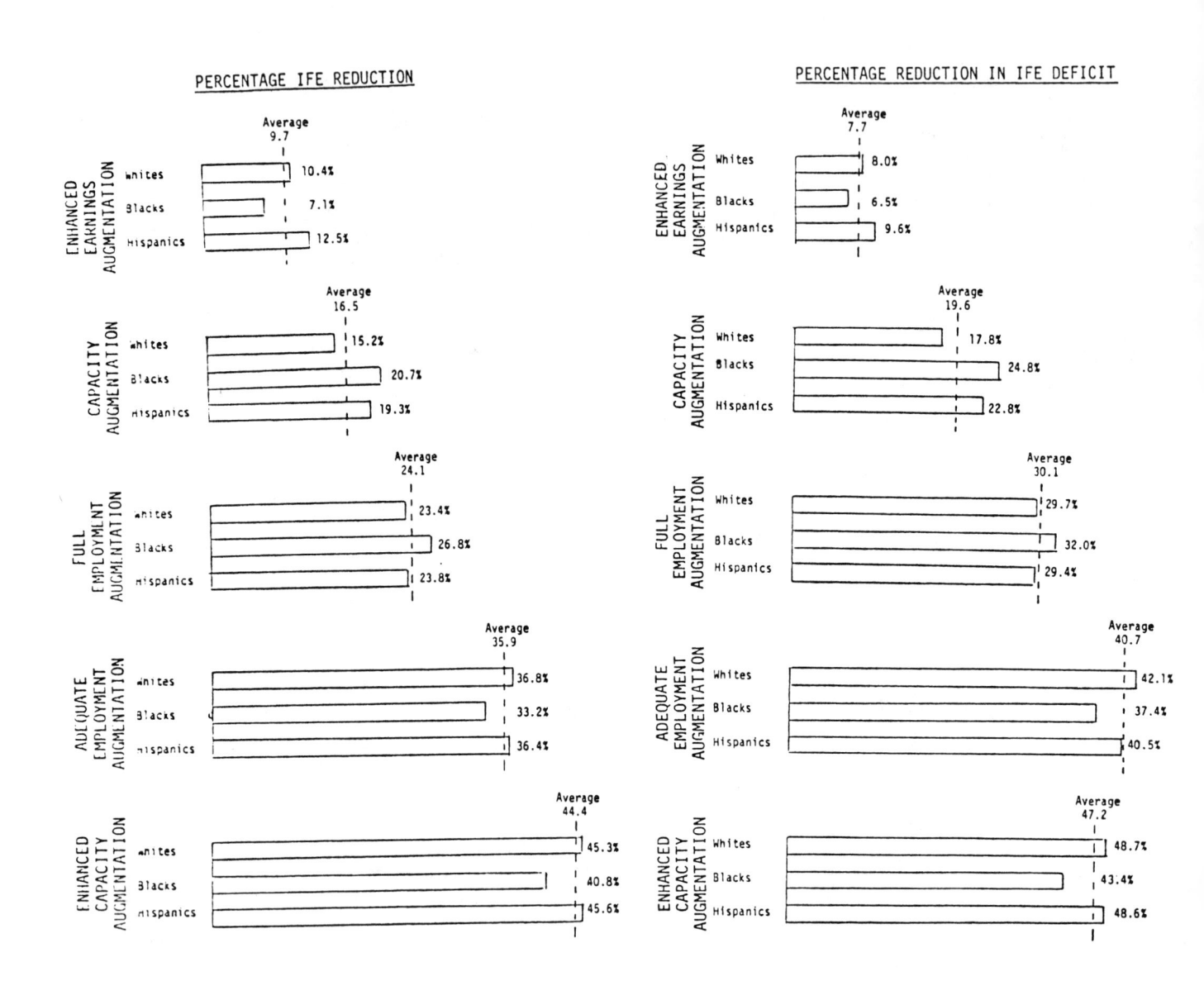

Chart 5.5. IMPACTS OF EARNINGS AUGMENTATION ON WHITES, BLACKS AND HISPANICS

PERCENTAGE IFE REDUCTION

ENHANCED EARNINGS AUGMENTATION (Average 9.7)
- Whites: 10.4%
- Blacks: 7.1%
- Hispanics: 12.5%

CAPACITY AUGMENTATION (Average 16.5)
- Whites: 15.2%
- Blacks: 20.7%
- Hispanics: 19.3%

FULL EMPLOYMENT AUGMENTATION (Average 24.1)
- Whites: 23.4%
- Blacks: 26.8%
- Hispanics: 23.8%

ADEQUATE EMPLOYMENT AUGMENTATION (Average 35.9)
- Whites: 36.8%
- Blacks: 33.2%
- Hispanics: 36.4%

ENHANCED CAPACITY AUGMENTATION (Average 44.4)
- Whites: 45.3%
- Blacks: 40.8%
- Hispanics: 45.6%

PERCENTAGE REDUCTION IN IFE DEFICIT

ENHANCED EARNINGS AUGMENTATION (Average 7.7)
- Whites: 8.0%
- Blacks: 6.5%
- Hispanics: 9.6%

CAPACITY AUGMENTATION (Average 19.6)
- Whites: 17.8%
- Blacks: 24.8%
- Hispanics: 22.8%

FULL EMPLOYMENT AUGMENTATION (Average 30.1)
- Whites: 29.7%
- Blacks: 32.0%
- Hispanics: 29.4%

ADEQUATE EMPLOYMENT AUGMENTATION (Average 40.7)
- Whites: 42.1%
- Blacks: 37.4%
- Hispanics: 40.5%

ENHANCED CAPACITY AUGMENTATION (Average 47.2)
- Whites: 48.7%
- Blacks: 43.4%
- Hispanics: 48.6%

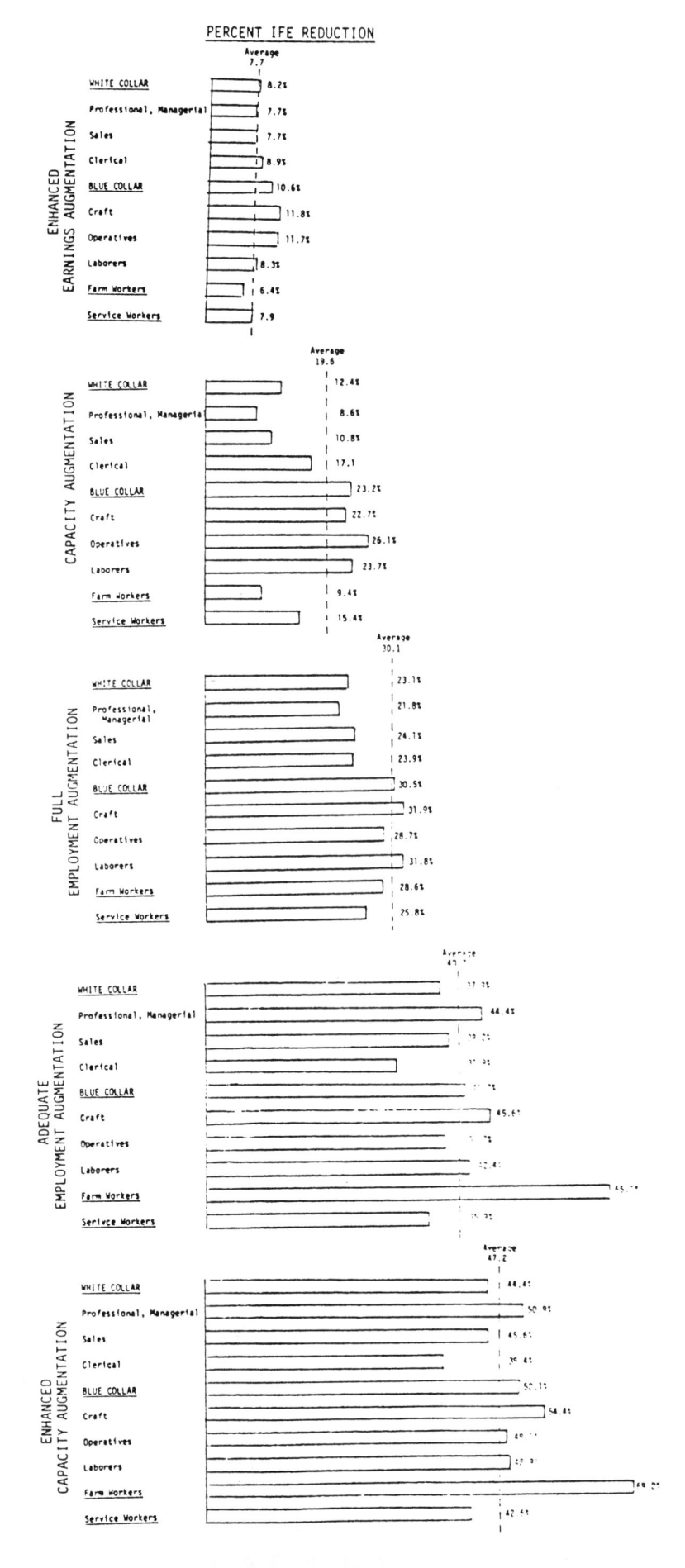

Chart 5.6. IMPACTS OF EARNINGS AUGMENTATION BY OCCUPATION OF PRIMARY EMPLOYMENT

PERCENT IFE REDUCTION

ENHANCED EARNINGS AUGMENTATION (Average 7.7)

Occupation	%
WHITE COLLAR	8.2%
Professional, Managerial	7.7%
Sales	7.7%
Clerical	8.9%
BLUE COLLAR	10.6%
Craft	11.8%
Operatives	11.7%
Laborers	8.3%
Farm Workers	6.4%
Service Workers	7.9

CAPACITY AUGMENTATION (Average 19.6)

Occupation	%
WHITE COLLAR	12.4%
Professional, Managerial	8.6%
Sales	10.8%
Clerical	17.1
BLUE COLLAR	23.2%
Craft	22.7%
Operatives	26.1%
Laborers	23.7%
Farm Workers	9.4%
Service Workers	15.4%

FULL EMPLOYMENT AUGMENTATION (Average 30.1)

Occupation	%
WHITE COLLAR	23.1%
Professional, Managerial	21.8%
Sales	24.1%
Clerical	23.9%
BLUE COLLAR	30.5%
Craft	31.9%
Operatives	28.7%
Laborers	31.8%
Farm Workers	28.6%
Service Workers	25.8%

ADEQUATE EMPLOYMENT AUGMENTATION (Average 42.7)

Occupation	%
WHITE COLLAR	37.2%
Professional, Managerial	44.4%
Sales	39.2%
Clerical	37.2%
BLUE COLLAR	43.2%
Craft	45.6%
Operatives	42.7%
Laborers	42.4%
Farm Workers	45.2%
Service Workers	39.2%

ENHANCED CAPACITY AUGMENTATION (Average 47.2)

Occupation	%
WHITE COLLAR	44.4%
Professional, Managerial	50.9%
Sales	45.6%
Clerical	39.4%
BLUE COLLAR	50.1%
Craft	54.8%
Operatives	48.2%
Laborers	48.3%
Farm Workers	49.2%
Service Workers	42.4%

Chart 5.7. IMPACTS OF EARNINGS AUGMENTATION BY AREA OF RESIDENCE

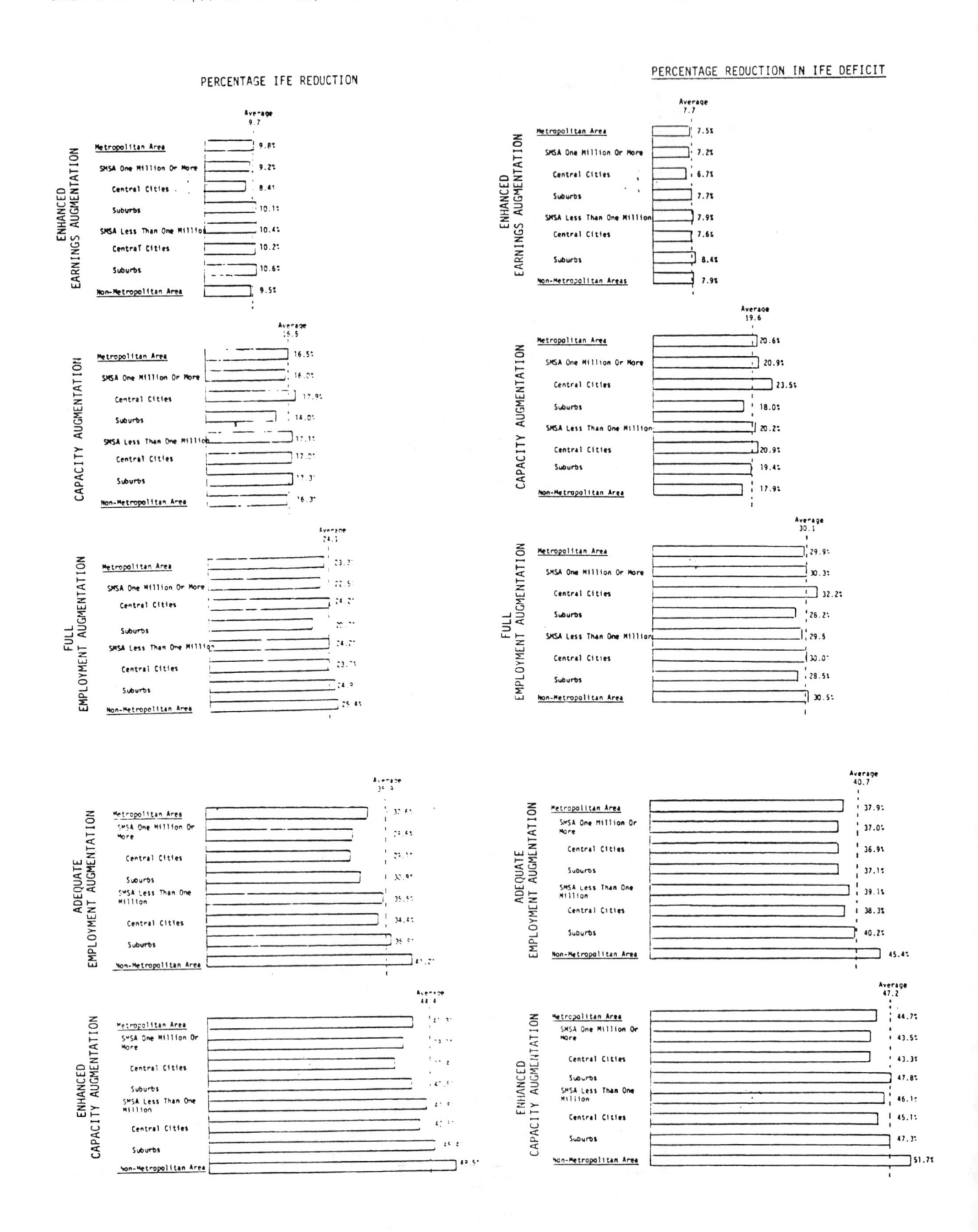

PERCENTAGE IFE REDUCTION

ENHANCED EARNINGS AUGMENTATION (Average 9.7)
- Metropolitan Area: 9.8%
- SMSA One Million Or More: 9.2%
- Central Cities: 8.4%
- Suburbs: 10.1%
- SMSA Less Than One Million: 10.4%
- Central Cities: 10.2%
- Suburbs: 10.6%
- Non-Metropolitan Area: 9.5%

CAPACITY AUGMENTATION (Average 16.5)
- Metropolitan Area: 16.5%
- SMSA One Million Or More: 16.0%
- Central Cities: 17.9%
- Suburbs: 14.0%
- SMSA Less Than One Million: 17.1%
- Central Cities: 17.0%
- Suburbs: 17.3%
- Non-Metropolitan Area: 16.3%

FULL EMPLOYMENT AUGMENTATION (Average 24.1)
- Metropolitan Area: 23.2%
- SMSA One Million Or More: 22.5%
- Central Cities: 24.2%
- Suburbs: —
- SMSA Less Than One Million: 24.2%
- Central Cities: 23.7%
- Suburbs: 24.9%
- Non-Metropolitan Area: 25.4%

ADEQUATE EMPLOYMENT AUGMENTATION (Average 36.0)
- Metropolitan Area: 37.6%
- SMSA One Million Or More: 23.6%
- Central Cities: 25.1%
- Suburbs: 30.9%
- SMSA Less Than One Million: 35.5%
- Central Cities: 34.4%
- Suburbs: 36.0%
- Non-Metropolitan Area: 40.2%

ENHANCED CAPACITY AUGMENTATION (Average 44.4)
- Metropolitan Area: 43.3%
- SMSA One Million Or More: 43.0%
- Central Cities: 44.2%
- Suburbs: 42.5%
- SMSA Less Than One Million: 43.0%
- Central Cities: 42.0%
- Suburbs: 44.0%
- Non-Metropolitan Area: 49.5%

PERCENTAGE REDUCTION IN IFE DEFICIT

ENHANCED EARNINGS AUGMENTATION (Average 7.7)
- Metropolitan Area: 7.5%
- SMSA One Million Or More: 7.2%
- Central Cities: 6.7%
- Suburbs: 7.7%
- SMSA Less Than One Million: 7.9%
- Central Cities: 7.6%
- Suburbs: 8.4%
- Non-Metropolitan Areas: 7.9%

CAPACITY AUGMENTATION (Average 19.6)
- Metropolitan Area: 20.6%
- SMSA One Million Or More: 20.9%
- Central Cities: 23.5%
- Suburbs: 18.0%
- SMSA Less Than One Million: 20.2%
- Central Cities: 20.9%
- Suburbs: 19.4%
- Non-Metropolitan Area: 17.9%

FULL EMPLOYMENT AUGMENTATION (Average 30.1)
- Metropolitan Area: 29.9%
- SMSA One Million Or More: 30.3%
- Central Cities: 32.2%
- Suburbs: 28.2%
- SMSA Less Than One Million: 29.5%
- Central Cities: 30.0%
- Suburbs: 28.5%
- Non-Metropolitan Area: 30.5%

ADEQUATE EMPLOYMENT AUGMENTATION (Average 40.7)
- Metropolitan Area: 37.9%
- SMSA One Million Or More: 37.0%
- Central Cities: 36.9%
- Suburbs: 37.1%
- SMSA Less Than One Million: 39.1%
- Central Cities: 38.3%
- Suburbs: 40.2%
- Non-Metropolitan Area: 45.4%

ENHANCED CAPACITY AUGMENTATION (Average 47.2)
- Metropolitan Area: 44.7%
- SMSA One Million Or More: 43.5%
- Central Cities: 43.3%
- Suburbs: 47.8%
- SMSA Less Than One Million: 46.1%
- Central Cities: 45.1%
- Suburbs: 47.3%
- Non-Metropolitan Area: 51.7%

benefited more than the suburbs from the Full Employment and Capacity Earnings augmentations compensating for forced idleness, while the suburbs benefited more from the Enhanced Earnings, Adequate Employment and Enhanced Capacity augmentations which compensated for low earnings relative to breadwinning responsibilities and which affected part-time workers significantly.

The Safety Net for the Working Poor

Since the alleviation of employment and earnings problems will not, alone, assure adequate family incomes because of limited family work force participation relative to support responsibilities, work and welfare must inevitably overlap if hardship is to be eliminated among the working poor. This overlap has increased over the years. In 1974, 28 percent of all families reported no income other than earnings, while 11 percent reported no earnings, leaving 61 percent who combined earnings with other income. 2/ By 1979, the proportion with earnings supplements had increased to 74 percent. Among unrelated individuals, the proportion with earnings supplements rose from 35 to 47 percent. The overlap increased among the poor, as well as the nonpoor:

	Families		Unrelated individuals		Poor families		Poor unrelated individuals	
	1974	1979	1974	1979	1974	1979	1974	1979
No earnings	11%	13%	38%	35%	38%	41%	65%	57%
Earnings only	28	13	27	18	24	16	19	15
Earnings supplemented by other income	61	74	35	47	38	43	16	28

How well do these earnings supplements protect those whose individual and family earnings are inadequate? Are transfer benefits equitably distributed and, in particular, do they reward individuals and families exhibiting greater work effort? Do in-kind benefits fill the gaps in the cash transfer system? Did the growth of social welfare expenditures over the 1970s improve the safety net and perhaps even justify some retrenchment at the outset of the 1980s? The hardship measures provide some perspective on these vital questions, and the answers in many cases contradict conventional wisdoms.

Poverty Has Not Been Eliminated

Cash transfers and other nonearned income significantly mitigate labor market-related hardship. In 1979 and 1980, the IFE was reduced by a fifth by nontransfer earnings supplements, such as pension benefits, alimony, interest and dividends (Table 5.4). Cash transfers subtracted a third from the number with family earnings and other nontransfer income below the poverty level, reducing the IFI Net-of-Transfers Deficit by 47 percent in 1979 and 45 percent in 1980. Nevertheless, 7.0 million work force participants slipped through the safety net in 1979, and 8.5 million in 1980. An additional $14.6 billion in transfers or other income would have been required to eliminate cash income poverty among work force participants in 1979 and $17.5 billion in 1980.

It has been argued, however, that in-kind aid makes up much, if not all, of this shortfall. In fiscal 1980, $8.7 billion worth of food stamps were provided to the needy, along with $1.8 billion in free or reduced price school lunches for children from poor or near-poor families. Housing assistance subsidies totaled $5.4 billion. Federal contributions for health care programs provided an estimated $16.2 billion in aid to the poor. 3/ With a poverty deficit of just $17.5 billion for poor households with work force participants, and a total poverty deficit of $29.7 billion for all poor households, these in-kind aid programs were of obvious importance. Yet the evidence suggests that these benefits did not eliminate hardship.

While the exact impact of in-kind aid depends on the value assigned to such benefits, it is clear that only a minority of the working poor escape poverty even when in-kind benefits other than health care are "cashed out" and added to other income. Health care is a special case, since it is so difficult to value and allocate benefits. For instance, the person on kidney dialysis has no lesser food, shelter, or even other medical care needs because he or she is receiving $50,000 or $100,000 in treatment annually. It is much clearer, however, that the family receiving food stamps does not have to spend its own income on food, and there is anecdotal evidence that food stamps circulate much like cash in some poverty areas. The value of food stamps, at least when used directly for food purchases, is printed on each coupon. Since food stamps have more liberal eligibility criteria than cash welfare and probably less of a stigma, they might also be expected to have a significant impact on the working poor. In fact, however, when the coupon value of food stamps is added to the cash incomes of the working poor, only half a million were lifted above the poverty threshold in 1979 and 1980. Food stamps reduced the severe hardship IFI Deficit by $2.2 billion in 1979 and $2.6 billion in 1980. Total food stamp benefits to workers were approximated by the reduction in the moderate hardship IFI Deficit (assuming that the quarter of a million work force participants raised above the moderate hardship level remained only a little above it because of the needs-based formula used to determine benefit levels). Thus, the total benefits received by the families of working poor participants in hardship was on the order of $3.6 to $3.7 billion in 1980, representing around two-fifths of total food stamp benefits. The remainder, presumably, went to dependent families with no work force participants.

Table 5.4. REDUCTION IN HARDSHIP RESULTING FROM CASH TRANSFERS AND IN-KIND AID, 1979 AND 1980

	Severe Hardship				Intermediate Hardship				Moderate Hardship			
	Count (000) 1979	1980	Deficit (1980$M) 1979	1980	Count (000) 1979	1980	Deficit (1980$M) 1979	1980	Count (000) 1979	1980	Deficit (1980$M) 1979	1980
IFE	13,280	15,111	$35,929	$41,000	17,190	19,462	$55,111	$62,416	21,553	24,255	$79,073	$89,142
− Reduction in hardship resulting from non-transfer income	-2,823	-2,953	-8,683	-9,278	-3,045	-3,146	-12,016	-12,709	-3,348	-3,322	-13,534	-16,249
= IFI Net-of-Transfers	10,457	12,158	27,246	31,723	14,145	16,316	43,096	49,708	18,205	20,933	63,539	72,893
− Reduction in hardship resulting from cash transfers	-3,402	-3,693	-12,690	-14,270	-3,621	-4,043	-16,974	-18,895	-3,851	-4,227	-21,348	-23,649
= IFI	7,055	8,465	14,556	17,452	10,524	12,273	26,122	30,812	14,354	16,706	42,192	49,294
− Reduction in hardship resulting from food stamps	-533	-513	-2,175	-2,573	-335	-385	-2,742	-3,148	-251	-220	-3,115	-3,515
= IFI Including Food Stamps	6,522	7,952	12,381	14,880	10,189	11,888	23,380	27,665	14,103	16,486	39,077	45,729
− Reduction in hardship resulting from school lunches and housing subsidies	-281	-319	-601	-721	-280	-254	-1,081	-1,163	-245	-235	-1,516	-1,618
= IFI Including In-Kind Aid (other than health care)	6,241	7,633	11,780	14,158	9,909	11,634	22,299	26,502	13,858	16,251	37,561	44,112

Valuing free school lunches at the cost per meal provided in the poverty budget, and housing subsidies by the differential between the proportion of cash incomes paid by subsidized and unsubsidized low-income residents of rental housing, and adding these values to the combined food stamp and cash incomes, reduced the severe hardship IFI Including Food Stamps counts by 281,000 in 1979 and 319,000 in 1980. The IFI Deficit was reduced by $0.6 billion in 1979, and by $0.7 billion in 1980. The moderate hardship IFI Including Food Stamps Deficit was reduced $1.5 billion in 1979 and $1.6 billion in 1980 by the addition of the estimated value of free school lunches and subsidized housing. Assuming that the quarter of a million work force participants lifted above moderate hardship standards by the receipt of such aid were only marginally above the adequacy levels, the total value of school lunches and housing subsidies for working families in 1980 was on the order of $1.8 billion, or a fourth of the estimated government subsidies for school lunches and housing. While it is inappropriate to conclude that the remaining three-fourths of benefits went to the nonworking low-income families, since both the school lunches and the subsidized housing were valued at somewhat less than their cost of provision, it is fair to say that the preponderance of such benefits went to families whose members were outside the work force.

Families with no earners received the bulk of both cash and in-kind aid, and the nonworking poor who received aid were more likely to escape poverty as a result:

	Persons in families with no work force participants in 1980 (000)	Persons in families with at least one work force participant in 1980 (000)
Below poverty incomes without cash transfers	20,970	25,875
Below poverty incomes after cash transfers	10,683	18,495
Lifted out of poverty by cash transfers	10,287	7,380
Percent lifted out of poverty by cash transfers	49.1%	28.5%
Below poverty incomes counting food stamps	10,196	17,046
Lifted out of cash poverty by food stamps	487	1,449
Percent reduction in poverty resulting from food stamps	4.6%	8.5%
Lifted out of net-of-transfer poverty by food stamps and cash transfers	10,774	8,829
Percent reduction in poverty net-of-transfers resulting from cash transfers and food stamps	51.4%	34.1%
Below poverty incomes counting food stamps, school lunches and housing	9,621	16,237
Lifted out of cash poverty by food stamps, school lunches and housing	1,062	2,258
Percent reduction in cash poverty from in-kind aid	9.9%	30.6%
Lifted out of net-of-transfer poverty by cash and in-kind aid	11,349	9,638
Percent reduction in poverty net-of-transfers from cash transfers and in-kind aid	54.1%	37.2%

Is Work Effort Rewarded?

Most cash transfers and in-kind aid are means-tested, so that benefits decline as earnings increase. But if a worker or working family is not able to achieve minimal self-sufficiency from earnings, it might be expected or desirable that those working more and yet falling short would be rewarded for their effort. The evidence suggests, however, that individuals and families whose earnings remain below the poverty level despite significant participation in the work force are no better protected than those with lesser work effort.

In 1980, the full-year work force participants with earnings and other nontransfer supplements below the poverty level were less likely to escape poverty through transfers than total work force participants (i.e., including those participating less than full-year), even though the average IFI Net-of-Transfers Deficits for full-year and total participants were very nearly the same, leaving the same margin to be made up by transfers:

	Total work force	Full-year work force
Reduction in IFI Net-of-Transfers resulting from cash benefits	-30.4%	-29.9%
Reduction in IFI Net-of-Transfer resulting from cash and in-kind aid	-37.2	-37.3
Reduction in IFI Net-of-Transfer Deficit resulting from cash transfers	-45.0	-41.3
Reduction in IFI Net-of-Transfer Deficit resulting from cash and in-kind aid	-55.4	-51.7

Likewise, transfers were more likely to alleviate the poverty of voluntary part-time workers than to meet the income shortfalls of full-time workers (Table 5.5). Half of the 1979 voluntary part-time workers in poverty before receipt of cash transfers had incomes above poverty after cash and in-kind aid. In contrast, the Net-of-Transfers IFI for persons employed full-time during all weeks in the work force was reduced only a third by cash and in-kind transfers. The reductions in the 1979 IFI Net-of-Transfers Deficits for full-time and voluntary part-time workers were 61 and 45 percent, respectively, reflecting the fact that more of the latter probably received benefits in excess of their IFI Net-of-Transfer Deficits. Similarly, workers who were unemployed some or all weeks in the work force were only slightly less likely to escape net-of-transfer poverty through transfers than those employed all weeks (either part-time or full-time); the exit rates were 38 and 42 percent, respectively. The IFI Net-of-Transfers Deficit of workers who experienced some joblessness was reduced 60 percent, but that of workers employed all weeks in the work force was reduced only 55 percent.

Workers who had greater individual earnings, hence smaller IIE Deficits, were somewhat more likely to escape poverty as a result of cash and in-kind transfers than were persons with lesser earnings or greater IIE Deficits. This was primarily because their average IFI Net-of-Transfer Deficits were lower, leaving less ground to be made up by benefits. Even so, the differences in protection rates were surprisingly small. Among all work force participants with IIE Deficits under $1,000 and family incomes below the poverty level before transfers, cash and in-kind aid raised 39 percent above the poverty level. For those with IIE Deficits above $1,000, cash and in-kind aid raised 34 percent above the the poverty threshold. The IFI Net-of-Transfers Deficit reductions were very similar, i.e., 60 and 50 percent, respectively.

Table 5.5. WORK EFFORT AND TRANSFER BENEFIT IMPACTS, 1979

	Percent reduction IFI Net-of-Transfers as result of cash transfers	Percent reduction IFI Net-of-Transfers as result of cash and in-kind aid	Percent reduction IFI Net-of-Transfers Deficit as result of cash transfers	Percent reduction IFI Net-of-Transfers Deficit as result of cash and in-kind aid	Average IFI Net-of-Transfers Deficit
Total work force	32.5%	40.3%	46.6%	54.8%	$2,296
Employed full-time	25.3	33.8	35.8	44.6	2,140
Employed part-time voluntarily	42.5	47.5	54.8	61.3	1,977
Employed part-time involuntarily	31.6	40.8	44.8	58.1	2,423
Intermittently employed	29.9	39.5	45.5	57.4	2,247
Mostly employed	25.9	35.7	39.8	52.5	1,828
Mixed	34.3	44.1	49.1	60.4	2,251
Mostly unemployed	31.3	40.1	48.4	60.2	3,105
Not employed	23.7	32.8	50.4	63.9	3,984
Full-year work force	55.9	40.9	40.9	51.3	2,311
Employed full-time	23.7	33.1	27.7	35.9	2,294
Employed part-time voluntarily	43.8	48.7	50.1	57.1	1,883
Employed part-time involuntarily	29.8	40.2	35.7	49.0	2,312
Intermittently employed	34.5	43.1	45.6	57.5	2,353
Mostly employed	30.9	41.3	38.7	52.6	1,940
Mixed	39.1	46.6	49.6	59.6	2,207
Mostly unemployed	32.8	40.5	47.1	59.3	3,090
Not employed	19.9	24.1	46.6	60.8	4,892
Individual earnings deficit					
$0-249	39.0	47.7	54.5	65.1	1,882
250-500	32.9	41.3	51.4	62.9	2,428
500-999	33.0	42.2	48.3	60.1	2,326
1,000-1,499	32.1	40.3	49.6	60.9	2,234
1,500-1,999	29.6	38.9	47.4	59.4	2,082
2,000-2,499	32.8	39.4	43.8	55.6	2,047
2,500-2,999	32.3	37.2	47.9	56.9	2,255
3,000-3,999	23.5	31.5	40.4	50.2	2,449
4,000+	22.0	27.0	34.6	42.4	3,300
Individual earnings					
$0-499	26.8	34.5	46.9	56.7	3,308
500-999	31.0	37.9	48.6	58.0	2,535
1,000-1,499	30.9	36.6	45.7	54.0	2,640
1,500-1,999	30.2	39.2	45.1	52.7	2,173
2,000-2,999	37.5	43.3	49.2	58.1	1,831
3,000-3,999	36.0	42.9	44.2	56.2	1,217
4,000-4,999	40.0	48.9	47.5	60.5	1,632
5,000-6,999	35.9	49.5	41.6	58.5	1,585
7,000-8,999	28.5	54.9	40.8	67.2	1,073

Finally, increased numbers of family work force participants did not uniformly increase the probability of escaping net-of-transfer poverty. For example, among three-person families with earnings and nontransfer incomes below the poverty level, 57 percent of those with no work force participants were lifted out of poverty by cash and in-kind transfers, compared to only 54 percent of those with three work force participants, 47 percent of those with two participants and 49 percent of those with one participant (Chart 5.8). The IFI Net-of-Transfers Deficit averaged only $2,115 for three-worker, three-person families, compared to $2,542 for those with two workers and $3,334 for those with one worker. In other words, there was less of a deficit to make up by transfers when there were more earners, yet the chances that transfers would fill the gaps were not substantially greater. The IFI Net-of-Transfers Deficit of three-person families with three in the work force was reduced by only 48 percent, compared to 58 percent when there were just two in the work force, and 68 percent when there was only one participant.

The impacts of cash and in-kind aid varied by the sex and family relationship, education, race, occupation and area residence of work force participants (Table 5.6):

● Female family heads were less likely than male family heads to exit from poverty as a result of cash transfers alone, but the inclusion of in-kind benefits evened the exit rates. Wives and other family members who participated in the work force had a relatively greater chance of being lifted out of poverty by transfers. Female unrelated individuals were more likely to be protected than male unrelated individuals. Overall, female workers who were poor before transfers were only slightly more likely than males to be lifted out of poverty by benefits.

● Prime age workers who did not achieve minimally adequate income from earnings and nontransfer supplements were less likely than younger or older workers to escape poverty through transfers and in-kind aid. Out-of-school 20- to 24-year-olds often fell through the safety net.

● Workers with limited education were more likely to be protected by transfers; 43 percent of dropouts in the IFI Net-of-Transfers received cash and in-kind aid which raised their families out of poverty. Just 26 percent of college graduates who were unsuccessful in the labor market were lifted out of poverty by transfers.

● Sales, clerical and service workers, as well as operatives, who were in poverty before transfers were far more likely than other working poor to be cushioned by cash benefits and in-kind aid which lifted them out of poverty.

● Blacks in the IFI Net-of-Transfers were less likely than whites in similar straits to be lifted out of poverty by the receipt of cash assistance, although the chances equalized with the inclusion of in-kind aid. The IFI Net-of-Transfers Deficit for blacks was reduced more by transfers than that of whites. Transfers had a lesser impact on Hispanic workers. Although their average IFI Net-of-Transfers Deficit was similar to that of blacks, they were far less likely to escape poverty and experienced a far smaller deficit reduction.

Chart 5.8. REDUCTION IN PRE-TRANSFER POVERTY AMONG ADULTS AGE 16 AND OVER RESULTING FROM CASH TRANSFERS AND IN-KIND AID

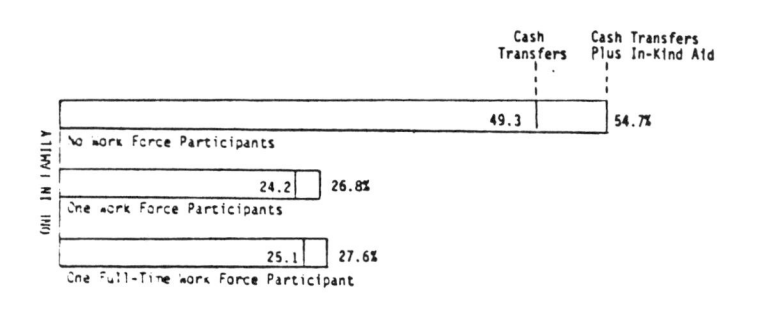

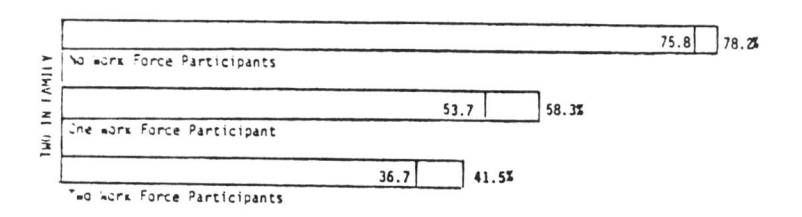

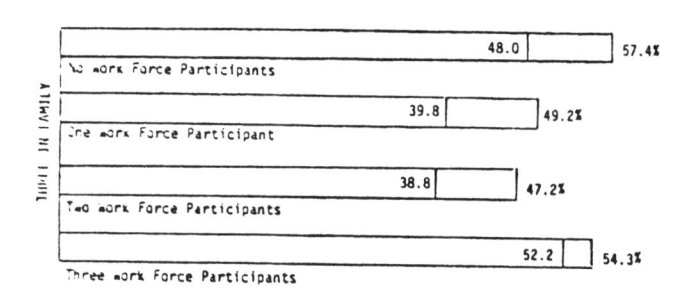

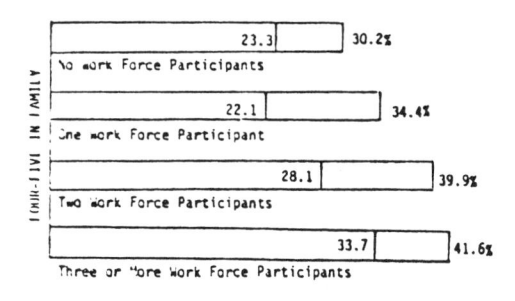

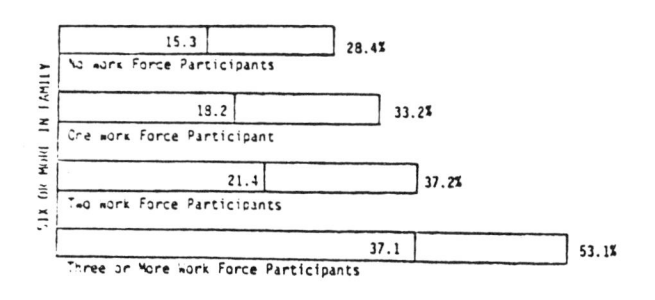

Cash Transfers | Cash Transfers Plus In-Kind Aid

ONE IN FAMILY
- No Work Force Participants: 49.3 | 54.7%
- One Work Force Participants: 24.2 | 26.8%
- One Full-Time Work Force Participant: 25.1 | 27.6%

TWO IN FAMILY
- No Work Force Participants: 75.8 | 78.2%
- One Work Force Participant: 53.7 | 58.3%
- Two Work Force Participants: 36.7 | 41.5%

THREE IN FAMILY
- No Work Force Participants: 48.0 | 57.4%
- One Work Force Participant: 39.8 | 49.2%
- Two Work Force Participants: 38.8 | 47.2%
- Three Work Force Participants: 52.2 | 54.3%

FOUR IN FAMILY
- No Work Force Participants: 23.3 | 30.2%
- One Work Force Participant: 22.1 | 34.4%
- Two Work Force Participants: 28.1 | 39.9%
- Three or More Work Force Participants: 33.7 | 41.6%

FIVE OR MORE IN FAMILY
- No Work Force Participants: 15.3 | 28.4%
- One Work Force Participant: 19.2 | 33.2%
- Two Work Force Participants: 21.4 | 37.2%
- Three or More Work Force Participants: 37.1 | 53.1%

Table 5.6. IMPACTS OF INCOME TRANSFERS ON SUBGROUPS IN THE NET-OF-TRANSFERS IFI IN 1979

	Percent reduction in IFI Net-of-Transfers resulting from cash transfers	Percent reduction in IFI Net-of-Transfers resulting from cash and in-kind transfers	Percent reduction in IFI Net-of-Transfers Deficit resulting from cash transfers	Percent reduction in IFI Net-of-Transfers Deficit resulting from cash and in-kind transfers	Average IFI Net-of-Transfers Deficit
Sex/relationship					
Total male	32.0%	39.0%	43.6%	52.3%	$2,318
Male family householders	33.4	39.9	39.0	48.7	2,474
Male unrelated individual	18.9	21.7	24.7	29.3	1,911
Other male	43.4	56.5	69.6	79.6	2,443
Total female	33.0	41.5	49.3	60.9	2,276
Female family householders	24.5	38.7	45.0	62.3	3,247
Wife	40.7	47.5	59.0	65.8	1,500
Female unrelated individual	29.0	31.2	39.3	42.3	1,818
Other female	44.8	54.7	64.7	76.2	2,315
Age					
16-19	26.5	37.8	48.3	60.5	2,222
16-19 student	(32.1)	(43.0)	(55.7)	(68.6)	(2,067)
20-24	21.8	29.3	41.0	50.4	2,155
20-24 student	(26.6)	(31.8)	(49.3)	(53.0)	(1,751)
25-44	22.5	33.1	38.8	52.6	2,604
45-64	37.2	41.2	47.1	53.1	2,143
65+	81.0	82.4	88.1	88.8	1,867
Race					
White	35.2	40.6	46.2	53.6	2,123
Black	25.8	40.7	48.4	64.9	2,925
Hispanic	21.2	30.5	39.0	52.4	2,360
Education					
High school student	32.6	45.6	56.9	70.2	2,259
Post-secondary student	28.8	32.5	46.5	52.2	1,795
Dropout	34.6	43.2	50.0	61.6	2,495
High school graduate only	32.5	39.7	43.1	52.7	2,193
Post-secondary 1-3 years	30.7	37.0	43.1	52.7	2,177
College and beyond	21.2	25.6	28.9	32.9	1,958
Occupation					
White collar	33.7	40.0	44.3	51.4	2,050
Professional, technical and managerial	26.9	31.5	33.9	39.0	2,190
Sales	41.7	48.4	50.6	56.9	1,895
Clerical	35.8	43.3	51.1	60.2	2,012
Blue collar	33.0	41.7	45.7	55.9	2,163
Craft and kindred	30.8	37.6	41.8	49.5	2,123
Operatives	35.1	44.2	47.3	58.8	2,070
Laborers	31.8	41.5	47.0	57.6	2,356
Farm workers	27.4	33.9	36.7	47.3	2,337
Service workers	34.6	42.9	50.2	61.5	2,193
SMSA status					
Inside SMSA	30.7	39.0	45.7	56.0	2,352
SMSA 1 million +	29.6	37.6	47.3	56.2	2,453
Central city	27.0	38.1	49.2	59.7	2,633
Suburb	32.6	37.1	44.7	51.5	2,246
SMSA under 1 million	31.9	40.7	43.8	55.8	2,235
Central city	29.7	40.8	43.8	55.3	2,322
Suburb	34.7	40.4	48.2	56.4	2,124
Outside SMSA	35.4	42.3	47.9	58.0	2,210
Division					
New England	38.2	46.4	56.4	65.6	2,195
Middle Atlantic	38.9	49.5	55.4	64.0	2,430
East North Central	36.6	43.3	50.6	59.4	2,432
West North Central	35.0	39.2	49.1	55.5	2,074
South Atlantic	30.2	39.2	42.7	56.0	2,195
East South Central	33.6	43.9	43.3	58.1	2,360
West South Central	25.8	33.4	37.8	50.6	2,347
Mountain	26.6	32.8	35.9	44.5	2,107
Pacific	29.1	34.7	47.0	53.3	2,247

The Unraveling Safety Net

Despite the increasing overlap between welfare and workfare, and the absolute growth of transfer payments over the 1970s, the safety net became _less_, rather than _more_, effective in reducing poverty among the working poor. To begin with, the real and relative growth of transfers are frequently exaggerated. Between 1974 and 1979, for instance, transfers _declined_ as a share of cash income reported for families and for unrelated individuals, while earnings increased: 4/

	Share of total reported cash income			
	Families		Unrelated individuals	
	Total	Poor	Total	Poor
Earnings				
1974	86.1%	41.8%	69.4%	24.6%
1979	84.0	43.8	72.8	26.2
Transfers				
1974	8.3	52.5	18.4	66.4
1979	6.9	50.0	13.1	64.3
Nontransfer income other than earnings				
1974	5.6	5.7	12.2	9.0
1979	9.1	6.2	14.1	9.5

In 1974, there were 9.8 million work force participants in families with before-transfer incomes below the poverty level, with 6.3 million remaining after receipt of cash benefits, a reduction of 35.3 percent. In 1979, the reduction caused by transfers had dropped to 32.5 percent. In 1975, the transfer impact was greater than in 1974 because of counter-cyclical benefits, but in 1980, when the unemployment rate was also high, the absolute and percentage reduction in the IFI Net-of-Transfer was substantially lower than in 1975:

	1974	1979	1975	1980
IFI Net-of-Transfers	9,806	10,457	11,531	12,158
IFI	6,346	7,055	7,252	8,465
Reduction from cash transfers	3,460	3,402	4,279	3,693
Percent reduction	-35.3%	-32.5%	-37.1%	-30.4%

When transfer impacts are measured in terms of percentage reductions in net-of-transfers poverty deficits, the same picture emerges. In 1975, for instance, the IFI Deficit was 52.5 percent below the IFI Net-of-Transfer Deficit. In 1980, it was only 45.0 percent lower.

There was evidence of declining rewards for work effort. Compared to the 6.7 percentage drop between 1975 and 1980 in the share of the total work force Net-of-Transfer IFI lifted out of poverty by cash benefits, there was a decline of 9.7 percentage points for full-year participants (Table 5.7). Likewise, the effectiveness of the safety net diminished for the nonworking poor, but the decline was less than for the working poor. For instance, 61.0 percent of all persons age 16 and over in households with no work force participants and with below-poverty net-of-transfer incomes in 1974 were lifted out of poverty by cash benefits; this compared to a 57.2 percent reduction in 1980. But the 3.8 percentage point decline in transfer effectiveness for the nonworking poor was far less than the 6.7 percentage point decline for the working poor:

	All individuals age 16 and in households with no work force participants			
	1974	1979	1975	1980
Below poverty without transfers	14,254	17,222	15,187	17,453
Below poverty with transfers	5,552	7,269	6,151	7,476
Reduction resulting from transfers	8,702	9,953	9,036	9,977
Percentage reduction	-61.0%	-57.8%	-59.5%	-57.2%

Neither the changing composition and work experience patterns of the work force, nor increased earnings shortfalls, explained the declining impacts of the cash transfers. The average IFE Deficit, and the average IFI Net-of-Transfer Deficit, both declined in real terms between 1974 and 1979, as well as between 1975 and 1980; in other words, there was less ground to make up by transfers so that the same level of real benefits should have lifted <u>more</u> rather than <u>fewer</u> of the working poor out of poverty:

	1974	1979	1979-1974	1975	1980	1980-1975
Average IFE Deficit (1980 $)	$2,742	$2,706	$-36	$2,771	$2,713	$-58
Average IFE Net-of-Transfer Deficit (1980 $)	2,652	2,606	-46	2,663	2,609	-54

The declining transfer impacts were evident among the long-term unemployed, the short-term unemployed, those employed part-time whether voluntarily or involuntarily, as well as among full-time workers who experienced no joblessness (Table 5.8). Weighting the 1979 Earnings Supplementation Rates-Transfers for each work experience pattern subgroup by its 1974 share of the severe hardship IFE for the total work force, and

Table 5.7. DECLINING EFFECTIVENESS OF TRANSFERS IN REDUCING POVERTY AMONG WORK FORCE PARTICIPANTS

	1974	1979	1979-1974	1975	1980	1980-1975
IFI Net-of-Transfers Minus IFI ÷ IFI						
Total Work Force	54.5%	48.2%	-6.3%	59.0%	43.6%	-15.4%
Full-Year Work Force	55.5	49.2	-6.3	64.1	42.6	-21.5
IFI Net-of-Transfers Minus IFI ÷ IFI Net-of-Transfers						
Total Work Force	35.3	32.5	-2.8	37.1	30.4	-6.7
Full-Year Work Force	35.7	33.0	-2.7	39.1	29.9	-9.2
IFI Net-of-Transfers Deficit Minus IFI Deficit ÷ IFI Deficit						
Total Work Force	101.8	87.2	-14.6	110.3	81.8	-28.5
Full-Year Work Force	78.3	69.3	-9.0	99.8	70.3	-29.5
IFI Net-of-Transfers Deficit Minus IFI Deficit ÷ IFI Net-of-Transfers Deficit						
Total Work Force	50.4	46.6	-3.8	52.5	45.0	-7.5
Full-Year Work Force	43.9	40.9	-3.0	49.9	41.3	-8.6
Earnings Supplementation Rate						
Total Work Force	47.1	46.9	-0.2	47.3	44.0	-3.3
Full-Year Work Force	46.2	45.4	-0.8	48.1	42.0	-6.1
Earnings Supplementation Rate - Nontransfers						
Total Work Force	18.3	21.3	+3.0	16.2	19.5	+3.3
Full-Year Work Force	16.4	18.6	+2.2	14.9	17.3	+2.4
Earnings Supplementation Rate - Transfers						
Total Work Force	28.8	25.6	-3.2	31.1	24.5	-6.6
Full-Year Work Force	29.8	26.8	-3.0	33.2	24.7	-8.5
IFE Deficit Minus IFI Deficit ÷ IFE Deficit						
Total Work Force	60.8	59.5	-1.3	61.7	57.4	-4.3
Full-Year Work Force	54.3	52.6	-1.7	58.1	52.5	-5.6
IFE Deficit Minus IFI Net-of-Transfers Deficit ÷ IFE Deficit						
Total Work Force	21.0	24.2	+3.2	19.5	22.6	+3.1
Full-Year Work Force	18.6	19.7	+1.1	16.3	19.0	+2.7
IFI Net-of-Transfers Minus IFI Deficit ÷ IFE Deficit						
Total Work Force	39.8	35.3	-4.5	42.2	34.8	-7.4
Full-Year Work Force	35.7	32.9	-2.8	41.8	33.5	-8.3

Table 5.8. CHANGE IN EARNINGS SUPPLEMENTATION RATE-TRANSFERS BY WORK EXPERIENCE PATTERN, AGE AND SEX/RELATIONSHIP

	1974	1975	1975-1974	1975	1980	1980-1975
Total work force						
Not employed	25.2%	21.0%	-4.2%	31.0%	17.0%	-14.0%
Mostly unemployed	29.0	28.4	-0.6	37.6	26.6	-11.0
Mixed	28.8	29.9	+1.1	39.0	28.1	-0.9
Mostly employed	25.2	22.0	-3.2	27.7	22.6	-5.1
Part-time involuntary	26.4	26.5	+0.1	27.6	24.4	-3.2
Part-time voluntary	34.5	19.3	-5.2	33.8	28.4	-5.4
Employed full-time	25.1	20.3	-4.8	24.3	19.9	-4.4
Full-year work force						
Not employed	30.3	16.7	-13.6	39.8	19.6	-20.2
Mostly unemployed	31.5	29.8	-1.7	39.9	27.4	-2.5
Mixed	31.4	34.4	+3.0	43.9	31.8	-12.1
Mostly employed	28.2	26.7	-1.5	30.5	24.6	-5.9
Part-time involuntary	27.2	27.5	-0.7	26.4	22.6	-3.8
Part-time voluntary	39.0	29.5	-9.5	34.6	28.2	-6.4
Employed full-time	21.7	20.3	-1.4	21.7	16.7	-5.2
Age						
16-19	24.9	22.4	-2.5	23.7	23.7	0
20-24	20.6	17.7	-2.9	23.5	17.7	-5.8
25-44	21.8	19.7	-2.1	27.5	18.2	-9.3
45-64	29.5	26.6	-2.9	32.6	27.3	-5.3
65+	51.7	50.1	-1.6	52.4	47.3	-5.1
Sex/relationship						
Male family heads	27.6	25.3	-2.3	32.6	23.7	-8.9
Male unrelated individuals	20.5	14.4	-5.1	23.9	17.1	-6.8
Other males	36.0	35.0	-1.0	37.1	31.8	-5.3
Female family heads	24.5	21.5	-3.0	24.6	16.8	-7.8
Wives	34.2	29.8	-4.4	36.8	30.0	-6.8
Female unrelated individuals	26.4	22.4	-4.0	25.7	22.5	-3.5
Other gemales	34.4	34.0	-0.4	34.2	33.0	-1.2

the 1980 rates by each subgroup's 1975 share, suggests that work experience pattern changes were a neutral factor:

Actual 1979 Earnings Supplementation Rate-Transfers	25.6%
1979 Earnings Supplementation Rates-Transfers for work experience groups weighted by their 1974 shares of the IFE	25.6
Effect of 1974-1979 work experience pattern changes	0
Actual 1980 Earnings Supplementation Rate-Transfers	24.5%
1980 Earnings Supplmentation Rates-Transfers for each work experience pattern group weighted by 1975 share of the IFE	24.2
Increase in Earnings Supplementation Rates-Transfers associated with 1975-1980 changes in work experience patterns	+0.3

Changes in the sex and family relationship composition of the severe hardship IFE for the total work force were relatively neutral in their potential impacts on transfer effects:

1979 Earnings Supplementation Rates-Transfers for sex/relationship groups weighted by 1974 share of the IFE	25.9%
Actual 1979 Earnings Supplementation Rate-Transfers	25.6
Decline in Earnings Supplementation Rate-Transfers associated with 1974-1979 sex/relationship changes in composition of IFE	-0.3
Actual 1980 Earnings Supplementation Rate-Transfers	24.5%
1980 Earnings Supplementation Rate-Transfers for sex/relationship groups weighted by 1975 IFE share	23.9
Increase in Earnings Supplementation Rate-Transfers associated with 1975-1980 changes in sex/relationship composition of IFE	+0.6

Moreover, the Earning Supplementation Rates-Transfers declined among male family heads, female family heads, wives, male unrelated individuals, as well as female unrelated individuals.

The only factor which may have contributed to reduced transfer supplementation was the declining share of older workers in the severe hardship IFE. However, the impacts could have accounted for only a minor portion of the 3.2 percentage point drop in the severe hardship Earnings Supplementation Rate-Transfers between 1974 and 1979, or the 6.6 percentage point drop between 1975 and 1980:

1979 Earnings Supplementation Rates-Transfers for each age group weighted by 1974 IFE share for each age group	26.4%
Actual 1979 Earnings Supplementation Rate-Transfers	25.6
Decline in Earnings Supplementation Rate-Transfers associated with 1974-1979 age changes	-0.8
Actual 1980 Earnings Supplementation Rate-Transfers	24.5%
1980 Earnings Supplementation Rate-Transfers for each age group weighted by 1975 IFE share for each age group	25.3
Decline in Earnings Supplementation Rate-Transfers associated with 1975-1980 age changes	-0.8

By implication, then, the primary cause of declining transfer impacts had to be reductions in the availability and level of transfer benefits for the working poor. There is direct as well as indirect evidence that this was the case. Much of the decline occurred among unemployed workers, and there is no doubt that unemployment insurance protections deteriorated. In 1975, 37.6 percent of persons with at least some unemployment who would have been poor in the absence of transfers were lifted out of poverty by receipt of cash benefits. In 1980, only 26.5 percent were protected by transfers:

	1974	1979	1975	1980
Participants employed all weeks				
IFI Net-of-Transfers (000)	6,186	6,795	6,681	7,097
IFI (000)	3,813	4,438	4,223	4,744
Reduction (000)	2,373	2,357	2,458	2,353
Percentage reduction	-38.4%	-34.7%	-36.8%	-33.2%
Participants who experienced unemployment				
IFI Net-of-Transfers (000)	3,620	3,662	4,851	5,062
IFI (000)	2,533	2,618	3,029	3,720
Reduction (000)	1,087	1,044	1,822	1,342
Percentage reduction	-30.0%	-28.5%	-37.6%	-26.5%

Paralleling these trends was a drop in unemployment insurance beneficiaries and benefit levels. Average weekly beneficiaries equalled 43.1 percent of the average annual unemployment in 1975, but only 38.2 percent in 1980. Moreover, the average weekly benefit in 1980 was 8 percent lower in real terms than in 1975: 5/

	1974	1979	1979-1974	1975	1980	1980-1975
Average weekly unemployment insurance beneficiaries (000)	1,881	2,040	+159	3,371	2,844	-527
Average annual unemployed (000)	5,076	5,963	+887	7,830	7,448	-382
Beneficiaries ÷ unemployed	37.1%	34.2%	-2.9%	43.1%	38.2%	-4.9%
Average weekly benefit (1980 $)	$107	$102	-$5	$108	$99	-$9

There were retrenchments in other transfer programs. Several states completely eliminated Aid to Families with Dependent Children-Unemployed Parents, thus, restricting AFDC payments to single parents and usually female heads. Yet the proportion of female-headed families receiving public assistance also dropped from 32.8 percent in 1974 to 27.1 percent in 1979. 6/ Average real AFDC benefits per recipient declined significantly. 7/ Because the size of recipient families dropped, real average benefits per recipient would have had to increase in order to maintain the effectiveness of AFDC in reducing poverty since family income needs rise less than proportionately with each additional family member: 8/

	1974	1979	1975	1980
AFDC monthly benefit per person in recipient families (1980 $)	$108	$105	$109	$100
Recipients per family	3.32	2.92	3.20	2.89

The enormous regional disparity in transfer levels and their availability declined, but this resulted more from diminished transfer protections in the high benefit areas rather than marked improvements in the low benefit areas (Table 5.9). For instance, between 1975 and 1980, the standard deviation in the proportions of the regional IFI Net-of-Transfers who escaped poverty as a result of cash benefits declined from 6.3 percentage points to 4.5 percentage points. Yet the poverty reduction impacts of transfers declined in all three regions with the lowest poverty reduction rates in 1975.

Practical Applications

The most practical and politically sensitive application of labor market and poverty statistics is their use in allocating federal funds to state and local areas, and in prioritizing the needs of eligible subgroups within these areas. As federal grants-in-aid grew rapidly during the

Table 5.9. CHANGING IMPACTS OF TRANSFERS BY CENSUS DIVISION

	1974	1979	1979-1974	1975	1980	1980-1975
IFI Net-of-Transfers Minus IFI ÷ IFI						
New England	82.7%	61.9%	-20.8%	85.6%	55.9%	-29.7%
Middle Atlantic	66.1	63.7	-2.4	77.0	58.4	-18.6
East North Central	63.3	57.7	-5.6	78.0	49.7	-28.3
West North Central	71.6	53.7	-17.9	69.8	44.5	-25.3
South Atlantic	43.2	43.3	+0.1	44.5	38.9	-5.6
East South Central	44.5	50.7	+6.2	50.9	33.4	-17.5
West South Central	38.7	34.7	-4.0	44.2	36.8	-7.4
Mountain	47.9	36.3	-11.6	44.2	32.6	-11.6
Pacific	64.7	41.1	-23.6	57.0	45.5	-11.5
Variability						
Standard Deviation	15.0	10.9	-4.1	16.5	9.4	-7.1
Standard Deviation ÷ Mean	25.9	22.1	-3.8	27.0	21.3	-5.7
IFI Net-of-Transfers Minus IFI ÷ IFI Net-of-Transfers						
New England	45.3	38.2	-7.1	46.1	35.9	-10.2
Middle Atlantic	39.8	38.9	-0.9	43.5	36.9	-6.6
East North Central	38.7	36.6	-2.1	43.8	33.2	-10.6
West North Central	41.7	34.9	-6.8	41.1	30.8	-10.3
South Atlantic	30.2	30.2	0	30.8	28.0	-2.8
East South Central	30.8	33.6	+2.8	33.7	25.0	-8.7
West South Central	27.9	25.8	-1.9	30.7	26.9	-3.8
Mountain	32.4	26.6	-5.8	30.7	24.6	-6.1
Pacific	39.3	29.1	-10.2	36.3	31.3	-5.0
Variability						
Standard Deviation	6.0	4.9	-1.1	6.3	4.5	-1.8
Standard Deviation ÷ Mean	16.6	15.1	-1.5	16.8	14.9	-1.9
IFI Net-of-Transfer Deficit Minus IFI Deficit ÷ IFI Net-of-Transfer Deficit						
New England	57.7	56.4	-1.3	65.5	54.2	-11.3
Middle Atlantic	58.6	55.4	-3.2	58.9	53.5	-5.4
East North Central	59.2	50.6	-8.6	60.4	51.2	-9.2
West North Central	53.2	49.1	-4.1	51.8	43.5	-8.3
South Atlantic	43.7	42.6	-1.1	46.0	40.7	-5.3
East South Central	46.1	43.3	-2.8	49.1	41.3	-7.8
West South Central	42.0	37.8	-4.2	41.8	37.7	-4.1
Mountain	40.8	35.9	-4.9	43.1	32.5	-10.6
Pacific	52.5	47.0	-5.5	54.7	45.7	-9.0
Variability						
Standard Deviation	7.4	7.2	-0.2	9.2	7.4	-0.8
Standard Deviation ÷ Mean	14.7	15.5	+0.8	15.6	16.6	+1.0
IFI Net-of-Transfer Deficit Minus IFI Deficit ÷ IFI Deficit						
New England	136.7	129.2	-7.5	190.2	118.6	-71.6
Middle Atlantic	141.5	124.3	-17.2	143.6	115.1	-28.5
East North Central	145.3	102.4	-42.9	152.5	105.0	-47.5
West North Central	113.8	96.5	-17.3	107.6	77.0	-30.6
South Atlantic	77.8	74.4	-3.4	85.2	68.5	-16.7
East South Central	85.9	76.3	-9.2	96.5	70.3	-26.2
West South Central	72.3	60.8	-11.5	71.7	60.4	-11.3
Mountain	69.1	56.0	-13.1	75.7	48.2	-27.5
Pacific	110.2	88.6	-21.6	120.6	84.1	-36.5
Variability						
Standard Deviation	30.7	25.9	-4.8	39.7	24.8	-14.9
Standard Deviation ÷ Mean	29.0	28.8	-0.2	34.2	29.9	-4.3

1970s, and in particular, the federally-funded employment and training programs addressed to the problems of the economically disadvantaged, the unemployment and poverty rates were adopted as "scientific" and "equitable" ways of distributing funds, in contrast to the discretionary approach more frequently used in the 1960s. Likewise, state and local planning procedures were often mandated in federal legislation. The funds allocated to states and localities were to be distributed according to the relative needs of residents as judged by their comparative unemployment and poverty rates. As the outlays for the Comprehensive Employment and Training Act grew, the statistics used in allocation and planning became more important issues. In the late 1970s, when CETA outlays were over $10 billion, a change in a few tenths of a percentage point in an area's unemployment rate might cost it hundreds of thousands of dollars under the CETA allocation formulae. Each time CETA was amended there was debate over the relative weight to be given to area unemployment and poverty in fund allocation, since poor areas were not always those with high unemployment, and since allocation formulae based on shares of excess unemployment above a certain level distributed resources to different areas than if shares of total unemployment were used. Revisions of the estimation procedures for local unemployment rates in 1978 led to court challenges about the techniques used in deriving state and local estimates.

Allocating Resources According to Hardship Shares

In concept, the hardship measures are preferable to the unemployment and poverty rates as a basis for allocating federal employment and training resources and other grants-in-aid addressed to labor market-related problems. The purpose of CETA (and its renamed successor) is "to provide job training and employment opportunities for economically disadvantaged, unemployed, or underemployed persons . . . ." Yet the unemployment rate does not count the underemployed, i.e., low income persons working part-time but seeking full-time work and those working full-time but earning poverty wages, and includes many--in fact, a large majority--who are not from low-income families. On the other hand, only a fourth of all poor persons, and two-fifths of those age 15 and over, are in the work force, while many individuals marginally above and not counted by the poverty level are transfer recipients who might be self-supporting if they received training and employment assistance, so that areas with generous transfer benefits are penalized in the allocation of federal manpower dollars where poverty is the criteria. The hardship measures, particularly the IFE and the IFE Deficit, focus on those who are in the work force and unable to achieve adequate earnings to support themselves and their families, whether the individuals are unemployed or underemployed. In other words, they focus on the legislatively-specified universe of need for remedial employment and training programs.

If hardship measures, rather than unemployment and poverty rates, or combinations of the two, were used to allocate funds, there would be some substantial changes in the shares provided to different areas:

Nonmetropolitan areas account for a substantially larger share of the hardship counts and deficits than of unemployment (Table 5.10). Aver-

Table 5.10. HARDSHIP AND UNEMPLOYMENT SHARES OF METROPOLITAN AND NONMETROPOLITAN AREAS AVERAGED FOR 1974 THROUGH 1980

	Average Annual Unemployment	Persons Experiencing Unemployment During Year	Persons Predominantly Unemployed During Year	Persons In Poverty	IIE	IIE Deficit	IFE	IFE Deficit	IFI	IFI Deficit
Metropolitan Areas	70.5%	68.7%	68.8%	61.0%	61.0%	57.5%	59.6%	61.1%	59.3%	59.8%
Nonmetropolitan Areas	29.5	31.3	31.2	39.0	39.0	42.5	40.4	38.9	40.7	40.2
Central Cities of Metropolitan Areas	34.1	31.2	33.3	37.0	26.8	26.3	32.1	34.5	34.1	35.4
Suburbs of Metropolitan Areas	36.5	37.6	35.6	24.0	34.2	31.2	27.5	26.6	25.2	25.0
Larger Metropolitan Areas[1]	--	39.2	39.8	33.8	32.3	30.5	31.7	33.3	31.4	31.6
Smaller Metropolitan Areas	--	29.6	28.9	27.2	28.7	27.1	27.9	27.8	27.9	28.2
Central Cities in Larger Metropolitan Areas	--	16.6	18.6	20.7	13.1	13.3	16.4	18.4	17.4	18.4
Central Cities in Smaller Metropolitan Areas	--	14.6	14.7	16.3	13.7	13.0	15.6	16.1	16.7	17.0
Suburbs in Larger Metropolitan Areas	--	22.6	21.2	13.1	19.3	17.1	15.3	15.0	14.0	13.7
Suburbs in Smaller Metropolitan Areas	--	15.0	14.2	10.9	14.9	14.1	12.2	11.7	11.2	11.2

SEVERE HARDSHIP - TOTAL WORK FORCE

[1] SMSA's with a population of over one million.

aging the hardship, poverty and unemployment rates over the 1974-1980 period (in order to average out the year-to-year changes in shares) and assuming equal resources to be allocated each year, the allocations to nonmetropolitan areas would have been 37 percent higher if IFE shares were used in the allocation formulae rather than shares of national average annual unemployment (Table 5.11). Because these nonmetropolitan areas accounted for a larger share of poverty than of unemployment, they would have received only 4 percent more if IFE shares were used in allocation rather than poverty shares. Compared to an allocation formula giving 50 percent weight to the share of average annual unemployment and 50 percent weight to the poverty share, an IFE-based allocation would have increased nonmetropolitan area resources by 18 percent.

Central cities would have received 6 percent less if allocation were according to IFE shares rather than shares of average annual unemployment, or 10 percent less relative to a formula giving equal weight to unemployment and poverty shares. The decrements would have been smaller if IFE Deficit shares were utilized for allocation rather than the IFE counts. Large central cities (those in metropolitan areas with over 1 million population) would have lost more than smaller central cities if the IFE share were used.

The suburban areas would have received a fourth less under an IFE-based formula compared to an unemployment share formula, and 9 percent less compared to a formula weighting unemployment and poverty shares equally. If the IFE Deficit shares were used in allocation, the suburbs would have received 12 percent less than under the unemployment-poverty formula.

● Over the 1974-1980 period, the West North Central, South Atlantic, East South Central, West South Central and Mountain states averaged a substantially larger share of the IFE than of persons experiencing unemployment or of persons unemployed over a third of their weeks in the work force (Table 5.12). If IFE shares rather than unemployment shares or equally weighted poverty and unemployment shares were used to distribute resources, the states in these regions would have received a fourth and a tenth _more_ respectively (Table 5.13). In contrast, the New England, Middle Atlantic and East North Central states would have received a fifth and an eighth _less_, respectively. Use of the IFI rather than the IFE shares would have exacerbated this tendency, since the New England, Middle Atlantic and East North Central states had more liberal transfer systems and higher Earnings Supplementation Rates so that their combined IFI share (30.6 percent averaged for the 1974-1980 period) was even lower than their combined IFE share (33.7 percent).

● For specific states and localities, alterations in the allocation basis can have even more dramatic impacts. To illustrate the feasibility of state level estimation, the complete array of hardship measures were calculated for Ohio, North Carolina, Georgia, California and New York. The impacts of hardship-based allocation varied significantly between these states. Ohio's share of national unemployment was much larger than its share of the IFE, and its IFI share was even smaller because its Earnings Supplementation Rate was far above average (Table 5.14). Ohio's IFI share matched its poverty share. In contrast, Georgia's IFE share was much larger than its unemployment share, and its IFI share was larger still

Table 5.11. PERCENT INCREASE OR DECREASE IN ALLOCATION RESULTING FROM USE OF HARDSHIP SHARE FOR ALLOCATION RATHER THAN UNEMPLOYMENT OR POVERTY SHARE

	\multicolumn{6}{c}{HARDSHIP SHARE ALLOCATION COMPARED TO ANNUAL AVERAGE UNEMPLOYMENT SHARE ALLOCATION}	\multicolumn{6}{c}{HARDSHIP SHARE ALLOCATION COMPARED TO POVERTY SHARE ALLOCATION}
	IIE	IIE Deficit	IFE	IFE Deficit	IFI	IFI Deficit	IIE	IIE Deficit	IFE	IFE Deficit	IFI	IFI Deficit
Metropolitan Areas	-13%	-18%	-15%	-13%	-16%	-15%	0	-6%	-2%	0	-3%	-2%
Nonmetropolitan Areas	+32	+44	+37	+32	+38	+36	0	+9	+4	0	+4	+3
Central Cities of Metropolitan Areas	-21	-23	-6	+1	0	+4	-28	-29	-13	-7	-8	-4
Suburbs of Metropolitan Areas	-6	-15	-25	-17	-31	-32	+43	+30	+15	+11	+5	+4
Larger Metropolitan Areas	--	--	--	--	--	--	-4	-10	-6	-1	-7	-7
Smaller Metropolitan Areas	--	--	--	--	--	--	+5	-1	+2	+2	+2	+4
Central Cities in Larger Metropolitan Areas	--	--	--	--	--	--	-37	-36	-21	-11	-16	-11
Central Cities in Smaller Metropolitan Areas	--	--	--	--	--	--	-15	-20	-4	-1	+2	+4
Suburbs in Larger Metropolitan Areas	--	--	--	--	--	--	+44	+31	+9	+14	+7	+5
Suburbs in Smaller Metropolitan Areas	--	--	--	--	--	--	+36	+29	+12	+7	+3	+3

	\multicolumn{6}{c}{HARDSHIP SHARE ALLOCATION COMPARED TO ALLOCATION BASED ON SHARE OF PERSONS EXPERIENCING UNEMPLOYMENT}	\multicolumn{6}{c}{HARDSHIP SHARE ALLOCATION COMPARED TO EQUALLY WEIGHTED POVERTY AND ANNUAL UNEMPLOYMENT SHARE ALLOCATION}
	IIE	IIE Deficit	IFE	IFE Deficit	IFI	IFI Deficit	IIE	IIE Deficit	IFE	IFE Deficit	IFI	IFI Deficit
Metropolitan Areas	-11%	-16%	-13%	-11%	-14%	-13%	-7%	-13%	-9%	-7%	-10%	-9%
Nonmetropolitan Areas	+25	+36	+29	+24	+30	+29	+14	+24	+18	+14	+19	+17
Central Cities of Metropolitan Areas	-14	-16	+3	+11	+9	+14	+25	-26	-10	-3	-4	0
Suburbs of Metropolitan Areas	-9	-17	-27	-29	-33	-34	+13	+3	-9	-12	-17	-16
Larger Metropolitan Areas	-17	-22	-19	-15	-20	-21	--	--	--	--	--	--
Smaller Metropolitan Areas	-3	-8	-6	-6	-4	-2	--	--	--	--	--	--
Central Cities in Larger Metropolitan Areas	-21	-20	-1	+11	-7	-1	--	--	--	--	--	--
Central Cities in Smaller Metropolitan Areas	-14	-11	+7	+11	+13	+17	--	--	--	--	--	--
Suburbs in Larger Metropolitan Areas	-6	-24	-32	+34	-38	-39	--	--	--	--	--	--
Suburbs in Smaller Metropolitan Areas	-1	-7	-19	+22	-25	-25	--	--	--	--	--	--

Table 5.12. AVERAGE SHARES OF UNEMPLOYMENT, POVERTY AND HARDSHIP FOR CENSUS DIVISIONS OVER 1974-1980 PERIOD

| | | | | Severe Hardship - Total Work Force ||||||
Division[1]	Persons Experiencing Unemployment	Persons Predominantly Unemployed	Poverty	IIE	IIE Deficit	IFE	IFE Deficit	IFI	IFI Deficit
New England	5.84%	6.01%	4.34%	5.43%	5.21%	4.96%	4.84%	4.44%	3.80%
Middle Atlantic	16.59	18.81	15.15	14.20	14.19	13.07	13.97	11.67	11.66
East North Central	19.87	20.30	15.34	17.93	17.74	15.62	16.49	14.51	14.29
West North Central	6.79	5.70	6.53	9.14	10.10	8.61	7.96	7.91	7.81
South Atlantic	15.30	15.01	18.32	16.64	16.07	17.83	17.39	19.27	19.49
East South Central	6.16	6.24	9.97	7.50	7.27	8.39	8.54	9.41	9.90
West South Central	8.77	7.99	13.90	11.13	11.09	12.31	12.17	13.87	14.74
Mountain	4.86	4.01	4.59	5.16	5.30	5.23	4.80	5.46	5.46
Pacific	15.74	15.73	11.88	12.81	12.99	13.94	13.90	13.46	12.90

[1]New England: Connecticut, Maine, Massachusetts New Hampshire, Rhode Island and Vermont
Middle Atlantic: New Jersey, New York and Pennsylvania
East North Central: Illinois, Indiana, Michigan, Ohio and Wisconsin
West North Central: Iowa, Kansas, Minnesota, Missouri, Nebraska, North and South Dakota
South Atlantic: Delaware, District of Columbia, Florida, Georgia, Maryland, Pennsylvania, Virginia, West Virginia
East South Central: Alabama, Kentucky, Mississippi and Tennessee
West South Central: Arkansas, Louisiana, Oklahoma and Texas
Mountain: Arizona, Colorado, Idaho, Montana, Nevada, New Mexico, Utah and Wyoming
Pacific: Alaska, California, Hawaii, Oregon and Washington

Table 5.13. PERCENTAGE CHANGE IN ALLOCATION RESULTING FROM USE OF ALTERNATIVE ALLOCATION BASES

Division	USE OF HARDSHIP SHARE COMPARED TO USE OF SHARE OF PERSONS EXPERIENCING UNEMPLOYMENT						USE OF HARDSHIP SHARE COMPARED TO USE OF POVERTY SHARE						USE OF HARDSHIP SHARE COMPARED AVERAGE OF SHARES OF POVERTY AND PERSONS EXPERIENCING UNEMPLOYMENT					
	IIE	IIE Deficit	IFE	IFE Deficit	IFI	IFI Deficit	IIE	IIE Deficit	IFE	IFE Deficit	IFI	IFI Deficit	IIE	IIE Deficit	IFE	IFE Deficit	IFI	IFI Deficit
New England	-7%	-11%	-15%	-17%	-24%	-35%	+25%	+20%	+14%	+12%	+2%	-12%	+7%	+2%	-3%	-5%	-13%	-25%
Middle Atlantic	-14	-9	-21	-16	-30	-30	-6	-9	-14	-8	-23	-23	-11	-11	-18	-12	-26	-27
East North Central	-10	-11	-21	-17	-27	-28	+17	+16	+2	+7	-5	-7	+2	+1	-11	-6	-18	-19
West North Central	+35	+49	+27	+17	+18	+15	+40	+55	+32	+22	+22	+20	+37	+52	+29	+20	+20	+17
South Atlantic	+9	+5	+17	+14	+26	+27	-9	-12	-3	-5	+5	+6	-1	-4	+6	+3	+15	+16
East South Central	+22	+18	+36	+39	+53	+61	-25	-27	-16	-14	-6	-1	-7	-10	+4	+6	+17	+23
West South Central	+27	+26	+40	+39	+58	+68	-20	-20	-11	-12	-2	+6	-2	-2	+9	+7	+22	+30
Mountain	+6	+9	+8	-1	+12	+12	+12	+15	-14	+5	+19	+19	+9	+12	+11	+1	+15	+15
Pacific	-19	-17	-11	-12	-14	-18	+8	+9	+17	+17	+13	+9	-7	-6	+1	+1	-3	-7

Table 5.14. STATE SHARES OF UNEMPLOYMENT, POVERTY AND HARDSHIP AVERAGED FOR 1974-1980 PERIOD

	Annual Average Unemployment	Persons Experiencing Unemployment	Predominantly Unemployed	Poverty	Severe Hardship - Total Work Force					
					IIE	IIE Deficit	IFE	IFE Deficit	IFI	IFI Deficit
Ohio	4.94%	4.86%	4.88%	3.77%	4.56%	4.36%	3.78%	3.93%	3.59%	3.54%
North Carolina	2.30	2.58	2.34	3.05	3.01	2.92	3.19	2.83	3.58	3.15
Georgia	2.24	2.30	2.25	3.21	2.66	2.58	2.98	2.95	3.42	3.66
California	12.02	11.42	11.75	8.93	9.33	9.46	10.31	10.26	10.00	9.61
New York	9.71	7.78	9.20	7.97	6.55	6.66	6.40	6.72	5.85	5.76

because of its below average Earnings Supplementation Rate. Yet Georgia's hardship share was below its poverty share.

Under an IFE-based allocation, North Carolina and Georgia would have gained nearly a fifth and a tenth, respectively, compared to a poverty/unemployment allocation formula. California's allocations would have changed little while Ohio's would have declined by an eighth and New York's by over a fourth (Table 5.15).

Another possible consequence of substituting a hardship-based allocation for an unemployment-based allocation is to stabilize funding and activity levels. Year-to-year fluctuations in allocations undermine operational effectiveness because of the difficulties of phasing programs up and down, or trying to plan when likely funding is uncertain. It obviously makes a difference whether federal budgeting responds to changes in the unemployment rate or in hardship incidence, since the fluctuations in hardship are less severe than the fluctuations in unemployment:

	Standard deviation in annual incidence as percentage 1974-1980 mean incidence
Unemployment rate	15.8%
Poverty and unemployment rate equally weighted	8.3
Severe hardship IIE rate	6.5
Severe hardship IFE rate	5.8
Severe hardship IFI rate	6.8

But the choice of statistics used for allocating whatever funds are made available nationally can also affect the stability of funding received by states and localities. Although the percentage fluctuations in hardship rates are less than the percentage fluctuations in unemployment or combined poverty and unemployment rates, hardship shares are only slightly more stable than unemployment, or poverty and unemployment, shares. For regions, states and areas, the coefficients of variation in IIE shares over the 1974-1980 period were slightly less than those for poverty or unemployment shares. In most, but not all cases, the IFE shares were more stable than unemployment shares, but the combined poverty/unemployment allocation shares were frequently more stable (Table 5.16). Since the IFI rate is not cyclically sensitive and has experienced differing trends in different areas, largely as a result of differentially changing transfer policies, the coefficients of variation for the IFI rate were larger than those for unemployment and/or poverty.

The resources addressed to the labor market problems of the disadvantaged are subdivided at the national level into categories addressed to different segments of the work force, and then are subdivided at the state and local levels according to shares of the universe of need. Each year the state or local decisionmaking agent must submit a plan detailing the composition of the eligible population and must indicate the priorities for service based on objective locally established criteria to assure services

Table 5.15. PERCENTAGE CHANGE IN ALLOCATION RESULTING FROM USE OF ALTERNATIVE ALLOCATION BASES

	\multicolumn{6}{c	}{USE OF HARDSHIP SHARE RATHER THAN SHARE OF AVERAGE ANNUAL UNEMPLOYMENT}	\multicolumn{6}{c	}{USE OF HARDSHIP SHARE RATHER THAN POVERTY SHARE}	\multicolumn{6}{c}{USE OF HARDSHIP SHARE RATHER THAN AVERAGE OF POVERTY AND UNEMPLOYMENT SHARES}
	IIE	IIE Deficit	IFE	IFE Deficit	IFI	IFI Deficit	IIE	IIE Deficit	IFE	IFE Deficit	IFI	IFI Deficit	IIE	IIE Deficit	IFE	IFE Deficit	IFI	IFI Deficit
Ohio	-8%	-12%	-23%	-20%	-27%	-28%	+21%	+16%	0	+4%	-5%	-6%	+5%	0	-13%	-10%	-18%	-19%
North Carolina	+31	+27	+39	+23	+56	+37	-1	-6	+5	-7	+17	+3	+13	+9	+19	+6	+34	+18
Georgia	+19	+15	+33	+32	+53	+63	-17	-20	-12	-8	+7	+14	-3	-6	+9	+8	+25	+34
California	-22	-11	-14	-15	-17	-20	+4	+6	+15	+15	+12	+8	-11	-10	-2	-2	-5	-8
New York	-33	-31	-34	-30	-40	-41	-18	-16	-20	-15	-27	-28	-26	-25	-28	-23	-7	-35

Table 5.16. YEAR-TO-YEAR FLUCTUATIONS IN HARDSHIP, UNEMPLOYMENT AND POVERTY SHARES AS MEASURED BY COEFFICIENTS OF VARIATION IN RATES FOR DIFFERENT AREAS OVER THE 1974-1980 PERIOD

	Unemployment share	Poverty share	Average share poverty and unemployment	Severe hardship - total work force		
				IIE share	IFE share	IFI share
Inside SMSA	1.9%	1.9%	0.8%	0.8%	2.0%	2.9%
Central city	2.3	4.7	2.4	2.0	3.3	5.8
Suburb	2.9	4.3	1.9	2.4	4.5	6.3
Outside SMSA	4.5	2.9	1.6	1.3	2.9	4.2
New England	10.3	7.5	14.0	7.0	7.4	11.5
Middle Atlantic	5.7	5.5	5.6	4.5	5.1	5.6
East North Central	5.1	3.4	6.6	1.7	4.1	6.0
West North Central	6.4	7.4	6.2	3.4	8.8	10.1
South Atlantic	2.7	2.5	6.0	2.5	2.5	5.1
East South Central	5.1	3.7	6.7	4.8	5.9	8.8
West South Central	3.9	6.8	6.1	3.6	4.0	6.8
Mountain	4.6	4.2	9.3	3.1	3.9	5.8
Pacific	4.9	3.6	5.1	2.7	4.4	3.6
Ohio	9.1	7.0	5.3	4.1	9.3	11.9
North Carolina	14.0	7.9	5.4	6.1	7.7	11.3
Georgia	10.2	14.6	12.3	4.5	10.6	16.5
California	9.0	4.0	5.5	3.7	6.2	4.7
New York	9.1	8.6	6.4	4.4	8.5	11.3

to those most in need. Yet even though the eligible population includes the unemployed and underemployed in low-income families, planning and client priorities are usually based on available unemployment and poverty data. These data may yield quite different client priorities than the hardship data:

- If the severe hardship IFE share for the total work force were used to target resources in 1979, males would have received marginally less than females, while if unemployment shares were used, they would have received slightly more (Chart 5.9). However, male family heads would have received substantially *more* under a hardship-based distribution. Female family heads would have gained enormously, since their share of the IFE was double their share of the average annual unemployed. The big losers would have been wives and other family members:

	Share average annual unemployment	Average of unemployment and poverty share	IFE share
Males	50.6%	43.5%	47.5%
Females	49.4	56.5	52.5
Male family heads	18.8	17.7	24.5
Female family heads	6.9	11.9	15.2
Wives	19.7	17.6	14.1
Other family members	40.5	28.7	19.8
Unrelated individuals	14.1	24.2	26.4

- High school dropouts would have received a much larger share of resources under an IFE-based distribution than under an unemployment-based distribution (Chart 5.10). Students would have received somewhat more while high school graduates and persons with some post-secondary education would have received much less. The IFE shares among the education subgroups very nearly matched the average of the unemployment and adult poverty shares:

	Share of workers who experienced unemployment	Average of share experiencing unemployment and poverty share	IFE share
Students	10.7%	10.8%	11.9%
High school dropouts	28.8	42.0	39.9
High school graduates only	38.4	30.7	30.2
Completed some post-secondary education	22.9	17.1	18.1

Chart 5.9. SHARES OF HARDSHIP, UNEMPLOYMENT AND POVERTY IN 1979 BY SEX AND FAMILY RELATIONSHIP

Chart 5.9. (Continued)

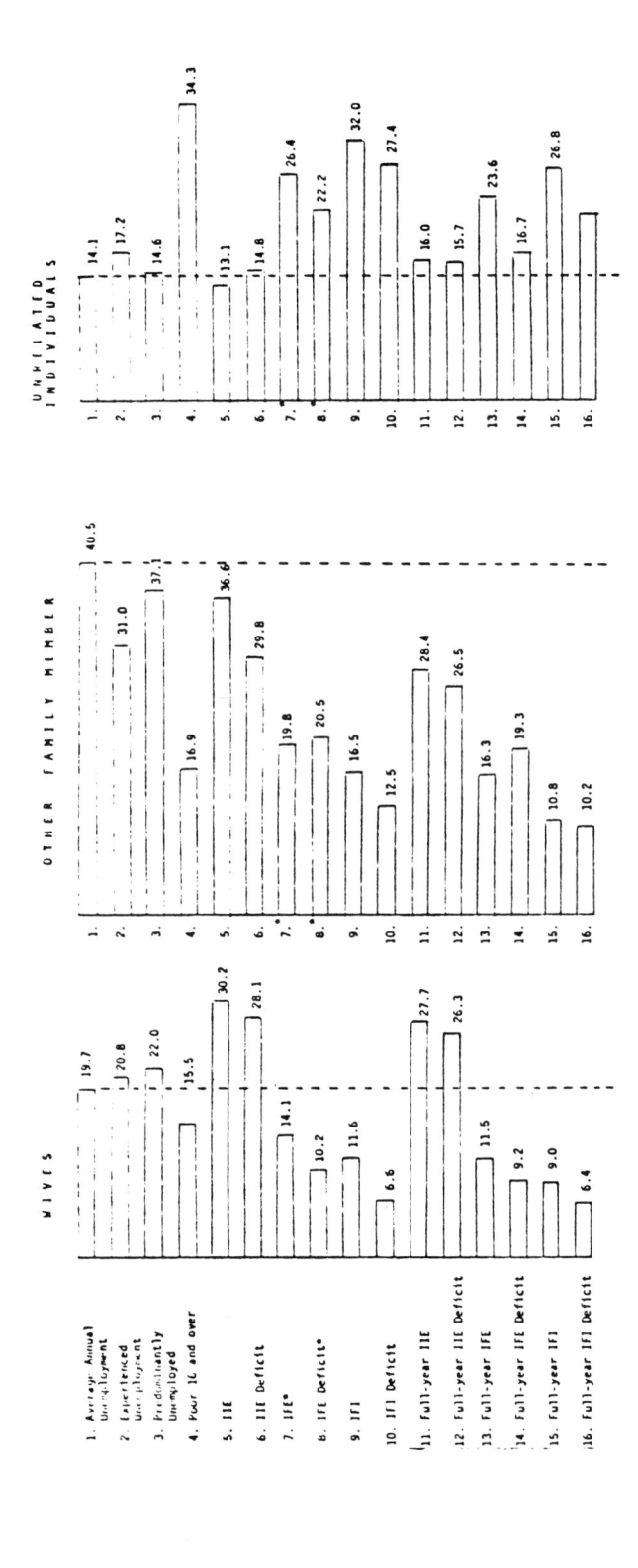

WIVES

1. Average Annual Unemployment — 19.7
2. Experienced Unemployment — 20.8
3. Predominantly Unemployed — 22.0
4. Poor 1C and over — 15.5
5. IIE — 30.2
6. IIE Deficit — 28.1
7. IIE* — 14.1
8. IIE Deficit* — 10.2
9. IFI — 11.6
10. IFI Deficit — 6.6
11. Full-year IIE — 27.7
12. Full-year IIE Deficit — 26.3
13. Full-year IFE — 11.5
14. Full-year IFE Deficit — 9.2
15. Full-year IFI — 9.0
16. Full-year IFI Deficit — 6.4

OTHER FAMILY MEMBER

1. — 40.5
2. — 31.0
3. — 37.1
4. — 16.9
5. — 36.6
6. — 29.8
7. — 19.8
8. — 20.5
9. — 16.5
10. — 12.5
11. — 28.4
12. — 26.5
13. — 16.3
14. — 19.3
15. — 10.8
16. — 10.2

UNRELATED INDIVIDUALS

1. — 14.1
2. — 17.2
3. — 14.6
4. — 34.3
5. — 13.1
6. — 14.8
7. — 26.4
8. — 22.2
9. — 32.0
10. — 27.4
11. — 16.0
12. — 15.7
13. — 23.6
14. — 16.7
15. — 26.8
16. —

Chart 5.10. SHARES OF HARDSHIP, UNEMPLOYMENT AND POVERTY IN 1979 BY EDUCATIONAL ATTAINMENT

STUDENTS

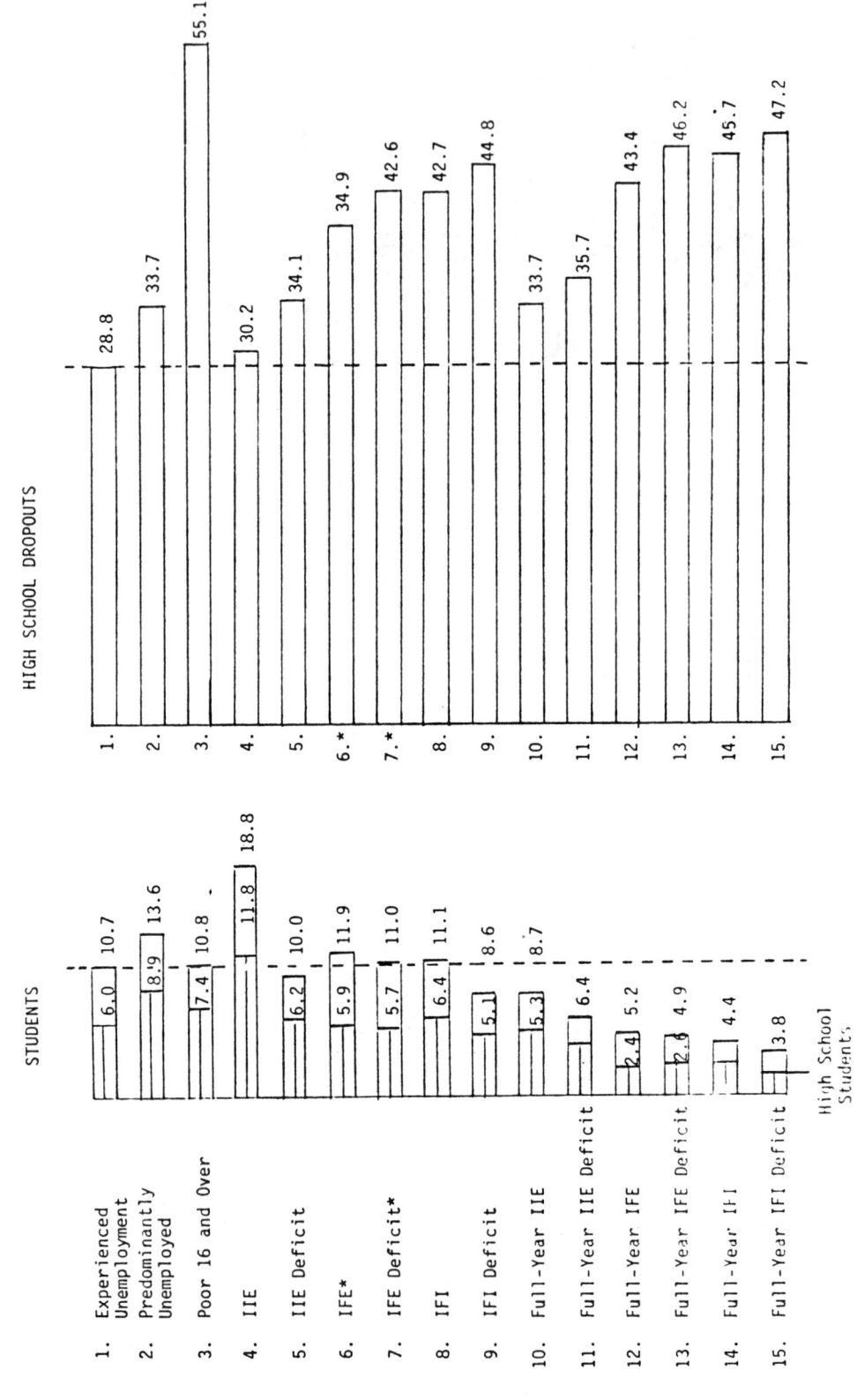

1. Experienced Unemployment	6.0	10.7
2. Predominantly Unemployed	8.9	13.6
3. Poor 16 and Over	7.4	10.8
4. IIE	11.8	18.8
5. IIE Deficit	6.2	10.0
6. IFE*	5.9	11.9
7. IFE Deficit*	5.7	11.0
8. IFI	6.4	11.1
9. IFI Deficit	5.1	8.6
10. Full-Year IIE	5.3	8.7
11. Full-Year IIE Deficit	6.4	
12. Full-Year IFE	2.4	5.2
13. Full-Year IFE Deficit	2.6	4.9
14. Full-Year IFI	4.4	
15. Full-Year IFI Deficit	3.8	

High School Students

HIGH SCHOOL DROPOUTS

1. 28.8
2. 33.7
3. 55.1
4. 30.2
5. 34.1
6.* 34.9
7.* 42.6
8. 42.7
9. 44.8
10. 33.7
11. 35.7
12. 43.4
13. 46.2
14. 45.7
15. 47.2

Chart 5.10. (Continued)

HIGH SCHOOL GRADUATES ONLY

NONSTUDENTS COMPLETED ONE OR MORE YEARS POST-SECONDARY EDUCATION (College Graduate)

#	Category	HS Grads Only	Nonstudents Post-Secondary (low / high)
1.	Experienced Unemployment	38.4	9.0 / 22.9
2.	Predominantly Unemployed	36.2	6.5 / 16.6
3.	Poor 16 and Over	22.9	6.9 / 11.2
4.	IIE	33.8	6.6 / 17.3
5.	IIE Deficit	36.4	8.1 / 19.5
6.	IFE*	30.2	7.4 / 18.1
7.	IFE Deficit*	28.9	7.0 / 17.5
8.	IFI	30.2	6.1 / 16.1
9.	IFI Deficit	30.6	5.9 / 16.1
10.	Full-Year IIE	37.6	7.3 / 19.1
11.	Full-Year IIE Deficit	37.6	11.7 / 20.2
12.	Full-Year IFE	33.0	7.5 / 18.1
13.	Full-Year IFE Deficit	31.2	7.1 / 17.8
14.	Full-Year IFI	32.9	6.6 / 17.0
14.	Full-Year IFI Deficit	33.1	6.6 / 16.8

- Minorities would have received about the same share whether targeting were based on IFE shares or shares of average annual unemployment (Chart 5.11). They would have received less under an IFE-based distribution than one based on the average of the unemployment and adult poverty shares. Minorities would have benefited more if the focus were only on full-year work force participants, if targeting were based on hardship deficits rather than counts, or if allocation used the IFI rather than the IFE share:

	Whites	Blacks	Hispanics
IFE share ÷ share average unemployed	99%	101%	103%
IFE Deficit share ÷ share average annual unemployed	94	121	104
IFI share ÷ share average annual unemployed	90	130	139
IFI Deficit share ÷ share average annual unemployed	88	140	139

- If hardship were the only consideration in targeting, youth would have received substantially less priority, while older workers would have received substantially more (Chart 5.12):

	Share average annual unemployment	Average shares of annual unemployment and poverty	IFE Share
16-19	25.6%	19.7%	13.4%
20-24	23.1	18.5	17.1
25-44	34.8	32.5	33.3
45+	16.5	29.4	36.2

State-Level Planning Strategies

The hardship measures can be used to plan intervention strategies as well as client priorities. For instance, the new legislation which replaces the Comprehensive Employment and Training Act puts greater emphasis on state level planning and decisionmaking. The baseline hardship measures, which have been calculated for five states, suggest that the underlying labor market problems and patterns differ significantly from one state to another. While disaggregations for each state would be needed to make refined judgments, the summary data provide a basis for better strategizing employment and training as well as income maintenance strategies at the state level:

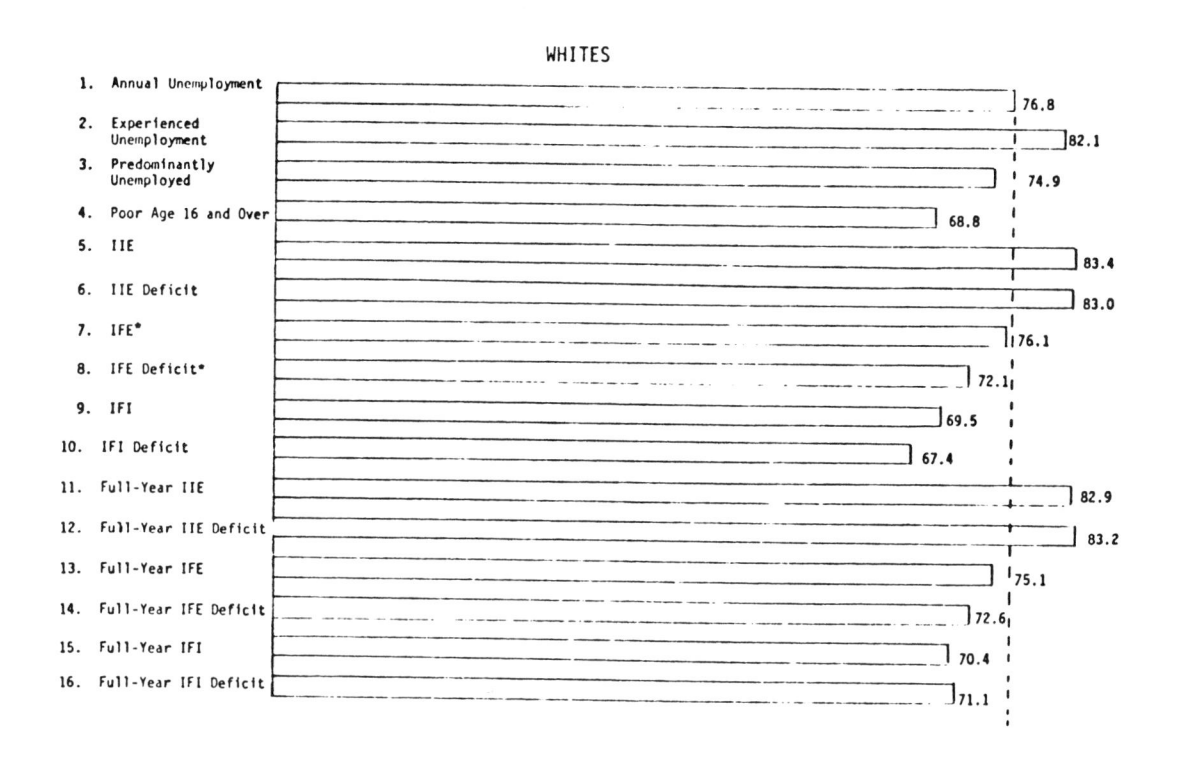

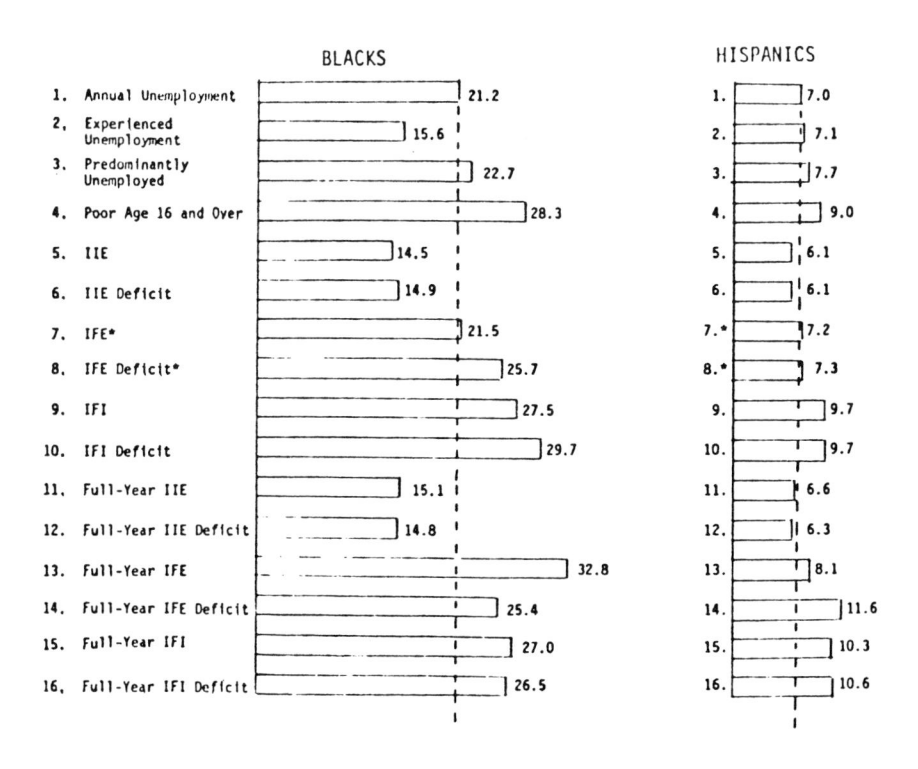

Chart 5.11. SHARES OF HARDSHIP, UNEMPLOYMENT AND POVERTY IN 1979 BY RACE

WHITES

#	Category	Value
1.	Annual Unemployment	76.8
2.	Experienced Unemployment	82.1
3.	Predominantly Unemployed	74.9
4.	Poor Age 16 and Over	68.8
5.	IIE	83.4
6.	IIE Deficit	83.0
7.	IFE*	76.1
8.	IFE Deficit*	72.1
9.	IFI	69.5
10.	IFI Deficit	67.4
11.	Full-Year IIE	82.9
12.	Full-Year IIE Deficit	83.2
13.	Full-Year IFE	75.1
14.	Full-Year IFE Deficit	72.6
15.	Full-Year IFI	70.4
16.	Full-Year IFI Deficit	71.1

BLACKS

#	Category	Value
1.	Annual Unemployment	21.2
2.	Experienced Unemployment	15.6
3.	Predominantly Unemployed	22.7
4.	Poor Age 16 and Over	28.3
5.	IIE	14.5
6.	IIE Deficit	14.9
7.	IFE*	21.5
8.	IFE Deficit*	25.7
9.	IFI	27.5
10.	IFI Deficit	29.7
11.	Full-Year IIE	15.1
12.	Full-Year IIE Deficit	14.8
13.	Full-Year IFE	32.8
14.	Full-Year IFE Deficit	25.4
15.	Full-Year IFI	27.0
16.	Full-Year IFI Deficit	26.5

HISPANICS

#	Value
1.	7.0
2.	7.1
3.	7.7
4.	9.0
5.	6.1
6.	6.1
7.*	7.2
8.*	7.3
9.	9.7
10.	9.7
11.	6.6
12.	6.3
13.	8.1
14.	11.6
15.	10.3
16.	10.6

Chart 5.12. SHARES OF HARDSHIP, UNEMPLOYMENT AND POVERTY IN 1979 BY AGE

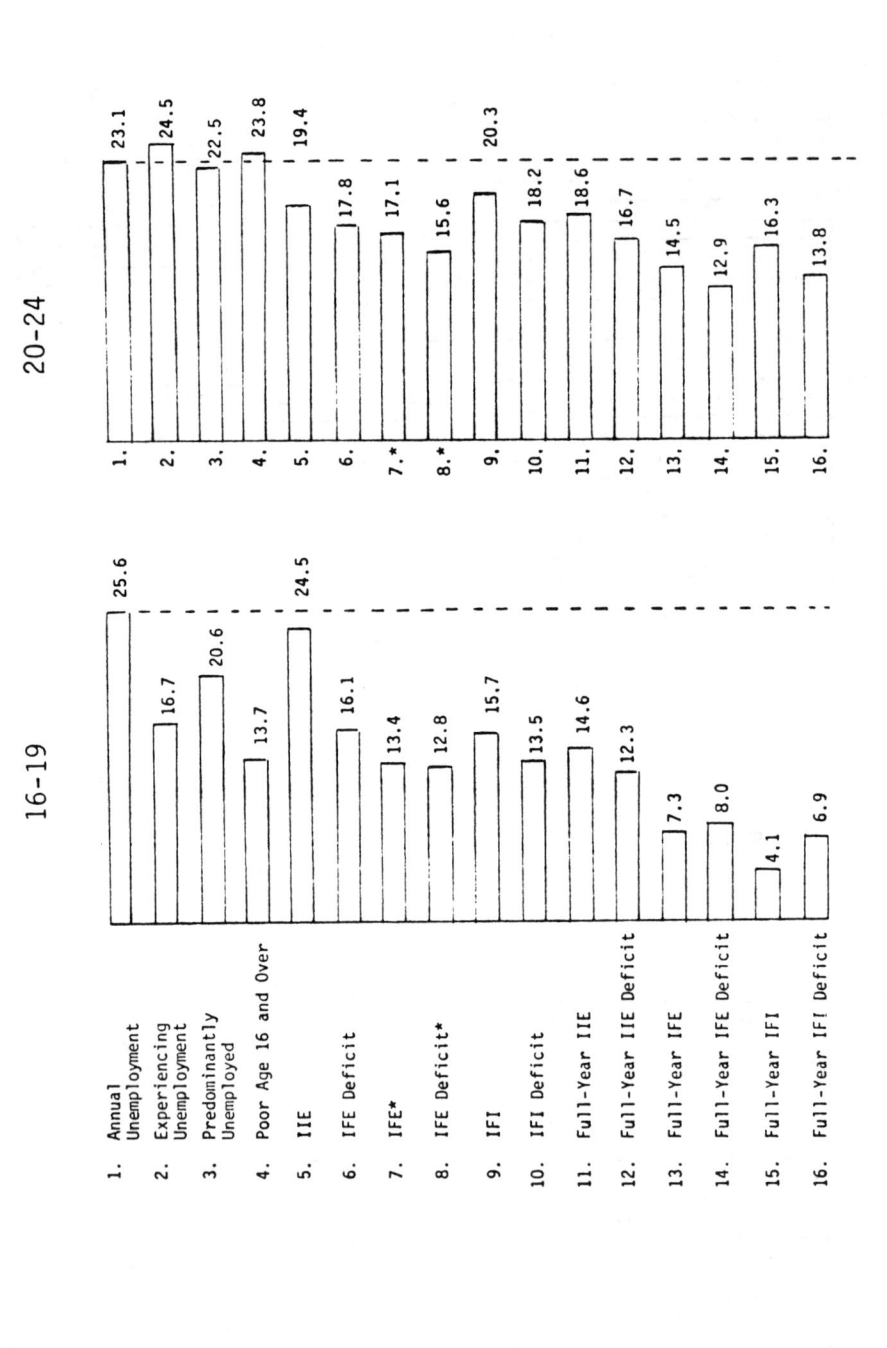

16-19

1.	Annual Unemployment	25.6
2.	Experiencing Unemployment	16.7
3.	Predominantly Unemployed	20.6
4.	Poor Age 16 and Over	13.7
5.	IIE	24.5
6.	IFE Deficit	16.1
7.	IFE*	13.4
8.	IFE Deficit*	12.8
9.	IFI	15.7
10.	IFI Deficit	13.5
11.	Full-Year IIE	14.6
12.	Full-Year IIE Deficit	12.3
13.	Full-Year IFE	7.3
14.	Full-Year IFE Deficit	8.0
15.	Full-Year IFI	4.1
16.	Full-Year IFI Deficit	6.9

20-24

1.	23.1
2.	24.5
3.	22.5
4.	23.8
5.	19.4
6.	17.8
7.*	17.1
8.*	15.6
9.	20.3
10.	18.2
11.	18.6
12.	16.7
13.	14.5
14.	12.9
15.	16.3
16.	13.8

Chart 5.12. (Continued)

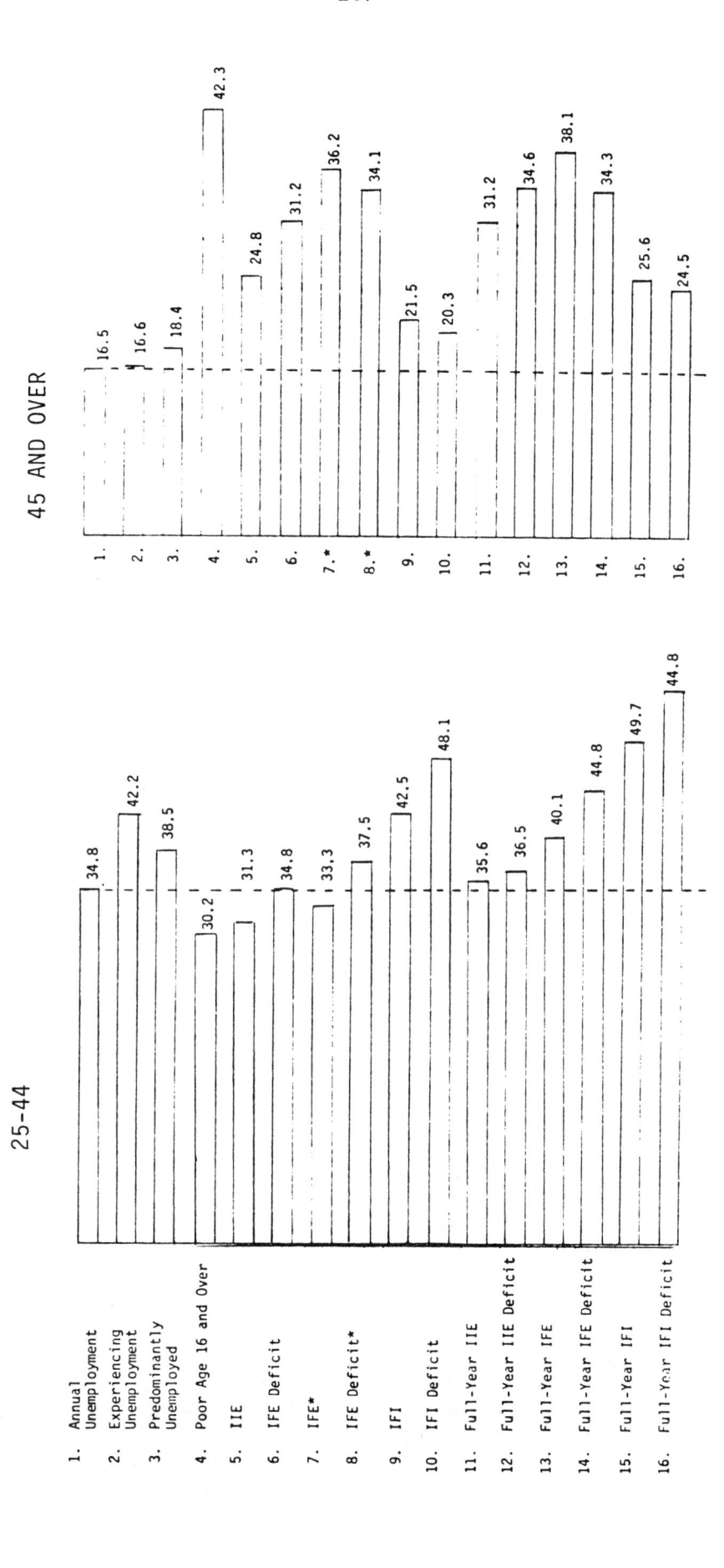

25-44

#	Label	Value
1.	Annual Unemployment	34.8
2.	Experiencing Unemployment	42.2
3.	Predominantly Unemployed	38.5
4.	Poor Age 16 and Over	30.2
5.	IIE	31.3
6.	IFE Deficit	34.8
7.	IFE*	33.3
8.	IFE Deficit*	37.5
9.	IFI	42.5
10.	IFI Deficit	48.1
11.	Full-Year IIE	35.6
12.	Full-Year IIE Deficit	36.5
13.	Full-Year IFE	40.1
14.	Full-Year IFE Deficit	44.8
15.	Full-Year IFI	49.7
16.	Full-Year IFI Deficit	44.8

45 AND OVER

#	Value
1.	16.5
2.	16.6
3.	18.4
4.	42.3
5.	24.8
6.	31.2
7.*	36.2
8.*	34.1
9.	21.5
10.	20.3
11.	31.2
12.	34.6
13.	38.1
14.	34.3
15.	25.6
16.	24.5

Georgia: With the highest hardship rates among the five sample states, and with relatively high average hardship deficits, Georgia would have received a large share of any funds distributed by hardship formulae (Table 5.17). These severe conditions did not reflect a depressed labor market. The percent of the Georgia work force experiencing unemployment in 1979 was far below the national average and the unemployment incidence in the other four states in the sample (although the percent employed part-time involuntarily was higher in Georgia). The proportion of the work force employed full-year was typical for the nation, so that this was not an explanation for the hardship rates. Persons with Inadequate Individual Earnings were more likely to have Inadequate Family Earnings, and represented a larger share of the IFE, than in other states; in other words, individual labor market problems were relatively more of a factor in explaining family hardship.

The clear culprit, then, was low wages. The IIE and IFE rates among workers employed all weeks were 20.7 and 10.8 percent, respectively, or 2.0 and 1.7 percentage points above the national averages (Table 5.18). Persons employed full-time, full-year represented 16.2 percent of the severe hardship IFE in Georgia compared to just 10.5 percent of the severe hardship IFE for the total work force nationwide, and 12.3, 11.3, 10.1 and 7.2 percent, respectively, in North Carolina, Ohio, New York and California. A ten percent increase in earnings for all Georgia workers would have reduced the IFE by 13.7 percent--or a greater amount than similar augmentation in other states or nationwide. In contrast Full Employment augmentation providing minimum wages for all hours of forced idleness had a lesser effect in Georgia than nationwide or in the other states in the sample. Finally, the cash and in-kind transfer system in Georgia was relatively ineffective in reducing poverty among the working poor. Only a fourth of workers in Georgia's IFI Net-of-Transfers were raised out of poverty by cash benefits, compared to nearly a third nationwide.

To alleviate hardship in Georgia, relatively more emphasis would be needed on the underemployed, vis-a-vis the unemployed. Attention might be placed on training and upgrading the skills of those already employed, with a focus on those forced to work part-time involuntarily. Supplementing these labor market strategies, the state might increase the exemptions under state income taxes or provide an earned income tax credit of some sort so as not to discourage work.

North Carolina: Like Georgia, North Carolina had comparatively high hardship rates despite low unemployment. However, there were some quite significant contrasts between the two states. The work force participation rate was higher in North Carolina, and the number of dependents per worker lower, apparently reflecting a greater number of secondary earners. The state was below the national average, and ranked lowest in the state sample, in the proportion of its work force employed full-time. As a result, hardship was not as "hard" in North Carolina as elsewhere; the state had the lowest average severe hardship deficits in the sample, far below those in Georgia. A comparatively small share of its IIE and IFE were full-year work force participants unemployed over one-third of their weeks in the work force, i.e., those likely to have the greatest average deficits. They represented only 8.6 percent of the North Carolina severe

Table 5.17. HARDSHIP AND RELATED SUMMARY INDICATORS FOR STATE PLANNING, 1979

	NATIONAL AVERAGE		GEORGIA		NORTH CAROLINA		OHIO		CALIFORNIA		NEW YORK	
	Indicator	Rank	Indicator	Rank	Indicator	Rank	Indicator	Rank	Indicator	Rank	Indicator	Rank
Severe Hardship Rates For Total Work Force												
IIE	24.2	(3)	26.2	(1)	25.6	(2)	22.5	(4)	20.4	(6)	21.5	(5)
IFE	11.4	(3)	12.9	(1)	12.9	(2)	9.5	(6)	10.5	(5)	10.6	(4)
IFI	6.0	(3)	8.1	(1)	7.9	(2)	5.0	(6)	5.7	(4)	5.4	(5)
Intermediate Hardship Rates For Total Work Force												
IIE	35.0	(3)	39.7	(2)	40.0	(1)	31.6	(5)	30.5	(6)	31.7	(4)
IFE	14.7	(3)	16.3	(2)	17.9	(1)	12.0	(6)	14.2	(4)	13.6	(5)
IFI	9.9	(4)	10.9	(2)	12.1	(1)	6.9	(6)	9.1	(3)	6.5	(5)
Moderate Hardship Rates For Total Work Force												
IIE	44.0	(3)	49.6	(2)	53.0	(1)	40.1	(4)	38.7	(6)	39.5	(5)
IFE	18.4	(3)	21.0	(2)	23.0	(1)	15.3	(6)	18.1	(4)	17.4	(5)
IFI	12.3	(4)	14.9	(2)	17.5	(1)	9.4	(4)	12.4	(3)	5.2	(5)
Intermediate + Severe Hardship For Total Work Force												
IIE	1.45	(5)	1.52	(2)	1.56	(1)	1.40	(6)	1.49	(3)	1.48	(4)
IFE	1.29	(3)	1.27	(6)	1.39	(1)	1.27	(5)	1.36	(2)	1.28	(4)
IFI	1.49	(4)	1.35	(6)	1.53	(3)	1.37	(5)	1.60	(1)	1.57	(2)
Moderate + Severe Hardship For Total Work Force												
IIE	1.82	(5)	1.89	(3)	2.07	(1)	1.78	(6)	1.90	(2)	1.83	(4)
IFE	1.62	(5)	1.63	(4)	1.79	(1)	1.61	(6)	1.73	(2)	1.64	(3)
IFI	2.03	(4)	1.85	(6)	2.23	(1)	1.89	(5)	2.18	(2)	2.08	(3)

Table 5.17. (Continued)

	NATIONAL AVERAGE		GEORGIA		NORTH CAROLINA		OHIO		CALIFORNIA		NEW YORK	
	Indicator	Rank	Indicator	Rank	Indicator	Rank	Indicator	Rank	Indicator	Rank	Indicator	Rank
Severe Hardship Rates For Full-Year Work Force												
IIE	17.0	(3)	19.8	(1)	18.9	(2)	14.5	(5)	14.5	(5)	14.5	(5)
IFE	6.8	(3)	8.1	(1)	8.0	(2)	5.1	(6)	5.3	(5)	5.9	(4)
IFI	3.7	(3)	5.1	(1)	4.7	(2)	3.2	(5)	3.0	(6)	3.2	(4)
Full-Year ÷ Total Work Force												
Work Force	71.8	(4)	71.9	(3)	69.7	(6)	74.1	(2)	70.4	(5)	75.6	(1)
IIE	50.4	(4)	54.6	(1)	51.3	(2)	47.7	(6)	50.1	(5)	50.9	(3)
IFE	42.7	(3)	45.5	(1)	43.5	(2)	39.8	(5)	35.5	(6)	44.5	(3)
IFI	43.9	(4)	45.3	(2)	41.5	(5)	47.2	(1)	37.3	(6)	44.5	(3)
Average Severe Hardship Deficits For Total Work Force												
IIE	$1,839	(4)	$1,868	(2)	$1,422	(6)	$1,971	(1)	$1,743	(5)	$1,851	(3)
IFE	2,384	(4)	2,422	(3)	2,028	(6)	2,437	(2)	2,330	(5)	2,630	(1)
IFI	1,818	(2)	1,833	(1)	1,431	(6)	1,810	(3)	1,670	(5)	1,791	(4)
Average Severe Hardship Deficits For Full-Year Work Force												
IIE	$2,698	(3)	$2,683	(4)	$2,350	(6)	$3,057	(1)	$2,529	(5)	$2,736	(2)
IFE	2,345	(5)	2,544	(2)	1,716	(6)	2,587	(1)	2,386	(4)	2,425	(3)
IFI	2,036	(2)	2,311	(1)	1,491	(6)	2,009	(3)	1,948	(4)	1,827	(5)
Work Force Participation Rate Persons 16+	70.1	(4)	71.8	(2)	74.0	(1)	67.9	(5)	70.8	(3)	64.6	(6)
Persons Per Work Force Participant	1.90	(4)	1.90	(3)	1.86	(5)	1.97	(2)	1.85	(6)	2.03	(1)
Persons Per Full-Year Work Force Participant	2.65	(4)	2.63	(6)	2.67	(2)	2.66	(3)	2.64	(5)	2.69	(1)

Table 5.17. (Continued)

	NATIONAL AVERAGE		GEORGIA		NORTH CAROLINA		OHIO		CALIFORNIA		NEW YORK	
	Indicator	Rank	Indicator	Rank	Indicator	Rank	Indicator	Rank	Indicator	Rank	Indicator	Rank
Persons in Families With Member in IIE Per Person in IIE	1.98	(5)	2.08	(1)	2.02	(4)	2.03	(3)	1.89	(6)	2.06	(2)
Percent IIE In IFE	32.2	(4)	33.9	(1)	33.1	(3)	29.8	(6)	31.0	(5)	33.5	(2)
Persons With IIE As Percent IFE	68.6	(3)	69.0	(2)	65.9	(5)	70.8	(1)	60.5	(6)	68.0	(4)
Percent Not In IIE Who Are In IFE	4.7	(4)	5.4	(2)	5.9	(1)	3.6	(6)	5.2	(3)	4.3	(5)
Earnings Supplementation Rates												
Total	46.9	(3)	37.2	(6)	38.8	(5)	47.1	(2)	45.6	(4)	49.2	(1)
Non-transfers	21.3	(4)	21.6	(3)	13.2	(6)	23.2	(1)	23.2	(2)	17.4	(5)
Transfers	25.6	(2)	15.5	(6)	25.6	(3)	23.9	(4)	22.4	(5)	31.8	(1)
Percent Reduction in Net-of-Transfers IFI												
From Cash Transfers	32.5	(2)	25.7	(6)	29.5	(4)	31.2	(3)	29.1	(5)	38.6	(1)
From Cash and In-Kind Aid	40.3	(3)	33.7	(6)	41.2	(2)	38.6	(4)	34.9	(5)	51.7	(1)
Percent Reduction in IFE From Augmentation												
Enhanced Earnings	9.7	(3)	13.7	(1)	11.1	(2)	7.8	(4)	7.6	(5)	5.8	(6)
Capacity Earnings	16.5	(3)	15.6	(5)	16.3	(4)	19.9	(1)	15.5	(6)	17.3	(2)
Full Employment	24.1	(2)	20.9	(6)	26.9	(1)	23.4	(4)	21.5	(5)	24.0	(3)
Adequate Employment	35.9	(2)	34.6	(4)	34.9	(3)	40.4	(1)	30.0	(6)	30.2	(5)
Enhanced Capacity	44.4	(3)	45.0	(2)	43.2	(4)	48.3	(1)	38.5	(5)	37.8	(6)

Table 5.17. (Continued)

	NATIONAL AVERAGE		GEORGIA		NORTH CAROLINA		OHIO		CALIFORNIA		NEW YORK	
	Indicator	Rank	Indicator	Rank	Indicator	Rank	Indicator	Rank	Indicator	Rank	Indicator	Rank
Percent Reduction In IFE Deficit From Augmentation												
Enhanced Earnings	7.7	(5)	8.3	(2)	10.4	(1)	6.5	(6)	8.2	(3)	7.8	(4)
Capacity Earnings	19.6	(3)	16.8	(5)	16.6	(6)	20.7	(2)	19.0	(4)	21.9	(1)
Full Employment	30.1	(3)	26.6	(6)	26.7	(5)	30.6	(2)	29.1	(4)	32.4	(1)
Adequate Employment	40.7	(3)	42.7	(2)	36.9	(4)	46.0	(1)	36.4	(5)	36.1	(6)
Enhanced Capacity	47.3	(3)	49.9	(2)	44.9	(4)	51.4	(1)	43.6	(5)	42.9	(6)
Work Experience Pattern Distribution												
Total Unemployed	15.8	(4)	13.9	(6)	14.8	(5)	15.8	(3)	17.0	(1)	15.9	(2)
Not Employed	1.7	(4)	1.8	(3)	1.6	(6)	1.8	(2)	1.6	(5)	2.2	(1)
Mostly Unemployed	1.4	(3)	1.2	(6)	1.3	(5)	1.3	(4)	1.5	(2)	1.7	(1)
Mixed	3.3	(3)	3.2	(5)	3.2	(5)	3.2	(5)	3.5	(2)	4.1	(1)
Mostly Employed	9.4	(3)	7.8	(6)	8.6	(4)	9.6	(2)	10.5	(1)	7.9	(5)
Total Employed	84.2	(3)	86.1	(1)	85.2	(2)	84.2	(4)	83.0	(6)	84.1	(5)
Involuntary Part-Time	6.1	(3)	6.7	(2)	7.8	(1)	5.9	(4)	5.7	(5)	5.2	(6)
Voluntary Part-Time	23.1	(2)	21.4	(4)	21.9	(3)	20.8	(5)	23.3	(1)	18.2	(6)
Employed Full-Time	55.0	(5)	57.8	(2)	55.5	(4)	57.5	(3)	54.0	(6)	60.6	(1)

Table 5.18. VARYING WORK EXPERIENCE PATTERNS AMONG TOTAL WORK FORCE PARTICIPANTS IN SEVERE HARDSHIP IN 1979 FOR FIVE STATES AND THE NATION

IIE Incidence

	National	Georgia	North Carolina	Ohio	California	New York
Total Unemployed	53.5%	59.8%	61.8%	49.6%	48.8%	51.0%
Not Employed	99.4	100.0	100.0	100.0	97.0	100.0
Mostly Unemployed	95.1	100.0	100.0	90.3	94.2	94.8
Mixed	69.1	70.1	75.0	68.5	63.6	68.9
Mostly Employed	33.5	40.0	44.2	28.5	30.3	30.8
Total Employed	18.7	20.7	19.3	17.4	14.6	14.8
Involuntary Part-Time	44.6	52.1	45.9	45.0	31.7	53.5
Voluntary Part-Time	32.6	33.9	29.2	35.5	26.6	28.5
Employed Full-Time	10.0	12.1	11.7	8.0	7.6	7.4

IIE Share

	National	Georgia	North Carolina	Ohio	California	New York
Total Unemployed	34.9	31.9	35.7	34.8	40.8	42.1
Not Employed	7.0	5.5	6.3	7.9	7.4	10.4
Mostly Unemployed	5.4	5.5	5.1	5.1	6.8	7.4
Mixed	9.5	7.6	9.3	9.6	10.8	13.0
Mostly Employed	13.0	8.9	14.9	12.2	15.6	11.4
Total Employed	65.1	68.1	64.3	65.2	59.2	57.9
Involuntary Part-Time	11.3	14.4	14.0	11.8	8.9	13.0
Voluntary Part-Time	31.1	30.6	25.0	32.9	30.4	24.1
Employed Full-Time	22.7	27.4	25.2	20.5	20.2	20.9

IIE Deficit Share

	National	Georgia	North Carolina	Ohio	California	New York
Total Unemployed	40.5	37.6	39.8	38.7	35.2	50.7
Not Employed	7.5	4.7	4.2	9.4	7.5	12.4
Mostly Unemployed	10.9	10.7	10.3	9.2	12.6	16.0
Mixed	11.4	12.5	11.4	11.2	13.1	13.8
Mostly Employed	10.5	9.7	14.0	8.8	12.0	8.5
Total Employed	59.8	62.4	60.2	61.3	54.8	49.3
Involuntary Part-Time	11.2	12.7	15.5	11.8	9.1	12.2
Voluntary Part-Time	17.9	18.6	15.5	17.2	19.6	12.2
Employed Full-Time	30.6	31.1	29.3	32.3	26.1	24.9

Table 5.18. (Continued)

IFE Incidence

	National	Georgia	North Carolina	Ohio	California	New York
Total Unemployed	22.8%	25.5%	26.2%	17.8%	20.8%	20.2%
Not Employed	46.8	39.3	33.4	44.1	49.8	46.4
Mostly Unemployed	42.4	58.9	52.7	32.9	37.6	34.9
Mixed	28.1	30.8	29.1	20.6	21.6	26.2
Mostly Employed	13.7	14.8	19.6	10.1	13.7	12.4
Total Employed	9.2	10.8	10.6	7.9	8.3	8.3
Involuntary Part-Time	19.8	26.9	20.7	19.3	17.4	27.3
Voluntary Part-Time	17.5	18.4	21.0	16.4	16.6	18.3
Employed Full-Time	4.5	6.1	5.0	3.6	3.8	3.6

IFE Share

	National	Georgia	North Carolina	Ohio	California	New York
Total Unemployed	31.7	27.5	30.0	29.7	33.7	34.5
Not Employed	7.0	5.5	4.2	8.3	7.4	9.7
Mostly Unemployed	5.1	5.5	5.4	4.4	5.3	5.5
Mixed	8.3	7.6	7.2	6.9	7.2	10.0
Mostly Employed	11.3	8.9	13.2	10.2	13.8	9.3
Total Employed	68.3	72.5	70.0	70.7	66.3	65.5
Involuntary Part-Time	10.7	14.4	12.6	12.0	9.5	13.4
Voluntary Part-Time	35.6	30.6	35.8	36.2	36.9	31.4
Employed Full-Time	20.0	27.4	21.6	22.0	19.9	20.7

IFE Deficit Share

	National	Georgia	North Carolina	Ohio	California	New York
Total Unemployed	36.2	31.7	32.6	32.6	38.5	39.2
Not Employed	12.3	6.5	3.8	12.2	13.4	16.3
Mostly Unemployed	7.1	9.6	10.6	5.0	6.2	6.7
Mixed	7.9	7.2	5.7	8.1	6.6	9.3
Mostly Employed	8.9	8.3	12.5	7.4	12.3	6.9
Total Employed	63.8	68.3	67.4	67.4	61.5	60.8
Involuntary Part-Time	11.2	15.6	13.0	16.0	8.7	15.2
Voluntary Part-Time	32.3	30.6	33.2	29.8	35.9	28.1
Employed Full-Time	20.3	22.3	21.2	22.6	16.9	17.5

Table 5.18. (Continued)

IFI Incidence

	National	Georgia	North Carolina	Ohio	California	New York
Total Unemployed	14.2%	7.5%	15.5%	11.6%	13.6%	14.2%
Not Employed	31.6	28.6	21.2	20.3	37.2	31.4
Mostly Unemployed	26.3	33.6	31.7	24.0	25.2	20.2
Mixed	16.0	17.0	19.2	15.0	12.3	15.1
Mostly Employed	8.6	12.6	10.4	7.3	9.0	7.7
Total Employed	4.5	6.6	6.6	3.8	4.1	3.7
Involuntary Part-Time	11.4	21.2	18.3	12.2	11.3	12.4
Voluntary Part-Time	6.9	9.9	11.2	5.6	6.6	7.0
Employed Full-Time	2.7	3.6	3.1	2.2	2.2	2.0

IFI Share

	National	Georgia	North Carolina	Ohio	California	New York
Total Unemployed	37.1	30.2	28.6	36.7	40.7	42.0
Not Employed	8.9	6.4	4.3	7.2	10.2	13.0
Mostly Unemployed	6.0	5.1	5.3	6.1	6.5	6.3
Mixed	8.9	6.7	7.8	9.4	7.5	11.4
Mostly Employed	13.3	12.1	11.4	14.0	16.6	11.3
Total Employed	62.9	69.8	71.4	63.3	59.3	58.0
Involuntary Part-Time	11.6	18.1	18.2	14.3	11.3	12.0
Voluntary Part-Time	26.6	26.1	31.3	23.2	26.9	23.8
Employed Full-Time	24.8	25.6	21.6	25.7	21.1	22.0

IFI Deficit Share

	National	Georgia	North Carolina	Ohio	California	New York
Total Unemployed	39.8	33.2	32.4	35.5	41.8	42.2
Not Employed	12.7	6.5	5.1	9.8	14.5	17.9
Mostly Unemployed	7.7	7.7	7.2	7.8	6.0	6.6
Mixed	8.5	8.7	6.8	9.2	7.4	9.6
Mostly Employed	10.9	10.3	13.4	8.6	13.4	8.0
Total Employed	60.2	66.8	67.6	64.5	58.2	57.8
Involuntary Part-Time	12.4	20.7	19.8	19.6	12.6	13.8
Voluntary Part-Time	22.7	24.8	24.5	16.1	26.1	21.3
Employed Full-Time	25.1	21.3	23.3	28.8	19.5	22.8

hardship IIE and 6.2 percent of the IFE for the total work force, compared to 11.3 and 10.6 percent nationwide, and 9.2 percent for both in Georgia. On the other hand, the unemployed represented 14.9 percent of the North Carolina IIE and 13.2 percent of its IFE compared to 8.9 percent of both the IIE and IFE counts in Georgia. IIE and IFE rates for the intermittently unemployed who were jobless less than a third of their weeks in the work force were higher in North Carolina than elsewhere.

The safety net in North Carolina was far more effective than in Georgia and compared favorably with California and Ohio. Over two-fifths of North Carolina's IFI Net-of-Transfers escaped poverty by the receipt of cash and in-kind aid, a percentage exceeded only by New York among the sample states.

Finally, both intermediate and moderate hardship were relatively more prevalent compared to severe hardship. Put another way, there were comparatively more persons just above the severe hardship cutoff compared to those falling below.

Based on these data, North Carolina should probably put relatively more emphasis on helping the less-than-full-year workers, the short-term unemployed and those employed part-time involuntarily. The state should serve relatively more secondary family earners. It might be politically prudent to offer less intensive services to greater numbers in order not to lift workers and families from just below severe hardship to a level significantly ahead of those just above severe hardship, since there is already a concentration just above the severe hardship margin.

Ohio: The severe hardship IFE and IFI rates in 1979 were lower in Ohio than in any of the other states in the sample, but the average IIE and IFE Deficits of those in hardship were quite high. A larger share of the persons in Ohio's IFE had Inadequate Individual Earnings than in the other states, so that the elimination of individual earnings problems as simulated by Adequate Employment and Enhanced Capacity augmentation would have substantial impacts in reducing the Ohio IFE and the IFE Deficit—greater than in any of the other states.

Moderate and intermediate hardship were also low in Ohio, both relative to other states and relative to the Ohio severe hardship total. Put another way, there were proportionately fewer Ohio work force participants just above the severe hardship level who would be affected by measures to substantially upgrade those with the most severe labor market problems.

California: A relatively large portion of the California work force experienced unemployment, mostly of a short-term nature. The severe hardship IIE and IFE incidence rates were extremely low among work force participants employed all weeks, so that the unemployed accounted for a large share of the IFE and the IIE. Many of these individuals in hardship participated less than full-year. While the hardship incidence rates were extremely low among Calfornia's full-year workers, they were comparatively high among less than full-year participants. California was lowest among the states in the percentage of the IFE represented by full-time, full-year workers, while the full-year participants who were predominantly unemployed represented only 9.6 percent of the California IFE, compared to 10.6 percent of the national IFE.

While the average deficits of persons in the IIE and IFE were comparatively low, the Earnings Supplementation Rate-Transfers, as well as the percentage reduction in the IFI Net-of-Transfers resulting from cash and in-kind aid, were only slightly above those in Georgia. California cannot be characterized as generous to its working poor.

Based on these data, California should focus relatively more on job creation for the short-term unemployed. But the basic problem is one of limited work force participation relative to family income needs. The percent of the IFE who had Inadequate Individual Earnings was lower in California than any other state, and providing all individuals in the severe hardship IFE with minimally adequate employment would have reduced the IFE by only 30.0 percent compared to the 35.9 percent drop in the IFE nationwide with Adequate Employment augmentation. Transfer improvements, perhaps rewarding work force attachment, would be necessary to substantially reduce the IFI.

New York: Hardship rates were relatively low in New York, particularly among full-year workers and those employed full-time all weeks in the work force. But New York had a high unemployment level, and a particularly large share of its unemployed were jobless more than a third of their weeks in the work force. The predominantly unemployed accounted for 8.0 percent of the New York work force compared to 6.4 percent of the national work force, and 25.2 percent of New York's severe hardship IFE compared to 20.4 percent of the national IFE. The average IFE Deficit was, therefore, quite high. Capacity Earnings and Full Employment augmentation, i.e., the augmentation strategies focused on unemployment problems, had a much more significant relative impact in New York than elsewhere in the nation. Despite the high average IFE Deficit, the Earnings Supplementation Rate-Transfers was higher in New York than any of the other states.

In order to address these conditions, New York should probably put more emphasis on job creation and significant training for the long-term unemployed from low-income families. Given the high transfer levels, job creation could provide a relatively effective alternative to dependency.

The Practicality of These Applications

In concept, then, the hardship measures, particularly the severe hardship IFE and the IFE Deficit, would be ideal as a basis for allocating, targeting and strategizing the use of resources addressed to the unemployed and underemployed from low-income families. There are, however, some practical constraints, and these could become quite formidable when combined with the political constraints. Unemployment rates for states and labor market areas are derived from the Current Population Survey. There is an accepted--if technically questionable--method of adjusting the CPS with decennial Census data and annual unemployment insurance and other data in order to derive estimates for labor market areas where the CPS sample alone is too small to make reliable estimates. Similar adjustment procedures could be derived to estimate hardship shares for all states and labor market areas. However, the unemployment rates would be inherently more dependable estimates because they are based on the average of the monthly CPS counts rather than a once-a-year survey.

The poverty rates for states and substate areas are no more dependable than the hardship rates, since they are also derived from the March Current Population Survey. Like the hardship measures, they understate the severity of problems in high-cost areas because there is no adjustment for cost variations other than the 15 percent lower poverty levels used for rural areas. Yet the inadequacies of the uniform poverty levels were already accepted before large amounts of funds were allocated by poverty-based formulae. Were a hardship approach to be seriously considered, the cost variation issue would be opened up again by areas threatened with a reduction in funds. Moreover, an allocation formula which weights both poverty and unemployment rates in some sense balances the estimation problems, since areas with low costs and high poverty rates probably have more disguised unemployment, so that their gains under one measurement anomaly are offset by their losses under another.

Both the poverty and hardship measures could be improved by adopting an area cost-of-living adjustment as is used in the Bureau of Labor Statistics lower living standard budget. But what is needed in addition is an expansion of the annual survey of work experience and income in order to provide more accurate estimates for states and subareas. Until cost variations are adopted in poverty and hardship measures, and statistical basis for state and local estimates improved, it is almost assured that the losers under a hardship allocation scheme would thwart any change, defending the familiar, if flawed, unemployment and poverty allocation procedures.

The hardship data could, however, be utilized to determine the aggregate annual funding levels. Both the poverty and annual average unemployment rates presumably considered in the annual budget process have unavoidable lags, so that "old" data must be used in projecting the budget level for the coming year. Yet hardship measures tend to fluctuate less than unemployment rates, so that this lag is of less consequence. In fact, a main advantage of the hardship formulation would be to concentrate attention on continuing structural problems. Realistically, it does not matter much which conceptual and measurement basis is used, because there is little evidence that need levels or changes are the primary determinants of congressional budgeting decisions.

The hardship measures would be of more use in prioritizing target groups nationally and locally and in determining intervention strategies. The 1980 census and the CPS could be combined to achieve estimates and disaggregations for states and large substate labor market areas. These data could be extremely useful for planning. While need should not be the only rationale for prioritizing target groups, the hardship measures are more meaningful than either unemployment or poverty to the extent need is considered the determining factor in targeting.

In summary, the national hardship data could be useful for national budgetary decisions. With refinements, including cost-of-living adjustments, disaggregated data could serve as the basis for allocating funds for state and labor market areas, although formidable political obstacles would have to be overcome. They would be useful for state and labor market area planning. While the CPS data could only be disaggregated adequately for the larger states, variants of the measures can be calculated from the 1980 census information.

Notes

1. *Report of the Minimum Wage Study Commission* (Washington: U.S. Government Printing Office, 1981), pp. 18-19.

2. *Money Income in 1975 of Families and Persons in the United States*, Series P-60, No. 105 (Washington: U.S. Government Printing Office, 1976); and *Money Income of Families and Persons in the United States: 1979*, Series P-60, No. 124 (Washington: U.S. Government Printing Office, 1981).

3. Sar A. Levitan, *Programs in Aid of the Poor for the 1980s* (Baltimore, Md.: The Johns Hopkins University Press, 1981).

4. *Money Income in 1975 of Families and Persons in the United States*, op. cit.; and *Money Income of Families and Persons in the United States:* op. cit.

5. *Social Security Bulletin*, June 1982, pp. 50-51; and *Employment and Training Report of the President, 1981* (Washington: U.S. Government Printing Office, 1981), p. 119.

6. *Money Income in 1975 of Families and Persons in the United States*, op. cit.; and *Money Income of Families and Persons in the United States:* op. cit.

7. *Social Security Bulletin*, June 1981, p. 42.

8. To escape poverty, the real average benefit per recipient in recipient families must increase as average family size declines, since the per person poverty level is larger in smaller families. For instance, the 1979 per person poverty level for one adult and one child was $2,467, compared to $1,935 for one parent and two children and $1,839 for one parent and three children.

CHAPTER 6. HARDSHIP--A MATTER OF PERSPECTIVE

Who Needs New Measures?

A Parable

An ancient parable recounts the story of six blind men of Hindustan who come upon an elephant in the road. One grasps a tusk and thinks it a spear; the next a knee which he presumes to be a tree; two others touch the trunk and tail, which to them feel like a snake and a rope; the fifth brushes against the elephant's ear which seems like a fan; while the last bumps into the belly and thinks he has hit a wall. Each believes his own perception is reality, and they walk on arguing vehemently whether an "elephant" is like a spear, a tree, a rope, a snake, a fan or a wall:

> These men of Hindustan
> Disputed loud and long,
> Each of his own opinion,
> Exceedingly stiff and strong.
> Though each was partly right,
> And all were in the wrong.

Policymakers, technical experts and laymen who seek to understand and improve the structure and operations of the labor market to assure that it provides adequately for those willing and able to work are, in many ways, like these blind men. Unable to encompass reality, we must grope, using statistical measures to determine the size, shape and texture of each appendage. Depending on what we touch and how we feel, as well as our preconceptions and referents, we may reach quite different judgments about the nature of the beast.

Most often we encounter the underbelly of the labor market--its inability to provide jobs for all those wanting to work. We focus on the unemployment problem and the unemployment measures, reasoning, correctly, that a person without work is a person without a paycheck, so that joblessness affects well-being. Where unemployment is concentrated among certain groups or areas, and when it rises nationwide, there is no doubt that, on average, the jobless, their families and their communities suffer. For most of us, this is all we understand about the labor market, and perhaps all we need to know.

Others focus on the underpinnings rather than the underbelly, considering unemployment only a problem when it affects household heads and primary breadwinners. An increasing share of the jobless are secondary family earners, and their joblessness may have minimal consequences for family well-being. Without the goad of dire necessity, some workers may be lacksadaisical in their search for jobs. It might reasonably be argued from this perspective that the aggregate unemployment statistics provide a very bloated impression of the hardship which prevails among work force participants.

Some of us concentrate only on the tail of unemployment which remains after transfers and other nonearned income have cushioned its negative earnings impacts. In view of the explosive growth of transfers and in-kind aid, it is often assumed that the truly needy among the unemployed will be protected against the consequences of joblessness. Some would wag the elephant by the tail--arguing that unemployment is high because the available benefits encourage malingering, and that a reduction in the benefits would, in fact, trim the fat from the underbelly.

Those who meet the elephant head-on may perceive it to be a quite different animal. Appended to the corpus of measured unemployment are a number of individuals who move in and out of the labor force in response to their changing employment prospects. Some individuals who are not looking for work report that they would take jobs if any were available. Others turn their attention to school or housekeeping when jobs are scarce. Because they are not actively looking for work, or are presumed unavailable because of other activities, they are not counted in the official unemployment statistics even though experience shows that they will work when jobs become more available. There are also many workers who want full-time employment but can find only part-time jobs. Though less palpable or stable than the other parts of the elephant, these appendages are large and growing relative to measured unemployment.

Just as the tusk is the elephant's most dangerous feature, it might be argued that wages, not unemployment, are the pointed factor in determining well-being. If earnings rates are high enough, even long periods of joblessness can be weathered. If pay is low, even full-time work will not provide an adequate standard of living. The majority of work force participants are fully employed whether the job market is good or bad, so that their well-being is determined more by wage levels than unemployment levels. Low wages are more dangerous still when combined with intermittent or involuntary part-time employment, and those who are gored by low earnings are also most likely to be trampled by involuntary idleness.

The trunk of the elephant, used for foraging and feeding, may be its most characteristic and certainly its most vital feature. A large elephant must have a longer and stronger trunk, and must keep it constantly at work, to assure sustenance. Likewise, the adequacy of earnings depends on the size and composition of the household which must be supported. The adequacy of household earnings depends not only on hourly wage levels, but also on the number of earners and their hours of availability. The amount of work which is needed depends on whether food is being provided from income other than earnings. Those who focus on the trunk of the labor market problem have little interest in wage levels or earnings statistics alone, but concentrate on the poverty numbers which tell whether family units of differing composition are able to earn enough, or adequately supplement earnings, in order to maintain well-being.

Like the blind men in the parable, we are prone to "disputing loud and long" that the part of the elephant we touch, measure, or care about, is, in truth, its essence. And like those men of Hindustan, each of us is partly right. Unemployment does have serious consequences for many of its victims. Hardship is prevalent when the unemployment rate is high, and hardship rises when joblessness increases. Yet it is also true that many of the unemployed suffer little as a result of their idleness because the earnings of other family members, or transfer payments and other earnings supplements, mitigate the consequences. This is not to deny that many who are excluded from the unemployment counts want to be and could be more self-sufficient, or that many with jobs are paid so little that they cannot afford the barest essentials. Poverty rises when wages do not keep pace with inflation, when unemployment increases and when individuals are discouraged and leave the labor force, so that the poverty rate reflects the severity of labor market problems.

But also like the men of Hindustan, each of us who concentrates on only a part of the animal can never grasp its totality. In order to determine who suffers seriously as a result of labor market problems, we must look at hidden as well as measured unemployment, and earnings as well as unemployment. Individual earning levels do not mean much unless considered in light of breadwinning responsibilities and family status. The well-being of workers depends on whether any earnings shortfalls are filled by transfers and other supplements. Yet the poverty data do not provide a really good picture of the consequences of labor market problems because so many of the poor cannot or do not work, while many of those who escape poverty through the receipt of transfers and other income would or could be more self-sufficient if they were more successful in the labor market.

Just as the blind men might have reasoned together to integrate their separate perceptions, it is possible to simultaneously consider all the detailed statistics on income levels and sources, wages, poverty, work attachment and family status, in order to get a better sense of the dimensions, causes and cures for labor market-related hardship. Yet few have the patience or capability to piece together these disparate statistics. Thus, the hardship measurement system was developed to provide a unifying perspective by restructuring the data elements and concepts of existing data sets within a framework designed specifically to measure the welfare consequences of labor market problems.

All Measures Are Arbitrary

It is not always easy to accept one's limitations. Many of us would rather continue groping than admit that our vision is limited and that what we perceive is a distortion of reality. It is no surprise, then, that new measures requiring new perspectives are rarely greeted with easy acceptance. The labor force and poverty measures, now entrenched and resistant to change, were once as controversial and confusing as the hardship notions may seem today. The unemployment rate has become so commonplace that we sometimes forget that "unemployment" was neither defined, in the current sense, nor reliably measured, until 1940. In fact, prevailing economic theory prior to the Great Depression actually denied its existence. Workers without jobs were supposed to bid down the wage rate until all were employed for less pay, so that any joblessness was voluntary, reflecting wage rigidities, or else merely transitory. It took the massive dislocations of the 1930s to upset this neoclassicial, full-employment equilibrium theory. With at least one of every four labor force participants unable to find a job--most of whom were previously stable workers--unemployment could not be written off as a temporary aberration or the fault of those standing in breadlines.

When President Roosevelt took office to provide a New Deal, the pervasiveness of unemployment was undeniable, but the exact dimensions of the problem were uncertain. The National Industrial Conference Board estimated that 2.9 million persons were unemployed in 1930, while the Works Progress Administration studies put the figure at 4.8 million. Estimates in 1936 ranged between 5.4 and 8.1 million. This uncertainty reflected the lack of agreement about how to define unemployment and the absence of any systematic efforts to measure it. Prior to the 1930 census, the only labor force data was a decennial count of "gainful workers." Individuals were asked what jobs they normally held when they worked. Those looking for work but without previous job experience were not counted as gainful workers, while those without jobs or forced to accept employment in a different line of work were included as gainful workers in their usual occupation. The aim was to measure the productive work force rather than variations in employment or unemployment, since it was assumed that all those seeking jobs would be fully employed in their usual line of work if they were flexible in their wage demands. In the Great Depression, however, when millions were willing and able to work at almost any wage and the most menial jobs, the gainful worker count was of little relevance. Necessity proved the mother of statistical invention, and one of the first tasks of the Works Progress Administration was a national post-card registration of the unemployed in 1937 and the initiation of a monthly household survey in 1939. Three years later, responsibility for the monthly survey was transferred to the Census Bureau, where sophisticated sampling techniques were gradually implemented and improved. In these surveys, persons 14 years of age and over in the noninstitutional population were classified as either "employed," "unemployed," or "not in the labor force." To be counted as "employed," the individual had to have worked for pay at least one hour during the preceding week, or for 15 hours without pay in a family enterprise. Those with jobs but not working because of illness, vacation, bad weather, a strike, or a layoff of no more than 30 days, were included with the employed, on the assumption that they had some job attachment. The unemployed were those not employed, who were willing and able to work, and had looked for a job in the last month.

Critics of these labor market definitions charged that they were both arbitrary and inaccurate. A major issue was their dependence on the household member's subjective assessment of willingness and ability to work, and the self-reporting of job search. It was noted that higher wages, or reduced income, or increased job availability, might all increase the desire to hold a job, consequently affecting reported levels of unemployment. The subjectivity of the measures was considered especially problematic for secondary family earners. To the extent that their incomes were not vital for their families' survival, wives and teenagers might easily be discouraged by bad times. On the other hand, other family members might seek work if the head lost his or her job. Thus, the size of the labor force would change and so would the measured unemployment rate, obscuring the distinction between unemployment and nonparticipation.

There were many early critics who charged that the unemployment measures understated the degree of involuntary idleness. Workers employed part-time but wanting full-time jobs were counted as employed even if they worked only one hour. Thus, the worker doing a few odd jobs because of the dearth of full-time positions would be included among the employed. It was also noted that self-employment might disguise unemployment, as persons wanting wage-paying jobs would be absorbed into family enterprises, such as farms. The employment measure did not differentiate between adequate and substandard employment. Only hours and not types of work were considered; only the receipt of wages and not their levels. A worker would be counted as employed even if he or she were skilled but working in an unskilled job, doing "make-work" or eking out a meager living despite full-time employment.

There was a running debate about data gathering techniques and the purity of monthly surveys. The issue always heated up in bad times. For instance, with the sluggish decline in unemployment from its 1958 post-War peak, the messenger was blamed for the message. The Joint Economic Committee issued analyses of frictional and structural unemployment in 1959 and 1960, and another on employment concepts in 1961. At the other extreme, a Reader's Digest article attacked the data and the statisticians, asserting that unemployment figures were more a creation of government bureaucrats than a reflection of real economic conditions.

But more was involved than political posturing or technical debate over the fine points to divert attention from the stark reality of unemployment. Important changes had occurred in the labor market and new theoretical perspectives and public policy issues had emerged over the two decades since the labor market statistics had been introduced. The question was not only whether labor market statistics provided embarrassing proof of the slow recovery, but also whether they were appropriate after twenty years of labor market changes.

One major development was the increase in secondary workers. Female labor force participation, which jumped dramatically in World War II, continued upward throughout the 1950s. Though the products of the post-war baby boom had not entered the labor force by 1960, structural changes were occurring, intensifying the relative unemployment problems of teenagers. The average unemployment rate of youths aged 16 to 19 years rose from 2.3 times the overall rate in 1950 to 2.7 times as high in 1960. In 1954, males age 20 years and over accounted for 65 percent of the labor force and 58 percent of the unemployed. Six years later, the adult male shares had dropped to 62 percent and 54 percent, respectively.

Several other structural problems emerged in the late 1950s. There was an apparent acceleration of technological change. The impacts were concentrated geographically as well as socioeconomically, intensifying structural problems in the match-up of labor supply and demand. Depressed areas were an increasing concern. Most significantly, the disparity between the unemployment rates of whites and blacks increased. In 1948, the unemployment rate for nonwhites was 1.7 times that for whites. It rose to 2.0 times as high in 1954, and 2.2 times by 1959. The major factor in this increase was the exodus of rural and frequently underemployed blacks to the cities, where they became more visible as unemployed and where they also came into direct and uneven competition with whites for available jobs.

It was also becoming apparent by the late 1950s that millions of workers, in addition to the blacks and the technologically displaced, were unable to earn an adequate livelihood. Poverty was not new, but it remained to be "discovered." As with unemployment three decades earlier, there were no agreed definitions of what constituted deprivation and no dependable statistics measuring its dimensions, so that many were willing to believe that poverty did not exist. It was not until 1964 that Mollie Orshansky of the Social Security Administration developed a generally accepted poverty index derived by multiplying the costs of a nutritionally minimum diet by a factor of three based on crude estimates of the proportion of low income budgets spent for food. These poverty measures were adopted as logistical and statistical support for the War on Poverty-- mapping its strategy, targeting its resources and benchmarking its progress.

Like the unemployment concepts, these measures generated a good deal of controversy. There was much debate over whether the poverty line really constituted the margin of deprivation. The War on Poverty's critics noted that the U.S. poverty standards exceeded the average living standards in most of the world. With the introduction of Medicaid in the mid-1960s, and the expansion of housing programs later in the decade, detractors argued that many needs were being met by in-kind aid, reducing cash requirements so that the poverty counts overstated the dimensions of deprivation. Other critics with a more liberal disposition charged that the poverty standards had been wrongly defined in absolute rather than relative terms simply to demonstrate progress in the War on Poverty as the nation's living standards rose over time. Poverty warriors felt that the poverty definition was too strict, and that the "near poor" with incomes 125 percent of the poverty thresholds should have been included in the universe of need.

The poverty measures were challenged on a range of technical grounds. Based on a once-a-year survey no larger than the monthly survey used to generate labor force statistics, the poverty numbers were of less reliability than annual average labor force estimates. There was serious underreporting of income, particularly nonearned income including cash transfers. The measures did not adjust for regional cost-of-living differences other than by lowering the poverty lines a fixed percent for residents of rural areas. Poverty standards were adjusted each year by the cost-of-living index, but it was debatable whether the CPI reflected the costs of the items in a poverty level "market basket."

Over time, however, the labor force and poverty measures gradually gained acceptance. Two national commissions were appointed by Presidents Kennedy and Carter to assess the challenges to the labor force statistics. For the most part, these commissions endorsed both the concepts and the data gathering procedures, calling for only minor refinements and increased disaggregations. The Bureau of Labor Statistics tried to overcome some of the shortcomings of the poverty measures by developing a lower living standard budget based on surveys of consumption patterns of low income families and the costs in different areas of the country. While these new standards gained some acceptance and application, the poverty measure remained the primary indicator of deprivation. In other words, despite the arbitrariness of the concepts, despite continuing debate over the underlying normative issues, statistical procedures and technical details, the poverty and labor force measures have become familiar through usage, enshrined in the law, incorporated into countless textbooks, theories and models, and packaged for public consumption by the media.

The Resistance to Hardship Measures

Ironically, as the poverty and labor force statistics became accepted and enshrined, secular changes in the labor market and in the social welfare system were continuing to undermine their effectiveness for one of their primary applications--measuring the welfare consequences of labor market problems. In the 1960s and early 1970s, the post-war babies and their mothers flooded into the labor market, increasing the share of the unemployed who were second and third family earners while dramatically expanding part-time employment and reducing poverty by increased family work participation. Cash transfers and in-kind aid grew rapidly in the 1960s and early 1970s, extending the overlap between work and welfare. The riots in Watts in 1965, followed by similar disturbances in other cities, focused national attention on the structural labor market problems which had not been eliminated by a booming economy. The National Advisory Commission on Civil Disorders found that "more than 20 percent of the rioters in Detroit were unemployed and many who were employed held intermittent, low status, unskilled jobs which they regarded as below their education and ability." The Commission concluded that "pervasive unemployment and underemployment are the most persistent and serious grievances of minority areas. They are inextricably linked to the problems of civil disorders." The War on Poverty also focused attention on those at the end of the labor queue who continued to experience difficulties even in a full employment economy. The newly introduced poverty data revealed that many families remained poor despite quite substantial work effort.

Thus, in 1966, President Johnson directed the Department of Labor to develop "subemployment" statistics which would measure not only the availability of employment, but its adequacy in providing for self-support and family maintenance. Subemployment measures for poverty areas were developed in 1967 and national estimates were presented in the 1968 Manpower Report of the President. The Comprehensive Employment and Training Act of 1973 required the Department of Labor and its Bureau of Labor Statistics to calculate and publish measures assessing the adequacy of employment and earnings. The 1976 CETA amendments, which established the National Commission on Employment and Unemployment Statistics, charged NCEUS with developing and refining hardship measures. The 1978 CETA amendments repeated the instruction to the Department of Labor to develop and publish such measures.

Despite the increasing need for hardship measures, as well as repeated legislative and administrative prodding, we remain today without accepted and regularly published statistics measuring the welfare consequences of labor market problems. The resistance to hardship measures has been as great, or greater, than the earlier resistance to unemployment and poverty measures.

Just as the unemployment measures were resisted because they would document that millions were involuntarily idle, and the poverty measures were resisted because they would document the existence of deprivation in our affluent nation, hardship measures are opposed because they will show that there are millions of Americans, both employed and unemployed, who are failing in or are failed by the labor market despite their significant work effort. To actually measure the extent of such problems would shatter the ideological detente between conservative pundits who criticize the labor force and poverty data for the many ways the numbers overstate problems, and the liberal experts who can point to the many ways in which existing measures understate the dimensions and degree of suffering. Though the ideology of the left and the right coincide on the notion of targeting resources to those most in need, the political and practical interests of both conservatives and liberals are better served when resources are widely dispersed. Thus, it is convenient to accept the unemployment rate as the primary measure of labor market problems—since its rise to publicly unacceptable levels usually means that mobilization occurs only when the middle class is being hurt—and to adopt the poverty measures as a basis for transfers, which are focused primarily on the nonworking poor, mainly the oldsters, who are a potent political force.

However, the intransigence towards hardship measures resulted more from entropy than ideology. The unemployment measures and concepts were adopted in a statistical vacuum. In the 1930s there were hundreds—not millions—of college graduates who had studied the gainful worker concept and its underlying neoclassical economic theory. Few of these scholars had staked their academic careers on quantitative interpretations of reality. There were no computers or econometric models demanding an unvarying statistical diet. Reporters did not crowd into the Department of Labor each month to get a hot story about the latest body count. By the time the poverty measures were introduced, statistics, statistical analyses and statistical analysts were already increasing in prominence. Yet income data and their applications were still relatively virgin territory. War had not yet been declared on deprivation, and billions of dollars did not rest on the levels and fluctuations of area poverty and unemployment rates.

Today, any new set of measures faces the resistance of a formidable array of vested interests—including the academicians who have developed their quantitative models around poverty and unemployment data, the statisticians who have spent their lives refining current measures, the elected officials and client groups who stand to lose money if alternative measures are used in resource allocation, the press and television commentators who can make a story each month from statistical blips in the unemployment rate, and the informed public, which has a general notion of what poverty and unemployment mean, and has little interest in learning a new statistical language.

There are also formidable problems inherent to hardship measurement. Complexity is unavoidable since the measures must consider underemployment as well as unemployment, both earned and nonearned income, individual earnings alone but also in relation to family size and needs, as well as both individual and family earnings in light of work force attachment.

As the National Commission on Employment and Unemployment Statistics concluded: "It is not realistic to try to incorporate all the dimensions into a summary survey statistic such as the unemployment rate and the poverty rate. A single indicator cannot give individual attention to the components of labor market-related hardship . . ., deal with multiple classifications of labor force status during a year, or give separate attention to the individual's status or to his or her family's economic status."

The hardship measures proposed in this volume, therefore, include three primary indicators: one counting the work force participants with inadequate individual earnings, another counting those with inadequate family earnings, and the third counting participants with inadequate family incomes. These counts of persons falling below earnings and income standards are paralleled by measures of the size of the earnings and income shortfalls, yielding an indication of the severity as well as incidence of hardship. Because of the difficulty, if not impossibility, of achieving consensus on standards of earnings and income adequacy, three different sets of hardship standards are utilized. Likewise, because of disagreement about the duration of work attachment which demonstrates a "real" commitment to work, all the measures are derived for full-year and half-year, as well as total, work force participants. Variants of these baseline measures are used to address certain "what if" questions which are important for policy. Detailed disaggregations are derived, paralleling the primary disaggregations of poverty, unemployment and work experience data, in order to provide more insight into the composition and distribution of labor market-related hardship. In other words, there is no one hardship measure, but rather a comprehensive, and far from simple, measurement system.

This measurement system is composited from the same data and definitional elements utilized in the labor force and poverty statistical systems, thus subsuming the problems and controversies of each separate system. For instance, the work experience data published each year by the Bureau of Labor Statistics rely on the ability of the household member interviewed in March to accurately reconstruct the weeks of employment and unemployment, as well as the usual hours of work, of each family member over the preceding calendar year. The income data collected in this same survey, which are the basis of the poverty counts, assume that income levels and sources are accurately reported. Since there is demonstrable underreporting, adjustments must be made which may be accurate in the aggregate, but are not as accurate in allocating underreported income types to different households in the survey. The hardship data integrate the work experience information reported for each family with its income and earnings information, so that errors in either or both will be reflected in the hardship measures.

However, the complexity of the hardship measurement system, or the intractability of the technical issues, can easily be exaggerated. The hardship nomenclatures and the corresponding acronyms are unfamiliar and perhaps unwieldy, while the disaggregated hardship data are formidable in their detail. Yet for someone equally unfamiliar with labor force concepts or with income and poverty definitions, the Bureau of Labor Statistics' annual reports on work experience and monthly reports on employment and earnings, or the Bureau of Census' annual reports on income and poverty, would be just as challenging in complexity and detail.

Technical adjustments over decades were required to finetune the weighting and sampling procedures, undercount adjustments, reliability estimates and other statistical aspects of the labor force and poverty measures. This work still continues. Similar efforts will be needed over many years to assure dependable and accurate hardship statistics. The hardship measures proposed in this volume were developed to utilize information gathered in the March Current Population Survey. But the survey instrument is not sacrosanct, nor is the survey approach. A few new questions, for instance, might improve the estimates of hours of availability for work over the year. Current Population Survey procedures were developed primarily to generate statistically reliable unemployment and employment counts each month. If annual income and earnings adequacy were considered of greater importance, it might be possible to expand the sample size for the March survey, or to supplement this with an alternative sample, perhaps a mail survey instrument accompanying income tax returns.

It is understandable if many of the data gatherers and technical experts who developed and refined the current concepts and survey procedures through years of hard work are less than enthusiastic about changes, particularly in a period when budget stringencies are threatening the already existing measurement systems and when staff are unavailable to handle even the rudimentary procedures required to insure the integrity of current data systems, much less to undertake the detailed technical work necessary to refine a new measurement system. Yet the obstacles are not insurmountable. The hardship measures used in this volume cost only a few thousand dollars to tabulate from already-gathered survey data for each year. The measures certainly meet the legislative charge to the Department of Labor, as well as the recommendation of the National Commission on Employment and Unemployment Statistics "that the Bureau of Labor Statistics prepare an annual report containing measures of the different types of labor market-related economic hardships resulting from low wages, unemployment and insufficient participation in the labor force" with data presented "which refer to individuals . . . in conjunction with the family relationship and the household income status of the individual . . . ." Without disputing the need for refinements, the benefits of larger samples, or the desirability of more precise survey questions as a basis for hardship estimates, there is no doubt that hardship measurement is technically feasible and that the measurement system proposed in this volume is at least one reasonable approach.

The real issue is not the feasibility of the hardship measures, but whether they are worth the trouble. Social statistics and statistical concepts are clearly not immutable, but rather a set of conventions useful only to the extent that they describe existing conditions, organize and quantify these in light of perceived theory, and generate information needed in addressing policy issues. The labor force and poverty measures have been accepted because they have served these purposes in the past. They still may serve these purposes for those who are knowledgeable enough to integrate the detailed and disaggregated labor force and income data in light of changing family patterns and labor force participation, and the increased overlap of work and welfare. But the hardship measures seek to simplify this integration, helping blind men to see the whole of the elephant, not just its separate appendages. The true test of the proposed measurement system is whether it provides this unifying perspective, increases understanding and improves policy.

A Summary of Findings

If the blind men of Hindustan could see, they would realize that the "elephant" is not a spear, a tree, a rope, a snake, a fan or a wall. It is a large and lumbering creature, with an uneven footfall and serious consequences for those who cross its path. It can be harnessed or caged, but hardly ignored. Analogously, the new measures reveal that labor market-related hardship is an immense problem, serious in both good times and bad. The consequences of hardship are distributed unevenly, and for those affected, the burdens are serious indeed. Hardship cannot be easily eliminated. A combination of macroeconomic measures, actions targeted to structural labor market problems, and coordinated income transfer policies, are necessary to make significant progress. In almost every feature, the welfare consequences of labor market problems look different when assessed from the hardship perspective rather than from the unemployment and poverty perspectives.

The Dimensions and Distribution of Hardship

* <u>The number who suffer severe hardship as a result of labor market problems experienced during the year far exceeds average annual unemployment. While many of the unemployed are affected little by their weeks of idleness, millions of workers who are able to find jobs all weeks they are in the work force earn less than what is necessary to support themselves and their families.</u>

Because of low wages and involuntary part-time employment, in addition to unemployment, one-fourth of the 117.0 million work force participants in 1979 had annual earnings below the minimum wage multiplied by their hours of availability. This 28.3 million with Inadequate Individual Earnings dwarfed the 6.0 million annual unemployed. There were 41.0 million work force participants who earned less than 125 percent of the minimum wage for their annual hours in the work force, while a staggering 51.0 million earned less than 150 percent of the minimum wage equivalent in 1979. To put this in perspective, a family of four with the head working full-time, full-year, and a secondary worker employed half-time, full-year, would have just earned enough to maintain what the Bureau of Labor Statistics defined as a lower living standard budget if both received 150 percent of the minimum wage or $4.50 per hour in 1979.

While many of these workers with Inadequate Individual Earnings resided in families with other, better paid workers and, therefore, reasonably adequate family earnings, half lived in families with total earnings below the poverty level. There were another 4.2 million workers who earned more than the minimum wage equivalent for their hours in the work force, yet lived in families with earnings below the poverty level because of limited work force participation or large family size.

Cash transfers and other earnings supplements protected some of these low earning individuals and families from hardship. Yet among the 13.3 million with Inadequate Family Earnings in 1979, 7.1 million had Inadequate Family Income, i.e., they remained in poverty after the receipt of cash transfers and other earnings supplements. There were 10.5 million work force participants in families with incomes less than 125 percent of the poverty level, and 14.4 million in families with incomes less than 150 percent of the poverty level:

	Numbers (000)	Percent of work force	Number in hardship divided by average annual unemployment
Inadequate Individual Earnings (IIE)			
Severe Hardship: Earned less than 100 percent of the minimum wage for hours of availability.	28,269	24.2%	4.7
Intermediate Hardship: Earned less than 125 percent of the minimum wage for hours of availability.	40,961	35.0	6.9
Moderate Hardship: Earned less than 150 percent of the minimum wage for hours of availability.	51,426	44.0	8.6
Inadequate Family Earnings (IFE)			
Severe Hardship: Work force participants in families with combined earnings below the poverty level.	13,280	11.4	2.2
Intermediate Hardship: Work force participants in families with combined earnings less than 125 percent of the poverty level.	17,190	14.7	2.9
Moderate Hardship: Work force participants in families with combined earnings less than 150 percent of poverty level.	21,553	18.4	3.6
Inadequate Family Income (IFI)			
Severe Hardship: Work force participants in poor families.	7,055	6.0	1.2
Intermediate Hardship: Work force participants in families with incomes less than 125 percent of poverty level.	10,524	9.0	1.8
Moderate Hardship: Work force participants in families with incomes less than 150 percent of poverty level.	14,354	12.3	2.4

These hardship counts for the total work force included some individuals with very limited work force attachment. Yet even if concern is limited to workers participating 50 weeks or more, the numbers with inadequate earnings and incomes are sobering:

	Hardship among full-year work force participants		
	Severe (000)	Intermediate (000)	Moderate (000)
Inadequate Individual Earnings	14,248	22,047	29,442
Inadequate Family Earnings	5,675	8,088	10,981
Inadequate Family Income	3,098	5,075	7,383

<u>Many individuals in the severe hardship IIE have earnings only a few dollars below the minimum wage equivalent, and many families in the severe hardship IFE and IFI have earnings and incomes very close to the poverty level. Yet the aggregate and average deficits of persons in hardship are substantial. Unlike the unemployed, the hardship population is concentrated at the bottom of the income distribution.</u>

To raise all work force participants up to minimum wage equivalent earnings for their hours of availability would have required $52.0 billion in 1979, which represented 4.0 percent of the nation's reported wages and salaries. The individual earnings shortfall for all work force participants in the severe hardship IIE was $1,839. The IIE Deficit for full-year work force participants was $38.0 billion and averaged $2,698.

To raise family earnings to the poverty level for all families with work force participants would have required $31.7 billion in 1979, or $2,384 for each work force participant in the IFE. To eliminate poverty among families with work force participants would have required $12.8 billion in additional earnings, or $1,818 per work force participant in the severe hardship IFI.

The wage bills needed to eliminate intermediate and moderate hardship were even larger:

	Hardship deficits (millions)		
	Severe	Intermediate	Moderate
IIE Deficit	$51,998	$87,442	$136,402
IFE Deficit	31,656	48,556	66,668
IFI Deficit	12,825	23,015	37,173

	Hardship deficits as percent of total wages and salaries		
	Severe	Intermediate	Moderate
IIE Deficit	4.0%	6.7%	10.5%
IFE Deficit	2.4	3.7	5.3
IFI Deficit	0.9	1.6	2.6

	Average hardship deficits		
	Severe	Intermediate	Moderate
IIE Deficit	$1,839	$2,135	$2,652
IFE Deficit	2,384	2,825	3,232
IFI Deficit	1,818	2,187	2,590

There can be no doubt, then, that the hardship measures focus on those workers whose employment problems have the most serious consequences:

	Percent in families with incomes below $8,000	Percent in families with incomes over $15,000
Total in work force in 1979	11.2%	70.0%
Persons experiencing unemployment	23.2	53.0
Workers with Inadequate Individual Earnings	29.5	48.6
Workers with Inadequate Family Earnings	66.1	8.0
Workers with Inadequate Family Incomes	93.8	0.0

- <u>Hardship, like unemployment, is most likely to affect women, minorities, younger and older workers, those with limited education, workers in blue collar and service jobs, and residents of nonmetropolitan areas and large central cities. As a general rule, the burdens of hardship are even more maldistributed than the burdens of unemployment.</u>

--The incidence of unemployment among females in the work force during 1979 was 104 percent of the incidence among males. In contrast, the female IFI rate was 135 percent that for males, the IFE incidence was 137 percent as high, while the IIE rate among women was 186 percent of the rate among men. Comparing male and female family heads who were the sole breadwinners for their households, the unemployment, IIE, IFE and IFI rates for women were, respectively, 208, 307, 242, and 355 percent those among males:

	Average annual unemployment	Percent experiencing unemployment	IIE incidence	IFE incidence	IFI incidence
Males	5.1%	15.5%	17.5%	9.7%	5.2%
Females	6.8	16.1	32.4	13.4	7.1
Male family heads (No wife in work force)	3.4	9.8	9.7	13.8	6.2
Female family heads	5.2	20.4	29.8	33.4	22.0

--Black workers were two-thirds more likely than whites to experience unemployment during 1979, and half again as likely to have Inadequate Individual Earnings. But the IFE rate among blacks was two and a half times that among whites, while the IFI rate was nearly three and a half times that of whites. Similarly, Hispanic workers were half again as likely to experience unemployment, two-thirds more likely to have Inadequate Family Earnings, and 2.4 times as likely to be poor:

	Average annual unemployment	Unemployment incidence	IIE incidence	IFE incidence	IFI incidence
Whites	5.1%	14.7%	22.9%	9.8%	4.8%
Blacks	12.2	24.2	34.6	24.1	16.4
Hispanics	8.3	22.0	28.5	16.0	15.5

--Workers age 65 and over were twice as likely as those age 25 to 44 to have Inadequate Individual Earnings during 1979 and 5.4 times as likely to have Inadequate Family Earnings, although income transfers equalized IFI rates. Teenage workers were three and a half times as likely as prime age workers to have Inadequate Individual Earnings. The IFE rate among teenagers was three-fifths higher, while their IFI incidence was 28 percent above that for 25-to-44-year-olds:

	Average annual unemployment	Unemployment incidence	IIE incidence	IFE incidence	IFI incidence
16-19	16.1%	26.5%	59.4%	15.2%	9.2%
20-24	9.0	25.5	30.8	12.7	8.0
25-44	4.5	14.9	16.9	8.4	5.7
45-64	3.1	9.1	17.5	9.2	4.2
65 and over	3.4	5.8	35.7	45.1	4.3

--The chances of experiencing unemployment during 1979 were 2.6 times higher among high school dropouts than among college graduates, but the IIE, IFE and IFI rates for dropouts were, respectively, 3.7, 4.3 and 5.5 times those for college graduates:

	Unemployment incidence	IIE incidence	IFE incidence	IFI incidence
Students	20.3%	54.7%	16.2%	8.0%
Dropouts	22.0	34.6	21.5	12.1
High school graduates, no further education	15.9	21.3	8.9	4.7
Post-secondary (1-3 years)	13.0	16.2	7.6	3.8
College graduates	8.5	9.4	4.9	2.2

--Workers employed primarily as operatives, laborers, farm workers and service workers were 2.8 times as likely to experience unemployment as workers in professional, technical, managerial and administrative jobs, but their IIE, IFE and IFI rates were 3.4, 2.9 and 3.5 times as large:

	Average annual unemployment	Unemployment incidence	IIE incidence	IFE incidence	IFI incidence
Professional, technical and managerial	2.3%	7.1%	10.2%	5.6%	2.6%
Sales	3.9	10.8	29.4	10.8	4.4
Clerical	4.6	12.1	21.3	8.5	4.4
Craft and kindred	4.5	17.3	11.5	7.5	4.3
Operatives	7.7	22.0	19.6	10.1	5.6
Laborers	10.8	27.4	35.2	16.6	9.7
Farm workers	3.8	11.0	58.4	25.7	15.7
Service workers	7.1	16.8	44.8	20.2	10.9

--Workers residing in nonmetropolitan areas had the same chance of experiencing unemployment as those in metropolitan areas, but they were two-fifths more likely to have Iadequate Individual Earnings, while their IFE and IFI rates were 50 and 46 percent higher, respectively. The unemployment incidence in central cities of SMSA's with over one million population was 1.3 times the incidence in surrounding suburbs; the large central city IFE and IFI rates were 1.8 and 2.3 times those of suburban areas:

	Average annual unemployment	Unemployment incidence	IIE incidence	IFE incidence	IFI incidence
Metropolitan area	5.8%	15.7%	21.4%	10.1%	5.4%
Central city	7.1	17.6	23.0	13.1	7.7
Suburbs	5.0	14.3	20.1	8.1	4.0
Nonmetropolitan area	5.7	15.7	29.8	13.9	7.3

Causal Factors

<u>Unemployment is not always, or even usually, associated with hardship. Underemployment--including, low wage full-time or voluntary part-time work, as well as involuntary part-time employment--is a more frequent cause of hardship than unemployment. Full-time, full-year employment is no guarantee of self-sufficiency. And while the individual earnings deficits of part-time workers are less than those of full-time workers and the unemployed, the earnings shortfalls of part-time workers contribute significantly to family earnings problems.</u>

Almost half of the 18.5 million work force participants who experienced some unemployment during 1979 had annual earnings above the minimum wage equivalent for their hours of availability. Less than a fourth resided in families with below-poverty earnings. Just one in seven of the unemployed resided in a poor family.

While the incidence of hardship was lower among those workers who were able to find and keep jobs for all their weeks in the work force, the employed with inadequate individual and family earnings and income outnumbered the unemployed in hardship:

	Severe hardship incidence			Severe hardship share		
	IIE	IFE	IFI	IIE	IFE	IFI
Employed all weeks	<u>12.6%</u>	<u>5.8%</u>	<u>3.6%</u>	<u>65.1%</u>	<u>68.3%</u>	<u>62.9%</u>
Employed full-time all weeks	10.0	4.5	2.7	22.7	22.0	24.8
Employed part-time voluntarily some or all weeks	32.6	17.5	6.9	31.1	35.6	22.6
Employed part-time involuntarily some weeks	44.6	19.8	11.4	11.3	10.7	11.6
Unemployed some weeks	<u>53.5</u>	<u>22.8</u>	<u>14.2</u>	<u>34.9</u>	<u>31.7</u>	<u>37.1</u>

The hardship deficits for participants with different patterns of work experience provide a measure of the relative consequences of different labor market problems. The average IIE Deficit for part-time workers was less than that for full-time workers, or for the unemployed, yet the part-timers still accounted for 29 percent of the 1979 aggregate IIE Deficit. The IFE and IFI Deficits are allocated among family work force participants in relation to the degree that their individual earnings problems contribute to the family earnings or income shortfall. Part-time workers accounted for 43 percent of the IFE Deficit and 35 percent of the IFI Deficit in 1979. In other words, part-time workers accounted for a substantial share of potential earnings for families with inadequate earnings and incomes, and their low wages, as well as limited hours of availability, were a major cause of hardship:

	Average deficit of subgroup as percent of average deficit for all in severe hardship			Share of total severe hardship deficit		
	IIE	IFE	IFI	IIE	IFE	IFI
Not employed	107%	175%	143%	8%	12%	13%
Intermittently employed	117	97	96	33	24	27
Part-time involuntary	100	105	107	11	11	12
Part-time voluntary	56	91	85	18	32	23
Employed full-time	135	92	102	31	20	25

* <u>Because needs increase with family size, the welfare consequences of low earnings are more serious for breadwinners who must support large families. Assuring minimally adequate individual earnings for all persons in hardship would alleviate, but not eliminate, Inadequate Family Earnings.</u>

Among the 13.3 million total work force participants with below-poverty family earnings in 1979, and the 5.7 million in the work force full-year, 4.2 million and 1.2 million, respectively, had individual earnings above the minimum wage equivalent for their usual hours of availability. Conversely, among the 28.7 million total work force participants in the severe hardship IIE, of whom 14.2 million were full-year participants, only 9.1 and 4.5 million, respectively, were in families with below-poverty earnings.

The probabilities that Inadequate Individual Earnings will be associated with Inadequate Family Earnings, or that family earnings will be inadequate despite adequate individual earnings, increase with the number of dependents per worker. For instance, the IFE incidence among workers in families with two work force participants was as follows:

	Severe hardship IFE incidence among workers with Inadequate Individual Earnings	Severe hardship IFE incidence among workers with adequate individual earnings
Two family members	18.9%	1.4%
Three family members	17.9	1.2
Four or five family members	26.7	2.3
Six or more family members	46.9	9.3

The likelihood of having Inadequate Family Earnings declines when there are more breadwinners with greater labor force attachment. For instance, workers from families with four or five members had the following IFE rates:

	Severe hardship IFE rate among workers in four or five member families
Three or more full-year participants in family	1.6%
Three or more in work force at least one week	3.0
Two full-year participants	5.5
Two in work force at least one week	8.6
One full-year participant	12.3
One in work force at least one week	20.5

Eliminating the IIE Deficits of all persons with below-poverty family earnings would have reduced the 1979 IFE count by only 36 percent, and the IFE Deficit by 41 percent. Among full-year work force participants, the IFE would have been reduced less than three-fifths by the elimination of

Inadequate Individual Earnings. Even if all the unemployed and involuntary part-time workers in the IFE were provided their usual wage for any hours of forced idleness <u>and</u> if everyone's earnings were then increased by 10 percent, the IFE would have been reduced by only 45 percent and the IFE Deficit by 47 percent. Similar augmentation of the earnings of full-year workers would have left a third of the full-year IFE with below-poverty family earnings.

<u>Income transfers mitigate the welfare consequences of labor market problems, but many work force participants and their families, including millions with substantial work force attachment, fall through the safety net. In-kind aid provides further relief, but adding the estimated value of in-kind aid (other than health care) to cash income only modestly reduces the number of work force participants in poverty.</u>

Of the 13.3 million work force participants in families with earnings below the poverty level in 1979, 2.8 million were lifted out of poverty by nontransfer earnings supplements such as private pensions, alimony, dividends and interest. Cash transfers then raised a third of the remaining 10.5 million out of poverty. If the value of food stamps were added to the cash incomes of recipient families, and this combined amount were compared to the poverty level for the family, another 0.5 million workers would have been lifted out of poverty. If the value of free school lunches and housing subsidies were added to cash income and food stamps, the working poor would have been reduced by an additional 0.3 million. In other words, the Net-of-Transfers IFI declined by a third as a result of cash transfers alone, while cash and in-kind transfers (excluding health care) together reduced the number of working poor by almost half. The IFI Net-of-Transfers Deficit was reduced $11.2 billion by cash transfers, while the cash equivalent of food stamps, school lunches and housing subtracted an additional $2.4 billion, representing reductions of 47 and 57 percent respectively:

Transfer impacts on the number of the working poor	(000)	Transfer impacts on poverty deficit of the working poor	($000)
Work force participants in families with below poverty earnings (IFE)	13,280	Family earnings deficit of work force participants in families with below poverty earnings (IFE Deficit)	$31,656
-Lifted out of poverty by nontransfer earnings supplements	- 2,823	-Reduction in family earnings deficit resulting from non-transfer earnings supplements	- 7,650
=Work force participants who would be poor without transfers (IFI Net-of-Transfers)	10,457	=Poverty deficit of families with work force participants if cash transfers excluded (IFI Net-of-Transfers Deficit)	24,006
-Lifted out of poverty by cash transfers	- 3,402	-Reduction in poverty deficit resulting from cash transfers	-11,181
=Work force participants in poverty (IFI)	7,055	=Poverty deficit of families with work force participants (IFI Deficit)	12,825
-Lifted out of poverty by addition of value of food stamps to cash income	- 533	-Reduction in poverty deficit if food stamps counted as cash income	- 1,916
-Lifted out of poverty by addition of value of housing subsidies and school lunches to cash income and food stamps	- 281	-Further reduction in poverty deficit if value of housing subsidies and school lunches added to cash income and food stamps	- 530
=Work force participants in poverty counting in-kind aid as income (IFI Including In-Kind Aid)	6,241	=Poverty deficit of families with work force participants when in-kind aid value included with cash income (IFI Including In-Kind Aid Deficit)	10,379

Hardship Trends

For the total work force, there was a noticeable decline in IIE incidence over the 1974-1980 period. The severe hardship IFE rate declined modestly, while the severe hardship IFI rate changed little, actually rising between 1975 and 1980. The moderate and intermediate hardship IIE and IFE counts increased relative to the severe hardship totals, while the moderate and intermediate hardship IFI totals declined relative to the severe hardship IFI.

Comparisons between the two low unemployment years, 1974 and 1979, and the two high unemployment years, 1975 and 1980, are the best indicators of multi-year trends. The severe hardship IIE rate dropped by 1.6 percentage points between 1974 and 1979, and 1.4 percentage points between 1975 and 1980. In contrast, the intermediate hardship IIE rate declined only 0.3 percentage points over the first period and 0.5 percentage points over the second; while the moderate hardship IIE declined 0.3 percentage points between 1974 and 1979 but rose 0.7 percentage points between 1975 and 1980. The number with individual earnings above the severe hardship level but below the intermediate hardship level increased from 37 of the severe hardship IIE in 1974 to 45 percent in 1979, or from 32 to 37 percent between 1975 and 1980. This suggests that wage increases, declining unemployment or other factors raised some individuals out of severe hardship without having the same proportionate impacts on those with less severe, but still significant, labor market problems:

	Hardship incidence for total work force						
	1974	1979	1979-1974	1975	1980	1980-1975	1980-1974
Severe Hardship							
IIE	25.8%	24.2%	-1.6%	29.1%	27.7%	-1.4%	+1.9%
IFE	11.6	11.4	-0.2	13.2	12.8	-0.4	+1.2
IFI	6.1	6.0	-0.1	6.9	7.2	+0.3	+1.1
Intermediate Hardship							
IIE	35.3	35.0	-0.3	38.4	37.9	-0.5	+2.6
IFE	14.9	14.7	-0.2	16.8	16.4	-0.4	+1.5
IFI	9.2	9.0	-0.2	10.3	10.4	+0.1	+1.2
Moderate Hardship							
IIE	44.3	44.0	-0.3	46.6	47.3	+0.7	+3.0
IFE	18.5	18.4	-0.1	20.9	20.5	-0.4	+2.0
IFI	12.8	12.3	-0.5	14.3	14.1	-0.3	+1.3

The severe hardship IFE rate dropped 0.2 percentage points between 1974 and 1979, and 0.4 percentage points between 1975 and 1980. The declines in the intermediate and moderate hardship IFE rates were of similar magnitude, so that both the intermediate and moderate hardship IFE counts increased in relation to the severe hardship IFE count.

The patterns were reversed in the case of the IFI, where the severe hardship rate declined only 0.1 percentage point between 1974 and 1979, while rising 0.3 percentage points between 1975 and 1980. In contrast, the moderate hardship IFI incidence declined by 0.5 percentage points in the first period and 0.3 percentage points in the second, reducing the moderate hardship IFI relative to the severe hardship IFI. The relative labor market gains of the worst off were thus offset by changes in the relative distribution of nonearned income.

• <u>The IFI incidence did not improve between 1974 and 1979, and actually rose between 1975 and 1980, because of the declining effectiveness of the safety net for the working poor. The impact of nontransfer earnings supplements increased significantly over the period. Changes in the composition of the IFE were favorable and the average IFE Deficit declined, but the diminished impact of cash transfers more than offset these favorable developments. The safety net for the working poor had unraveled prior to the massive cutbacks in social programs in the early 1980s.</u>

Nontransfer earnings supplements raised 18.3 percent of the severe hardship IFE out of poverty in 1974 but 21.3 percent in 1979. This "Earnings Supplementation Rate-Nontransfers" increased from 16.2 percent in 1975 to 19.5 percent in 1980. Yet the Earnings Supplementation Rate-Total, which considered transfer as well as nontransfer earnings supplements, declined from 47.1 to 46.9 percent in the first period, and from 47.3 to 44.0 percent in the second. The reason is that cash benefits lifted 35.3 percent of the Net-of-Transfers IFI out of poverty in 1974, but only 32.5

percent in 1979, with an even greater drop, from 37.1 to 30.4 percent, between 1975 and 1980.

The impacts of cash transfers on the nonworking poor declined as well, but the slippage in benefits was greatest for the working poor. For instance, 50.7 percent of all persons in households without any work force participant in 1975 were lifted out of poverty by cash benefits compared to 49.1 percent in 1980. This 1.6 percentage point drop compared to a 6.7 percentage point drop in the proportion of otherwise poor families with at least one work force participant who were lifted out of poverty by transfers.

This drop occurred despite a slight decline in the constant dollar average Net-of-Transfer IFI Deficit. It was not explained by changing work force composition or work experience patterns. For almost all subgroups in the work force, there was a noticeable decline in the Earnings Supplementation Rate-Transfers. As a result of favorable changes in work experience patterns of persons with Inadequate Family Earnings, the Earnings Supplementation Rate-Transfers should have risen 0.3 percentage points between 1975 and 1980. Favorable changes in the sex and family relationship composition of the IFE should have increased the transfer impact by 0.6 percentage points, offsetting the 0.8 percentage point decline which might have been expected from the reduced proportion of older workers (who more frequently receive transfers).

- <u>Changes in work attachment and experience patterns were relatively neutral, as increased full-year participation reduced hardship probabilities, offsetting the negative effects of increased part-time employment. On the other hand, changes in the composition of the total work force were, on balance, quite favorable, contributing to the decline of the severe hardship IIE and IFE rates.</u>

The proportion of the total work force who were full-year participants increased from 70.2 in 1974 to 71.8 percent in 1979, while the proportion participating at least half year increased from 83.0 to 84.4 percent. The incidence of unemployment dropped by 2.1 percentage points, while among the unemployed, the proportion who were jobless for over one-third of their weeks of participation dropped from 41.8 to 40.6 percent. These labor market developments reduced hardship probabilities, since the short-term work force participants, those experiencing unemployment, and particularly those predominantly unemployed, had significantly higher IIE and IFE likelihoods.

The percent of the total work force employed voluntarily or involuntarily part-time for some or all weeks in the work force and who experienced no weeks of unemployment, increased from 22.5 percent in 1974 to 29.2 percent in 1979. Since the severe hardship IIE rate among part-time workers was three-fourths higher than for the rest of the work force, while the IFE rate was three-fifths higher, increased part-time work raised the IIE and IFE probabilities for the total work force.

On balance, these changes in work experience patterns and work force attachment contributed to a 0.3 percentage point increase in the severe hardship IIE rate and a 0.1 percentage point increase in the IFE rate between 1974 and 1979 (as judged by weighting the 1979 incidence for each work experience/attachment subgroup by its 1974 share, and comparing the weighted hardship rates with the actuals for 1979). However, labor market changes should have reduced the IIE rate by 1.0 percentage points between 1975 and 1980, and the IFE by 0.6 percentage points, since unemployment was lower in the latter year.

The changing composition of the labor force contributed to declining hardship incidence:

Teenagers and older workers (45 and above)--those more likely to have inadequate individual and family earnings--represented 44.8 percent of the 1974 work force, but 40.3 percent of the 1979 work force. All else being equal, this decline should have reduced the severe hardship IIE rate by 0.6 percentage points and the IFE rate by 0.2 percentage points.

Dropouts declined from 28.7 percent of the work force in 1974 to 20.9 percent in 1979, while persons who had completed some post-secondary education increased from 28.1 to 32.7 percent. Given the lower hardship incidence among the better educated, this upgrading of the work force's educational attainment should have reduced the severe hardship IIE rate by 2.6 percentage points and the IFE rate by 1.5 percentage points, all else being equal.

White collar workers increased from 46.2 to 49.3 percent of the work force, while farm and service workers, laborers and operatives--those workers most likely to have inadequate individual and family earnings--dropped from 39.7 of the work force in 1974 to 36.7 percent in 1979. All else being equal, this should have contributed to a 0.9 percentage point drop in the severe hardship IIE rate and a 0.5 percentage point drop in the IFE rate.

The negative impacts of the population shift to those regions where severe hardship was more prevalent were offset by the movement to the suburbs where hardship was less prevalent. All else being equal, the regional shifts would have increased both the severe hardship IIE and IFE rates by less than 0.1 percentage points while the suburbanization would have reduced both by less than 0.1 percentage points.

- <u>As a result of substantial changes in family size and composition, as well as in family work patterns, female family heads and unrelated individuals represented a larger share of the hardship counts and deficits in 1980 than in 1974. Conversely, male family heads, wives and other family earners constituted a declining share. The favorable effects of reduced family size and increased participation by second and third family earners were offset by the growth of female-headed families and single-person families.</u>

Unrelated individuals increased from 11.2 percent of the work force in 1974 to 14.6 percent in 1979, while workers in larger families with six or more members declined from 12.4 to 9.4 percent. The number of earners also increased, so that 81.4 percent of the work force participants in multiple-member families in 1979 also had other workers in their families, compared to 79.2 percent in 1974. Weighting the severe hardship IFE and IFI share rates for each family size/number of earners category by its 1974 share suggests that these changes subtracted 0.4 percentage points from the IFE rate and 0.3 percentage points from the IFI rate.

Male family heads accounted for 39.5 percent of the work force in 1974 but only 35.9 percent in 1979. Working wives increased only marginally from 24.4 to 24.6 percent, while other family members declined from 20.6 to 19.8 percent of the work force. Female family heads increased from 4.4 to 5.1 percent. Because the severe hardship IFE and IFI rates tend to be lower among male family heads and wives, and unrelated individuals and female family heads, the changing sex/family relationship composition of the work force contributed 0.3 percentage points to the IFE rate and 0.3 percentage points to the IFI rate.

The composition of the hardship population changed as a result of shifting family patterns. Male family heads accounted for 24.5 percent of the 1979 severe hardship IFE, down from 26.9 percent in 1974, while female family heads accounted for 15.2 percent, up from a 14.6 percent share of the 1974 IFE. Male family heads dropped from 25.9 to 23.2 percent of the IFI, mirrored by an increase from 17.2 to 18.9 percent for female family heads. Wives and other family members declined from 35.4 percent of the IFE and 30.7 percent of the IFI in 1974, to 33.9 and 28.1 percent, respectively, in 1979.

<u>Despite a deterioration in the relative unemployment status of black workers during the 1974-1980 period, they realized at least modest absolute and relative gains as judged from the hardship perspective, although the pace of these gains was far below that of the preceding decade. For blacks, intermediate and moderate hardship improved more than severe hardship. Hispanics made substantial absolute and relative progress in escaping severe hardship, but the intermediate and moderate hardship gains were more limited.</u>

The annual unemployment rate for blacks was 2.1 times that of whites in 1974, with a gap of 5.4 percentage points; by 1979, the unemployment rate ratio had increased to 2.4 as the gap widened to 7.1 percentage points. Nevertheless, the severe hardship IIE rate of blacks declined from 1.6 to 1.5 times that of whites, while the black/white IFE incidence ratio fell from 2.6 to 2.5, and the IFI ratio from 3.6 to 3.5. This relative progress was derailed by the 1980 decline, which affected blacks relatively more than the 1975 recession, but the 1980 black/white hardship incidence ratios still remained below the 1974 levels. The improvements for minorities during the 1974-1980 period were far slower than in the preceding decade. According to the hardship measure developed by the National Commission on Employment and Unemployment Statistics, the hardship incidence among nonwhites fell from 3.9 times that for whites in 1967 to 3.2 times as high in 1971, and then improved only marginally to 3.0 times the white rate in 1979.

The intermediate and moderate hardship IFE and IFI rates for blacks declined relative to the severe hardship IFE and IFI rates. Among white work force participants, the exact opposite was true:

	IIE		IFE		IFI	
	Whites	Blacks	Whites	Blacks	Whites	Blacks
Intermediate ÷ Severe						
1974	1.38	1.29	1.29	1.26	1.54	1.44
1979	1.46	1.36	1.31	1.24	1.53	1.39
1974-1979	+.08	+.07	+.02	-.02	-.01	-.05
Moderate ÷ Severe						
1974	1.75	1.54	1.62	1.50	2.19	1.87
1979	1.85	1.62	1.66	1.49	2.14	1.77
1974-1979	+.10	+.08	+.04	-.01	-.05	-.10

Though the ratio of Hispanic to white unemployment remained unchanged, the Hispanic severe hardship IIE rate declined slightly from 1.32 times the white rate in 1974 to 1.28 as high in 1979, while the Hispanic/white IFE incidence ratio dropped noticeably from 1.82 to 1.66, and the IFI incidence ratio declined from 2.73 to 2.42. Moderate and intermediate hardship improved less than severe hardship. For instance, the number of Hispanics in the moderate hardship IFE was 1.69 times the number in the severe hardship IFE in 1974 and 1.80 times as high in 1979, an increase of 0.11 percentage points compared to the 0.04 percentage point increase among whites and the 0.01 percentage point decline among blacks. Apparently, the severe hardship reductions were achieved by the movement of many Hispanic workers and their families to just above the severe hardship levels, rather than reflecting across-the-board improvements.

Hardship in Good Times and Bad

● Hardship rises in recessions and declines during periods of economic growth. However, the cyclicality of hardship is less extreme than the cyclicality of unemployment. Hardship is a continuing structural problem which persists even in periods of economic growth and low unemployment.

Over the 1974-1980 period, there was a significant correlation between unemployment and hardship rates:

	Correlation between average annual unemployment rate and severe hardship incidence	Correlation between unemployment incidence among work force participants and severe hardship incidence
IIE incidence	.92	.91
IFE incidence	.94	.87
IFE incidence	.78	.69

However, the proportionate fluctuations in hardship were less severe, since many of the job losers during recessions were already in hardship, and their conditions simply became worse:

	1974-1975		1979-1980	
	Absolute increase (000)	Percentage increase	Absolute increase (000)	Percentage increase
Average annual unemployment	2,754	54	1,485	25
Persons experiencing unemployment	2,568	14	2,942	16
Severe hardship IIE	3,589	13	4,478	16
Severe hardship IFE	1,760	15	1,831	14
Severe hardship IFI	906	14	1,410	20

The standard deviation of the average annual unemployment rate over the 1974-1980 period was 15 percent of the mean; the standard deviation in the severe hardship IFE, IFE and IFI rates were 7, 7 and 9 percent of their respective means. Simple regression analysis suggests that each 1.00 percentage point increase in the average annual unemployment rate was associated with a 1.25 percentage point increase in the severe hardship IIE rate, a 0.54 percentage point increase in the IFE rate, and a 0.26 percentage point increase in IFI incidence.

● <u>Though recessions exacerbate conditions for the victims of structural employment problems, they also undermine the well-being of the more advantaged segments of the labor force who rarely suffer under normal circumstances. This was particularly true of the 1974-1975 recession. Yet the work force was also better protected by income transfers in the 1974-1975 downturn, so that the incidence of Inadequate Family Income among work force participants was lower in 1975 than 1980 despite higher unemployment. The disadvantaged were affected relatively more by the latter recession and suffered more because of reduced protections.</u>

Recessions cause hardship for the more advantaged segments of the work force:

--Prime age (25-to-44-year-old) workers accounted for only 29 percent of the 1974 severe hardship IFE but 43 percent of the 1974-1975 IFE increment.

--Male family heads accounted for 27 percent of the 1974 IFE but for 40 percent of the 1974-1975 IFE increment.

--Work force participants who had completed some post-secondary education accounted for 14 percent of the 1974 IFE but 25 percent of the recessionary increment.

--Whites accounted for 76 percent of the IFE but 92 percent of the 1974-1975 IFE increment.

In the 1979-1980 recession, the more advantaged segments were hurt, but to a lesser degree, as suggested by the ratio of each advantaged subgroup's share of the recession increment in the severe hardship IFE divided by its share of the pre-recession IFE:

	Share 1974-1975 IFE increment / Share 1974 IFE	Share 1979-1980 IFE increment / Share 1979 IFE
Male family heads	1.47	1.15
Work force participants who had completed some post-secondary education	1.79	1.27
Whites	1.21	1.04
Prime age workers (25-to-44-years-old)	1.47	1.58

The unemployment rate was a fifth higher in 1975 than in 1980 (8.5 percent versus 7.1 percent). The severe hardship IIE incidence was marginally higher (29.1 percent versus 27.7 percent), as was the IFE rate (13.2 percent versus 12.8 percent). Yet despite the relatively worse labor market conditions, the IFI rate was lower in 1975 than in 1980 (7.2 percent versus 6.9 percent). The reason is clear. Income transfers reduced the Net-of-Transfer IFI by 37 percent in the 1975 recession year, compared to just 30 percent in 1980, even though the average Net-of-Transfer IFI Deficit was, in real terms, lower in 1980 than 1975, leaving less ground to be made up by cash benefits.

The most disadvantaged in the work force were the most adversely affected by declining transfers. The IFI rate among blacks in 1980 was 1.4 percentage points above the 1975 level compared to the 0.3 percentage point increase in the IFI rate for the total work force. The IFI incidence among female family heads rose by 1.1 percentage points, and among high school dropouts by 1.7 percentage points.

Some Implications

To significantly alleviate labor market-related hardship will require a combination of macroeconomic and targeted structural measures, combined with expanded income transfers for the working poor. Full employment and increased minimum wages are necessary but far from sufficient, since only a portion of the benefits of more jobs or higher wages go to persons otherwise in hardship. Even if full employment and increased wages could

<u>be achieved by all work force participants with Inadequate Family Earnings, earnings supplements would still be needed by millions of work force participants in order to escape poverty.</u>

Since less than a fourth of the 1979 unemployed were in families with inadequate earnings, and only one in seven in poor families, and since just a third of workers with Inadequate Individual Earnings were in families with below-poverty earnings, reductions in unemployment or increases in the minimum wage which would reduce the IIE incidence would also affect many workers not suffering hardship. Regressions using 1974-1980 annual data suggest that a 10 percentage point increase in the legislated minimum wage (as measured relative to the the real minimum wage averaged for the 1967-1980 period) was associated with a 1.9 percentage point reduction in the IIE, a 0.6 percentage point drop in the IFE and a 0.3 percentage point drop in the IFI. Since the ratio of the legislated minimum divided by the average real minimum ranged only from 94 percent in 1977 to 102 percent in 1978, or a swing of 8 percentage points, changes in the minimum were not a central factor in hardship trends. A 1 percentage point decline in average annual unemployment was associated with a 1.2 percentage point drop in the severe hardship IIE rate, a 0.5 percentage point drop in the IFE rate, and a 0.3 percentage point drop in the IFI rate.

Projecting 1982 hardship levels based on this simple regression model for 1974 through 1980, and assuming, most plausibly, that unemployment will average 9 percent and inflation will erode only 5 percent from the unchanging legislated minimum wage, the severe hardship IIE rate will be 30.7 percent, the IFE rate, 14.2 percent, and the IFI rate, 8.0 percent (or even higher, as retrenchment in transfer benefits is greater than the 1970s downtrend). These projected levels would contrast unfavorably with the 1979 lows of 24.2, 11.4 and 6.0 percent, respectively. Yet even if unemployment had miraculously dropped to a 7.0 percent level, and even if inflation had declined to a 2.5 percent annual rate, the IFE rate would have remained at 13.0 percent, almost the same as in 1975--while the IFI rate would have been 7.2 percent, in contrast to 6.9 percent in 1975. In other words, large-scale hardship will remain at high levels even if economic conditions improve.

If all workers were provided minimally adequate individual earnings, hardship would not be eliminated and transfers would still be needed to alleviate deprivation among work force participants and their families. The severe hardship IFE count would have been reduced by only 36 percent in 1979, and the IFE Deficit by 41 percent, if the earnings of all persons were augmented up to the minimum wage equivalent for all hours of availability. If every person living in families with below-poverty earnings in 1979 were provided employment at the usual wage for any hours of forced idleness, and their earnings were then increased by 10 percent, 56 percent would have remained with Inadequate Family Earnings, and they would have needed $22.1 billion in earnings supplements to reach the poverty level. Thus, targeted manpower programs providing minimum wage employment or marginal earnings improvements would not eliminate the need for income transfers.

<u>If the hardship measures were used, rather than unemployment and poverty rates, as the basis for allocating and targeting resources in-</u>

tended for the unemployed and underemployed from low-income families, the distribution among geographic areas and population segments would change significantly. Nonmetropolitan areas would benefit substantially and so would the Southern states. Family heads, both males and females, would receive greater priority. There would be much more emphasis on helping older workers and less on youth employment problems. Dropouts would receive far more attention.

The nonmetropolitan-area share of the severe hardship IFE, averaged for the 1974-1980 period, was nearly two-fifths higher than the nonmetropolitan-area share of average annual unemployment, and a fifth above the nonmetropolitan share of poverty and unemployment, each equally weighted. If funds were allocated based on IFE shares, the suburban rings of metropolitan areas would have received a fourth less than if unemployment shares were the determining factor, or a tenth less than if equally weighted unemployment and poverty shares were used in allocation.

The West North Central, South Atlantic, East South Central, West South Central, and Mountain states would have received a fourth more under an IFE-based allocation than an unemployment-based allocaton, and a tenth more than under a poverty and unemployment share basis.

If resources were allocated according to need, and need were based on the IFE share rather than unemployment, the following work force groups would have been the big winners and losers in 1979:

Winners

	Share of unemployed	Share of poverty and unemployment	IFE share
Male family heads	18.8%	17.7%	24.5%
Female family heads	6.9	11.9	15.2
Unrelated individuals	14.1	24.2	26.4
Dropouts	28.8	42.0	39.9
45 and over	16.5	29.4	36.2

Losers

	Share of unemployed	Share of poverty and unemployment	IFE share
Wives	19.7%	17.6%	14.1%
Other family members	40.5	28.7	19.8
High school graduates	38.4	30.7	30.2
Completers of some post-secondary education	22.9	17.1	19.1
16-19	25.6	19.7	13.4
20-24	23.1	18.5	17.1

Adding A Third Leg to Social Statistics

These assorted findings challenge many conventional wisdoms about how many and who are suffering as a result of labor market problems. The same general conclusions might be reached by careful analysis of the detailed and disaggregated labor force and income data, but the hardship measures provide a systematic integration which offers new perspectives to the public and policymakers who have not been able to piece together the hodgepodge of existing statistics. Yet the demonstrated utility and sensibility of the proposed measures does not assure their acceptance. Those who do not like what they see from the hardship perspective may argue that the measures distort reality because of the value judgments, assumptions and technical problems implicit in the measures. Indeed, it is sobering to recognize that so many millions of Americans are unable to support themselves and their families even when they are lucky enough to find and hold jobs, that there has been little or no progress in alleviating hardship over recent years, that the burdens of labor market-related hardship are even more maldistributed than the burdens of unemployment, that the greater public concern with cyclical rather than structural problems may be misplaced, that a rising tide will not lift all boats, and that welfare and workfare must continue to overlap if hardship is to be alleviated for those failing in or failed by the labor market. It may be equally difficult to admit that the unemployment and poverty statistics, which are the foundation of public policy and public understanding, are not effective in perhaps their primary application--measuring who and how many suffer as a result of labor market problems. It is certainly no easy task to learn an entirely new nomenclature, or to adjust and supplement libraries of econometric studies and esoteric analyses which have been based on the assumption that unemployment and poverty rates were good proxies for labor market-related hardship. It will also be a formidable challenge to finetune the hardship measures and to modify the underlying survey instruments and approaches in order to improve the accuracy and reliability of hardship statistics. Yet if we are seriously committed to understanding and alleviating the welfare consequences of labor market problems, then the unemployment and poverty statistics must be supplemented by new measures developed to integrate earnings, work experience and income data in a systematic way, recognizing the complexities of varying family status, labor force attachment and patterns of work experience. Social policies must, then, be redirected in light of these new perspectives.

We have spent too many years "disputing loud and long" whether the "elephant" is like a spear, a tree, a rope, a snake, a fan, or a wall. There is no need to continue groping, conjecturing and disputing. With the help of hardship measures, we can see, understand and perhaps better harness the beast.

APPENDIX A. HARDSHIP MEASURES--TECHNICAL DETAILS

The hardship measures are calculated from the data gathered in the March Current Population Survey covering the earnings, income and work experience of individuals over the previous calendar year, as well as their labor market, education and family status in the survey week (Table A-1). Each of the hardship measures is derived by manipulation of several CPS questionnaire responses. The information elements required for the calculation of the hardship measures have only been gathered since the introduction of a more comprehensive questionnaire in March 1975, so that the measures can only be tabulated for the years 1974 forward. A supplement was added to the March 1980 CPS to measure the receipt of in-kind aid. The adequacy of family income after "cashing out" in-kind benefits can only be estimated for 1979 and 1980.

The complete hardship measures are presented in a 44 row/17 column data matrix (Table A-2). In this matrix (which is even more inclusive than the streamlined version outlined in Chapter 1), there are 19 "baseline measures" (rows 1 through 19). The first seven (rows 1-7) concern the adequacy of each individual's employment and earnings over the previous year. The adequacy of family earnings are considered in the next six measures (rows 8-13). The adequacy of family income is considered by the following six measures (rows 14-19). There are twenty-five "interpretative measures" (rows 20-44) which vary the baseline measures by augmenting earnings, income and employment in different ways or which relate one baseline measure to another. Ten of these interpretative measures (rows 20-29) are designed to focus on the labor force pathologies which cause hardship. Eight of the interpretative measures (rows 30-37) focus on the interrelationships between hardship and family composition. Seven of the interpretative measures (rows 38-44) focus on the impacts of cash and in-kind transfers in mitigating hardship.

Each measure is divided into components based on the pattern of work force experience of the individuals who are counted by the measure, i.e, whether they were employed full-time, part-time, intermittently, or not at all, during their period of participation (as indicated in columns 1 through 12). There is separate categorization of persons not in the work force according to their age and armed forces status (columns 13 through 17).

This matrix of hardship measures is calculated under nine different combinations of hardship severity and duration of work force participation: (1) using the severe hardship standards and counting all work force participants; (2) using severe hardship standards and counting only those participants in the work force half year or more; (3) using severe hardship standards and counting only full-year work force participants; (4) using intermediate hardship standards and including all work force participants;

Table A-1. CURRENT POPULATION SURVEY, MARCH 1981 QUESTIONNAIRE

Table A-1. (Continued)

Table A-1. (Continued)

Table A-1. (Continued)

Table A-1. (Continued)

Table A-1. (Continued)

Table A-1. (Continued)

	Page 3	Page 4	Page 5	Page 6
NAME (Optional)				
LINE NUMBER (Item 18A)				
	0 0	0 0	0 0	0 0
	1 1	1 1	1 1	1 1
	2 2	2 2	2 2	2 2
	3 3	3 3	3 3	3 3
	■ 4	■ 4	■ 4	■ 4
	5	5	5	5
	6	6	6	6
	7	7	7	7
	8	8	8	8
	9	9	9	9

56 DURING 1980 DID ANYONE IN THIS HOUSEHOLD RECEIVE:

56A Any Social Security payments from the U.S. Government?
   Yes ⌐7   No ○ (Skip to 57A)

56B. Who received Social Security payments either for themselves or as combined payments with other family members?

	Yes ○ No ○	Yes ○ No ○	Yes ○ No ○	Yes ○ No ○

Complete 56C & 56D for each person with a "Yes" in 56B

56C. In how many months of 1980 did ... receive Social Security payments?

	Months	Months	Months	Months
	0 1	0 1	0 1	0 1
	0 1 2 3 4 5 6 7 8 9	0 1 2 3 4 5 6 7 8 9	0 1 2 3 4 5 6 7 8 9	0 1 2 3 4 5 6 7 8 9

56D. How much did ... receive in Social Security payments during 1980?
(separate combined payments)

NOTE: Social Security checks are green-colored checks.

	$ 0 0 0 0	$ 0 0 0 0	$ 0 0 0 0	$ 0 0 0 0
	1 1 1 1	1 1 1 1	1 1 1 1	1 1 1 1
	2 2 2 2	2 2 2 2	2 2 2 2	2 2 2 2
	3 3 3 3	3 3 3 3	3 3 3 3	3 3 3 3
	○ Already included 4 4 4 4	○ Already included 4 4 4 4	○ Already included 4 4 4 4	○ Already included 4 4 4 4
	5 5 5 5	5 5 5 5	5 5 5 5	5 5 5 5
	6 6 6 6	6 6 6 6	6 6 6 6	6 6 6 6
	7 7 7 7	7 7 7 7	7 7 7 7	7 7 7 7
	8 8 8 8	8 8 8 8	8 8 8 8	8 8 8 8
	9 9 9 9	9 9 9 9	9 9 9 9	9 9 9 9

56E. INTERVIEWER CHECK ITEM

   Children under 23 present — *(Ask 56F)*

   No children under 23 present — *(Skip to 57)*

56F Did anyone in this household receive any separate Social Security payments which we have not talked about for the children in this household?

   Yes   No

(If "Yes," make necessary changes to include this amount in 56D for person receiving)

57 DURING 1980 DID ANYONE IN THIS HOUSEHOLD RECEIVE:

57A Any SSI payments, that is, Supplemental Security Income?
   Yes ⌐7   No (Go to next page)

57B Who received SSI? *(Anyone else?)*

	Yes No	Yes No	Yes No	Yes No

(Complete 57C for each person with "Yes" in 57B)

57C. How much did ... receive in Supplemental Security Income during 1980? *(Include both Federal and State SSI)*

NOTE: SSI checks from the U.S. Government, are pale gold in color. The color of state checks may vary.

	$ 0 0 0 0	$ 0 0 0 0	$ 0 0 0 0	$ 0 0 0 0
	1 1 1 1	1 1 1 1	1 1 1 1	1 1 1 1
	2 2 2 2	2 2 2 2	2 2 2 2	2 2 2 2
	3 3 3 3	3 3 3 3	3 3 3 3	3 3 3 3
	4 4 4 4	4 4 4 4	4 4 4 4	4 4 4 4
	5 5 5	5 5 5 5	5 5 5	5 5 5
	6 6 6	6 6 6	6 6 6	6 6 6
	7 7 7	7 7 7	7 7 7	7 7 7
	8 8 8	8 8 8	8 8 8	8 8 8
	9 9 9	9 9 9	9 9 9	9 9 9

(Go to 57C for next person with "Yes" in 57B or go to next page)

Annual Total = last check x 11.25   Medicare Deduction: $9/month

Table A-2. HARDSHIP MEASURE DATA MATRIX

	2. Employed Full-Time During Period in Work Force	3. Part-Time Workers Some or All Weeks Employed	4. Voluntarily Part-Time	5. Involuntarily Part-Time	6. Intermittently Employed (All Who Experienced Some Employment and Unemployment)	7. Mostly Employed (More Than Two-Thirds of Weeks Employed)	8. Mixed	9. Mostly Unemployed (More Than Two-Thirds of Weeks Unemployed)	10. Not Employed at All	11. Discouraged	12. Unemployed	13. Out-of-Work Force	14. Armed Forces	15. Age 0-15	16. Age 16+	17. Total In and Out of Work Force

Baseline Measures -- Individual Earnings Adequacy

1. <u>Work Experience</u> (all persons 16 and over)
2. <u>Inadequate Individual Earnings</u> (subset of work force who earned less than minimum wage standard times hours of availability for work)
3. <u>IIE Incidence</u> (proportion individuals in each work force experience category who had Inadequate Individual Earnings)
4. <u>IIE Distribution</u> (persons with Inadequate Individual Earnings in each work force status category divided by total work force with Inadequate Individual Earnings)
5. <u>IIE Total Deficit</u> (minimum wage standard times hours of availability minus actual earnings for all persons with Inadequate Individual Earnings)
6. <u>IIE Average Deficit</u> (total IIE Deficit divided by number with Inadequate Individual Earnings)
7. <u>IIE Deficit Distribution</u> (share of total deficit for individuals in different work force experience category)

Baseline Measures -- Family Earnings Adequacy

8. <u>Inadequate Family Earnings</u> (persons in families whose total earnings were below family income standard)
9. <u>IFE Incidence</u> (proportion individuals in each work force experience category who were in families with inadequate earnings)
10. <u>IFE Distribution</u> (persons in each work force experience category who were in families with inadequate earnings divided by total with Inadequate Family Earnings)
11. <u>IFE Total Deficit</u> (aggregate of income standards for all families with inadequate earnings minus their aggregated earnings)
12. <u>IFE Average Deficit</u> (IFE Total Deficit divided by number in IFE)
13. <u>IFE Deficit Distribution</u> (share of IFE Total Deficit accounted for by family members in different work force experience categories)

Baseline Measures -- Family Income Adequacy

14. <u>Inadequate Family Income</u> (persons in families whose total income was below family income standard)
15. <u>IFI Incidence</u> (proportion individuals in each work force experience category who were in families with inadequate income)
16. <u>IFI Distribution</u> (persons in each work force experience category who were in families with inadequate income divided by total with Inadequate Family Income)
17. <u>IFI Total Deficit</u> (aggregate of income standards for all families with inadequate income minus their aggregated earnings)
18. <u>IFI Average Deficit</u> (IFI Total Deficit divided by number in IFI)
19. <u>IFI Deficit Distribution</u> (share of IFI Total Deficit accounted for by family members in different work force experience categories)

Table A-2. (Continued)

Interpretative Measures -- Labor Force Pathology

20. Full Employment IFE (IFE if every individual were employed at minimum wage standard for all hours of availability not employed)
21. Full Employment IFE Deficit (IFE Deficit if every individual were employed at minimum wage standard for all hours of availability not employed)
22. Adequate Employment IFE (IFE if every individual were employed at least at minimum wage standard for all hours of availability)
23. Adequate Employment IFE Deficit (IFE Deficit if every individual were employed at minimum wage standard for all hours of availability)
24. Capacity Employment IFE (IFE if every individual earned as much for hours of availability not worked as during each of those worked)
25. Capacity Employment IFE Deficit (IFE Deficit if each individual earned as much for hours of availability not worked as during each of those worked)
26. Enhanced Earnings IFE (IFE if each individual's earnings were increased by 10 percent)
27. Enhanced Earnings IFE Deficit (IFE Deficit if each individual's earnings were increased by 10 percent)
28. Enhanced Capacity IFE (IFE if each individual earned 110 percent of minimum wage standard for all hours of availability)
29. Enhanced Capacity IFE Deficit (IFE Deficit if each individual earned 110 percent of minimum wage standard for all hours of availability)

Interpretative Measures -- Family Composition

30. Marginally Augmented Full Employment IFE (IFE if subgroup earnings increased by minimum wage standard for each hour of availability not employed)
31. Marginally Augmented Full Employment IFE Deficit (IFE Deficit if subgroup earnings increased by minimum wage standard for each hour of availability not employed)
32. Marginally Augmented Adequate Employment IFE (IFE if subgroup earnings increased to at least minimum wage standard for all hours of availability)
33. Marginally Augmented Adequate Employment IFE Deficit (IFE Deficit if subgroup earnings increased to minimum wage standard for all hours of availability)
34. Marginally Augmented Capacity Employment IFE (IFE if subgroup earnings were increased so earnings in each hour not employed same as for hours employed)
35. Marginally Augmented Capacity Employment IFE Deficit (IFE Deficit if subgroup earnings increased so earnings in each hour not employed same as for hours employed)
36. Persons with Inadequate Individual Earnings in Families with Inadequate Family Earnings
37. Earnings Supplementation Rate (proportion persons with IFE who were in families with adequate income)

Interpretative Measures -- Transfer Impacts

38. Earnings Supplementation Rate-Nontransfers (proportion persons with IFE who were in families with adequate incomes net of transfers)
39. IFI Net-of-Transfers (IFI when cash transfers subtracted from income)
40. IFI Net-of-Transfers Deficit (IFI Deficit when cash transfers subtracted from income)
41. IFI Including Food Stamps (IFI when value of food stamps added to cash income)
42. IFI Including Food Stamps Deficit (IFI Deficit when value of food stamps added to cash income)
43. IFI Including In-Kind Aid (IFI when value of food stamps, housing subsidies and school lunches added to cash income)
44. IFI Including In-Kind Aid Deficit (IFI Deficit when value of food stamps, housing subsidies and school lunches added to cash income)

(5) using intermediate hardship standards and counting only those participants in the work force a half year or more; (6) using intermediate hardship standards and counting full-year work force participants; (7) using moderate hardship standards and counting all work force participants; (8) using moderate hardship standards and counting only those participants in the work force half year or more; and (9) using moderate hardship standards and counting just the full-year work force participants. The severe, intermediate, and moderate hardship standards for the measures of individual earnings adequacy are 100, 125, and 150 percent of the average real minimum wage for the 1967-1980 period, adjusted each year by the CPI less housing costs. The respective standards for the family earnings and income measures are 100, 125, and 150 percent of the poverty level for each family. Half-year participation is defined as 27 weeks or more and full-year participation as 50 weeks or more.

For each of the nine combinations of hardship severity and duration of work force participation, the hardship data matrix is calculated for all individuals, as well as selected subgroups. The disaggregations, selected on the basis of analytical importance, are as follows:

-- Region of residence:

1. New England
2. Middle Atlantic
3. East North Central
4. West North Central
5. South Atlantic
6. East South Central
7. West South Central
8. Mountain
9. Pacific

-- Area of residence:

1. Inside SMSA

    a. SMSA 1 million or more

        (1) Central city
        (2) Balance of SMSA

    b. SMSA under 1 million

        (1) Central city
        (2) Balance of SMSA

2. Outside SMSA

    a. Farm

-- State of residence (selected from those with adequate CPS sample size for tabulation of hardship measures)

    California
    Georgia
    New York
    North Carolina
    Ohio

-- Family size and earners

1. One person in work force

    a. 1 person in family
    b. 2 persons in family
    c. 3 persons in family
    d. 4-5 persons in family
    e. 6+ persons in family

2. Two persons in work force

    a. 2 persons in family
    b. 3 persons in family
    c. 4-5 persons in family
    d. 6+ persons in family

3. Three or more persons in work force

    a. 3 persons in family
    b. 4-5 persons in family
    c. 6+ persons in family

-- Race/origin of individual

1. White
2. Black
3. Hispanic (includes blacks and whites, as well as those identified neither as blacks or whites)

-- Sex of individual and family relationship

1. Male family head

    a. Wife in work force
    b. Wife not in work force
    c. Wife not present

2. Male unrelated individual
3. Female family head
4. Wife
5. Female unrelated individual
6. Other male
7. Other female

-- Age/student status

   1. 16-19 total
   2. 16-19 student as major activity in survey week
   3. 20-24 total
   4. 20-24 student as major activity in survey week
   5. 25-44
   6. 45-64
   7. 65+

-- Educational attainment

   1. High school student (primary activity in survey week)
   2. Post-secondary student (primary activity in survey week)
   3. High school dropout
   4. Out-of-school high school graduate with no further education
   5. Out-of-school high school graduate with 1-3 years of college
   6. Out-of-school high school graduate with 4 or more years of college

-- Occupation of longest job in last year

   1. None reported
   2. White collar

      a. Professional, technical, managerial and administrative
      b. Sales
      c. Clerical

   3. Blue collar

      a. Craftsmen
      b. Operatives
      c. Nonfarm laborers

   4. Farmworkers
   5. Service workers

-- Individual earnings deficit (minimum wage or multiple times hours availability for work minus annual earnings)

   1. $0-249
   2. $250-$499
   3. $500-$999
   4. $1000-$1499
   5. $1500-$1999
   6. $2000-$2499
   7. $2500-$2999
   8. $3000-$3999
   9. $4000+

-- Annual earnings

1. $0-$499
2. $500-$999
3. $1000-$1499
4. $1500-$1999
5. $2000-$2999
6. $3000-$3999
7. $4000-$4999
8. $5000-$6999
9. $7000-$8999
10. $9000+

-- Family income

1. Under $2000
2. $2000-$3999
3. $4000-$5999
4. $6000-$7999
5. $8000-$9999
6. $10000-$14999
7. $15000-$24999
8. $25000-$34999
9. $35000+

Appendix B provides detailed hardship data for 1979, but only a subpart of the full data matrix available with each disaggregation are presented. As an example of the comprehensive information which has been computed from the March CPS tapes covering 1974 through 1980, the intermediate hardship matrix is presented for female family heads in the work force full-year (Table A-3). To illustrate the interpretation of this matrix, there were 9,009,000 female family heads in March 1979 (Row 1, Column 17) of whom 4,267,000 participated 50 weeks or more in the work force (Row 1, Column 1). Among these full-year participants, 649,000 experienced at least a week of unemployment (Row 1, Column 6 plus Column 10). Among all female family heads participating full-year, 34.5 percent had earnings less than 125 percent of the minimum wage for their hours of availability (Row 3, Column 1); of these individuals 37.0 percent were employed full-time, full-year (Row 4, Column 2). There were 1,140,000 female family heads in the work force full-year whose family earnings were below 125 percent of the poverty level (Row 8, Column 1) and a total of 3,771,000 other female family heads in the work force less than full-year or not at all who had family earnings less than 125 percent of the poverty level (Row 8, Column 13). A total of 3,485,000 female family heads lived in near poverty (Row 14, Column 14), although the number would be reduced to 3,202,000 if the value of food stamps, school lunches and housing were added to cash income (Row 43, Column 17). Among the near poor, 772,000 were full-year work force participants (Row 14, Column 1). If all full-year participants in the work force had their earnings increased to 125 percent of the minimum wage for all hours of availability, the number of female family heads with family earnings less than 125 percent of poverty would have dropped from 1,140,000 (Row 8, Column 1) to 618,000 (Row 22, Column 1). If the earnings of only female family heads in the work force full-year were increased to 125 percent of the minimum wage level for all

Table A-3. INTERMEDIATE HARDSHIP MEASURES FOR FEMALE FAMILY HEADS IN WORK FORCE FULL-YEAR

	(1) Total In Work Force	(2) Employed Full-Time	(3) Employed Part-Time	(4) Employed Part-Time Voluntarily	(5) Employed Part-Time Involuntarily	(6) Intermittently Employed	(7) Mostly Employed	(8) Mixed	(9) Mostly Unemployed	(10) Not Employed	(11) Discouraged	(12) Unemployed	(13) Out of Work Force	(14) Armed Forces	(15) Age 0-15	(16) Age 16+	(17) Total In and Out of Work Force
1. Work Experience	4,267	2,622	966	714	282	624	382	169	73	25	19	6	4,742	0	0	4,742	9,009
2. IIE	1,470	544	484	311	173	418	212	139	66	25	19	6	523	0	0	523	1,994
3. IIE Incidence	34.5	20.7	48.6	43.6	61.1	66.9	55.7	82.1	90.7	100.0	100.0	100.0	11.0	0	0	11.0	22.1
4. IIE Distribution	100.0	37.0	32.9	21.2	11.7	28.4	14.4	9.5	4.5	1.7	1.3	0.4	--	--	--	--	--
5. IIE Deficit	3,752	1,176	1,002	497	505	1,388	508	519	361	187	141	47	--	--	--	--	--
6. IIE Average Deficit	2,552	2,161	2,071	1,599	2,023	3,323	2,391	3,374	5,443	7,441	7,434	7,462	--	--	--	--	--
7. IIE Deficit Distribution	100.0	31.3	26.7	13.3	13.4	37.0	13.5	13.8	9.6	5.0	3.8	1.2	--	--	--	--	--
8. IFE	1,140	324	420	296	125	375	182	126	67	21	15	6	3,771	0	0	3,771	4,911
9. IFE Incidence	26.7	12.3	42.2	41.4	44.2	60.1	47.7	74.4	91.5	84.0	78.8	100.0	79.5	0	0	79.5	54.5
10. IFE Distribution	100.0	28.4	36.9	25.9	10.9	32.9	16.0	11.1	5.9	1.9	1.3	0.5	--	--	--	--	--
11. IFE Deficit	3,606	838	1,287	917	371	1,315	513	445	358	164	112	52	--	--	--	--	--
12. IFE Average Deficit	3,163	2,591	3,062	3,101	2,971	3,510	2,821	3,527	5,355	7,772	7,509	8,401	--	--	--	--	--
13. IFE Deficit Distribution	100.0	23.3	35.7	25.4	10.3	36.5	14.2	12.3	9.9	4.6	3.1	1.5	--	--	--	--	--
14. IFI	772	218	261	173	87	272	129	87	56	21	15	6	2,713	0	0	2,713	3,485
15. IFI Incidence	18.1	8.3	26.2	24.3	30.9	43.6	33.8	51.1	77.3	84.0	78.8	100.0	57.2	0	0	57.2	39.7
16. IFI Distribution	100.0	28.2	33.8	22.5	11.3	35.1	16.7	11.2	7.3	2.7	1.9	0.8	--	--	--	--	--
17. IFI Deficit	2,036	480	709	483	225	736	309	239	188	111	72	39	--	--	--	--	--
18. IFI Average Deficit	2,639	2,207	2,719	2,787	2,584	2,705	2,394	2,756	3,336	5,246	4,851	6,191	--	--	--	--	--
19. IFI Deficit Distribution	100.0	23.6	34.8	23.7	11.1	36.1	15.2	11.7	9.2	5.5	3.6	1.9	--	--	--	--	--
20. Full Employment IFE	869	304	327	244	83	228	137	53	39	9	7	2	--	--	--	--	--
21. Full Employment IFE Deficit	2,263	892	828	615	213	519	326	101	92	24	13	11	3,681	--	--	--	4,550
22. Adequate Employment IFE	618	151	281	240	41	176	96	48	32	9	7	2	--	--	--	--	--
23. Adequate Employment IFE Deficit	1,502	386	730	615	115	364	219	89	56	22	11	11	3,595	--	--	--	4,213
24. Capacity Employment IFE	922	306	382	286	96	225	137	53	35	9	7	2	--	--	--	--	--
25. Capacity Employment IFE Deficit	2,780	900	1,255	986	268	604	376	134	94	22	11	11	3,709	--	--	--	4,631
26. Enhanced Earnings IFE	993	257	363	257	107	351	164	121	67	21	15	6	--	--	--	--	--
27. Enhanced Earnings IFE Deficit	3,388	743	1,220	865	355	1,260	477	431	353	164	112	53	3,685	--	--	--	4,678
28. Enhanced Capacity IFE	488	114	227	193	34	140	78	37	25	7	5	2	--	--	--	--	--
29. Enhanced Capacity IFE Deficit	1,123	255	593	506	87	258	164	58	36	17	7	10	3,512	--	--	--	4,000
30. Marginally Augmented Full Employment IFE	7,837	2,368	2,880	2,152	728	2,399	1,008	843	547	191	154	37	--	--	--	--	--
31. Marginally Augmented Full Employment IFE Deficit	23,086	6,614	7,735	5,488	2,247	7,590	2,744	2,619	2,227	7,735	2,247	5,488	54,366	101	14,717	39,547	62,202
32. Marginally Augmented Adequate Employment IFE	7,575	2,209	2,835	2,149	686	2,342	961	839	542	188	153	35	--	--	--	--	--
33. Marginally Augmented Adequate Employment IFE Deficit	22,278	6,090	7,628	5,484	2,144	7,417	2,631	2,599	2,187	1,143	966	177	53,994	101	14,420	39,473	61,569
34. Marginally Augmented Capacity Employment IFE	7,893	2,368	2,935	2,194	741	2,399	1,013	843	543	190	154	37	--	--	--	--	--
35. Marginally Augmented Capacity Employment IFE Deficit	23,617	6,615	8,166	5,864	2,302	7,689	2,797	2,657	2,234	1,147	968	179	54,516	101	14,726	39,589	62,309
36. Persons in Both IIE and IFE	967	265	342	220	122	339	153	124	63	21	15	6	--	--	--	--	--
37. Earnings Supplementation Rate	32.3	32.7	38.0	41.3	30.1	27.4	29.0	31.3	15.5	0	0	0	--	--	--	--	--
38. Earnings Supplementation Rate-Nontransfers	14.4	16.7	16.4	18.9	10.5	10.9	16.9	8.0	0.2	0	0	0	--	--	--	--	--
39. IFI Net-of-Transfers	976	269	352	240	112	334	151	116	67	21	15	6	3,397	0	0	3,397	4,373
40. IFI Net-of-Transfers Deficit	3,104	697	1,100	771	329	1,144	423	408	313	163	112	52	--	--	--	--	--
41. IFI Including Food Stamps	732	207	244	159	86	259	123	84	52	21	11	6	2,597	0	0	2,597	3,329
42. IFI Including Food Stamps Deficit	1,698	403	593	405	188	616	260	205	152	87	56	31	--	--	--	--	--
43. IFI Including In-Kind Aid	679	188	234	155	79	235	113	74	49	21	15	6	2,523	0	0	2,523	3,202
44. IFI Including In-Kind Aid Deficit	1,513	353	536	368	168	546	226	183	137	79	49	30	--	--	--	--	--

hours of availability, the 8,088,000 IFE total for all full-year work force participants in 1979 would have been reduced to 7,575,000 (Row 23, Column 1).

There are a number of assumptions which must be made, given limitations in the information available from the March Current Population Survey questionnaire, in order to derive the hardship measures for individuals with differing work experience patterns. The detailed definitions and calculation procedures for each measure in the hardship data matrix are contained in Table A-4. Because the concepts behind each measure are consistent, but must be derived separately depending on an individual's work experience pattern, Table A-4 presents definitions for all measures (Rows 1-44) for each separate work experience pattern category. For instance, all 44 measures are first defined for persons working full-time all weeks in the work force. They are next defined for persons working part-time voluntarily some or all weeks in the work force, and so forth for the other categories. The hardship counts for the total work force are defined as the sum of these separately calculated elements. Column 1, Total Work Force, is thus excluded from the definitional table because it represents the sum of Columns 2 through 12. Column 2, Employed Part-Time, is excluded since this is simply the sum of Columns 4 and 5, Employed Part-Tme Voluntarily and Involuntarily. Likewise, Column 10, Not Employed, is excluded, since it is the sum of Column 11, Discouraged, and Column 12, Unemployed. Columns 7, 8 and 9 are also excluded, since they are subclassifications of, and calculated in the same way as Column 6, Intermittently Employed, simply classifying each individual according to whether they were unemployed less than a third of their weeks in the work force (Column 7, Mostly Employed), over two-thirds of their weeks in the work force (Column 9, Mostly Unemployed) or had intermediate unemployment (Column 8, Mixed). Finally Columns 14 through 17 are excluded. Column 14, Armed Forces, Column 15, Persons Age 0-15, and Column 16, Persons Age 16 and Over are subclassifications of Column 13, while Column 17 is the sum of Columns 1 and 13. Columns 13 through 17 are only calculated for Rows 1-3, 8, 9, 14, 15, 39, 41 and 43. It might be noted that when the hardship measures are restricted to full-year or to half-year participants, the less-than-full-year or less-than-half-year participants are then added to the out-of-the-work-force categories.

A key step in the derivation of these definitions is the calculation of an "individual earnings standard" for every work force participant using questions about weeks of participation, usual weekly hours, and the number of weeks when the individual worked more or worked less than usual hours, in order to estimate hours of availability for work during the year and the earnings that would have been provided at a minimum wage hourly rate or its multiple. The IIE compares actual earnings for each work force participant to this individual earnings standard. Where actual earnings are below this standard, the IIE Deficit is the difference between them. The Adequate Employment IFE augments the earnings of each individual in the IFE up to the "individual earnings standard" if their earnings are below this level.

Table A-4. DETAILED DEFINITIONS OF HARDSHIP MEASURES

(2). Employed Full-Time

#	Measure	Definition
1.	Work Force Experience	1(2) = Employed all weeks in labor force with no weeks of less than 35 hours employment
2.	Inadequate Individual Earnings (IIE)	2(2) = 1(2) minus persons with annual earnings above an individual earnings standard equal to product of weeks in labor force times minimum hourly wage or multiple times hours usually worked per week
3.	IIE Incidence	3(2) = 100 times 2(2) ÷ 1(2)
4.	IIE Distribution	4(2) = 100 times 2(2) ÷ 2(1)
5.	IIE Total Deficit	5(2) = Sum of differences between annual earnings of persons in 2(2) and individual earnings standards as specified in 2(2)
6.	IIE Average Deficit	6(2) = 5(2) ÷ 2(2)
7.	IIE Deficit Distribution	7(2) = 100 times 5(2) ÷ 5(1)
8.	Inadequate Family Earnings (IFE)	8(2) = 1(2) minus persons in families with sum of annual earnings of all members above poverty threshold or multiple
9.	IFE Incidence	9(2) = 100 times 8(2) ÷ 1(2)
10.	IFE Distribution	10(2) = 100 times 8(2) ÷ 8(1)
11.	IFE Total Deficit	11(2) = For unrelated individuals and persons in 8(2) who are sole work force participants in families, sum of differences between annual earnings and appropriate poverty standard or multiple. For persons in families with two or more adjusted work force participants and whose combined IIE Deficit is equal to or greater than difference between poverty standard and aggregate family earnings, sum of differences between appropriate poverty standard or multiple and aggregate family earnings, times share of combined family IIE Deficit accounted for by persons in 8(2). For persons in families with two or more adjusted work force participants and whose family IIE Deficit is less than difference between poverty standard and aggregate family earnings, sum of IIE Deficits for family members in 8(2) plus these members' share of combined individual earnings standards (or earnings if higher) for family members times the difference between the poverty standard or multiple minus aggregate family earnings, and the combined family IIE Deficit
12.	IFE Average Deficit	12(2) = 11(2) ÷ 8(2)
13.	IFE Deficit Distribution	13(2) = 100 times 11(2) ÷ 11(1)
14.	Inadequate Family Income (IFI)	14(2) = 8(2) minus persons in families with total income above poverty threshold or multiple
15.	IFI Incidence	15(2) = 100 times 14(2) ÷ 1(2)
16.	IFI Distribution	16(2) = 100 times 14(2) ÷ 14(1)
17.	IFI Total Deficit	17(2) = For unrelated individuals and persons in 14(2) who are sole work force participants in families, sum of differences between family income and poverty standard or multiple. For persons in families with two or more persons in adjusted work force and whose combined IIE Deficit is equal to or greater than difference between poverty standard and family income, sum of differences between appropriate poverty standard or multiple and aggregate family income, times share of combined family IIE Deficit accounted for by persons in 14(2). For persons in families with two or more persons in adjusted work force and where combined family IIE Deficit is less than difference between poverty standard and family income, sum of IIE Deficit for family members in 14(2) plus these members' share of combined individual earnings standards (or earnings if higher) for family members times the difference between the poverty standard or multiple minus family income, and the combined family IIE Deficit
18.	IFI Average Deficit	18(2) = 17(2) ÷ 14(2)
19.	IFI Deficit Distribution	19(2) = 100 times 17(2) ÷ 17(1)
20.	Full Employment IFE	20(2) = 8(2) minus persons in families with augmented earnings of all family members in 1(1) plus actual earnings of family members not in 1(1) greater than poverty threshold (augmented earnings for persons in 8(2) are same as actual earnings)
21.	Full Employment IFE Deficit	21(2) = Calculated similar to 11(2) for persons in 20(2) with sum of augmented and actual earnings of family members as specified in 20(2) through 20(12) instead of actual earnings compared to poverty standard or multiple

Table A-4. (Continued)

22.	Adequate Employment IFE	22(2) = Calculated similar to 20(2) with augmented earnings for persons in 8(2) equal to individual earnings standard as specified in 2(2) or actual earnings, whichever is larger
23.	Adequate Employment IFE Deficit	23(2) = Calculated similar to 21(2) with augmented earnings as specified in 22(2) through 22(12)
24.	Capacity Employment IFE	24(2) = Calculated similar to 20(2) with augmented earnings for persons in 8(2) equal to actual earnings
25.	Capacity Employment IFE Deficit	25(2) = Calculated similar to 21(2) with augmented earnings as specified in 24(2) through 24(12)
26.	Enhanced Earnings IFE	26(2) = Calculated similar to 20(2) with augmented earnings for persons in 8(1) equal to 110 percent of actual earnings
27.	Enhanced Earnings IFE Deficit	27(2) = Calculated similar to 20(2) with augmented earnings as specified in 26(2)
28.	Enhanced Capacity IFE	28(2) = Calculated similar to 20(2) with earnings augmented to 110 percent those specified in 24(2) through 24(12)
29.	Enhanced Capacity IFE Deficit	29(2) = Calculated similar to 21(2) with earnings augmented to 110 percent those specified in 24(2) through 24(12)
30.	Marginally Augmented Full Employment IFE (calculated only for sex, family relationship and age disaggregations)	30(2) = 8(2) minus persons in families with augmented earnings of all family members in 1(1) as disaggregated plus actual earnings of family members not in 1(1) as disaggregated greater than poverty threshold (augmented earnings for disaggregated subgroup members in 8(2) are same as actual earnings)
31.	Marginally Augmented Full Employment IFE Deficit (calculated only for sex/family relationship and age disaggregations)	31(2) = Calculated similar to 11(2) with sum of augmented and actual earnings of family members as specified in 30(2) through 30(12) instead of actual earnings compared to poverty standard or multiple
32.	Marginally Augmented Adequate Employment IFE (calculated only for sex/family relationship and age disaggregations)	32(2) = Calculated similar to 30(2) with augmented earnings for disaggregated subgroup members in 8(1) equal to individual earnings standards as specified in 2(2) through 2(12) or actual earnings, whichever are larger
33.	Marginally Augmented Adequate Employment IFE Deficit (calculated only for sex, family relationship and age disaggregations)	33(2) = Calculated similar to 21(2) with augmented earnings as specified in 32(2) through 32(12)
34.	Marginally Augmented Capacity Employment IFE (calculated only for sex/family relationship and age disaggregations)	34(2) = Calculated similar to 30(2) with augmented earnings for disaggregated subgroup members in 8(2) equal to actual earnings, and augmented earnings of other disaggregated subgroup members in 8(1) as specified in 8(3) through 8(12)
35.	Marginally Augmented Capacity Employment IFE Deficit (calculated only for sex/family relationship and age disaggregations)	35(2) = Calculated similar to 31(2) with augmented earnings as specified in 34(2) through 34(12)
36.	Persons with Earnings Deficits in Families with Earnings Deficits	36(2) = 8(2) minus persons not included in 2(2)
37.	Earnings Supplementation Rate	37(2) = [1 - 14(2)/8(2)] times 100
38.	Earnings Supplementation Rate-Nontransfers	38(2) = [1 - 39(2)/8(2)] times 100
39.	IFI Net-of-Transfers	39(2) = 8(2) minus persons in families with income excluding cash transfers above poverty standard or multiple
40.	IFI Net-of-Transfers Deficit	40(2) = Calculated similar to 17(2) except using family income excluding cash transfers
41.	IFI Including Food Stamps (calculated only for 1979 and 1980)	41(2) = 8(2) minus persons in families with cash income plus value of food stamps above poverty standard or multiple
42.	IFI Including Food Stamps Deficit (calculated only for 1979 and 1980)	42(2) = Calculated similar to 17(2) except using family cash income plus food stamp value
43.	IFI Including In-Kind Aid (calculated only for 1979 and 1980)	43(2) = 8(2) minus persons in families with cash income plus value of food stamps received plus number of family members receiving free or reduced price lunches times .044 poverty threshold for family, and, if resident of subsidized housing, plus 40 percent of cash income if cash income less than $3000; 25 percent if $3000-$6999; 10 percent if $7000-$9999; and 5 percent if $10,000 or more, is above poverty standard or multiple
44.	IFI Including In-Kind Aid Deficit (calculated only for 1979 and 1980)	44(2) = Calculated similar to 17(2) except using cash and including income for family as specified in 43(2)

Table A-4. (Continued)

(4). Employed Part-Time Voluntarily

1.	Work Force Experience	1(4) = Worked throughout period of labor force participation; some weeks less than 35 hours; main reason was that wanted to work part-time, could only work part-time or other
2.	Inadequate Individual Earnings (IIE)	2(4) = 1(4) minus persons earning more than an individual earnings standard equal to hours usually worked times minimum wage or multiple times weeks in labor force if usual hours less than 35 unless weeks worked less than 35 are less than weeks worked in which case 40 hours are ascribed to the weeks worked more than part-time; if usual hours more than 35 but some weeks voluntarily less than 35, these weeks are ascribed 20 hours while others are ascribed usual hours
3.	IIE Incidence	3(4) = 100 times 2(4) ÷ 1(4)
4.	IIE Distribution	4(4) = 100 times 2(4) ÷ 2(1)
5.	IIE Total Deficit	5(4) = Sum of differences between annual earnings of persons in 2(4) and individual earnings standards as specified in 2(4)
6.	IIE Average Deficit	6(4) = 5(4) ÷ 2(4)
7.	IIE Deficit Distribution	7(4) = 100 times 5(4) ÷ 5(1)
8.	Inadequate Family Earnings (IFE)	8(4) = 1(4) minus persons in families with sum of annual earnings of all members above poverty threshold or multiple
9.	IFE Incidence	9(4) = 100 times 8(4) ÷ 1(4)
10.	IFE Distribution	10(4) = 100 times 8(4) ÷ 8(1)
11.	IFE Total Deficit	11(4) = For unrelated individuals and persons in 8(4) who are sole work force participants in families, sum of differences between annual earnings and appropriate poverty standard or multiple. For persons in families with two or more adjusted work force participants and whose combined IIE Deficit is equal to or greater than difference between poverty standard and aggregate family earnings, sum of differences between appropriate poverty standard or multiple and aggregate family earnings, times share of combined family IIE Deficit accounted for by persons in 8(4). For persons in families with two or more adjusted work force participants and whose family IIE Deficit is less than difference between poverty standard and aggregate family earnings, sum of IIE Deficits for family members in 8(4) plus these members' share of combined individual earnings standards (or earnings if higher) for family members times the difference between the poverty standard or multiple minus aggregate family earnings, and the combined family IIE Deficit
12.	IFE Average Deficit	12(4) = 11(4) ÷ 8(4)
13.	IFE Deficit Distribution	13(4) = 100 times 11(4) ÷ 11(1)
14.	Inadequate Family Income (IFI)	14(4) = 8(4) minus persons in families with total income above poverty threshold or multiple
15.	IFI Incidence	15(4) = 100 times 14(4) ÷ 1(4)
16.	IFI Distribution	16(4) = 100 times 14(4) ÷ 14(1)
17.	IFI Total Deficit	17(4) = For unrelated individuals and persons in 14(4) who are sole work force participants in families, sum of differences between family income and poverty standard or multiple. For persons in families with two or more persons in adjusted work force and whose combined IIE Deficit is equal to or greater than difference between poverty standard and family income, sum of differences between appropriate poverty standard or multiple and aggregate family income, times share of combined family IIE Deficit accounted for by persons in 14(4). For persons in families with two or more persons in adjusted work force and where combined family IIE Deficit is less than difference between poverty standard and family income, sum of IIE Deficit for family members in 14(4) plus these members' share of combined individual earnings standards (or earnings if higher) for family members times the difference between the poverty standard or multiple minus family income, and the combined family IIE Deficit
18.	IFI Average Deficit	18(4) = 17(4) ÷ 14(4)
19.	IFI Deficit Distribution	19(4) = 100 times 17(4) ÷ 17(1)
20.	Full Employment IFE	20(4) = 8(4) minus persons in families with augmented earnings of all family members in 1(1) plus actual earnings of family members not in 1(1) greater than poverty threshold (augmented earnings for persons in 8(4) equal actual earnings)
21.	Full Employment IFE Deficit	21(4) = Calculated similar to 11(4) with sum of augmented and actual earnings of family members as specified in 20(2) through 20(12) instead of actual earnings compared to poverty standard or multiple
22.	Adequate Employment IFE	22(4) = Calculated similar to 20(4) with augmented earnings of all family members in 8(4) equal to individual earnings standard as specified in 2(4)

Table A-4. (Continued)

#	Name	Definition
23.	Adequate Employment IFE Deficit	23(4) = Calculated similar to 21(4) with augmented earnings as specified in 22(2) through 22(13)
24.	Capacity Employment IFE	24(4) = Calculated similar to 20(4) with augmented earnings for persons in 8(4) same as actual earnings
25.	Capacity Employment IFE Deficit	25(4) = Calculated similar to 21(4) with augmented earnings as specified in 24(2) through 24(12)
26.	Enhanced Earnings IFE	26(4) = Calculated similar to 20(4) with augmented earnings for persons in 8(1) equal to 110 percent of actual earnings
27.	Enhanced Earnings IFE Deficit	27(4) = Calculated similar to 21(4) with augmented earnings for all persons in 8(1) equal to 110 percent of actual earnings
28.	Enhanced Capacity IFE	28(4) = Calculated similar to 20(4) with earnings augmented to 110 percent those specified in 24(2) through 24(12)
29.	Enhanced Capacity IFE Deficit	29(4) = Calculated similar to 21(4) with earnings augmented to 110 percent those specified in 24(2) through 24(12)
30.	Marginally Augmented Full Employment IFE (calculated only for sex/family relationship and age disaggregations)	30(4) = 8(4) minus persons in families with augmented earnings of all family members in 1(1) as disaggregated plus actual earnings of family members not in 1(1) as disaggregated greater than poverty threshold (augmented earnings for disaggregated subgroup members in 8(4) equal actual earnings)
31.	Marginally Augmented Full Employment IFE Deficit (calculated only for sex/family relationship and age disaggregations)	31(4) = Calculated similar to 11(4) with sum of augmented and actual earnings of family members as specified in 30(2) through 30(12) instead of actual earnings compared to poverty standard or multiple
32.	Marginally Augmented Adequate Employment IFE (calculated only for sex/family relationship and age disaggregations)	32(4) = Calculated similar to 30(4) with augmented earnings of all disaggregated subgroup members in 8(4) equal to individual earnings standard as specified in 2(4)
33.	Marginally Augmented Adequate Employment IFE Deficit (calculated only for sex/family relationship and age disaggregations)	33(4) = Calculated similar to 31(4) with augmented earnings as specified in 32(2) through 32(12)
34.	Marginally Augmented Capacity Employment IFE (calculated only for sex/family relationship and age disaggregations)	34(4) = Calculated similar to 30(4) with augmented earnings for disaggregated subgroup members in 8(4) same as actual earnings
35.	Marginally Augmented Capacity Employment IFE Deficit (calculated only for sex/family relationship and age disaggregations)	35(4) = Calculated similar to 31(4) with augmented earnings as specified in 34(2) through 34(12)
36.	Persons with Earnings Deficits in Families with Earnings Deficits	36(4) = 8(4) minus persons not included in 2(4)
37.	Earnings Supplementation Rate	37(4) = [1 - 14(4)/8(4)] times 100
38.	Earnings Supplementation Rate-Nontransfers	38(4) = [1 - 39(4)/8(4)] times 100
39.	IFI Net-of-Transfers	39(4) = 8(4) minus persons in families with income excluding cash transfers above poverty standard or multiple
40.	IFI Net-of-Transfers Deficit	40(4) = Calculated similar to 17(4) except using family income excluding cash transfers
41.	IFI Including Food Stamps (calculated only for 1979 and 1980)	41(4) = 8(4) minus persons in families with cash income plus value of food stamps above poverty standard or multiple
42.	IFI Including Food Stamps Deficit (calculated only for 1979 and 1980)	42(4) = Calculated similar to 17(4) except using family cash income plus food stamp value
43.	IFI Including In-Kind Aid (calculated only for 1979 and 1980)	43(4) = 8(4) minus persons in families with cash income supplemented as noted in 43(2) is above poverty standard or multiple
44.	IFI Including In-Kind Aid Deficit (calculated only for 1979 and 1980)	44(4) = Calculated similar to 17(4) except using cash and including income for family as specified in 43(2)

Table A-4. (Continued)

(5). Employed Part-Time Involuntarily

1. **Work Force Experience**

   1(5) = Worked throughout period of labor force participation; some or all weeks less than 35 hours; main reason for reduced hours was that could only find part-time jobs, slack work or materials shortage

2. **Inadequate Individual Earnings (IIE)**

   2(5) = 1(5) minus persons earning more than an individual earnings standard equal to 40 times minimum wage or multiple times weeks in labor force if usually worked less than 35; although add 40 times weeks involuntary part-time to usual hours times weeks full-time

3. **IIE Incidence**

   3(5) = 100 times 2(5) ÷ 1(5)

4. **IIE Distribution**

   4(5) = 100 times 2(5) ÷ 2(1)

5. **IIE Total Deficit**

   5(5) = Sum of differences between annual earnings of persons in 2(5) and individual earnings standards as specified in 2(5)

6. **IIE Average Deficit**

   6(5) = 5(5) ÷ 2(5)

7. **IIE Deficit Distribution**

   7(5) = 100 times 5(5) ÷ 5(1)

8. **Inadequate Family Earnings (IFE)**

   8(5) = 1(5) minus persons in families with sum of annual earnings of all members above poverty threshold or multiple

9. **IFE Incidence**

   9(5) = 100 times 8(5) ÷ 1(5)

10. **IFE Distribution**

    10(5) = 100 times 8(5) ÷ 8(1)

11. **IFE Total Deficit**

    11(5) = For unrelated individuals and person in 8(5) who are sole work force participants in families, sum of differences between annual earnings and appropriate poverty standard or multiple. For persons in families with two or more adjusted work force participants and whose combined IIE Deficit is equal to or greater than difference between poverty standard and aggregate family earnings, sum of differences between appropriate poverty standard or multiple and aggregate family earnings, times share of combined family IIE Deficit accounted for by persons in 8(5). For persons in families with two or more adjusted work force participants and whose family IIE Deficit is less than difference between poverty standard and aggregate family earnings, sum of IIE Deficits for family members in 8(5) plus these members' share of combined individual earnings standards (or earnings if higher) for family members times the difference between the poverty standard or multiple minus aggregate family earnings, and the combined family IIE Deficit

12. **IFE Average Deficit**

    12(5) = 11(5) ÷ 8(5)

13. **IFE Deficit Distribution**

    13(5) = 100 times 11(5) ÷ 11(1)

14. **Inadequate Family Income (IFI)**

    14(5) = 8(5) minus persons in families with total income above poverty threshold or multiple

15. **IFI Incidence**

    15(5) = 100 times 14(5) ÷ 1(5)

16. **IFI Distribution**

    16(5) = 100 times 14(5) ÷ 14(1)

17. **IFI Total Deficit**

    17(5) = For unrelated individuals and persons in 14(5) who are sole work force participants in families, sum of differences between family income and poverty standard or multiple. For persons in families with two or more persons in adjusted work force and whose combined IIE Deficit is equal to or greater than difference between poverty standard and family income, sum of differences between appropriate poverty standard or multiple and aggregate family income, times share of combined family IIE Deficit accounted for by persons in 14(5). For persons in families with two or more persons in adjusted work force and where combined family IIE Deficit is less than difference between poverty standard and family income, sum of IIE Deficit for family members in 14(5) plus these members' share of combined individual earnings standards (or earnings if higher) for family members times the difference between the poverty standard or multiple minus family income, and the combined family IIE Deficit

18. **IFI Average Deficit**

    18(5) = 17(5) ÷ 14(5)

19. **IFI Deficit Distribution**

    19(5) = 100 times 17(5) ÷ 17(1)

20. **Full Employment IFE**

    20(5) = 8(5) minus persons in families with augmented earnings of all family members in 1(1) plus actual earnings of family members not in 1(1) greater than poverty threshold (augmented earnings for persons in 8(5) equal earnings plus minimum wage or multiple times 40 minus usual hours times weeks worked less than 35 involuntarily where usual less than 35 or plus minimum wage or multiple times usual hours minus 20 times weeks worked less than 35 involuntarily where usual hours more than 35)

21. **Full Employment IFE Deficit**

    21(5) = Calculated similar to 11(5) for persons in 20(5) with sum of augmented and actual earnings of family members as specified in 20(2) through 20(12) instead of actual earnings compared to poverty standard or multiple

Table A-4. (Continued)

22.	Adequate Employment IFE	22(5) = Calculated similar to 20(5) with augmented earnings of all family members in 8(5) equal to individual earnings standard as specified in 2(5)
23.	Adequate Employment IFE Deficit	23(5) = Calculated similar to 21(5) with augmented earnings as specified in 22(2) through 22(12)
24.	Capacity Employment IFE	24(5) = Calculated similar to 20(5) with augmented earnings for persons in 8(5) if usual hours less than 35 and no weeks greater than 35, 40 times annual earnings ÷ usual weekly hours; if usual less than 35 and some weeks greater than 35, usual hours times annual earnings times weeks worked ÷ [usual hours times weeks part-time plus 40 times weeks full-time]; is usual hours 35 or more, usual hours times annual earnings times weeks worked ÷ [40 times weeks full-time plus 20 times weeks part-time]
25.	Capacity Employment IFE Deficit	25(5) = Calculated similar to 21(5) with augmented earnings as specified in 24(2) through 24(12)
26.	Enhanced Earnings IFE	26(5) = Calculated similar to 20(5) with augmented earnings for all persons in 8(1) equal to 110 percent of actual earnings
27.	Enhanced Earnings IFE Deficit	27(5) = Calculated similar to 21(5) with augmented earnings for all persons in 8(1) equal to 110 percent of actual earnings
28.	Enhanced Capacity IFE	28(5) = Calculated similar to 20(5) with earnings augmented to 110 percent those specified in 24(2) through 24(12)
29.	Enhanced Capacity IFE Deficit	29(5) = Calculated similar to 21(5) with earnings augmented to 110 percent those specified in 24(2) through 24(12)
30.	Marginally Augmented Full Employment IFE (calculated only for sex/family relationship and age disaggregations)	30(5) = 8(5) minus persons in families with augmented earnings of all family members in 1(1) as disaggregated plus actual earnings of all family members not in 1(1) as disaggregated greater than poverty threshold (augmented earnings for disaggregated subgroup members in 8(5) equal earnings plus minimum wage or multiple times 40 minus usual hours times weeks worked less than 35 where usual less than 35 or plus minimum wage or multiple times usual hours minus 20 times weeks worked less than 35 where usual hours more than 35)
31.	Marginally Augmented Full Employment IFE Deficit (calculated only for sex/family relationship and age disaggregations)	31(5) = Calculated similar to 11(5) with sum of augmented and actual earnings of family members as specified in 30(2) through 30(12) instead of actual earnings compared to poverty standard or multiple
32.	Marginally Augmented Adequate Employment IFE (calculated only for sex/family relationship and age disaggregations)	32(5) = Calculated similar to 30(5) with augmented earnings of all disaggregated subgroup members in 8(5) equal to individual earnings standard as specified in 2(5)
33.	Marginally Augmented Adequate Employment IFE Deficit (calculated only for sex/family relationship and age disaggregations)	33(5) = Calculated similar to 31(5) with augmented earnings as specified in 32(2) through 32(12)
34.	Marginally Augmented Capacity Employment IFE (calculated only for sex/family relationship and age disaggregations)	34(5) = Calculated similar to 30(5) with augmented earnings for disaggregated subgroup members in 8(5) if usual hours less than 35 and no weeks greater than 35, 40 times annual earnings ÷ usual weekly hours; if usual less than 35 and some weeks greater than 35, usual hours times annual earnings times weeks worked ÷ [usual hours times weeks part-time plus 40 times weeks full-time]; if usual hours 35 or more, usual hours times annual earnings times weeks worked ÷ [40 times weeks full-time plus 20 times weeks part-time]
35.	Marginally Augmented Capacity Employment IFE Deficit (calculated only for sex/family relationship and age disaggregations)	35(5) = Calculated similar to 31(5) with augmented earnings as specified in 34(2) through 34(12)
36.	Persons with Earnings Deficits in Families with Earnings Deficits	36(5) = 8(5) minus persons not included in 2(5)
37.	Earnings Supplementation Rate	37(5) = [1 - 14(5)/8(5)] times 100
38.	Earnings Supplementation Rate-Nontransfers	38(5) = [1 - 39(5)/8(5)] times 100
39.	IFI Net-of-Transfers	39(5) = 8(5) minus persons in families with income excluding cash transfers above poverty standard or multiple
40.	IFI Net-of-Transfers Deficit	40(5) = Calculated similar to 17(5) except using family income excluding cash transfers
41.	IFI Including Food Stamps (calculated only for 1979 and 1980)	41(5) = 8(5) minus persons in families with cash income plus value of food stamps above poverty standard or multiple
42.	IFI Including Food Stamps Deficit (calculated only for 1979 and 1980)	42(5) = Calculated similar to 17(5) except using family cash income plus food stamp value
43.	IFI Including In-Kind Aid (calculated only for 1979 and 1980)	43(5) = 8(5) minus persons in families with cash income supplemented as noted in 43(2) is above poverty standard or multiple
44.	IFI Including In-Kind Aid Deficit (calculated only for 1979 and 1980)	44(5) = Calculated similar to 17(5) except using cash and including income for family as specified in 43(2)

Table A-4. (Continued)

(6). Intermittently Employed

1. **Work Force Experience** — 1(6) = Experienced weeks of both employment and unemployment while in the work force

2. **Inadequate Individual Earnings (IIE)** — 2(6) = 1(6) minus persons with annual earnings in excess of an individual earnings standard equal to the product of weeks in labor force times minimum wage or multiple times usual hours worked, except in case where usual hours less than 35 and main reason less than 35 was slack work or could only find part-time job, in which case 40 hours substitutes for usual hours, and except where some weeks employment were at less than 35 hours because wanted part-time work or could only work part-time while usual hours were above 35 hours, in which case weeks less than 35 hours are assigned 20 hours, other weeks employed are assigned usual hours, and weeks unemployed are assigned 20 or usual hours in proportion to weeks employed part-time voluntarily to weeks employed full-time

3. **IIE Incidence** — 3(6) = 100 times 2(6) ÷ 1(6)

4. **IIE Distribution** — 4(6) = 100 times 2(6) ÷ 2(1)

5. **IIE Total Deficit** — 5(6) = Sum of differences between annual earnings of persons in 2(6) and individual earnings standards as specified in 2(6)

6. **IIE Average Deficit** — 6(6) = 5(6) ÷ 2(6)

7. **IIE Deficit Distribution** — 7(6) = 100 times 5(6) ÷ 5(1)

8. **Inadequate Family Earnings (IFE)** — 8(6) = 1(6) minus persons in families with sum of annual earnings of all members above poverty threshold or multiple

9. **IFE Incidence** — 9(6) = 100 times 8(6) ÷ 2(6)

10. **IFE Distribution** — 10(6) = 100 times 8(6) ÷ 8(1)

11. **IFE Total Deficit** — 11(6) = For unrelated individuals and persons in 8(6) who are sole work force participants in families, sum of differences between annual earnings and appropriate poverty standard or multiple. For persons in families with two or more adjusted work force participants and whose combined IIE Deficit is equal to or greater than difference between poverty standard and aggregate family earnings, sum of differences between appropriate poverty standard or multiple and aggregate family earnings, times share of combined family IIE Deficit accounted for by persons in 8(6). For persons in families with two or more adjusted work force participants and whose family IIE Deficit is less than difference between poverty standard and aggregate family earnings, sum of IIE Deficits for family members in 8(6) plus these members' share of combined individual earnings standards (or earnings if higher) for family members times the difference between the poverty standard or multiple minus aggregate family earnings, and the combined family IIE Deficit

12. **IFE Average Deficit** — 12(6) = 11(6) ÷ 8(6)

13. **IFE Deficit Distribution** — 13(6) = 100 times 11(6) ÷ 11(1)

14. **Inadequate Family Income (IFI)** — 14(6) = 8(6) minus persons in families with total income above poverty threshold or multiple

15. **IFI Incidence** — 15(6) = 100 times 14(6) ÷ 1(6)

16. **IFI Distribution** — 16(6) = 100 times 14(6) ÷ 14(1)

17. **IFI Total Deficit** — 17(6) = For unrelated individuals and persons in 14(6) who are sole work force participants in families, sum of differences between family income and poverty standard or multiple. For persons in families with two or more persons in adjusted work force and whose combined IIE Deficit is equal to or greater than difference between poverty standard and family income, sum of differences between appropriate poverty standard or multiple and aggregate family income, times share of combined family IIE Deficit accounted for by persons in 14(6). For persons in families with two or more persons in adjusted work force and where combined family IIE Deficit is less than difference between poverty standard and family income, sum of IIE Deficit for family members in 14(6) plus these members' share of combined individual earnings standards (or earnings if higher) for family members times the difference between the poverty standard or multiple minus family income, and the combined family IIE Deficit

18. **IFI Average Deficit** — 18(6) = 17(6) ÷ 14(6)

19. **IFI Deficit Distribution** — 19(6) = 100 times 17(6) ÷ 17(1)

20. **Full Employment IFE** — 20(6) = 8(6) minus persons in families with augmented earnings of all family members in 1(1) plus actual earnings of family members not in 1(1) greater than poverty threshold (augmented earnings for persons in 8(6) are actual earnings plus weeks unemployed times usual hours worked times minimum wage or multiple except where some weeks employed part-time involuntarily in which case earnings also augmented by minimum wage or multiple times 40 minus usual hours times weeks less than 35 where usual is less than 35, or by minimum wage or multiple times usual hours minus 20 times weeks worked less than 35 hours where usual more than 35)

Table A-4. (Continued)

#	Name	Definition
21.	Full Employment IFE Deficit	21(6) = Calculated similar to 11(6) for persons in 20(6) with sum of augmented and actual earnings of family members as specified in 20(2) through 20(12) instead of actual earnings compared to poverty standard or multiple
22.	Adequate Employment IFE	22(6) = Calculated similar to 20(6) with augmented earnings of all family members in 8(6) equal to individual earnings standard as specified in 2(6)
23.	Adequate Employment IFE Deficit	23(6) = Calculated similar to 21(6) with augmented earnings as specified in 22(2) through 22(12)
24.	Capacity Employment IFE	24(6) = Calculated similar to 20(6) with augmented earnings for persons in 8(6) equal to weekly earnings for weeks employed times weeks in labor force; where some weeks employed part-time involuntarily, equal annual earnings ÷ weeks full-time and 1/2 weeks part-time, times weeks in labor force
25.	Capacity Employment IFE Deficit	25(6) = Calculated similar to 21(6) with augmented earnings as specified in 24(2) through 24(12)
26.	Enhanced Earnings IFE	26(6) = Calculated similar to 20(6) with augmented earnings for persons in 8(1) equal to 110 percent of actual earnings
27.	Enhanced Earnings IFE Deficit	27(6) = Calculated similar to 21(6) with augmented earnings for persons in 8(1) equal to 110 percent of actual earnings
28.	Enhanced Capacity IFE	28(6) = Calculated similar to 20(6) with earnings augmented to 110 percent those specified in 24(2) through 24(12)
29.	Enhanced Capacity IFE Deficit	29(6) = Calculated similar to 21(6) with earnings augmented to 110 percent those specified in 24(2) through 24(12)
30.	Marginally Augmented Full Employment IFE (calculated only for sex/family relationship and age disaggregations)	30(6) = 8(6) minus persons in families with augmented earnings of all family members in 1(1) as disaggregated plus actual earnings of family members not in 1(1) as disaggregated greater than poverty threshold (augmented earnings for disaggregated subgroup members in 8(6) are actual earnings plus weeks unemployed times usual hours worked times minimum wage or multiple except where some weeks employed part-time involuntarily in which case earnings also augmented by minimum wage or multiple times 40 minus usual hours times weeks less than 35 where usual is less than 35, or by minimum wage or multiple times usual hours minus 20 times weeks worked less than 35 hours where usual more than 35)
31.	Marginally Augmented Full Employment IFE Deficit (calculated only for sex/family relationship and age disaggregations)	31(6) = Calculated similar to 11(6) with sum of augmented and actual earnings of family members as specified in 30(2) through 30(12) instead of actual earnings compared to poverty standard or multiple
32.	Marginally Augmented Adequate Employment IFE (calculated only for sex/family relationship and age disaggregations)	32(6) = Calculated similar to 30(6) with augmented earnings of all disaggregated subgroup members in 8(1) equal to individual earnings standards as specified in 2(2) through 2(12) or actual earnings, whichever are larger
33.	Marginally Augmented Adequate Employment IFE Deficit (calculated only for sex/family relationship and age disaggregations)	33(6) = Calculated similar to 31(6) with augmented earnings as specified in 32(2) through 32(12)
34.	Marginally Augmented Capacity Employment IFE (calculated only for sex/family relationship and age disaggregations)	34(6) = Calculated similar to 30(6) with augmented earnings for disaggregated subgroup members as specified in 34(2) through 34(12); for subgroup members in 8(6), augmented earnings equal to weekly earnings for weeks employed times weeks in labor force; where some weeks employed part-time involuntarily, equal annual earnings ÷ weeks full-time and 1/2 weeks part-time times weeks in labor force
35.	Marginally Augmented Capacity Employment IFE Deficit (calculated only for sex/family relationship and age disaggregations)	35(6) = Calculated similar to 31(6) with augmented earnings as specified in 34(2) through 34(12)
36.	Persons with Earnings Deficits in Families with Earnings Deficits	36(6) = 8(6) minus persons not included in 2(6)
37.	Earnings Supplementation Rate	37(6) = [1 - 14(6)/8(6)] times 100
38.	Earnings Supplementation Rate-Nontransfers	38(6) = [1 - 39(6)/8(6)] times 100
39.	IFI Net-of-Transfers	39(6) = 8(6) minus persons in families with income excluding cash transfers above poverty standard or multiple
40.	IFI Net-of-Transfers Deficit	40(6) = Calculated similar to 17(6) except using family income excluding cash transfers
41.	IFI Including Food Stamps (calculated only for 1979 and 1980)	41(6) = 8(6) minus persons in families with cash income plus value of food stamps above poverty standard or multiple
42.	IFI Including Food Stamps Deficit (calculated only for 1979 and 1980)	42(6) = Calculated similar to 17(6) except using family cash income plus food stamp value
43.	IFI Including In-Kind Aid (calculated only for 1979 and 1980)	43(6) = 8(6) minus persons in families with cash income supplemented as noted in 43(2) is above poverty standard or multiple
44.	IFI Including In-Kind Aid Deficit (calculated only for 1979 and 1980)	44(6) = Calculated similar to 17(6) except using cash and including income for family as specified in 43(2)

Table A-4. (Continued)

(11). Discouraged

1. **Work Force Experience** — 1(11) = Did not work in previous year; main reason could not find work; unemployed at least 4 weeks

2. **Inadequate Individual Earnings (IIE)** — 2(11) = 1(11) minus persons with annual earnings (despite no reported work) above individual earnings standard equal to 2000 hours times minimum wage or multiple

3. **IIE Incidence** — 3(11) = 100 times 2(11) ÷ 1(11)

4. **IIE Distribution** — 4(11) = 100 times 2(11) ÷ 2(1)

5. **IIE Total Deficit** — 5(11) = Sum of individual earnings standards of persons in 2(11) where individual earning standards equal 40 times minimum wage or multiple times week of participation

6. **IIE Average Deficit** — 6(11) = 5(11) ÷ 2(11)

7. **IIE Deficit Distribution** — 7(11) = 100 times 5(11) ÷ 5(1)

8. **Inadequate Family Earnings (IFE)** — 8(11) = 1(11) minus persons in families with sum of annual earnings of all members above poverty threshold or multiple

9. **IFE Incidence** — 9(11) = 100 times 8(11) ÷ 1(11)

10. **IFE Distribution** — 10(11) = 100 times 8(11) ÷ 8(1)

11. **IFE Total Deficit** — 11(11) = For unrelated individuals and persons in 8(11) who are sole work force participants in families, sum of differences between annual earnings and appropriate poverty standard or multiple. For persons in families with two or more adjusted work force participants and whose combined IIE Deficit is equal to or greater than difference between appropriate poverty standard or multiple and aggregate family earnings, times share of combined family IIE Deficit accounted for by persons in 8(11). For persons in families with two or more adjusted work force participants and whose family IIE Deficit is less than difference between poverty standard and aggregate family earnings, sum of IIE Deficits for family members in 8(11) plus these members' share of combined individual earnings standards (or earnings if higher) for family members times the difference between the poverty standard or multiple minus aggregate family earnings, and the combined family IIE Deficit

12. **IFE Average Deficit** — 12(11) = 11(11) ÷ 8(11)

13. **IFE Deficit Distribution** — 13(11) = 100 times 11(11) ÷ 11(1)

14. **Inadequate Family Income (IFI)** — 14(11) = 8(11) minus persons in families with total income above poverty threshold or multiple

15. **IFI Incidence** — 15(11) = 100 times 14(11) ÷ 1(11)

16. **IFI Distribution** — 16(11) = 100 times 14(11) ÷ 14(1)

17. **IFI Total Deficit** — 17(11) = For unrelated individuals and persons in 14(11) who are sole work force participants in families, sum of differences between family income and poverty standard or multiple. For persons in families with two or more persons in adjusted work force and whose combined IIE Deficit is equal to or greater than difference between poverty standard and family income, sum of differences between appropriate poverty standard or multiple and aggregate family income, times share of combined family IIE Deficit accounted for by persons in 14(11). For persons in families with two or more persons in adjusted work force and where combined family IIE Deficit is less than difference between poverty standard and family income, sum of IIE Deficit for family members in 14(11) plus these members' share of combined individual earnings standards (or earnings if higher) for family members times the difference between the poverty standard or multiple minus family income, and the combined family IIE Deficit

18. **IFI Average Deficit** — 18(11) = 17(11) ÷ 14(11)

19. **IFI Deficit Distribution** — 19(11) = 100 times 17(11) ÷ 17(1)

20. **Full Employment IFE** — 20(11) = 8(11) minus persons in families with augmented earnings of all family members in 1(1) plus actual earnings of family members not in 1(1) greater than poverty threshold (augmented earnings for persons in 8(11) equal minimum wage times 40 times 50)

21. **Full Employment IFE Deficit** — 21(11) = Calculated similar to 11(11) for persons in 20(11) with sum of augmented and actual earnings of family members as specified in 20(2) through 20(12) instead of actual earnings compared to poverty standard or multiple

22. **Adequate Employment IFE** — 22(11) = Calculated similar to 20(11) with augmented earnings of all family members in 8(11) equal to individual earnings standard as specified in 2(11)

23. **Adequate Employment IFE Deficit** — 23(11) = Calculated similar to 21(11) with augmented earnings as specified in 22(2) through 22(12)

Table A-4. (Continued)

24.	Capacity Employment IFE	24(11) = Calculated similar to 20(11) with augmented earnings for persons in 8(11) equal to individual earnings standard as specified in 2(11)
25.	Capacity Employment IFE Deficit	25(11) = Calculated similar to 21(11) with augmented earnings as specified in 24(2) through 24(12)
26.	Enhanced Earnings IFE	26(11) = Calculated similar to 20(11) with augmented earnings for persons in 8(1) equal to 110 percent of actual earnings
27.	Enhanced Earnings IFE Deficit	27(11) = Calculated similar to 21(11) with augmented earnings for all persons in 8(1) equal to 110 percent of actual earnings
28.	Enhanced Capacity IFE	28(11) = Calculated similar to 20(11) with earnings augmented to 110 percent those specified in 24(2) through 24(12)
29.	Enhanced Capacity IFE Deficit	29(11) = Calculated similar to 21(11) with earnings augmented to 110 percent those specified in 24(2) through 24(12)
30.	Marginally Augmented Full Employment IFE (calculated only for sex/family relationship and age disaggregations)	30(11) = 8(11) minus persons in families with augmented earnings of all family members in 1(1) as disaggregated plus actual earnings of family members not in 1(1) as disaggregated greater than poverty threshold (augmented earnings for disaggregated subgroup members in 8(11) equal minimum wages times 40 times 50)
31.	Marginally Augmented Full Employment IFE Deficit (calculated only for sex/family relationship and age disaggregations)	31(11) = Calculated similar to 11(11) with sum of augmented and actual earnings of family members as specified in 30(2) through 30(12) instead of actual earnings compared to poverty standard or multiple
32.	Marginally Augmented Adequate Employment IFE (calculated only for sex/family relationship and age disaggregations)	32(11) = Calculated similar to 30(11) with augmented earnings of all disaggregated subgroup members in 8(11) equal to individual earnings standard as specified in 2(11)
33.	Marginally Augmented Adequate Employment IFE Deficit (calculated only for sex/family relationship and age disaggregations)	33(11) = Calculated similar to 31(11) with augmented earnings as specified in 32(2) through 32(12)
34.	Marginally Augmented Capacity Employment IFE (calculated only for sex/family relationship and age disaggregations)	34(11) = Calculated similar to 30(11) with augmented earnings for disaggregated subgroup members in 8(11) equal to individual earnings standard as specified in 2(11)
35.	Marginally Augmented Capacity Employment IFE Deficit (calculated only for sex/family relationship and age disaggregations)	35(11) = Calculated similar to 31(11) with augmented earnings as specified in 34(2) through 34(12)
36.	Persons with Earnings Deficits in Families with Earnings Deficits	36(11) = 8(11) minus persons not included in 2(11)
37.	Earnings Supplementation Rate	37(11) = [1 - 14(11)/8(11)] times 100
38.	Earnings Supplementation Rate-Nontransfers	38(11) = [1 - 39(11)/8(11)] times 100
39.	IFI Net-of-Transfers	39(11) = 8(11) minus persons in families with income excluding cash transfers above poverty standard or multiple
40.	IFI Net-of-Transfers Deficit	40(11) = Calculated similar to 17(11) except using family income excluding cash transfers
41.	IFI Including Food Stamps (calculated only for 1979 and 1980)	41(11) = 8(11) minus persons in families with cash income plus value of food stamps above poverty standard or multiple
42.	IFI Including Food Stamps Deficit (calculated only for 1979 and 1980)	42(11) = Calculated similar to 17(11) except using family cash income plus food stamp value
43.	IFI Including In-Kind Aid (calculated only for 1979 and 1980)	43(11) = 8(11) minus persons in families with cash income supplemented as noted in 43(2) is above poverty standard or multiple
44.	IFI Including In-Kind Aid Deficit (calculated only for 1979 and 1980)	44(11) = Calculated similar to 17(11) except using cash and including income for family as specified in 43(2)

Table A-4. (Continued)

(12). Unemployed

1. Work Force Experience — 1(12) = Unemployed throughout period of participation, and any weeks nonparticipation in period due to reasons other than inability to find work or unemployed less than 4 weeks and discouraged throughout remainder of period

2. Inadequate Individual Earnings (IIE) — 2(12) = 1(12) minus persons with annual earnings above an individual earnings standard equal to weeks in labor force times minimum wage or multiple times 40

3. IIE Incidence — 3(12) = 100 times 2(12) ÷ 1(12)

4. IIE Distribution — 4(12) = 100 times 2(12) ÷ 2(1)

5. IIE Total Deficit — 5(12) = Sum of individual earnings standards in 2(12) where individual earnings standards equal 40 hours times minimum wage or multiple times weeks of participation

6. IIE Average Deficit — 6(12) = 5(12) ÷ 2(12)

7. IIE Deficit Distribution — 7(12) = 100 times 5(12) ÷ 5(1)

8. Inadequate Family Earnings (IFE) — 8(12) = 1(12) minus persons in families with sum of annual earnings of all members above poverty threshold or multiple

9. IFE Incidence — 9(12) = 100 times 8(12) ÷ 1(12)

10. IFE Distribution — 10(12) = 100 times 8(12) ÷ 8(1)

11. IFE Total Deficit — 11(12) = For unrelated individuals and persons in 8(12) who are sole work force participants in families, sum of differences between annual earnings and appropriate poverty standard or multiple. For persons in families with two or more adjusted work force participants and whose combined IIE Deficit is equal to or greater than difference between appropriate poverty standard or multiple and aggregate family earnings, times share of combined family IIE Deficit accounted for by persons in 8(12). For persons in families with two or more adjusted work force participants and whose family IIE Deficit is less than difference between poverty standard and aggregate family earnings, sum of IIE Deficits for family members in 8(12) plus these members' share of combined individual earnings standards (or earnings if higher) for family members times the difference between the poverty standard or multiple minus aggregate family earnings, and the combined family IIE Deficit

12. IFE Average Deficit — 12(12) = 11(12) ÷ 8(12)

13. IFE Deficit Distribution — 13(12) = 100 times 11(12) ÷ 11(1)

14. Inadequate Family Income (IFI) — 14(12) = 8(12) minus persons in families with total income above poverty threshold or multiple

15. IFI Incidence — 15(12) = 100 times 14(12) ÷ 1(12)

16. IFI Distribution — 16(12) = 100 times 14(12) ÷ 14(1)

17. IFI Total Deficit — 17(12) = For unrelated individuals and persons in 14(12) who are sole work force participants in families, sum of differences between family income and poverty standard or multiple. For persons in families with two or more persons in adjusted work force and whose combined IIE Deficit is equal to or greater than difference between poverty standard and family income, sum of differences between appropriate poverty standard or multiple and aggregate family income, times share of combined family IIE Deficit accounted for by persons in 14(12). For persons in families with two or more persons in adjusted work force and where combined family IIE Deficit is less than difference between poverty standard and family income, sum of IIE Deficit for family members in 14(12) plus these members' share of combined individual earnings standards (or earnings if higher) for family members times the difference between the poverty standard or multiple minus family income, and the combined family IIE Deficit

18. IFI Average Deficit — 18(12) = 17(12) ÷ 14(12)

19. IFI Deficit Distribution — 19(12) = 100 times 17(12) ÷ 17(1)

20. Full Employment IFE — 20(12) = 8(12) minus persons in families with augmented earnings of all family members in 1(1) plus actual earnings of family members not in 1(1) greater than poverty threshold (augmented earnings for persons in 8(12) equal minimum wage times 40 times weeks in labor force)

21. Full Employment IFE Deficit — 21(12) = Calculated similar to 11(12) for persons in 20(12) with sum of augmented and actual earnings of family members as specified in 20(2) through 20(12) instead of actual earnings compared to poverty standard or multiple

22. Adequate Employment IFE — 22(12) = Calculated similar to 20(12) with augmented earnings of all family members in 8(12) equal to individual earnings standard as specified in 2(12)

23. Adequate Employment IFE Deficit — 23(12) = Calculated similar to 21(12) with augmented earnings as specified in 22(2) through 22(12)

Table A-4. (Continued)

24.	Capacity Employment IFE	24(12) = Calculated similar to 20(12) with augmented earnings for persons in 8(12) equal to individual earnings standard as specified in 2(12)
25.	Capacity Employment IFE Deficit	25(12) = Calculated similar to 21(12) with augmented earnings as specified in 24(2) through 24(12)
26.	Enhanced Earnings IFE	26(12) = Calculated similar to 20(12) with augmented earnings for persons in 8(1) equal to 110 percent of actual earnings
27.	Enhanced Earnings IFE Deficit	27(12) = Calculated similar to 21(12) with augmented earnings for all persons in 8(1) equal to 110 percent of actual earnings
28.	Enhanced Capacity IFE	28(12) = Calculated similar to 20(12) with earnings augmented to 110 percent those specified in 24(2) through 24(12)
29.	Enhanced Capacity IFE Deficit	29(12) = Calculated similar to 21(12) with earnings augmented to 110 percent those specified in 24(2) through 24(12)
30.	Marginally Augmented Full Employment IFE (calculated only for sex/family relationship and age disaggregations)	30(12) = 8(12) minus persons in families with augmented earnings of all family members in 1(1) as disaggregated plus actual earnings of family members not in 1(1) as disaggregated greater than poverty threshold (augmented earnings for disaggregated subgroup members in 8(12) equal minimum wage times 40 times weeks in labor force)
31.	Marginally Augmented Full Employment IFE Deficit (calculated only for sex/family relationship and age disaggregations)	31(12) = Calculated similar to 11(12) with sum of augmented and actual earnings of family members as specified in 30(2) through 30(12) instead of actual earnings compared to poverty standard or multiple
32.	Marginally Augmented Adequate Employment IFE (calculated only for sex/family relationship and age disaggregations)	32(12) = Calculated similar to 30(12) with augmented earnings of all disaggregated subgroup members in 8(12) equal to individual earnings standard as specified in 2(12)
33.	Marginally Augmented Adequate Employment IFE Deficit (calculated only for sex/family relationship and age disaggregations)	33(12) = Calculated similar to 31(12) with augmented earnings as specified in 32(2) through 32(12)
34.	Marginally Augmented Capacity Employment IFE (calculated only for sex/family relationship and age disaggregations)	34(12) = Calculated similar to 30(12) with augmented earnings for disaggregated subgroup members in 8(12) equal to individual earnings standard as specified in 2(12)
35.	Marginally Augmented Capacity Employment IFE Deficit (calculated only for sex/family relationship and age disaggregations)	35(12) = Calculated similar to 31(12) with augmented earnings as specified in 34(2) through 34(12)
36.	Persons with Earnings Deficits in Families with Earnings Deficits	36(12) = 8(12) minus persons not included in 2(12)
37.	Earnings Supplementation Rate	37(12) = [1 - 14(12)/8(12)] times 100
38.	Earnings Supplementation Rate-Nontransfers	38(12) = [1 - 39(12)/8(12)] times 100
39.	IFI Net-of-Transfers	39(12) = 8(12) minus persons in families with income excluding cash transfers above poverty standard or multiple
40.	IFI Net-of-Transfers Deficit	40(12) = Calculated similar to 17(12) except using family income excluding cash transfers
41.	IFI Including Food Stamps (calculated only for 1979 and 1980)	41(12) = 8(12) minus persons in families with cash income plus value of food stamps above poverty standard or multiple
42.	IFI Including Food Stamps Deficit (calculated only for 1979 and 1980)	42(12) = Calculated similar to 17(12) except using family cash income plus food stamp value
43.	IFI Including In-Kind Aid (calculated only for 1979 and 1980)	43(12) = 8(12) minus persons in families with cash income supplemented as noted in 43(2) is above poverty standard or multiple
44.	IFI Including In-Kind Aid Deficit (calculated only for 1979 and 1980)	44(12) = Calculated similar to 17(12) except using cash and including income for family as specified in 43(2)

Table A-4. (Continued)

(13). Total Out of Work Force

1.	Work Force Experience	1(13) = Total population minus 1(1)
2.	Inadequate Individual Earnings (IIE)	2(13) = 1(13) minus persons in families with no member in 2(1)
3.	IIE Incidence	3(13) = 2(13) ÷ 1(13)
4.	IIE Distribution	4(13) = N.A.
5.	IIE Total Deficit	5(13) = N.A.
6.	IIE Average Deficit	6(13) = N.A.
7.	IIE Deficit Distribution	7(13) = N.A.
8.	Inadequate Family Earnings (IFE)	8(13) = 1(13) minus persons in families with earnings above poverty level or multiple
9.	IFE Incidence	9(13) = 100 times 8(13) ÷ 1(13)
10.	IFE Distribution	10(13) = N.A.
11.	IFE Total Deficit	11(13) = N.A.
12.	IFE Average Deficit	12(13) = N.A.
13.	IFE Deficit Distribution	13(13) = N.A.
14.	Inadequate Family Income (IFI)	14(13) = 1(13) minus persons in families with cash incomes above poverty level or multiple
15.	IFI Incidence	15(13) = 100 times 14(13) ÷ 1(13)
16.	IFI Distribution	16(13) = N.A.
17.	IFI Total Deficit	17(13) = N.A.
18.	IFI Average Deficit	18(13) = N.A.
19.	IFI Deficit Distribution	19(13) = N.A.
20.	Full Employment IFE	20(13) = Persons in families with earnings below poverty level or multiple after earnings of all family members augmented as specified in 20(2) through 20(12), minus 20(1)
21.	Full Employment IFE Deficit	21(13) = N.A.
22.	Adequate Employment IFE	22(13) = Persons in families with earnings below poverty level or multiple after earnings of all family members augmented as specified in 22(2) through 22(12), minus 22(1)
23.	Adequate Employment IFE Deficit	23(13) = N.A.
24.	Capacity Employment IFE	24(13) = Persons in families with earnings below poverty level or multiple after earnings of all family members augmented as specified in 24(2) through 24(2), minus 24(1)
25.	Capacity Employment IFE Deficit	25(13) = N.A.
26.	Enhanced Earnings IFE	26(13) = Persons in families with earnings below poverty level or multiple after earnings of all family members augmented as specified in 26(2) through 26(12), minus 26(1)
27.	Enhanced Earnings IFE Deficit	27(13) = N.A.
28.	Enhanced Capacity IFE	28(13) = Persons in families with earnings below poverty level or multiple after earnings of all family members augmented as specified in 28(2) through 28(12), minus 28(1)
29.	Enhanced Capacity IFE Deficit	29(13) = N.A.
30.	Marginally Augmented Full Employment IFE (calculated only for sex/family relationship and age disaggregations)	30(13) = Persons in families with earnings below poverty level or multiple after earnings of subgroup augmented as specified in 30(2) through 30(12), minus 30(1)
31.	Marginally Augmented Full Employment IFE Deficit (calculated only for sex/family relationship and age disaggregations)	31(13) = N.A.
32.	Marginally Augmented Adequate Employment IFE (calculated only for sex/family relationship and age disaggregations)	32(13) = Persons in families with earnings below poverty level or multiple after earnings of subgroup augmented as specified in 32(2) through 30(12), minus 32(1)
33.	Marginally Augmented Adequate Employment IFE Deficit (calculated only for sex/family relationship and age disaggregations)	33(13) = N.A.

Table A-4. (Continued)

34.	Marginally Augmented Capacity Employment IFE (calculated only for sex/family relationship and age disaggregations)	34(13) = Persons in families with earnings below poverty level or multiple after earnings of subgroup augmented as specified in 34(2) through 34(12), minus 34(1)
35.	Marginally Augmented Capacity Employment IFE Deficit (calculated only for sex/family relationship and age disaggregations)	35(13) = N.A.
36.	Persons with Earnings Deficits in Families with Earnings Deficits	36(13) = N.A.
37.	Earnings Supplementation Rate	37(13) = N.A.
38.	Earnings Supplementation Rate-Nontransfers	38(13) = N.A.
39.	IFI Net-of-Transfers	39(13) = Persons in families with incomes excluding cash transfers below poverty level or multiple, minus 39(1)
40.	IFI Net-of-Transfers Deficit	40(13) = N.A.
41.	IFI Including Food Stamps (calculated only for 1979 and 1980)	41(13) = Persons in families with cash incomes plus food stamps below poverty level or multiple, minus 41(1)
42.	IFI Including Food Stamps Deficit (calculated only for 1979 and 1980)	42(13) = N.A.
43.	IFI Including In-Kind Aid (calculated only for 1979 and 1980)	43(13) = Persons in families with cash incomes and in-kind aid valued as specified in 43(2) below poverty level or multiple, minus persons in 43(1)
44.	IFI Including In-Kind Aid Deficit (calculated only for 1979 and 1980)	44(13) = N.A.

APPENDIX B. DETAILED HARDSHIP DATA FOR 1979
(Using 1980 Census Weights)

Table B-1.   Hardship by Work Experience Pattern in 1979

Table B-2.   Race/Ethnic Origin and Hardship

Table B-3.   Sex, Family Relationship and Hardship

Table B-4.   Hardship by Family Size and Number of Earners

Table B-5.   Hardship and Family Income in 1979

Table B-6.   Hardship in 1979 and Age at Interview

Table B-7.   Hardship in 1979 by Educational Attainment at Interview

Table B-8.   Hardship and Individual Earnings in 1979

Table B-9.   Hardship and Individual Earnings Deficit in 1979

Table B-10.   Hardship and Occupation of Longest Job in 1979

Table B-11.   Hardship in Metropolitan and Nonmetropolitan Areas in 1979

Table B-12.   Hardship in 1979 Disaggregated by Geographic Region

Table B-13.   Hardship in 1979 in a Sample of States

Table B-1. HARDSHIP BY WORK EXPERIENCE PATTERN IN 1979

SEVERE HARDSHIP: TOTAL WORK FORCE

	Total Work Force	Not Employed	(Discouraged)	(Unemployed)	Intermittently Employed	(Mostly Unemployed)	(Mixed)	(Mostly Employed)
Work Force (000)	116,983	1,990	811	1,179	16,478	1,607	3,895	10,976
IIE (000)	28,269	1,979	811	1,167	7,898	1,529	2,691	3,679
IIE Incidence (%)	24.2	99.4	100.0	99.0	47.9	95.1	69.1	33.5
IIE Deficit ($ Millions)	51,998	3,906	2,684	1,222	17,039	5,675	5,926	5,437
IIE Average Deficit ($)	1,839	1,974	3,309	1,046	2,157	3,712	2,203	1,478
IFE (000)	13,280	931	409	523	3,219	681	1,096	1,502
IFE Incidence (%)	11.4	46.8	50.4	44.3	19.9	42.4	28.1	13.7
IFE Deficit ($ Millions)	31,656	3,889	1,857	2,032	7,587	2,258	2,499	2,830
IFE Average Deficit ($)	2,384	4,176	4,544	3,888	2,314	3,314	2,280	1,884
IFI (000)	7,055	629	293	336	1,989	423	625	941
IFI Incidence (%)	6.0	31.6	36.1	28.5	12.1	26.3	16.0	8.6
IFI Deficit ($ Millions)	12,825	1,629	768	861	3,475	986	1,092	1,397
IFI Average Deficit ($)	1,818	2,591	2,621	2,565	1,747	2,329	1,748	1,485
Full Employment IFE (000)	10,078	570	118	452	1,886	284	518	1,084
Full Employment IFE Deficit ($ Millions)	22,115	1,721	761	1,461	3,596	650	969	1,977
Adequate Employment IFE (000)	8,513	690	247	443	1,658	262	496	901
Adequate Employment IFE Deficit ($ Millions)	18,769	2,244	766	1,478	3,093	567	974	1,552
Capacity Employment IFE (000)	11,093	709	255	454	1,898	261	515	1,122
Capacity Employment IFE Deficit	25,451	2,243	765	1,477	3,847	654	1,057	2,136
Enhanced Earnings IFE (000)	11,998	912	402	510	2,936	652	1,008	1,276
Enhanced Earnings IFE Deficit ($ Millions)	29,231	3,886	1,848	2,039	6,853	2,155	2,242	2,457
Enhanced Capacity IFE (000)	7,379	660	231	428	1,342	219	401	722
Enhanced Capacity IFE Deficit ($ Millions)	16,690	2,133	707	1,426	2,545	478	812	1,255
IIE in IFE (000)	9,116	931	409	522	2,777	664	1,002	1,111
Earnings Supplementation Rate-Total ($)	46.9	32.5	28.3	35.8	39.4	37.9	43.0	37.4
Earnings Supplementation Rate-Net of Transfers (%)	21.3	11.5	8.9	13.5	13.4	9.5	13.1	15.4
IFI Net of Transfers (000)	10,457	824	372	452	2,838	616	952	1,270
IFI Net of Transfers Deficit ($ Millions)	24,006	1,629	1,608	1,675	6,377	1,913	2,143	2,322
IFI Including Food Stamps (000)	6,522	582	280	302	1,811	385	561	865
IFI Including Food Stamps Deficit ($ Millions)	10,907	1,261	600	661	2,882	801	901	1,180
IFI Including In-Kind Aid (000)	6,241	554	267	288	1,718	369	532	817
IFI Including In-Kind Aid Deficit ($ Millions)	10,379	1,185	565	621	2,714	762	849	1,103

Table B-1. (Continued)

SEVERE HARDSHIP: TOTAL WORK FORCE (continued)

	Employed Part-Time	(Employed Part-Time Involuntarily)	(Employed Part-Time Voluntarily)	Employed Full-Time	Out Of Work Force
Work Force (000)	34,156	7,172	26,985	64,359	106,177
IIE (000)	11,983	3,196	8,788	6,408	27,622
IIE Incidence (%)	35.1	44.6	32.6	10.0	26.0
IIE Deficit ($ Millions)	15,162	5,849	9,313	15,891	--
IIE Average Deficit ($)	1,265	1,830	1,060	2,480	--
IFE (000)	6,151	1,419	4,732	2,919	41,466
IFE Incidence (%)	18.0	19.8	17.5	4.5	39.1
IFE Deficit ($ Millions)	13,770	3,556	10,214	6,410	--
IFE Average Deficit ($)	2,239	2,506	2,159	2,196	--
IFI (000)	2,690	815	1,875	1,748	19,027
IFI Incidence (%)	7.9	11.4	6.9	2.7	17.9
IFI Deficit ($ Millions)	4,505	1,593	2,911	3,217	--
IFI Average Deficit ($)	1,675	1,959	1,553	1,840	--
Full Employment IFE (000)	4,942	1,048	3,894	2,679	39,493
Full Employment IFE Deficit ($ Millions)	10,549	2,516	8,033	6,249	--
Adequate Employment IFE (000)	4,529	794	3,735	1,635	38,388
Adequate Employment IFE Deficit ($ Millions)	10,022	1,954	8,065	3,411	--
Capacity Employment IFE (000)	5,720	1,147	4,573	2,767	--
Capacity Employment IFE Deficit	13,011	2,817	10,194	6,351	--
Enhanced Earnings IFE (000)	5,596	1,282	4,314	2,555	40,126
Enhanced Earnings IFE Deficit ($ Millions)	12,754	3,273	9,481	5,737	--
Enhanced Capacity IFE (000)	4,000	683	3,316	1,378	36,971
Enhanced Capacity IFE Deficit ($ Millions)	9,104	1,743	7,361	2,909	--
IIE in IFE (000)	3,602	1,171	2,431	1,806	--
Earnings Supplementation Rate-Total ($)	56.3	42.5	60.4	40.1	54.1
Earnings Supplementation Rate-Net of Transfers (%)	27.6	16.0	31.1	19.8	20.6
IFI Net of Transfers (000)	4,454	1,192	3,262	2,341	32,943
IFI Net of Transfers Deficit ($ Millions)	9,336	2,888	6,448	5,009	--
IFI Including Food Stamps (000)	2,518	747	1,771	1,611	11,471
IFI Including Food Stamps Deficit ($ Millions)	3,889	1,288	2,601	2,877	--
IFI Including In-Kind Aid (000)	2,419	706	1,713	1,550	16,400
IFI Including In-Kind Aid Deficit ($ Millions)	3,705	1,210	2,495	2,774	--

Table B-1. (Continued)

SEVERE HARDSHIP: HALF-YEAR WORK FORCE

	Total Work Force	Not Employed	(Discouraged)	(Unemployed)	Intermittently Employed	(Mostly Unemployed)	(Mixed)	(Mostly Employed)
Work Force (000)	98,733	436	359	77	14,449	1,452	3,272	9,725
IIE (000)	19,299	436	359	77	6,517	1,377	2,182	2,957
IIE Incidence (%)	19.5	99.0	100.0	99.6	45.1	94.8	66.7	30.4
IIE Deficit ($ Millions)	46,403	2,442	2,021	421	15,970	5,506	5,469	4,995
IIE Average Deficit ($)	2,404	5,605	5,627	5,503	2,451	3,999	2,506	1,689
IFE (000)	8,014	242	189	54	2,630	609	877	1,144
IFE Incidence (%)	8.1	55.5	52.5	69.8	18.2	41.9	26.8	11.8
IFE Deficit ($ Millions)	17,891	1,230	974	256	6,084	2,073	1,918	2,094
IFE Average Deficit ($)	2,232	5,078	5,163	4,777	2,313	3,403	2,186	1,830
IFI (000)	4,276	169	136	34	1,545	375	474	696
IFI Incidence (%)	4.3	38.8	37.8	43.7	10.7	25.8	14.5	7.2
IFI Deficit ($ Millions)	8,064	540	419	120	2,787	901	821	1,065
IFI Average Deficit ($)	1,885	3,189	3,091	3,582	1,804	2,404	1,732	1,531
Full Employment IFE (000)	5,434	82	64	18	1,336	226	338	773
Full Employment IFE Deficit ($ Millions)	10,957	199	163	36	2,580	558	570	1,452
Adequate Employment IFE (000)	3,959	82	68	14	1,143	207	324	612
Adequate Employment IFE Deficit ($ Millions)	7,261	218	181	36	2,104	476	574	1,054
Capacity Employment IFE (000)	6,193	88	70	18	1,325	201	325	799
Capacity Employment IFE Deficit ($ Millions)	13,503	218	182	36	2,807	558	668	1,582
Enhanced Earnings IFE (000)	7,000	237	184	53	2,320	580	797	942
Enhanced Earnings IFE Deficit ($ Millions)	16,597	1,237	982	255	5,658	2,027	1,772	1,860
Enhanced Capacity IFE (000)	3,122	76	63	13	871	172	232	467
Enhanced Capacity IFE Deficit ($ Millions)	5,631	171	143	28	1,572	384	398	790
IIE in IFE (000)	6,099	242	189	53	2,274	594	815	865
Earnings Supplementation Rate-Total (%)	46.6	30.1	28.1	37.3	41.3	38.5	46.0	39.2
Earnings Supplementation Rate-Net of Transfers (%)	20.5	12.2	9.2	22.6	13.8	9.6	13.4	16.3
IFI Net of Transfers (000)	6,372	213	171	42	2,268	551	760	957
IFI Net-of-Transfers Deficit ($ Millions)	14,029	1,042	842	200	5,150	1,760	1,655	1,735
IFI Including Food Stamps (000)	3,944	160	129	31	1,398	343	422	633
IFI Including Food Stamps Deficit ($ Millions)	6,963	427	327	101	2,312	732	687	894
IFI Including In-Kind Aid (000)	3,788	156	125	31	1,339	331	405	603
IFI Including In-Kind Deficit ($ Millions)	6,658	402	304	98	2,186	691	652	837

Table B-1. (Continued)

SEVERE HARDSHIP:
HALF-YEAR WORK FORCE (continued)

	Employed Part-Time	(Employed Part-Time Involuntarily)	(Employed Part-Time Voluntarily)	Employed Full-Time	Out Of Work Force
Work Force (000)	24,603	5,425	19,178	59,245	124,426
IIE (000)	7,592	1,932	5,659	4,756	21,994
IIE Incidence (%)	30.9	35.6	29.5	8.0	17.7
IIE Deficit ($ Millions)	13,119	4,945	8,174	14,872	--
IIE Average Deficit ($)	1,728	2,559	1,444	3,127	--
IFE (000)	3,417	805	2,612	1,725	46,732
IFE Incidence (%)	13.9	14.8	13.6	2.9	37.6
IFE Deficit ($ Millions)	6,704	1,801	4,903	3,873	--
IFE Average Deficit ($)	1,962	2,238	1,877	2,245	--
IFI (000)	1,462	475	987	1,102	21,804
IFI Incidence (%)	5.9	8.8	5.1	1.9	17.5
IFI Deficit ($ Millions)	2,439	899	1,539	2,299	--
IFI Average Deficit ($)	1,668	1,891	1,560	2,087	--
Full Employment IFE (000)	2,437	498	1,940	1,578	44,764
Full Employment IFE Deficit ($ Millions)	4,241	1,053	3,188	3,938	--
Adequate Employment IFE (000)	2,121	279	1,842	614	43,411
Adequate Employment IFE Deficit ($ Millions)	3,707	516	3,191	1,233	--
Capacity Employment IFE (000)	3,130	583	2,547	1,649	44,937
Capacity Employment IFE Deficit ($ Millions)	6,448	1,365	5,083	4,029	--
Enhanced Earnings IFE (000)	3,017	712	2,305	1,426	45,124
Enhanced Earnings IFE Deficit ($ Millions)	6,168	1,656	4,512	3,533	--
Enhanced Capacity IFE (000)	1,743	212	1,530	433	41,777
Enhanced Capacity IFE Deficit ($ Millions)	3,023	376	2,647	864	--
IIE in IFE (000)	2,259	704	1,555	1,324	--
Earnings Supplementation Rate-Total (%)	57.2	40.9	62.2	36.1	53.3
Earnings Supplementation Rate-Net of Transfers (%)	28.7	15.1	32.9	15.6	20.8
IFI Net of Transfers (000)	2,436	684	1,753	1,455	37,028
IFI Net of Transfers Deficit ($ Millions)	4,615	1,460	3,155	3,216	--
IFI Including Food Stamps (000)	1,369	434	935	1,016	20,049
IFI Including Food Stamps Deficit ($ Millions)	2,141	748	1,393	2,082	--
IFI Including In-Kind Aid (000)	1,319	412	907	974	18,854
IFI Including In-Kind Aid Deficit ($ Millions)	2,057	717	1,341	2,013	--

Table B-1. (Continued)

SEVERE HARDSHIP: FULL-YEAR WORK FORCE

	Total Work Force	Not Employed	(Discouraged)	(Unemployed)	Intermittently Employed	(Mostly Unemployed)	(Mixed)	(Mostly Employed)
Work Force (000)	83,979	354	298	55	10,997	1,221	2,609	7,167
IIE (000)	14,248	354	298	55	4,769	1,154	1,690	1,925
IIE Incidence (%)	17.0	100.0	100.0	100.0	43.4	94.5	64.8	26.9
IIE Deficit ($ Millions)	38,446	2,108	1,778	330	12,973	4,822	4,557	3,595
IIE Average Deficit ($)	2,698	5,960	5,961	5,953	2,720	4,178	2,697	1,867
IFE (000)	5,675	192	153	39	1,894	501	701	682
IFE Incidence (%)	6.8	54.4	51.4	70.0	17.2	41.0	27.2	9.5
IFE Deficit ($ Millions)	13,306	974	801	173	4,565	1,655	1,574	1,336
IFE Average Deficit ($)	2,345	5,069	5,221	4,470	2,411	3,305	2,216	1,957
IFI (000)	3,098	133	112	21	1,094	305	382	407
IFI Incidence (%)	3.7	37.7	37.7	38.0	9.9	25.0	14.6	5.7
IFI Deficit ($ Millions)	6,308	434	358	78	2,139	742	697	700
IFI Average Deficit ($)	2,036	3,253	3,167	3,709	1,956	2,433	1,826	1,720
Full Employment IFE (000)	3,667	60	53	6	832	160	254	418
Full Employment IFE Deficit ($ Millions)	8,142	158	143	16	1,782	397	464	921
Adequate Employment IFE (000)	2,408	51	45	6	685	138	234	313
Adequate Employment IFE Deficit ($ Millions)	4,766	148	132	16	1,393	323	442	628
Capacity Employment IFE (000)	4,278	53	47	6	837	152	249	436
Capacity Employment IFE Deficit ($ Millions)	10,231	148	132	16	2,016	402	588	1,026
Enhanced Earnings IFE (000)	4,935	189	150	39	1,672	473	645	554
Enhanced Earnings IFE Deficit ($ Millions)	12,854	1,000	826	174	4,464	1,675	1,554	1,234
Enhanced Capacity IFE (000)	1,882	47	41	6	531	116	172	243
Enhanced Capacity IFE Deficit ($ Millions)	3,578	114	102	121	1,016	257	304	455
IIE in IFE (000)	4,524	192	153	39	1,678	486	659	533
Earnings Supplementation Rate-Total (%)	45.4	30.6	26.8	45.7	42.2	39.1	46.2	40.4
Earnings Supplementation Rate-Net of Transfers (%)	18.6	13.9	9.8	30.0	11.8	9.3	11.8	13.7
IFI Net of Transfers (000)	4,621	166	138	27	1,670	454	627	589
IFI Net of Transfers Deficit ($ Millions)	10,681	812	689	123	3,930	1,403	1,384	1,143
IFI Including Food Stamps (000)	2,891	130	110	21	986	279	345	362
IFI Including Food Stamps Deficit ($ Millions)	5,439	341	275	66	1,763	598	583	582
IFI Including In-Kind Aid (000)	2,733	126	105	21	951	270	335	346
IFI Including In-Kind Aid Deficit ($ Millions)	5,206	319	254	64	1,672	571	559	542

Table B-1. (Continued)

SEVERE HARDSHIP:
FULL-YEAR WORK FORCE (continued)

	Employed Part-Time	(Employed Part-Time Involuntarily)	(Employed Part-Time Voluntarily)	Employed Full-Time	Out Of Work Force
Work Force (000)	17,671	4,160	13,511	54,956	139,181
IIE (000)	5,064	1,345	3,720	4,060	18,136
IIE Incidence (%)	28.7	32.3	27.5	7.4	13.0
IIE Deficit ($ Millions)	9,928	3,800	6,128	13,437	--
IIE Average Deficit ($)	1,960	2,825	1,648	3,309	--
IFE (000)	2,194	542	1,652	1,395	49,071
IFE Incidence (%)	12.4	13.0	12.2	2.5	35.3
IFE Deficit ($ Millions)	4,512	1,306	3,205	3,256	--
IFE Average Deficit ($)	2,056	2,409	1,940	2,334	--
IFI (000)	962	337	625	909	22,984
IFI Incidence (%)	5.4	8.1	4.6	1.7	16.5
IFI Deficit ($ Millions)	1,758	775	1,044	1,977	--
IFI Average Deficit ($)	1,828	2,120	1,670	2,176	--
Full Employment IFE (000)	1,462	327	1,135	1,313	47,271
Full Employment IFE Deficit ($ Millions)	2,735	810	1,925	3,467	--
Adequate Employment IFE (000)	1,221	152	1,069	451	45,854
Adequate Employment IFE Deficit ($ Millions)	2,290	366	1,924	936	--
Capacity Employment IFE (000)	2,035	418	1,617	1,353	47,481
Capacity Employment IFE Deficit ($ Millions)	4,528	1,065	3,463	3,540	--
Enhanced Earnings IFE (000)	1,929	483	1,446	1,145	47,189
Enhanced Earnings IFE Deficit ($ Millions)	4,313	1,257	3,057	3,076	--
Enhanced Capacity IFE (000)	992	123	869	312	44,056
Enhanced Capacity IFE Deficit ($ Millions)	1,824	266	1,557	624	--
IIE in IFE (000)	1,551	480	1,071	1,103	--
Earnings Supplementation Rate-Total (%)	56.2	37.9	62.2	34.8	53.2
Earnings Supplementation Rate-Net of Transfers (%)	27.4	11.4	32.7	14.5	21.0
IFI Net of Transfers (000)	1,592	480	1,112	1,192	38,779
IFI Net of Transfers Deficit ($ Millions)	3,204	1,110	2,094	2,735	--
IFI Including Food Stamps (000)	889	306	583	835	21,152
IFI Including Food Stamps Deficit ($ Millions)	1,528	592	936	1,807	--
IFI Including In-Kind Aid (000)	857	287	571	798	19,909
IFI Including In-Kind Aid Deficit ($ Millions)	1,464	566	898	1,752	--

Table B-1. (Continued)

INTERMEDIATE HARDSHIP: TOTAL WORK FORCE

	Total Work Force	Not Employed	(Discouraged)	(Unemployed)	Intermittently Employed	(Mostly Unemployed)	(Mixed)	(Mostly Employed)
Work Force (000)	116,983	1,990	811	1,179	16,478	1,607	3,895	10,976
IIE (000)	40,961	1,979	811	1,168	9,857	1,563	3,087	5,207
IIE Incidence (%)	35.0	99.4	100.0	99.0	59.8	97.3	79.3	47.4
IIE Deficit ($ Millions)	87,442	4,882	3,355	1,527	27,574	7,642	9,412	10,520
IIE Average Deficit ($)	2,135	2,467	4,136	1,308	2,797	4,888	3,049	2,021
IFE (000)	17,190	1,014	455	559	4,203	769	1,364	2,069
IFE Incidence (%)	14.7	50.9	56.0	47.4	25.5	47.9	35.0	18.8
IFE Deficit ($ Millions)	48,556	4,980	2,395	2,585	12,151	3,171	4,023	4,957
IFE Average Deficit ($)	2,825	4,912	5,269	4,622	2,891	4,122	2,949	2,396
IFI (OOO)	10,524	764	350	414	2,919	556	937	1,425
IFI Incidence (%)	9.0	38.4	43.2	35.1	17.7	34.6	24.1	13.0
IFI Deficit ($ Millions)	23,015	2,478	1,189	1,290	6,503	1,624	2,072	2,806
IFI Average Deficit ($)	2,187	3,244	3,394	3,117	2,228	2,919	2,212	1,969
Full Employment IFE (000)	12,802	593	118	475	2,406	313	617	1,476
Full Employment IFE Deficit ($ Millions)	33,203	2,198	327	1,871	5,570	879	1,424	3,267
Adequate Employment IFE Deficit	10,006	722	260	461	1,915	269	531	1,115
Adequate Employment IFE Deficit ($ Millions)	26,570	2,862	968	1,895	4,392	732	1,305	2,355
Capacity Employment IFE (000)	14,610	762	278	483	2,617	334	681	1,601
Capacity Employment IFE Deficit	39,600	2,862	967	1,894	6,431	1,044	1,731	3,656
Enhanced Earnings IFE (000)	15,422	979	439	540	3,816	729	1,255	1,832
Enhanced Earnings IFE Deficit ($ Millions)	44,605	4,988	2,385	2,603	11,012	3,039	3,651	4,321
Enhanced Capacity IFE (000)	8,623	678	239	439	1,570	225	437	908
Enhanced Capacity IFE Deficit ($ Millions)	23,373	2,695	889	1,807	3,598	619	1,083	1,895
IIE in IFE (000)	13,470	1,012	455	557	3,729	756	1,300	1,674
Earnings Supplementation Rate-Total (%)	38.8	24.7	23.0	26.0	30.5	27.7	31.3	31.1
Earnings Supplementation Rate-Net of Transfers (%)	17.7	9.4	9.9	9.0	10.9	8.3	9.3	12.8
IFI Net of Transfers (000)	14,145	919	410	509	3,747	706	1,238	1,803
IFI Net-of-Transfers Deficit	37,970	4,287	2,013	2,184	10,418	2,744	3,512	4,163
IFI Including Food Stamps (000)	10,189	743	344	399	2,822	538	913	1,371
IFI Including Food Stamps Deficit ($ Millions)	20,599	2,085	1,009	1,076	5,728	1,406	1,817	2,506
IFI Including In-Kind Aid (000)	9,909	722	329	392	2,739	526	873	1,340
IFI Including In-Kind Aid Deficit ($ Millions)	19,646	1,968	953	1,015	5,426	1,339	1,717	2,370

Table B-1. (Continued)

INTERMEDIATE HARDSHIP:
TOTAL WORK FORCE (continued)

	Employed Part-Time	(Employed Part-Time Involuntarily)	(Employed Part-Time Voluntarily)	Employed Full-Time	Out Of Work Force
Work Force (000)	34,156	7,172	26,985	64,359	106,177
IIE (000)	17,211	4,078	13,133	11,914	36,347
IIE Incidence (%)	50.4	56.9	48.7	18.5	34.2
IIE Deficit ($ Millions)	26,208	9,632	16,576	28,778	--
IIE Average Deficit ($)	1,523	2,362	1,262	2,415	--
IFE (000)	7,646	1,789	5,858	4,327	45,623
IFE Incidence (%)	22.4	24.9	21.7	6.7	43.0
IFE Deficit ($ Millions)	20,701	5,429	15,272	10,725	--
IFE Average Deficit ($)	2,707	3,035	2,607	2,478	--
IFI (000)	4,029	1,216	2,812	2,812	26,116
IFI Incidence (%)	11.8	17.0	10.4	4.4	24.6
IFI Deficit ($ Millions)	8,004	2,841	5,163	6,030	--
IFI Average Deficit ($)	1,987	2,335	1,836	2,144	--
Full Employment IFE (000)	5,903	1,333	4,570	3,901	43,186
Full Employment IFE Deficit ($ Millions)	15,018	3,807	11,211	10,417	--
Adequate Employment IFE (000)	5,196	889	4,308	2,172	40,961
Adequate Employment IFE Deficit ($ Millions)	13,929	2,677	11,252	5,387	--
Capacity Employment IFE (000)	7,146	1,500	5,646	4,086	43,833
Capacity Employment IFE Deficit ($ Millions)	19,665	4,395	15,270	10,642	--
Enhanced Earnings IFE (000)	6,972	1,604	5,368	3,654	43,758
Enhanced Earnings IFE Deficit ($ Millions)	19,186	5,000	14,186	9,419	--
Enhanced Capacity IFE (000)	4,592	763	3,829	1,782	39,053
Enhanced Capacity IFE Deficit ($ Millions)	12,609	2,374	10,235	4,471	--
IIE in IFE (000)	5,527	1,582	3,944	3,203	--
Earnings Supplementation Rate-Total (%)	47.3	32.0	52.0	35.0	42.8
Earnings Supplementation Rate-Net of Transfers (%)	22.7	13.5	25.6	17.4	16.6
IFI Net of Transfers (000)	5,907	1,546	4,361	3,573	38,034
IFI Net of Transfers Deficit ($ Millions)	14,647	4,515	10,131	8,618	--
IFI Including Food Stamps (000)	3,887	1,176	2,711	2,736	25,415
IFI Including Food Stamps Deficit ($ Millions)	7,255	2,479	4,776	5,530	--
IFI Including In-Kind Aid (000)	3,801	1,138	2,663	2,647	24,640
IFI Including In-Kind Aid Deficit ($ Millions)	6,941	2,341	4,600	5,311	--

Table B-1. (Continued)

MODERATE HARDSHIP: TOTAL WORK FORCE

	Total Work Force	Not Employed	(Discouraged)	(Unemployed)	Intermittently Employed	(Mostly Unemployed)	(Mixed)	(Mostly Employed)
Work Force (000)	116,983	1,990	811	1,179	16,478	1,607	3,895	10,976
IIE (000)	51,426	1,979	811	1,168	11,220	1,578	3,299	6,343
IIE Incidence (%)	44.0	99.4	100.0	99.0	68.1	98.2	84.7	57.8
IIE Deficit ($ Millions)	136,402	5,859	4,026	1,833	40,154	9,641	13,265	17,247
IIE Average Deficit ($)	2,652	2,961	4,964	1,570	3,579	6,110	4,021	2,719
IFE (000)	21,553	1,109	493	616	5,195	858	1,613	2,724
IFE Incidence (%)	18.4	55.7	60.7	52.2	31.5	53.4	41.4	24.8
IFE Deficit ($ Millions)	69,668	6,118	2,958	3,160	17,709	4,163	5,790	7,756
IFE Average Deficit ($)	3,232	5,519	6,005	5,130	3,409	4,855	3,589	2,847
IFI (000)	14,354	873	394	479	3,829	640	1,149	2,040
IFI Incidence (%)	12.3	43.9	48.6	40.6	23.2	39.8	29.5	18.6
IFI Deficit ($ Millions)	37,123	3,423	1,660	1,763	10,579	2,367	3,336	4,876
IFI Average Deficit ($)	2,590	3,920	4,210	3,680	2,763	3,701	2,903	2,390
Full Employment IFE (000)	15,660	623	122	501	2,930	332	727	1,871
Full Employment IFE Deficit ($ Millions)	46,871	2,676	394	2,282	8,077	1,110	1,983	4,984
Adequate Employment IFE (000)	11,275	747	267	480	2,116	274	562	1,279
Adequate Employment IFE Deficit ($ Millions)	34,926	3,490	1,181	2,309	5,766	890	1,632	3,243
Capacity Employment IFE (000)	18,480	813	298	515	3,405	412	879	2,114
Capacity Employment IFE Deficit ($ Millions)	57,747	3,490	1,181	2,309	9,944	1,507	2,629	5,808
Enhanced Earnings IFE (000)	19,078	1,042	464	577	4,639	816	1,472	2,351
Enhanced Earnings IFE Deficit ($ Millions)	63,820	6,158	2,949	3,209	16,129	3,988	5,308	6,832
Enhanced Capacity IFE (000)	9,602	700	244	456	1,730	227	462	1,041
Enhanced Capacity IFE Deficit ($ Millions)	30,471	3,299	1,076	2,223	4,692	755	1,354	2,584
IIE in IFE (000)	17,974	1,106	493	614	4,731	847	1,546	2,338
Earnings Supplementation Rate-Total (%)	33.4	21.2	20.0	22.2	26.3	25.4	28.8	25.1
Earnings Supplementation Rate-Net of Transfers (%)	15.4	7.6	7.7	7.6	9.9	7.7	8.6	11.3
IFI Net of Transfers (000)	18,205	1,024	455	569	4,683	792	1,474	2,417
IFI Net-of-Transfers Deficit ($ Millions)	55,982	5,351	2,622	2,729	15,479	3,669	5,129	6,682
IFI Including Food Stamps (000)	14,103	861	388	473	3,748	632	1,123	1,993
IFI Including Food Stamps Deficit ($ Millions)	34,429	3,019	1,472	1,547	9,704	2,134	3,054	4,516
IFI Including In-Kind Aid (000)	13,858	850	383	467	3,713	625	1,116	1,973
IFI Including In-Kind Aid Deficit ($ Millions)	33,093	2,885	1,410	1,476	9,306	2,051	2,920	4,335

Table B-1. (Continued)

MODERATE HARDSHIP:
TOTAL WORK FORCE (continued)

	Employed Part-Time	(Employed Part-Time Involuntarily)	(Employed Part-Time Voluntarily)	Employed Full-Time	Out Of Work Force
Work Force (000)	34,156	7,172	26,985	64,359	106,177
IIE (000)	20,742	4,731	16,011	17,485	42,784
IIE Incidence (%)	60.7	66.0	59.3	27.2	40.3
IIE Deficit ($ Millions)	40,758	14,351	26,407	49,631	--
IIE Average Deficit ($)	1,965	3,033	1,649	2,839	--
IFE (000)	9,142	2,189	6,954	6,107	50,112
IFE Incidence (%)	26.8	30.5	25.8	9.5	47.2
IFE Deficit ($ Millions)	28,912	7,701	21,211	16,929	--
IFE Average Deficit ($)	3,162	3,518	3,050	2,772	--
IFI (000)	5,489	1,622	3,867	4,163	32,648
IFI Incidence (%)	16.1	22.6	14.3	6.5	30.7
IFI Deficit ($ Millions)	12,822	4,528	8,294	10,350	--
IFI Average Deficit ($)	2,336	2,791	2,145	2,486	--
Full Employment IFE (000)	6,699	1,597	5,102	5,409	46,955
Full Employment IFE Deficit ($ Millions)	19,787	5,337	14,450	16,331	--
Adequate Employment IFE (000)	5,680	963	4,718	2,732	43,340
Adequate Employment IFE Deficit ($ Millions)	17,931	3,429	14,501	7,739	--
Capacity Employment IFE (000)	8,495	1,808	6,687	5,768	48,147
Capacity Employment IFE Deficit ($ Millions)	27,512	6,333	21,180	16,800	--
Enhanced Earnings IFE (000)	8,302	1,953	6,349	5,095	47,585
Enhanced Earnings IFE Deficit ($ Millions)	26,878	7,127	19,750	14,656	--
Enhanced Capacity IFE (000)	4,996	832	4,165	2,176	40,997
Enhanced Capacity IFE Deficit ($ Millions)	16,165	3,015	13,150	6,315	--
IIE in IFE (000)	7,328	2,018	5,310	4,810	--
Earnings Supplementation Rate-Total (%)	40.0	25.9	44.4	31.8	34.9
Earnings Supplementation Rate-Net of Transfers (%)	19.3	11.1	21.9	16.1	13.9
IFI Net of Transfers (000)	7,375	1,945	5,430	5,122	43,149
IFI Net of Transfers Deficit ($ Millions)	21,259	6,531	14,728	13,892	--
IFI Including Food Stamps (000)	5,406	1,596	3,809	4,088	32,254
IFI Including Food Stamps Deficit ($ Millions)	11,964	4,128	7,835	9,742	--
IFI Including In-Kind Aid (000)	5,297	1,563	3,734	3,997	31,712
IFI Including In-Kind Aid Deficit ($ Millions)	11,520	3,941	7,579	9,383	--

Table B-2. RACE/ETHNIC ORIGIN AND HARDSHIP

	Severe Hardship: Total Work Force			Severe Hardship: Half-Year Work Force			Severe Hardship: Full-Year Work Force		
	White	Black	Hispanic	White	Black	Hispanic	White	Black	Hispanic
Work Force (000)	102,761	11,702	5,872	87,032	9,643	4,922	74,023	8,220	4,150
IIE (000)	23,584	4,101	1,718	16,128	2,780	1,234	11,807	2,145	946
IIE Incidence (%)	22.9	35.0	29.3	18.5	28.8	25.1	16.0	26.1	22.8
IIE Deficit ($ Millions)	43,174	7,732	3,173	38,673	6,794	2,848	31,981	5,677	2,425
IIE Average Deficit ($)	1,831	1,886	1,847	2,398	2,444	2,308	2,709	2,646	2,564
IFE (000)	10,111	2,851	957	6,104	1,743	623	4,261	1,294	459
IFE Incidence (%)	9.8	24.4	16.3	7.0	18.1	12.7	5.8	15.7	11.1
IFE Deficit ($ Millions)	22,831	8,129	2,311	13,040	4,507	1,486	9,654	3,384	1,151
IFE Average Deficit ($)	2,258	2,851	2,415	2,136	2,586	2,386	2,266	2,615	2,508
IFI (000)	4,902	1,943	682	3,037	1,130	435	2,182	836	318
IFI Incidence (%)	4.8	16.6	11.6	3.5	11.7	8.8	2.9	10.2	7.7
IFI Deficit ($ Millions)	8,640	3,805	1,246	5,718	2,147	846	4,483	1,673	671
IFI Average Deficit ($)	1,762	1,958	1,827	1,883	1,900	1,947	2,055	2,000	2,107
Full Employment IFE (000)	7,750	2,086	729	4,154	1,163	441	2,774	811	321
Full Employment IFE Deficit ($ Millions)	16,058	5,531	1,631	8,053	2,676	997	5,979	1,990	823
Adequate Employment IFE (000)	6,391	1,905	609	2,929	938	332	1,715	631	228
Adequate Employment IFE Deficit ($ Millions)	13,232	5,090	1,376	5,029	2,072	731	3,135	1,519	566
Capacity Employment IFE (000)	8,578	2,260	772	4,812	1,257	470	3,295	896	343
Capacity Employment IFE Deficit ($ Millions)	18,771	6,109	1,785	10,238	3,000	1,113	7,740	2,285	899
Enhanced Earnings IFE (000)	9,062	2,648	837	5,285	1,570	529	3,691	1,139	387
Enhanced Earnings IFE Deficit ($ Millions)	20,998	7,600	2,088	12,117	4,164	1,364	9,313	3,279	1,130
Enhanced Capacity IFE (000)	5,526	1,687	521	2,280	775	266	1,313	524	178
Enhanced Capacity IFE Deficit ($ Millions)	11,713	4,597	1,187	3,855	1,662	557	2,306	1,190	409
IIE in IFE (000)	6,777	2,156	628	4,613	1,375	433	3,407	1,031	328
Earnings Supplementation Rate-Total (%)	51.5	31.8	28.8	50.2	35.2	30.2	48.8	35.3	30.6
Earnings Supplementation Rate-Net of Transfers (%)	25.2	8.1	9.5	23.9	9.2	8.8	22.0	8.1	7.8
IFI Net of Transfers (000)	7,567	2,616	866	4,646	1,582	568	3,325	1,188	423
IFI Net-of-Transfers Deficit ($ Millions)	16,063	7,376	2,043	9,699	4,024	1,338	7,370	3,068	1,048
IFI Including Food Stamps (000)	4,416	1,706	627	2,854	985	398	2,042	724	290
IFI Including Food Stamps Deficit ($ Millions)	7,684	2,873	1,029	5,131	1,649	697	4,025	1,277	554
IFI Including In-Kind Aid (000)	4,496	1,553	602	2,786	900	377	1,996	663	277
IFI Including In-Kind Aid Deficit ($ Millions)	7,450	2,589	972	4,987	1,497	657	3,914	1,163	520

Table B-2. (Continued)

	Intermediate Hardship: Total Work Force			Moderate Hardship: Total Work Force		
	White	Black	Hispanic	White	Black	Hispanic
Work Force (000)	102,761	11,702	5,872	102,761	11,702	5,872
IIE (000)	34,493	5,561	2,639	43,636	6,645	3,242
IIE Incidence (%)	33.6	47.5	44.9	42.5	56.8	55.2
IIE Deficit ($ Millions)	72,862	12,692	5,629	114,181	19,198	8,996
IIE Average Deficit ($)	2,112	2,282	2,133	2,617	2,889	2,775
IFE (000)	13,224	3,540	1,301	16,743	4,243	1,720
IFE Incidence (%)	12.9	30.3	22.2	16.3	36.3	29.3
IFE Deficit ($ Millions)	35,401	12,046	3,733	51,303	16,718	5,593
IFE Average Deficit ($)	2,677	3,403	2,868	3,064	3,940	3,252
IFI (000)	7,518	2,700	1,040	10,501	3,435	1,431
IFI Incidence (%)	7.3	23.1	17.7	10.2	29.4	24.4
IFI Deficit ($ Millions)	15,580	6,756	2,373	25,539	10,543	3,931
IFI Average Deficit ($)	2,072	2,502	2,281	2,432	3,069	2,746
Full Employment IFE (000)	9,891	2,592	980	12,203	3,047	1,250
Full Employment IFE Deficit ($ Millions)	24,333	8,038	2,601	34,567	11,116	3,864
Adequate Employment IFE (000)	7,586	2,148	758	8,607	2,354	894
Adequate Employment IFE Deficit ($ Millions)	19,019	6,890	2,037	25,215	8,813	2,752
Capacity Employment IFE (000)	11,356	2,894	1,090	14,463	3,534	1,423
Capacity Employment IFE Deficit ($ Millions)	29,386	9,281	2,943	43,121	13,242	4,495
Enhanced Earnings IFE (000)	11,828	3,228	1,148	14,755	3,840	1,495
Enhanced Earnings IFE Deficit ($ Millions)	32,343	11,243	3,345	46,707	15,596	4,992
Enhanced Capacity IFE (000)	6,542	1,850	640	7,340	2,006	753
Enhanced Capacity IFE Deficit ($ Millions)	16,627	6,173	1,732	21,900	7,808	2,298
IIE in IFE (000)	10,180	2,979	1,020	13,774	3,747	1,446
Earnings Supplementation Rate-Total (%)	43.2	23.7	20.1	37.3	19.1	16.8
Earnings Supplementation Rate-Net of Transfers (%)	20.7	6.7	6.1	18.1	5.5	5.9
IFI Net of Transfers (000)	10,490	3,302	1,222	13,705	4,009	1,619
IFI Net-of-Transfers Deficit	26,002	11,046	3,383	39,134	15,461	5,151
IFI Including Food Stamps (000)	7,307	2,579	1,003	10,339	3,351	1,401
IFI Including Food Stamps Deficit ($ Millions)	14,344	5,616	2,109	24,107	9,277	3,630
IFI Including In-Kind Aid (000)	7,163	2,453	976	10,200	3,259	1,366
IFI Including In-Kind Aid Deficit ($ Millions)	13,911	5,118	2,006	23,465	8,615	3,473

Table B-3. SEX, FAMILY RELATIONSHIP AND HARDSHIP

SEVERE HARDSHIP: TOTAL WORK FORCE

	Male Family Head	(Male Family Head-Wife In Work Force)	(Male Family Head-Wife Not In Work Force)	(Male Family Head Wife Not Present)	Male Unrelated Individual	Female Family Head	Wife	Female Unrelated Individual	Other Male	Other Female
Work Force (000)	42,051	26,571	14,118	1,362	9,263	5,976	28,814	7,777	13,424	9,676
IIE (000)	3,901	2,393	1,281	227	1,744	1,795	8,534	1,963	5,706	4,624
IIE Incidence (%)	9.3	9.0	9.1	16.7	18.8	30.0	29.6	25.2	42.5	47.8
IIE Deficit ($ Millions)	11,270	7,087	3,605	578	4,255	2,943	14,628	3,443	9,665	5,815
IIE Average Deficit ($)	2,889	2,961	2,814	2,549	2,440	1,639	1,712	1,754	1,694	1,257
IFE (000)	3,250	1,098	1,969	182	1,592	2,012	1,875	1,913	1,463	1,175
IFE Incidence (%)	7.7	4.1	13.9	13.4	17.2	337	65	24.6	10.9	12.1
IFE Deficit ($ Millions)	8,284	1,952	5,882	450	3,252	6,657	3,222	3,756	3,626	2,859
IFE Average Deficit ($)	2,549	1,777	2,987	2,465	2,043	3,308	1,718	1,964	2,479	2,434
IFI (000)	1,638	670	860	108	1,058	1,330	815	1,055	667	492
IFI Incidence (%)	3.9	2.5	6.1	7.9	11.4	22.3	2.8	13.6	5.0	5.1
IFI Deficit ($ Millions)	3,713	1,208	2,294	212	1,878	3,147	845	1,640	874	728
IFI Average Deficit ($)	2,267	1,802	2,668	1,963	1,774	2,367	1,037	1,554	1,311	1,480
Full Employment IFE (000)	2,540	684	1,723	133	1,099	1,663	1,343	1,484	1,053	896
Full Employment IFE Deficit ($ Millions)	5,983	1,059	4,626	298	2,054	4,868	2,270	2,625	2,266	2,050
Adequate Employment IFE (000)	2,032	440	1,486	105	868	1,592	1,053	1,292	914	763
Adequate Employment IFE Deficit ($ Millions)	4,422	519	3,710	192	1,561	4,711	1,924	2,286	2,015	1,850
Capacity Employment IFE (000)	2,766	843	1,778	144	1,247	1,714	1,528	1,704	1,162	973
Capacity Employment IFE Deficit ($ Millions)	6,847	1,426	5,091	330	2,461	5,326	2,713	3,232	2,609	2,263
Enhanced Earnings IFE (000)	2,898	936	1,793	166	1,453	1,860	1,656	1,759	1,303	1,069
Enhanced Earnings IFE Deficit ($ Millions)	7,454	1,708	5,335	410	2,990	6,250	2,965	3,481	3,395	2,696
Enhanced Capacity IFE (000)	1,715	323	1,315	77	770	1,425	866	1,163	765	675
Enhanced Capacity IFE Deficit ($ Millions)	3,732	384	3,187	161	1,399	4,272	1,695	2,079	1,810	1,703
IIE in IFE (000)	1,948	804	1,010	133	1,154	1,426	1,271	1,365	1,091	860
Earnings Supplementation Rate-Total (%)	49.6	39.0	56.4	40.8	33.5	33.9	56.5	44.8	54.4	58.1
Earnings Supplementation Rate-Net of Transfers (%)	24.3	18.4	28.2	17.0	18.1	12.4	26.7	22.4	19.4	24.1
IFI Net of Transfers (000)	2,461	896	1,414	151	1,304	1,762	1,375	1,485	1,178	892
IFI Net-of-Transfers Deficit ($ Millions)	6,088	1,641	4,063	384	2,492	5,721	2,063	2,699	2,878	2,065
IFI Including Food Stamps (000)	1,524	617	806	101	1,029	1,190	747	1,043	558	432
IFI Including Food Stamps Deficit ($ Millions)	3,236	1,079	1,965	192	1,780	2,396	733	1,574	647	542
IFI Including In-Kind Aid (000)	1,479	599	783	97	1,021	1,080	722	1,022	513	404
IFI Including In-Kind Aid Deficit ($ Millions)	3,120	1,050	1,883	186	1,763	2,155	706	1,556	587	491

Table B-3. (Continued)

SEVERE HARDSHIP: HALF-YEAR WORK FORCE

	Male Family Head	(Male Family Head-Wife In Work Force)	(Male Family Head-Wife Not In Work Force)	(Male Family Head-Wife Not Present)	Male Unrelated Individual	Female Family Head	Wife	Female Unrelated Individual	Other Male	Other Female
Work Force (000)	40,346	25,783	13,306	1,258	8,460	5,038	22,861	6,839	9,196	5,992
IIE (000)	3,500	2,183	1,129	188	1,461	1,191	5,744	1,485	3,485	2,436
IIE Incidence (%)	8.7	8.5	8.15	14.9	17.3	23.6	25.1	21.7	37.9	40.6
IIE Deficit ($ Millions)	10,949	6,899	3,491	559	4,048	2,505	12,901	3,136	8,262	4,603
IIE Average Deficit ($)	3,128	3,160	3,092	2,978	2,770	2,103	2,247	2,112	2,371	1,890
IFE (000)	2,369	867	1,379	123	1,012	1,186	1,031	1,107	797	513
IFE Incidence (%)	5.9	3.4	10.4	9.8	12.0	23.5	4.5	16.2	8.7	8.6
IFE Deficit ($ Millions)	6,075	1,824	3,930	320	1,763	3,050	1,827	1,691	2,145	1,340
IFE Average Deficit ($)	2,564	2,105	2,849	2,594	1,743	2,572	1,772	1,528	2,693	2,610
IFI (000)	1,364	577	716	71	668	715	420	618	322	171
IFI Incidence (%)	3.4	2.2	5.4	4.7	7.9	14.2	1.8	9.0	3.5	2.8
IFI Deficit ($ Millions)	3,258	1,195	1,892	172	1,100	1,438	553	883	495	338
IFI Average Deficit ($)	2,389	2,072	2,643	2,402	1,645	2,011	1,318	1,429	1,537	1,979
Full Employment IFE (000)	1,764	533	1,150	81	534	894	652	710	532	349
Full Employment IFE Deficit ($ Millions)	4,244	1,204	2,858	182	751	1,924	1,192	831	1,204	812
Adequate Employment IFE (000)	1,273	302	911	60	291	805	429	495	397	270
Adequate Employment IFE Deficit ($ Millions)	2,559	564	1,917	79	278	1,577	824	507	902	614
Capacity Employment IFE (000)	1,946	652	1,203	91	674	910	792	904	570	396
Capacity Employment IFE Deficit ($ Millions)	5,019	1,536	3,267	216	1,093	2,161	1,537	133	1,411	950
Enhanced Earnings IFE (000)	2,058	732	1,215	111	893	1,040	887	974	693	455
Enhanced Earnings IFE Deficit ($ Millions)	5,665	1,824	3,544	297	1,573	2,804	1,728	1,493	2,046	1,289
Enhanced Capacity IFE (000)	998	201	760	36	219	651	330	390	314	221
Enhanced Capacity IFE Deficit ($ Millions)	1,898	366	1,476	55	207	1,225	674	403	737	4,870
IIE in IFE (000)	1,679	705	870	104	871	858	764	891	642	394
Earnings Supplementation Rate-Total (%)	42.4	33.4	48.1	42.1	33.9	39.7	59.3	44.2	59.6	66.7
Earnings Supplementation Rate-Net of Transfers (%)	19.5	14.3	23.1	16.1	17.1	15.4	27.6	22.4	19.3	26.6
IFI Net of Transfers (000)	1,906	743	1,060	103	838	1,003	746	859	643	377
IFI Net-of-Transfers Deficit ($ Millions)	4,894	1,585	3,017	292	1,385	2,549	1,230	1,285	1,704	978
IFI Including Food Stamps (000)	1,271	533	668	70	648	619	391	616	257	142
IFI Including Food Stamps Deficit ($ Millions)	2,839	1,067	1,613	159	1,030	1,108	489	863	379	256
IFI Including In-Kind Aid (000)	1,233	520	645	68	642	552	378	606	244	132
IFI Including In-Kind Aid Deficit ($ Millions)	2,738	1,040	1,543	155	1,022	980	467	856	355	240

Table B-3. (Continued)

SEVERE HARDSHIP: FULL-YEAR WORK FORCE

	Male Family Head	(Male Family Head-Wife In Work Force)	(Male Family Head-Wife Not In Work Force)	(Male Family Head-Wife Not Present)	Male Unrelated Individual	Female Family Head	Wife	Female Unrelated Individual	Other Male	Other Female
Work Force (000)	37,575	24,063	12,379	1,133	7,264	4,267	17,596	5,664	7,225	4,387
IIE (000)	3,085	1,926	1,002	157	1,196	888	3,950	1,085	2,528	1,516
IIE Incidence (%)	8.2	8.0	8.1	13.9	16.5	20.8	22.4	19.2	35.0	34.5
IIE Deficit ($ Millions)	10,057	6,304	3,258	494	3,505	2,038	10,116	2,528	6,768	3,433
IIE Average Deficit ($)	3,260	3,273	3,252	3,148	2,932	2,295	2,561	2,330	2,677	2,265
IFE (000)	1,946	722	1,127	97	683	811	655	661	568	351
IFE Incidence (%)	5.2	3.0	9.1	8.5	9.4	19.0	3.7	11.7	7.9	8.0
IFE Deficit ($ Millions)	5,188	1,609	3,335	244	1,256	2,099	1,222	973	1,590	979
IFE Average Deficit ($)	2,666	2,227	2,960	2,529	1,840	2,589	1,865	1,472	2,797	2,786
IFI (000)	1,158	488	618	53	477	496	280	353	229	106
IFI Incidence (%)	3.1	2.0	5.0	4.7	6.6	11.6	1.6	6.2	3.2	2.4
IFI Deficit ($ Millions)	2,882	1,060	1,696	126	856	1,023	406	499	818	225
IFI Average Deficit ($)	2,488	2,173	2,746	2,385	1,797	2,062	1,450	1,415	1,825	2,124
Full Employment IFE (000)	1,448	464	925	60	276	571	405	358	362	247
Full Employment IFE Deficit ($ Millions)	3,759	1,200	2,432	178	424	1,299	773	405	817	605
Adequate Employment IFE (000)	974	236	699	39	88	475	235	209	251	174
Adequate Employment IFE Deficit ($ Millions)	2,030	471	1,522	37	75	954	459	195	621	431
Capacity Employment IFE (000)	1,582	544	972	66	411	595	497	521	400	272
Capacity Employment IFE Deficit ($ Millions)	4,445	1,494	2,801	150	717	1,501	1,036	741	1,065	726
Enhanced Earnings IFE (000)	1,681	602	995	84	608	706	565	578	487	310
Enhanced Earnings IFE Deficit ($ Millions)	5,103	1,810	3,063	203	1,135	1,978	1,202	853	1,592	992
Enhanced Capacity IFE (000)	755	155	581	19	67	329	182	165	200	134
Enhanced Capacity IFE Deficit ($ Millions)	1,466	2,981	1,146	22	53	780	362	151	484	332
IIE in IFE (000)	1,447	608	754	85	653	619	506	562	469	269
Earnings Supplementation Rate-Total (%)	40.5	32.5	45.2	45.1	30.2	38.8	57.3	46.7	59.8	69.9
Earnings Supplementation Rate-Net of Transfers (%)	17.7	11.8	21.5	17.7	13.9	14.2	25.1	22.5	17.0	25.9
IFI Net-of-Transfers (000)	1,601	637	884	80	588	696	490	513	472	260
IFI Net-of-Transfers Deficit ($ Millions)	4,255	1,417	2,618	220	1,039	1,798	861	753	1,289	685
IFI Including Food Stamps (000)	1,076	447	576	53	458	425	260	351	181	89
IFI Including Food Stamps Deficit ($ Millions)	2,521	948	1,455	118	802	774	356	486	329	172
IFI Including In-Kind Aid (000)	1,045	437	557	51	456	376	252	345	176	84
IFI Including In-Kind Aid Deficit ($ Millions)	2,434	925	1,394	115	797	683	340	483	309	160

Table B-3. (Continued)

INTERMEDIATE HARDSHIP: TOTAL WORK FORCE

	Male Family Head	(Male Family Head-Wife in Work Force)	(Male Family Head-Wife Not In Work Force)	(Male Family Head-Wife Not Present)	Male Unrelated Individual	Female Family Head	Wife	Female Unrelated Individual	Other Male	Other Female
Work Force (000)	42,051	26,571	14,118	1,362	9,263	5,976	28,814	7,777	13,424	9,676
IIE (000)	5,926	3,671	1,925	330	2,490	2,631	12,783	2,979	7,723	6,430
IIE Incidence (%)	14.1	13.8	13.6	24.2	26.9	44.0	44.4	38.3	57.5	66.4
IIE Deficit ($ Millions)	18,845	11,955	5,932	958	7,135	5,239	24,718	6,170	15,589	9,747
IIE Average Deficit ($)	3,180	3,257	3,082	2,902	2,866	1,991	1,934	2,071	2,019	1,516
IFE (000)	4,493	1,682	2,564	248	1,928	2,454	2,655	2,305	1,881	1,475
IFE Incidence (%)	10.7	6.3	18.2	18.2	20.8	41.1	9.2	29.6	14.0	15.2
IFE Deficit ($ Millions)	13,423	3,383	9,334	706	2,964	9,783	5,166	5,645	5,401	4,174
IFE Average Deficit ($)	2,988	2,012	3,641	2,849	2,575	3,987	1,946	2,449	2,871	2,831
IFI (000)	2,655	1,121	1,373	161	1,447	1,768	1,355	1,479	1,036	784
IFI Incidence (%)	6.3	4.2	9.7	11.8	15.6	29.6	4.7	19.0	7.7	8.1
IFI Deficit ($ Millions)	6,893	2,207	4,301	385	3,113	5,423	1,675	2,777	1,756	1,378
IFI Average Deficit ($)	2,596	1,969	3,133	2,387	2,152	3,068	1,236	1,878	1,695	1,757
Full Employment IFE (000)	3,442	999	2,259	184	1,336	2,040	1,840	1,750	1,309	1,085
Full Employment IFE Deficit ($ Millions)	9,601	1,847	7,281	473	3,028	7,047	3,536	3,791	3,306	2,894
Adequate Employment IFE (000)	2,602	591	1,880	132	987	1,788	1,296	1,437	1,039	856
Adequate Employment IFE Deficit ($ Millions)	6,880	877	5,717	285	2,197	6,377	2,796	3,117	2,739	2,465
Capacity Employment IFE (000)	3,864	1,312	2,349	203	1,558	2,157	2,204	2,072	1,501	1,254
Capacity Employment IFE Deficit ($ Millions)	11,136	2,502	8,102	532	3,793	7,976	4,484	4,887	3,976	3,348
Enhanced Earnings IFE (000)	3,914	1,387	2,308	220	1,767	2,256	2,270	2,159	1,718	1,338
Enhanced Earnings IFE Deficit ($ Millions)	11,953	2,905	8,411	638	4,562	9,153	4,774	5,213	5,015	3,935
Enhanced Capacity IFE (000)	2,173	430	1,650	93	859	1,593	1,056	1,299	888	754
Enhanced Capacity IFE Deficit ($ Millions)	5,725	640	4,847	237	1,966	5,740	2,419	2,821	2,440	2,263
IIE in IFE (000)	3,059	1,311	1,558	190	1,552	1,990	2,128	1,868	1,594	1,279
Earnings Supplementation Rate-Total (%)	40.9	33.4	46.4	35.0	24.9	28.0	48.9	35.8	44.9	46.8
Earnings Supplementation Rate-Net of Transfers (%)	19.6	16.0	22.6	13.1	13.6	11.9	22.0	17.5	17.0	20.6
IFI Net of Transfers (000)	3,613	1,412	1,985	215	1,665	2,161	2,072	1,901	1,560	1,171
IFI Net-of-Transfers Deficit	10,332	2,895	6,825	611	3,941	8,515	3,520	4,214	4,346	3,102
IFI Including Food Stamps (000)	2,588	1,089	1,341	158	1,430	1,680	1,315	1,474	973	729
IFI Including Food Stamps Deficit ($ Millions)	6,287	2,040	3,889	358	2,989	4,527	1,531	2,699	1,433	1,133
IFI Including In-Kind Aid (000)	2,526	1,058	1,315	153	1,411	1,595	1,278	1,460	941	699
IFI Including In-Kind Aid Deficit ($ Millions)	6,074	1,980	3,751	343	2,958	4,117	1,466	2,665	1,320	1,048

Table B-3. (Continued)

MODERATE HARDSHIP: TOTAL WORK FORCE

	Male Family Head	(Male Family Head-Wife in Work Force)	(Male Family Head-Wife Not in Work Force)	(Male Family Head-Wife Not Present)	Male Unrelated Individual	Female Family Head	Wife	Female Unrelated Individual	Other Male	Other Female
Work Force (000)	42,051	26,571	14,118	1,362	9,263	5,976	28,814	7,777	13,424	9,076
IIE (000)	8,218	5,214	2,582	423	3,237	3,315	16,284	3,885	9,078	7,409
IIE Incidence (%)	19.5	19.6	18.3	31.0	34.9	55.5	56.5	50.0	67.6	76.6
IIE Deficit ($ Millions)	29,753	19,114	9,169	1,470	11,013	8,495	39,029	10,149	23,106	14,857
IIE Average Deficit ($)	3,620	3,666	3,552	3,479	3,402	2,563	2,397	2,612	2,545	2,005
IFE (000)	5,849	2,354	3,186	309	2,349	2,882	3,508	2,723	2,417	1,825
IFE Incidence (%)	13.9	8.9	22.6	22.7	25.4	48.2	12.2	35.0	18.0	18.9
IFE Deficit ($ Millions)	20,216	5,418	13,762	1,035	7,078	13,463	7,778	7,889	7,536	5,709
IFE Average Deficit ($)	3,456	2,302	4,320	3,344	3,014	4,672	2,217	2,897	3,117	3,128
IFI (000)	3,849	1,668	1,974	207	1,873	2,198	2,036	1,907	1,422	1,069
IFI Incidence (%)	9.2	6.3	14.0	15.2	20.2	36.8	7.1	24.5	10.6	11.0
IFI Deficit ($ Millions)	11,625	3,738	7,264	623	4,749	8,283	2,990	4,293	2,974	2,260
IFI Average Deficit ($)	3,020	2,241	3,680	3,001	2,536	3,768	1,468	2,251	2,092	2,115
Full Employment IHE (000)	4,417	1,381	2,814	221	1,573	2,432	2,352	2,009	1,574	1,305
Full Employment IIE Deficit ($ Millions)	14,387	2,955	10,733	699	4,201	9,662	5,163	5,094	4,500	3,864
Adequate Employment IFE (000)	3,145	747	2,244	154	1,082	1,924	1,501	1,527	1,154	943
Adequate Employment IFE Deficit ($ Millions)	9,767	1,320	8,057	390	2,865	8,056	3,738	3,945	3,468	3,087
Capacity Employment IFE (000)	5,077	1,875	2,937	265	1,883	2,627	2,932	2,471	1,928	1,562
Capacity Employment IFE Deficit ($ Millions)	16,987	4,092	12,084	811	5,457	11,257	6,860	6,876	5,651	4,659
Enhanced Earnings IFE (000)	5,098	1,974	2,848	276	2,177	2,620	3,015	2,444	2,104	1,618
Enhanced Earnings IFE Deficit ($ Millions)	17,877	4,615	12,325	936	6,469	12,554	7,333	7,270	6,965	5,352
Enhanced Capacity IFE (000)	2,589	538	1,942	109	969	1,705	1,224	1,366	943	807
Enhanced Capacity IFE Deficit ($ Millions)	8,015	939	6,755	320	2,556	7,207	3,253	3,565	3,077	2,799
IIE in IFE (000)	4,207	1,856	2,095	256	2,017	2,498	3,037	2,381	2,174	1,661
Earnings Supplementation Rate-Total (%)	34.2	29.1	38.0	33.0	20.3	23.7	42.0	30.0	41.2	41.4
Earnings Supplementation Rate-Net of Transfers (%)	16.5	14.9	18.1	12.8	11.0	11.0	19.1	14.8	17.4	17.3
IFI Net of Transfers (000)	4,883	2,003	2,610	270	2,091	2,565	2,839	2,320	1,997	1,509
IFI Net-of-Transfers Deficit ($ Millions)	16,190	4,705	10,569	916	5,798	11,819	5,575	6,095	6,148	4,357
IFI Including Food Stamps (000)	3,792	1,645	1,944	204	1,855	2,155	2,009	1,900	1,341	1,050
IFI Including Food Stamps Deficit ($ Millions)	10,913	3,529	6,792	593	4,601	7,310	2,827	4,206	2,590	1,980
IFI Including In-Kind Aid (000)	3,731	1,621	1,907	203	1,836	2,095	1,981	1,880	1,316	1,020
IFI Including In-Kind Aid Deficit ($ Millions)	10,589	3,434	6,581	573	4,550	6,761	2,733	4,156	2,441	1,864

Table B-4. HARDSHIP BY FAMILY SIZE AND NUMBER OF EARNERS

SEVERE HARDSHIP: TOTAL WORK FORCE

	Total	One In Work Force				Total	Two In Work Force		
		1 Member	2 Members	3 Members	4-5 Members	6+ Members		2 Members	3 Members	4-5 Members	6+ Members
Work Force (000)	35,655	17,041	8,287	4,701	5,215	411	51,073	19,448	13,359	15,927	2,338
IIE (000)	7,341	3,707	1,709	904	761	199	11,165	3,746	2,874	3,759	786
IIE Incidence (%)	20.6	21.8	21.4	21.5	14.6	21.8	21.9	19.3	21.5	23.6	33.6
IIE Deficit ($ Millions)	15,190	7,698	3,573	1,873	1,606	441	20,965	7,810	5,186	6,598	1,372
IIE Average Deficit ($)	2,069	2,076	2,019	2,072	2,110	2,218	1,878	2,085	1,805	1,755	1,745
IFE (000)	8,457	3,505	2,375	1,119	1,077	381	3,628	975	676	1,381	595
IFE Incidence (%)	23.7	20.6	28.7	26.6	20.7	41.8	7.1	5.0	5.1	8.7	25.4
IFE Deficit ($ Millions)	24,467	7,009	6,555	3,731	4,803	2,369	5,924	1,110	860	2,409	1,572
IFE Average Deficit ($)	2,893	2,000	2,760	3,334	4,458	6,223	1,633	1,083	1,271	1,744	2,644
IFI (000)	4,450	2,114	733	536	767	301	2,014	404	306	874	431
IFI Incidence (%)	12.5	12.4	8.8	12.7	14.7	33.0	3.9	2.1	2.3	5.5	18.4
IFI Deficit ($ Millions)	9,618	3,518	1,462	1,183	2,304	1,151	2,695	362	278	1,159	896
IFI Average Deficit ($)	2,161	1,664	1,995	2,209	3,005	3,824	1,338	897	909	1,327	2,080
Full Employment IFE (000)	6,929	2,583	1,957	968	1,042	379	2,515	597	401	1,015	502
Full Employment IFE Deficit ($ Millions)	18,149	4,679	4,826	2,678	3,883	2,083	3,398	5,920	404	1,341	1,060
Adequate Employment IFE (000)	6,151	2,160	1,765	825	1,026	375	1,947	410	267	811	459
Adequate Employment IFE Deficit ($ Millions)	15,956	3,847	4,332	2,321	3,501	1,955	2,440	3,821	268	924	866
Capacity Employment IFE (000)	7,375	2,951	2,075	959	1,016	373	2,868	768	488	1,101	510
Capacity Employment IFE Deficit ($ Millions)	20,413	5,694	5,532	2,997	4,070	2,121	4,184	813	565	1,649	1,157
Enhanced Earnings IFE (000)	7,819	3,212	2,226	1,043	992	346	3,207	881	611	1,184	531
Enhanced Earnings IFE Deficit ($ Millions)	22,850	6,470	6,140	3,502	4,514	2,224	5,297	974	762	2,146	1,414
Enhanced Capacity IFE (000)	5,523	1,933	1,602	726	925	338	1,564	360	222	618	366
Enhanced Capacity IFE Deficit ($ Millions)	1,437	3,478	3,979	2,109	3,049	1,760	2,007	330	225	731	722
IIE in IFE (000)	5,639	2,520	1,467	794	665	193	2,603	708	512	1,009	374
Earnings Supplementation Rate-Total (%)	47.4	39.7	69.1	52.1	28.8	21.0	44.5	58.6	54.8	36.7	27.5
Earnings Supplementation Rate-Net of Transfers (%)	21.8	20.4	33.4	20.5	8.6	3.4	20.0	34.6	26.1	12.0	7.8
IFI Net of Transfers (000)	6,613	2,788	1,582	890	985	368	2,903	638	500	1,216	548
IFI Net of Transfers Deficit ($ Millions)	18,306	5,192	4,006	2,750	4,142	2,216	4,716	684	581	1,989	1,462
IFI Including Food Stamps (000)	4,215	2,072	698	482	702	261	1,801	375	277	777	372
IFI Including Food Stamps Deficit ($ Millions)	8,242	3,354	1,292	949	1,817	829	2,280	343	248	994	695
IFI Including In-Kind Aid (000)	4,045	2,042	659	452	646	246	1,713	373	264	731	344
IFI Including In-Kind Aid Deficit ($ Millions)	7,852	3,319	1,235	875	1,661	762	2,165	339	241	946	638

Table B-4. (Continued)

SEVERE HARDSHIP:
TOTAL WORK FORCE

| | Total | Three Or More In Work Force |||
		3 Members	4-5 Members	6+ Members
Work Force (000)	30,255	6,503	15,977	7,775
IIE (000)	9,762	1,785	5,030	2,948
IIE Incidence (%)	32.3	27.4	31.5	37.9
IIE Deficit ($ Millions)	15,842	3,144	7,868	4,830
IIE Average Deficit ($)	1,623	1,762	1,564	1,638
IFE (000)	1,195	137	479	579
IFE Incidence (%)	4.0	2.1	3.0	7.4
IFE Deficit ($ Millions)	1,265	963	480	689
IFE Average Deficit ($)	1,059	705	1,001	1,190
IFI (000)	591	44	244	303
IFI Incidence (%)	2.0	.7	1.5	3.9
IFI Deficit ($ Millions)	512	34	173	305
IFI Average Deficit ($)	866	770	710	1,006
Full Employment IFE (000)	634	58	264	311
Full Employment IFE Deficit ($ Millions)	568	32	223	312
Adequate Employment IFE (000)	415	37	162	216
Adequate Employment IFE Deficit ($ Millions)	374	15	155	204
Capacity Employment IFE (000)	851	104	348	399
Capacity Employment IFE Deficit ($ Millions)	854	71	341	441
Enhanced Earnings IFE (000)	972	125	366	480
Enhanced Earnings IFE Deficit ($ Millions)	1,084	82	421	582
Enhanced Capacity IFE (000)	291	20	126	146
Enhanced Capacity IFE Deficit ($ Millions)	309	11	134	164
IIE in IFE (000)	873	106	352	415
Earnings Supplementation Rate-Total (%)	50.5	67.8	49.1	47.7
Earnings Supplementation Rate-Net of Transfers (%)	21.2	32.4	23.3	16.8
IFI Net of Transfers (000)	941	92	368	482
IFI Net of Transfers Deficit ($ Millions)	984	64	347	573
IFI Including Food Stamps (000)	506	42	232	232
IFI Including Food Stamps Deficit ($ Millions)	387	33	143	211
IFI Including In-Kind Aid (000)	483	42	215	226
IFI Including In-Kind Aid Deficit ($ Millions)	362	33	132	196

Table B-4. (Continued)

SEVERE HARDSHIP: HALF-YEAR WORK FORCE

	Total	One In Work Force				Total	Two In Work Force			
		1 Member	2 Members	3 Members	4-5 Members	6+ Members		2 Members	3 Members	4-5 Members	6+ Members
Work Force (000)	32,044	15,030	7,299	3,853	4,980	882	43,039	17,054	11,121	13,090	1,775
IIE (000)	5,612	2,879	1,329	686	563	155	1,497	2,794	1,892	2,357	455
IIE Incidence (%)	17.5	19.2	18.2	17.8	11.3	17.5	17.4	16.4	17.0	18.0	25.6
IIE Deficit ($ Millions)	14,055	6,939	3,341	1,771	1,590	413	18,378	6,954	4,547	5,727	1,150
IIE Average Deficit ($)	2,504	2,410	2,514	2,582	2,824	2,667	2,451	2,489	2,403	2,430	2,530
IFE (000)	5,150	2,058	1,362	714	729	286	2,092	514	385	815	378
IFE Incidence (%)	16.1	13.7	18.7	18.5	14.6	32.4	4.9	3.0	3.5	6.2	21.3
IFE Deficit ($ Millions)	12,260	3,364	2,992	1,908	2,594	1,402	4,359	700	644	1,811	1,204
IFE Average Deficit ($)	2,381	1,635	2,196	2,671	3,558	4,901	2,084	1,360	1,673	2,222	3,188
IFI (000)	2,687	1,241	421	306	505	215	1,192	227	178	517	270
IFI Incidence (%)	8.4	8.3	5.8	7.9	10.1	24.3	2.8	1.3	1.6	4.0	15.2
IFI Deficit ($ Millions)	5,364	1,919	768	590	1,349	738	2,149	260	232	950	708
IFI Average Deficit ($)	1,996	1,547	1,824	1,930	2,671	3,441	1,803	1,143	1,302	1,838	2,621
Full Employment IFE (000)	3,729	1,207	983	567	688	283	1,301	255	200	545	301
Full Employment IFE Deficit ($ Millions)	7,348	1,539	1,665	1,093	1,850	1,200	2,816	387	346	1,187	897
Adequate Employment IFE (000)	2,886	760	753	422	673	277	857	123	93	378	263
Adequate Employment IFE Deficit ($ Millions)	5,001	764	1,116	669	1,412	1,040	1,758	165	164	718	711
Capacity Employment IFE (000)	4,102	1,530	1,068	560	665	278	1,565	382	259	613	310
Capacity Employment IFE Deficit ($ Millions)	9,028	2,355	2,180	1,312	1,982	1,199	3,433	582	485	1,397	968
Enhanced Earnings IFE (000)	4,582	1,816	1,229	639	647	252	1,794	443	339	682	330
Enhanced Earnings IFE Deficit ($ Millions)	10,992	2,986	2,691	1,721	2,334	1,260	4,350	727	674	1,792	1,158
Enhanced Capacity IFE (000)	2,342	589	604	328	582	240	629	93	66	269	201
Enhanced Capacity IFE Deficit ($ Millions)	3,947	595	909	524	1,056	863	1,288	124	125	478	560
IIE in IFE (000)	3,863	1,714	997	566	454	132	1,627	439	324	637	227
Earnings Supplementation Rate-Total (%)	47.8	39.7	69.1	57.2	30.8	25.0	43.0	55.8	53.8	36.6	28.5
Earnings Supplementation Rate-Net of Transfers (%)	21.3	20.1	32.2	23.9	8.6	4.5	18.5	33.0	26.0	11.3	6.9
IFI Net of Transfers (000)	4,051	1,645	923	543	666	273	1,704	345	285	723	352
IFI Net of Transfers Deficit ($ Millions)	9,428	2,595	1,929	1,339	2,231	1,334	3,608	497	459	1,538	1,114
IFI Including Food Stamps (000)	2,535	1,222	400	272	452	188	1,057	207	164	461	224
IFI Including Food Stamps Deficit ($ Millions)	4,074	1,837	702	483	1,103	549	1,856	247	210	832	566
IFI Including In-Kind Aid (000)	2,429	1,207	374	257	414	177	1,014	205	157	443	208
IFI Including In-Kind Aid Deficit ($ Millions)	4,461	1,822	623	446	1,015	505	1,782	244	205	803	530

333

Table B-4. (Continued)

SEVERE HARDSHIP:
HALF-YEAR WORK FORCE

	Total	Three Or More In Work Force		
		3 Members	4-5 Members	6+ Members
Work Force (000)	23,040	5,304	12,155	5,581
IIE (000)	6,016	1,196	3,052	1,769
IIE Incidence (%)	26.1	22.5	25.1	31.7
IIE Deficit ($ Millions)	13,369	2,744	6,563	4,062
IIE Average Deficit ($)	2,222	2,795	2,150	2,297
IFE (000)	664	82	244	337
IFE Incidence (%)	2.9	1.6	2.0	6.0
IFE Deficit ($ Millions)	1,025	827	351	592
IFZ Average Deficit ($)	1,545	1,004	1,436	1,757
IFI (000)	332	33	129	170
IFI Incidence (%)	1.4	.6	1.1	3.1
IFI Deficit ($ Millions)	440	33	153	253
IFI Average Deficit ($)	1,324	1,026	1,187	1,484
Full Employment IFE (000)	336	32	121	184
Full Employment IFE Deficit ($ Millions)	660	34	234	392
Adequate Employment IFE (000)	169	15	59	95
Adequate Employment IFE Deficit ($ Millions)	414	17	14	26
Capacity Employment IFE (000)	447	67	170	211
Capacity Employment IFE Deficit ($ Millions)	859	79	319	461
Enhanced Earnings IFE (000)	526	74	184	268
Enhanced Earnings IFE Deficit ($ Millions)	1,017	81	38	560
Enhanced Capacity HFE (000)	111	8	34	69
Enhanced Capacity IFE Deficit ($ Millions)	323	14	103	206
IIE in IFE (000)	516	67	200	249
Earnings Supplementation Rate-Total (%)	49.9	60.4	47.1	49.4
Earnings Supplementation Rate-Net of Transfers (%)	21.2	24.5	22.3	19.6
IFI Net of Transfers (000)	523	62	190	271
IFI Net of Transfers Deficit ($ Millions)	788	56	26	477
IFI Including Food Stamps (000)	292	31	128	132
IFI Including Food Stamps Deficit ($ Millions)	342	33	131	178
IFI Including In-Kind Aid (000)	289	31	128	129
IFI Including In-Kind Aid Deficit ($ Millions)	324	33	126	165

Table B-4. (Continued)

SEVERE HARDSHIP: FULL-YEAR WORK FORCE

		One In Work Force						Two In Work Force			
	Total	1 Member	2 Members	3 Members	4-5 Members	6+ Members	Total	2 Members	3 Members	4-5 Members	6+ Members
Work Force (000)	27,745	12,717	6,298	3,337	4,597	796	36,796	14,793	9,486	11,027	1,490
IIE (000)	4,356	2,223	1,039	506	464	123	5,551	2,136	1,432	1,646	337
IIE Incidence (%)	15.7	17.5	16.5	15.2	10.1	15.5	15.1	14.4	15.1	14.9	22.6
IIE Deficit ($ Millions)	11,883	5,610	2,860	1,464	1,400	348	15,352	5,848	3,913	4,619	972
IIE Average Deficit ($)	2,728	2,614	2,753	2,893	3,015	2,829	2,766	2,738	2,733	2,805	2,885
IIE (000)	3,565	1,303	952	497	569	244	1,554	365	286	610	293
IIE Incidence (%)	12.8	10.2	15.1	14.9	12.4	30.7	4.2	2.5	3.0	5.5	19.6
IIE Deficit ($ Millions)	8,735	2,164	2,126	1,312	1,996	1,135	3,598	533	513	1,519	1,033
IIE Average Deficit ($)	2,450	1,662	2,234	2,639	3,508	4,644	2,316	1,462	1,795	2,488	3,530
IFI (000)	1,894	796	313	210	394	181	915	175	143	387	211
IFI Incidence (%)	6.8	6.3	5.0	6.3	8.6	22.8	2.5	1.2	1.5	3.5	14.1
IFI Deficit ($ Millions)	4,000	1,304	569	420	1,085	622	1,865	216	204	816	628
IFI Average Deficit ($)	2,112	1,639	1,816	2,002	2,756	3,427	2,038	1,239	1,430	2,107	2,984
Full Employment IFE (000)	2,389	613	635	367	531	242	985	184	141	423	237
Full Employment IFE Deficit ($ Millions)	4,914	805	1,098	686	1,359	966	2,533	318	269	1,084	862
Adequate Employment IFE (000)	1,664	288	415	209	515	236	603	64	45	294	201
Adequate Employment IFE Deficit ($ Millions)	2,934	265	615	294	937	824	1,466	102	76	601	686
Capacity Employment IFE (000)	2,734	900	713	373	510	237	1,168	267	189	464	248
Capacity Employment IFE Deficit ($ Millions)	6,221	1,410	1,514	873	1,462	963	3,120	482	431	1,304	903
Enhanced Earnings IFE (000)	3,169	1,151	860	446	501	210	1,324	313	253	504	253
Enhanced Earnings IFE Deficit ($ Millions)	7,831	1,930	1,924	1,178	1,790	1,009	3,963	599	587	1,720	1,057
Enhanced Capacity IFE (000)	1,345	224	335	149	438	199	442	50	29	205	157
Enhanced Capacity IFE Deficit ($ Millions)	2,250	200	502	224	653	670	1,070	85	56	377	551
IIE in IPE (000)	2,836	1,175	745	427	380	108	1,237	318	255	494	171
Earnings Supplementation Rate-Total (%)	46.9	38.9	67.1	57.8	30.8	25.8	41.1	52.1	50.0	36.5	28.1
Earnings Supplementation Rate-Net of Transfers (%)	19.8	18.4	31.4	21.8	7.9	5.3	15.8	28.5	22.6	9.8	6.0
IFI Net of Transfers (000)	2,860	1,063	653	389	524	232	1,308	261	221	551	275
IFI Net of Transfers Deficit	6,874	1,736	1,389	913	1,757	1,080	3,047	403	386	1,304	954
IFI Including Food Stamps (000)	1,775	779	296	188	351	161	811	162	131	345	173
IFI Including Food Stamps Deficit ($ Millions)	3,481	1,243	520	357	901	460	1,608	207	184	717	499
IFI Including In-Kind Aid (000)	1,702	770	281	181	319	151	778	160	126	335	157
IFI Including In-Kind Aid Deficit ($ Millions)	3,326	1,236	501	335	834	421	1,546	205	180	696	466

Table B-4. (Continued)

SEVERE HARDSHIP: FULL-YEAR WORK FORCE

	Total	Three Or More In Work Force		
		3 Members	4-5 Members	6+ Members
Work Force (000)	18,950	4,442	9,981	4,528
IIE (000)	4,203	874	2,080	1,249
IIE Incidence (%)	22.2	19.7	20.8	27.6
IIE Deficit ($ Millions)	10,681	2,258	5,184	3,238
IIE Average Deficit ($)	2,541	2,585	2,492	2,592
IFE (000)	481	56	164	261
IFE Incidence (%)	2.5	1.3	1.6	5.8
IFE Deficit ($ Millions)	809	639	262	483
IFE Average Deficit ($)	1,683	1,136	1,600	1,852
IFI (000)	243	20	92	131
IFI Incidence (%)	1.3	.4	.9	2.9
IFI Deficit ($ Millions)	360	27	131	202
IFI Average Deficit ($)	1,479	1,354	1,419	1,542
Full Employment IFE (000)	253	21	90	142
Full Employment IFE Deficit ($ Millions)	624	28	214	381
Adequate Employment IFE (000)	120	10	37	73
Adequate Employment IFE Deficit ($ Millions)	335	3	103	23
Capacity Employment IFE (000)	326	45	112	169
Capacity Employment IFE Deficit ($ Millions)	780	68	285	43
Enhanced Earnings IFE (000)	375	50	121	205
Enhanced Earnings IFE Deficit ($ Millions)	900	73	300	53
Enhanced Capacity IFE (000)	78	5	25	49
Enhanced Capacity IFE Deficit ($ Millions)	23	-0-	72	162
IIE in IFE (000)	380	50	137	193
Earnings Supplementation Rate-Total (%)	49.4	64.6	43.7	49.8
Earnings Supplementation Rate-Net of Transfers (%)	19.7	25.7	19.7	18.3
IFI Net of Transfers (000)	386	42	131	213
IFI Net of Transfers Deficit ($ Millions)	624	48	201	374
IFI Including Food Stamps (000)	212	19	91	101
IFI Including Food Stamps Deficit ($ Millions)	282	27	109	146
IFI Including In-Kind Aid (000)	211	19	91	100
IFI Including In-Kind Aid Deficit ($ Millions)	267	26	105	136

Table B-4. (Continued)

INTERMEDIATE HARDSHIP: TOTAL WORK FORCE

	Total	One In Work Force					Total	Two In Work Force			
		1 Member	2 Members	3 Members	4-5 Members	6+ Members		2 Members	3 Members	4-5 Members	6+ Members
Work Force (000)	35,655	17,041	8,287	4,201	5,215	911	51,073	19,448	13,359	15,927	2,388
IIE (000)	10,648	5,468	2,557	1,306	1,055	261	16,457	5,807	4,206	5,397	1,047
IIE Incidence (%)	29.9	32.1	30.9	31.1	20.2	28.7	32.2	29.9	31.5	33.9	44.8
IIE Deficit ($ Millions)	25,743	13,304	5,938	3,137	2,654	709	35,379	13,396	879	10,994	2,200
IIE Average Deficit ($)	2,418	2,433	2,322	2,401	2,516	2,712	2,150	2,307	2,090	2,037	2,101
IFE (000)	10,303	4,232	2,833	1,396	1,380	462	5,073	1,360	1,012	1,941	760
IFE Incidence (%)	28.9	24.8	34.2	33.2	26.5	50.7	9.9	7.0	7.6	12.2	32.5
IFE Deficit ($ Millions)	36,440	10,609	9,589	5,528	7,193	3,521	9,776	1,753	1,461	4,040	2,522
IFE Average Deficit ($)	3,537	2,507	3,385	3,959	5,213	7,621	1,927	1,289	1,444	2,081	3,320
IFI (000)	6,275	2,926	1,059	807	1,080	403	3,129	605	541	1,360	623
IFI Incidence (%)	17.6	17.2	12.8	19.2	20.7	44.2	6.1	3.1	4.1	8.5	26.7
IFI Deficit ($ Millions)	16,789	5,891	2,531	2,143	4,105	2,120	5,110	663	571	2,237	1,639
IFI Average Deficit ($)	2,676	2,013	2,389	2,657	3,800	5,264	1,633	1,096	1,055	1,645	2,630
Full Employment IFE (000)	8,508	3,086	2,380	1,234	1,346	462	3,378	767	555	1,405	651
Full Employment IFE Deficit ($ Millions)	26,694	6,819	6,925	3,926	5,889	3,135	5,517	908	650	2,237	1,722
Adequate Employment IFE (000)	7,080	2,424	1,967	941	1,296	452	2,414	495	325	1,021	573
Adequate Employment IFE Deficit ($ Millions)	22,356	5,313	5,955	3,156	5,070	2,862	3,655	558	398	1,386	1,314
Capacity Employment IFE (000)	9,210	3,630	2,564	1,236	1,320	459	4,065	1,072	726	1,592	676
Capacity Employment IFE Deficit ($ Millions)	30,886	8,679	8,179	4,522	6,288	3,218	7,120	1,327	973	2,872	1,948
Enhanced Earnings IFE (000)	9,490	3,926	2,635	1,260	1,231	439	4,361	1,139	849	1,671	702
Enhanced Earnings IFE Deficit ($ Millions)	33,957	9,775	8,971	5,158	6,748	3,305	8,670	1,565	1,275	3,557	2,273
Enhanced Capacity IFE (000)	6,303	2,158	1,793	800	1,127	423	1,944	426	267	762	489
Enhanced Capacity IFE Deficit ($ Millions)	19,952	4,786	5,458	2,842	4,322	2,543	2,974	481	334	1,077	1,082
IIE in IFE (000)	7,840	3,420	2,078	1,148	934	259	4,112	1,096	867	1,579	570
Earnings Supplementation Rate-Total (%)	39.1	30.9	62.6	42.2	21.7	12.8	38.3	55.5	46.5	29.9	17.9
Earnings Supplementation Rate-Net of Transfers (%)	18.0	15.7	28.4	18.3	8.2	3.2	16.8	30.2	18.7	11.2	4.2
IFI Net of Transfers (000)	8,451	3,567	2,029	1,141	1,267	447	4,223	949	823	1,723	727
IFI Net of Transfers Deficit ($ Millions)	28,138	8,155	6,107	4,208	6,337	3,331	7,983	1,147	1,050	3,431	2,356
IFI Including Food Stamps (000)	6,128	2,904	1,027	769	1,039	389	3,028	601	511	1,303	613
IFI Including Food Stamps Deficit ($ Millions)	15,093	5,688	2,318	1,841	3,522	1,724	4,573	637	523	2,021	1,391
IFI Including In-Kind Aid (000)	5,978	2,870	995	718	1,015	380	2,960	588	491	1,277	604
IFI Including In-Kind Aid Deficit ($ Millions)	14,428	5,623	2,226	1,696	3,267	1,616	4,345	627	502	1,921	1,294

Table B-4. (Continued)

INTERMEDIATE HARDSHIP: TOTAL WORK FORCE

	Total	Three Or More In Work Force 3 Members	4-5 Members	6+ Members
Work Force (000)	30,255	6,503	15,977	7,775
IIE (000)	13,856	2,568	7,205	4,083
IIE Incidence (%)	45.8	39.5	45.1	52.5
IIE Deficit ($ Millions)	26,320	5,281	13,170	7,870
IIE Average Deficit ($)	1,900	2,056	1,828	1,928
IFE (000)	1,874	213	765	836
IFE Incidence (%)	6.0	3.3	4.8	10.8
IFE Deficit ($ Millions)	2,341	1,846	871	1,284
IFE Average Deficit ($)	1,290	867	1,139	1,536
IFI (000)	1,120	98	443	579
IFI Incidence (%)	3.7	1.5	2.8	7.4
IFI Deficit ($ Millions)	1,116	69	331	876
IFI Average Deficit ($)	996	708	836	1,168
Full Employment IFE (000)	916	82	385	450
Full Employment IFE Deficit ($ Millions)	992	56	374	562
Adequate Employment IFE (000)	512	38	202	272
Adequate Employment IFE Deficit ($ Millions)	559	22	228	309
Capacity Employment IFE (000)	1,335	163	574	598
Capacity Employment IFE Deficit ($ Millions)	1,593	137	616	840
Enhanced Earnings IFE (000)	1,571	198	648	725
Enhanced Earnings IFE Deficit ($ Millions)	1,979	155	735	1,089
Enhanced Capacity IFE (000)	376	24	167	185
Enhanced Capacity IFE Deficit ($ Millions)	446	17	190	239
IIE in IFE (000)	1,518	180	625	714
Earnings Supplementation Rate-Total (%)	38.3	54.2	42.0	30.8
Earnings Supplementation Rate-Net of Transfers (%)	18.9	23.1	24.0	13.2
IFI Net of Transfers (000)	1,471	164	581	726
IFI Net of Transfers Deficit ($ Millions)	1,849	128	642	1,078
IFI Including Food Stamps (000)	1,033	89	413	532
IFI Including Food Stamps Deficit ($ Millions)	933	68	330	535
IFI Including In-Kind Aid (000)	971	89	385	497
IFI Including In-Kind Aid Deficit ($ Millions)	873	67	310	496

Table B-4. (Continued)

MODERATE HARDSHIP: TOTAL WORK FORCE

	Total	One In Work Force					Total	Two In Work Force			
		1 Member	2 Members	3 Members	4-5 Members	6+ Members		2 Members	3 Members	4-5 Members	6+ Members
Work Force (000)	35,655	17,041	8,287	4,201	5,215	911	51,073	19,448	13,359	15,927	2,338
IIE (000)	13,616	7,122	3,214	1,628	1,330	322	21,118	7,653	5,438	6,770	1,258
IIE Incidence (%)	38.2	41.8	38.8	38.7	25.5	35.4	41.3	39.4	40.7	42.5	53.8
IIE Deficit ($ Millions)	40,337	21,162	9,143	4,860	4,117	1,056	55,757	21,465	13,899	17,087	3,306
IIE Average Deficit ($)	2,962	2,971	2,845	2,986	3,095	3,277	2,640	2,805	2,556	2,524	2,628
IFE (000)	12,224	5,072	3,223	1,663	1,738	528	6,633	1,705	1,385	2,580	963
IFE Incidence (%)	34.3	29.8	38.9	39.6	33.3	57.9	13.0	8.8	10.4	16.2	41.2
IFE Deficit ($ Millions)	50,871	14,966	13,099	7,708	10,225	4,873	14,895	2,652	2,316	6,230	3,696
IFE Average Deficit ($)	4,162	2,951	4,064	4,636	5,882	9,230	2,246	1,556	1,673	2,415	3,837
IFI (000)	8,205	3,779	1,439	1,074	1,428	483	4,425	851	809	1,953	812
IFI Incidence (%)	23.0	22.2	17.4	25.6	27.4	53.0	8.7	4.4	6.1	12.3	34.7
IFI Deficit ($ Millions)	26,440	9,041	4,018	3,494	6,550	3,336	8,601	1,110	1,047	3,833	2,610
IFI Average Deficit ($)	3,223	2,392	2,792	3,253	4,586	6,903	1,944	1,304	1,295	1,963	3,214
Full Employment IFE (000)	10,031	3,581	2,743	1,488	1,692	526	4,363	900	796	1,833	834
Full Employment IFE Deficit ($ Millions)	36,994	9,295	9,345	5,477	8,511	4,366	8,299	1,296	1,002	3,461	2,539
Adequate Employment IFE (000)	7,803	2,609	2,051	1,020	1,608	515	2,824	555	371	1,202	696
Adequate Employment IFE Deficit ($ Millions)	29,185	6,810	7,563	4,006	6,928	3,877	4,981	750	537	1,900	1,794
Capacity Employment IFE (000)	11,040	4,354	2,974	1,508	1,680	524	5,477	1,349	1,075	2,178	875
Capacity Employment IFE Deficit ($ Millions)	43,850	12,333	11,371	6,464	9,166	4,516	11,180	2,007	1,597	4,631	2,944
Enhanced Earnings IFE (000)	11,153	4,622	2,985	1,483	1,556	507	5,738	1,512	1,188	2,198	840
Enhanced Earnings IFE Deficit ($ Millions)	47,415	13,738	12,283	7,193	9,636	4,565	13,133	2,352	1,998	5,455	3,328
Enhanced Capacity IFE (000)	6,943	2,335	1,874	856	1,388	490	2,237	484	304	906	543
Enhanced Capacity IFE Deficit ($ Millions)	25,882	6,121	6,947	3,585	5,779	3,450	4,001	644	447	1,456	1,453
IIE in IFE (000)	9,968	4,398	2,606	1,444	1,201	317	5,623	1,453	1,226	2,187	756
Earnings Supplementation Rate-Total (%)	32.9	25.5	55.3	35.4	17.8	8.5	33.3	50.1	41.6	24.3	15.7
Earnings Supplementation Rate-Net of Transfers (%)	15.2	13.0	23.8	16.7	8.0	2.8	15.4	25.3	19.3	10.6	5.3
IFI Net of Transfers (000)	10,365	4,412	2,455	1,386	1,599	513	5,611	1,274	1,117	2,307	913
IFI Net of Transfers Deficit ($ Millions)	40,413	11,893	8,720	6,010	9,146	4,644	12,422	1,817	1,748	5,386	3,471
IFI Including Food Stamps (000)	8,117	3,754	1,422	1,054	1,409	478	4,346	846	804	1,906	790
IFI Including Food Stamps Deficit ($ Millions)	24,561	8,807	3,776	3,157	5,911	2,910	7,981	1,081	990	3,571	2,338
IFI Including In-Kind Aid (000)	7,984	3,716	1,381	1,024	1,393	471	4,285	839	790	1,880	776
IFI Including In-Kind Aid Deficit ($ Millions)	23,629	8,706	3,633	2,939	5,583	2,767	7,673	1,065	959	3,435	2,214

Table B-4. (Continued)

MODERATE HARDSHIP: TOTAL WORK FORCE

	Total	Three Or More In Work Force		
		3 Members	4-5 Members	6+ Members
Work Force (000)	30,255	6,503	15,977	7,775
JIE (000)	16,692	3,177	8,715	4,801
JIE Incidence (%)	55.2	48.8	54.5	61.7
JIE Deficit ($ Millions)	40,309	8,170	20,308	11,830
JIE Average Deficit ($)	2,415	2,572	2,330	2,464
IFE (000)	2,696	306	1,114	1,275
IFE Incidence (%)	8.9	4.7	7.0	16.4
IFE Deficit ($ Millions)	3,902	301	1,457	2,144
IFE Average Deficit ($)	1,447	982	1,308	1,681
IFI (000)	1,725	165	701	859
IFI Incidence (%)	5.7	2.5	4.4	11.0
IFI Deficit ($ Millions)	2,133	130	726	1,277
IFI Average Deficit ($)	1,237	788	1,036	1,488
Full Employment IFE (000)	1,267	102	508	657
Full Employment IFE Deficit ($ Millions)	1,578	84	584	911
Adequate Employment IFE (000)	649	49	256	344
Adequate Employment IFE Deficit ($ Millions)	760	30	307	423
Capacity Employment IFE (000)	1,962	213	839	910
Capacity Employment IFE Deficit ($ Millions)	2,717	222	1,041	1454
Enhanced Earnings IFE (000)	2,186	243	909	1,034
Enhanced Earnings IFE Deficit ($ Millions)	3,271	256	1,219	1,796
Enhanced Capacity IFE (000)	423	28	190	205
Enhanced Capacity IFE Deficit ($ Millions)	588	22	248	318
IIE in IFE (000)	2,384	271	1,006	1,107
Earnings Supplementation Rate-Total (%)	36.0	46.0	37.1	32.7
Earnings Supplementation Rate-Net of Transfers (%)	17.3	27.1	19.5	13.1
IFI Net of Transfers (000)	2,229	223	897	1,109
IFI Net of Transfers Deficit ($ Millions)	3,147	212	1,103	1,831
IFI Including Food Stamps (000)	1,640	165	657	817
IFI Including Food Stamps Deficit ($ Millions)	1,887	126	659	1,103
IFI Including In-Kind Aid (000)	1,589	158	636	796
IFI Including In-Kind Aid Deficit ($ Millions)	1,791	125	628	1,039

Table B-5. HARDSHIP AND FAMILY INCOME IN 1979

SEVERE HARDSHIP: TOTAL WORK FORCE

	Under $2,000	$2,000-3,999	$4,000-5,999	$6,000-7,999	$8,000-9,999	$10,000-14,999	$15,000-24,999	$25,000-34,999	$35,000+
Work Force (000)	1,605	2,702	3,885	5,009	5,504	16,720	35,340	24,523	22,696
IIE (000)	1,383	2,119	2,704	2,120	1,806	4,433	6,487	5,988	5,087
IIE Incidence (%)	86.2	78.4	69.6	42.3	32.8	26.5	18.9	24.4	22.4
IIE Deficit ($ Millions)	4,719	5,089	5,167	4,133	3,692	8,344	10,671	10,030	7,928
IIE Average Deficit ($)	3,412	2,401	1,911	1,950	2,045	1,882	1,645	1,675	1,558
IFE (000)	1,600	2,645	2,459	2,048	1,400	2,048	824	273	88
IFE Incidence (%)	99.7	97.9	63.3	40.9	25.4	12.2	2.4	1.1	.4
IFE Deficit ($ Millions)	5,712	6,459	5,899	4,389	2,819	4,018	1,732	716	260
IFE Average Deficit ($)	3,570	2,442	2,399	2,143	2,014	1,962	2,102	2,627	2,942
IFI (000)	1,600	2,485	1,464	846	447	213	-0-	-0-	-0-
IFI Incidence (%)	99.7	92.0	37.7	16.9	8.1	1.3	-0-	-0-	-0-
IFI Deficit ($ Millions)	5,353	3,933	2,040	1,011	359	128	-0-	-0-	-0-
IFI Average Deficit ($)	3,345	1,583	1,394	1,155	804	598	-0-	-0-	-0-
Full Employment IFE (000)	1,319	1,914	1,846	1,543	1,064	1,572	664	207	72
Full Employment IFE Deficit ($ Millions)	3,855	4,246	4,092	3,209	2,010	2,898	1,323	557	182
Adequate Employment IFE (000)	953	1,518	1,554	1,383	973	1,368	575	174	62
Adequate Employment IFE Deficit ($ Millions)	2,566	3,521	3,631	2,917	1,847	2,611	1,235	491	158
Capacity Employment IFE (000)	1,472	2,156	2,021	1,670	1,154	1,687	709	227	84
Capacity Employment IFE Deficit ($ Millions)	4,755	4,982	4,631	3,556	2,246	3,240	1,488	628	231
Enhanced Earnings IFE (000)	1,600	2,507	2,281	1,784	1,163	1,726	704	229	83
Enhanced Earnings IFE Deficit ($ Millions)	5,616	6,035	5,451	3,918	2,498	3,562	1,569	651	237
Enhanced Capacity IFE (000)	885	1,385	1,393	1,161	786	1,116	484	157	57
Enhanced Capacity IFE Deficit ($ Millions)	2,411	3,203	3,252	2,505	1,573	2,247	1,102	442	136
IIE in IFE (000)	1,381	2,084	1,816	1,323	808	1,166	408	172	54
Earnings Supplementation Rate-Total (%)	-0-	6.1	40.5	58.7	68.1	89.6	100.0	100.0	100.0
Earnings Supplementation Rate-Net of Transfers (%)	-0-	1.8	11.5	17.5	23.6	45.6	77.1	872	998
IFI Net of Transfers (000)	1,600	2,596	2,176	1,690	1,070	1,115	189	35	-0-
IFI Net-of-Transfers Deficit	5,627	5,843	5,053	3,350	1,890	1,845	325	108	-0-
IFI Including Food Stamps (000)	1,599	2,436	1,316	717	317	138	-0-	-0-	-0-
IFI Including Food Stamps Deficit ($ Millions)	5,101	3,332	1,504	690	213	682	-0-	-0-	-0-
IFI Including In-Kind Aid (000)	1,599	2,372	1,228	667	259	115	-0-	-0-	-0-
IFI Including In-Kind Aid Deficit ($ Millions)	5,056	3,155	1,329	602	178	576	-0-	-0-	-0-

Table B-5. (Continued)

SEVERE HARDSHIP: FULL-YEAR WORK FORCE

	Under $2,000	$2,000-3,999	$4,000-5,999	$6,000-7,999	$8,000-9,999	$10,000-14,999	$15,000-24,999	$25,000-34,999	$35,000+
Work Force (000)	643	1,127	2,021	3,111	3,646	11,977	25,776	18,599	17,078
IIE (000)	627	1,057	1,714	1,300	1,040	2,390	3,066	1,708	1,346
IIE Incidence (%)	97.4	93.7	84.8	41.8	28.5	20.0	11.9	9.2	7.9
IIE Deficit ($ Millions)	3,639	3,820	4,156	3,291	2,875	6,385	7,514	3,868	2,899
IIE Average Deficit ($)	5,807	3,615	2,424	2,532	2,763	2,672	2,450	2,264	2,154
IFE (000)	641	1,088	1,040	935	643	932	307	59	31
IFE Incidence (%)	99.6	96.5	51.5	30.0	17.6	7.8	1.2	.3	.2
IFE Deficit ($ Millions)	2,481	2,490	2,353	1,956	1,254	1,888	634	163	88
IFE Average Deficit ($)	3,872	2,289	2,262	2,092	1,950	2,026	2,065	2,766	2,870
IFI (000)	641	1,011	666	426	232	121	-0-	-0-	-0-
IFI Incidence (%)	99.6	89.7	33.0	13.7	6.4	1.0	-0-	-0-	-0-
IFI Deficit ($ Millions)	2,390	1,804	1,109	659	248	98	-0-	-0-	-0-
IFI Average Deficit ($)	3,731	1,783	1,664	1,546	1,069	810	-0-	-0-	-0-
Full Employment IFE (000)	457	587	623	638	450	629	211	49	23
Full Employment IFE Deficit ($ Millions)	1,418	1,214	1,318	1,322	889	1,368	437	136	45
Adequate Employment IFE (000)	141	270	414	492	365	506	161	39	19
Adequate Employment IFE Deficit ($ Millions)	244	498	788	1,003	687	1,071	332	112	31
Capacity Employment IFE (000)	538	755	750	693	500	727	235	54	27
Capacity Employment IFE Deficit ($ Millions)	1,941	1,675	1,649	1,556	1,029	1,625	522	150	85
Enhanced Earnings IFE (000)	641	1,016	931	766	508	747	252	49	25
Enhanced Earnings IFE Deficit ($ Millions)	2,466	2,389	2,252	1,878	1,168	1,821	610	171	99
Enhanced Capacity IFE (000)	119	222	342	380	271	383	121	31	14
Enhanced Capacity IFE Deficit ($ Millions)	191	394	619	739	487	781	257	87	24
IIE in IFE (000)	621	1,030	940	695	406	575	193	35	24
Earnings Supplementation Rate-Total (%)	-0-	7.0	35.9	54.4	63.9	87.1	100.0	100.0	100.0
Earnings Supplementation Rate-Net of Transfers (%)	-0-	1.7	9.5	13.6	22.3	40.2	68.1	89.2	100.0
IFI Net of Transfers (000)	641	1,070	941	807	500	557	94	6	-0-
IFI Net-of-Transfers Deficit ($ Millions)	2,472	2,311	2,096	1,667	904	1,010	192	27	-0-
IFI Including Food Stamps (000)	641	988	600	368	167	77	-0-	-0-	-0-
IFI Including Food Stamps Deficit ($ Millions)	2,305	1,595	859	472	154	54	-0-	-0-	-0-
IFI Including In-Kind Aid (000)	641	967	574	342	142	67	-0-	-0-	-0-
IFI Including In-Kind Aid Deficit ($ Millions)	2,294	1,534	785	419	130	45	-0-	-0-	-0-

Table B-5. (Continued)

INTERMEDIATE HARDSHIP: TOTAL WORK FORCE

	Under $2,000	$2,000-3,999	$4,000-5,999	$6,000-7,999	$8,000-9,999	$10,000-14,999	$15,000-24,999	$25,000-34,999	$35,000+
Work Force (000)	1,605	2,702	3,885	5,009	5,504	16,720	34,340	24,523	22,696
IIE (000)	1,486	2,361	3,204	3,716	2,702	6,746	9,040	3,862	3,355
IIE Incidence (%)	92.6	87.4	82.5	74.2	49.1	38.7	28.9	15.7	14.8
IIE Deficit ($ Millions)	6,107	7,327	8,578	7,758	6,385	14,375	18,935	5,677	4,505
IIE Average Deficit ($)	4,110	3,103	2,677	2,088	2,363	2,220	1,907	1,470	1,343
IFE (000)	1,600	2,700	3,164	2,782	2,152	3,185	1,245	184	72
IFE Incidence (%)	99.7	99.9	81.5	55.5	39.1	19.0	3.6	.7	.3
IFE Deficit ($ Millions)	7,386	9,277	8,972	7,189	4,923	6,992	2,842	461	167
IFE Average Deficit ($)	4,616	3,436	2,835	2,584	2,287	2,195	2,282	2,507	2,342
IFI (000)	1,600	2,700	2,605	1,557	1,078	972	10	-0-	-0-
IFI Incidence (%)	99.7	99.9	67.1	31.1	19.6	5.8	-0-	-0-	-0-
IFI Deficit ($ Millions)	7,027	6,723	4,362	2,602	1,374	925	2	-0-	-0-
IFI Average Deficit ($)	4,392	2,490	1,674	1,671	1,274	952	180	-0-	-0-
Full Employment IFE (000)	1,323	2,038	2,338	2,037	1,583	2,280	926	157	58
Full Employment IFE Deficit ($ Millions)	4,976	5,979	6,035	5,000	3,454	4,935	2,085	365	118
Adequate Employment IFE (000)	953	1,541	1,750	1,592	1,288	1,896	751	136	53
Adequate Employment IFE Deficit ($ Millions)	3,243	4,631	4,896	4,162	2,939	4,193	1,857	338	103
Capacity Employment IFE (000)	1,506	2,341	2,652	2,337	1,775	2,644	1,044	157	68
Capacity Employment IFE Deficit ($ Millions)	6,262	7,312	7,142	5,829	4,029	5,751	2,416	406	148
Enhanced Earnings IFE (000)	1,600	2,698	2,882	2,447	1,814	2,619	1,050	168	65
Enhanced Earnings IFE Deficit ($ Millions)	7,291	8,807	8,264	6,461	4,292	6,085	2,518	428	154
Enhanced Capacity IFE (000)	885	1,437	1,543	1,382	1,032	1,508	622	123	47
Enhanced Capacity IFE Deficit ($ Millions)	3,052	4,241	4,390	3,603	2,414	3,465	1,629	309	88
IIE in IFE (000)	1,482	2,360	2,613	2,306	1,541	2,124	817	95	33
Earnings Supplementation Rate-Total (%)	-0-	-0-	17.7	44.0	49.9	69.5	99.2	100.0	100.0
Earnings Supplementation Rate-Net of Transfers (%)	-0-	-0-	5.1	11.7	16.5	32.1	68.7	89.4	99.8
IFI Net of Transfers (000)	1,600	2,700	3,001	2,456	1,797	2,163	390	20	-0-
IFI Net-of-Transfers Deficit ($ Millions)	7,302	8,654	7,908	5,812	3,655	3,847	683	72	-0-
IFI Including Food Stamps (000)	1,600	2,694	2,559	1,470	998	859	10	-0-	-0-
IFI Including Food Stamps Deficit ($ Millions)	6,775	6,097	3,721	2,169	1,103	732	2	-0-	-0-
IFI Including In-Kind Aid (000)	1,599	2,683	2,473	1,410	941	793	10	-0-	-0-
IFI Including In-Kind Aid Deficit ($ Millions)	6,726	5,874	3,420	1,985	990	650	-0-	-0-	-0-

Table B-6. HARDSHIP IN 1979 AND AGE AT INTERVIEW

SEVERE HARDSHIP: TOTAL WORK FORCE

	16-19	(16-19 Student)	20-24	(20-24 Student)	25-44	45-64	65 +
Work Force (000)	11,648	6,314	17,787	2,636	52,100	31,175	4,272
IIE (000)	6,923	3,977	5,489	1,071	8,857	5,474	1,526
IIE Incidence (%)	59.4	63.0	30.9	40.6	17.0	17.6	35.7
IIE Deficit ($ Millions)	8,369	3,655	9,264	1,087	18,120	13,360	2,886
IIE Average Deficit ($)	1,209	919	1,688	1,016	2,046	2,461	1,891
IFE (000)	1,782	840	2,268	474	4,421	2,880	1,929
IFE Incidence (%)	15.3	13.3	12.8	18.0	8.5	9.2	45.1
IFE Deficit ($ Millions)	4,055	1,788	4,940	931	11,884	6,442	4,335
IFE Average Deficit ($)	2,275	2,129	2,178	1,964	2,688	2,237	2,247
IFI (000)	1,108	460	1,432	201	2,998	1,291	227
IFI Incidence (%)	9.5	7.3	8.1	7.6	5.8	4.1	5.3
IFI Deficit ($ Millions)	1,733	621	2,328	2,433	6,129	2,329	266
IFI Average Deficit ($)	1,564	1,348	1,626	1,213	2,058	1,805	1,171
Full Employment IFE (000)	1,357	685	1,646	396	3,309	2,131	1,635
Full Employment IFE Deficit ($ Millions)	2,839	1,428	3,326	724	8,055	4,432	3,463
Adequate Employment IFE (000)	1,207	621	1,430	371	2,802	1,603	1,471
Adequate Employment IFE Deficit ($ Millions)	2,659	1,367	2,879	293	6,796	3,284	3,151
Capacity Employment IFE (000)	1,513	742	1,849	438	3,539	2,396	1,796
Capacity Employment IFE Deficit ($ Millions)	3,246	1,569	3,778	826	9,056	5,330	4,042
Enhanced Earnings IFE (000)	1,638	777	2,019	429	3,916	2,601	1,823
Enhanced Earnings IFE Deficit ($ Millions)	3,852	1,713	4,532	860	10,872	5,911	4,064
Enhanced Capacity IFE (000)	1,072	560	1,226	322	2,344	1,359	1,378
Enhanced Capacity IFE Deficit ($ Millions)	2,465	1,295	2,555	629	5,862	2,901	2,907
IIE in IFE (000)	1,341	595	1,617	289	3,093	2,017	1,048
Earnings Supplementation Rate-Total (%)	37.8	45.2	36.9	57.7	32.2	55.2	88.2
Earnings Supplementation Rate-Net of Transfers (%)	15.4	19.4	19.2	42.2	12.5	28.6	38.1
IFI Net of Transfers (000)	1,507	677	1,832	274	3,868	2,056	1,194
IFI Net-of-Transfers Deficit ($ Millions)	3,348	1,399	3,948	480	10,074	4,406	2,229
IFI Including Food Stamps (000)	983	408	1,350	193	2,746	1,225	219
IFI Including Food Stamps Deficit	1,403	480	2,035	229	5,092	2,121	257
IFI Including In-Kind Aid (000)	938	386	1,296	187	2,589	1,208	210
IFI Including In-Kind Aid Deficit ($ Millions)	1,321	439	1,960	225	4,780	2,068	250

Table B-6. (Continued)

SEVERE HARDSHIP: HALF-YEAR WORK FORCE

	16-19	(16-19 Student)	20-24	(20-24 Student)	25-44	45-64	65 +
Work Force (000)	5,885	2,398	14,050	1,262	47,047	28,685	3,066
IIE (000)	3,335	1,526	3,779	540	6,606	4,490	1,090
IIE Incidence (%)	56.7	63.6	26.9	42.8	14.0	15.7	35.5
IIE Deficit ($ Millions)	6,346	2,401	8,150	813	16,603	12,653	2,651
IIE Average Deficit ($)	1,903	1,574	2,157	1,507	2,513	2,818	2,432
IFE (000)	681	223	1,278	203	3,051	1,930	1,068
IFE Incidence (%)	11.7	9.3	9.1	16.1	6.5	6.7	34.8
IFE Deficit ($ Millions)	1,654	503	2,529	328	7,595	4,123	1,990
IFE Average Deficit ($)	2,408	2,252	1,979	1,618	2,489	2,136	1,863
IFI (000)	431	119	782	78	2,026	927	111
IFI Incidence (%)	7.3	5.0	5.6	6.1	4.3	3.2	3.6
IFI Deficit ($ Millions)	701	154	1,231	81	4,206	1,790	136
IFI Average Deficit ($)	1,624	1,293	1,574	1,050	2,076	1,932	1,226
Full Employment IFE (000)	442	161	797	142	2,104	1,286	804
Full Employment IFE Deficit ($ Millions)	915	340	1,395	214	4,757	2,581	1,308
Adequate Employment IFE (000)	341	137	598	128	1,609	759	652
Adequate Employment IFE Deficit ($ Millions)	731	299	936	181	3,246	1,337	1,011
Capacity Employment IFE (000)	523	192	943	179	2,271	1,502	954
Capacity Employment IFE Deficit ($ Millions)	1,159	435	1,728	289	5,474	3,338	1,805
Enhanced Earnings IFE (000)	616	207	1,085	176	2,629	1,691	979
Enhanced Earnings IFE Deficit ($ Millions)	1,595	489	2,324	294	6,972	3,868	1,838
Enhanced Capacity IFE (000)	288	125	438	93	1,252	569	575
Enhanced Capacity IFE Deficit ($ Millions)	612	266	686	140	2,431	1,051	850
IIE in IFE (000)	564	170	1,010	138	2,279	1,557	688
Earnings Supplementation Rate-Total (%)	37.2	46.7	38.8	61.8	33.6	52.0	89.6
Earnings Supplementation Rate-Net of Transfers (%)	15.6	21.0	18.7	47.2	12.8	25.8	38.4
IFI Net of Transfers (000)	580	177	1,039	107	2,662	1,432	658
IFI Net-of-Transfers Deficit ($ Millions)	1,372	382	2,079	166	6,480	3,010	1,084
IFI Including Food Stamps (000)	377	100	720	75	1,862	877	107
IFI Including Food Stamps Deficit	576	114	1,078	78	3,536	1,640	134
IFI Including In-Kind Aid (000)	364	96	696	74	1,761	863	104
IFI Including In-Kind Aid Deficit ($ Millions)	552	106	1,046	77	3,331	1,597	131

Table B-6. (Continued)

SEVERE HARDSHIP: FULL-YEAR WORK FORCE

	16-19	(16-19 Student)	20-24	(20-24 Student)	25-44	45-64	65 +
Work Force (000)	3,762	1,355	11,251	717	41,103	25,506	2,356
IIE (000)	2,086	871	2,648	291	5,073	3,603	837
IIE Incidence (%)	55.4	64.3	23.5	40.6	12.3	14.1	35.5
IIE Deficit ($ Millions)	4,717	1,730	6,408	502	14,041	11,062	2,218
IIE Average Deficit ($)	2,261	1,986	2,420	1,722	2,767	3,070	2,651
IFE (000)	415	132	821	114	2,277	1,421	741
IFE Incidence (%)	11.0	9.7	7.3	15.9	5.5	5.6	31.4
IFE Deficit ($ Millions)	1,069	297	1,712	205	5,959	3,183	1,383
IFE Average Deficit ($)	2,579	2,250	2,085	1,794	2,617	2,239	1,867
IFI (000)	259	77	505	36	1,540	714	80
IFI Incidence (%)	6.9	5.7	4.5	5.0	3.7	2.8	3.4
IFI Deficit ($ Millions)	433	97	872	4.3	3,459	1,444	99
IFI Average Deficit ($)	1,677	1,258	1,727	1,207	2,246	2,021	1,249
Full Employment IFE (000)	236	87	454	73	1,535	915	527
Full Employment IFE Deficit ($ Millions)	571	203	913	121	3,768	2,028	862
Adequate Employment IFE (000)	168	69	303	61	1,078	458	401
Adequate Employment IFE Deficit ($ Millions)	437	172	552	102	2,282	876	619
Capacity Employment IFE (000)	297	110	574	104	1,662	1,086	659
Capacity Employment IFE Deficit ($ Millions)	753	273	1,175	193	4,398	2,633	1,272
Enhanced Earnings IFE (000)	374	120	693	101	1,946	1,243	678
Enhanced Earnings IFE Deficit ($ Millions)	1,110	323	1,619	188	5,704	3,114	1,305
Enhanced Capacity IFE (000)	141	64	226	44	817	347	351
Enhanced Capacity IFE Deficit ($ Millions)	355	154	386	75	1,657	668	512
IIE in IFE (000)	356	104	674	84	1,790	1,191	513
Earnings Supplementation Rate-Total (%)	37.6	41.9	38.5	68.5	32.4	49.7	89.2
Earnings Supplementation Rate-Net of Transfers (%)	13.9	20.0	15.8	51.1	10.4	25.2	36.7
IFI Net of Transfers (000)	357	106	692	56	2,040	1,064	468
IFI Net-of-Transfers Deficit ($ Millions)	868	226	1,472	98	5,216	2,346	779
IFI Including Food Stamps (000)	226	64	452	34	1,413	673	76
IFI Including Food Stamps Deficit ($ Millions)	350	679	749	39	2,931	1,311	98
IFI Including In-Kind Aid (000)	220	62	437	34	1,339	662	75
IFI Including In-Kind Aid Deficit ($ Millions)	334	617	726	38	2,774	1,276	96

Table B-7. HARDSHIP IN 1979 BY EDUCATIONAL ATTAINMENT AT INTERVIEW

SEVERE HARDSHIP: TOTAL WORK FORCE

	High School Student	Post-Secondary Student	High School Dropout	High School Graduate-No More Education	Post-Secondary 1-3 Years	College 4 or More Years
Work Force (000)	5,070	4,643	24,488	44,542	18,524	19,716
IIE (000)	3,325	1,984	8,537	9,543	3,021	1,858
IIE Incidence (%)	65.6	42.7	34.9	21.4	16.3	9.4
IIE Deficit ($ Millions)	3,214	1,979	17,716	18,923	5,933	4,233
IIE Average Deficit ($)	966	997	2,075	1,983	1,964	2,278
IFE (000)	779	793	5,297	4,014	1,415	982
IFE Incidence (%)	15.4	17.1	21.6	9.0	7.6	5.0
IFE Deficit ($ Millions)	1,799	1,680	13,483	9,153	3,322	2,219
IFE Average Deficit ($)	2,311	2,119	2,545	2,280	2,348	2,259
IFI (000)	449	331	3,011	2,133	702	431
IFI Incidence (%)	8.9	7.1	12.3	4.8	3.8	2.2
IFI Deficit ($ Millions)	648	447	5,745	3,921	1,303	761
IFI Average Deficit ($)	1,444	1,351	1,908	1,839	1,857	1,768
Full Employment IFE (000)	630	662	3,979	2,937	1,106	764
Full Employment IFE Deficit ($ Millions)	1,408	1,308	9,178	6,251	2,365	1,606
Adequate Employment IFE (000)	578	611	3,406	2,382	918	618
Adequate Employment IFE Deficit ($ Millions)	1,331	1,256	7,937	5,076	1,876	1,294
Capacity Employment IFE (000)	681	714	4,399	3,223	1,214	862
Capacity Employment IFE Deficit ($ Millions)	1,532	1,449	10,668	7,204	2,691	1,907
Enhanced Earnings IFE (000)	718	731	4,857	3,551	1,268	873
Enhanced Earnings IFE Deficit ($ Millions)	1,733	1,563	12,485	8,340	3,055	2,056
Enhanced Capacity IFE (000)	521	548	2,965	2,009	800	537
Enhanced Capacity IFE Deficit ($ Millions)	1,259	1,150	7,050	4,442	1,653	1,136
IIE in IFE (000)	571	475	3,810	2,739	916	605
Earnings Supplementation Rate-Total (%)	42.4	58.3	43.2	46.9	50.4	56.1
Earnings Supplementation Rate-Net of Transfers (%)	14.4	41.3	13.0	21.3	28.4	44.3
IFI Net of Transfers (000)	666	465	4,607	3,159	1,013	547
IFI Net-of-Transfers Deficit ($ Millions)	1,505	835	11,493	6,896	2,205	1,071
IFI Including Food Stamps (000)	390	326	2,729	1,993	668	416
IFI Including Food Stamps Deficit ($ Millions)	493	412	4,678	3,413	1,185	729
IFI Including In-Kind Aid (000)	362	314	2,615	1,905	638	407
IFI Including In-Kind Aid Deficit ($ Millions)	448	399	4,413	3,264	1,135	719

Table B-7. (Continued)

SEVERE HARDSHIP: HALF-YEAR WORK FORCE

	High School Student	Post-Secondary Student	High School Dropout	High School Graduate-No More Education	Post Secondary 1-3 Years	College 4 or More Years
Work Force (000)	1,921	2,191	20,304	39,551	16,565	18,201
IIE (000)	1,265	937	6,187	7,200	2,265	1,445
IIE Incidence (%)	65.9	42.8	30.5	18.2	13.7	7.9
IIE Deficit ($ Millions)	2,140	1,427	16,170	17,269	5,429	3,969
IIE Average Deficit ($)	1,691	1,523	2,614	2,399	2,397	2,746
IFE (000)	212	333	3,330	2,635	878	627
IFE Incidence (%)	11.0	15.2	16.4	6.7	5.3	3.4
IFE Deficit ($ Millions)	537	603	7,931	5,605	1,951	1,265
IFE Average Deficit ($)	2,530	1,812	2,382	2,127	2,222	2,017
IFI (000)	115	130	1,880	1,415	448	290
IFI Incidence (%)	6.0	5.9	9.3	3.6	2.7	1.6
IFI Deficit ($ Millions)	146	170	3,688	2,702	832	527
IFI Average Deficit ($)	1,271	1,306	1,962	1,909	1,858	1,816
Full Employment IFE (000)	151	230	2,277	1,737	601	438
Full Employment IFE Deficit ($ Millions)	350	370	4,708	3,474	1,227	827
Adequate Employment IFE (000)	128	206	1,679	1,237	418	291
Adequate Employment IFE Deficit ($ Millions)	288	331	3,274	2,216	701	451
Capacity Employment IFE (000)	175	279	2,558	1,961	699	520
Capacity Employment IFE Deficit ($ Millions)	431	482	5,794	4,218	1,525	1,054
Enhanced Earnings IFE (000)	196	299	2,977	2,239	751	538
Enhanced Earnings IFE Deficit ($ Millions)	521	554	7,346	5,177	1,823	1,176
Enhanced Capacity IFE (000)	116	163	1,350	936	329	227
Enhanced Capacity IFE Deficit ($ Millions)	251	271	2,565	1,655	544	345
IIE in IFE (000)	164	227	2,596	1,987	662	464
Earnings Supplementation Rate-Total (%)	46.0	61.0	43.5	46.3	49.0	53.7
Earnings Supplementation Rate-Net of Transfers (%)	15.5	44.0	13.0	20.6	26.6	40.5
IFI Net of Transfers (000)	179	186	2,898	2,091	644	373
IFI Net-of-Transfers Deficit ($ Millions)	435	294	6,886	4,373	1,334	702
IFI Including Food Stamps (000)	95	128	1,691	1,322	428	280
IFI Including Food Stamps Deficit ($ Millions)	102	157	3,052	2,387	760	505
IFI Including In-Kind Aid (000)	89	125	1,624	1,266	408	275
IFI Including In-Kind Aid Deficit ($ Millions)	92	153	2,888	2,296	730	498

Table B-7. (Continued)

SEVERE HARDSHIP: FULL-YEAR WORK FORCE

	High School Student	Post-Secondary Student	High School Dropout	High School Graduate-No More Education	Post-Secondary 1-3 Years	College 4 or More Years
Work Force (000)	1,138	1,178	16,970	34,211	14,469	16,013
IIE (000)	762	482	4,808	5,473	1,678	1,044
IIE Incidence (%)	67.0	40.9	28.3	16.0	11.6	6.5
IIE Deficit ($ Millions)	1,619	858	13,752	14,438	4,502	3,278
IIE Average Deficit ($)	2,124	1,778	2,860	2,638	2,683	2,140
IFE (000)	141	161	2,461	1,889	600	424
IFE Incidence (%)	12.4	13.7	14.5	5.5	4.1	2.6
IFE Deficit ($ Millions)	341	304	6,152	4,145	1,422	943
IFE Average Deficit ($)	2,422	1,887	2,500	2,195	2,368	2,227
IFI (000)	83	52	1,417	1,020	321	205
IFI Incidence (%)	7.3	4.4	8.3	3.0	2.2	1.3
IFI Deficit ($ Millions)	1,156	70	2,977	2,085	642	418
IFI Average Deficit ($)	1,393	1,347	2,102	2,044	2,001	2,038
Full Employment IFE (000)	93	91	1,633	1,197	367	287
Full Employment IFE Deficit ($ Millions)	219	166	3,723	2,567	855	613
Adequate Employment IFE (000)	74	76	1,114	762	219	164
Adequate Employment IFE Deficit ($ Millions)	161	146	2,420	1,388	372	278
Capacity Employment IFE (000)	111	127	1,871	1,359	457	354
Capacity Employment IFE Deficit ($ Millions)	277	250	4,608	3,170	1,119	808
Enhanced Earnings IFE (000)	129	144	2,188	1,599	509	366
Enhanced Earnings IFE Deficit ($ Millions)	356	286	5,960	3,979	1,374	900
Enhanced Capacity IFE (000)	68	55	888	575	168	128
Enhanced Capacity IFE Deficit ($ Millions)	136	116	1,836	1,008	2,745	208
IIE in IFE (000)	115	122	1,967	1,504	489	328
Earnings Supplementation Rate-Total (%)	41.0	67.6	42.4	46.0	46.6	51.6
Earnings Supplementation Rate-Net of Transfers (%)	15.5	44.3	11.8	19.8	23.6	36.9
IFI Net of Transfers (000)	119	90	2,171	1,515	459	267
IFI Net-of-Transfers Deficit ($ Millions)	267	162	5,420	3,262	1,016	553
IFI Including Food Stamps (000)	70	50	1,266	955	302	196
IFI Including Food Stamps Deficit ($ Millions)	82	64	2,445	1,863	584	401
IFI Including In-Kind Aid (000)	67	50	1,221	914	289	191
IFI Including In-Kind Aid Deficit ($ Millions)	74	62	2,309	1,799	564	397

Table B-8. HARDSHIP AND INDIVIDUAL EARNINGS IN 1979

SEVERE HARDSHIP: TOTAL WORK FORCE

	$0-499	$500-999	$1,000-1,499	$1,500-1,999	$2,000-2,999	$3,000-3,999	$1,000-4,999	$5,000-6,999	$7,000-8,999	$9,000+
Work Force (000)	9,198	4,613	4,098	3,297	6,006	6,045	4,814	10,185	10,422	58,303
IIE (000)	7,737	3,292	2,722	1,920	3,471	3,134	2,455	2,863	480	194
IIE Incidence (%)	84.1	71.4	66.4	58.2	57.8	51.8	51.0	28.1	4.6	.3
IIE Deficit ($ Millions)	17,155	4,886	5,121	3,802	7,115	6,049	3,624	3,159	792	295
IIE Average Deficit ($)	2,217	1,484	1,881	1,980	2,050	1,930	1,476	1,103	1,649	1,519
IPE (000)	3,505	1,437	1,310	1,075	1,996	1,943	788	819	310	97
IPE Incidence (%)	38.1	31.2	32.0	32.6	33.2	32.1	16.4	8.0	3.0	.2
IPE Deficit ($ Millions)	12,313	4,053	3,733	2,552	3,870	2,315	1,157	1,261	322	79
IPE Average Deficit ($)	3,513	2,820	2,849	2,375	1,939	1,192	1,469	1,540	1,037	820
IFI (000)	2,128	789	743	560	945	876	351	438	168	57
IFI Incidence (%)	23.1	17.1	18.1	17.0	15.7	14.5	7.3	4.3	1.6	.1
IFI Deficit ($ Millions)	5,106	1,490	1,543	1,008	1,408	929	501	632	163	45
IFI Average Deficit ($)	2,399	1,887	2,075	1,800	1,491	1,061	1,429	1,442	969	790
Full Employment IFE (000)	2,757	1,205	1,047	868	1,457	1,258	540	607	258	81
Full Employment IFE Deficit ($ Millions)	8,350	3,009	2,655	1,772	2,578	1,438	837	1,075	319	82
Adequate Employment IFE (000)	2,349	1,050	853	715	1,179	1,039	457	558	235	77
Adequate Employment IFE Deficit ($ Millions)	7,040	2,681	2,134	1,486	2,077	1,205	725	1,031	311	79
Capacity Employment IFE (000)	3,108	1,274	1,138	929	1,610	1,432	597	643	277	85
Capacity Employment IFE Deficit ($ Millions)	10,023	3,405	3,075	2,023	2,946	1,632	860	1,093	315	79
Enhanced Earnings IFE (000)	3,391	1,366	1,263	1,034	1,931	1,576	584	631	180	41
Enhanced Earnings IFE Deficit ($ Millions)	12,221	3,946	3,566	2,370	3,408	1,758	878	897	165	23
Enhanced Capacity IFE (000)	2,192	957	779	668	1,064	791	342	421	136	29
Enhanced Capacity IFE Deficit ($ Millions)	6,760	2,547	1,975	1,323	1,751	859	533	742	174	27
IIE in IFE (000)	2,973	1,043	983	723	1,313	1,177	502	373	28	-0-
Earnings Supplementation Rate-Total (%)	39.3	45.1	43.3	47.9	52.7	54.9	55.5	46.5	45.8	41.5
Earnings Supplementation Rate-Net of Transfers (%)	17.1	20.4	17.9	21.3	24.2	29.5	25.8	16.6	17.2	19.2
IFI Net of Transfers (000)	2,906	1,144	1,076	845	1,513	1,369	585	683	257	78
IFI Net-of-Transfers Deficit ($ Millions)	9,613	2,900	2,841	1,836	2,771	1,665	955	1,082	276	66
IFI Including Food Stamps (000)	1,994	741	697	520	891	809	316	380	133	42
IFI Including Food Stamps Deficit ($ Millions)	4,332	1,273	1,361	900	1,213	781	417	495	106	35
IFI Including In-Kind Aid (000)	1,902	710	682	514	856	782	299	345	116	36
IFI Including In-Kind Aid Deficit ($ Millions)	4,158	1,220	1,307	868	1,161	729	377	439	91	28

Table B-8. (Continued)

SEVERE HARDSHIP: FULL-YEAR WORK FORCE

	$0-499	$500-999	$1,000-1,499	$1,500-1,999	$2,000-2,999	$3,000-3,999	$4,000-4,999	$5,000-6,999	$7,000-8,999	$9,000+
Work Force (000)	2,197	765	1,023	993	2,378	3,145	2,881	7,512	8,752	54,333
IIE (000)	2,185	725	929	860	1,959	2,214	2,042	2,686	461	186
IIE Incidence (%)	99.4	94.7	90.8	86.6	82.4	70.4	70.9	35.8	5.3	.3
IIE Deficit ($ Millions)	11,805	2,646	3,346	2,744	5,438	5,100	3,309	3,016	752	291
IIE Average Deficit ($)	5,404	3,649	3,601	3,191	2,775	2,303	1,620	1,123	1,632	1,560
IFE (000)	958	316	464	410	932	1,092	510	642	260	89
IFE Incidence (%)	43.6	41.6	45.3	41.3	39.2	34.7	17.7	8.5	3.0	.2
IFE Deficit ($ Millions)	3,980	1,016	1,448	1,126	1,964	1,455	792	1,118	318	88
IFE Average Deficit ($)	4,154	3,194	3,123	2,744	2,108	1,333	1,533	1,741	1,223	996
IFI (000)	648	192	259	236	489	490	236	349	147	53
IFI Incidence (%)	29.5	25.1	25.3	23.8	20.6	15.6	8.2	4.6	1.7	.1
IFI Deficit ($ Millions)	2,082	4,594	660	497	867	615	354	559	162	52
IFI Average Deficit ($)	3,216	2,390	2,549	2,106	1,774	1,257	1,502	1,603	1,102	970
Full Employment IFE (000)	620	202	303	266	558	588	331	488	234	78
Full Employment IFE Deficit ($ Millions)	2,165	459	798	640	1,092	803	593	1,104	379	110
Adequate Employment IFE (000)	205	131	180	166	343	404	247	440	216	76
Adequate Employment IFE Deficit ($ Millions)	518	278	405	393	646	561	452	1,033	371	110
Capacity Employment IFE (000)	754	240	365	319	694	717	356	508	244	82
Capacity Employment IFE Deficit ($ Millions)	2,948	710	1,114	855	1,437	963	610	1,106	379	110
Enhanced Earnings IFE (000)	936	306	455	390	904	887	369	501	150	37
Enhanced Earnings IFE Deficit ($ Millions)	4,148	1,042	1,500	1,143	1,906	1,244	679	931	219	42
Enhanced Capacity IFE (000)	185	104	151	153	293	309	178	346	129	35
Enhanced Capacity IFE Deficit ($ Millions)	419	234	349	330	521	406	313	748	216	42
IIE in IFE (000)	952	299	431	374	801	871	415	353	28	-0-
Earnings Supplementation Rate-Total (%)	32.4	39.6	44.2	42.5	47.5	55.1	53.8	45.7	43.6	39.7
Earnings Supplementation Rate-Net of Transfers (%)	14.2	14.9	15.0	14.6	20.9	25.6	22.3	14.9	15.7	18.9
IFI Net of Transfers (000)	822	271	394	351	737	812	397	547	220	72
IFI Net-of-Transfers Deficit ($ Millions)	3,245	786	1,140	879	1,528	1,103	688	962	277	72
IFI Including Food Stamps (000)	624	181	242	217	459	448	209	304	116	39
IFI Including Food Stamps Deficit ($ Millions)	1,894	391	593	430	747	520	280	445	219	37
IFI Including In-Kind Aid (000)	606	181	240	215	447	438	195	276	100	34
IFI Including In-Kind Aid Deficit ($ Millions)	1,852	380	573	416	719	494	262	394	86	31

Table B-8. (Continued)

INTERMEDIATE HARDSHIP: TOTAL WORK FORCE

	$0-499	$500-999	$1,000-1,499	$1,500-1,999	$2,000-2,999	$3,000-3,999	$4,000-4,999	$5,000-6,999	$7,000-8,999	$9,000+
Work Force (000)	9,198	4,613	4,098	3,297	6,006	6,045	4,814	10,185	10,422	58,303
IIE (000)	8,417	3,881	3,323	2,456	4,370	4,303	3,321	7,202	2,806	881
IIE Incidence (%)	91.5	84.1	81.1	74.5	72.8	71.2	69.0	70.7	26.9	1.5
IIE Deficit ($ Millions)	21,702	6,754	7,299	5,684	11,226	10,719	7,669	11,679	3,100	1,610
IIE Average Deficit ($)	2,578	1,740	2,196	2,315	2,569	2,491	2,309	1,622	1,105	1,827
IIE (000)	3,887	1,636	1,413	1,194	2,195	2,343	1,630	1,689	745	460
IFE Incidence (%)	42.3	35.5	34.5	36.2	36.5	38.8	33.9	16.6	7.1	.8
IIE Deficit ($ Millions)	15,909	5,471	5,143	3,720	6,123	4,688	2,668	3,116	1,149	568
IIE Average Deficit ($)	4,093	3,345	3,641	3,117	2,789	2,001	1,637	1,845	1,543	1,235
IFI (000)	2,649	1,062	949	724	1,253	1,281	875	960	477	295
IFI Incidence (%)	28.8	23.0	23.1	21.9	20.9	21.2	18.2	9.4	4.6	.5
IFI Deficit ($ Millions)	7,606	2,364	2,471	1,708	2,638	2,168	1,284	1,723	679	373
IFI Average Deficit ($)	2,871	2,227	2,605	2,361	2,106	1,692	1,468	1,795	1,422	1,262
Full Employment IFE (000)	2,990	1,308	1,112	948	1,628	1,559	1,093	1,191	590	383
Full Employment IFE Deficit ($ Millions)	10,706	3,966	3,593	2,506	3,955	2,736	1,795	2,307	1,062	578
Adequate Employment IFE (000)	2,470	1,100	887	751	1,211	1,161	772	825	480	348
Adequate Employment IFE Deficit ($ Millions)	8,924	3,426	2,758	1,965	2,931	2,022	1,266	1,752	972	555
Capacity Employment IFE (000)	3,474	1,456	1,242	1,067	1,852	1,866	1,275	1,328	632	418
Capacity Employment IFE Deficit ($ Millions)	13,094	4,694	4,372	3,053	4,820	3,433	2,048	2,454	1,063	570
Enhanced Earnings IFE (000)	3,699	1,556	1,361	1,146	2,107	2,232	1,260	1,273	534	253
Enhanced Earnings IFE Deficit ($ Millions)	15,819	5,325	4,996	3,502	5,600	3,930	2,070	2,355	734	276
Enhanced Capacity IFE (000)	2,297	1,009	810	694	1,108	997	556	603	357	191
Enhanced Capacity IFE Deficit ($ Millions)	8,557	3,249	2,544	1,767	2,544	1,570	927	1,285	642	287
IIE in IFE (000)	3,579	1,376	1,188	961	1,702	1,784	1,194	1,344	303	38
Earnings Supplementation Rate-Total (%)	31.8	35.1	32.9	39.4	42.9	45.3	46.4	43.2	35.9	35.8
Earnings Supplementation Rate-Net of Transfers (%)	14.2	16.2	13.9	18.2	19.0	21.3	22.1	20.7	16.5	14.0
IFI Net of Transfers (000)	3,335	1,370	1,216	976	1,777	1,844	1,221	1,339	622	396
IFI Net-of-Transfers Deficit ($ Millions)	12,736	4,064	4,053	2,796	4,593	3,483	2,132	2,639	978	497
IFI Including Food Stamps (000)	2,584	1,025	932	702	1,214	1,255	841	908	447	281
IFI Including Food Stamps Deficit ($ Millions)	6,769	2,113	2,260	1,567	2,387	1,959	1,146	1,488	572	338
IFI Including In-Kind Aid (000)	2,528	998	917	686	1,190	1,234	816	860	425	255
IFI Including In-Kind Aid Deficit ($ Millions)	6,500	2,027	2,177	1,511	2,295	1,861	1,074	1,377	519	305

Table B-9. HARDSHIP AND INDIVIDUAL EARNINGS DEFICITS IN 1979

SEVERE HARDSHIP: TOTAL WORK FORCE

	$0-249	$250-499	$500-999	$1,000-1,499	$1,500-1,999	$2,000-2,499	$2,500-2,999	$3,000-3,999	$4,000+
Work Force (000)	93,636	3,664	5,151	3,159	2,209	1,646	1,644	1,925	3,949
IIE (000)	4,921	3,664	5,151	3,159	2,209	1,646	1,644	1,925	3,949
IIE Incidence (%)	5.3	100.0	100.0	100.0	100.0	100.0	100.0	100.0	100.0
IIE Deficit ($ Millions)	575	1,382	3,934	3,961	3,925	3,709	4,601	6,756	23,156
IIE Average Deficit ($)	117	377	764	1,254	1,777	2,253	2,798	3,510	5,864
IFE (000)	5,470	982	1,300	875	713	595	637	819	1,889
IFE Incidence (%)	5.8	26.8	25.2	27.7	32.3	36.1	38.7	42.5	47.8
IFE Deficit ($ Millions)	10,929	2,526	3,143	2,106	1,516	1,278	1,546	2,066	6,546
IFE Average Deficit ($)	1,998	2,572	2,417	2,407	2,126	2,149	2,427	2,522	3,466
IFI (000)	2,354	549	714	489	407	338	373	541	1,291
IFI Incidence (%)	2.5	15.0	13.9	15.5	18.4	20.5	22.7	28.1	32.7
IFI Deficit ($ Millions)	3,305	965	1,281	811	633	579	648	1,033	3,571
IFI Average Deficit ($)	1,404	1,758	1,794	1,660	1,556	1,713	1,737	1,910	2,765
Full Employment IFE (000)	5,057	833	990	607	423	331	306	417	1,113
Full Employment IFE Deficit ($ Millions)	10,804	2,113	2,228	1,233	761	614	555	790	3,018
Adequate Employment IFE (000)	4,903	829	981	570	347	212	227	197	245
Adequate Employment IFE Deficit ($ Millions)	10,833	2,201	2,302	1,214	614	439	419	310	437
Capacity Employment IFE (000)	5,175	859	1,103	720	504	408	407	537	1,381
Capacity Employment IFE Deficit ($ Millions)	10,786	2,264	2,656	1,642	1,048	901	872	1,184	4,098
Enhanced Earnings IFE (000)	4,801	900	1,190	795	621	519	597	762	1,811
Enhanced Earnings IFE Deficit ($ Millions)	9,812	2,411	2,918	1,952	1,367	1,150	1,412	1,895	6,315
Enhanced Capacity IFE (000)	4,280	745	867	507	291	174	202	142	171
Enhanced Capacity IFE Deficit ($ Millions)	9,723	2,073	2,089	1,071	496	363	336	2,249	316
IIE in IFE (000)	1,306	982	1,300	875	713	595	637	819	1,889
Earnings Supplementation Rate-Total (%)	57.0	44.1	45.1	44.2	43.0	43.2	41.4	34.0	31.6
Earnings Supplementation Rate-Net of Transfers (%)	29.5	16.7	18.1	17.7	19.0	15.4	13.5	13.7	12.3
IFI Net of Transfers (000)	3,858	818	1,065	720	578	503	551	707	1,656
IFI Net-of-Transfers Deficit ($ Millions)	7,262	1,986	2,477	1,608	1,204	1,030	1,243	1,731	5,465
IFI Including Food Stamps (000)	2,121	516	654	452	377	314	354	502	1,232
IFI Including Food Stamps Deficit ($ Millions)	2,715	900	1,059	660	522	487	558	890	3,219
IFI Including In-Kind Aid (000)	2,016	480	616	430	353	305	346	484	1,209
IFI Including In-Kind Aid Deficit ($ Millions)	2,535	737	987	629	489	457	536	863	3,145

Table B-9. (Continued)

SEVERE HARDSHIP: FULL-YEAR WORK FORCE

	$0-249	$250-400	$500-999	$1,000-$1,499	$1,500-1,999	$2,000-2,499	$2,500-2,999	$3,000-3,999	$4,000+
Work Force (000)	70,648	1,041	2,287	1,458	1,294	1,055	1,141	1,409	3,605
IIE (000)	957	1,041	2,287	1,458	1,294	1,055	1,141	1,409	3,605
IIE Incidence (%)	1.4	100.0	100.0	100.0	100.0	100.0	100.0	100.0	100.0
IIE Deficit ($ Millions)	131	405	1,834	1,856	2,324	2,388	3,208	4,981	21,319
IIE Average Deficit ($)	137	389	802	1,273	1,795	2,763	2,811	3,535	5,914
IFE (000)	1,304	178	403	316	374	344	428	610	1,718
IFE Incidence (%)	1.8	17.1	17.6	21.6	28.9	32.6	37.5	43.3	47.7
IFE Deficit ($ Millions)	1,884	302	814	573	681	621	871	1,490	6,070
IFE Average Deficit ($)	1,444	1,690	2,021	1,815	1,822	1,806	2,036	2,443	3,533
IFI (000)	499	89	195	148	192	188	221	393	1,172
IFI Incidence (%)	.7	8.6	8.5	10.1	14.8	17.8	19.4	27.9	32.5
IFI Deficit ($ Millions)	626	111	339	195	285	278	367	772	3,334
IFI Average Deficit ($)	1,255	1,249	1,740	1,317	1,482	1,477	1,659	1,963	2,846
Full Employment IFE (000)	1,193	125	276	186	181	180	190	290	1,046
Full Employment IFE Deficit ($ Millions)	2,115	257	642	374	315	289	352	611	3,187
Adequate Employment IFE (000)	1,153	133	264	158	149	101	107	121	223
Adequate Employment IFE Deficit ($ Millions)	2,128	277	600	316	266	217	205	288	470
Capacity Employment IFE (000)	1,233	132	312	244	237	227	248	379	1,266
Capacity Employment IFE Deficit ($ Millions)	2,124	281	752	495	474	463	557	914	4,172
Enhanced Earnings IFE (000)	985	139	343	267	308	281	398	567	1,646
Enhanced Earnings IFE Deficit ($ Millions)	1,562	279	736	530	608	585	811	1,482	6,261
Enhanced Capacity IFE (000)	874	105	212	135	124	84	91	88	169
Enhanced Capacity IFE Deficit ($ Millions)	1,552	224	495	243	202	161	154	217	330
IIE in IFE (000)	154	178	403	316	374	344	428	610	1,718
Earnings Supplementation Rate-Total (%)	61.7	50.1	51.6	53.2	48.6	45.2	48.3	35.5	31.8
Earnings Supplementation Rate-Net of Transfers (%)	29.4	17.2	21.5	19.5	19.9	16.0	16.7	12.7	12.5
IFI Net of Transfers (000)	921	148	316	254	299	289	357	533	1,504
IFI Net-of-Transfers Deficit ($ Millions)	1,329	241	651	432	541	481	663	1,285	5,059
IFI Including Food Stamps (000)	410	80	177	136	170	175	208	365	1,121
IFI Including Food Stamps Deficit ($ Millions)	455	92	281	161	233	236	323	659	2,999
IFI Including In-Kind Aid (000)	374	74	166	130	164	172	204	351	1,099
IFI Including In-Kind Aid Deficit ($ Millions)	404	83	256	151	218	218	309	637	2,929

Table B-9. (Continued)

INTERMEDIATE HARDSHIP: TOTAL WORK FORCE

	$0-249	$250-499	$500-999	$1,000-$1,499	$1,500-1,999	$2,000-2,499	$2,500-2,999	$3,000-3,999	$4,000+
Work Force (000)	81,655	5,077	6,739	5,240	3,226	2,899	2,003	3,151	6,993
IIE (000)	5,633	5,077	6,739	5,240	3,266	2,899	2,003	3,151	6,993
IIE Incidence (%)	6.9	100.0	100.0	100.0	100.0	100.0	100.0	100.0	100.0
IIE Deficit ($ Millions)	651	1,927	4,980	6,621	5,623	6,608	5,510	11,002	45,520
IIE Average Deficit ($)	116	380	739	1,264	1,743	2,279	2,751	3,491	6,367
IFE (000)	5,311	1,274	1,773	1,362	949	916	714	1,330	3,560
IFE Incidence (%)	6.5	25.1	26.3	26.0	29.4	31.6	35.7	42.2	50.9
IFE Deficit ($ Millions)	12,332	3,635	5,081	3,621	2,678	2,380	1,836	3,702	13,291
IFE Average Deficit ($)	2,322	2,854	2,866	2,658	2,821	2,598	2,570	2,783	3,733
IFI (000)	2,628	803	1,105	821	632	604	418	919	2,593
IFI Incidence (%)	3.2	15.8	16.4	15.7	19.6	20.8	20.9	29.2	37.1
IFI Deficit ($ Millions)	4,240	1,644	2,352	1,656	1,352	1,226	805	1,959	7,781
IFI Average Deficit ($)	1,613	2,047	2,128	2,016	2,140	2,030	1,928	2,131	3,000
Full Employment IFE (000)	4,834	1,102	1,426	1,025	680	581	405	737	2,012
Full Employment IFE Deficit ($ Millions)	12,283	3,250	3,968	2,427	1,573	1,376	874	1,612	5,840
Adequate Employment IFE (000)	4,618	1,002	1,350	885	573	400	264	397	517
Adequate Employment IFE Deficit ($ Millions)	12,235	3,224	4,010	2,257	1,367	934	539	927	1,077
Capacity Employment IFE (000)	5,017	1,162	1,616	1,179	811	721	525	956	2,622
Capacity Employment IFE Deficit ($ Millions)	12,310	3,394	4,646	3,062	2,150	1,887	1,353	2,390	8,408
Enhanced Earnings IFE (000)	4,553	1,149	1,635	1,184	875	816	626	1,227	3,357
Enhanced Earnings IFE Deficit ($ Millions)	10,980	3,415	4,775	3,292	2,441	2,142	1,642	3,336	12,582
Enhanced Capacity IFE (000)	3,980	919	1,210	769	488	337	217	325	377
Enhanced Capacity IFE Deficit ($ Millions)	10,898	3,005	3,648	1,962	1,164	766	423	739	768
IIE in IFE (000)	1,591	1,274	1,773	1,362	949	916	714	1,330	3,560
Earnings Supplementation Rate-Total (%)	50.1	36.9	37.7	39.7	33.4	34.1	41.5	30.9	27.2
Earnings Supplementation Rate-Net of Transfers (%)	26.3	15.6	16.3	16.2	15.3	14.1	19.8	9.8	11.1
IFI Net of Transfers (000)	3,914	1,075	1,485	1,142	804	787	573	1,199	3,166
IFI Net-of-Transfers Deficit ($ Millions)	8,220	2,885	4,035	2,840	2,127	2,000	1,408	3,148	11,306
IFI Including Food Stamps (000)	2,520	773	1,062	787	611	585	401	897	2,552
IFI Including Food Stamps Deficit ($ Millions)	3,780	1,413	2,063	1,455	1,189	1,086	715	1,746	7,153
IFI Including In-Kind Aid (000)	2,431	754	1,020	769	587	574	384	874	2,516
IFI Including In-Kind Aid Deficit ($ Millions)	3,584	1,331	1,937	1,358	1,130	1,019	669	1,663	6,957

Table B-10. HARDSHIP AND OCCUPATION OF LONGEST JOB IN 1979

SEVERE HARDSHIP: TOTAL WORK FORCE

	White Collar	Professional, Technical, and Managerial	(Sales)	(Clerical)	Blue Collar	(Craft and Kindred)	(Operatives)	(Laborers)	Farm Workers	Service Workers	No Employment
Work Force (000)	57,675	29,175	7,123	21,377	37,141	14,330	16,603	6,209	3,209	16,968	1,990
IIE (000)	9,639	2,977	2,099	4,564	7,151	1,661	3,297	2,193	1,874	7,625	1,979
IIE Incidence (%)	16.7	10.2	29.5	21.3	19.3	11.6	19.9	35.3	58.4	44.9	99.4
IIE Deficit ($ Millions)	17,454	7,579	3,148	6,728	13,057	3,692	5,744	3,616	6,008	11,579	3,906
IIE Average Deficit ($)	1,811	2,546	1,500	1,474	1,825	2,222	1,742	1,649	3,205	1,519	1,974
IFE (000)	4,246	1,640	775	1,832	3,818	1,080	1,709	1,029	827	3,458	931
IFE Incidence (%)	7.4	5.6	10.9	8.6	10.3	7.5	10.3	16.6	25.8	20.4	46.8
IFE Deficit ($ Millions)	9,354	3,861	1,670	3,823	8,618	2,378	3,741	2,500	2,004	7,791	3,889
IFE Average Deficit ($)	2,203	2,355	2,156	2,087	2,257	2,202	2,189	2,428	2,423	2,253	4,176
IFI (000)	1,877	757	314	806	2,171	622	951	599	508	1,870	629
IFI Incidence (%)	3.3	2.6	4.4	3.8	5.8	4.3	5.7	9.6	15.8	11.0	31.6
IFI Deficit ($ Millions)	3,233	1,492	505	1,236	3,807	1,112	1,597	1,098	1,035	3,121	1,629
IFI Average Deficit ($)	1,722	1,971	1,605	1,534	1,754	1,788	1,680	1,834	2,037	1,669	2,591
Full Employment IFE (000)	3,398	1,316	611	1,471	2,766	757	1,257	752	608	2,735	570
Full Employment IFE Deficit ($ Millions)	7,194	3,018	1,268	2,908	5,992	1,619	2,669	1,704	1,430	5,778	1,721
Adequate Employment IFE (000)	2,782	985	497	1,300	2,391	627	1,113	651	328	2,321	690
Adequate Employment IFE Deficit ($ Millions)	5,806	2,147	1,015	2,643	5,026	1,293	2,295	1,439	7,002	4,993	2,244
Capacity Employment IFE (000)	3,718	1,489	686	1,543	2,960	820	1,328	812	732	2,925	709
Capacity Employment IFE Deficit ($ Millions)	8,190	3,529	1,490	3,171	6,610	1,836	2,865	1,908	1,815	6,594	2,243
Enhanced Earnings IFE (000)	3,757	1,434	697	1,626	3,406	951	1,508	947	761	3,162	912
Enhanced Earnings IFE Deficit ($ Millions)	8,588	3,565	1,542	3,481	7,704	2,097	3,315	2,292	1,876	7,176	3,886
Enhanced Capacity IFE (000)	2,381	848	443	1,090	2,033	528	940	565	283	2,022	660
Enhanced Capacity IFE Deficit ($ Millions)	5,158	1,895	908	2,356	4,302	1,085	1,940	1,277	625	4,471	2,133
IIE in IFE (000)	2,614	1,010	512	1,092	2,438	673	1,062	703	698	2,434	931
Earnings Supplementation Rate-Total (%)	55.8	53.8	59.4	56.0	43.1	42.4	44.4	41.8	38.5	45.9	32.5
Earnings Supplementation Rate-Net of Transfers (%)	33.3	36.9	30.4	31.4	15.1	16.8	14.3	14.6	15.3	17.3	11.5
IFI Net of Transfers (000)	2,831	1,035	539	1,256	3,242	899	1,465	879	700	2,859	824
IFI Net-of-Transfers Deficit ($ Millions)	5,804	2,256	1,021	2,527	7,012	1,909	3,032	2,071	1,636	6,270	3,283
IFI Including Food Stamps (000)	1,771	727	288	756	1,977	575	853	549	472	1,720	582
IFI Including Food Stamps Deficit ($ Millions)	2,927	1,404	455	1,068	3,249	993	1,334	922	882	2,589	1,261
IFI Including In-Kind Aid (000)	1,700	709	278	712	1,891	561	817	514	463	1,632	554
IFI Including In-Kind Aid Deficit ($ Millions)	2,822	1,377	440	1,005	3,093	964	1,250	879	862	2,415	1,185

Table B-10. (Continued)

SEVERE HARDSHIP: FULL-YEAR WORK FORCE

	White Collar	(Professional, Technical, and Managerial)	(Sales)	(Clerical)	Blue Collar	(Craft and kindred)	(Operatives)	(Laborers)	Farm Workers	Service Workers	No Employment
Work Force (000)	43,615	23,892	4,844	14,879	28,228	11,962	12,511	3,756	2,260	9,522	354
IIE (000)	5,045	1,804	1,008	2,232	4,112	1,155	1,923	1,034	1,297	3,441	354
IIE Incidence (%)	11.6	7.6	20.8	15.0	14.6	9.7	15.4	27.5	57.4	36.1	100.0
IIE Deficit ($ Millions)	13,087	6,028	2,299	4,760	10,005	3,034	4,393	2,577	5,336	7,910	2,108
IIE Average Deficit ($)	2,594	3,341	2,280	2,132	2,433	2,626	2,284	2,493	4,116	2,299	5,960
IFE (000)	1,727	731	338	658	1,826	584	797	445	525	1,405	192
IFE Incidence (%)	4.0	3.1	7.0	4.4	6.5	4.9	6.4	11.8	23.2	14.8	54.4
IFE Deficit ($ Millions)	3,638	1,791	688	1,160	4,261	1,325	1,824	1,112	1,395	3,037	974
IFE Average Deficit ($)	2,107	2,448	2,035	1,763	2,334	2,268	2,290	2,500	2,659	2,161	5,069
IFI (000)	783	391	129	262	1,111	384	446	281	325	746	133
IFI Incidence (%)	1.8	1.6	2.7	1.8	3.9	3.2	3.6	7.5	14.4	7.8	37.7
IFI Deficit ($ Millions)	1,540	893	235	413	2,245	771	891	583	810	1,278	434
IFI Average Deficit ($)	1,967	2,282	1,815	1,572	2,021	2,009	1,999	2,074	2,496	1,714	3,253
Full Employment IFE (000)	1,188	533	238	417	1,119	345	499	275	374	927	60
Full Employment IFE Deficit ($ Millions)	2,489	1,355	461	672	2,571	818	1,148	605	1,000	1,924	158
Adequate Employment IFE (000)	719	256	148	315	832	241	399	192	121	685	51
Adequate Employment IFE Deficit ($ Millions)	1,253	502	248	504	1,720	494	833	394	253	1,391	148
Capacity Employment IFE (000)	1,417	646	286	484	1,233	381	533	298	469	1,107	53
Capacity Employment IFE Deficit ($ Millions)	3,212	1,733	652	826	3,036	990	1,295	751	1,342	2,494	148
Enhanced Earnings IFE (000)	1,448	612	291	544	1,580	503	676	401	477	1,242	189
Enhanced Earnings IFE Deficit ($ Millions)	3,472	1,757	665	1,051	4,038	1,275	1,682	1,081	1,387	2,957	1,000
Enhanced Capacity IFE (000)	525	192	117	215	658	186	314	157	94	559	47
Enhanced Capacity IFE Deficit ($ Millions)	948	380	194	374	1,229	358	587	284	197	1,090	114
IIE in IFE (000)	1,316	593	256	467	1,414	473	589	351	486	1,116	192
Earnings Supplementation Rate-Total (%)	54.7	46.5	61.7	60.1	39.2	34.3	44.0	36.8	38.1	46.9	30.6
Earnings Supplementation Rate-Net of Transfers (%)	30.2	28.2	32.9	31.2	11.0	11.0	11.7	9.6	17.0	15.4	13.9
IFI Net of Transfers (000)	1,205	525	227	453	1,626	520	703	402	436	1,189	166
IFI Net-of-Transfers Deficit ($ Millions)	2,474	1,255	442	778	3,732	1,173	1,564	995	1,146	2,517	812
IFI Including Food Stamps (000)	725	370	114	240	1,006	350	394	262	309	670	130
IFI Including Food Stamps Deficit ($ Millions)	1,435	852	220	363	1,890	691	721	477	716	1,058	341
IFI Including In-Kind Aid (000)	706	363	114	229	961	340	372	249	305	634	126
IFI Including In-Kind Aid Deficit ($ Millions)	1,404	840	218	346	1,801	674	672	456	704	979	319

Table B-10. (Continued)

INTERMEDIATE HARDSHIP: TOTAL WORK FORCE

	White Collar	(Professional Technical, and Managerial)	(Sales)	(Clerical)	Blue Collar	(Craft and Kindred)	(Operatives)	(Laborers)	Farm Workers	Service Workers	No Employment
Work Force (000)	57,675	29,175	7,123	21,377	37,141	14,330	16,603	6,209	3,209	16,968	1,990
IIE (000)	15,309	4,531	2,994	7,784	10,977	2,509	5,453	3,015	2,202	10,494	1,979
IIE Incidence (%)	26.5	15.5	42.0	36.4	29.6	17.5	32.8	48.6	68.6	61.8	99.4
IIE Deficit ($ Millions)	30,464	12,480	5,420	12,564	23,543	6,442	11,007	6,093	8,819	19,734	4,882
IIE Average Deficit ($)	1,990	2,754	1,810	1,614	2,145	2,568	2,018	2,021	4,006	1,880	2,467
IFE (000)	5,586	2,200	984	2,402	5,196	1,470	2,385	1,341	1,053	4,340	1,014
IFE Incidence (%)	9.7	7.5	13.8	11.2	14.0	10.3	14.4	21.6	32.8	25.6	50.9
IFE Deficit ($ Millions)	14,558	5,976	2,548	6,035	14,103	4,001	6,250	3,852	2,999	11,915	4,980
IFE Average Deficit ($)	2,606	2,716	2,591	2,512	2,714	2,721	2,621	2,873	2,847	2,745	4,912
IFI (000)	2,897	1,150	489	1,257	3,388	971	1,516	902	713	2,761	764
IFI Incidence (%)	5.0	3.9	6.9	5.9	9.1	6.8	9.1	14.5	22.2	16.3	38.4
IFI Deficit ($ Millions)	5,812	2,588	895	2,329	7,351	2,190	3,170	1,991	1,703	5,670	2,478
IFI Average Deficit ($)	2,006	2,250	1,830	1,852	2,169	2,257	2,091	2,207	2,389	2,053	3,244
Full Employment IFE (000)	4,339	1,728	745	1,866	3,737	1,043	1,731	963	758	3,375	593
Full Employment IFE Deficit ($ Millions)	10,835	4,574	1,833	4,428	9,533	2,653	4,369	2,511	2,088	8,549	2,198
Adequate Employment IFE (000)	3,321	1,230	556	1,535	2,975	821	1,392	762	378	2,610	722
Adequate Employment IFE Deficit ($ Millions)	8,375	3,181	1,410	3,784	7,524	2,053	3,463	2,009	962	6,847	2,862
Capacity Employment IFE (000)	4,928	1,997	864	2,068	4,170	1,157	1,923	1,089	949	3,801	762
Capacity Employment IFE Deficit ($ Millions)	12,831	5,474	2,256	5,101	10,908	3,057	4,884	2,967	2,714	10,285	2,862
Enhanced Earnings IFE (000)	4,960	1,917	894	2,149	4,579	1,283	2,091	1,205	977	3,927	979
Enhanced Earnings IFE Deficit ($ Millions)	13,306	5,472	2,346	5,489	12,548	3,512	5,519	3,517	2,777	10,985	4,988
Enhanced Capacity IFE (000)	2,876	1,051	509	1,317	2,460	687	1,139	634	319	2,289	678
Enhanced Capacity IFE Deficit ($ Millions)	7,383	2,800	1,257	3,326	6,358	1,692	2,900	1,766	853	6,083	2,695
IIE in IFE (000)	4,088	1,502	785	1,801	3,825	974	1,783	1,068	947	3,599	1,012
Earnings Supplementation Rate-Total (%)	48.1	47.7	50.3	47.7	34.8	34.0	36.4	32.7	32.3	36.4	24.7
Earnings Supplementation Rate-Net of Transfers (%)	28.6	32.0	27.3	26.0	12.1	13.5	11.6	11.2	13.2	13.6	9.4
IFI Net of Transfers (000)	3,991	1,497	716	1,778	4,569	1,271	2,108	1,190	915	3,751	919
IFI Net-of-Transfers Deficit ($ Millions)	9,491	3,706	1,637	4,148	11,875	3,339	5,258	3,278	2,504	9,814	4,287
IFI Including Food Stamps (000)	2,827	1,129	481	1,218	3,268	932	1,460	876	694	2,656	743
IFI Including Food Stamps Deficit ($ Millions)	5,404	2,469	822	2,113	6,583	2,015	2,806	1,761	1,525	5,002	2,085
IFI Including In-Kind Aid (000)	2,759	1,112	469	1,178	3,166	917	1,413	836	686	2,576	722
IFI Including In-Kind Aid Deficit ($ Millions)	5,209	2,418	796	1,996	6,290	1,957	2,649	1,684	1,491	4,687	1,968

Table B-11. HARDSHIP IN METROPOLITAN AND NONMETROPOLITAN AREAS IN 1979

SEVERE HARDSHIP: TOTAL WORK FORCE

	Inside SMSA	SMSA 1 Million +	Large SMSA Central City	Large SMSA Suburbs	SMSA Less Than 1 Million	Small SMSA Central City	Small SMSA Suburbs	Outside SMSA	Farm
Work Force (000)	80,692	46,103	16,592	29,510	34,590	15,905	18,684	36,291	3,315
IIE (000)	17,389	9,122	3,679	5,443	8,267	3,974	4,293	10,880	1,418
IIE Incidence (%)	21.5	19.8	22.2	18.4	23.9	25.0	23.0	30.0	42.8
IIE Deficit ($ Millions)	29,500	15,456	6,772	8,684	14,044	6,633	7,411	22,498	4,711
IIE Average Deficit ($)	1,696	1,694	1,841	1,595	1,699	1,669	1,726	2,068	3,322
IHE (000)	8,197	4,359	2,199	2,159	3,838	2,073	1,765	5,083	501
IHE Incidence (%)	10.2	9.5	13.3	7.3	11.1	13.0	9.4	14.0	15.1
IHE Deficit ($ Millions)	19,857	10,974	5,905	5,069	8,883	5,045	3,838	11,798	1,023
IHE Average Deficit ($)	2,423	2,518	2,685	2,347	2,315	2,434	2,174	2,321	2,040
IFI (000)	4,385	2,371	1,320	1,051	2,014	1,176	839	2,670	265
IFI Incidence (%)	5.4	5.1	8.0	3.6	5.8	7.4	4.5	7.4	8.0
IFI Deficit ($ Millions)	8,072	4,355	2,418	1,937	3,717	2,304	1,414	4,753	568
IFI Average Deficit ($)	1,841	1,837	1,832	1,843	1,845	1,959	1,686	1,780	2,144
Full Employment IFE (000)	6,287	3,379	1,666	1,713	2,908	1,582	1,325	3,791	374
Full Employment IFE Deficit ($ Millions)	13,910	7,646	4,004	3,642	6,264	3,530	2,734	8,205	703
Adequate Employment IFE (000)	5,525	3,050	1,559	1,491	2,475	1,359	1,116	2,988	152
Adequate Employment IFE Deficit ($ Millions)	12,325	6,916	3,727	3,190	5,408	3,114	2,294	6,445	233
Capacity Employment IFE (000)	6,842	3,661	1,805	1,856	3,181	1,721	1,459	4,252	465
Capacity Employment IFE Deficit ($ Millions)	15,763	8,676	4,518	4,158	7,087	3,992	3,095	9,689	938
Enhanced Earnings IFE (000)	7,397	3,957	2,015	1,942	3,440	1,862	1,578	4,601	458
Enhanced Earnings IFE Deficit ($ Millions)	18,368	10,189	5,510	4,678	8,180	4,664	3,515	10,862	955
Enhanced Capacity IFE (000)	4,812	2,655	1,377	1,278	2,157	1,193	964	2,567	120
Enhanced Capacity IFE Deficit ($ Millions)	10,986	6,195	3,350	2,845	4,791	2,769	2,022	5,704	200
IIE in IFE (000)	5,432	2,846	1,504	1,342	2,586	1,428	1,158	3,684	415
Earnings Supplementation Rate-Total (%)	46.5	45.6	40.0	51.3	47.5	43.3	52.5	47.5	47.1
Earnings Supplementation Rate-Net of Transfers (%)	22.8	22.7	17.8	27.8	22.9	19.4	27.1	18.7	22.5
IFI Net of Transfers (000)	6,325	3,368	1,807	1,560	2,958	1,672	1,286	4,131	389
IFI Net-of-Transfers Deficit ($ Millions)	14,874	8,260	4,757	3,503	6,614	3,882	2,731	9,131	780
IFI Including Food Stamps (000)	4,062	2,215	1,210	1,006	1,847	1,064	782	2,460	261
IFI Including Food Stamps Deficit ($ Millions)	6,904	3,783	2,036	1,747	3,120	1,882	1,239	4,005	528
IFI Including In-Kind Aid (000)	3,857	2,101	1,119	982	1,755	989	766	2,384	260
IFI Including In-Kind Aid Deficit ($ Millions)	6,542	3,617	1,917	1,699	2,926	1,735	1,191	3,837	523

Table B-11. (Continued)

SEVERE HARDSHIP: FULL-YEAR WORK FORCE

	Inside SMSA	SMSA 1 Million +	Large SMSA Central City	Large SMSA Suburbs	SMSA Less Than 1 Million	Small SMSA Central City	Small SMSA Suburbs	Outside SMSA	Farm
Work Force (000)	58,296	33,422	12,101	21,321	24,874	11,352	13,522	75,682	2,522
IIE (000)	8,346	4,332	1,873	2,459	4,014	1,948	2,066	5,901	1,026
IIE Incidence (%)	14.3	13.0	15.5	11.5	16.1	17.2	15.3	23.0	40.7
IIE Deficit ($ Millions)	20,964	10,937	4,929	6,008	10,027	4,775	5,252	17,481	4,224
IIE Average Deficit ($)	2,512	2,525	2,631	2,443	2,498	2,451	2,542	2,962	4,116
IFE (000)	3,275	1,694	858	836	1,581	841	740	2,400	344
IFE Incidence (%)	5.6	5.1	7.1	3.9	6.4	7.4	5.5	9.3	13.6
IFE Deficit ($ Millions)	7,607	4,133	2,175	1,958	3,474	1,877	1,597	56,994	847
IFE Average Deficit ($)	2,323	2,439	2,534	2,342	2,197	2,231	2,159	2,375	2,462
IFI (000)	1,768	912	511	401	856	468	387	1,330	194
IFI Incidence (%)	3.0	2.7	4.2	1.9	3.4	4.1	2.9	5.2	7.7
IFI Deficit ($ Millions)	3,525	1,870	1,002	868	1,655	932	723	2,784	505
IFI Average Deficit ($)	1,994	2,049	1,959	2,165	1,934	1,990	1,867	2,093	2,604
Full Employment IFE (000)	2,067	1,063	512	550	1,005	533	472	1,600	254
Full Employment IFE Deficit ($ Millions)	4,473	2,356	1,155	1,201	2,117	1,090	1,026	3,670	640
Adequate Employment IFE (000)	1,455	786	398	388	670	356	314	952	64
Adequate Employment IFE Deficit ($ Millions)	2,855	1,551	827	724	1,304	696	609	1,911	122
Capacity Employment IFE (000)	2,391	1,226	586	640	1,165	612	554	1,887	322
Capacity Employment IFE Deficit	5,542	2,863	1,371	1,492	2,679	1,382	1,297	4,690	860
Enhanced Earnings IFE (000)	2,817	1,473	749	724	1,344	706	637	2,118	314
Enhanced Earnings IFE Deficit ($ Millions)	7,311	3,975	2,068	1,908	3,336	1,806	1,530	5,542	854
Enhanced Capacity IFE (000)	1,141	606	318	288	534	278	257	742	47
Enhanced Capacity IFE Deficit	2,136	1,163	640	523	973	506	467	1,442	91
IIE in IFE (000)	2,559	1,328	686	643	1,231	663	568	1,965	324
Earnings Supplementation Rate-Total (%)	46.0	46.2	40.4	52.0	45.9	44.3	47.7	44.6	43.6
Earnings Supplementation Rate-Net of Transfers (%)	20.4	20.4	14.3	26.6	20.4	17.7	23.5	16.1	21.9
IFI Net of Transfers (000)	2,607	1,349	736	613	1,258	692	566	2,014	268
IFI Net-of-Transfers Deficit ($ Millions)	6,030	3,292	1,858	1,434	2,738	1,533	1,205	4,651	670
IFI Including Food Stamps (000)	1,608	844	459	385	764	406	357	1,233	191
IFI Including Food Stamps Deficit ($ Millions)	3,045	1,633	851	782	1,412	770	642	2,396	475
IFI Including In-Kind Aid (000)	1,537	817	442	375	720	374	346	1,196	191
IFI Including In-Kind Aid Deficit ($ Millions)	2,901	1,571	810	760	1,331	713	618	2,305	472

Table B-11. (Continued)

INTERMEDIATE HARDSHIP: TOTAL WORK FORCE

	Inside SMSA	SMSA 1 Million +	Large SMSA Central City	Large SMSA Suburbs	SMSA Less Than 1 Million	Small SMSA Central City	Small SMSA Suburbs	Outside SMSA	Farm
Work Force (000)	80,692	46,103	16,592	29,510	34,590	15,905	18,684	36,291	3,315
IIE (000)	25,666	13,589	5,400	8,189	12,077	5,817	6,260	15,295	1,787
IIE Incidence (%)	31.8	29.5	32.5	27.7	34.9	36.6	33.5	42.1	53.9
IIE Deficit ($ Millions)	50,641	26,347	11,383	14,964	24,294	11,582	12,712	36,801	6,951
IIE Average Deficit ($)	1,973	1,939	2,108	1,827	2,012	1,991	2,031	2,406	3,890
IFE (000)	10,537	5,529	2,824	2,705	5,007	2,729	2,278	6,653	659
IFE Incidence (%)	13.1	12.0	17.0	9.2	14.5	17.2	12.2	18.3	19.9
IFE Deficit ($ Millions)	30,359	16,589	8,832	7,758	13,770	7,759	6,011	18,197	1,534
IFE Average Deficit ($)	2,881	3,000	3,127	2,868	2,750	2,843	2,639	2,735	2,327
IFI (000)	6,462	3,431	1,849	1,582	3,031	1,779	1,252	4,042	408
IFI Incidence (%)	8.0	7.4	11.1	5.4	8.8	11.2	6.7	11.2	12.3
IFI Deficit ($ Millions)	14,424	7,785	4,343	3,442	6,639	4,039	2,600	8,592	870
IFI Average Deficit ($)	2,232	2,269	2,349	2,176	2,190	2,270	2,077	2,115	2,130
Full Employment IIE (000)	7,914	4,209	2,113	2,096	3,705	2,046	1,659	4,888	489
Full Employment IFE Deficit ($ Millions)	20,895	11,393	5,904	5,488	9,502	5,322	4,180	12,308	1,039
Adequate Employment IFE (000)	6,471	3,537	1,801	1,735	2,935	1,616	1,319	3,534	174
Adequate Employment IFE Deficit ($ Millions)	17,468	9,789	5,206	4,582	7,679	4,378	3,301	9,103	324
Capacity Employment IFE (000)	8,918	4,682	2,334	2,348	4,236	2,294	1,942	5,692	638
Capacity Employment IFE Deficit ($ Millions)	24,545	13,326	6,849	6,477	11,218	6,234	4,984	15,055	1,416
Enhanced Earnings IFE (000)	9,493	4,981	2,544	2,437	4,513	2,463	2,050	5,928	598
Enhanced Earnings IFE Deficit ($ Millions)	27,947	15,315	8,166	7,149	12,632	7,137	5,495	16,658	1,417
Enhanced Capacity IFE (000)	5,604	3,086	1,575	1,511	2,518	1,386	1,132	3,019	139
Enhanced Capacity IFE Deficit ($ Millions)	15,408	8,671	4,639	4,032	6,737	3,865	2,872	7,964	278
IIE in IFE (000)	8,074	4,177	2,182	1,995	3,897	2,147	1,748	5,396	576
Earnings Supplementation Rate-Total (%)	38.7	37.9	34.5	41.5	39.5	34.8	45.0	39.0	38.1
Earnings Supplementation Rate-Net of Transfers (%)	19.0	19.0	16.3	21.9	19.0	16.0	22.7	15.6	18.8
IFI Net of Transfers (000)	8,532	4,479	2,365	2,114	4,054	2,294	1,760	5,612	535
IFI Net-of-Transfers Deficit ($ Millions)	23,420	12,827	7,250	5,577	10,592	6,163	4,430	14,550	1,192
IFI Including Food Stamps (000)	6,254	3,331	1,797	1,534	2,923	1,700	1,223	3,935	394
IFI Including Food Stamps Deficit ($ Millions)	12,926	7,044	3,859	3,185	5,882	3,511	2,371	7,673	823
IFI Including In-Kind Aid (000)	6,044	3,226	1,725	1,501	2,818	1,624	1,194	3,865	392
IFI Including In-Kind Aid Deficit ($ Millions)	12,278	6,729	3,629	3,100	5,549	3,257	2,292	7,369	815

Table B-12. HARDSHIP IN 1979 DISAGGREGATED BY GEOGRAPHIC REGION

SEVERE HARDSHIP: TOTAL WORK FORCE

	New England	Middle Atlantic	East North Central	West North Central	South Atlantic	East South Central	West South Central	Mountain	Pacific
Work Force (000)	6,856	18,407	21,808	9,522	18,710	7,032	11,825	6,011	16,812
IIE (000)	1,569	3,948	4,975	2,575	4,848	2,033	3,152	1,576	3,593
IIE Incidence (%)	22.9	21.4	22.8	27.0	25.9	28.9	26.7	26.2	21.4
IIE Deficit ($ Millions)	2,580	7,197	8,999	5,278	8,910	3,726	5,892	3,050	6,366
IIE Average Deficit ($)	1,644	1,823	1,809	2,050	1,838	1,832	1,869	1,936	1,772
IFE (000)	645	1,812	2,032	1,102	2,462	1,079	1,654	689	1,805
IFE Incidence (%)	9.4	9.8	9.3	11.6	13.2	15.3	14.0	11.5	10.7
IFE Deficit ($ Millions)	1,477	4,629	5,139	2,377	5,638	2,670	3,950	1,527	4,249
IFE Average Deficit ($)	2,289	2,554	2,529	2,158	2,290	2,475	2,388	2,215	2,355
IFI (000)	294	891	1,007	532	1,345	602	1,008	383	993
IFI Incidence (%)	4.3	4.8	4.6	5.6	7.2	8.6	8.5	6.4	5.9
IFI Deficit ($ Millions)	456	1,613	1,907	863	2,415	1,214	1,982	705	1,670
IFI Average Deficit ($)	1,548	1,811	1,894	1,622	1,795	2,017	1,966	1,842	1,682
Full Employment IFE (000)	486	1,351	1,540	840	1,853	793	1,280	525	1,409
Full Employment IFE Deficit ($ Millions)	1,008	3,076	3,390	1,722	4,091	1,837	2,910	1,095	299
Adequate Employment IFE (000)	424	1,221	1,336	660	1,536	670	1,028	410	1,228
Adequate Employment IFE Deficit ($ Millions)	875	2,838	3,032	1,344	3,354	1,591	2,311	815	2,611
Capacity Employment IFE (000)	542	1,468	1,686	947	2,018	904	1,425	593	1,512
Capacity Employment IFE Deficit ($ Millions)	1,185	3,501	3,995	2,070	4,597	2,165	3,268	1,249	3,421
Enhanced Earnings IFE (000)	582	1,646	1,865	999	2,171	985	1,465	618	1,665
Enhanced Earnings IFE Deficit ($ Millions)	1,368	4,289	4,788	2,203	5,169	2,458	3,633	1,402	3,923
Enhanced Capacity IFE (000)	371	1,064	1,187	589	1,277	578	891	353	1,070
Enhanced Capacity IFE Deficit ($ Millions)	784	2,534	2,714	1,211	2,952	1,420	2,047	711	2,315
IIE in IFE (000)	432	1,209	1,457	770	1,732	751	1,159	469	1,135
Earnings Supplementation Rate-Total (%)	54.4	50.8	50.4	51.7	45.4	44.2	39.1	44.5	45.0
Earnings Supplementation Rate-Net of Transfers (%)	26.3	19.5	21.9	25.7	21.7	15.9	17.9	24.3	22.3
IFI Net of Transfers (000)	476	1,459	1,588	818	1,928	907	1,358	522	1,401
IFI Net-of-Transfers Deficit ($ Millions)	1,045	3,618	3,859	1,696	4,212	2,140	3,187	1,100	3,149
IFI Including Food Stamps (000)	274	780	948	511	1,234	528	938	358	950
IFI Including Food Stamps Deficit ($ Millions)	378	1,372	1,652	776	1,964	960	1,655	630	1,521
IFI Including In-Kind Aid (000)	255	737	901	497	1,172	509	905	351	915
IFI Including In-Kind Aid Deficit ($ Millions)	349	1,303	1,565	755	1,855	897	1,573	611	1,470

Table B-12. (Continued)

SEVERE HARDSHIP: HALF-YEAR WORK FORCE

	New England	Middle Atlantic	East North Central	West North Central	South Atlantic	East South Central	West South Central	Mountain	Pacific
Work Force (000)	5,808	15,779	18,574	8,031	15,782	5,864	9,732	5,006	14,156
IIE (000)	1,035	2,649	3,327	1,849	3,394	1,412	2,110	1,085	2,437
IIE Incidence (%)	17.8	16.8	17.9	23.0	21.5	24.1	21.7	21.7	17.2
IIE Deficit ($ Millions)	2,304	6,377	7,945	4,842	7,962	3,362	5,230	2,783	5,598
IIE Average Deficit ($)	2,225	2,408	2,388	2,619	2,346	2,380	2,478	2,565	2,297
IFE (000)	383	1,086	1,192	655	1,563	667	1,011	441	1,016
IFE Incidence (%)	6.6	6.9	6.4	8.2	9.9	11.4	10.4	8.8	7.2
IFE Deficit ($ Millions)	838	2,563	2,816	1,323	3,280	1,591	2,304	936	2,241
IFE Average Deficit ($)	2,188	2,361	2,361	2,020	2,098	2,385	2,278	2,121	2,206
IFI (000)	169	528	596	314	861	363	607	258	581
IFI Incidence (%)	2.9	3.3	3.2	3.9	5.5	6.2	6.2	5.2	4.1
IFI Deficit ($ Millions)	293	946	1,132	553	1,546	807	1,278	499	1,010
IFI Average Deficit ($)	1,729	1,791	1,899	1,764	1,795	2,224	2,106	1,934	1,737
Full Employment IFE (000)	251	723	807	436	1,047	449	716	306	700
Full Employment IFE Deficit ($ Millions)	488	1,457	1,581	830	2,121	980	1,584	584	1,332
Adequate Employment IFE (000)	187	594	603	282	755	334	475	190	539
Adequate Employment IFE Deficit ($ Millions)	344	1,110	1,115	455	1,371	670	956	323	917
Capacity Employment IFE (000)	295	789	899	529	1,190	524	825	362	781
Capacity Employment IFE Deficit ($ Millions)	631	1,727	1,981	1,133	2,503	1,237	1,892	726	1,673
Enhanced Earnings IFE (000)	334	953	1,059	571	1,331	602	859	383	908
Enhanced Earnings IFE Deficit ($ Millions)	791	2,372	2,616	1,245	3,006	1,469	2,144	866	2,087
Enhanced Capacity IFE (000)	150	469	471	234	577	273	376	148	425
Enhanced Capacity IFE Deficit ($ Millions)	276	860	880	362	1,041	526	746	250	690
IIE in IFE (000)	288	780	941	526	1,201	507	780	339	736
Earnings Supplementation Rate-Total (%)	55.7	51.3	50.0	52.1	44.9	45.6	40.0	41.5	42.8
Earnings Supplementation Rate-Net of Transfers (%)	25.6	19.1	21.5	26.7	21.1	14.6	17.4	22.0	20.4
IFI Net of Transfers (000)	285	878	936	480	1,234	570	835	344	809
IFI Net-of-Transfers Deficit ($ Millions)	604	2,067	2,145	937	2,542	1,321	1,927	727	1,754
IFI Including Food Stamps (000)	159	457	565	305	782	317	559	240	559
IFI Including Food Stamps Deficit ($ Millions)	253	807	1,019	507	1,257	653	1,095	449	923
IFI Including In-Kind Aid (000)	151	438	537	299	736	304	543	236	545
IFI Including In-Kind Aid Deficit ($ Millions)	236	775	975	499	1,188	612	1,047	435	890

Table B-12. (Continued)

SEVERE HARDSHIP: FULL-YEAR WORK FORCE

	New England	Middle Atlantic	East North Central	West North Central	South Atlantic	East South Central	West South Central	Mountain	Pacific
Work Force (000)	4,926	13,797	15,857	6,780	13,530	5,036	8,200	4,105	11,747
IIE (000)	729	1,988	2,400	1,405	2,551	1,089	1,549	781	1,756
IIE Incidence (%)	14.8	14.4	15.1	20.7	18.9	21.6	18.9	19.0	14.9
IIE Deficit ($ Millions)	1,848	5,333	6,471	4,152	6,642	2,844	4,282	2,310	4,563
IIE Average Deficit ($)	2,536	2,683	2,696	2,955	2,603	2,613	2,764	2,957	2,598
IFE (000)	267	792	862	459	1,106	486	738	300	665
IFE Incidence (%)	5.4	5.7	5.4	6.8	8.2	9.7	9.0	7.3	5.7
IFE Deficit ($ Millions)	627	1,900	2,104	956	2,378	1,228	1,789	714	1,609
IFE Average Deficit ($)	2,350	2,400	2,441	2,082	2,151	2,526	2,425	2,380	2,418
IFI (000)	126	397	425	232	618	278	446	193	382
IFI Incidence (%)	2.6	2.9	2.7	3.4	4.6	5.5	5.4	4.7	3.2
IFI Deficit ($ Millions)	244	746	855	459	1,191	661	995	408	748
IFI Average Deficit ($)	1,933	1,877	2,011	1,977	1,927	2,381	2,230	2,112	1,962
Full Employment IFE (000)	158	497	540	290	725	322	525	192	418
Full Employment IFE Deficit ($ Millions)	357	1,039	1,163	583	1,564	786	1,299	461	891
Adequate Employment IFE (000)	109	384	376	143	473	213	325	95	290
Adequate Employment IFE Deficit ($ Millions)	227	745	723	219	919	483	726	199	524
Capacity Employment IFE (000)	199	553	633	361	824	387	589	237	496
Capacity Employment IFE Deficit ($ Millions)	473	1,255	1,484	825	1,897	1,028	1,540	563	1,167
Enhanced Earnings IFE (000)	230	690	768	394	924	435	625	264	605
Enhanced Earnings IFE Deficit ($ Millions)	633	1,831	1,973	920	2,302	1,209	1,744	696	1,546
Enhanced Capacity IFE (000)	88	303	292	112	351	181	259	76	221
Enhanced Capacity IFE Deficit ($ Millions)	181	561	553	160	669	364	559	146	385
IIE in IFE (000)	213	601	702	404	861	385	580	252	526
Earnings Supplementation Rate-Total (%)	52.7	49.8	50.7	49.4	44.1	42.8	39.5	35.6	42.7
Earnings Supplementation Rate-Net of Transfers (%)	21.3	16.1	20.8	24.8	20.1	13.0	15.6	18.3	18.2
IFI Net of Transfers (000)	210	664	683	365	884	423	622	245	544
IFI Net-of-Transfers Deficit ($ Millions)	476	1,569	1,615	712	1,909	1,041	1,508	581	1,270
IFI Including Food Stamps (000)	118	349	400	226	554	243	409	178	362
IFI Including Food Stamps Deficit ($ Millions)	216	636	766	420	943	543	871	363	680
IFI Including In-Kind Aid (000)	112	332	391	221	577	234	397	174	353
IFI Including In-Kind Aid Deficit ($ Millions)	202	609	738	414	890	508	837	353	655

Table B-13. HARDSHIP IN 1979 IN A SAMPLE OF STATES

SEVERE HARDSHIP: TOTAL WORK FORCE

	California	Georgia	New York	North Carolina	Ohio
Work Force (000)	12,440	2,786	8,581	3,150	5,416
IIE (000)	2,538	729	1,848	807	1,219
IIE Incidence (%)	20.4	26.2	21.5	25.6	22.5
IIE Deficit ($ Millions)	4,424	1,362	3,421	1,422	2,402
IIE Average Deficit ($)	1,743	1,868	1,851	1,762	1,971
IFE (000)	1,300	358	912	405	513
IFE Incidence (%)	10.5	12.9	10.6	12.9	9.5
IFE Deficit ($ Millions)	3,029	867	2,398	822	1,249
IFE Average Deficit ($)	2,330	2,422	2,630	2,028	2,437
IFI (000)	708	225	463	248	271
IFI Incidence (%)	5.7	8.1	5.4	7.9	5.0
IFI Deficit ($ Millions)	1,182	412	829	355	491
IFI Average Deficit ($)	1,670	1,833	1,791	1,431	1,810
Full Employment IFE (000)	1,020	283	693	296	393
Full Employment IFE Deficit ($ Millions)	2,143	636	1,621	604	867
Adequate Employment IFE (000)	910	234	637	264	306
Adequate Employment IFE Deficit ($ Millions)	1,924	497	1,532	519	675
Capacity Employment IFE (000)	1,098	302	754	339	411
Capacity Employment IFE Deficit ($ Millions)	2,450	721	1,872	685	991
Enhanced Earnings IFE (000)	1,201	309	859	360	473
Enhanced Earnings IFE Deficit ($ Millions)	2,777	795	2,211	736	1,168
Enhanced Capacity IFE (000)	800	197	567	230	265
Enhanced Capacity IFE Deficit ($ Millions)	1,708	434	1,369	453	607
IIE in IFE (000)	787	247	620	267	363
Earnings Supplementation Rate-Total (%)	45.6	37.2	49.2	38.8	47.1
Earnings Supplementation Rate-Net of Transfers (%)	23.2	15.5	17.4	13.2	23.2
IFI Net of Transfers (000)	999	303	754	352	394
IFI Net of Transfers Deficit ($ Millions)	2,239	681	1,915	660	855
IFI Including Food Stamps (000)	677	210	396	215	255
IFI Including Food Stamps Deficit ($ Millions)	1,075	341	706	300	424
IFI Including In-Kind Aid (000)	650	201	364	207	242
IFI Including In-Kind Aid Deficit ($ Millions)	1,042	325	668	287	404

Table B-13. (Continued)

	SEVERE HARDSHIP: HALF-YEAR WORK FORCE					SEVERE HARDSHIP: FULL-YEAR WORK FORCE				
	North Carolina	Ohio	California	Georgia	New York	North Carolina	Ohio	California	Georgia	New York
Work Force (000)	2,629	4,669	8,755	2,005	6,485	2,197	4,013	10,547	2,336	7,343
IIE (000)	572	816	1,272	398	941	414	581	1,741	505	1,215
IIE Incidence (%)	21.7	17.5	14.5	19.8	14.5	18.9	14.5	16.5	21.6	16.5
IIE Deficit ($ Millions)	1,289	2,177	3,216	1,067	2,574	974	1,778	3,906	1,199	3,037
IIE Average Deficit ($)	2,255	2,667	2,529	2,683	2,736	2,350	3,057	2,243	2,373	2,500
IFE (000)	264	296	462	163	385	176	204	720	214	538
IFE Incidence (%)	10.0	6.3	5.3	8.1	5.9	8.0	5.1	6.8	9.2	7.3
IFE Deficit ($ Millions)	518	684	1,103	413	934	302	529	1,552	499	1,300
IFE Average Deficit ($)	1,961	2,309	2,386	2,544	2,425	1,716	2,587	2,157	2,327	2,417
IFI (000)	166	174	264	102	206	103	128	404	135	273
IFI Incidence (%)	6.3	3.7	3.0	5.1	3.2	4.7	3.2	3.8	5.8	3.7
IFI Deficit ($ Millions)	244	314	515	239	376	154	256	687	267	475
IFI Average Deficit ($)	1,473	1,802	1,948	2,331	1,827	1,491	2,009	1,699	1,971	1,740
Full Employment IFE (000)	180	200	292	122	244	117	126	505	159	361
Full Employment IFE Deficit ($ Millions)	349	390	610	305	537	214	310	946	337	788
Adequate Employment IFE (000)	139	127	203	76	191	84	72	398	115	306
Adequate Employment IFE Deficit ($ Millions)	268	195	385	175	390	133	115	692	195	610
Capacity Employment IFE (000)	206	214	349	131	279	138	139	567	175	398
Capacity Employment IFE Deficit ($ Millions)	418	487	799	363	674	371	388	1,173	412	937
Enhanced Earnings IFE (000)	225	266	418	130	353	143	190	643	177	495
Enhanced Earnings IFE Deficit ($ Millions)	473	645	1,061	408	907	279	510	1,447	455	1,196
Enhanced Capacity IFE (000)	114	90	157	57	162	66	51	322	85	253
Enhanced Capacity IFE Deficit ($ Millions)	212	147	286	124	302	92	85	518	142	483
IIE in IFE (000)	196	242	361	128	300	132	175	499	164	391
Earnings Supplementation Rate-Total (%)	37.3	41.2	42.8	36.9	46.6	41.4	37.6	43.9	36.8	49.2
Earnings Supplementation Rate-Net of Transfers (%)	13.8	22.0	18.3	16.1	14.4	14.2	18.2	20.8	16.1	18.0
IFI Net of Transfers (000)	228	231	378	136	330	151	167	570	180	441
IFI Net of Transfers Deficit ($ Millions)	416	496	880	347	779	259	388	1,214	410	1,060
IFI Including Food Stamps (000)	144	162	248	96	178	86	117	386	128	232
IFI Including Food Stamps Deficit ($ Millions)	207	279	464	198	323	123	225	623	223	401
IFI Including In-Kind Aid (000)	136	154	240	90	169	80	116	374	123	220
IFI Including In-Kind Aid Deficit ($ Millions)	196	268	449	189	310	115	219	602	211	385

Table B-13. (Continued)

INTERMEDIATE HARDSHIP: TOTAL WORK FORCE / MODERATE HARDSHIP: TOTAL WORK FORCE

	California	Georgia	New York	North Carolina	Ohio	California	Georgia	New York	North Carolina	Ohio
Work Force (000)	12,440	2,786	8,581	3,150	5,416	12,440	2,786	8,581	3,150	5,416
IIE (000)	3,793	1,105	2,723	1,260	1,712	4,810	1,381	3,389	1,670	2,170
IIE Incidence (%)	30.5	39.7	31.7	40.0	31.6	38.7	49.6	39.5	53.0	40.1
IIE Deficit ($ Millions)	7,652	2,384	5,704	2,540	3,853	12,149	3,790	8,870	4,195	5,927
IIE Average Deficit ($)	2,017	2,157	2,095	2,016	2,250	2,526	2,744	2,617	2,512	2,731
IFE (000)	1,762	453	1,169	562	651	2,246	585	1,494	724	827
IFE Incidence (%)	14.2	16.3	13.6	17.9	12.0	18.1	21.0	17.4	23.0	15.3
IFE Deficit ($ Millions)	4,721	1,332	3,636	1,342	1,859	6,892	1,911	5,188	2,032	2,642
IFE Average Deficit ($)	2,680	2,942	3,109	2,387	2,855	3,068	3,266	3,472	2,805	3,197
IFI (000)	1,135	303	727	380	372	1,545	416	962	552	511
IFI Incidence (%)	9.1	10.9	8.5	12.1	6.9	12.4	14.9	11.2	17.5	9.4
IFI Deficit ($ Millions)	2,228	730	1,564	681	844	3,722	1,155	2,602	1,183	1,327
IFI Average Deficit ($)	1,963	2,408	2,153	1,794	2,270	2,409	2,779	2,703	2,144	2,595
Full Employment IFE (000)	1,336	361	887	430	502	1,627	441	1,141	552	613
Full Employment IFE Deficit ($ Millions)	3,304	962	2,429	963	1,269	4,724	1,379	3,454	1,453	1,778
Adequate Employment IFE (000)	1,108	258	756	319	366	1,224	303	875	368	417
Adequate Employment IFE Deficit ($ Millions)	2,815	699	2,172	760	945	3,744	914	2,880	1,003	1,272
Capacity Employment IFE (000)	1,478	396	972	494	546	1,905	499	1,271	647	689
Capacity Employment IFE Deficit ($ Millions)	3,919	1,111	2,867	1,148	1,502	5,755	1,628	4,150	1,779	2,170
Enhanced Earnings IFE (000)	1,574	410	1,033	483	581	1,985	504	1,307	628	734
Enhanced Earnings IFE Deficit ($ Millions)	4,330	1,223	3,343	1,195	1,724	6,284	1,744	4,725	1,837	2,412
Enhanced Capacity IFE (000)	951	224	651	262	311	1,070	243	741	296	363
Enhanced Capacity IFE Deficit ($ Millions)	2,446	613	1,925	646	838	3,262	796	2,522	853	1,107
IIE in IFE (000)	1,286	368	874	435	506	1,799	504	1,196	622	663
Earnings Supplementation Rate-Total (%)	35.6	33.0	37.9	32.5	42.9	31.2	29.0	35.6	23.8	38.1
Earnings Supplementation Rate-Net of Transfers (%)	18.7	13.4	15.6	12.3	23.4	15.6	11.0	16.4	11.7	18.6
IFI Net of Transfers (000)	1,433	392	986	493	498	1,895	521	1,249	640	673
IFI Net of Transfers Deficit ($ Millions)	3,613	1,088	2,963	1,119	1,331	5,443	1,608	4,299	1,734	1,962
IFI Including Food Stamps (000)	1,112	298	693	360	365	1,516	412	942	530	494
IFI Including Food Stamps Deficit ($ Millions)	2,082	646	1,389	603	766	3,554	1,063	2,386	1,076	1,244
IFI Including In-Kind Aid (000)	1,085	272	656	356	363	1,499	408	899	516	489
IFI Including In-Kind Aid Deficit ($ Millions)	2,006	614	1,309	574	730	3,448	1,013	2,257	1,030	1,195

APPENDIX C. SUMMARY HARDSHIP DATA FOR 1974 THROUGH 1980

Table C-1. Summary Hardship Measures, 1974 Through 1980, for Total, Half-Year and Full-Year Work Force Under Severe, Intermediate and Moderate Hardship Standards

Table C-2. Summary Severe Hardship Measures, 1974 Through 1980, for Total and Full-Year Work Force, Disaggregated by Work Experience Pattern

Table C-3. Summary Severe Hardship Measures, 1974 Through 1980, for Total Work Force, Disaggregated by Sex and Family Relationship

Table C-4. Summary Severe Hardship Measures, 1974 Through 1980, for Total Work Force, Disaggregated by Family Size and Number of Earners

Table C-5. Summary Severe Hardship Measures, 1974 Through 1980, for Total Work Force, Disaggregated by Educational Attainment

Table C-6. Summary Severe Hardship Measures, 1974 Through 1980, for Total Work Force, Disaggregated by Age

Table C-7. Summary Severe Hardship Measures, 1974 Through 1980, for Total Work Force, Disaggregated by Race/Ethnic Origin

Table C-8. Summary Severe Hardship Measures, 1974 Through 1980, for Total Work Force, Disaggregated by Geographic Region

Table C-9. Summary Severe Hardship Measures, 1974 Through 1980, for Total Work Force, Disaggregated by Area of Residence

Table C-10. Severe Hardship Inadequate Family Earnings and Related Deficits After Augmentation of Subgroup Earnings, 1974 Through 1980.

Table C-1. SUMMARY HARDSHIP MEASURES 1974 THROUGH 1980, FOR TOTAL, HALF-YEAR AND FULL-YEAR WORK FORCE UNDER SEVERE, INTERMEDIATE AND MODERATE HARDSHIP STANDARDS

	1974	1975	1976	1977	1978	1979	1979R	1980
WORK EXPERIENCE MEASURES								
Work Force								
Total	103,601	104,442	107,148	109,663	112,363	114,648	116,983	118,348
Half-Year	85,969	88,017	89,701	91,886	94,521	96,887	98,733	101,120
Full-Year	72,761	75,887	76,575	78,036	80,205	82,471	83,979	87,454
Unemployed								
Total	18,537	21,105	20,447	19,512	17,738	17,972	18,486	21,410
Half-Year	14,473	16,906	16,306	15,329	13,870	14,504	14,885	17,619
Full-Year	10,796	13,634	12,668	11,600	10,282	11,072	11,351	13,984
Unemployment Incidence								
Total	17.9	20.2	19.1	17.8	15.8	15.6	15.8	18.1
Half-Year	16.8	19.2	18.2	16.7	14.7	15.0	15.1	17.4
Full-Year	14.8	18.0	16.5	14.9	12.8	13.4	13.5	16.0
Predominantly Unemployed								
Total	7,740	10,941	10,255	9,132	7,750	7,276	7,492	10,348
Half-Year	5,222	8,011	7,380	6,318	5,274	5,019	5,160	7,643
Full-Year	4,120	6,785	5,975	5,099	4,220	4,072		
Incidence Predominantly Unemployed								
Total	7.5	10.4	9.6	8.3	6.9	6.3	6.4	8.7
Half-Year	6.1	9.1	8.2	6.9	5.6	5.2	5.2	7.6
Full-Year	5.7	8.9	7.8	6.5	5.3	4.9	5.0	7.2
IIE								
Severe Hardship								
Total	26,756	30,345	29,894	30,325	28,660	27,575	28,269	32,747
Half-Year	17,844	21,059	20,419	20,814	19,491	18,836	19,299	23,246
Full-Year	13,103	16,173	15,332	15,693	14,282	13,913	14,248	17,921
Intermediate Hardship								
Total	36,572	40,057	39,948	40,541	39,902	39,960	40,961	44,810
Half-Year	25,386	28,938	28,395	28,939	28,221	28,537	29,232	33,120
Full-Year	18,893	22,443	21,587	21,920	21,027	21,534	22,047	25,949
Moderate Hardship								
Total	45,925	48,689	49,532	49,728	50,443	50,184	51,426	55,933
Half-Year	33,226	36,322	36,598	36,815	37,307	37,238	38,130	43,036
Full-Year	25,305	28,700	28,534	28,405	28,590	28,771	29,442	34,553
IIE INCIDENCE								
Severe Hardship								
Total	25.8	29.1	27.9	27.7	25.5	24.1	24.2	27.7
Half-Year	20.8	23.9	22.8	22.7	20.6	19.4	19.5	23.0
Full-Year	18.0	21.3	20.0	20.1	17.8	16.9	17.0	20.5
Intermediate Hardship								
Total	35.3	38.4	37.3	37.0	35.5	34.9	35.0	37.9
Half-Year	29.5	32.9	31.7	31.5	29.9	29.5	29.6	32.8
Full-Year	26.0	29.6	28.2	28.1	26.2	26.1	26.3	29.7
Moderate Hardship								
Total	44.3	46.6	46.2	45.3	44.9	43.8	44.0	47.3
Half-Year	38.6	41.3	40.8	40.1	39.5	38.4	38.6	42.6
Full-Year	34.8	37.8	37.3	36.4	35.6	34.9	35.1	39.5

Table C-1. (Continued)

IIE DEFICIT

Severe Hardship

Total	34,029	46,093	47,467	49,284	46,631	50,830	51,998	70,668
Half-Year	30,085	41,402	42,319	43,924	41,379	45,404	46,403	63,835
Full-Year	24,901	35,189	35,473	36,710	34,071	37,621	38,446	53,973

Intermediate Hardship

Total	55,725	73,466	76,082	79,818	77,995	85,417	87,442	115,773
Half-Year	49,603	66,408	68,291	71,661	69,758	76,897	78,659	105,350
Full-Year	40,813	56,274	57,051	59,683	57,226	63,610	65,053	89,036

Moderate Hardship

Total	85,243	109,140	113,944	120,201	120,847	133,218	136,402	175,988
Half-Year	76,543	99,338	103,076	108,802	109,073	120,996	123,804	161,321
Full-Year	63,106	84,315	86,339	90,755	89,845	100,509	102,809	136,884

IIE DEFICIT (1980 $)

Severe Hardship

Total	56,862	70,568	68,732	67,026	58,895	57,692	59,018	70,648
Half-Year	50,272	67,527	61,278	59,736	52,262	51,534	52,668	63,835
Full-Year	41,610	53,874	51,364	49,925	43,031	42,700	43,636	53,973

Intermediate Hardship

Total	93,116	112,476	110,166	108,553	98,508	96,948	99,247	115,773
Half-Year	82,887	101,671	98,885	97,459	88,105	87,278	89,277	105,350
Full-Year	68,199	86,155	82,610	81,169	72,277	72,197	73,835	89,036

Moderate Hardship

Total	142,441	167,093	164,991	163,473	152,630	151,202	154,816	175,988
Half-Year	127,903	152,086	149,254	147,971	137,759	137,330	140,518	161,321
Full-Year	105,450	129,086	125,019	123,426	113,474	114,078	116,688	136,884

IIE AVERAGE DEFICIT

Severe Hardship

Total	1,272	1,519	1,588	1,625	1,627	1,843	1,839	2,157
Half-Year	1,686	1,966	2,073	2,110	2,123	2,410	2,404	2,746
Full-Year	1,900	2,176	2,314	2,339	2,386	2,704	2,698	3,012

Intermediate Hardship

Total	1,524	1,834	1,905	1,969	1,955	2,138	2,135	2,584
Half-Year	1,954	2,295	2,405	2,476	2,472	2,695	2,691	3,181
Full-Year	2,160	2,507	2,643	2,723	2,722	2,954	2,951	3,431

Moderate Hardship

Total	1,856	2,242	2,300	2,417	2,396	2,655	2,652	3,146
Half-Year	2,304	2,735	2,816	2,955	2,924	3,249	3,247	3,748
Full-Year	2,494	2,938	3,026	3,195	3,142	3,493	3,492	3,962

IIE AVERAGE DEFICIT (1980 $)

Severe Hardship

Total	2,126	2,326	2,299	2,210	2,055	2,092	2,087	2,157
Half-Year	2,817	3,010	3,002	2,870	2,681	2,735	2,729	2,746
Full-Year	3,175	3,331	3,351	3,181	3,014	3,069	3,062	3,012

Intermediate Hardship

Total	2,547	2,808	2,758	2,678	2,469	2,426	2,423	2,584
Half-Year	3,265	3,514	3,482	3,367	3,122	3,059	3,054	3,181
Full-Year	3,609	3,838	3,827	3,703	3,438	3,353	3,349	3,431

Moderate Hardship

Total	3,101	3,433	3,330	3,287	3,026	3,013	3,010	3,146
Half-Year	3,850	4,187	4,078	4,019	3,693	3,688	3,685	3,748
Full-Year	4,167	4,498	4,382	4,345	3,968	3,965	3,963	3,962

Table C-1. (Continued)

IIE DEFICIT AS PERCENT TOTAL WAGES AND SALARIES

Severe Hardship

Total	4.3	5.5	5.2	4.9	4.1	4.0	4.0	5.0
Half-Year	3.8	4.9	4.6	4.4	3.6	3.6	3.6	4.5
Full-Year	3.1	4.2	3.9	3.6	3.0	3.0	3.0	3.8

Intermediate Hardship

Total	7.1	8.8	8.3	7.9	6.8	6.7	6.7	8.2
Half-Year	6.3	8.0	7.5	7.1	6.1	6.0	6.0	7.5
Full-Year	5.2	6.7	6.2	5.9	5.0	5.0	5.0	6.3

Moderate Hardship

Total	10.9	13.1	12.5	12.0	10.5	10.4	10.5	12.4
Half-Year	9.5	11.9	11.3	10.8	9.5	9.4	9.5	11.4
Full-Year	8.1	10.1	9.5	9.0	7.8	7.8	7.9	9.7

IFE

Severe Hardship

Total	12,008	13,768	13,402	13,494	13,020	12,914	13,280	15,111
Half-Year	7,222	8,887	8,547	8,366	7,953	7,818	8,014	9,761
Full-Year	5,162	6,719	6,259	6,141	5,505	5,546	5,675	7,264

Intermediate Hardship

Total	15,426	17,516	17,262	17,257	16,688	16,697	17,190	19,462
Half-Year	9,924	11,886	11,592	11,327	10,843	10,834	11,128	13,314
Full-Year	7,243	9,149	8,622	8,442	7,684	7,886	8,088	10,157

Moderate Hardship

Total	19,134	21,852	21,561	21,372	20,732	20,944	21,553	24,255
Half-Year	12,874	15,451	15,072	14,625	14,085	14,313	14,699	17,350
Full-Year	9,583	12,080	11,420	11,035	10,232	10,706	10,981	13,452

IFE INCIDENCE

Severe Hardship

Total	11.6	13.2	12.5	12.3	11.6	11.3	11.4	12.8
Half-Year	8.4	10.1	9.5	9.1	8.4	8.1	8.1	9.7
Full-Year	7.1	8.9	8.2	7.9	6.9	6.7	6.8	8.3

Intermediate Hardship

Total	14.9	16.8	16.1	15.7	14.9	14.6	14.7	16.4
Half-Year	11.5	13.5	12.9	12.3	11.5	11.2	11.3	13.2
Full-Year	10.0	12.1	11.3	10.8	9.6	9.6	9.6	11.6

Moderate Hardship

Total	18.5	20.9	20.1	19.5	18.5	18.3	18.4	20.5
Half-Year	15.0	17.6	16.8	15.9	14.9	14.8	14.9	17.2
Full-Year	13.2	15.9	14.9	14.1	12.8	13.0	13.1	15.4

IFE DEFICIT

Severe Hardship

Total	19,700	24,925	25,455	26,902	27,770	30,801	31,656	41,000
Half-Year	11,591	16,060	15,978	16,184	16,121	17,491	17,891	25,749
Full-Year	8,468	12,491	12,203	12,254	11,486	13,038	13,306	19,981

Intermediate Hardship

Total	30,111	37,853	38,667	40,853	42,430	47,223	48,556	62,416
Half-Year	19,167	25,967	25,938	26,406	26,763	29,338	30,053	42,049
Full-Year	14,263	20,465	20,060	20,272	19,422	22,171	22,665	33,027

Moderate Hardship

Total	43,128	53,980	55,248	58,255	60,709	67,737	69,668	89,142
Half-Year	29,224	38,953	39,115	39,897	40,823	45,058	46,195	63,474
Full-Year	22,209	31,179	30,749	31,104	30,258	34,642	35,456	50,616

Table C-1. (Continued)

IFE DEFICIT (1980 $)

Severe Hardship

Total	32,919	38,160	36,858	36,586	35,073	34,959	35,929	41,000
Half-Year	19,369	24,588	23,136	22,010	20,361	19,852	20,306	25,749
Full-Year	14,150	19,124	17,669	16,666	14,507	14,798	15,102	19,981

Intermediate Hardship

Total	50,315	57,953	55,990	55,559	53,589	53,598	55,111	62,416
Half-Year	32,028	39,755	37,558	35,912	33,802	33,299	34,652	42,049
Full-Year	23,833	31,332	29,046	27,569	24,530	25,164	25,725	33,027

Moderate Hardship

Total	72,067	86,643	80,000	79,227	76,675	76,881	79,073	89,142
Half-Year	48,833	59,637	56,639	54,260	51,559	51,141	52,431	63,474
Full-Year	37,111	47,735	44,524	42,301	38,215	39,319	40,243	50,616

IFE AVERAGE DEFICIT

Severe Hardship

Total	1,641	1,810	1,899	1,994	2,133	2,385	2,384	2,713
Half-Year	1,605	1,807	1,870	1,934	2,027	2,237	2,232	2,638
Full-Year	1,641	1,859	1,950	1,994	2,087	2,351	2,345	2,751

Intermediate Hardship

Total	1,952	2,161	2,240	2,367	2,542	2,828	2,825	3,207
Half-Year	1,931	2,185	2,238	2,331	2,468	2,708	2,701	3,158
Full-Year	1,969	2,237	2,327	2,401	2,528	2,811	2,802	3,252

Moderate Hardship

Total	2,254	2,470	2,562	2,726	2,928	3,234	3,232	3,675
Half-Year	2,270	2,521	2,595	2,728	2,898	3,148	3,143	3,658
Full Year	2,318	2,581	2,693	2,819	2,957	3,236	3,229	3,763

IFE AVERAGE DEFICIT (1980 $)

Severe Hardship

Total	2,742	2,771	2,750	2,712	2,694	2,707	2,706	2,713
Half-Year	2,682	2,767	2,708	2,630	2,560	2,539	2,533	2,638
Full-Year	2,742	2,846	2,824	2,715	2,636	2,668	2,662	2,751

Intermediate Hardship

Total	3,262	3,308	3,244	3,219	3,211	3,210	3,210	3,207
Half-Year	3,227	3,345	3,241	3,170	3,117	3,074	3,066	3,158
Full-Year	3,290	3,425	3,369	3,265	3,193	3,190	3,180	3,252

Moderate Hardship

Total	3,766	3,782	3,710	3,707	3,572	3,671	3,668	3,675
Half-Year	3,793	3,860	3,757	3,710	3,660	3,573	3,567	3,658
Full-Year	3,873	3,952	3,899	3,834	3,735	3,673	3,665	3,763

IFE DEFICIT AS PERCENT TOTAL WAGES AND SALARIES

Severe Hardship

Total	2.5	3.0	2.8	2.7	2.4	2.4	2.4	2.9
Half-Year	1.5	1.9	1.8	1.6	1.4	1.4	1.4	1.8
Full-Year	1.1	1.5	1.4	1.2	1.0	1.0	1.0	1.4

Intermediate Hardship

Total	3.8	4.6	4.2	4.0	3.7	3.7	3.7	4.4
Half-Year	2.4	3.1	2.8	2.6	2.3	2.3	2.3	3.0
Full-Year	1.8	2.5	2.2	2.0	1.7	1.7	1.7	2.3

Moderate Hardship

Total	5.5	6.5	6.1	5.8	5.3	5.3	5.3	6.3
Half-Year	3.7	4.7	4.3	4.0	3.5	3.5	3.6	4.5
Full-Year	2.8	3.7	3.4	3.1	2.6	2.7	2.7	3.6

Table C-1. (Continued)

IFI

Severe Hardship

Total	6,346	7,252	7,033	6,998	7,012	6,853	7,055	8,465
Half-Year	3,790	4,576	4,443	4,305	4,198	4,172	4,278	5,504
Full-Year	2,776	3,485	3,313	3,233	3,009	3,026	3,098	4,213

Intermediate Hardship

Total	9,558	10,756	10,395	10,532	10,253	10,214	10,524	12,273
Half-Year	6,046	7,172	6,873	6,879	6,585	6,624	6,804	8,369
Full-Year	4,520	5,570	5,147	5,254	4,785	4,947	5,075	6,480

Moderate Hardship

Total	13,219	14,955	14,587	14,500	14,022	13,934	14,354	16,706
Half-Year	8,829	10,476	10,093	9,891	9,441	9,512	9,776	11,910
Full-Year	6,687	8,284	7,698	7,601	6,987	7,193	7,383	9,367

IFI INCIDENCE

Severe Hardship

Total	6.1	6.9	6.6	6.4	6.2	6.0	6.0	7.2
Half-Year	4.4	5.2	5.0	4.7	4.4	4.3	4.3	5.4
Full-Year	3.8	4.6	4.3	4.1	3.8	3.7	3.7	4.8

Intermediate Hardship

Total	9.2	10.3	9.7	9.6	9.1	8.9	9.0	10.4
Half-Year	7.0	8.1	7.7	7.5	7.0	6.8	6.9	8.3
Full-Year	6.2	7.3	6.7	6.7	6.0	6.0	6.0	7.4

Moderate Hardship

Total	12.8	14.3	13.6	13.2	12.5	12.2	12.3	14.1
Half-Year	10.3	11.9	11.3	10.8	10.0	9.8	9.9	11.8
Full-Year	9.2	10.9	10.1	9.7	8.7	8.7	8.8	10.7

IFI DEFICIT

Severe Hardship

Total	7,713	9,538	9,573	10,357	11,027	12,499	12,825	17,452
Half-Year	5,033	6,599	6,442	6,770	6,817	7,895	8,064	11,778
Full-Year	3,867	5,233	5,074	5,308	5,064	6,189	6,308	9,499

Intermediate Hardship

Total	14,021	17,316	17,420	18,716	19,894	22,387	23,015	30,812
Half-Year	9,636	12,525	12,341	12,860	13,187	15,026	15,391	21,965
Full-Year	7,479	10,032	9,794	10,181	9,921	11,811	12,077	17,796

Moderate Hardship

Total	22,944	28,333	28,554	30,503	32,180	36,120	37,173	49,244
Half-Year	16,549	21,382	21,146	21,981	22,588	25,557	26,227	36,752
Full-Year	13,048	17,371	16,988	17,621	17,292	20,307	20,808	30,109

IFI DEFICIT (1980 $)

Severe Hardship

Total	12,889	14,603	13,862	14,085	13,927	14,186	14,556	17,452
Half-Year	8,410	10,103	9,328	9,207	8,610	8,961	9,153	11,778
Full-Year	6,462	8,012	7,347	7,219	6,396	7,025	7,160	9,499

Intermediate Hardship

Total	23,429	26,511	25,224	25,453	25,127	25,409	26,122	30,812
Half-Year	16,102	19,176	17,870	17,490	16,655	17,055	17,469	21,965
Full-Year	12,497	15,359	14,181	13,846	12,530	13,405	13,708	17,796

Moderate Hardship

Total	38,339	43,378	41,346	41,484	40,643	40,996	42,192	49,244
Half-Year	27,653	32,736	30,619	29,894	28,528	29,007	29,767	36,752
Full-Year	21,803	26,596	24,599	23,965	21,839	23,048	23,617	30,109

Table C-1. (Continued)

IFI AVERAGE DEFICIT

Severe Hardship

Total	1,215	1,315	1,361	1,480	1,573	1,824	1,818	2,062
Half-Year	1,328	1,442	1,450	1,573	1,624	1,892	1,885	2,140
Full-Year	1,393	1,509	1,532	1,642	1,683	2,045	2,036	2,255

Intermediate Hardship

Total	1,467	1,610	1,676	1,777	1,940	2,192	2,187	2,511
Half-Year	1,594	1,746	1,796	1,870	2,003	2,268	2,262	2,624
Full-Year	1,655	1,801	1,903	1,938	2,074	2,388	2,380	2,746

Moderate Hardship

Total	1,736	1,895	1,957	2,104	2,295	2,592	2,590	2,948
Half-Year	1,874	2,041	2,095	2,222	2,393	2,687	2,683	3,086
Full-Year	1,951	2,097	2,207	2,318	2,475	2,823	2,818	3,214

IFI AVERAGE DEFICIT (1980 $)

Severe Hardship

Total	2,030	2,013	1,971	2,013	1,987	2,070	2,063	2,062
Half-Year	2,219	2,208	2,100	2,139	2,051	2,147	2,139	2,140
Full-Year	2,328	2,310	2,218	2,233	2,126	2,321	2,311	2,255

Intermediate Hardship

Total	2,451	2,465	2,427	2,417	2,450	2,488	2,482	2,511
Half-Year	2,664	2,673	2,601	2,543	2,530	2,574	2,567	2,624
Full-Year	2,766	2,757	2,756	2,636	2,619	2,710	2,701	2,746

Moderate Hardship

Total	2,901	2,901	2,834	2,861	2,899	2,942	2,940	2,948
Half-Year	3,131	3,125	3,034	3,022	3,022	3,050	3,045	3,086
Full-Year	3,260	3,211	3,196	3,152	3,126	3,204	3,198	3,214

IFI DEFICIT AS PERCENT TOTAL WAGES AND SALARIES

Severe Hardship

Total	.9	1.1	1.0	.9	.9	.9	.9	1.1
Half-Year	.6	.8	.7	.7	.6	.6	.6	.8
Full-Year	.5	.6	.6	.5	.4	.4	.5	.7

Intermediate Hardship

Total	1.7	1.9	1.9	1.7	1.6	1.6	1.6	2.0
Half-Year	1.2	1.5	1.4	1.3	1.1	1.1	1.2	1.6
Full-Year	1.0	1.2	1.1	1.0	.9	.8	.9	1.3

Moderate Hardship

Total	2.7	3.1	3.1	3.0	2.6	2.6	2.6	3.2
Half-Year	2.1	2.6	2.3	2.2	2.0	1.8	2.0	2.6
Full-Year	1.7	2.1	1.0	1.8	1.5	1.5	1.6	2.1

FULL EMPLOYMENT IFE

Severe Hardship

Total	9,034	9,399	9,246	9,598	9,684	9,801	10,078	10,564
Half-Year	4,942	5,407	5,233	5,315	5,356	5,298	5,434	6,154
Full-Year	3,378	3,824	3,597	3,715	3,516	3,583	3,667	4,334

Intermediate Hardship

Total	11,471	11,823	11,778	12,097	12,170	12,496	12,802	13,390
Half-Year	6,878	7,342	7,239	7,223	7,288	7,445	7,647	8,546
Full-Year	4,847	5,424	5,197	5,199	4,995	5,258	5,393	6,292

Moderate Hardship

Total	14,115	15,571	14,527	14,797	14,744	15,246	15,660	16,606
Half-Year	8,998	9,666	9,495	9,392	9,422	9,729	9,991	11,257
Full-Year	6,629	7,319	7,095	6,974	6,707	7,135	7,318	8,611

Table C-1. (Continued)

FULL EMPLOYMENT IFE AS PERCENT IFE

Severe Hardship

Total	75.2	68.3	69.0	71.1	74.4	75.9	75.9	69.9
Half-Year	68.4	60.8	61.2	63.5	67.3	67.8	67.8	63.0
Full-Year	65.4	56.9	57.5	60.5	63.9	64.6	64.6	59.7

Intermediate Hardship

Total	74.4	67.5	68.2	79.1	72.9	74.8	74.5	68.8
Half-Year	69.3	61.8	62.4	63.8	67.2	68.7	68.7	87.6
Full-Year	66.9	59.3	60.3	61.6	65.0	66.7	66.7	61.9

Moderate Hardship

Total	73.8	66.7	67.4	69.2	71.1	72.8	72.7	68.5
Half-Year	69.9	62.6	63.0	64.2	66.9	68.0	68.0	64.9
Full-Year	69.2	60.6	62.1	63.2	65.5	66.6	66.6	64.0

ADEQUATE EMPLOYMENT IFE

Severe Hardship

Total	7,349	7,872	7,781	7,899	8,082	8,252	8,513	8,742
Half-Year	3,389	3,923	3,814	3,721	3,828	3,844	3,959	4,369
Full-Year	2,079	2,555	2,371	2,303	2,238	2,346	2,408	2,817

Intermediate Hardship

Total	8,673	9,205	9,218	9,297	9,536	9,693	10,006	10,347
Half-Year	4,432	4,952	4,869	4,736	4,878	4,961	5,110	5,620
Full-Year	2,817	3,371	3,174	3,047	3,025	3,154	3,235	3,845

Moderate Hardship

Total	9,924	10,413	10,479	10,514	10,697	10,925	11,275	11,552
Half-Year	5,410	5,951	5,836	5,673	5,781	5,902	6,079	6,600
Full-Year	3,636	4,212	3,999	3,815	3,726	3,915	4,018	4,703

ADEQUATE EMPLOYMENT IFE AS PERCENT IFE

Severe Hardship

Total	61.2	57.2	58.1	58.5	62.1	63.9	64.1	57.9
Half-Year	46.9	44.1	44.6	44.5	48.1	49.2	49.4	44.8
Full-Year	40.3	38.0	37.9	37.5	40.7	42.3	42.4	38.8

Intermediate Hardship

Total	56.2	52.6	53.4	53.9	57.1	58.1	58.2	53.2
Half-Year	44.7	41.7	42.0	41.8	45.0	45.8	45.9	42.2
Full-Year	38.9	36.8	36.8	36.1	39.4	40.0	40.0	37.9

Moderate Hardship

Total	51.9	47.7	48.6	49.2	51.6	52.2	52.3	47.6
Half-Year	42.0	38.5	38.7	38.8	41.0	41.2	41.4	38.0
Full-Year	37.9	34.9	35.0	34.6	36.4	36.6	36.6	35.0

CAPACITY EMPLOYMENT IFE

Severe Hardship

Total	9,864	10,549	10,384	10,796	10,740	10,796	11,093	11,658
Half-Year	5,482	6,198	6,069	6,198	6,133	6,051	6,193	6,905
Full-Year	3,826	4,424	4,268	4,381	4,106	4,190	4,278	4,928

Intermediate Hardship

Total	12,923	13,624	13,665	14,032	13,923	14,207	14,610	15,489
Half-Year	7,882	8,667	8,599	8,738	8,607	8,803	9,022	10,009
Full-Year	5,635	6,430	6,227	6,323	5,953	6,259	6,397	7,478

Moderate Hardship

Total	16,213	17,191	17,397	17,643	17,446	17,971	18,480	19,825
Half-Year	10,514	11,571	11,654	11,544	11,488	11,930	12,232	13,650
Full-Year	7,780	8,822	8,693	8,559	8,280	8,809	9,014	10,447

Table C-1. (Continued)

CAPACITY EMPLOYMENT IFE AS PERCENT IFE

Severe Hardship

Total	82.1	76.6	77.5	80.0	82.5	83.6	83.5	77.1
Half-Year	75.9	69.7	71.0	74.1	77.1	77.3	77.3	70.7
Full-Year	74.1	65.8	68.2	71.3	74.6	75.5	75.4	66.5

Intermediate Hardship

Total	83.8	77.8	79.2	81.3	83.4	85.1	85.0	79.6
Half-Year	79.4	72.9	74.2	77.1	79.4	81.3	81.1	75.2
Full-Year	77.8	70.3	72.2	74.9	77.5	79.4	79.1	73.6

Moderate Hardship

Total	84.7	78.7	80.7	82.6	84.2	85.8	85.7	81.7
Half-Year	81.7	74.9	77.3	78.9	81.6	83.4	83.2	78.7
Full-Year	81.2	73.0	76.1	77.6	80.9	82.3	82.1	77.7

ENHANCED EARNINGS IFE

Severe Hardship

Total	10,900	12,434	12,162	12,051	11,703	11,674	11,998	13,638
Half-Year	6,371	7,826	7,575	7,231	6,933	6,835	7,000	8,582
Full-Year	4,499	5,869	5,503	5,289	4,738	4,827	4,935	6,343

Intermediate Hardship

Total	13,884	15,763	15,636	15,447	14,939	14,990	15,422	17,400
Half-Year	8,673	10,499	10,292	9,893	9,434	9,483	9,728	11,602
Full-Year	6,267	8,033	7,631	7,319	6,605	6,847	7,010	8,765

Moderate Hardship

Total	17,054	19,337	19,265	19,015	18,502	18,540	19,078	21,532
Half-Year	11,226	13,366	13,206	12,719	12,272	12,337	12,663	15,034
Full-Year	8,278	10,367	9,936	9,524	8,792	9,096	9,323	11,551

ENHANCED EARNINGS IFE AS PERCENT IFE

Severe Hardship

Total	90.8	90.3	90.7	89.3	89.9	90.4	90.3	90.3
Half-Year	88.2	88.1	88.6	86.4	87.2	87.4	87.3	87.9
Full-Year	87.2	87.3	87.9	86.1	86.1	87.0	87.0	87.3

Intermediate Hardship

Total	90.0	90.0	90.6	89.5	89.5	89.8	89.7	89.4
Half-Year	87.4	88.3	88.8	87.3	87.0	87.5	87.4	87.1
Full-Year	86.5	87.8	88.5	86.7	86.0	86.8	86.7	86.3

Moderate Hardship

Total	89.1	88.5	89.4	89.0	89.2	88.5	88.5	88.8
Half-Year	87.2	86.5	87.6	87.0	87.1	86.2	86.2	86.7
Full-Year	86.4	85.8	87.0	86.3	85.9	85.0	84.9	85.9

ENHANCED CAPACITY IFE

Severe Hardship

Total	6,468	6,839	6,802	6,895	7,028	7,157	7,379	7,657
Half-Year	2,754	3,188	3,090	2,970	3,027	3,030	3,122	3,533
Full-Year	1,670	2,029	1,886	1,834	1,719	1,836	1,882	2,241

Intermediate Hardship

Total	7,545	8,039	7,957	8,010	8,185	8,354	8,623	8,831
Half-Year	3,540	4,062	3,926	3,755	3,834	3,931	4,054	4,455
Full-Year	2,246	2,720	2,547	2,420	2,324	2,482	2,550	2,986

Moderate Hardship

Total	8,467	8,945	8,930	8,991	9,165	9,308	9,602	9,870
Half-Year	4,287	4,774	4,682	4,533	4,624	4,686	4,827	5,249
Full-Year	2,825	3,316	3,179	3,024	2,913	3,057	3,136	3,629

Table C-1. (Continued)

**ENHANCED CAPACITY IFE
AS PERCENT IFE**

Severe Hardship

Total	53.9	49.7	50.7	51.1	54.0	55.4	55.6	50.7
Half-Year	38.1	35.9	36.2	35.5	38.1	38.8	39.0	36.2
Full-Year	32.4	30.2	30.1	29.9	31.2	33.1	33.2	30.9

Intermediate Hardship

Total	48.9	45.9	46.1	46.5	49.0	50.0	50.2	45.4
Half-Year	35.7	34.2	33.9	33.2	35.4	36.3	36.4	33.5
Full-Year	31.0	29.7	29.5	28.7	30.2	31.5	31.5	29.4

Moderate Hardship

Total	44.3	40.9	41.4	42.1	44.2	44.4	44.6	40.7
Half-Year	33.3	30.9	31.1	31.0	32.8	32.7	32.8	30.3
Full-Year	29.5	27.5	27.8	27.4	28.5	28.6	28.6	27.0

IIE IN IFE

Severe Hardship

Total	8,383	10,287	9,828	9,913	9,290	8,884	9,116	11,407
Half-Year	5,580	7,162	6,793	6,735	6,241	5,962	6,099	7,949
Full-Year	4,137	5,632	5,154	5,143	4,506	4,431	4,524	6,150

Intermediate Hardship

Total	11,986	14,151	13,815	13,820	13,335	13,090	13,470	15,914
Half-Year	8,146	10,043	9,727	9,615	9,105	9,001	9,238	11,350
Full-Year	6,059	7,864	7,368	7,299	6,592	6,698	6,867	8,769

Moderate Hardship

Total	15,786	18,471	18,189	17,884	17,613	17,471	17,974	20,942
Half-Year	10,956	13,393	13,086	12,703	12,378	12,374	12,703	15,431
Full-Year	8,217	10,547	9,978	9,658	9,099	9,371	9,610	12,050

IIE IN IFE AS PERCENT IIE

Severe Hardship

Total	31.3	33.9	32.9	32.7	32.4	32.2	32.2	34.8
Half-Year	31.3	34.0	33.3	32.4	32.0	31.7	31.6	34.2
Full-Year	31.5	34.8	33.6	32.8	31.6	31.8	31.8	34.3

Intermediate Hardship

Total	32.8	35.3	34.6	34.1	33.4	32.8	32.9	35.5
Half-Year	32.1	34.7	34.3	33.2	32.3	31.5	31.6	34.3
Full-Year	32.1	35.0	34.1	33.3	31.4	31.1	31.1	33.8

Moderate Hardship

Total	34.4	36.7	36.7	36.0	34.9	34.8	35.0	37.4
Half-Year	33.0	36.9	35.8	34.5	33.2	33.2	33.3	35.9
Full-Year	32.5	36.7	35.0	34.0	31.8	32.5	32.6	34.9

**IN IFE BUT NOT IIE
AS PERCENT NOT IN IIE**

Severe Hardship

Total	4.7	4.7	4.6	4.5	4.5	4.6	4.7	4.3
Half-Year	2.4	2.6	2.5	2.3	2.3	2.4	2.4	2.3
Full-Year	1.7	1.8	1.8	1.6	1.5	1.6	1.7	1.6

Intermediate Hardship

Total	5.1	5.2	5.1	5.0	4.6	4.8	4.8	4.8
Half-Year	2.9	3.1	3.0	2.7	2.6	2.7	2.7	2.9
Full-Year	2.3	2.4	2.3	2.0	1.8	1.9	2.0	2.3

Moderate Hardship

Total	5.8	6.1	5.9	5.8	5.0	5.4	5.5	5.3
Half-Year	3.6	4.0	37.4	3.5	3.0	3.3	3.3	3.3
Full-Year	3.2	3.2	3.0	2.8	2.2	2.5	2.5	2.7

Table C-1. (Continued)

EARNINGS SUPPLEMENTATION RATE - TOTAL

Severe Hardship

Total	47.1	47.3	47.5	48.1	46.1	46.9	46.9	44.0
Half-Year	47.5	48.5	48.0	48.5	47.2	46.6	46.6	43.6
Full-Year	46.2	48.1	47.1	47.3	45.3	45.4	45.4	42.0

Intermediate Hardship

Total	38.0	38.6	39.8	39.0	38.6	38.8	38.8	36.9
Half-Year	39.1	39.7	40.7	39.3	39.3	38.9	38.9	37.1
Full-Year	37.6	39.1	40.3	37.8	37.7	37.3	37.2	36.2

Moderate Hardship

Total	30.9	31.6	32.3	32.2	32.4	33.5	33.4	31.1
Half-Year	31.4	32.2	33.0	32.4	33.0	33.5	33.5	31.4
Full-Year	30.2	31.4	32.6	31.1	31.7	32.8	32.8	30.4

EARNINGS SUPPLEMENTATION RATE - TRANSFERS

Severe Hardship

Total	28.8	31.1	30.0	29.9	26.1	25.7	25.6	24.5
Half-Year	29.4	32.3	31.8	30.3	27.2	26.2	26.1	24.4
Full-Year	29.8	33.2	31.6	30.5	27.1	26.9	26.8	24.7

Intermediate Hardship

Total	23.5	25.0	25.5	23.3	22.5	21.2	21.1	20.7
Half-Year	24.9	26.2	27.0	23.7	23.4	21.7	21.6	21.1
Full-Year	24.6	26.4	27.2	23.4	23.2	21.8	21.5	21.7

Moderate Hardship

Total	18.5	20.4	20.6	19.0	18.7	18.0	17.9	17.4
Half-Year	19.2	21.1	21.8	19.2	19.6	18.1	18.0	17.9
Full-Year	18.6	21.1	22.2	18.8	19.1	18.2	18.1	18.0

Table C-2. SUMMARY SEVERE HARDSHIP MEASURES, 1974 THROUGH 1980, FOR TOTAL AND FULL-YEAR WORK FORCE, DISAGGREGATED BY WORK EXPERIENCE PATTERN

WORK FORCE

WORK EXPERIENCE PATTERN	1974	1975	1976	1977	1978	1979	1979R	1980
Total								
Not Employed	2,129	3,202	2,929	2,568	2,072	1,927	1,990	2,597
Discouraged	846	1,577	1,342	1,042	,788	780	811	1,269
Unemployed	1,283	1,624	1,587	1,526	1,284	1,146	1,179	1,328
Intermittently Employed	16,408	17,903	17,518	16,944	15,666	16,045	16,478	18,813
Mostly Unemployed	1,616	2,568	2,479	2,136	1,541	1,548	1,607	2,568
Mixed	3,995	5,171	4,847	4,428	4,137	3,801	3,895	5,183
Mostly Employed	10,797	10,164	10,192	10,381	9,987	10,696	10,976	11,063
Part-Time Employed	23,311	26,322	28,690	30,374	32,020	33,439	34,156	32,591
Involuntary	3,986	6,160	6,495	6,319	6,273	7,027	7,172	7,644
Voluntary	19,325	20,162	22,195	24,054	25,747	26,412	26,985	24,948
Employed Full-Time	61,753	57,016	58,011	59,777	62,604	63,238	64,359	64,347
Total	103,601	104,442	107,148	109,663	112,363	114,648	116,983	118,348
Full-Year								
Not Employed	379	945	785	558	403	339	354	665
Discouraged	313	831	683	499	333	285	298	578
Unemployed	66	114	101	108	71	53	55	87
Intermittently Employed	10,417	12,689	11,883	11,042	9,879	10,733	10,997	13,319
Mostly Unemployed	1,163	2,038	1,860	1,511	1,131	1,179	1,221	1,983
Mixed	2,578	3,802	3,330	3,030	2,686	2,554	2,609	3,687
Mostly Employed	6,675	6,849	6,693	6,500	6,062	7,000	7,167	7,649
Part-Time Employed	10,366	13,480	14,307	15,502	16,478	11,323	17,671	17,615
Involuntary	2,198	3,615	3,725	3,676	3,569	4,076	4,160	4,705
Voluntary	8,168	9,865	10,682	11,826	12,909	13,247	13,511	12,910
Employed Full-Time	51,599	48,773	49,501	50,935	53,445	54,076	54,956	55,856
Total	72,761	75,887	76,575	78,036	80,205	82,471	83,979	87,454

DISTRIBUTION WORK FORCE

WORK EXPERIENCE PATTERN	1974	1975	1976	1977	1978	1979	1979R	1980
Total								
Not Employed	2.1	3.1	2.7	2.3	1.8	1.7	1.7	2.2
Discouraged	.8	1.5	1.3	1.0	.7	.7	.7	1.1
Unemployed	1.2	1.6	1.4	1.3	1.1	1.0	1.0	1.1
Intermittently Employed	15.8	17.1	16.3	15.5	13.9	14.0	14.1	15.9
Mostly Unemployed	1.6	2.5	2.3	1.9	1.4	1.4	1.4	2.2
Mixed	3.9	5.0	4.5	4.0	3.7	3.3	3.3	4.4
Mostly Employed	10.4	9.7	9.5	9.5	8.9	9.3	9.4	9.3
Part-Time Employed	22.5	25.2	26.8	27.7	28.5	29.2	29.2	27.5
Involuntary	3.8	5.9	6.1	5.8	5.7	6.1	6.1	6.5
Voluntary	18.7	19.3	20.7	21.9	22.9	23.0	23.1	21.1
Employed Full-Time	59.6	54.6	54.1	54.5	55.7	55.2	55.0	54.4
Total	100.0	100.0	100.0	100.0	100.0	100.0	100.0	100.0
Full-Year								
Not Employed	.5	1.2	1.0	.7	.5	.4	.4	.8
Discouraged	.4	1.1	.9	.6	.4	.3	.4	.7
Unemployed	.1	.2	.1	.1	.1	.1	.1	.1
Intermittently Employed	14.3	16.7	15.5	14.1	12.3	13.0	13.1	15.2
Mostly Unemployed	1.6	2.7	2.4	1.9	1.4	1.4	1.5	2.3
Mixed	3.5	5.0	4.3	3.9	3.3	3.1	3.1	4.2
Mostly Employed	9.2	9.0	8.7	8.3	7.6	8.5	8.5	8.7
Part-Time Employed	14.2	17.8	18.8	19.9	20.5	21.0	21.0	20.1
Involuntary	3.0	4.8	4.9	4.7	4.4	4.9	5.0	5.4
Voluntary	11.2	13.0	13.9	15.2	16.1	16.1	16.1	14.8
Employed Full-Time	70.9	64.3	64.6	65.3	66.6	65.6	65.4	63.9
Total	100.0	100.0	100.0	100.0	100.0	100.0	100.0	100.0

Table C-2. (Continued)

IIE

WORK EXPERIENCE PATTERN	1974	1975	1976	1977	1978	1979	1979R	1980
Total								
Not Employed	2,084	3,146	2,894	2,531	2,030	1,915	1,979	2,586
Discouraged	842	1,574	1,340	1,042	788	780	811	1,269
Unemployed	1,242	1,573	1,554	1,490	1,242	135	1,167	1,317
Intermittently Employed	7,970	9,491	9,303	9,036	8,023	7,663	7,898	10,177
Mostly Unemployed	1,524	2,410	2,308	2,001	1,453	1,471	1,529	2,447
Mixed	2,760	3,508	3,337	3,098	2,958	2,621	2,691	3,673
Mostly Employed	3,687	3,573	3,659	3,937	3,612	3,571	3,679	4,057
Part-Time Employed	9,481	10,991	11,441	11,812	11,832	11,728	11,983	12,726
Involuntary	2,113	2,994	3,158	3,015	2,908	3,131	3,196	3,656
Voluntary	7,368	7,996	8,283	8,797	8,923	8,597	8,788	9,070
Employed Full-Time	7,220	6,717	6,256	6,946	6,775	6,268	6,408	7,258
Total	26,756	30,345	29,894	30,325	28,660	27,575	28,269	32,747
Full-Year								
Not Employed	379	945	785	558	403	339	354	665
Discouraged	313	831	683	449	333	285	298	578
Unemployed	66	114	101	108	71	53	55	87
Intermittently Employed	4,338	6,174	5,687	5,338	4,576	4,630	4,769	6,665
Mostly Unemployed	1,098	1,908	1,737	1,425	1,065	1,112	1,154	1,886
Mixed	1,625	2,411	2,098	1,974	1,808	1,649	1,690	2,475
Mostly Employed	1,616	1,855	1,852	1,939	1,703	1,869	1,925	2,303
Part-Time Employed	3,919	4,829	4,955	5,280	5,116	4,963	5,064	5,856
Involuntary	897	1,321	1,387	1,391	1,274	1,319	1,345	1,781
Voluntary	3,022	3,508	3,569	3,888	3,842	3,643	3,720	4,075
Employed Full-Time	4,467	4,225	3,905	4,517	4,186	3,981	4,060	4,736
Total	13,103	16,173	15,332	15,693	14,282	13,913	14,248	17,921

IIE DISTRIBUTION

WORK EXPERIENCE PATTERN	1974	1975	1976	1977	1978	1979	1979R	1980
Total								
Not Employed	7.8	10.4	9.7	8.3	7.1	6.9	7.0	7.9
Discouraged	3.1	5.2	4.5	3.4	2.7	2.8	2.9	3.9
Unemployed	4.6	5.2	5.2	4.9	4.3	4.1	4.1	4.0
Intermittently Employed	29.8	31.3	31.1	29.8	28.0	27.8	27.9	31.1
Mostly Unemployed	5.7	7.9	7.7	6.6	5.1	5.3	5.4	7.5
Mixed	10.3	11.6	11.2	10.2	10.3	9.5	9.5	11.2
Mostly Employed	13.8	11.8	12.2	13.0	12.6	13.0	13.0	12.4
Part-Time Employed	35.4	36.2	38.3	39.0	41.3	42.5	42.4	38.9
Involuntary	7.9	9.9	10.6	9.9	10.1	11.4	11.3	11.2
Voluntary	27.5	26.4	27.7	29.0	31.1	31.2	31.1	27.7
Employed Full-Time	27.0	22.1	20.9	22.9	23.6	22.7	22.7	22.2
Total	100.0	100.0	100.0	100.0	100.0	100.0	100.0	100.0
Full-Time								
Not Employed	2.9	5.8	5.1	3.6	2.8	2.4	2.5	3.7
Discouraged	2.4	5.1	4.5	2.9	2.3	2.1	2.1	3.2
Unemployed	.5	.7	.7	.7	.5	.4	.4	.5
Intermittently Employed	33.1	38.2	37.1	34.0	32.0	33.3	33.5	37.2
Mostly Unemployed	8.4	11.8	11.3	9.1	7.5	8.0	8.1	10.5
Mixed	12.4	14.9	13.7	12.6	12.7	11.9	11.9	13.8
Mostly Employed	12.3	11.5	12.1	12.4	11.9	13.4	13.5	12.9
Part-Time Employed	29.9	29.9	32.3	33.6	35.8	35.7	35.5	32.7
Involuntary	6.8	8.2	9.0	8.9	8.9	9.5	9.4	9.9
Voluntary	23.1	21.7	23.3	24.8	26.9	26.2	26.1	22.7
Employed Full-Time	34.1	26.1	25.5	28.8	29.3	28.6	28.5	26.9
Total	100.0	100.0	100.0	100.0	100.0	100.0	100.0	100.0

Table C-2. (Continued)

IIE INCIDENCE

WORK EXPERIENCE PATTERN	1974	1975	1976	1977	1978	1979	1979R	1980
Total								
Not Employed	97.9	98.3	98.8	98.6	98.0	99.4	99.4	99.6
Discouraged	99.6	99.7	99.9	100.0	100.0	100.0	100.0	100.0
Unemployed	96.7	96.8	97.9	97.6	96.7	99.0	99.0	99.2
Intermittently Employed	48.6	53.0	53.1	53.3	51.2	47.8	47.9	54.1
Mostly Unemployed	94.3	93.9	93.1	93.7	94.3	95.0	95.1	95.3
Mixed	69.1	67.8	68.8	70.0	71.5	69.0	69.1	70.9
Mostly Employed	34.1	35.2	35.9	37.9	36.2	33.4	33.5	36.7
Part-Time Employed	40.7	41.8	39.9	38.9	37.0	35.1	35.1	39.0
Involuntary	53.0	48.6	48.6	47.7	46.4	44.6	44.6	47.8
Voluntary	38.1	39.7	37.3	36.6	34.7	32.6	32.6	36.4
Employed Full-Time	11.7	11.8	10.8	11.6	10.8	9.9	10.0	11.3
Total	25.8	29.1	27.9	27.7	25.5	24.1	24.2	27.7
Full-Year								
Not Employed	100.0	100.0	100.0	100.0	100.0	100.0	100.0	100.0
Discouraged	100.0	100.0	100.0	100.0	100.0	100.0	100.0	100.0
Unemployed	100.0	100.0	100.0	100.0	100.0	100.0	100.0	100.0
Intermittently Employed	41.6	48.7	47.9	48.3	46.3	43.1	43.4	50.0
Mostly Unemployed	94.3	93.7	93.4	94.3	94.2	94.3	94.5	95.1
Mixed	63.0	63.4	63.0	65.1	67.3	64.6	64.8	67.1
Mostly Employed	24.2	27.1	27.7	29.8	28.1	26.7	26.9	30.1
Part-Time Employed	37.8	35.8	34.4	34.1	31.0	28.6	28.7	33.2
Involuntary	40.8	36.5	37.2	37.9	35.7	32.4	32.3	37.9
Voluntary	37.0	35.6	33.4	32.9	29.8	27.5	27.5	31.6
Employed Full-Time	8.7	8.7	7.9	8.9	7.8	7.4	7.4	8.5
Total	18.0	21.3	20.0	20.1	17.8	16.9	17.0	20.5

IIE DEFICIT

WORK EXPERIENCE PATTERN	1974	1975	1976	1977	1978	1979	1979R	1980
Total								
Not Employed	2,897	6,375	5,872	4,913	4,027	3,767	3,906	7,205
Discouraged	2,002	4,883	4,353	3,314	2,625	2,577	2,684	5,401
Unemployed	895	1,492	1,520	1,599	1,402	1,190	1,222	1,804
Intermittently Employed	11,305	16,853	17,212	16,566	14,987	16,532	17,039	26,739
Mostly Unemployed	3,802	6,719	6,798	6,173	4,838	5,462	5,675	10,383
Mixed	4,013	6,180	6,186	5,660	5,582	5,789	5,926	9,433
Mostly Employed	3,490	3,953	4,228	4,733	4,567	5,281	5,437	6,922
Part-Time Employed	7,618	10,430	11,594	13,049	13,210	14,882	15,162	17,811
Involuntary	2,716	4,140	4,572	4,884	4,517	5,763	5,849	7,723
Voluntary	4,902	6,290	7,022	8,165	8,693	9,120	9,313	10,088
Employed Full-Time	12,209	12,434	12,789	14,756	14,407	15,648	15,891	18,894
Total	34,029	46,093	47,467	49,284	46,631	50,830	51,998	70,648
Full-Year								
Not Employed	1,565	4,239	3,730	2,823	2,182	2,018	2,108	4,430
Discouraged	1,293	3,727	3,248	2,274	1,801	1,700	1,778	3,851
Unemployed	272	512	482	550	381	318	330	579
Intermittently Employed	8,122	13,429	13,177	12,454	11,027	12,593	12,973	21,130
Mostly Unemployed	3,146	5,857	5,748	5,057	4,062	4,649	4,822	8,971
Mixed	2,959	5,008	4,706	4,380	4,141	4,457	4,557	7,384
Mostly Employed	2,017	2,564	2,723	3,018	2,824	3,486	3,595	4,774
Part-Time Employed	5,000	6,966	7,684	8,899	8,740	9,754	9,928	12,406
Involuntary	1,752	2,697	2,991	3,316	2,954	3,744	3,800	5,452
Voluntary	3,248	4,269	4,693	5,583	5,787	6,010	6,128	6,954
Employed Full-Time	10,213	10,554	10,881	12,533	12,121	13,257	13,437	16,007
Total	24,901	35,189	35,473	36,710	34,071	37,621	38,446	53,973

Table C-2. (Continued)

IIE DEFICIT (1980 $)

WORK EXPERIENCE PATTERN	1974	1975	1976	1977	1978	1979	1979R	1980
Total								
Not Employed	4,841	9,760	8,503	6,682	5,086	4,276	4,433	7,205
Discouraged	3,345	7,476	6,303	4,507	3,315	2,925	3,047	5,401
Unemployed	1,496	2,284	2,200	2,175	1,771	1,351	1,387	1,804
Intermittently Employed	18,891	25,802	24,922	22,529	18,928	18,764	19,339	26,739
Mostly Unemployed	6,353	10,287	9,844	8,395	6,110	6,199	6,442	10,383
Mixed	6,705	9,462	8,957	7,698	7,050	6,571	6,726	9,433
Mostly Employed	5,832	6,052	6,122	6,437	5,768	5,994	6,171	6,922
Part-Time Employed	12,730	15,968	16,788	17,747	16,684	16,891	17,209	17,811
Involuntary	4,538	6,338	6,620	6,642	5,704	6,541	6,639	7,723
Voluntary	8,191	9,630	10,168	11,105	10,979	10,351	10,570	10,088
Employed Full-Time	20,401	19,036	18,519	20,068	18,197	17,760	18,037	18,894
Total	56,862	70,568	68,732	67,162	58,895	57,692	59,018	70,648
Full-Time								
Not Employed	2,615	6,490	5,402	3,840	2,756	2,290	2,392	4,430
Discouraged	2,160	5,706	4,703	3,092	2,275	1,930	2,018	3,871
Unemployed	455	784	698	748	481	361	374	579
Intermittently Employed	13,572	20,560	19,080	16,938	13,927	14,293	14,725	2,113
Mostly Unemployed	5,257	8,967	8,323	6,877	5,130	5,277	5,473	8,971
Mixed	4,944	7,667	6,814	5,956	5,231	5,059	5,172	7,384
Mostly Employed	3,370	3,925	3,943	4,105	3,567	3,957	4,080	4,774
Part-Time Employed	8,355	10,665	11,126	12,102	11,039	11,071	11,268	12,406
Involuntary	2,928	4,129	4,331	4,510	3,730	4,247	4,313	5,452
Voluntary	5,427	6,536	6,795	7,592	7,309	6,821	6,956	6,954
Employed Full-Time	17,066	16,158	15,756	17,045	15,308	15,047	15,250	16,007
Total	41,610	53,874	51,364	49,925	43,031	42,700	43,636	53,973

IIE DEFICIT DISTRIBUTION

WORK EXPERIENCE PATTERN	1974	1975	1976	1977	1978	1979	1979R	1980
Total								
Not Employed	8.5	13.8	12.4	10.0	8.6	7.4	7.5	10.2
Discouraged	5.9	10.6	9.2	6.7	5.6	5.1	5.2	7.6
Unemployed	2.6	3.2	3.2	3.2	3.0	2.3	2.3	2.6
Intermittently Employed	33.2	36.6	36.3	33.6	32.1	32.5	32.8	37.8
Mostly Unemployed	11.2	14.6	14.3	12.5	10.4	10.7	10.9	14.7
Mixed	11.8	13.4	13.0	11.5	12.0	11.4	11.4	13.4
Mostly Employed	10.3	8.6	8.9	9.6	9.8	10.4	10.5	9.8
Part-Time Employed	22.4	22.6	24.4	26.5	28.3	29.3	29.2	25.2
Involuntary	8.0	9.0	9.6	9.9	9.7	11.3	11.2	10.9
Voluntary	14.4	13.6	14.8	16.6	18.6	17.9	17.9	14.3
Employed Full-Time	35.9	27.0	26.9	29.9	30.9	30.8	30.6	26.7
Total	100.0	100.0	100.0	100.0	100.0	100.0	100.0	100.0
Full-Year								
Not Employed	6.3	12.0	10.5	7.7	6.4	5.4	5.5	8.2
Discouraged	5.2	10.6	9.2	6.2	5.3	4.5	4.6	7.1
Unemployed	1.1	1.5	1.4	1.5	1.1	.8	.9	1.1
Intermittently Employed	32.6	38.2	37.1	33.9	32.4	33.5	33.7	39.1
Mostly Unemployed	12.6	16.6	16.2	13.8	11.9	12.4	12.5	16.6
Mixed	11.9	14.2	13.3	11.9	12.2	11.8	11.9	13.7
Mostly Employed	8.1	7.3	7.7	8.2	8.3	9.3	9.3	8.8
Part-Time Employed	20.1	19.8	21.7	24.2	25.7	25.9	25.8	23.0
Involuntary	7.0	7.7	8.4	9.0	8.7	10.0	9.9	10.1
Voluntary	13.0	12.1	13.2	15.2	17.0	16.0	15.9	12.9
Employed Full-Time	41.0	30.0	30.7	34.1	35.6	35.2	34.9	29.7
Total	100.0	100.0	100.0	100.0	100.0	100.0	100.0	100.0

Table C-2. (Continued)

IIE AVERAGE DEFICIT

WORK EXPERIENCE PATTERN	1974	1975	1976	1977	1978	1979	1979R	1980
Total								
Not Employed	1,390	2,026	2,029	1,941	1,984	1,967	1,974	2,786
Discouraged	2,377	3,103	3,248	3,182	3,331	3,302	3,309	4,257
Unemployed	721	949	978	1,074	1,129	1,048	1,046	1,369
Intermittently Employed	1,418	1,776	1,850	1,833	1,868	2,157	2,157	2,627
Mostly Unemployed	2,495	2,788	2,946	3,084	3,329	3,713	3,712	4,244
Mixed	1,454	1,762	1,854	1,827	1,887	2,208	2,203	2,568
Mostly Employed	947	1,107	1,156	1,202	1,264	1,479	1,478	1,706
Part-Time Employed	803	949	1,013	1,105	1,116	1,269	1,265	1,400
Involuntary	1,285	1,383	1,448	1,620	1,553	1,841	1,830	2,113
Voluntary	665	787	848	928	974	1,061	1,060	1,112
Employed Full-Time	1,691	1,851	2,044	2,124	2,126	2,496	2,480	2,603
Total	1,272	1,519	1,588	1,625	1,627	1,843	1,839	2,157
Full-Year								
Not Employed	4,129	4,485	4,755	5,062	5,413	5,959	5,960	6,667
Discouraged	4,128	4,486	4,755	5,060	5,417	5,961	5,961	6,668
Unemployed	4,131	4,480	4,752	5,069	5,393	5,953	5,953	6,658
Intermittently Employed	1,872	2,175	2,317	2,333	2,410	2,720	2,720	3,170
Mostly Unemployed	2,867	3,069	3,309	3,549	3,814	4,182	4,178	4,756
Mixed	1,821	2,077	2,243	2,218	2,290	2,702	2,697	2,983
Mostly Employed	1,248	1,382	1,470	1,557	1,658	1,865	1,867	2,073
Part-Time Employed	1,276	1,443	1,551	1,685	1,708	1,965	1,960	2,118
Involuntary	1,954	2,042	2,157	2,383	2,318	2,838	2,825	3,061
Voluntary	1,075	1,217	1,315	1,436	1,506	1,650	1,648	1,706
Employed Full-Time	2,286	2,498	2,787	2,775	2,895	3,330	3,309	3,380
Total	1,900	2,176	2,314	2,339	2,386	2,704	2,698	3,012

IIE AVERAGE DEFICIT (1980 $)

WORK EXPERIENCE PATTERN	1974	1975	1976	1977	1978	1979	1979R	1980
Total								
Not Employed	2,323	3,102	2,938	2,640	2,506	2,233	2,240	2,786
Discouraged	3,972	4,751	4,703	4,328	4,207	3,748	3,756	4,257
Unemployed	1,205	1,453	1,416	1,461	1,426	1,189	1,187	1,369
Intermittently Employed	2,369	2,719	2,679	2,493	2,359	2,448	2,448	2,627
Mostly Unemployed	4,169	4,268	4,266	4,194	4,205	4,214	4,213	4,244
Mixed	2,430	2,698	2,685	2,485	2,383	2,506	2,500	2,568
Mostly Employed	1,582	1,695	1,674	1,635	1,596	1,677	1,678	1,706
Part-Time Employed	1,342	1,453	1,467	1,504	1,410	1,440	1,436	1,400
Involuntary	2,147	2,117	2,097	2,203	1,961	2,090	2,077	2,113
Voluntary	1,111	1,205	1,228	1,262	1,230	1,204	1,203	1,112
Employed Full-Time	2,826	2,834	2,960	2,889	2,685	2,833	2,818	2,603
Total	2,126	2,326	2,299	2,210	2,055	2,092	2,087	2,157
Full-Year								
Not Employed	6,900	6,867	6,885	6,884	6,837	6,763	6,765	6,667
Discouraged	6,898	6,868	6,885	6,882	6,842	6,766	6,766	6,668
Unemployed	6,903	6,859	6,881	6,894	6,811	6,757	6,767	6,658
Intermittently Employed	3,128	3,330	3,355	3,173	3,044	3,087	3,087	3,170
Mostly Unemployed	4,791	4,699	4,791	4,827	4,817	4,747	4,742	4,756
Mixed	3,043	3,180	3,248	3,016	2,892	3,067	3,061	2,983
Mostly Employed	2,085	2,116	2,129	2,118	2,094	2,117	2,119	2,073
Part-Time Employed	2,132	2,209	2,246	2,292	2,157	2,230	2,225	2,118
Involuntary	3,265	3,126	3,123	3,241	2,928	3,221	3,206	3,061
Voluntary	1,796	1,863	1,904	1,953	1,902	1,873	1,870	1,706
Employed Full-Time	3,820	3,824	4,036	3,774	3,656	3,780	3,756	3,380
Total	3,175	3,331	3,351	3,181	3,014	3,069	3,062	3,012

Table C-2. (Continued)

IFE

WORK EXPERIENCE PATTERN	1974	1975	1976	1977	1978	1979	1979R	1980
Total								
Not Employed	972	1,517	1,379	1,296	1,050	902	931	1,343
Discouraged	457	826	745	605	458	392	409	719
Unemployed	515	691	633	691	592	510	523	624
Intermittently Employed	3,086	3,887	3,661	3,522	3,307	3,179	3,279	4,343
Mostly Unemployed	713	1,090	1,062	934	655	657	681	1,217
Mixed	1,015	1,457	1,289	1,163	1,203	1,069	1,096	1,533
Mostly Employed	1,358	1,341	1,310	1,425	1,449	1,454	1,502	1,593
Part-Time Employed	4,771	5,304	5,503	5,623	5,680	5,988	6,151	6,329
Involuntary	888	1,233	1,250	1,218	1,150	1,384	1,419	1,546
Voluntary	3,883	4,072	4,252	4,405	4,529	4,605	4,732	4,783
Employed Full-Time	3,179	3,060	2,859	3,053	2,983	2,845	2,919	3,095
Total	12,008	13,768	13,402	13,494	13,020	12,914	13,280	15,111
Full-Year								
Not Employed	236	545	476	356	280	183	192	404
Discouraged	194	474	427	293	232	146	153	352
Unemployed	42	71	50	63	48	37	39	52
Intermittently Employed	1,695	2,600	2,263	2,076	1,794	1,844	1,894	2,806
Mostly Unemployed	522	878	815	692	491	485	501	961
Mixed	608	1,041	838	729	691	698	710	1,012
Mostly Employed	564	681	611	654	612	661	682	833
Part-Time Employed	1,713	2,127	2,107	2,185	2,061	2,144	2,194	2,529
Involuntary	362	530	484	511	446	530	542	723
Voluntary	1,351	1,597	1,623	1,674	1,615	1,614	1,652	1,806
Employed Full-Time	1,519	1,447	1,412	1,524	1,370	1,374	1,395	1,525
Total	5,162	6,719	6,259	6,141	5,505	5,546	5,675	7,264

IFE INCIDENCE

WORK EXPERIENCE PATTERN	1974	1975	1976	1977	1978	1979	1979R	1980
Total								
Not Employed	45.6	47.4	47.1	50.5	50.7	46.8	46.8	51.7
Discouraged	54.1	52.3	55.5	58.1	58.2	50.2	50.4	56.7
Unemployed	40.1	42.6	39.9	45.3	46.1	44.5	44.3	47.0
Intermittently Employed	18.8	21.7	20.9	20.8	21.1	19.8	19.9	23.1
Mostly Unemployed	44.1	42.5	42.6	43.7	42.5	42.4	42.4	47.4
Mixed	25.4	28.2	26.6	26.3	29.1	28.1	28.1	29.6
Mostly Employed	12.6	13.2	12.9	13.7	14.5	13.6	13.7	14.4
Part-Time Employed	20.5	20.2	19.2	18.5	17.7	17.9	18.0	19.4
Involuntary	22.3	20.0	19.2	19.3	18.3	19.7	19.8	20.2
Voluntary	20.1	20.2	19.2	18.3	17.6	17.4	17.5	19.2
Employed Full-Time	5.1	5.4	4.9	5.1	4.8	4.5	4.5	4.8
Total	11.6	13.2	12.5	12.3	11.6	11.3	11.4	12.8
Full-Year								
Not Employed	62.2	57.7	60.7	63.9	69.5	54.2	54.4	60.8
Discouraged	61.9	57.1	62.4	65.2	69.8	51.3	51.4	61.0
Unemployed	63.8	61.9	48.8	58.4	67.8	69.6	70.0	59.5
Intermittently Employed	16.3	20.5	19.0	18.8	18.2	17.2	17.2	21.1
Mostly Unemployed	44.9	43.1	43.8	45.8	43.4	41.1	41.0	48.5
Mixed	23.6	27.4	25.2	24.1	25.7	27.3	27.2	27.5
Mostly Employed	8.4	9.9	9.1	10.1	10.1	9.4	9.5	10.9
Part-Time Employed	16.5	15.8	14.6	14.1	12.5	12.4	12.4	14.4
Involuntary	16.5	14.7	13.0	13.9	12.5	13.0	13.0	15.4
Voluntary	16.5	16.2	15.2	14.2	12.5	12.2	12.2	14.0
Employed Full-Time	2.9	3.0	2.9	3.0	2.6	2.5	2.5	2.7
Total	7.1	8.9	8.2	7.9	6.9	6.7	6.8	8.3

Table C-2. (Continued)

IFE DISTRIBUTION

WORK EXPERIENCE PATTERN	1974	1975	1976	1977	1978	1979	1979R	1980
Total								
Not Employed	10.1	11.0	10.3	9.6	8.1	7.0	7.0	8.9
Discouraged	4.6	6.0	5.6	4.5	3.5	3.0	3.1	4.8
Unemployed	5.4	5.0	4.7	5.1	4.5	3.9	3.9	4.1
Intermittently Employed	25.7	28.2	27.3	26.1	25.4	24.6	24.7	28.7
Mostly Unemployed	5.9	7.9	7.9	6.9	5.0	5.1	5.1	8.1
Mixed	8.5	10.6	9.6	8.6	9.2	8.3	8.3	10.1
Mostly Employed	11.3	9.7	9.8	10.6	11.1	11.3	11.3	10.5
Part-Time Employed	39.7	38.5	41.1	41.7	43.6	46.4	46.3	41.9
Involuntary	7.4	9.0	9.3	9.0	8.8	10.7	10.7	10.2
Voluntary	32.3	29.6	31.7	32.6	34.8	35.7	35.6	31.7
Employed Full-Time	26.5	22.2	21.3	22.6	22.9	22.0	22.0	20.5
Total	100.0	100.0	100.0	100.0	100.0	100.0	100.0	100.0
Full-Year								
Not Employed	4.6	8.1	7.6	5.8	5.1	3.3	3.4	5.6
Discouraged	3.8	7.1	6.8	4.8	4.2	2.6	2.7	4.8
Unemployed	.8	1.1	.8	1.0	.9	.7	.7	.7
Intermittently Employed	32.8	38.7	36.2	33.8	32.6	33.2	33.4	38.6
Mostly Unemployed	10.1	13.1	13.0	11.3	8.9	8.7	8.8	13.2
Mixed	11.8	15.5	13.4	11.9	12.5	12.6	12.5	13.9
Mostly Employed	10.9	10.1	9.8	10.7	11.1	11.9	12.0	11.5
Part-Time Employed	33.2	31.7	33.7	35.6	37.4	38.7	38.7	34.8
Involuntary	7.0	7.9	7.7	8.3	8.1	9.6	9.6	10.0
Voluntary	26.2	23.8	25.9	27.3	29.3	29.1	29.1	24.9
Employed Full-Time	29.4	21.5	22.6	24.8	24.9	24.8	24.6	21.0
Total	100.0	100.0	100.0	100.0	100.0	100.0	100.0	100.0

IFE DEFICIT

WORK EXPERIENCE PATTERN	1974	1975	1976	1977	1978	1979	1979R	1980
Total								
Not Employed	2,683	4,470	4,365	4,350	3,770	3,753	3,889	6,136
Discouraged	1,345	2,642	2,557	2,205	1,757	1,770	1,857	3,431
Unemployed	1,338	1,828	1,808	2,144	2,013	1,983	2,032	2,705
Intermittently Employed	5,091	7,103	7,038	6,977	7,204	7,369	7,587	12,169
Mostly Unemployed	1,550	2,701	2,556	2,411	1,987	2,178	2,258	4,650
Mixed	1,654	2,432	2,391	2,263	2,549	2,440	2,499	4,118
Mostly Employed	1,886	1,969	2,091	2,303	2,667	2,752	2,830	3,400
Part-Time Employed	7,163	8,462	9,348	10,098	11,032	13,417	1,377	15,279
Involuntary	1,595	2,220	2,425	2,377	2,462	3,469	3,556	3,798
Voluntary	5,568	6,242	6,922	7,721	8,569	9,948	10,214	11,481
Employed Full-Time	4,763	4,890	4,704	5,477	5,764	6,262	6,410	7,417
Total	19,700	24,925	25,455	26,902	27,770	30,801	31,656	41,000
Full-Year								
Not Employed	726	1,808	1,771	1,385	1,123	926	974	2,053
Discouraged	614	1,592	1,614	1,124	927	760	801	1,789
Unemployed	111	216	157	261	196	166	173	2,644
Intermittently Employed	2,963	4,847	4,512	4,236	4,017	4,458	4,565	8,236
Mostly Unemployed	1,178	2,158	2,009	1,850	1,551	1,602	1,655	3,757
Mixed	993	1,703	1,564	1,366	1,409	1,559	1,574	2,725
Mostly Employed	793	987	939	1,020	1,057	1,297	1,336	1,755
Part-Time Employed	2,393	3,295	3,459	3,813	3,689	4,422	4,512	5,794
Involuntary	619	902	950	1,002	918	1,285	1,306	1,840
Voluntary	1,774	2,393	2,508	2,811	2,771	3,136	3,205	3,954
Employed Full-Time	2,386	2,540	2,461	2,820	2,657	3,233	3,256	3,897
Total	8,468	12,491	12,203	12,254	11,486	13,038	13,306	19,981

Table C-2. (Continued)

IFE DEFICIT (1980 $)

WORK EXPERIENCE PATTERN	1974	1975	1976	1977	1978	1979	1979R	1980
Total								
Not Employed	4,483	6,844	6,321	5,916	4,762	4,260	4,414	6,136
Discouraged	2,247	4,045	3,703	2,999	2,219	2,009	2,108	3,431
Unemployed	2,236	2,799	2,618	2,916	2,542	2,251	2,306	2,705
Intermittently Employed	8,507	10,875	10,190	9,489	9,098	8,364	8,611	12,169
Mostly Unemployed	2,590	4,135	3,701	3,279	2,510	2,472	2,563	4,650
Mixed	2,764	3,723	3,462	3,078	3,219	2,769	2,836	4,118
Mostly Employed	3,152	3,015	3,027	3,132	3,369	3,124	3,212	3,400
Part-Time Employed	11,969	12,955	13,535	13,733	13,933	15,228	15,629	15,279
Involuntary	2,665	3,399	3,512	3,233	3,110	3,937	4,036	3,798
Voluntary	9,304	9,557	10,023	10,501	10,823	11,291	11,593	11,481
Employed Full-Time	7,959	7,487	6,812	7,448	7,280	7,107	7,276	7,417
Total	32,919	38,160	36,858	36,586	35,073	34,959	35,929	41,000
Full-Time								
Not Employed	1,213	2,768	2,564	1,884	1,419	1,051	1,106	2,053
Discouraged	1,026	2,437	2,336	1,529	1,171	863	909	1,789
Unemployed	185	331	228	355	247	188	197	264
Intermittently Employed	4,951	7,421	6,533	5,760	5,074	5,060	5,181	8,236
Mostly Unemployed	1,968	3,304	2,909	2,516	1,959	1,818	1,879	3,757
Mixed	1,659	2,607	2,265	1,858	1,779	1,769	1,786	2,725
Mostly Employed	1,325	1,511	1,360	1,387	1,335	1,472	1,516	1,755
Part-Time Employed	3,999	5,045	5,008	5,186	4,659	5,019	5,121	5,794
Involuntary	1,034	1,381	1,376	1,363	1,159	1,458	1,483	1,840
Voluntary	2,964	3,664	3,632	3,823	3,500	3,559	3,638	3,954
Employed Full-Time	3,987	3,889	3,564	3,835	3,356	3,669	3,695	3,892
Total	14,150	19,124	17,669	16,666	14,507	14,798	15,102	19,981

IFE DEFICIT DISTRIBUTION

WORK EXPERIENCE PATTERN	1974	1875	1976	1977	1978	1979	1979R	1980
Total								
Not Employed	13.6	17.9	17.1	16.2	13.6	12.2	12.3	15.0
Discouraged	6.8	10.6	10.0	8.2	6.3	5.7	5.9	8.4
Unemployed	6.8	7.3	7.1	8.0	7.2	6.4	6.4	6.6
Intermittently Employed	25.8	28.5	27.6	25.9	25.9	23.9	24.0	29.7
Mostly Unemployed	7.9	10.8	10.0	9.0	7.2	7.1	7.1	11.3
Mixed	8.4	9.8	9.4	8.4	9.2	7.9	7.9	10.0
Mostly Employed	9.6	7.9	8.2	8.6	9.6	8.9	8.9	8.3
Part-Time Employed	36.4	33.9	36.7	37.5	39.7	43.6	43.5	37.3
Involuntary	8.1	8.9	9.5	8.8	8.9	11.3	11.2	9.3
Voluntary	28.3	25.0	27.2	28.7	30.9	32.3	32.3	28.0
Employed Full-Time	24.2	19.6	18.5	20.4	20.8	20.3	20.3	18.1
Total	100.0	100.0	100.0	100.0	100.0	100.0	100.0	100.0
Full-Year								
Not Employed	8.6	14.5	14.5	11.3	9.8	7.1	7.3	10.3
Discouraged	7.3	12.7	13.2	9.2	8.1	5.8	6.0	9.0
Unemployed	1.3	1.7	1.3	2.1	1.7	1.3	1.3	1.3
Intermittently Employed	35.0	38.8	37.0	34.6	35.0	34.2	34.3	41.2
Mostly Unemployed	13.9	17.3	16.5	15.1	13.5	12.3	12.4	18.8
Mixed	11.7	13.6	12.8	11.1	12.3	12.0	11.8	13.6
Mostly Employed	9.4	7.9	7.7	8.3	9.2	9.9	10.0	8.8
Part-Time Employed	28.3	26.4	28.3	31.1	32.1	33.9	33.9	29.0
Involuntary	7.3	7.2	7.8	8.2	8.0	9.9	9.8	9.2
Voluntary	21.0	19.2	20.6	22.9	24.1	24.1	24.1	19.8
Employed Full-Time	28.2	20.3	20.2	23.0	23.1	24.8	24.5	19.5
Total	100.0	100.0	100.0	100.0	100.0	100.0	100.0	100.0

Table C-2. (Continued)

IFE AVERAGE DEFICIT

WORK EXPERIENCE PATTERN	1974	1975	1976	1977	1978	1979	1979R	1980
Total								
Not Employed	2,761	2,947	3,167	3,355	3,590	4,162	4,176	4,569
Discouraged	2,941	3,199	3,432	3,645	3,833	4,515	4,544	4,774
Unemployed	2,601	2,645	2,855	3,101	3,401	3,891	3,888	4,333
Intermittently Employed	1,649	1,827	1,922	1,981	2,178	2,318	2,314	2,802
Mostly Unemployed	2,175	2,478	2,406	2,580	3,033	3,317	3,314	3,822
Mixed	1,630	1,670	1,855	1,946	2,119	2,282	2,280	2,686
Mostly Employed	1,389	1,469	1,596	1,617	1,841	1,893	1,884	2,135
Part-Time Employed	1,501	1,595	1,699	1,796	1,942	2,241	2,239	2,414
Involuntary	1,796	1,801	1,940	1,952	2,141	2,506	2,506	2,456
Voluntary	1,434	1,533	1,628	1,753	1,892	2,161	2,159	2,400
Employed Full-Time	1,499	1,598	1,645	1,794	1,933	2,201	2,196	2,396
Total	1,641	1,810	1,899	1,994	2,133	2,385	2,384	2,713
Full-Year								
Not Employed	3,076	3,317	3,720	3,887	4,011	5,049	5,069	5,083
Discouraged	3,167	3,358	3,783	3,837	3,995	5,197	5,221	5,080
Unemployed	2,652	3,047	3,179	4,120	4,091	4,464	4,470	5,103
Intermittently Employed	1,749	1,864	1,993	2,041	2,239	2,418	2,411	2,935
Mostly Unemployed	2,257	2,457	2,464	2,674	3,157	3,306	3,305	3,908
Mixed	1,631	1,635	1,867	1,873	2,040	2,234	2,216	2,692
Mostly Employed	1,405	1,450	1,538	1,558	1,728	1,962	1,957	2,107
Part-Time Employed	1,397	1,549	1,641	1,745	1,790	2,062	2,056	2,291
Involuntary	1,711	1,702	1,964	1,963	2,058	2,424	2,409	2,546
Voluntary	1,314	1,498	1,545	1,679	1,716	1,943	1,940	2,189
Employed Full-Time	1,571	1,756	1,743	1,850	1,940	2,352	2,334	2,556
Total	1,641	1,859	1,950	1,996	2,087	2,351	2,345	2,751

IFE AVERAGE DEFICIT (1980 $)

WORK EXPERIENCE PATTERN	1974	1975	1976	1977	1978	1979	1979R	1980
Total								
Not Employed	4,614	4,512	4,586	4,835	4,534	4,724	4,740	4,569
Discouraged	4,914	4,898	4,970	4,957	4,841	5,124	5,157	4,774
Unemployed	4,346	4,049	4,134	4,217	4,295	4,416	4,413	4,333
Intermittently Employed	2,755	2,797	2,783	2,694	2,751	2,631	2,626	2,802
Mostly Unemployed	3,634	3,794	3,484	3,509	3,831	3,765	3,761	3,822
Mixed	2,724	2,557	2,686	2,647	2,676	2,590	2,588	2,686
Mostly Employed	2,321	2,249	2,311	2,199	2,325	2,149	2,138	2,135
Part-Time Employed	2,508	2,442	2,460	2,443	2,453	2,543	2,541	2,414
Involuntary	3,001	2,757	2,809	2,655	2,704	2,844	2,844	2,456
Voluntary	2,396	2,347	2,357	2,384	2,390	2,453	2,450	2,400
Employed Full-Time	2,505	2,447	2,382	2,440	2,441	2,498	2,492	2,396
Total	2,742	2,771	2,750	2,712	2,694	2,707	2,706	2,713
Full-Year								
Not Employed	5,140	5,078	5,387	5,286	5,066	5,731	5,753	5,083
Discouraged	5,292	5,141	5,478	5,218	5,046	5,899	5,926	5,080
Unemployed	4,431	4,665	4,603	5,603	5,167	5,067	5,073	5,103
Intermittently Employed	2,923	2,854	2,886	2,776	2,828	2,744	2,736	2,935
Mostly Unemployed	3,771	3,762	3,568	3,637	3,987	3,752	3,751	3,908
Mixed	2,725	2,503	2,703	2,547	2,577	2,536	2,515	2,692
Mostly Employed	2,348	2,220	2,227	2,119	2,182	2,227	2,221	2,107
Part-Time Employed	2,334	2,372	2,376	2,373	2,261	2,340	2,334	2,291
Involuntary	2,859	2,606	2,844	2,670	2,599	2,751	2,734	2,546
Voluntary	2,196	2,293	2,237	2,283	2,167	2,205	2,202	2,189
Employed Full-Time	2,625	2,688	2,524	2,516	2,450	2,670	2,649	2,556
Total	2,742	2,846	2,824	2,715	2,636	2,668	2,662	2,751

Table C-2. (Continued)

IFI

WORK EXPERIENCE PATTERN	1974	1975	1976	1977	1978	1979	1979R	1980
Total								
Not Employed	638	885	869	911	752	606	629	996
Discouraged	292	451	459	422	328	279	293	547
Unemployed	345	434	410	489	424	327	336	449
Intermittently Employed	1,895	2,144	2,046	1,954	2,017	1,933	1,989	2,724
Mostly Unemployed	435	579	544	508	388	413	423	789
Mixed	618	745	700	617	712	613	625	911
Mostly Employed	842	820	802	829	917	908	941	1,025
Part-Time Employed	2,020	2,443	2,480	2,392	2,473	2,617	2,690	2,875
Involuntary	541	756	763	711	714	793	815	925
Voluntary	1,480	1,687	1,716	1,681	1,759	1,824	1,875	1,951
Employed Full-Time	1,793	1,780	1,638	1,742	1,770	1,696	1,748	1,869
Total	6,346	7,252	7,033	6,998	7,012	6,853	7,055	8,465
Full-Year								
Not Employed	132	276	280	229	198	126	133	291
Discouraged	108	238	247	192	163	106	112	255
Unemployed	24	38	32	37	35	20	21	36
Intermittently Employed	1,004	1,324	1,181	1,092	1,021	1,071	1,094	1,717
Mostly Unemployed	307	448	391	370	282	298	305	622
Mixed	347	489	428	360	379	380	382	568
Mostly Employed	349	386	363	362	361	393	407	526
Part-Time Employed	687	976	955	903	901	939	962	1,167
Involuntary	229	337	326	283	285	329	337	448
Voluntary	458	640	629	620	616	610	625	719
Employed Full-Time	954	909	897	1,009	889	890	909	1,038
Total	2,776	3,485	3,313	3,233	3,009	3,026	3,098	4,213

IFI DISTRIBUTION

WORK EXPERIENCE PATTERN	1974	1975	1976	1977	1978	1979	1979R	1980
Total								
Not Employed	10.1	12.2	12.4	13.0	10.7	8.8	8.9	11.8
Discouraged	4.6	6.2	6.5	6.0	4.7	4.1	4.2	6.5
Unemployed	5.4	6.0	5.8	7.0	6.1	4.8	4.8	5.3
Intermittently Employed	29.9	29.6	29.1	27.9	28.8	28.2	28.2	32.2
Mostly Unemployed	6.9	8.0	7.7	7.3	5.5	6.0	6.0	9.3
Mixed	9.7	10.3	9.9	8.8	10.2	8.9	8.9	10.8
Mostly Employed	13.3	11.3	11.4	11.8	13.1	13.2	13.3	12.1
Part-Time Employed	31.8	33.7	35.3	34.2	35.3	38.2	38.1	34.0
Involuntary	8.5	10.4	10.9	10.2	10.2	11.6	11.6	10.9
Voluntary	23.3	23.3	24.4	24.0	25.1	26.6	26.6	23.0
Employed Full-Time	28.3	24.5	23.3	24.9	25.2	24.8	24.8	22.1
Total	100.0	100.0	100.0	100.0	100.0	100.0	100.0	100.0
Full-Year								
Not Employed	4.7	7.9	8.4	7.1	6.6	4.2	4.3	6.9
Discouraged	3.9	6.8	7.5	5.9	5.4	3.5	3.6	6.0
Unemployed	.9	1.1	1.0	1.2	1.2	.7	.7	.9
Intermittently Employed	36.2	38.0	35.7	33.8	33.9	35.4	35.3	40.8
Mostly Unemployed	11.1	12.9	11.8	11.4	9.4	9.8	9.8	14.8
Mixed	12.5	14.0	12.9	11.1	12.6	12.6	12.3	13.5
Mostly Employed	12.6	11.1	11.0	11.2	12.0	13.0	13.1	12.5
Part-Time Employed	24.7	28.0	28.8	27.9	29.9	31.0	31.1	27.7
Involuntary	8.2	9.7	9.9	8.7	9.5	10.9	10.9	10.6
Voluntary	16.5	18.4	19.0	19.2	20.5	20.2	20.2	17.1
Employed Full-Time	34.4	26.1	27.1	31.2	29.5	29.4	29.3	24.6
Total	100.0	100.0	100.0	100.0	100.0	100.0	100.0	100.0

Table C-2. (Continued)

IFI DEFICIT

WORK EXPERIENCE PATTERN	1974	1975	1976	1977	1978	1979	1979R	1980
Total								
Not Employed	937	1,387	1,402	1,613	1,507	1,568	1,629	2,770
Discouraged	442	754	794	788	689	734	768	1,575
Unemployed	495	632	607	825	809	834	861	1,195
Intermittently Employed	2,343	2,999	2,808	2,923	3,232	3,400	3,475	5,884
Mostly Unemployed	636	955	849	904	739	967	986	2,117
Mixed	793	1,057	967	928	1,140	1,072	1,092	1,903
Mostly Employed	914	987	991	1,091	1,352	1,361	1,397	1,863
Part-Time Employed	2,118	2,746	3,066	3,050	3,387	4,389	4,505	4,957
Involuntary	717	1,013	1,116	1,000	1,114	1,550	1,593	1,738
Voluntary	1,401	1,733	1,950	2,050	2,273	2,840	2,911	3,219
Employed Full-Time	2,315	2,407	2,297	2,771	2,901	3,142	3,217	3,842
Total	7,713	9,538	9,573	10,357	11,027	12,499	12,825	17,452
Full-Time								
Not Employed	213	448	524	420	424	408	434	890
Discouraged	179	393	460	345	362	334	356	759
Unemployed	34	55	64	75	62	74	78	131
Intermittently Employed	1,409	1,953	1,777	1,733	1,733	2,104	2,138	3,989
Mostly Unemployed	475	722	641	692	586	724	742	1,721
Mixed	479	705	651	566	630	699	697	1,239
Mostly Employed	455	526	485	475	516	681	700	1,028
Part-Time Employed	782	1,288	1,296	1,332	1,321	1,716	1,758	2,152
Involuntary	307	516	519	474	489	704	714	915
Voluntary	475	711	778	857	832	1,011	1,044	1,236
Employed Full-Time	1,464	1,544	1,476	1,824	1,587	1,962	1,977	2,469
Total	3,867	5,233	5,074	5,308	5,064	6,189	6,308	9,499

IFI INCIDENCE

WORK EXPERIENCE PATTERN	1974	1975	1976	1977	1978	1979	1979R	1980
Total								
Not Employed	30.0	27.6	29.7	35.5	36.3	31.4	31.6	38.4
Discouraged	34.6	28.6	34.2	40.5	41.6	35.8	36.1	43.1
Unemployed	26.9	26.7	25.9	32.0	33.0	28.5	28.5	33.8
Intermittently Employed	11.6	12.0	11.7	11.5	12.9	12.0	12.1	14.5
Mostly Unemployed	26.9	22.6	22.0	23.8	25.2	26.6	26.3	30.7
Mixed	15.5	14.4	14.4	13.9	17.2	16.1	16.0	17.6
Mostly Employed	7.8	8.1	7.9	8.0	9.2	8.5	8.6	9.3
Part-Time Employed	8.7	9.3	8.6	7.9	7.7	7.8	7.9	8.8
Involuntary	13.6	12.3	11.8	11.2	11.4	11.3	11.4	12.1
Voluntary	7.7	8.4	7.7	7.0	6.8	6.9	6.9	7.8
Employed Full-Time	2.9	3.1	2.8	2.9	2.8	2.7	2.7	2.9
Total	6.1	6.9	6.6	6.4	6.2	6.0	6.0	7.2
Full Year								
Not Employed	34.7	29.2	35.6	41.1	49.1	37.2	37.7	43.8
Discouraged	34.4	28.6	36.2	42.7	49.1	37.2	37.7	44.1
Unemployed	36.3	33.1	31.8	34.4	49.1	37.2	38.0	41.8
Intermittently Employed	9.6	10.4	9.9	9.9	10.3	10.0	9.9	12.9
Mostly Unemployed	26.4	22.0	21.0	24.5	24.9	25.2	25.0	31.4
Mixed	13.5	12.9	12.9	11.9	14.1	14.9	14.6	15.4
Mostly Employed	5.2	5.6	5.4	5.6	5.9	5.6	5.7	6.9
Part-Time Employed	6.6	7.2	6.6	5.8	5.5	5.4	5.4	6.6
Involuntary	10.4	9.3	8.8	7.7	8.0	8.1	8.1	9.5
Voluntary	5.6	6.5	5.9	5.2	4.8	4.6	4.6	5.6
Employed Full-Time	1.8	1.9	1.8	2.0	1.7	1.6	1.7	1.9
Total	3.8	4.6	4.3	4.1	3.8	3.7	3.7	4.8

Table C-2. (Continued)

IFI DEFICIT (1980 $)

WORK EXPERIENCE PATTERN	1974	1975	1976	1977	1978	1979	1979R	1980
Total								
Not Employed	1,566	2,123	2,029	2,194	1,903	1,780	1,849	2,770
Discouraged	739	1,154	1,150	1,071	881	833	872	1,575
Unemployed	827	968	875	1,122	1,022	947	977	1,195
Intermittently Employed	3,915	4,591	4,066	3,975	4,082	3,859	3,944	5,884
Mostly Unemployed	1,063	1,462	1,230	1,229	934	1,098	1,119	2,117
Mixed	1,325	1,618	1,401	1,262	1,440	1,217	1,239	1,903
Mostly Employed	1,527	1,511	1,436	1,484	1,708	1,545	1,586	1,863
Part-Time Employed	3,539	4,204	4,440	4,148	4,278	4,982	5,113	4,957
Involuntary	1,198	1,551	1,616	1,360	1,407	1,759	1,808	1,738
Voluntary	2,341	2,653	2,824	2,788	2,871	3,223	3,304	3,219
Employed Full-Time	3,868	3,685	3,326	3,768	3,664	3,563	3,651	3,842
Total	12,888	14,603	13,862	14,085	14,927	14,186	14,556	17,452
Full Year								
Not Employed	356	686	758	571	536	463	492	890
Discouraged	299	602	666	772	457	379	404	759
Unemployed	57	84	92	102	79	84	89	131
Intermittently Employed	2,354	2,990	2,574	2,356	2,188	2,388	2,428	3,989
Mostly Unemployed	794	1,105	928	941	741	822	842	1,721
Mixed	800	1,079	943	770	796	793	791	1,239
Mostly Employed	760	805	702	646	652	773	794	1,028
Part-Time Employed	1,307	1,972	1,877	1,811	1,668	1,948	1,996	2,152
Involuntary	513	790	751	645	618	799	810	915
Voluntary	794	1,180	1,126	1,166	1,050	1,147	1,185	1,236
Employed Full-Time	2,446	2,364	2,138	2,480	2,004	2,227	2,244	2,469
Total	6,462	8,012	7,347	7,219	6,396	7,025	7,160	9,499

IFI AVERAGE DEFICIT

WORK EXPERIENCE PATTERN	1974	1975	1976	1977	1978	1979	1979R	1980
Total								
Not Employed	1,469	1,567	1,612	1,771	2,004	2,588	2,591	2,780
Discouraged	1,512	1,673	1,730	1,867	2,130	2,629	2,621	2,878
Unemployed	1,433	1,456	1,480	1,689	1,907	2,554	2,565	2,661
Intermittently Employed	1,236	1,399	1,372	1,496	1,603	1,759	1,747	2,160
Mostly Unemployed	1,461	1,648	1,560	1,779	1,906	2,344	2,329	2,684
Mixed	1,283	1,419	1,383	1,505	1,602	1,749	1,748	2,089
Mostly Employed	1,086	1,204	1,236	1,316	1,475	1,499	1,485	1,819
Part-Time Employed	1,049	1,124	1,237	1,275	1,369	1,677	1,675	1,724
Involuntary	1,327	1,341	1,462	1,407	1,560	1,954	1,954	1,880
Voluntary	947	1,027	1,136	1,219	1,292	1,557	1,553	1,650
Employed Full-Time	1,291	1,352	1,402	1,591	1,639	1,852	1,840	2,056
Total	1,215	1,315	1,361	1,480	1,573	1,824	1,818	2,062
Full-Year								
Not Employed	1,620	1,625	1,873	1,833	2,142	3,239	3,253	3,061
Discouraged	1,667	1,654	1,861	1,797	2,217	3,148	3,167	2,981
Unemployed	1,411	1,443	1,970	2,016	1,792	3,729	3,709	3,617
Intermittently Employed	1,403	1,475	1,504	1,587	1,697	1,964	1,956	2,323
Mostly Unemployed	1,546	1,610	1,641	1,873	2,082	2,434	2,433	2,766
Mixed	1,378	1,442	1,522	1,574	1,664	1,836	1,826	2,182
Mostly Employed	1,302	1,361	1,337	1,310	1,431	1,731	1,720	1,953
Part-Time Employed	1,139	1,319	1,357	1,475	1,466	1,827	1,828	1,843
Involuntary	1,340	1,533	1,589	1,678	1,719	2,140	2,120	2,043
Voluntary	1,038	1,206	1,237	1,382	1,349	1,658	1,670	1,719
Employed Full-Time	1,534	1,698	1,646	1,807	1,785	2,204	2,176	2,379
Total	1,393	1,501	1,532	1,642	1,683	2,045	2,036	2,255

Table C-2. (Continued)

IFI AVERAGE DEFICIT (1980 $)

WORK EXPERIENCE PATTERN	1974	1975	1976	1977	1978	1979	1979R	1980
Total								
Not Employed	2,455	2,399	2,334	2,409	2,531	2,937	2,941	2,780
Discouraged	2,527	2,561	2,505	2,539	2,690	2,984	2,975	2,878
Unemployed	2,395	2,229	2,143	2,297	2,409	2,899	2,911	2,661
Intermittently Employed	2,065	2,142	1,987	2,035	2,025	1,996	1,983	2,160
Mostly Unemployed	2,441	2,523	2,259	2,419	2,407	2,660	2,643	2,684
Mixed	2,144	2,172	2,003	2,047	2,023	1,985	1,984	2,089
Mostly Employed	1,815	1,843	1,790	1,790	1,863	1,701	1,685	1,819
Part-Time Employed	1,753	1,721	1,792	1,734	1,729	1,903	1,901	1,724
Involuntary	2,217	2,053	2,117	1,914	1,970	2,218	2,218	1,880
Voluntary	1,582	1,572	1,645	1,658	1,632	1,767	1,763	1,650
Employed Full-Time	2,157	2,070	2,030	2,163	2,070	2,102	2,088	2,056
Total	2,030	2,013	1,971	2,013	1,987	2,070	2,063	2,062
Full-Year								
Not Employed	2,707	2,488	2,712	2,493	2,705	3,676	3,692	3,061
Discouraged	2,786	2,532	2,695	2,444	2,800	3,573	3,595	2,981
Unemployed	2,358	2,209	2,853	2,742	2,263	4,232	4,210	3,617
Intermittently Employed	2,344	2,258	2,178	2,158	2,143	2,229	2,220	2,323
Mostly Unemployed	2,583	2,465	2,376	2,547	2,630	2,763	2,761	2,766
Mixed	2,303	2,207	2,204	2,141	2,102	2,084	2,073	2,182
Mostly Employed	2,176	2,084	1,936	1,782	1,807	1,965	1,952	1,953
Part-Time Employed	1,903	2,019	1,965	2,006	1,852	2,074	2,075	1,843
Involuntary	2,239	2,347	2,301	2,282	2,171	2,429	2,406	2,043
Voluntary	1,734	1,846	1,791	1,880	1,704	1,882	1,895	1,719
Employed Full-Time	2,563	2,600	2,383	2,458	2,254	2,502	2,470	2,379
Total	2,328	2,298	2,218	2,233	2,126	2,321	2,311	2,255

PERCENT IIE IN IFE

WORK EXPERIENCE PATTERN	1974	1975	1976	1977	1978	1979	1979R	1980
Total								
Not Employed	46.3	48.0	47.4	50.8	51.6	47.0	47.0	51.9
Discouraged	54.3	52.4	55.6	58.1	58.1	50.3	50.4	56.7
Unemployed	40.8	43.7	40.2	45.8	47.4	44.8	44.7	47.4
Intermittently Employed	32.5	35.4	34.8	34.2	35.2	35.2	35.2	37.9
Mostly Unemployed	45.6	44.4	45.3	45.7	44.3	43.5	43.4	49.1
Mixed	33.6	37.7	36.1	35.1	36.8	37.4	37.2	38.8
Mostly Employed	26.4	27.2	26.9	27.6	30.1	30.2	30.2	30.4
Part-Time Employed	29.2	30.8	29.8	30.1	29.4	30.0	30.1	31.9
Involuntary	36.0	35.3	33.6	34.2	33.4	36.5	36.6	35.5
Voluntary	27.3	29.1	28.4	28.7	28.0	27.6	27.6	30.5
Employed Full-Time	28.5	30.2	28.9	28.5	28.7	28.2	28.2	29.5
Total	31.3	33.9	32.9	32.7	32.4	32.2	32.2	34.8
Full-Year								
Not Employed	62.3	57.7	60.6	63.8	69.5	54.0	54.2	60.8
Discouraged	62.0	57.0	62.5	65.3	69.7	51.2	51.3	60.9
Unemployed	63.6	62.3	49.5	58.3	67.6	69.8	70.9	59.8
Intermittently Employed	34.0	37.8	36.0	35.6	35.3	35.4	35.2	38.6
Mostly Unemployed	46.5	45.4	46.3	47.9	45.4	42.3	42.1	50.4
Mixed	34.2	39.4	37.2	34.8	35.4	39.4	39.0	38.8
Mostly Employed	25.3	27.8	25.1	27.3	28.9	27.7	27.7	28.7
Part-Time Employed	30.7	32.8	30.8	31.4	29.6	30.7	30.6	32.9
Involuntary	36.9	36.1	31.6	33.6	31.3	35.7	35.7	36.5
Voluntary	28.9	31.5	30.4	30.6	29.1	28.8	28.8	31.3
Employed Full-Time	27.4	27.8	28.3	27.2	26.1	27.4	27.2	26.4
Total	31.6	34.8	33.6	32.8	31.6	31.8	31.8	34.3

Table C-2. (Continued)

EARNINGS SUPPLEMENTATION RATE-TOTAL

WORK EXPERIENCE PATTERN	1974	1975	1976	1977	1978	1979	1979R	1980
Total								
Not Employed	34.4	41.7	36.9	29.7	28.4	32.8	32.5	25.8
Discouraged	36.0	45.4	38.4	30.3	28.5	28.8	28.3	23.9
Unemployed	32.9	37.2	35.4	29.3	28.3	35.9	35.8	28.0
Intermittently Employed	38.6	44.8	44.1	44.5	39.0	39.2	39.4	37.3
Mostly Unemployed	38.9	46.8	48.8	45.6	40.8	37.2	37.9	35.2
Mixed	39.1	48.9	45.7	47.0	40.8	42.7	43.0	40.6
Mostly Employed	38.0	38.8	38.8	41.8	36.7	37.6	37.4	35.7
Part-Time Employed	57.7	53.9	54.9	57.5	56.5	56.3	56.3	54.6
Involuntary	39.1	38.7	38.9	41.7	37.9	42.7	42.5	40.2
Voluntary	61.9	58.6	59.6	61.8	61.2	60.4	60.4	59.2
Employed Full-Time	43.6	41.8	42.7	42.9	40.7	40.4	40.1	39.6
Total	47.1	47.3	47.5	48.1	46.1	46.9	46.9	44.0
Full-Year								
Not Employed	44.2	49.4	41.3	35.7	29.3	31.4	30.6	28.0
Discouraged	44.5	49.8	42.0	34.5	29.7	27.5	26.8	27.7
Unemployed	43.1	46.5	34.8	41.2	27.5	46.6	45.7	29.9
Intermittently Employed	40.8	49.1	47.8	47.4	43.1	41.9	42.2	38.8
Mostly Unemployed	41.1	49.0	52.1	46.6	42.7	38.6	39.1	35.3
Mixed	42.9	53.1	48.9	50.7	45.2	45.5	46.2	43.9
Mostly Employed	38.1	43.2	40.6	44.6	41.1	40.5	40.4	36.8
Part-Time Employed	59.9	54.1	54.7	58.7	56.3	56.2	56.2	53.8
Involuntary	36.8	36.5	32.5	44.7	36.2	38.0	37.9	38.0
Voluntary	66.1	59.9	61.3	62.9	61.9	62.2	62.2	60.2
Employed Full-Time	37.2	37.2	36.5	33.8	35.1	35.3	34.8	31.9
Total	46.2	48.1	47.1	47.3	45.3	45.4	45.4	42.0

EARNINGS SUPPLEMENTATION RATE - TRANSFERS

WORK EXPERIENCE PATTERN	1974	1975	1976	1977	1978	1979	1979R	1980
Total								
Not Employed	25.2	31.1	29.2	23.4	19.6	21.2	21.0	17.0
Discouraged	25.5	36.7	31.0	24.3	18.6	19.9	19.4	16.8
Unemployed	24.9	24.4	27.1	22.8	20.4	22.3	22.3	17.2
Intermittently Employed	27.3	34.7	32.1	31.7	25.8	25.9	26.0	25.7
Mostly Unemployed	29.0	37.6	39.1	35.7	31.8	28.0	28.4	26.6
Mixed	28.8	39.0	34.2	34.8	28.7	29.8	29.9	28.1
Mostly Employed	25.2	27.7	24.5	26.7	20.6	22.1	22.0	22.6
Part-Time Employed	33.1	32.3	31.2	33.0	30.2	28.8	28.7	27.5
Involuntary	26.4	27.6	27.6	28.2	23.4	26.8	26.5	24.4
Voluntary	34.5	33.8	32.3	34.2	31.9	29.4	29.3	28.4
Employed Full-Time	25.1	24.3	25.3	25.0	21.3	20.6	20.3	19.9
Total	28.8	31.1	30.0	29.9	26.1	25.7	25.6	24.5
Full-Year								
Not Employed	30.3	39.8	35.3	30.0	18.4	17.4	16.7	19.6
Discouraged	32.1	40.6	35.8	28.2	18.0	17.6	17.0	19.5
Unemployed	22.5	33.8	30.3	38.5	20.6	16.6	15.7	19.6
Intermittently Employed	30.4	39.0	36.7	35.4	29.6	30.2	30.4	28.1
Mostly Unemployed	31.5	39.9	42.3	37.0	32.9	29.5	29.8	27.4
Mixed	31.4	43.9	37.8	38.8	32.8	34.1	34.4	31.8
Mostly Employed	28.2	30.5	27.7	29.9	23.3	26.6	26.7	24.6
Part-Time Employed	36.5	32.6	31.4	33.4	32.3	28.9	28.8	26.5
Involuntary	27.2	26.4	23.9	28.5	24.0	26.6	26.5	22.6
Voluntary	39.0	34.6	33.6	34.9	34.6	29.7	29.5	28.2
Employed Full-Time	21.7	21.5	22.3	20.2	17.8	20.6	20.3	16.7
Total	29.8	33.2	31.6	30.5	27.1	26.9	26.8	24.7

Table C-3. SUMMARY SEVERE HARDSHIP MEASURES, 1974 THROUGH 1980, FOR TOTAL WORK FORCE, DISAGGREGATED BY SEX AND FAMILY RELATIONSHIP

	1974	1975	1976	1977	1978	1979	1979R	1980
WORK FORCE								
Male Family Head	40,887	40,948	40,923	40,796	41,020	41,322	42,051	42,178
Wife In Work Force	23,287	23,483	24,329	24,615	25,318	26,128	26,571	26,768
Wife Not In Work Force	16,513	16,384	15,472	14,955	14,418	13,849	14,118	13,855
Wife Not Present	1,088	1,081	1,121	1,226	1,283	1,345	1,362	1,534
Male Unrelated Individual	6,087	6,384	6,994	7,838	8,430	9,120	9,263	9,638
Other Male	12,575	12,332	12,766	13,040	13,230	13,048	13,424	13,461
Total Male	59,489	59,664	60,683	61,674	62,680	63,490	64,739	65,277
Female Family Head	4,523	4,640	4,790	5,274	5,550	5,859	5,976	6,294
Wife	25,250	25,447	26,416	26,676	27,475	28,308	28,814	29,033
Female Unrelated Individual	5,551	6,047	6,372	6,906	7,395	7,566	7,777	8,082
Other Female	8,788	8,644	8,887	9,132	9,263	9,425	9,676	9,662
Total Female	44,112	44,778	46,465	47,988	49,683	51,158	52,244	53,071
SHARE WORK FORCE								
Male Family Head	39.5	39.2	38.2	37.2	36.5	36.0	35.9	35.6
Wife In Work Force	22.5	22.5	22.7	22.4	22.5	22.8	22.7	22.6
Wife Not In Work Force	15.9	15.7	14.4	13.6	12.8	12.1	12.1	11.7
Wife Not Present	1.1	1.0	1.0	1.1	1.1	1.2	1.2	1.3
Male Unrelated Individual	5.9	6.1	6.5	7.1	7.5	8.0	7.9	8.1
Other Male	12.1	11.8	11.9	11.9	11.8	11.4	11.5	11.4
Total Male	57.4	57.1	56.6	56.2	55.8	55.4	55.3	55.2
Female Family Head	4.4	4.4	4.5	4.8	4.9	5.1	5.1	5.3
Wife	24.4	24.4	24.7	24.3	24.5	24.7	24.6	24.5
Female Unrelated Individual	5.4	5.8	5.9	6.3	6.6	6.6	6.6	6.8
Other Female	8.5	8.3	8.3	8.3	8.3	8.2	8.3	8.2
Total Female	42.7	42.9	43.4	43.8	44.2	44.6	44.7	44.8
UNEMPLOYED								
Male Family Head	5,166	6,306	5,545	4,789	4,320	4,406	4,488	5,712
Wife In Work Force	3,203	3,868	3,466	3,012	2,927	2,922	2,975	3,751
Wife Not In Work Force	1,776	2,235	1,887	1,591	1,234	1,276	1,303	1,646
Wife Not Present	186	203	191	186	157	207	210	315
Male Unrelated Individual	1,368	1,642	1,801	1,862	1,738	1,909	1,947	2,162
Other Male	3,748	3,987	4,047	4,077	3,515	3,448	3,606	4,198
Total Male	10,282	11,935	11,393	10,728	9,573	9,764	10,041	12,072
Female Family Head	998	1,094	1,115	1,198	1,127	1,196	1,226	1,407
Wife	4,044	4,568	4,358	3,974	3,646	3,745	3,833	4,225
Female Unrelated Individual	916	1,112	1,145	1,168	1,191	1,204	1,238	1,366
Other Female	2,296	2,395	2,436	2,445	2,202	2,062	2,129	2,340
Total Female	8,254	9,169	9,054	8,785	8,166	8,208	8,426	9,338
UNEMPLOYMENT RATE								
Male Family Head	12.6	15.4	13.5	11.7	10.5	10.7	10.7	13.5
Wife In Work Force	13.8	16.5	14.2	12.2	11.6	11.2	11.2	14.0
Wife Not In Work Force	10.8	13.6	12.2	10.6	8.6	9.2	9.2	11.9
Wife Not Present	17.1	18.8	17.0	15.2	12.2	15.4	15.4	20.2
Male Unrelated Individual	22.5	25.7	25.8	23.8	20.6	20.9	21.0	22.4
Other Male	29.9	32.3	31.7	31.2	26.6	26.4	26.9	31.2
Total Male	17.3	20.0	18.8	17.4	15.3	15.5	15.5	18.5
Female Family Head	22.1	23.6	23.3	22.7	20.3	20.7	20.5	22.4
Wife	16.0	18.0	16.4	14.9	13.3	13.3	13.3	14.6
Female Unrelated Individual	16.5	18.4	18.0	16.9	16.1	15.9	15.9	16.9
Other Female	26.1	27.6	27.4	26.8	23.8	21.9	22.0	24.2
Total Female	18.7	20.5	19.5	18.3	16.4	16.0	16.1	17.6

Table C-3. (Continued)

SHARE OF UNEMPLOYED

Male Family Head	27.9	29.9	27.1	24.5	24.4	24.5	24.3	26.7
Wife In Work Force	17.3	18.3	17.0	15.4	16.5	16.3	16.1	17.5
Wife Not In Work Force	9.6	10.6	9.2	8.2	7.0	7.1	7.1	7.7
Wife Not Present	1.0	1.0	.9	1.0	.9	1.2	1.1	1.5
Male Unrelated Individual	7.4	7.8	8.8	9.5	9.8	10.6	10.5	10.1
Other Male	20.2	18.9	19.8	20.9	19.8	19.2	19.5	19.6
Total Male	55.5	56.6	55.7	55.0	54.0	54.3	54.4	56.4
Female Family Head	5.4	5.2	5.5	6.1	6.4	6.7	6.6	6.6
Wife	21.8	21.6	21.3	20.4	20.6	20.8	20.8	19.7
Female Unrelated Individual	4.9	5.3	5.6	6.0	6.7	6.7	6.7	6.4
Other Female	12.4	11.3	11.9	12.5	12.4	11.5	11.5	10.9
Total Female	44.5	43.4	44.3	45.0	46.0	45.7	45.6	43.6

PREDOMINANTLY UNEMPLOYED

Male Family Head	1,611	2,750	2,313	1,780	1,477	1,325	1,348	2,255
Wife In Work Force	921	1,660	1,379	1,067	947	833	846	1,440
Wife Not In Work Force	604	992	835	630	450	408	417	646
Wife Not Present	86	98	99	83	79	83	87	169
Male Unrelated Individual	521	777	865	787	683	678	687	1,013
Other Male	1,779	2,453	2,391	2,166	1,816	1,663	1,746	2,375
Total Male	3,911	5,980	5,569	4,733	3,976	3,666	3,781	5,643
Female Family Head	518	678	646	696	597	609	626	833
Wife	1,852	2,432	2,240	1,936	1,606	1,610	1,648	2,065
Female Unrelated Individual	355	514	481	483	459	396	406	535
Other Female	1,105	1,336	1,319	1,283	1,113	994	1,031	1,271
Total Female	3,830	4,960	4,686	4,398	3,775	3,609	3,711	4,704

INCIDENCE PREDOMINANTLY UNEMPLOYED

Male Family Head	3.9	6.7	5.7	4.4	3.6	3.2	3.2	5.3
Wife In Work Force	4.0	7.1	5.7	4.3	3.7	3.2	3.2	5.4
Wife Not In Work Force	3.7	6.1	5.4	4.2	3.1	2.9	3.0	4.7
Wife Not Present	7.9	9.1	8.8	6.8	6.2	6.2	6.4	10.9
Male Unrelated Individual	8.6	12.2	12.4	10.0	8.1	7.4	7.4	10.5
Other Male	14.2	19.9	18.7	16.6	13.7	12.7	13.0	17.6
Total Male	6.6	10.0	9.2	7.7	6.3	5.8	5.8	8.6
Female Family Head	11.5	14.6	13.5	13.2	10.8	10.4	10.4	13.2
Wife	7.3	9.6	8.5	7.3	5.8	5.7	5.7	7.1
Female Unrelated Individual	6.4	8.5	7.5	7.0	6.2	5.2	5.2	6.6
Other Female	12.6	15.5	14.8	14.0	12.0	10.5	10.7	13.2
Total Female	8.7	11.1	10.1	9.2	7.6	7.1	7.1	8.9

SHARE PREDOMINANTLY UNEMPLOYED

Male Family Head	20.8	25.1	22.6	19.5	19.1	18.2	18.0	21.8
Wife In Work Force	11.9	15.2	13.4	11.7	12.2	11.4	11.3	13.9
Wife Not In Work Force	7.8	9.1	8.1	6.9	5.8	5.6	5.6	6.2
Wife Not Present	1.1	.9	1.0	.9	1.0	1.1	1.2	1.6
Male Unrelated Individual	6.7	7.1	8.4	8.6	8.8	9.3	9.2	9.8
Other Male	23.0	22.4	23.3	23.7	23.4	22.9	23.3	23.0
Total Male	50.5	54.7	54.3	51.8	51.3	50.4	50.5	54.5
Female Family Head	6.7	6.2	6.3	7.6	7.7	8.4	8.4	8.0
Wife	23.9	22.2	21.8	21.2	20.7	22.1	22.0	20.0
Female Unrelated Individual	4.6	4.7	4.7	5.3	5.9	5.4	5.4	5.2
Other Female	14.3	12.2	12.9	14.0	14.4	13.7	13.8	12.3
Total Female	49.5	45.3	45.7	48.2	48.7	49.6	49.5	45.4

Table C-3. (Continued)

IIE

Male Family Head	3,981	4,885	4,476	4,324	4,036	3,807	3,901	4,892
Wife In Work Force	2,317	2,885	2,711	2,649	2,522	2,336	2,393	3,007
Wife Not In Work Force	1,487	1,798	1,550	1,478	1,319	1,251	1,281	1,561
Wife Not Present	177	201	215	196	196	220	227	324
Male Unrelated Individual	1,318	1,580	1,598	1,756	1,696	1,728	1,744	2,046
Other Male	5,371	6,197	6,247	6,224	5,763	5,519	5,706	6,666
Total Male	10,670	12,662	12,321	12,304	11,495	11,054	11,352	13,604
Female Family Head	1,567	1,722	1,660	1,780	1,774	1,748	1,795	2,196
Wife	8,377	8,979	9,043	9,170	8,687	8,372	8,534	9,344
Female Unrelated Individual	1,608	1,926	1,909	2,070	2,000	1,905	1,963	2,326
Other Female	4,533	5,057	4,960	5,004	4,703	4,497	4,624	5,277
Total Female	16,085	17,684	17,572	18,024	17,164	16,522	16,917	19,143

IIE INCIDENCE

Male Family Head	9.7	11.9	10.9	10.6	9.8	9.2	9.3	11.6
Wife In Work Force	9.9	12.3	11.1	19.8	10.0	8.9	9.0	11.2
Wife Not In Work Force	9.0	11.0	10.0	9.9	9.1	9.0	9.1	11.3
Wife Not Present	16.3	18.6	19.2	16.0	15.2	16.4	16.7	20.8
Male Unrelated Individual	21.7	24.7	22.9	22.4	20.1	18.9	18.8	21.2
Other Male	42.9	50.3	48.9	47.7	43.6	42.3	42.5	49.5
Total Male	17.9	21.2	20.3	20.0	18.3	17.4	17.5	20.8
Female Family Head	34.7	37.1	34.7	33.7	32.0	29.8	30.0	34.9
Wife	33.2	35.3	34.2	34.4	31.6	29.6	29.6	32.2
Female Unrelated Individual	29.0	31.8	30.0	30.0	27.0	25.2	25.2	28.8
Other Female	51.6	58.5	55.8	54.8	50.8	47.7	47.8	54.6
Total Female	36.5	39.5	37.8	37.6	34.5	32.3	32.4	36.1

IIE SHARE

Male Family Head	14.9	16.1	15.0	14.3	14.1	13.8	13.8	14.9
Wife In Work Force	8.7	9.5	9.1	8.7	8.8	8.5	8.5	9.2
Wife Not In Work Force	5.6	5.9	5.2	4.9	4.6	4.5	4.5	4.8
Wife Not Present	.7	.7	.7	.6	.7	.8	.8	1.0
Male Unrelated Individual	4.9	5.2	5.3	5.8	5.9	6.3	6.2	6.2
Other Male	20.1	20.4	20.9	20.5	20.1	20.0	20.2	20.4
Total Male	39.9	41.7	41.2	40.6	40.1	40.1	40.2	41.5
Female Family Head	5.9	5.7	5.6	5.9	6.2	6.4	6.3	6.7
Wife	31.3	29.6	30.3	30.2	30.3	30.4	30.2	28.5
Female Unrelated Individual	6.0	6.3	6.4	6.8	7.0	6.9	6.9	7.1
Other Female	16.9	16.7	16.6	16.5	16.4	16.3	16.4	16.1
Total Female	60.1	58.3	58.8	59.4	59.9	59.9	59.8	58.5

IIE DEFICIT

Male Family Head	8,214	11,143	11,172	11,254	10,708	11,058	11,270	16,254
Wife In Work Force	4,885	6,836	7,011	7,243	7,108	6,958	7,087	10,534
Wife Not In Work Force	2,979	3,911	3,667	3,498	3,127	3,539	3,605	4,737
Wife Not Present	351	396	494	514	473	561	578	982
Male Unrelated Individual	2,320	3,177	3,336	3,644	3,426	4,232	4,255	5,755
Other Male	6,239	8,594	9,574	9,215	8,368	9,329	9,665	13,524
Total Male	16,773	22,914	24,082	24,113	22,502	24,619	25,190	35,533
Female Family Head	1,931	2,460	2,424	2,802	2,771	2,857	2,943	4,788
Wife	9,522	12,374	12,648	13,642	12,842	14,396	14,608	17,798
Female Unrelated Individual	2,027	3,171	3,071	3,201	3,214	3,339	3,443	5,050
Other Female	3,775	5,174	5,243	5,527	5,302	5,619	5,815	7,478
Total Female	17,255	23,179	23,386	25,172	24,129	26,211	26,809	35,114

Table C-3. (Continued)

	1974	1975	1976	1977	1978	1979	1979R	1980
IIE DEFICIT (1980 $)								
Male Family Head	13,726	17,061	16,176	15,305	13,524	12,550	12,792	16,254
Wife In Work Force	8,101	10,466	10,153	9,850	8,977	7,897	8,044	10,534
Wife Not In Work Force	4,977	5,988	5,309	4,757	3,949	4,017	4,092	4,737
Wife Not Present	586	606	715	699	598	636	656	982
Male Unrelated Individual	3,877	4,864	4,830	4,956	4,327	4,804	4,829	5,755
Other Male	10,425	13,157	13,863	12,532	10,569	10,588	10,970	13,524
Total Male	28,028	35,081	34,871	32,794	28,420	27,943	28,591	35,533
Female Family Head	3,227	3,766	3,509	3,810	3,500	3,243	3,341	4,788
Wife	15,911	18,944	18,314	18,552	16,219	16,339	16,580	17,798
Female Unrelated Individual	3,387	4,855	4,446	4,354	4,059	3,789	3,908	5,050
Other Female	6,308	7,921	7,592	7,517	6,696	6,378	6,600	7,478
Total Female	28,833	35,487	33,863	3,423	30,475	29,749	30,428	35,114
IIE DEFICIT SHARE								
Male Family Head	24.1	24.2	23.5	22.8	23.0	21.8	21.7	23.0
Wife In Work Force	14.4	14.8	14.8	14.7	15.2	13.7	13.6	14.9
Wife Not In Work Force	8.8	8.5	7.7	7.1	6.7	7.0	6.9	6.7
Wife Not Present	1.0	.9	1.0	1.0	1.0	1.1	1.1	1.4
Male Unrelated Individual	6.8	6.9	7.0	7.4	7.3	8.3	8.2	8.1
Other Male	18.3	18.6	20.0	18.6	17.9	18.4	18.6	19.1
Total Male	49.3	49.7	50.7	48.9	48.3	48.4	48.4	50.3
Female Family Head	5.7	5.3	5.1	5.7	5.9	5.6	5.7	6.8
Wife	28.0	26.8	26.6	27.7	27.5	28.3	28.1	25.2
Female Unrelated Individual	6.0	6.9	6.5	6.5	6.9	6.6	6.6	7.1
Other Female	11.1	11.2	11.0	11.2	.11.4	11.1	11.2	10.6
Total Female	50.7	50.3	49.3	51.1	51.7	51.6	51.6	49.7
IIE AVERAGE DEFICIT								
Male Family Head	2,063	2,281	2,496	2,603	2,653	2,905	2,889	3,323
Wife In Work Force	2,108	2,369	2,587	2,734	2,818	2,979	2,961	3,503
Wife Not In Work Force	2,003	2,175	2,365	2,366	2,371	2,829	2,814	3,035
Wife Not Present	1,977	1,966	2,294	2,619	2,418	2,545	2,549	3,032
Male Unrelated Individual	1,760	2,011	2,087	2,076	2,020	2,449	2,440	2,813
Other Male	1,162	-1,387	1,533	1,481	1,452	1,690	1,694	2,029
Total Male	1,572	1,810	1,955	1,960	1,958	2,227	2,219	2,612
Female Family Head	1,232	1,429	1,460	1,574	1,562	1,634	1,639	2,180
Wife	1,137	1,378	1,399	1,488	1,478	1,719	1,712	1,905
Female Unrelated Individual	1,260	1,647	1,608	1,547	1,607	1,753	1,754	2,171
Other Female	833	1,023	1,057	1,105	1,127	1,250	1,257	1,417
Total Female	1,073	1,311	1,331	1,397	1,406	1,586	1,585	1,834
IIE AVERAGE DEFICIT (1980 $)								
Male Family Head	3,447	3,492	3,614	3,540	3,351	3,297	3,279	3,323
Wife In Work Force	3,522	3,627	3,746	3,718	3,559	3,381	3,361	3,503
Wife Not In Work Force	3,347	3,330	3,425	3,218	2,995	3,211	3,194	3,035
Wife Not Present	3,303	3,010	3,322	3,562	3,054	2,889	2,893	3,032
Male Unrelated Individual	2,941	3,079	3,022	2,823	2,551	2,780	2,769	2,813
Other Male	1,942	2,123	2,220	2,014	1,834	1,918	1,923	2,029
Total Male	2,627	2,771	2,831	2,666	2,473	2,528	2,519	2,612
Female Family Head	2,059	2,188	2,114	2,141	1,973	1,855	1,860	2,180
Wife	1,900	2,110	2,026	2,024	1,867	1,951	1,943	1,905
Female Unrelated Individual	2,105	2,522	2,328	2,104	2,030	1,990	1,991	2,171
Other Female	1,392	1,566	1,531	1,503	1,423	1,419	1,427	1,417
Total Female	1,793	2,007	1,927	1,900	1,776	1,800	1,799	1,834
IFE								
Male Family Head	3,234	3,933	3,406	3,366	3,056	3,170	3,250	3,764
Wife In Work Force	1,093	1,411	1,176	1,230	1,107	1,073	1,098	1,374
Wife Not In Work Force	2,001	2,381	2,084	1,990	1,799	1,919	1,969	2,146
Wife Not Present	139	141	146	146	150	178	182	243
Male Unrelated Individual	1,289	1,417	1,540	1,538	1,561	1,559	1,592	1,705
Other Male	1,460	1,636	1,647	1,618	1,528	1,405	1,463	1,789
Total Male	5,984	6,987	6,593	6,522	6,145	6,134	6,305	7,258
Female Family Head	1,748	1,751	1,791	1,880	1,902	1,959	2,012	2,212
Wife	1,739	2,065	1,929	1,972	1,845	1,828	1,875	2,177
Female Unrelated Individual	1,493	1,813	1,914	1,967	1,969	1,861	1,913	2,106
Other Female	1,043	1,151	1,175	1,152	1,160	1,132	1,175	1,359
Total Female	6,024	6,781	6,809	6,971	6,876	6,780	6,975	7,854

Table C-3. (Continued)

IFE INCIDENCE

Male Family Head	7.9	9.6	8.3	8.3	7.4	7.7	7.7	8.9
Wife In Work Force	4.7	6.0	4.8	5.0	4.4	4.1	4.1	5.1
Wife Not In Work Force	12.1	14.5	13.5	13.3	12.5	13.9	13.9	15.5
Wife Not Present	12.8	13.0	13.0	11.9	11.7	13.3	13.4	15.6
Male Unrelated Individual	21.2	22.2	22.0	19.6	18.5	17.1	17.2	17.7
Other Male	11.7	13.3	12.9	12.4	11.5	10.8	10.9	13.3
Total Male	10.1	11.7	10.9	10.6	9.8	9.7	9.7	11.1
Female Family Head	38.7	37.7	37.4	35.7	34.3	33.4	33.7	35.1
Wife	6.9	8.1	7.3	7.4	6.7	6.5	6.5	7.5
Female Unrelated Individual	26.9	30.0	30.0	28.5	26.6	24.6	24.6	26.1
Other Female	11.9	13.3	13.2	12.6	12.5	12.0	12.1	14.1
Total Female	13.9	15.1	14.7	14.5	13.8	13.3	13.4	14.8

IFE SHARE

Male Family Head	26.9	28.6	25.4	24.9	23.5	24.5	24.5	24.9
Wife In Work Force	9.1	10.2	8.8	9.1	8.5	8.3	8.3	9.1
Wife Not In Work Force	16.7	17.3	15.5	14.7	13.8	14.9	14.8	14.2
Wife Not Present	1.2	1.0	1.1	1.1	1.2	1.4	1.4	1.6
Male Unrelated Individual	10.7	10.3	11.5	11.4	12.0	12.1	12.0	11.3
Other Male	12.2	11.9	12.3	12.0	11.7	10.9	11.0	11.8
Total Male	49.8	50.7	49.2	48.3	45.5	47.5	47.5	48.0
Female Family Head	14.6	12.7	13.4	13.9	14.6	15.2	15.2	14.6
Wife	14.5	15.0	14.4	14.6	14.2	14.2	14.1	14.4
Female Unrelated Individual	12.4	13.2	14.3	14.6	15.1	14.4	14.4	13.9
Other Female	8.7	8.4	8.8	8.5	8.9	8.8	8.8	9.0
Total Female	50.2	49.3	50.8	51.7	54.5	52.5	52.5	52.0

IFE DEFICIT

Male Family Head	5,693	7,780	7,240	7,281	6,979	8,105	8,284	11,249
Wife In Work Force	1,339	1,885	1,735	1,909	1,742	1,917	1,952	2,937
Wife Not In Work Force	4,110	5,636	5,186	5,065	4,910	5,751	5,882	7,623
Wife Not Present	244	259	319	307	328	438	450	689
Male Unrelated Individual	1,793	2,298	2,597	2,723	2,784	3,194	3,252	4,144
Other Male	2,235	3,141	3,076	3,324	3,488	3,468	3,626	4,827
Total Male	9,721	13,219	12,913	13,328	13,251	14,767	15,162	20,220
Female Family Head	4,168	4,533	4,746	5,346	5,757	6,460	6,657	8,538
Wife	2,031	2,437	2,440	2,725	2,786	3,158	3,222	4,039
Female Unrelated Individual	2,129	2,864	3,084	3,249	3,442	3,656	3,756	4,722
Other Female	1,652	1,872	2,272	2,254	2,533	2,761	2,859	3,481
Total Female	9,980	11,706	12,542	13,574	14,518	16,035	16,494	20,780

IFE DEFICIT (1980 $)

Male Family Head	9,514	11,911	10,483	9,903	8,815	9,199	9,402	11,249
Wife In Work Force	2,237	2,886	2,512	2,596	2,220	2,175	2,215	2,937
Wife Not In Work Force	6,868	8,629	7,509	6,888	6,201	6,527	6,676	7,623
Wife Not Present	409	397	462	418	414	497	510	689
Male Unrelated Individual	2,996	3,518	3,761	3,704	3,516	3,625	3,691	4,144
Other Male	3,735	4,809	4,454	4,521	4,405	3,936	4,115	4,827
Total Male	16,244	20,238	18,698	18,126	16,736	16,761	17,209	20,220
Female Family Head	6,964	6,939	6,872	7,270	7,271	7,332	7,555	8,538
Wife	3,393	3,731	3,534	3,707	3,518	3,584	3,657	4,039
Female Unrelated Individual	3,558	4,385	4,465	4,418	4,347	4,149	4,264	4,722
Other Female	2,760	2,866	3,290	3,065	3,199	3,134	3,245	3,481
Total Female	16,677	17,922	18,161	18,461	18,336	18,200	18,721	20,780

Table C-3. (Continued)

IFE DEFICIT SHARE

Male Family Head	28.9	31.2	28.4	27.1	25.1	26.3	26.2	27.4
Wife In Work Force	6.8	7.6	6.8	7.1	6.3	6.2	6.2	7.2
Wife Not In Work Force	20.9	22.6	20.4	18.8	17.7	18.7	18.6	18.6
Wife Not Present	1.2	1.0	1.3	1.1	1.2	1.4	1.4	1.7
Male Unrelated Individual	9.1	9.2	10.2	10.1	10.0	10.4	10.3	10.1
Other Male	11.3	12.6	12.1	12.4	12.6	11.3	11.5	11.8
Total Male	49.3	53.0	50.7	49.5	47.7	47.9	47.9	49.3
Female Family Head	21.2	18.2	18.6	19.9	20.7	21.0	21.0	20.8
Wife	10.3	9.8	9.6	10.1	10.0	10.3	10.2	9.9
Female Unrelated Individual	10.8	11.5	12.1	12.1	12.4	11.9	11.9	11.5
Other Female	9.9	7.5	8.9	8.4	9.1	9.0	9.0	8.5
Total Female	50.7	47.0	49.3	50.5	52.3	52.1	52.1	50.7

IFE AVERAGE DEFICIT

Male Family Head	1,760	1,978	2,125	2,163	2,284	2,557	2,549	2,989
Wife In Work Force	1,225	1,335	1,476	1,552	1,574	1,786	1,777	2,137
Wife Not In Work Force	2,054	2,367	2,488	2,545	2,729	2,997	2,987	3,552
Wife Not Present	1,753	1,842	2,184	2,110	2,185	2,455	2,465	2,838
Male Unrelated Individual	1,391	1,621	1,687	1,771	1,783	2,048	2,043	2,431
Other Male	1,530	1,920	1,868	2,054	2,283	2,469	2,479	2,698
Total Male	1,625	1,892	1,959	2,044	2,156	2,407	2,405	2,786
Female Family Head	2,384	2,588	2,650	2,843	3,027	3,298	3,308	3,861
Wife	1,168	1,180	1,265	1,382	1,510	1,727	1,718	1,856
Female Unrelated Individual	1,426	1,580	1,611	1,651	1,749	1,965	1,964	2,242
Other Female	1,583	1,626	1,933	1,956	2,189	2,439	2,434	2,562
Total Female	1,657	1,726	1,842	1,973	2,111	2,365	2,365	2,574

IFE AVERAGE DEFICIT (1980 $)

Male Family Head	2,941	3,028	3,077	2,942	2,885	2,902	2,893	2,989
Wife In Work Force	2,047	2,044	2,137	2,111	1,987	2,027	2,017	2,137
Wife Not In Work Force	3,432	3,624	3,603	3,461	3,446	3,402	3,390	3,552
Wife Not Present	2,929	2,820	3,162	2,870	2,760	2,786	2,798	2,838
Male Unrelated Individual	2,324	2,482	2,443	2,409	2,252	2,324	2,319	2,431
Other Male	2,557	2,940	2,705	2,793	2,883	2,802	2,814	2,698
Total Male	2,715	2,897	2,837	2,780	2,723	2,732	2,730	2,786
Female Family Head	3,984	3,962	3,837	3,866	3,823	3,743	3,755	3,861
Wife	1,952	1,807	1,832	1,880	1,907	1,960	1,950	1,856
Female Unrelated Individual	2,383	2,419	2,333	2,245	2,209	2,230	2,228	2,242
Other Female	2,645	2,489	2,799	2,660	2,758	2,768	2,763	2,562
Total Female	2,769	2,643	2,667	2,683	2,666	2,684	2,684	2,574

IFI

Male Family Head	1,646	1,955	1,724	1,664	1,531	1,600	1,638	2,023
Wife In Work Force	628	782	710	719	664	656	670	834
Wife Not In Work Force	952	1,118	919	866	794	838	860	1,049
Wife Not Present	65	54	94	79	73	105	108	140
Male Unrelated Individual	829	903	980	1,017	1,053	1,043	1,058	1,173
Other Male	666	781	702	688	663	630	667	863
Total Male	3,141	3,638	3,406	3,369	3,247	3,273	3,363	4,059
Female Family Head	1,089	1,094	1,118	1,184	1,290	1,287	1,330	1,553
Wife	766	919	856	849	819	797	815	978
Female Unrelated Individual	839	1,051	1,096	1,062	1,109	1,026	1,055	1,230
Other Female	511	551	556	534	547	469	492	644
Total Female	3,205	3,614	3,626	3,629	3,765	3,579	3,692	4,405

Table C-3. (Continued)

IFI INCIDENCE

Male Family Head	4.0	4.8	4.2	4.1	3.7	3.9	3.9	4.8
Wife In Work Force	2.7	3.3	2.9	2.9	2.6	2.5	2.5	3.1
Wife Not In Work Force	5.8	6.8	5.9	5.8	5.5	6.1	6.1	7.6
Wife Not Present	6.0	5.0	8.4	6.4	5.7	7.8	7.9	9.0
Male Unrelated Individual	13.6	14.1	14.0	13.0	12.5	11.4	11.4	12.2
Other Male	5.3	6.3	5.5	5.3	5.0	4.8	5.2	6.4
Total Male	5.3	6.1	5.6	5.4	5.2	5.2	5.1	6.2
Female Family Head	24.1	23.6	23.3	22.4	23.2	22.0	22.3	24.7
Wife	3.0	3.6	3.2	3.2	3.0	2.8	2.8	3.4
Female Unrelated Individual	15.1	17.4	17.2	15.4	15.0	13.6	13.6	15.2
Other Female	5.8	6.4	6.3	5.8	5.9	5.0	5.1	6.7
Total Female	7.3	8.1	7.8	7.6	7.6	7.0	7.1	8.3

IFI SHARE

Male Family Head	25.9	27.0	24.5	23.8	21.8	23.3	23.2	23.9
Wife In Work Force	9.9	10.8	10.1	10.3	9.5	9.6	9.5	9.9
Wife Not In Work Force	15.0	15.4	13.1	12.4	11.3	12.2	12.2	12.4
Wife Not Present	1.0	.7	1.3	1.1	1.0	1.5	1.5	1.7
Male Unrelated Individual	13.1	12.5	13.9	14.5	15.0	15.2	15.0	13.9
Other Male	10.5	10.8	10.0	9.8	9.5	9.2	9.5	10.2
Total Male	49.5	50.2	48.4	48.1	46.3	47.8	47.7	48.0
Female Family Head	17.2	15.1	15.9	16.9	18.4	18.9	18.9	18.3
Wife	12.1	12.7	12.2	12.1	11.7	11.6	11.6	11.6
Female Unrelated Individual	13.2	14.5	15.6	15.2	15.8	15.0	15.0	14.5
Other Female	8.1	7.6	7.9	7.6	7.8	6.8	7.0	7.6
Total Female	50.5	49.8	51.6	51.9	53.7	52.2	52.3	52.0

IFI DEFICIT

Male Family Head	2,583	3,152	2,944	3,104	2,975	3,643	3,713	5,200
Wife in Work Force	738	10,025	987	1,082	983	1,184	1,208	1,731
Wife Not in Work Force	1,760	2,076	1,807	1,858	1,885	2,254	2,293	3,167
Wife Not Present	85	74	151	164	106	205	212	302
Male Unrelated Individual	961	1,170	1,298	1,496	1,477	1,865	1,878	2,914
Other Male	594	803	704	733	790	822	874	1,372
Total Male	4,138	5,125	4,946	5,333	5,242	6,330	6,465	8,986
Female Family Head	1,820	1,922	1,981	2,312	2,733	3,040	3,147	4,211
Wife	492	672	566	699	754	846	845	1,108
Female Unrelated Individual	842	1,294	1,473	1,371	1,524	1,591	1,640	2,172
Other Female	421	525	607	642	774	691	728	977
Total Female	3,575	4,413	4,627	5,024	5,785	6,168	6,360	8,467

IFI DEFICIT (1980$)

Male Family Head	4,316	4,826	4,263	4,221	3,757	4,135	4,214	5,200
Wife in Work Force	1,233	1,535	1,429	1,471	1,242	1,344	1,371	1,731
Wife Not in Work Force	2,940	3,178	2,616	2,527	2,381	2,558	2,603	3,167
Wife Not Present	142	114	219	223	134	233	241	302
Male Unrelated Individual	1,605	1,791	1,879	2,035	1,866	2,117	2,131	2,414
Other Male	992	1,229	820	997	998	933	992	1,372
Total Male	6,914	7,846	7,162	7,253	6,621	7,185	7,338	8,986
Female Family Head	3,041	2,942	2,868	3,144	3,451	3,451	3,572	4,211
Wife	823	705	820	951	953	960	959	1,108
Female Unrelated Individual	1,408	1,981	2,133	1,864	1,925	1,806	1,861	2,172
Other Female	704	804	879	873	978	784	826	977
Total Female	5,974	6,756	6,700	6,833	7,308	7,001	7,218	8,467

Table C-3. (Continued)

IFI DEFICIT SHARE

Male Family Head	33.5	33.1	30.8	30.0	27.0	29.1	29.0	29.8
Wife in Work Force	9.6	10.5	10.3	10.4	8.9	9.5	9.4	9.9
Wife Not in Work Force	22.8	21.8	18.9	17.9	17.1	18.0	17.9	18.1
Wife Not Present	1.1	.8	1.6	1.6	1.5	1.6	1.7	1.7
Male Unrelated Individual	12.5	12.3	13.6	14.4	13.4	14.9	14.6	13.8
Other Male	7.7	8.4	7.4	7.1	7.2	6.6	6.8	7.9
Total Male	52.6	53.7	51.7	51.5	47.5	50.6	50.4	51.5
Female Family Head	23.6	20.2	20.7	22.3	24.8	24.3	24.5	24.1
Wife	6.4	7.0	5.9	6.8	6.8	6.8	6.6	6.3
Female Unrelated Individual	10.9	13.6	15.4	13.2	13.8	12.7	12.8	12.4
Other Female	5.5	5.5	6.3	6.2	7.0	5.4	5.7	5.6
Total Female	47.4	46.3	48.3	48.5	52.5	49.4	49.6	48.5

IFI AVERAGE DEFICIT

Male Family Head	1,569	1,613	1,708	1,865	1,944	2,277	2,267	2,570
Wife in Work Force	1,175	1,281	1,389	1,504	1,481	1,804	1,802	2,076
Wife Not in Work Force	1,848	1,856	1,965	2,146	2,375	2,688	2,668	3,018
Wife Not Present	1,301	1,371	1,607	2,080	1,462	1,952	1,963	2,160
Male Unrelated Individual	1,158	1,296	1,324	1,471	1,403	1,788	1,774	2,057
Other Male	891	1,028	1,003	1,066	1,191	1,304	1,311	1,591
Total Male	1,291	1,408	1,452	1,583	1,618	1,934	1,922	2,214
Female Family Head	1,671	1,757	1,771	1,953	2,118	2,362	2,367	2,711
Wife	643	732	662	823	.921	1,062	1,037	1,132
Female Unrelated Individual	1,003	1,231	1,343	1,291	1,374	1,552	1,554	1,765
Other Female	826	954	1,090	1,202	1,416	1,473	1,480	1,516
Total Female	1,115	1,221	1,276	1,384	1,537	1,723	1,723	1,922

IFI AVERAGE DEFICIT (1980$)

Male Family Head	2,622	2,470	2,473	2,536	2,455	2,584	2,573	2,570
Wife in Fork Force	1,963	1,961	2,011	2,045	1,871	2,048	2,045	2,076
Wife Not in Work Force	3,088	2,842	2,845	2,919	3,000	3,051	3,028	3,018
Wife Not Present	2,174	2,099	2,327	2,829	1,847	2,216	2,228	2,160
Male Unrelated Individual	1,935	1,984	1,917	2,001	1,772	2,029	2,013	2,057
Other Male	1,489	1,574	1,452	1,450	1,504	1,480	1,488	1,591
Total Male	2,157	2,156	2,102	2,152	2,044	2,195	2,181	2,214
Female Family Head	2,792	2,690	2,564	2,656	2,675	2,681	2,687	2,711
Wife	1,074	1,121	959	1,119	1,163	1,205	1,177	1,132
Female Unrelated Individual	1,676	1,885	1,945	1,756	1,735	1,762	1,764	1,756
Other Female	1,380	1,461	1,578	1,635	1,788	1,672	1,680	1,516
Total Female	1,863	1,869	1,848	1,882	1,941	1,956	1,956	1,922

IIE IN IFE

Male Family Head	51.6	54.8	51.6	52.5	49.8	50.1	49.9	51.6
Wife in Work Force	35.5	37.4	33.9	37.1	33.7	33.7	33.6	35.6
Wife Not in Work Force	76.0	82.8	81.8	79.0	79.3	79.0	78.8	80.8
Wife Not Present	58.2	54.7	55.3	60.7	56.6	59.1	58.6	59.3
Male Unrelated Individual	68.3	69.7	72.8	67.0	66.6	65.9	66.1	66.3
Other Male	20.0	22.0	21.4	20.7	20.9	19.1	19.1	22.2
Total Male	37.7	40.6	39.0	38.5	37.8	37.1	36.9	39.5
Female Family Head	80.1	77.6	76.4	77.1	75.8	79.3	79.4	77.4
Wife	14.8	17.0	15.3	15.4	14.9	14.8	14.9	17.2
Female Unrelated Individual	67.5	69.8	72.9	70.3	71.6	69.7	69.5	69.8
Other Female	17.2	18.6	19.6	18.7	18.8	18.5	18.9	21.0
Total Female	27.1	29.1	28.6	28.7	28.8	29.0	29.1	31.6

Table C-3. (Continued)

EARNINGS SUPPLEMENTATION RATE - TOTAL

Male Family Head	49.1	50.3	49.4	50.6	49.9	49.5	49.6	46.3
Wife in Work Force	42.6	44.6	39.6	41.5	40.0	38.8	39.0	39.3
Wife Not in Work Force	52.4	53.1	55.9	56.5	55.9	58.3	56.4	51.1
Wife Not Present	53.1	61.5	35.6	46.0	51.6	41.1	40.8	42.5
Male Unrelated Individual	35.6	36.3	36.3	33.9	32.6	33.1	33.5	31.2
Other Male	54.4	52.3	57.4	57.5	56.6	55.1	54.4	51.8
Total Male	47.5	47.9	48.3	48.3	47.2	46.6	46.7	44.1
Female Family Head	37.7	37.6	37.5	37.1	32.1	34.3	33.9	29.8
Wife	56.0	55.5	55.6	56.9	55.6	56.4	56.5	55.1
Female Unrelated Individual	43.8	42.0	42.7	46.0	43.6	44.9	44.8	41.6
Other Female	51.0	52.2	53.7	53.6	52.9	58.5	58.1	52.6
Total Female	46.8	46.7	46.7	47.9	45.2	47.2	47.1	43.9

EARNINGS SUPPLEMENTATION RATE - TRANSFERS

Male Family Head	27.6	32.6	29.2	29.4	27.0	25.3	25.3	23.7
Wife in Work Force	24.3	30.6	25.4	23.9	19.7	20.4	20.6	20.6
Wife Not in Work Force	29.1	33.5	31.6	32.7	30.9	28.2	28.2	25.5
Wife Not Present	32.3	38.8	25.6	30.1	35.5	24.0	23.8	24.9
Male Unrelated Individual	20.5	23.9	21.1	22.0	18.1	15.4	15.4	17.1
Other Male	36.0	37.1	39.1	42.0	37.3	35.8	35.0	31.8
Total Male	28.1	31.9	30.4	30.7	27.3	25.3	25.0	24.1
Female Family Head	24.5	24.6	24.2	24.3	19.5	21.7	21.5	16.8
Wife	34.2	36.8	35.8	34.0	29.0	29.9	29.8	30.0
Female Unrelated Individual	26.4	25.7	24.6	25.7	23.0	22.5	22.4	22.5
Other Female	34.4	34.2	35.8	33.7	37.5	34.1	34.0	33.0
Total Female	29.5	30.3	29.6	29.2	25.1	26.2	26.1	24.8

Table C-4. SUMMARY SEVERE HARDSHIP MEASURES, 1974 THROUGH 1980, FOR TOTAL WORK FORCE DISAGGREGATED BY FAMILY SIZE AND NUMBER OF EARNERS

	1974	1975	1976	1977	1978	1979	1979R	1980
WORK FORCE								
One Family Member In Work Force	30,792	31,782	31,965	33,294	34,349	34,895	35,655	36,550
One In Family	11,638	12,431	13,366	14,744	15,825	16,686	17,041	17,720
Two In Family	7,673	7,813	7,604	7,802	8,004	8,106	8,287	8,340
Three In Family	4,228	4,208	4,239	4,168	492	4,107	4,201	4,427
Four Or Five In Family	5,860	5,942	5,577	5,474	5,359	5,101	5,215	5,190
Six Or More In Family	1,393	1,388	1,179	1,106	969	895	911	872
Two Family Members in Work Force	46,009	45,701	47,082	47,619	49,347	49,988	51,073	51,899
Two In Family	17,403	17,205	17,888	18,169	18,687	19,010	19,448	19,518
Three In Family	11,323	11,405	11,506	11,854	12,589	13,074	13,359	13,668
Four Or Five In Family	13,829	13,910	14,746	14,972	15,592	15,631	15,927	16,349
Six Or More In Family	3,455	3,181	2,942	2,623	2,478	2,273	2,338	2,364
Three Or More In Work Force	26,799	26,958	28,101	28,750	28,666	29,766	30,255	29,899
Three In Family	5,244	5,343	5,545	5,791	5,897	6,382	6,503	6,664
Four Or Five In Family	13,513	13,667	14,182	15,309	15,339	15,789	15,977	15,846
Six Or More Family	8,042	7,949	8,373	7,650	7,431	7,595	7,775	7,388
SHARE WORK FORCE								
One Family Member In Work Force	29.7	30.4	29.8	30.4	30.6	30.4	30.4	30.9
One In Family	11.2	11.9	12.5	13.4	14.1	14.6	14.6	15.0
Two In Family	7.4	7.5	7.1	7.1	7.1	7.1	7.1	7.0
Three In Family	4.1	4.0	4.0	3.8	3.7	3.6	3.6	3.7
Four Or Five In Family	5.7	5.7	5.2	5.0	4.8	4.4	4.5	4.4
Six Or More In Family	1.3	1.3	1.1	1.0	.9	.8	.8	.7
Two Family Members In Work Force	44.4	43.8	43.9	43.4	43.9	43.6	43.7	43.9
Two In Family	16.8	16.5	16.7	16.6	16.6	16.6	16.6	16.5
Three In Family	10.9	10.9	10.7	10.8	11.2	11.4	11.4	11.5
Four Or Five In Family	13.3	13.3	13.8	13.7	13.9	13.6	13.6	13.8
Six Or More In Family	3.3	3.0	2.7	2.4	2.2	2.0	2.0	2.0
Three Or More In Work Force	25.9	25.8	26.2	26.2	25.5	26.0	25.9	25.3
Three In Family	5.1	5.1	5.2	5.3	5.2	5.6	5.6	5.6
Four Or Five In Family	13.0	13.1	13.2	14.0	13.7	13.8	13.7	13.4
Six Or More In Family	7.8	7.6	7.8	7.0	6.6	6.6	6.6	6.2
UNEMPLOYED								
One Family Member In Work Force	5,217	6,333	6,193	6,010	5,602	5,786	5,935	6,788
One In Family	2,284	2,754	2,946	3,030	2,929	3,113	3,185	3,528
Two In Family	1,041	1,305	1,162	1,066	973	999	1,024	1,169
Three In Family	773	887	887	805	724	762	787	900
Four Or Five In Family	843	1,050	934	891	791	745	767	974
Six Or More In Family	275	336	264	217	187	167	171	216
Two Family Members in Work Force	8,083	8,789	8,453	7,812	7,272	7,287	7,490	8,802
Two In Family	2,838	3,140	3,115	2,738	2,534	2,600	2,663	2,974
Three In Family	2,132	2,225	2,095	2,058	1,936	1,980	2,040	2,442
Four Or Five In Family	2,372	2,689	2,595	2,476	2,304	2,272	2,332	2,841
Six Or More In Family	741	735	649	539	498	435	453	545
Three Or More In Work Force	5,236	5,983	5,800	5,690	4,863	4,898	5,042	5,819
Three In Family	851	1,103	980	1,033	850	886	914	1,108
Four Or Five In Family	2,574	2,907	2,754	2,922	2,496	2,494	2,560	2,959
Six Or More in Family	1,812	1,974	2,066	1,735	1,517	1,518	1,570	1,752
UNEMPLOYMENT RATE								
One Family Member In Work Force	16.9	19.9	19.4	18.1	16.3	16.6	16.6	18.6
One In Family	19.6	22.2	22.0	20.6	18.5	18.7	18.7	19.9
Two In Family	13.6	16.7	15.3	13.7	12.2	12.3	12.4	14.0
Three In Family	18.3	21.1	20.9	19.3	17.3	18.6	18.7	20.3
Four Or Five In Family	14.4	17.7	16.7	16.3	14.8	14.6	14.7	18.8
Six Or More In Family	19.7	24.2	22.4	19.6	19.3	18.7	18.8	24.8
Two Family Members In Work Force	17.6	19.2	18.0	16.4	14.7	14.6	14.7	17.0
Two In Family	16.3	18.3	17.4	15.1	13.6	13.7	13.7	15.2
Three In Family	18.8	19.5	18.2	17.4	15.4	15.1	15.3	17.9
Four Or Five In Family	17.1	19.3	17.6	16.5	14.8	14.5	14.6	17.4
Six Or More In Family	21.4	23.1	22.1	20.5	20.1	19.1	19.4	23.1
Three Or More In Work Force	19.5	22.2	20.6	19.8	17.0	16.5	16.7	19.5
Three In Family	16.2	20.6	17.7	17.8	14.4	13.9	14.1	16.6
Four Or Five In Family	19.0	21.3	19.4	19.1	16.3	15.8	16.0	18.7
Six Or More In Family	22.5	24.8	24.7	22.7	20.4	20.0	20.2	23.7

Table C-4. (Continued)

SHARE UNEMPLOYED

One Family Member In Work Force	28.1	30.0	30.3	30.8	31.6	32.2	32.1	31.7
One In Family	12.3	13.0	14.4	15.5	16.5	17.3	17.2	16.5
Two In Family	5.6	6.2	5.7	5.5	5.5	5.6	5.5	5.5
Three In Family	4.2	4.2	4.3	4.1	4.1	4.3	4.3	4.2
Four Or Five In Family	4.5	5.0	4.6	4.6	4.1	4.1	4.2	4.5
Six Or More In Family	1.5	1.6	1.3	1.1	1.1	.9	.9	1.0
Two Family Members in Work Force	43.6	41.6	41.3	40.0	41.0	40.5	40.6	41.1
Two In Family	15.2	14.9	15.2	14.0	14.3	15.0	14.4	13.9
Three In Family	11.5	10.5	10.2	10.5	10.9	11.0	11.0	11.4
Four Or Five In Family	12.8	12.7	12.7	12.7	13.0	12.6	12.6	13.3
Six Or More In Family	4.0	3.5	3.2	2.8	2.8	2.4	2.5	2.5
Three Or More In Work Force	28.2	28.3	28.4	29.2	27.4	27.3	27.3	27.2
Three In Family	4.6	5.2	4.8	5.3	4.8	4.9	4.9	5.2
Four Or Five In Family	13.9	13.8	13.5	15.0	14.1	13.9	13.9	13.8
Six Or More In Family	9.8	9.4	10.1	8.9	8.6	8.4	8.5	8.2

PREDOMINANTLY UNEMPLOYED

One Family Member In Work Force	2,168	3,206	3,055	2,780	2,423	2,270	2,327	3,257
One In Family	877	1,291	1,346	1,271	1,142	1,076	1,094	1,549
Two In Family	482	745	660	549	494	458	471	618
Three In Family	341	468	471	417	340	346	355	496
Four Or Five In Family	356	504	446	426	351	317	327	464
Six Or More In Family	113	196	131	119	96	77	82	129
Two Family Members In Work Force	3,292	4,528	4,224	3,554	3,098	2,852	2,942	4,179
Two In Family	1,037	1,522	1,479	1,137	959	956	980	1,319
Three In Family	875	1,195	1,091	958	837	750	779	1,199
Four Or Five In Family	1,020	1,391	1,297	1,169	1,029	944	969	1,348
Six Or More In Family	360	421	357	289	273	200	211	315
Three Or More In Work Force	2,278	3,206	2,976	2,796	2,231	2,154	2,222	2,911
Three In Family	369	591	507	494	400	367	379	520
Four Or Five In Family	1,119	1,497	1,383	1,404	1,107	1,076	1,106	1,439
Six Or More In Family	791	1,119	1,085	899	724	711	738	951

INCIDENCE PREDOMINANTLY UNEMPLOYED

One Family Member In Work Force	7.0	10.1	9.6	8.3	7.1	6.5	6.5	8.9
One In Family	7.5	10.4	10.1	8.6	7.2	6.4	6.4	8.7
Two In Family	6.3	8.6	8.7	7.0	6.2	5.7	5.7	7.4
Three In Family	8.1	11.1	11.1	10.0	8.1	8.4	8.5	11.2
Four Or Five In Family	6.1	8.5	8.0	7.8	6.5	6.2	6.3	8.9
Six Or More In Family	8.1	14.1	11.1	10.8	9.9	8.6	9.0	14.8
Two Family Members in Work Force	7.2	9.9	9.0	7.5	6.3	5.7	5.8	8.1
Two In Family	6.0	8.8	8.3	6.3	5.1	5.0	5.0	6.8
Three In Family	7.7	10.5	9.5	8.1	6.6	5.7	5.8	8.9
Four Or Five In Family	7.4	10.0	8.8	7.8	6.6	6.0	6.1	8.2
Six Or More In Family	10.4	13.2	12.1	11.0	11.0	8.8	9.0	13.3
Three Or More In Work Force	8.5	11.9	10.6	9.7	7.8	7.2	7.3	9.7
Three In Family	7.0	11.1	9.1	8.5	6.8	5.8	5.8	7.8
Four Or Five In Family	8.3	11.0	9.8	9.2	7.2	6.8	6.9	9.1
Six Or More In Family	9.8	14.1	13.0	11.8	9.7	9.4	9.5	12.9

SHARE PREDOMINANTLY UNEMPLOYED

One Family Member In Work Force	28.1	29.3	29.8	30.4	31.3	31.2	31.1	31.5
One In Family	11.3	11.8	13.1	13.9	14.7	14.8	14.6	15.0
Two In Family	6.2	6.8	6.4	6.0	6.4	6.3	6.3	6.0
Three In Family	4.4	4.3	4.6	4.6	4.4	4.8	4.7	4.8
Four Or Five In Family	4.6	4.6	4.3	4.7	4.5	4.4	4.4	4.5
Six Or More In Family	1.5	1.8	1.3	1.3	1.2	1.1	1.1	1.2
Two Family Members In Work Force	42.5	41.4	41.2	38.9	40.0	39.2	39.3	40.3
Two In Family	13.4	13.9	14.4	12.5	12.4	13.1	13.1	12.7
Three In Family	11.3	10.9	10.6	10.5	10.8	10.3	10.4	11.6
Four Or Five In Family	13.2	12.7	12.6	12.8	13.3	13.0	12.9	13.0
Six Or More In Family	4.4	3.8	3.5	3.2	3.5	2.7	2.8	3.0
Three Or More In Work Force	29.4	29.3	29.0	30.6	28.8	29.6	29.7	28.1
Three In Family	4.8	5.4	4.9	5.4	5.2	5.0	5.1	5.0
Four Or Five In Family	14.5	13.7	13.5	15.4	14.3	14.8	14.8	13.9
Six Or More In Family	10.2	15.4	10.6	9.8	10.3	9.8	9.9	9.2

Table C-4. (Continued)

IIE

One Family Member In Work Force	6,432	7,549	7,293	7,631	7,410	7,166	7,341	8,726
One In Family	2,926	3,505	3,508	3,825	3,696	3,633	3,707	4,372
Two In Family	1,697	1,946	1,786	1,799	1,825	1,724	1,769	2,087
Three In Family	852	919	954	930	934	877	904	1,079
Four Or Five In Family	716	858	806	829	752	743	761	949
Six Or More In Family	241	320	239	249	203	190	199	238
Two Family Members in Work Force	11,120	12,217	12,160	11,979	11,600	10,873	11,165	13,005
Two In Family	3,721	4,164	4,257	4,128	3,974	3,646	3,746	4,414
Three In Family	2,795	3,049	3,006	2,995	2,866	2,796	2,874	3,400
Four Or Five In Family	3,464	3,804	3,887	3,916	3,885	3,676	3,759	4,353
Six Or More In Family	1,140	1,200	1,010	940	876	754	786	839
Three Or More In Work Force	9,203	10,580	10,440	10,715	9,650	9,536	9,762	11,015
Three In Family	1,549	1,750	1,659	1,905	1,654	1,741	1,785	2,045
Four Or Five In Family	4,502	5,224	5,135	5,531	4,955	4,930	5,030	5,789
Six Or More In Family	3,152	3,606	3,646	3,279	3,041	2,865	2,948	3,181

IIE INCIDENCE

One Family Member In Work Force	20.9	23.8	22.8	22.9	21.6	20.5	20.6	23.9
One In Family	25.1	28.2	26.2	25.9	23.4	21.8	21.8	24.7
Two In Family	22.1	24.9	23.5	23.1	22.8	21.3	21.4	25.0
Three In Family	20.1	21.8	22.5	22.3	22.3	21.4	21.5	24.4
Four Or Five In Family	12.2	14.4	14.5	15.1	14.0	14.6	14.6	18.3
Six Or More In Family	17.3	23.0	20.3	22.5	20.9	21.2	21.8	27.3
Two Family Members In Work Force	24.2	26.7	25.8	25.2	23.5	21.8	21.9	25.1
Two In Family	21.4	24.2	23.8	22.7	21.3	19.2	19.3	22.6
Three In Family	24.7	26.7	26.1	25.3	22.8	21.4	21.9	24.9
Four Or Five In Family	25.0	27.3	26.4	26.2	24.9	23.5	23.6	26.6
Six Or More In Family	33.0	37.7	34.3	35.8	35.3	33.2	33.6	35.5
Three Or More In Work Force	34.3	39.2	37.2	37.3	33.7	32.0	32.3	36.8
Three In Family	29.5	32.8	29.9	32.9	28.0	27.3	27.4	30.7
Four Or Five In Family	33.3	38.2	36.2	36.1	32.3	31.2	31.5	36.5
Six Or More In Family	39.2	45.4	43.5	42.9	40.9	37.7	37.9	43.1

SHARE IIE

One Family Member In Work Force	24.0	24.9	24.4	25.2	25.9	26.0	26.0	26.6
One In Family	10.9	11.6	11.7	12.9	12.9	13.2	13.1	13.4
Two In Family	6.3	6.4	6.0	5.9	6.4	6.3	6.3	6.4
Three In Family	3.2	3.0	3.2	3.1	3.3	3.2	3.2	3.3
Four Or Five In Family	2.7	2.8	2.7	2.7	2.6	2.7	2.7	2.9
Six Or More In Family	.9	1.1	.8	.8	.7	.7	.7	.7
Two Family Members in Work Force	41.6	40.3	40.7	39.5	40.5	39.4	39.5	39.7
Two In Family	13.9	13.7	14.2	13.6	13.9	13.2	13.3	13.5
Three In Family	10.4	10.0	10.1	9.9	10.0	10.1	10.2	10.4
Four Or Five In Family	12.9	12.5	13.0	12.0	13.6	13.3	13.3	13.3
Six Or More In Family	4.3	4.0	3.4	3.1	3.1	2.7	2.8	2.6
Three Or More In Work Force	34.4	34.9	34.9	35.3	33.7	34.6	34.5	33.6
Three In Family	5.8	5.8	5.5	6.3	5.8	6.3	6.3	6.2
Four Or Five In Family	16.8	17.2	17.2	18.2	17.3	17.9	17.8	17.7
Six Or More in Family	11.8	11.9	12.2	10.8	10.6	10.4	10.4	9.7

IIE DEFICIT

One Family Member In Work Force	9,477	13,176	13,203	13,800	13,377	14,885	15,190	21,089
One In Family	4,347	6,348	6,407	6,845	6,640	7,571	7,698	10,806
Two In Family	2,417	3,243	3,188	3,237	3,283	3,466	3,573	4,797
Three In Family	1,194	1,498	1,690	1,747	1,735	1,838	1,873	2,469
Four Or Five In Family	1,125	1,483	1,443	1,526	1,326	1,586	1,606	2,463
Six Or More In Family	393	605	476	444	392	424	441	554
Two Family Members In Work-Force	14,326	18,806	19,959	19,969	19,532	20,431	20,965	28,638
Two In Family	5,533	7,085	7,788	7,954	7,625	7,599	7,810	10,641
Three In Family	3,585	4,587	4,862	4,633	4,841	5,044	5,186	7,118
Four Or Five In Family	3,972	5,438	5,846	5,921	5,734	6,489	6,598	9,106
Six Or More In Family	1,237	1,695	1,464	1,462	1,332	1,299	1,372	1,773
Three Or More In Work Force	10,226	14,110	14,304	15,515	13,723	15,514	15,842	20,921
Three In Family	2,017	2,723	2,625	3,327	2,789	3,069	3,144	4,259
Four Or Five In Family	4,757	6,877	6,936	7,413	6,813	7,717	7,868	10,530
Six Or More In Family	3,451	4,511	4,743	4,776	4,121	4,729	4,830	6,131

Table C-4. (Continued)

IIE DEFICIT (1980 $)

One Family Member In Work Force	15,836	20,173	19,119	18,767	16,895	16,894	17,241	21,089
One In Family	7,264	9,719	9,277	9,309	8,386	8,593	8,737	10,806
Two In Family	4,040	4,964	4,617	4,402	4,147	3,934	4,055	4,797
Three In Family	1,995	2,293	2,447	2,377	2,192	2,086	2,126	2,469
Four Or Five In Family	1,880	2,271	2,089	2,076	1,675	1,800	1,823	2,463
Six Or More In Family	657	926	689	604	495	481	500	554
Two Family Members in Work Force	23,938	28,792	28,901	27,158	24,669	23,189	23,796	28,638
Two In Family	9,245	10,848	11,277	10,817	9,630	8,624	8,864	10,641
Three In Family	5,990	7,023	7,040	6,300	6,114	5,725	5,886	7,118
Four Or Five In Family	6,636	8,326	8,464	8,053	7,242	7,365	7,488	9,106
Six Or More In Family	2,066	2,595	2,120	1,988	1,682	1,474	1,557	1,773
Three Or More In Work Force	17,087	21,603	20,712	21,101	17,332	17,609	17,981	20,921
Three In Family	3,371	4,169	3,801	4,525	3,522	3,483	3,568	4,259
Four Or Five In Family	7,949	10,529	10,043	10,081	8,605	8,759	8,931	10,530
Six Or More In Family	5,767	6,906	6,868	6,495	5,204	5,367	5,482	6,131

SHARE IIE DEFICIT

One Family Member In Work Force	27.9	28.6	27.8	28.0	28.7	29.3	29.2	29.9
One In Family	12.8	13.8	13.5	13.9	14.2	14.9	14.8	15.3
Two In Family	7.1	7.0	6.7	6.7	7.0	6.8	6.9	6.8
Three In Family	3.5	3.3	3.6	3.5	3.7	3.6	3.6	3.5
Four Or Five In Family	3.3	3.2	3.0	3.1	2.8	3.2	3.1	3.5
Six Or More In Family	1.2	1.3	1.0	.9	.8	.8	.8	.8
Two Family Members In Work Force	42.1	40.8	42.0	40.5	41.9	40.2	40.3	40.5
Two In Family	16.3	15.4	16.4	16.1	16.4	14.9	15.0	15.1
Three In Family	10.5	10.0	10.2	9.4	10.4	9.9	10.0	10.1
Four Or Five In Family	11.7	11.8	12.3	12.0	12.3	12.8	12.7	12.9
Six Or More In Family	3.6	3.7	3.1	3.0	2.9	2.6	2.6	2.5
Three Or More In Work Force	30.1	30.6	30.1	31.5	29.4	30.5	30.5	29.6
Three In Family	5.9	5.9	5.5	6.8	6.0	6.0	6.0	6.0
Four Or Five In Family	13.9	14.9	14.6	15.0	14.6	15.2	15.1	14.9
Six Or More In Family	10.1	9.8	10.0	9.7	8.8	9.3	9.3	8.7

IIE AVERAGE DEFICIT

One Family Member In Work Force	1,473	1,746	1,810	1,808	1,805	2,077	2,069	2,417
One In Family	1,486	1,811	1,827	1,789	1,797	2,084	2,076	2,471
Two In Family	1,424	1,667	1,785	1,800	1,799	2,011	2,019	2,298
Three In Family	1,402	1,629	1,771	1,879	1,858	2,096	2,072	2,289
Four Or Five In Family	1,573	1,728	1,789	1,842	1,763	2,135	2,110	2,595
Six Or More In Family	1,629	1,891	1,988	1,784	1,930	2,233	2,218	2,326
Two Family Members in Work Force	1,288	1,539	1,641	1,667	1,684	1,879	1,878	2,202
Two In Family	1,487	1,702	1,830	1,927	1,919	2,084	2,085	2,411
Three In Family	1,282	1,504	1,617	1,547	1,689	1,804	1,805	2,094
Four Or Five In Family	1,147	1,430	1,504	1,512	1,476	1,765	1,755	2,092
Six Or More In Family	1,085	1,413	1,449	1,555	1,521	1,723	1,745	2,112
Three Or More In Work Force	1,111	1,334	1,370	1,448	1,422	1,627	1,623	1,899
Three In Family	1,302	1,556	1,582	1,746	1,681	1,762	1,762	2,083
Four Or Five In Family	1,057	1,317	1,351	1,340	1,375	1,565	1,564	1,819
Six Or More In Family	1,095	1,251	1,301	1,456	1,355	1,651	1,638	1,927

IIE AVERAGE DEFICIT (1980 $)

One Family Member In Work Force	2,461	2,673	2,621	2,460	2,280	2,357	2,348	2,417
One In Family	2,483	2,773	2,645	2,433	2,270	2,365	2,356	2,471
Two In Family	2,380	2,552	2,585	2,448	2,272	2,685	2,292	2,298
Three In Family	2,343	2,494	2,564	2,555	2,347	2,379	2,352	2,289
Four Or Five In Family	2,628	2,646	2,590	2,505	2,227	2,423	2,395	2,595
Six Or More In Family	2,722	2,895	2,879	2,426	2,438	2,534	2,517	2,326
Two Family Members In Work Force	2,152	2,356	2,376	2,267	2,127	2,133	2,132	2,202
Two In Family	2,485	2,606	2,650	2,621	2,424	2,365	2,366	2,411
Three In Family	2,142	2,303	2,341	2,104	2,133	2,048	2,049	2,094
Four Or Five In Family	1,917	2,189	2,178	2,056	1,864	2,003	1,985	2,092
Six Or More In Family	1,813	2,163	2,098	2,115	1,921	1,955	1,981	2,112
Three Or More In Work Force	1,856	2,042	1,984	1,969	1,796	1,847	1,842	1,899
Three In Family	2,176	2,382	2,291	2,374	2,131	2,000	2,000	2,083
Four Or Five In Family	1,766	2,016	1,956	1,822	1,737	1,776	1,775	1,819
Six Or More In Family	1,830	1,915	1,884	1,980	1,711	1,874	1,859	1,927

Table C-4. (Continued)

IFE

One Family Member In Work Force	7,255	8,167	8,139	8,291	8,276	8,234	8,457	9,241
One In Family	2,782	3,230	3,454	3,505	3,530	3,420	3,505	3,811
Two In Family	2,116	2,231	2,187	2,250	2,224	2,310	2,375	2,505
Three In Family	977	1,050	1,032	1,030	1,124	1,086	1,119	1,264
Four Or Five In Family	925	1,118	1,060	1,106	1,035	1,047	1,077	1,269
Six Or More In Family	455	538	406	400	364	371	381	391
Two Family Members in Work Force	3,302	3,952	3,746	3,609	3,444	3,519	3,628	4,170
Two In Family	907	1,013	1,021	1,037	953	947	975	1,126
Three In Family	655	811	760	682	661	661	676	894
Four Or Five In Family	1,011	1,301	1,300	1,301	1,256	1,346	1,381	1,562
Six Or More In Family	729	826	665	589	574	565	595	588
Three Or More In Work Force	1,451	1,649	1,516	1,594	1,300	1,162	1,195	1,700
Three In Family	149	167	140	180	171	134	137	137
Four Or Five In Family	517	625	568	710	486	468	479	751
Six Or More In Family	785	856	809	704	642	560	579	813

IFE INCIDENCE

One Family Member In Work Force	23.6	25.7	25.5	24.9	24.1	23.6	23.7	25.3
One In Family	23.9	26.0	25.8	23.8	22.3	20.5	20.6	21.5
Two In Family	27.6	28.6	28.8	28.8	27.8	28.5	28.7	30.0
Three In Family	23.1	24.9	24.3	24.7	26.8	26.4	26.6	28.6
Four Or Five In Family	15.8	18.8	19.0	20.2	19.3	20.5	20.7	24.5
Six Or More In Family	32.6	38.8	34.5	36.1	37.5	41.5	41.8	44.8
Two Family Members In Work Force	7.2	8.6	8.0	7.6	7.0	7.0	7.1	8.0
Two In Family	5.2	5.9	5.7	5.7	5.1	5.0	5.0	5.8
Three In Family	5.8	7.1	6.6	5.8	5.2	5.1	5.1	6.5
Four Or Five In Family	7.3	9.4	8.8	8.7	8.1	8.6	8.7	9.6
Six Or More In Family	21.1	26.0	22.6	22.5	23.2	24.8	25.4	24.9
Three Or More In Work Force	5.4	6.1	5.4	5.5	4.5	3.9	4.0	5.7
Three In Family	2.8	3.1	2.5	3.1	2.9	2.1	2.1	2.1
Four Or Five In Family	3.8	4.6	4.0	4.6	3.2	3.0	3.0	4.7
Six Or More In Family	9.8	10.8	9.7	9.2	8.6	7.4	7.4	11.0

IFE SHARE

One Family Member In Work Force	60.4	59.3	60.7	61.4	63.6	63.8	63.7	61.2
One In Family	23.2	23.5	25.8	26.0	27.1	26.5	26.4	25.2
Two In Family	17.6	16.2	16.3	16.7	17.1	17.9	17.9	16.6
Three In Family	8.1	7.6	7.7	7.6	8.6	8.4	8.4	8.4
Four Or Five In Family	7.7	8.1	7.9	8.2	7.9	8.1	8.1	8.4
Six Or More In Family	3.8	3.9	3.0	3.0	2.8	2.9	2.9	2.6
Two Family Members in Work Force	27.5	28.7	28.0	26.7	26.5	27.2	27.3	27.6
Two In Family	7.6	7.4	7.6	7.7	7.3	7.3	7.3	7.5
Three In Family	5.5	5.9	5.7	5.1	5.1	5.1	5.1	5.9
Four Or Five In Family	8.4	9.4	9.7	9.6	9.6	10.4	10.4	10.3
Six Or More In Family	6.1	6.0	5.0	4.4	4.4	4.4	4.5	3.9
Three Or More In Work Force	12.1	12.0	11.3	11.8	10.0	9.0	9.0	11.3
Three In Family	1.2	1.2	1.0	1.3	1.3	1.0	1.0	.9
Four Or Five In Family	4.3	4.5	4.2	5.3	3.7	3.6	3.6	5.0
Six Or More In Family	6.5	6.2	6.0	5.2	4.9	4.3	4.4	5.4

IFE DEFICIT

One Family Member In Work Force	14,897	18,532	19,233	20,510	21,545	23,811	24,467	31,171
One In Family	3,922	5,162	5,681	5,972	6,227	6,850	7,009	8,865
Two In Family	3,858	4,571	4,802	5,230	5,577	6,376	6,555	7,893
Three In Family	2,288	2,703	2,954	3,145	3,473	3,628	3,731	4,830
Four Or Five In Family	2,884	3,624	3,817	4,051	4,164	4,674	4,803	6,584
Six Or More In Family	1,945	2,472	1,978	2,113	2,105	2,284	2,369	2,999
Two Family Members In Work Force	3,730	4,909	4,841	4,863	4,831	5,752	5,924	7,742
Two In Family	668	808	869	916	914	1,051	1,083	1,373
Three In Family	598	727	795	769	766	834	860	1,315
Four Or Five In Family	1,174	1,815	1,763	1,935	1,922	2,377	2,409	3,311
Six Or More In Family	1,289	1,559	1,414	1,243	1,229	1,490	1,572	1,742
Three Or More In Work Force	1,074	1,484	1,381	1,529	1,393	1,238	1,265	2,087
Three In Family	66	97	82	123	128	94	96	112
Four Or Five In Family	332	496	449	614	430	472	480	813
Six Or More In Family	676	891	850	792	835	672	689	1,161

Table C-4. (Continued)

IFE DEFICIT (1980 $)

One Family Member In Work Force	24,893	28,372	27,849	27,893	27,174	27,025	27,770	31,171
One In Family	6,553	7,903	8,226	8,122	7,864	7,774	7,955	8,865
Two In Family	6,446	6,997	6,953	7,112	7,043	7,236	7,440	7,893
Three In Family	3,824	4,138	4,278	4,277	4,387	4,118	4,235	4,830
Four Or Five In Family	4,819	5,548	5,527	5,509	5,259	5,305	5,451	6,584
Six Or More In Family	3,251	3,785	2,864	2,873	2,658	2,592	2,689	2,999
Two Family Members in Work Force	6,232	7,516	7,010	6,614	6,102	6,529	6,723	7,742
Two In Family	1,169	1,236	1,259	1,246	1,155	1,193	1,229	1,373
Three In Family	999	1,113	1,151	1,046	967	947	976	1,315
Four Or Five In Family	1,962	2,779	2,552	2,632	2,427	2,698	2,734	3,311
Six Or More In Family	2,153	2,387	2,048	1,690	1,552	1,692	1,785	1,742
Three Or More In Work Force	1,794	2,272	1,999	2,079	1,759	1,405	1,436	2,087
Three In Family	111	149	118	168	161	107	109	112
Four Or Five In Family	554	760	650	835	543	535	544	813
Six Or More In Family	1,129	1,364	1,231	1,077	1,055	762	782	1,161

IFE DEFICIT SHARE

One Family Member In Work Force	75.6	74.3	75.6	76.2	77.6	77.3	77.3	76.0
One In Family	19.9	20.7	22.3	22.2	22.4	22.2	22.1	21.6
Two In Family	19.6	18.3	18.9	19.4	20.1	20.7	20.7	19.3
Three In Family	11.6	10.8	11.6	11.7	12.5	11.8	11.8	11.8
Four Or Five In Family	14.6	14.5	15.0	15.1	15.0	15.2	15.2	16.1
Six Or More In Family	9.9	9.9	7.8	7.9	7.6	7.4	7.5	7.3
Two Family Members In Work Force	18.9	19.7	19.0	18.1	17.4	18.7	18.7	18.9
Two In Family	3.4	3.2	3.4	3.4	3.3	3.4	3.4	3.4
Three In Family	3.0	2.9	3.1	2.9	2.8	2.7	2.7	3.2
Four Or Five In Family	6.0	7.3	6.9	7.2	6.9	7.7	7.6	8.1
Six Or More In Family	6.5	6.3	5.6	4.6	4.4	4.8	5.0	4.2
Three Or More In Work Force	5.4	6.0	5.4	5.7	5.0	4.0	4.0	5.1
Three In Family	.3	.4	.3	.5	.5	.3	.3	.3
Four Or Five In Family	1.7	2.0	1.8	2.3	1.5	1.5	1.5	2.0
Six Or More In Family	3.4	3.6	3.3	2.9	3.0	2.2	2.2	2.8

IFE AVERAGE DEFICIT

One Family Member In Work Force	2,053	2,269	2,363	2,474	2,603	2,892	2,893	3,373
One In Family	1,410	1,598	1,645	1,704	1,764	2,003	2,000	2,326
Two In Family	1,823	2,049	2,196	2,324	2,508	2,759	2,760	3,151
Three In Family	2,343	2,574	2,862	3,055	3,089	3,342	3,334	3,820
Four Or Five In Family	3,118	3,241	3,600	3,661	4,023	4,465	4,458	5,187
Six Or More In Family	4,277	4,596	4,867	5,284	5,790	6,154	6,223	7,669
Two Family Members in Work Force	1,130	1,242	1,292	1,347	1,403	1,635	1,633	1,857
Two In Family	737	797	851	884	960	1,110	1,110	1,220
Three In Family	913	897	1,046	1,128	1,159	1,261	1,271	1,471
Four Or Five In Family	1,162	1,395	1,356	1,487	1,530	1,766	1,744	2,120
Six Or More In Family	1,767	1,887	2,127	2,109	2,140	2,639	2,644	2,963
Three Or More In Work Force	740	900	911	959	1,072	1,066	1,059	1,227
Three In Family	446	581	586	685	745	705	705	819
Four Or Five In Family	641	794	791	865	885	1,008	1,001	1,084
Six Or More In Family	860	1,040	1,050	1,125	1,300	1,200	1,190	1,429

IFE AVERAGE DEFICIT (1980 $)

One Family Member In Work Force	3,431	3,474	3,422	3,365	3,288	3,282	3,284	3,373
One In Family	2,356	2,447	2,382	2,317	2,228	2,273	2,270	2,326
Two In Family	3,046	3,137	3,180	3,161	3,168	3,131	3,133	3,151
Three In Family	3,915	3,941	4,144	4,155	3,901	3,793	3,784	3,820
Four Or Five In Family	5,211	4,962	5,213	4,979	5,081	5,068	5,060	5,187
Six Or More In Family	7,147	7,036	7,047	7,186	7,313	6,985	7,063	7,669
Two Family Members In Work Force	1,888	1,902	1,871	1,832	1,772	1,856	1,853	1,857
Two In Family	1,232	1,220	1,232	1,202	1,212	1,260	1,260	1,220
Three In Family	1,526	1,373	1,515	1,534	1,464	1,431	1,443	1,471
Four Or Five In Family	1,942	2,136	1,963	2,022	1,932	2,004	1,979	2,120
Six Or More In Family	2,953	2,889	3,080	2,868	2,703	2,995	3,001	2,963
Three Or More In Work Force	1,237	1,377	1,319	1,304	1,354	1,210	1,202	1,227
Three In Family	745	890	849	932	941	800	800	819
Four Or Five In Family	1,071	1,216	1,145	1,176	1,118	1,144	1,136	1,084
Six Or More In Family	1,437	1,592	1,520	1,530	1,642	1,362	1,351	1,429

Table C-4. (Continued)

IFI

One Family Member In Work Force	3,748	4,222	4,221	4,297	4,383	4,332	4,450	5,151
One In Family	1,669	1,954	2,077	2,079	2,162	2,069	2,114	2,403
Two In Family	623	663	652	664	712	710	733	874
Three In Family	473	507	485	517	539	518	536	661
Four Or Five In Family	626	696	682	723	668	744	767	882
Six Or More In Family	357	401	326	315	301	290	301	331
Two Family Members in Work Force	1,765	2,027	1,985	1,846	1,919	1,948	2,014	2,347
Two In Family	324	386	395	400	351	391	404	459
Three In Family	298	346	363	251	319	298	306	422
Four Or Five In Family	606	745	786	778	826	853	874	1,018
Six Or More In Family	536	549	442	417	422	406	431	448
Three Or More In Work Force	833	1,004	827	855	710	573	591	967
Three In Family	39	74	61	66	78	42	44	53
Four Or Five In Family	267	351	286	365	239	239	244	397
Six Or More In Family	527	579	480	423	393	292	303	517

IFI INCIDENCE

One Family Member In Work Force	12.2	13.3	13.2	12.9	12.8	12.4	12.5	14.1
One In Family	14.3	15.7	15.5	14.1	13.7	12.4	12.4	13.6
Two In Family	8.1	8.5	8.6	8.5	8.9	8.8	8.8	10.5
Three In Family	11.2	12.1	11.4	12.4	12.9	12.6	12.7	14.9
Four Or Five In Family	10.7	11.7	12.2	13.2	12.5	14.6	14.7	17.0
Six Or More In Family	25.6	28.9	27.6	28.5	31.1	32.4	33.0	37.9
Two Family Members In Work Force	3.8	4.4	4.2	3.9	3.9	3.9	3.9	4.5
Two In Family	1.9	2.2	2.2	2.2	1.9	2.1	2.1	2.4
Three In Family	2.6	3.0	3.2	2.1	2.5	2.3	2.3	3.1
Four Or Five In Family	4.4	5.4	5.3	5.2	5.3	5.5	5.5	6.2
Six Or More In Family	15.5	17.3	15.0	15.9	17.0	17.9	18.4	19.0
Three Or More In Work Force	3.1	3.7	2.9	3.0	2.5	1.9	2.0	3.2
Three In Family	.7	1.4	1.1	1.1	1.3	.7	.7	.8
Four Or Five In Family	2.0	2.6	2.0	2.4	1.6	1.5	1.5	2.5
Six Or More In Family	6.6	7.3	5.7	5.5	5.3	3.8	3.9	7.0

IFI SHARE

One Family Member In Work Force	59.1	58.2	60.0	61.4	62.5	63.2	63.1	60.9
One In Family	26.3	26.9	29.5	29.7	30.8	30.2	30.0	28.4
Two In Family	9.8	9.1	9.3	9.5	10.2	10.4	10.4	10.3
Three In Family	7.5	7.0	6.9	7.4	7.7	7.6	7.6	7.8
Four Or Five In Family	9.9	9.6	9.7	10.3	9.5	10.9	10.9	10.4
Six Or More In Family	5.6	5.5	4.6	4.5	4.3	4.2	4.3	3.9
Two Family Members in Work Force	27.8	28.0	28.2	26.4	27.4	28.4	28.5	27.7
Two In Family	5.1	5.3	5.6	5.7	5.0	5.7	5.7	5.4
Three In Family	4.7	4.8	5.2	3.6	4.5	4.3	4.3	5.0
Four Or Five In Family	9.5	10.3	11.2	11.1	11.8	12.4	12.4	12.1
Six Or More In Family	8.4	7.6	6.3	6.0	6.0	5.9	6.1	5.3
Three Or More In Work Force	13.1	13.8	11.8	12.2	10.1	8.4	8.4	11.4
Three In Family	.6	1.0	.9	.9	1.1	.6	.6	.6
Four Or Five In Family	4.2	4.8	4.1	5.2	3.4	3.5	3.5	4.7
Six Or More In Family	8.3	8.0	6.8	6.0	5.6	4.3	4.3	6.1

IFI DEFICIT

One Family Member In Work Force	5,571	6,764	6,989	7,659	8,269	9,390	9,618	12,812
One In Family	1,803	2,464	2,771	2,867	3,001	3,457	3,518	4,585
Two In Family	767	817	928	1,002	1,194	1,421	1,463	1,843
Three In Family	727	803	855	1,015	1,120	1,146	1,183	1,696
Four Or Five In Family	1,270	1,510	1,493	1,753	1,831	2,254	2,304	3,076
Six Or More In Family	1,004	1,170	943	1,022	1,124	1,112	1,151	1,611
Two Family Members In Work Force	1,619	2,049	1,969	1,997	2,162	2,606	2,695	3,676
Two In Family	208	265	276	347	276	351	362	454
Three In Family	553	246	270	227	307	270	278	528
Four Or Five In Family	396	771	792	852	948	1,142	1,159	1,731
Six Or More In Family	630	767	631	571	632	843	896	964
Three Or More In Work Force	523	725	615	701	595	503	512	965
Three In Family	21	32	35	49	51	33	34	42
Four Or Five In Family	130	234	193	311	186	172	173	318
Six Or More In Family	372	458	387	342	359	298	305	605

Table C-4. (Continued)

IFI DEFICIT (1980 $)

One Family Member In Work Force	9,309	10,356	10,120	10,416	10,444	10,657	10,916	12,812
One In Family	3,013	3,772	4,012	3,899	3,791	3,923	3,993	4,585
Two In Family	1,281	1,251	1,343	1,363	1,508	1,613	1,660	1,843
Three In Family	1,214	1,230	1,239	1,381	1,414	1,301	1,343	1,696
Four Or Five In Family	2,123	2,311	2,161	2,384	2,312	2,558	2,615	3,076
Six Or More In Family	1,678	1,792	1,365	1,390	1,420	1,262	1,306	1,611
Two Family Members in Work Force	2,705	3,137	2,851	2,716	2,731	2,958	3,059	3,676
Two In Family	347	406	400	472	348	398	411	454
Three In Family	381	377	392	308	388	307	315	528
Four Or Five In Family	924	1,181	1,146	1,159	1,197	1,296	1,315	1,731
Six Or More In Family	1,053	1,174	913	776	798	957	1,017	964
Three Or More In Work Force	874	1,110	891	953	752	571	581	965
Three In Family	35	50	51	66	64	37	38	42
Four Or Five In Family	217	358	280	423	235	196	197	318
Six Or More In Family	622	702	560	465	453	339	346	605

IFI DEFICIT SHARE

One Family Member In Work Force	72.2	70.9	73.0	74.0	75.0	75.1	75.0	73.4
One In Family	23.4	25.8	28.9	27.7	27.2	27.7	27.4	26.3
Two In Family	9.9	8.6	9.7	9.7	10.8	11.4	11.4	10.6
Three In Family	9.4	8.4	8.9	9.8	10.2	9.2	9.2	9.7
Four Or Five In Family	16.5	15.8	15.6	16.9	16.6	18.0	18.0	17.6
Six Or More In Family	13.0	12.3	9.8	9.9	10.2	8.9	9.0	9.2
Two Family Members In Work Force	21.0	21.5	20.6	19.3	19.6	20.8	21.0	21.1
Two In Family	2.7	2.8	2.9	3.4	2.5	2.8	2.8	2.6
Three In Family	3.0	2.6	2.8	2.2	2.8	2.2	2.2	3.0
Four Or Five In Family	7.2	8.1	8.3	8.2	8.6	9.1	9.0	9.9
Six Or More In Family	8.2	8.0	6.6	5.5	5.7	6.7	7.0	5.5
Three Or More In Work Force	6.8	7.6	6.4	6.8	5.4	4.0	4.0	5.5
Three In Family	.3	.3	.4	.5	.5	.3	.3	.2
Four Or Five In Family	1.7	2.5	2.0	3.0	1.7	1.4	1.4	1.8
Six Or More In Family	4.8	4.8	4.0	3.3	3.3	2.4	2.4	3.5

IFI AVERAGE DEFICIT

One Family Member In Work Force	1,486	1,602	1,656	1,782	1,887	2,168	2,161	2,487
One In Family	1,080	1,261	1,334	1,379	1,388	1,671	1,664	1,908
Two In Family	1,231	1,232	1,423	1,510	1,676	2,001	1,995	2,109
Three In Family	1,538	1,584	1,763	1,965	2,076	2,213	2,209	2,565
Four Or Five In Family	2,029	2,168	2,189	2,425	2,741	3,029	3,005	3,488
Six Or More In Family	2,810	2,916	2,894	3,244	3,730	3,831	3,824	4,872
Two Family Members in Work Force	917	1,011	992	1,082	1,127	1,337	1,338	1,566
Two In Family	640	686	700	868	785	897	897	988
Three In Family	764	712	746	904	961	907	909	1,251
Four Or Five In Family	912	1,035	1,008	1,095	1,147	1,339	1,327	1,699
Six Or More In Family	1,175	1,396	1,426	1,369	1,496	2,075	2,080	2,152
Three Or More In Work Force	628	722	744	820	839	879	866	998
Three In Family	549	441	578	735	650	790	770	794
Four Or Five In Family	485	666	675	851	777	721	710	800
Six Or More In Family	706	792	806	807	914	1,022	1,006	1,171

IFI AVERAGE DEFICIT (1980 $)

One Family Member In Work Force	2,483	2,453	2,398	2,424	2,383	2,461	2,453	2,487
One In Family	1,805	1,931	1,932	1,875	1,753	1,897	1,889	1,908
Two In Family	2,057	1,886	2,061	2,054	2,117	2,271	2,264	2,109
Three In Family	2,570	2,425	2,553	2,672	2,622	2,512	2,507	2,565
Four Or Five In Family	3,390	3,319	3,170	3,298	3,462	3,438	3,411	3,488
Six Or More In Family	4,696	4,464	4,191	4,412	4,711	4,348	4,340	4,872
Two Family Members In Work Force	1,532	1,548	1,436	1,472	1,423	1,517	1,519	1,566
Two In Family	1,069	1,050	1,014	1,180	991	1,018	1,018	988
Three In Family	1,277	1,090	1,080	1,229	1,214	1,029	1,032	1,251
Four Or Five In Family	1,524	1,585	1,460	1,489	1,449	1,520	1,506	1,699
Six Or More In Family	1,963	2,137	2,065	1,862	1,889	2,355	2,361	2,152
Three Or More In Work Force	1,049	1,105	1,077	1,115	1,060	998	983	998
Three In Family	917	675	837	1,000	821	897	874	794
Four Or Five In Family	810	1,020	977	1,157	981	818	806	800
Six Or More In Family	1,180	1,213	1,167	1,098	1,154	1,160	1,142	1,171

Table C-4. (Continued)

IIE IN IFE

One Family Member In Work Force	75.4	77.7	78.3	76.4	75.9	76.8	76.8	77.0
One In Family	67.9	69.8	72.8	68.8	69.3	67.9	68.0	68.1
Two In Family	77.9	81.1	80.1	80.7	78.4	83.1	82.9	82.3
Three In Family	84.3	86.7	84.3	84.6	85.6	88.0	87.8	88.9
Four Or Five In Family	83.1	87.3	86.5	87.0	84.7	87.5	87.4	88.0
Six Or More In Family	94.6	93.4	95.0	95.2	96.6	96.8	97.0	97.5
Two Family Members in Work Force	22.0	25.1	23.5	23.3	22.6	23.3	23.3	25.4
Two In Family	18.4	19.5	18.8	20.4	18.9	18.9	18.9	20.3
Three In Family	18.4	22.3	19.6	18.6	18.5	17.9	17.8	22.1
Four Or Five In Family	22.0	26.5	25.9	25.0	23.8	26.8	26.8	28.5
Six Or More In Family	42.9	47.6	46.0	43.9	48.1	46.9	47.6	49.9
Three Or More In Work Force	11.8	12.8	12.0	12.1	10.8	8.9	8.9	12.5
Three In Family	6.8	8.5	7.0	5.3	8.3	6.0	5.9	5.8
Four Or Five In Family	9.2	9.8	9.6	10.5	8.0	7.0	7.0	10.7
Six Or More In Family	18.0	19.1	17.7	16.9	16.6	14.0	14.1	20.2

EARNINGS SUPPLEMENTATION RATE—TOTAL

One Family Member In Work Force	48.3	48.3	48.1	48.2	47.0	47.4	47.4	44.3
One In Family	40.0	39.5	39.9	40.7	38.7	39.5	39.7	36.9
Two In Family	70.6	70.3	70.2	70.5	68.0	69.3	69.1	65.1
Three In Family	51.6	51.7	53.0	49.8	52.0	52.3	52.1	47.7
Four Or Five In Family	32.3	37.7	35.7	34.7	35.5	28.9	28.8	30.5
Six Or More In Family	21.4	25.4	19.9	21.2	17.1	21.8	21.0	15.4
Two Family Members In Work Force	46.5	48.7	47.0	48.8	44.3	44.6	44.5	43.7
Two In Family	64.2	61.9	61.3	61.4	63.2	58.7	58.6	59.2
Three In Family	54.4	57.3	52.3	63.2	51.7	54.9	54.8	52.8
Four Or Five In Family	40.0	42.7	39.6	40.2	34.2	36.6	36.7	34.8
Six Or More In Family	26.5	33.5	33.5	29.3	26.5	28.1	27.5	23.8
Three Or More In Work Force	42.6	39.1	45.5	46.4	45.4	50.7	50.5	43.1
Three In Family	74.0	56.0	56.6	63.3	54.5	68.9	67.8	61.4
Four Or Five In Family	48.3	43.8	49.5	48.5	50.8	48.9	49.1	47.1
Six Or More In Family	32.9	32.4	40.7	39.8	38.9	47.9	47.7	36.4

EARNINGS SUPPLEMENTATION RATE - TRANSFERS

One Family Member In Work Force	29.2	31.0	29.8	29.6	26.9	25.7	25.6	24.3
One In Family	23.7	24.9	24.4	24.1	20.8	19.3	19.3	20.0
Two In Family	40.8	42.3	41.2	41.0	37.7	36.1	35.7	32.5
Three In Family	31.7	34.2	34.4	33.3	30.9	31.8	31.6	26.4
Four Or Five In Family	21.6	28.0	25.5	24.4	24.7	20.3	20.2	22.1
Six Or More In Family	19.3	20.3	15.4	17.5	14.0	18.0	17.6	12.6
Two Family Members In Work Force	29.1	33.5	30.6	31.3	25.4	24.7	24.5	24.6
Two In Family	35.5	36.4	33.9	32.6	29.7	24.2	24.0	25.8
Three In Family	34.4	40.3	32.6	42.0	32.7	29.1	28.7	32.6
Four Or Five In Family	26.5	32.2	28.1	28.6	19.0	24.8	24.7	21.4
Six Or More In Family	21.6	25.3	27.9	23.1	18.6	20.2	19.7	18.6
Three Or More In Work Force	26.1	25.7	29.7	28.8	25.7	29.3	29.3	24.8
Three In Family	43.8	35.8	32.6	28.3	20.3	36.2	35.4	27.9
Four Or Five In Family	28.2	25.0	27.5	26.3	26.0	25.5	25.8	20.8
Six Or More In Family	21.2	24.4	30.7	31.3	26.9	30.8	30.9	28.1

Table C-5. SUMMARY SEVERE HARDSHIP MEASURES, 1974 THROUGH 1980, FOR TOTAL WORK FORCE, DISAGGREGATED BY EDUCATIONAL ATTAINMENT

	1974	1975	1976	1977	1978	1979	1979R	1980
TOTAL WORK FORCE								
High School Student	5,124	4,722	5,031	5,155	4,836	4,930	5,070	4,910
Post-Secondary Student	4,426	4,333	4,416	4,402	4,288	4,515	4,643	4,730
High School Dropout	27,008	25,900	25,729	25,454	24,451	24,050	24,488	23,713
High School Graduate Only	38,625	39,194	39,992	41,092	42,729	43,778	44,542	45,940
Post-Secondary 1-3 Years	13,793	14,576	15,412	16,428	17,618	18,081	18,524	18,880
College Graduate	14,624	15,716	16,568	17,133	18,439	19,295	19,714	20,175
SHARE TOTAL WORK FORCE								
High School Student	4.9	4.5	4.7	4.7	4.3	4.3	4.3	4.1
Post-Secondary Student	4.3	4.1	4.1	4.0	3.8	3.9	4.0	4.0
High School Dropout	28.7	24.8	24.0	23.2	24.1	21.0	20.9	20.0
High School Graduate Only	37.3	37.5	37.3	37.5	38.0	38.2	38.1	38.8
Post-Secondary 1-3 Years	14.0	14.0	14.4	15.0	15.7	15.8	15.8	16.0
College Graduate	14.1	15.0	15.5	15.6	16.4	16.8	16.9	17.0
UNEMPLOYED								
High School Student	1,455	1,343	1,376	1,428	1,155	1,070	1,112	1,331
Post-Secondary Student	1,059	1,096	1,052	1,053	820	849	870	972
High School Dropout	5,936	6,707	6,093	5,634	5,065	5,187	5,317	6,055
High School Graduate Only	6,772	7,875	7,592	7,328	6,763	6,914	7,093	8,609
Post-Secondary 1-3 Years	1,893	2,437	2,495	2,337	2,279	2,325	2,406	2,623
College Graduate	1,421	1,646	1,837	1,731	1,656	1,628	1,669	1,820
UNEMPLOYMENT RATE								
High School Student	28.4	28.4	27.4	27.7	23.9	21.7	21.9	27.1
Post-Secondary Student	23.9	25.3	23.8	23.9	19.1	18.8	18.7	20.5
High School Dropout	22.0	25.9	23.7	22.1	20.7	21.6	22.0	25.5
High School Graduate Only	17.5	20.1	19.0	17.8	15.8	15.8	15.9	18.7
Post-Secondary 1-3 Years	13.7	16.7	16.2	14.2	12.9	12.9	13.0	13.9
College Graduate	9.7	10.5	11.1	10.1	9.0	8.4	8.5	9.0
SHARE UNEMPLOYED								
High School Student	7.8	6.4	6.7	7.3	6.5	6.0	6.0	6.2
Post-Secondary Student	5.7	5.2	5.1	5.4	4.6	4.7	4.7	4.5
High School Dropout	32.0	31.8	29.8	28.9	28.6	28.9	28.8	28.3
High School Graduate Only	36.5	37.3	37.1	37.6	38.1	38.5	38.4	40.2
Post-Secondary 1-3 Years	10.2	11.5	12.2	12.0	12.8	12.9	13.0	12.3
College Graduate	7.7	7.8	9.0	8.9	9.3	9.1	9.0	8.5
PREDOMINANTLY UNEMPLOYED								
High School Student	815	863	950	898	668	641	668	862
Post-Secondary Student	381	575	499	441	351	345	352	481
High School Dropout	2,768	3,787	3,371	3,018	2,586	2,454	2,523	3,307
High School Graduate Only	2,621	3,941	3,512	3,225	2,822	2,637	2,709	3,990
Post-Secondary 1-3 Years	712	1,091	1,128	880	828	726	755	1,059
College Graduate	444	682	794	668	497	475	485	648

Table C-5. (Continued)

INCIDENCE PREDOMINANTLY UNEMPLOYED

High School Student	15.9	18.3	18.9	17.4	13.8	13.0	13.2	17.6
Post-Secondary Student	8.6	13.3	11.3	10.0	8.2	7.6	7.6	10.2
High School Dropout	10.2	14.6	13.1	11.9	10.6	10.2	10.3	13.9
High School Graduate Only	6.8	10.1	8.8	7.8	6.6	6.0	6.1	8.7
Post-Secondary 1-3 Years	5.2	7.5	7.3	5.4	4.7	4.0	4.1	5.6
College Graduate	3.0	4.3	4.8	3.9	2.7	2.5	2.5	3.2

SHARE PREDOMINANTLY UNEMPLOYED

High School Student	10.5	7.9	9.3	9.8	8.6	8.8	8.9	8.3
Post-Secondary Student	4.9	5.3	4.9	4.8	4.5	4.7	4.7	4.6
High School Dropout	35.8	34.6	32.9	33.0	33.4	33.7	33.7	32.0
High School Graduate Only	33.9	36.0	34.2	35.3	36.4	36.2	36.2	38.6
Post-Secondary 1-3 Years	9.2	10.0	11.0	9.6	10.7	10.0	10.1	10.2
College Graduate	5.7	6.2	7.7	7.3	6.4	6.5	6.5	6.3

IIE

High School Student	3,521	3,592	3,717	3,774	3,328	'3,236	3,325	3,634
Post-Secondary Student	1,842	2,217	2,113	2,067	1,829	1,938	1,984	2,321
High School Dropout	9,269	10,011	9,508	9,424	8,840	8,324	8,537	9,368
High School Graduate Only	8,471	9,914	9,712	10,203	9,711	9,328	9,543	11,785
Post-Secondary 1-3 Years	2,301	2,884	3,038	3,024	3,097	2,937	3,021	3,503
College Graduate	1,351	1,726	1,805	1,833	1,855	1,813	1,858	2,135

IIE INCIDENCE

High School Student	68.7	76.1	13.9	73.2	68.8	65.6	65.6	74.0
Post-Secondary Student	41.6	51.2	47.9	47.0	42.7	42.9	42.7	49.1
High School Dropout	34.3	38.7	37.0	37.0	36.2	34.6	34.9	39.5
High School Graduate Only	21.9	25.3	24.3	24.8	22.7	21.3	21.4	25.7
Post-Secondary 1-3 Years	16.7	19.8	19.7	18.4	17.6	16.2	16.3	18.6
College Graduate	9.2	11.0	10.9	10.7	10.1	9.4	9.4	10.6

IIE DISTRIBUTION

High School Student	13.2	11.8	12.4	12.4	11.6	11.7	11.8	11.1
Post-Secondary Student	6.9	7.3	7.1	6.8	6.4	7.0	7.0	7.1
High School Dropout	34.6	33.0	31.8	31.1	30.8	30.2	30.2	28.6
High School Graduate Only	31.7	32.7	32.5	33.6	33.9	33.8	33.8	36.0
Post-Secondary 1-3 Years	8.6	9.5	10.2	10.0	10.8	10.7	10.7	10.7
College Graduate	5.0	5.7	6.0	6.0	6.5	6.6	6.6	6.5

IIE DEFICIT

High School Student	2,324	2,802	3,216	3,252	2,821	3,112	3,214	4,233
Post-Secondary Student	1,242	1,783	1,906	1,802	1,626	1,929	1,979	2,572
High School Dropout	13,773	17,192	16,862	16,980	15,875	17,316	17,716	22,997
High School Graduate Only	11,495	16,443	17,085	18,269	17,049	18,552	18,923	27,454
Post-Secondary 1-3 Years	3,066	4,681	4,991	5,418	5,640	5,785	5,937	8,080
College Graduate	2,129	3,192	3,407	3,564	3,620	4,137	4,233	5,312

Table C-5. (Continued)

IIE DEFICIT (1980 $)

High School Student	3,883	4,290	4,657	4,422	3,563	3,532	3,648	4,233
Post-Secondary Student	2,075	2,729	2,760	2,451	2,053	2,189	2,247	2,572
High School Dropout	23,014	26,321	24,415	23,093	20,050	19,653	20,708	22,997
High School Graduate Only	19,209	25,174	24,739	24,845	21,533	21,056	21,478	27,454
Post-Secondary 1-3 Years	5,123	7,166	7,227	7,368	7,123	6,566	6,734	8,080
College Graduate	3,557	4,887	4,933	4,847	4,572	4,695	4,805	5,312

IIE DEFICIT DISTRIBUTION

High School Student	6.8	6.1	6.8	6.6	6.1	6.1	6.2	6.0
Post-Secondary Student	3.6	3.9	4.0	3.7	3.5	3.8	3.8	3.6
High School Dropout	40.5	37.3	35.5	34.5	34.0	34.1	34.1	32.6
High School Graduate Only	33.8	35.7	36.0	37.1	36.6	36.5	36.4	38.9
Post-Secondary 1-3 Years	9.0	10.2	10.5	11.0	12.1	11.4	11.4	11.4
College Graduate	6.3	6.9	1.2	7.2	7.8	8.1	8.1	7.5

IIE AVERAGE DEFICIT

High School Student	660	780	865	862	848	962	966	1,165
Post-Secondary Student	674	804	902	872	889	995	997	1,108
High School Dropout	1,486	1,117	1,773	1,802	1,796	2,080	2,075	2,455
High School Graduate Only	1,357	1,659	1,759	1,791	1,756	1,989	1,983	2,330
Post-Secondary 1-3 Years	1,333	1,623	1,643	1,791	1,821	1,970	1,964	2,306
College Graduate	1,490	1,849	1,887	1,945	1,951	2,282	2,278	2,488

IIE AVERAGE DEFICIT (1980 $)

High School Student	1,103	1,194	1,253	1,172	1,071	1,092	1,096	1,165
Post-Secondary Student	1,126	1,231	1,306	1,186	1,123	1,129	1,132	1,108
High School Dropout	2,483	2,629	2,567	2,451	2,268	2,361	2,355	2,455
High School Graduate Only	2,268	2,540	2,547	2,436	2,218	2,258	2,251	2,330
Post-Secondary 1-3 Years	2,227	2,485	2,379	2,436	2,300	2,236	2,229	2,306
College Graduate	2,490	2,831	2,732	2,645	2,464	2,590	2,585	2,488

IFE

High School Student	812	844	881	931	786	754	779	862
Post-Secondary Student	684	751	772	723	737	764	793	869
High School Dropout	5,705	6,209	5,733	5,652	5,274	5,162	5,297	5,802
High School Graduate Only	3,143	3,867	3,818	4,013	3,859	3,909	4,014	4,947
Post-Secondary 1-3 Years	1,000	1,287	1,395	1,366	1,442	1,374	1,415	1,607
College Graduate	663	810	803	809	921	952	982	1,023

IFE INCIDENCE

High School Student	15.9	17.9	17.5	18.1	16.3	15.3	15.4	17.6
Post-Secondary Student	15.4	17.3	17.5	16.4	17.2	16.9	17.1	18.4
High School Dropout	21.1	24.0	22.3	22.2	21.6	21.5	21.6	24.5
High School Graduate Only	8.1	9.9	9.5	9.8	9.0	8.9	9.0	10.8
Post-Secondary 1-3 Years	1.3	8.8	9.1	8.3	8.2	7.6	7.6	8.5
College Graduate	4.5	5.2	4.8	4.7	5.0	4.9	5.0	5.1

Table C-5. (Continued)

IFE DISTRIBUTION

High School Student	6.8	6.1	6.6	6.9	6.0	5.8	5.9	5.7
Post-Secondary Student	5.9	5.5	5.8	5.4	5.7	5.9	6.0	5.8
High School Dropout	47.5	45.1	42.8	41.9	40.5	40.0	39.9	38.4
High School Graduate Only	26.2	28.1	28.4	29.7	29.6	30.3	30.2	32.7
Post-Secondary 1-3 Years	8.3	9.3	10.4	10.1	11.1	10.6	10.7	10.6
College Graduate	5.5	5.9	6.0	6.0	7.1	7.4	7.4	6.8

IFE DEFICIT

High School Student	1,329	1,505	1,707	1,918	1,791	1,743	1,799	2,238
Post-Secondary Student	947	1,257	1,236	1,288	1,457	1,632	1,680	2,196
High School Dropout	9,902	11,746	11,719	11,960	12,005	13,112	13,483	17,250
High School Graduate Only	5,007	6,896	6,987	7,838	7,841	8,927	9,153	12,850
Post-Secondary 1-3 Years	1,528	2,199	2,405	2,427	2,907	3,232	3,322	3,997
College Graduate	987	1,321	1,402	1,471	1,768	2,155	2,219	2,469

IFE DEFICIT (1980 $)

High School Student	2,221	2,304	2,471	2,609	2,262	1,978	2,042	2,238
Post-Secondary Student	1,583	1,925	1,790	1,751	1,841	1,853	1,907	2,196
High School Dropout	16,546	17,984	16,969	16,266	15,162	14,882	15,303	17,250
High School Graduate Only	8,367	10,558	10,117	10,660	9,903	10,132	10,388	12,850
Post-Secondary 1-3 Years	2,554	3,366	3,482	3,300	3,671	3,668	3,770	3,997
College Graduate	1,650	2,023	2,030	2,001	2,234	2,446	2,519	2,469

IFE DEFICIT DISTRIBUTION

High School Student	6.7	6.0	6.7	7.1	6.5	5.6	5.7	5.5
Post-Secondary Student	5.7	5.0	4.9	4.8	5.2	5.3	5.3	5.4
High School Dropout	50.3	47.1	46.0	44.5	43.2	42.6	42.6	42.1
High School Graduate Only	25.4	27.7	27.4	29.1	28.2	29.0	28.9	31.3
Post-Secondary 1-3 Years	7.8	8.8	9.4	9.0	10.5	10.5	10.5	9.7
College Graduate	5.0	5.3	5.5	5.5	6.4	7.0	7.0	6.0

IFE AVERAGE DEFICIT

High School Student	1,635	1,783	1,937	2,060	2,278	2,313	2,311	2,596
Post-Secondary Student	1,385	1,674	1,602	1,782	1,977	2,137	2,119	2,527
High School Dropout	1,736	1,892	2,044	2,116	2,276	2,540	2,545	2,973
High School Graduate Only	1,641	1,783	1,830	1,953	2,032	2,284	2,280	2,597
Post-Secondary 1-3 Years	1,528	1,708	1,643	1,777	2,016	2,352	2,348	2,487
College Graduate	1,490	1,631	1,746	1,818	1,919	2,263	2,259	2,414

IFE AVERAGE DEFICIT (1980 $)

High School Student	2,732	2,730	2,805	2,802	2,877	2,625	2,623	2,596
Post-Secondary Student	2,314	2,563	2,320	2,423	2,497	2,425	2,405	2,527
High School Dropout	2,901	2,897	2,960	2,878	2,875	2,883	2,889	2,973
High School Graduate Only	2,742	2,730	2,650	2,656	2,566	2,592	2,588	2,597
Post-Secondary 1-3 Years	2,553	2,615	2,379	2,417	2,546	2,670	2,665	2,487
College Graduate	2,490	2,497	2,528	2,412	2,424	2,569	2,564	2,414

Table C-5. (Continued)

IFI

High School Student	498	532	507	525	467	434	449	524
Post-Secondary Student	318	395	404	364	351	321	331	416
High School Dropout	3,153	3,400	3,147	3,013	2,993	2,920	3,011	3,500
High School Graduate Only	1,627	1,932	1,943	1,984	2,047	2,076	2,133	2,731
Post-Secondary 1-3 Years	480	615	653	712	758	685	702	805
College Graduate	270	377	379	399	395	417	431	491

IFI INCIDENCE

High School Student	9.7	11.3	10.1	10.2	9.7	8.8	8.9	10.7
Post-Secondary Student	7.2	9.1	9.1	8.3	8.2	7.1	7.1	8.8
High School Dropout	11.7	13.1	12.2	11.8	12.9	12.1	12.3	14.8
High School Graduate Only	4.2	4.2	4.9	4.8	4.8	4.7	4.8	5.9
Post-Secondary 1-3 Years	3.5	4.2	4.2	4.3	4.3	3.8	3.8	4.3
College Graduate	1.8	2.4	2.3	2.3	2.1	2.2	2.2	2.4

IFI DISTRIBUTION

High School Student	7.8	7.3	7.2	7.5	6.7	6.3	6.4	6.2
Post-Secondary Student	5.0	5.4	5.7	5.2	5.0	4.7	4.7	4.9
High School Dropout	49.7	46.9	44.7	43.1	42.7	42.6	42.7	41.3
High School Graduate Only	25.6	26.6	27.6	28.4	29.2	30.3	30.2	32.3
Post-Secondary 1-3 Years	7.6	8.5	9.3	10.2	10.8	10.0	10.0	9.5
College Graduate	4.3	5.2	5.4	5.7	5.6	6.1	6.1	5.8

IFI DEFICIT

High School Student	463	540	582	631	644	626	648	863
Post-Secondary Student	287	442	484	458	453	440	447	699
High School Dropout	4,035	4,633	4,496	4,618	4,992	5,585	5,745	7,952
High School Graduate Only	2,013	2,602	2,608	2,966	3,166	3,836	3,921	5,413
Post-Secondary 1-3 Years	599	822	877	1,050	1,178	1,272	1,303	1,623
College Graduate	316	499	525	634	593	739	761	902

IFI DEFICIT (1980 $)

High School Student	774	827	843	858	814	711	735	863
Post-Secondary Student	479	677	701	623	572	499	507	699
High School Dropout	6,742	7,093	6,510	6,280	6,305	6,339	6,520	7,952
High School Graduate Only	3,363	3,984	3,776	4,034	3,999	4,354	4,451	5,413
Post-Secondary 1-3 Years	1,001	1,258	1,270	1,428	1,488	1,444	1,479	1,623
College Graduate	528	764	761	862	749	839	864	902

IFI DEFICIT DISTRIBUTION

High School Student	6.0	5.7	6.1	6.1	5.8	5.0	5.1	4.9
Post-Secondary Student	3.7	4.6	5.1	4.4	4.1	3.5	3.5	4.0
High School Dropout	52.3	48.6	47.0	44.6	45.3	44.7	44.8	45.6
High School Graduate Only	26.1	27.3	27.2	28.6	28.7	30.7	30.6	31.0
Post-Secondary 1-3 Years	7.6	8.6	9.2	10.1	10.7	10.2	10.2	9.3
College Graduate	4.1	5.2	5.5	6.1	5.4	5.9	5.9	5.2

Table C-5. (Continued)

IFI AVERAGE DEFICIT

High School Student	930	1,015	1,147	1,201	1,379	1,444	1,444	1,647
Post-Secondary Student	901	1,119	1,200	1,258	1,292	1,370	1,351	1,682
High School Dropout	1,280	1,363	1,429	1,532	1,668	1,913	1,908	2,272
High School Graduate Only	1,237	1,347	1,342	1,495	1,547	1,848	1,839	1,982
Post-Secondary 1-3 Years	1,247	1,336	1,343	1,474	1,554	1,858	1,857	2,017
College Graduate	1,172	1,322	1,387	1,588	1,501	1,771	1,768	1,840

IFI AVERAGE DEFICIT (1980 $)

High School Student	1,554	1,554	1,661	1,633	1,742	1,639	1,639	1,647
Post-Secondary Student	1,506	1,713	1,738	1,711	1,632	1,555	1,533	1,682
High School Dropout	2,139	2,087	2,069	2,083	2,107	2,171	2,166	2,272
High School Graduate Only	2,067	2,062	1,943	2,033	1,954	2,097	2,087	1,982
Post-Secondary 1-3 Years	2,084	2,045	1,945	2,005	1,962	2,109	2,108	2,017
College Graduate	1,958	2,024	2,008	2,160	1,896	2,010	2,007	1,840

PERCENT IIE IN IFE

High School Student	18.1	20.1	20.1	20.2	18.9	17.1	17.2	19.6
Post-Secondary Student	19.8	20.9	21.8	21.4	21.5	23.8	23.9	24.3
High School Dropout	44.2	47.5	45.3	44.9	44.6	44.6	44.6	48.3
High School Graduate Only	25.9	28.9	29.1	29.1	28.0	28.7	28.7	32.2
Post-Secondary 1-3 Years	29.9	32.4	31.6	32.3	32.1	30.5	30.3	33.1
College Graduate	30.0	31.6	29.2	29.4	32.8	32.5	32.5	30.6

EARNINGS SUPPLEMENTION RATE - TOTAL

High School Student	38.7	37.0	42.4	43.6	40.6	42.5	42.4	39.2
Post-Secondary Student	53.5	47.4	47.7	49.7	52.4	58.0	58.3	52.2
High School Dropout	44.7	45.2	45.1	46.7	43.2	43.4	43.2	39.7
High School Graduate Only	48.2	50.0	49.1	50.6	46.9	46.9	46.9	44.8
Post-Secondary 1-3 Years	52.0	52.2	53.2	47.8	47.4	50.2	50.4	49.9
College Graduate	59.3	53.4	52.8	50.7	57.1	56.2	56.1	52.0

EARNINGS SUPPLEMENTATION RATE - TRANSFERS

High School Student	25.7	27.2	30.5	31.0	25.1	28.2	28.0	26.5
Post-Secondary Student	25.4	22.9	20.8	24.1	18.5	16.6	17.0	15.9
High School Dropout	32.7	34.1	33.7	33.9	30.7	30.3	30.2	28.2
High School Graduate Only	27.7	33.2	30.8	30.4	26.1	25.6	25.6	24.8
Post-Secondary 1-3 Years	23.3	25.2	26.9	23.3	21.3	22.2	22.0	21.8
College Graduate	15.8	18.0	14.5	15.9	14.8	11.9	11.8	11.3

Table C-6. SUMMARY SEVERE HARDSHIP MEASURES, 1974 THROUGH 1980, FOR TOTAL WORK FORCE, DISAGGREGATED BY AGE

	1974	1975	1976	1977	1978	1979	1979R	1980
Work Force								
16-19	11,401	11,062	11,268	11,374	11,319	11,347	11,648	10,955
16-19 Student	6,486	6,098	6,337	6,450	6,054	6,166	6,314	6,218
20-24	15,564	15,709	16,259	16,673	17,347	17,232	17,787	18,051
20-24 Student	2,456	2,390	2,444	2,420	2,411	2,557	2,636	2,572
25-44	41,635	43,061	44,889	46,632	48,653	50,971	52,100	53,840
45-64	30,752	30,478	30,696	30,845	30,813	30,905	31,175	31,284
65+	4,198	4,132	4,036	4,139	4,230	4,193	4,272	4,218
Work Force Distribution								
16-19	11.0	10.6	10.5	10.4	10.1	9.9	10.0	9.3
16-19 Student	6.3	5.8	5.9	5.9	5.4	5.4	5.4	5.3
20-24	15.0	15.0	15.2	15.2	15.4	15.0	15.2	15.3
20-24 Student	2.4	2.3	2.3	2.2	2.1	2.2	2.3	2.2
25-44	40.2	41.2	41.9	42.5	43.3	44.5	44.5	45.5
45-64	29.7	29.2	28.6	28.1	27.4	27.0	26.6	26.4
65+	4.1	4.0	3.8	3.8	3.8	3.7	3.7	3.6
Unemployment								
16-19	3,604	3,595	3,481	3,519	3,088	2,990	3,085	3,235
16-19 Student	1,741	1,620	1,624	1,644	1,329	1,298	1,341	1,509
20-24	4,655	5,107	5,042	5,025	4,548	4,382	4,532	5,196
20-24 Student	599	642	601	591	486	449	462	539
25-44	6,637	8,013	7,890	7,461	7,026	7,533	7,785	9,412
45-64	3,291	3,976	3,670	3,224	2,743	2,822	2,827	3,327
65+	348	414	364	283	333	244	247	238
Share of Unemployment								
16-19	19.4	17.0	17.0	18.0	17.4	16.6	16.7	15.1
16-19 Student	9.4	7.7	7.9	8.4	7.5	7.2	7.3	7.0
20-24	25.1	24.2	24.7	25.8	25.6	24.4	24.5	24.3
20-24 Student	3.2	3.0	2.9	3.0	2.7	2.5	2.5	2.5
25-44	35.8	38.0	38.6	38.2	39.6	41.9	42.2	44.0
45-64	17.8	18.8	17.9	16.5	15.5	15.7	15.3	15.5
65+	1.9	1.9	1.8	1.5	1.9	1.4	1.3	1.1
Unemployment Rate								
16-19	31.6	32.5	30.9	30.9	27.3	24.6	26.5	29.5
16-19 Student	26.8	26.6	25.6	25.5	22.0	21.1	21.2	24.3
20-24	29.9	32.5	31.0	30.1	26.2	25.4	25.5	28.8
20-24 Student	24.4	26.9	24.6	24.4	20.2	17.6	17.5	21.0
25-44	15.9	18.6	17.6	16.0	14.4	14.8	14.9	17.5
45-64	10.7	13.0	12.0	10.5	8.9	9.1	9.1	10.6
65+	8.3	10.0	9.0	6.8	7.9	5.8	5.8	5.6
Predominantly Unemployed								
16-19	1,793	2,137	2,013	1,837	1,601	1,490	1,544	1,861
16-19 Student	909	994	1,045	928	713	695	721	890
20-24	1,736	2,561	2,337	2,197	1,828	1,636	1,683	2,447
20-24 Student	211	342	276	267	218	182	188	285
25-44	2,554	3,844	3,712	3,343	2,767	2,773	2,884	4,362
45-64	1,448	2,089	1,914	1,566	1,338	1,220	1,222	1,522
65+	208	310	279	188	217	157	160	155
Incidence Predominantly Unemployed								
16-19	15.7	19.3	17.9	16.2	14.1	13.1	13.3	17.0
16-19 Student	14.0	16.3	16.5	14.4	11.8	11.3	11.4	14.3
20-24	11.2	16.3	14.4	13.2	10.5	9.5	9.5	13.6
20-24 Student	8.6	14.3	11.2	11.0	9.0	7.1	7.1	11.1
25-44	6.1	8.9	8.3	7.2	5.7	5.4	5.5	8.1
45-64	4.7	6.9	6.2	5.1	4.3	3.9	3.9	4.9
65+	5.0	7.5	6.9	4.5	5.1	3.7	3.7	3.7

Table C-6. (Continued)

Share of Predominantly Unemployed								
16-19	23.2	19.5	19.6	20.1	20.7	20.5	20.6	18.0
16-19 Student	11.7	9.1	10.2	10.2	9.2	9.6	9.6	8.6
20-24	22.4	23.4	22.8	24.1	23.6	22.5	22.5	23.6
20-24 Student	2.7	3.1	2.7	2.9	2.8	2.5	2.5	2.8
25-44	33.0	35.1	36.2	36.6	35.7	38.1	38.5	42.2
45-64	18.7	19.0	18.7	17.1	17.3	16.8	16.3	14.7
65+	2.7	2.8	2.7	2.1	2.8	2.2	2.1	1.5
IIE								
16-19	6,985	7,665	7,547	7,477	6,870	6,740	6,923	7,360
16-19 Student	4,174	4,423	4,486	4,505	3,931	3,884	3,977	4,353
20-24	4,964	5,923	5,730	5,960	5,596	5,314	5,489	6,710
20-24 Student	1,001	1,178	1,096	1,076	983	1,041	1,071	1,242
25-44	7,463	8,699	8,894	9,134	8,961	8,607	8,857	10,989
45-64	5,733	6,337	6,119	6,075	5,606	5,415	5,474	6,084
65+	1,612	1,721	1,603	1,679	1,628	1,499	1,526	1,603
IIE INCIDENCE								
16-19	61.3	69.3	67.0	65.7	60.7	59.4	59.4	67.2
16-19 Student	64.4	72.5	70.8	69.8	64.9	63.0	63.0	70.0
20-24	31.9	37.7	35.2	35.7	32.3	30.8	30.9	37.2
20-24 Student	40.7	49.3	44.8	44.5	40.8	40.7	40.6	48.3
25-44	17.9	20.2	19.8	19.6	18.4	16.9	17.0	20.4
45-64	18.6	20.8	19.9	19.7	18.2	17.5	17.6	19.4
65+	38.4	41.6	39.7	40.6	38.5	35.7	35.7	38.0
IIE Share								
16-19	26.1	25.3	25.2	24.7	24.0	24.4	24.5	22.5
16-19 Student	15.6	14.6	15.0	14.9	13.7	14.1	14.1	13.3
20-24	18.6	19.5	19.2	19.7	19.5	19.3	19.4	20.5
20-24 Student	3.7	3.9	3.7	3.5	3.4	3.8	3.8	3.8
25-44	27.9	28.7	29.8	30.0	31.3	31.2	31.3	33.6
45-64	21.4	20.9	20.5	20.0	19.6	19.6	19.4	18.6
65+	6.0	5.7	5.4	5.5	5.7	5.4	5.4	4.9
IIE Deficit								
16-19	5,780	7,757	7,852	7,783	7,437	8,103	8,369	10,447
16-19 Student	2,656	3,312	3,640	3,693	3,183	3,551	3,655	4,694
20-24	5,536	8,384	8,494	8,855	8,046	8,968	9,264	13,310
20-24 Student	716	1,023	1,114	1,021	834	1,052	1,087	1,378
25-44	10,539	14,295	15,937	16,825	16,121	17,633	18,120	27,139
45-64	9,782	12,780	12,329	12,776	12,259	13,298	13,360	16,198
65+	2,392	2,876	2,854	3,044	2,768	2,827	2,886	3,554
IFI Incidence								
16-19	9.8	12.2	9.9	9.8	10.4	9.4	9.5	10.9
16-19 Student	8.4	10.0	8.5	8.4	8.0	7.3	7.3	8.5
20-24	7.7	9.4	9.4	8.9	8.7	8.0	8.1	10.0
20-24 Student	8.1	10.3	11.1	10.9	10.1	7.6	7.6	9.8
25-44	5.6	6.1	6.0	5.9	5.7	5.7	5.8	7.0
45-64	4.5	4.9	4.6	4.6	4.3	4.2	4.1	4.7
65+	7.1	7.2	7.2	6.1	4.7	5.3	5.3	6.2
IIE Deficit 1980 $								
16-19	9,658	11,876	11,370	10,586	9,393	9,197	9,499	10,447
16-19 Student	4,438	5,071	5,271	5,022	4,020	4,030	4,149	4,694
20-24	9,250	12,836	12,299	12,043	10,163	10,179	10,514	13,310
20-24 Student	1,197	1,567	1,613	1,388	1,053	1,194	1,234	1,378
25-44	17,611	21,886	23,076	22,882	20,360	20,013	20,566	27,139
45-64	16,345	19,566	17,853	17,375	15,483	15,093	15,163	16,198
65+	3,997	4,403	4,133	4,140	3,496	3,209	3,275	3,554
IIE Deficit Share								
16-19	17.0	16.8	16.5	15.8	15.9	15.9	16.1	14.8
16-19 Student	7.8	7.2	7.7	7.5	6.8	7.0	7.0	6.6
20-24	16.3	18.2	17.9	18.0	17.3	17.6	17.8	18.8
20-24 Student	2.1	2.2	2.3	2.1	1.8	2.1	2.1	2.0
25-44	31.0	31.0	33.6	34.1	34.6	34.7	34.8	38.4
45-64	28.7	27.7	26.0	25.9	26.3	26.2	25.7	22.9
65+	7.0	6.2	6.0	6.2	5.9	5.6	5.5	5.0

Table C-6. (Continued)

IIE Average Deficit

16-19	828	1,012	1,040	1,041	1,083	1,202	1,209	1,420
16-19 Student	636	749	811	820	810	914	919	1,078
20-24	115	1,416	1,482	1,486	1,438	1,688	1,688	1,984
20-24 Student	716	869	1,016	949	848	1,011	1,016	1,109
25-44	1,412	1,643	1,792	1,842	1,799	2,049	2,046	2,470
45-64	1,706	2,017	2,015	2,103	2,187	2,456	2,441	2,662
65+	1,484	1,671	1,781	1,813	1,701	1,886	1,891	2,216

IIE Average Deficit (1980 $)

16-19	1,384	1,549	1,506	1,416	1,368	1,364	1,372	1,420
16-19 Student	1,063	1,147	1,174	1,115	1,023	1,037	1,043	1,078
20-24	1,863	2,168	2,146	2,021	1,816	1,916	1,916	1,984
20-24 Student	1,196	1,330	1,471	1,291	1,071	1,147	1,153	1,109
25-44	2,359	2,515	2,595	2,505	2,272	2,326	2,322	2,470
45-64	2,851	3,088	2,918	2,860	2,762	2,788	2,771	2,662
65+	2,480	2,558	2,579	2,466	2,183	2,141	2,146	2,216

IFE

16-19	1,791	2,035	1,852	1,880	1,858	1,723	1,782	1,944
16-19 Student	947	977	967	1,008	873	816	840	952
20-24	1,857	2,275	2,331	2,279	2,310	2,188	2,268	2,676
20-24 Student	405	464	490	448	454	459	474	503
25-44	3,499	4,246	4,159	4,158	4,133	4,263	4,421	5,384
45-64	2,907	3,213	3,103	3,138	2,880	2,849	2,880	3,172
65+	1,953	1,999	1,957	2,039	1,839	1,891	1,929	1,935

IFE Share

16-19	14.9	14.8	13.8	13.9	14.3	13.3	13.4	12.9
16-19 Student	7.9	7.1	7.2	7.5	6.7	6.3	6.3	6.3
20-24	15.5	16.5	17.4	16.9	17.7	16.9	17.1	17.7
20-24 Student	3.4	3.4	3.7	3.3	3.5	3.6	3.6	3.3
25-44	29.1	30.8	31.0	30.8	31.7	33.0	33.3	35.6
45-64	24.2	23.3	23.2	23.3	72.1	22.0	21.7	21.0
65+	16.3	14.5	14.6	15.1	14.1	14.6	14.5	12.8

IFE Incidence

16-19	15.7	18.4	16.4	16.5	16.4	15.2	15.3	17.7
16-19 Student	14.6	16.0	15.3	15.6	14.4	13.2	13.3	15.3
20-24	11.9	14.5	14.3	13.7	13.3	12.7	12.8	14.8
20-24 Student	16.5	19.4	20.0	18.5	18.8	18.0	18.0	19.6
25-44	8.4	9.9	9.3	8.9	8.5	8.4	8.5	10.0
45-64	9.5	10.5	10.1	10.2	9.3	9.2	9.2	10.1
65+	46.5	48.4	48.5	49.3	43.5	45.1	45.1	45.9

IFE Deficit

16-19	2,820	3,459	3,310	3,599	3,949	3,937	4,055	4,850
16-19 Student	1,443	1,661	1,706	1,953	1,852	1,747	1,788	2,337
20-24	2,800	3,792	4,094	4,229	4,588	4,784	4,940	7,001
20-24 Student	565	763	811	825	891	903	931	1,246
25-44	6,555	8,796	8,991	9,520	9,952	11,444	11,884	16,322
45-64	4,508	5,547	5,577	5,744	5,655	6,394	6,442	7,900
65+	3,018	3,331	3,483	3,810	3,626	4,242	4,335	4,926

IFE Deficit (1980 $)

16-19	4,712	5,296	4,793	4,894	4,987	4,468	4,603	4,850
16-19 Student	2,411	2,544	2,470	2,656	2,339	1,983	2,029	2,337
20-24	4,678	5,806	5,928	5,752	5,794	5,430	5,607	7,001
20-24 Student	944	1,169	1,175	1,122	1,125	1,025	1,056	1,246
25-44	10,953	13,466	13,091	12,947	12,569	12,989	13,488	16,322
45-64	7,533	8,492	8,075	7,812	7,143	7,257	7,312	7,900
65+	5,043	5,100	5,044	5,181	4,580	4,815	4,920	4,926

Table C-6. (Continued)

IFE Deficit Share

16-19	14.3	13.9	13.0	13.4	14.2	12.8	12.8	11.8
16-19 Student	7.3	6.7	6.7	7.3	6.7	5.7	5.6	5.7
20-24	14.2	15.2	16.1	15.7	16.5	15.5	15.6	17.1
20-24 Student	2.9	3.1	3.2	3.1	3.2	2.9	2.9	3.0
25-44	33.3	34.5	35.3	35.4	35.8	37.2	37.5	39.8
45-64	22.9	22.3	21.9	21.4	20.4	20.8	20.4	19.3
65+	15.3	13.4	13.7	14.2	13.1	13.8	13.7	12.0

IFE Average Deficit

16-19	1,574	1,700	1,788	1,914	2,125	2,284	2,275	2,495
16-19 Student	1,525	1,700	1,764	1,938	2,122	2,140	2,129	2,454
20-24	1,508	1,667	1,756	1,855	1,986	2,186	2,178	2,617
20-24 Student	1,395	1,645	1,656	1,840	1,962	1,966	1,964	2,478
25-44	1,873	2,072	2,162	2,290	2,408	2,685	2,688	3,032
45-64	1,551	1,726	1,797	1,831	1,964	2,244	2,237	2,491
65+	1,545	1,667	1,780	1,868	1,972	2,244	2,247	2,546

IFE Average Deficit (1980 $)

16-19	2,630	2,603	2,589	2,603	2,684	2,592	2,582	2,495
16-19 Student	2,548	2,603	2,554	2,636	2,680	2,429	2,416	2,454
20-24	2,520	2,552	2,543	2,523	2,508	2,481	2,472	2,617
20-24 Student	2,331	2,518	2,398	2,502	2,478	2,231	2,229	2,478
25-44	3,130	3,172	3,131	3,114	3,041	3,047	3,051	3,032
45-64	2,592	2,643	2,602	2,490	2,481	2,547	2,539	2,491
65+	2,582	2,552	2,577	2,540	2,491	2,547	2,550	2,546

IFI

16-19	1,113	1,347	1,119	1,109	1,181	1,069	1,108	1,197
16-19 Student	547	609	540	541	482	447	460	528
20-24	1,204	1,470	1,531	1,488	1,505	1,378	1,432	1,803
20-24 Student	198	246	272	264	244	194	201	253
25-44	2,333	2,632	2,676	2,741	2,791	2,894	2,998	3,749
45-64	1,398	1,505	1,415	1,410	1,337	1,287	1,291	1,455
65+	299	299	291	251	199	224	227	261

IFI Share

16-19	17.5	18.6	15.9	15.8	16.8	15.6	15.7	14.1
16-19 Student	8.6	8.4	7.7	7.7	6.9	6.5	6.5	6.2
20-24	19.0	20.2	21.8	21.3	21.5	20.1	20.3	21.3
20-24 Student	3.1	3.4	3.9	3.8	3.5	2.8	2.8	3.0
25-44	36.8	36.3	38.0	39.2	39.8	42.2	42.5	44.3
45-64	22.0	20.8	20.1	20.1	19.1	18.8	18.3	17.2
65+	4.7	4.1	4.1	3.6	2.8	3.3	3.2	3.1

IFI Deficit

16-19	1,140	1,476	1,285	1,329	1,690	1,670	1,733	2,060
16-19 Student	473	618	582	623	619	604	621	792
20-24	1,354	1,725	1,940	2,173	2,171	2,254	2,328	3,582
20-24 Student	183	265	351	338	342	235	243	427
25-44	3,377	4,155	4,167	4,712	5,020	5,972	6,169	8,685
45-64	1,622	1,962	1,917	1,909	1,985	2,336	2,329	2,814
65+	220	221	264	233	161	267	266	311

IFI Deficit (1980 $)

16-19	1,905	2,259	1,860	1,807	2,135	1,896	1,967	2,060
16-19 Student	790	946	843	848	782	686	704	792
20-24	2,262	2,641	2,809	2,955	2,742	2,558	2,643	3,582
20-24 Student	306	405	509	460	432	267	276	427
25-44	5,642	6,361	6,034	6,409	6,340	6,778	7,001	8,685
45-64	2,711	3,004	2,776	2,597	2,507	2,651	2,644	2,814
65+	367	338	382	317	203	303	302	311

IFI Deficit Share

16-19	14.8	15.5	13.4	12.8	15.3	13.4	13.5	11.8
16-19 Student	6.1	6.5	6.1	6.0	5.6	4.8	4.8	4.5
20-24	17.6	18.1	20.3	21.0	19.7	18.0	18.2	20.5
20-24 Student	2.4	2.8	3.7	3.3	3.1	1.9	1.9	2.4
25-44	43.8	43.6	43.5	45.5	45.5	47.8	48.1	49.8
45-64	21.0	17.0	20.0	18.4	18.0	18.7	18.2	16.1
65+	2.8	2.3	2.8	2.3	1.5	2.1	2.1	1.8

Table C-6. (Continued)

	1974	1975	1976	1977	1978	1979	1979R	1980
IFI Average Deficit								
16-19	1,024	1,096	1,148	1,198	1,432	1,562	1,564	1,721
16-19 Student	864	1,015	1,078	1,153	1,284	1,351	1,348	1,500
20-24	1,129	1,173	1,267	1,460	1,443	1,636	1,626	1,986
20-24 Student	923	1,077	1,290	1,282	1,402	1,211	1,213	1,686
25-44	1,448	1,579	1,557	1,719	1,799	2,063	2,058	2,317
45-64	1,161	1,304	1,355	1,355	1,485	1,814	1,805	1,934
65+	735	739	905	930	808	1,196	1,171	1,193
IFI Average Deficit (1980 $)								
16-19	1,711	1,678	1,662	1,629	1,809	1,773	1,775	1,721
16-19 Student	1,444	1,554	1,561	1,568	1,622	1,533	1,530	1,500
20-24	1,878	1,796	1,835	1,986	1,823	1,857	1,846	1,986
20-24 Student	1,542	1,649	1,868	1,743	1,771	1,374	1,377	1,686
25-44	2,420	2,417	2,255	2,338	2,272	2,342	2,336	2,317
45-64	1,940	1,996	1,962	1,843	1,876	2,059	2,049	1,934
65+	1,228	1,131	1,310	1,265	1,021	1,357	1,329	1,193
IIE In IFE								
16-19	19.3	22.1	20.3	20.7	21.1	19.3	19.4	21.9
16-19 Student	16.9	18.0	17.5	18.2	16.8	14.9	15.0	17.3
20-24	26.8	29.1	30.2	28.3	29.4	29.4	29.5	31.9
20-24 Student	21.6	24.8	26.8	24.6	24.5	26.9	27.0	27.7
25-44	32.9	36.1	34.7	33.8	33.1	34.7	34.9	37.4
45-64	36.9	39.4	38.3	38.3	37.6	37.0	36.8	38.9
65+	70.6	71.6	70.9	75.6	69.0	68.7	68.7	73.2
Earnings Supplementation Rate - Total								
16-19	37.9	33.8	39.6	41.0	36.5	37.9	37.8	38.4
16-19 Student	42.2	37.7	44.1	46.4	44.7	45.2	45.2	44.6
20-24	35.1	35.4	34.3	34.7	34.9	37.0	36.9	32.6
20-24 Student	51.0	47.0	44.4	41.2	46.2	57.7	57.7	49.7
25-44	33.3	38.0	35.7	34.1	32.5	32.1	32.2	30.4
45-64	51.9	53.2	54.4	55.1	53.6	54.8	55.2	54.1
65+	84.7	85.0	85.1	87.7	89.2	88.2	88.2	86.5
Earnings Supplementation Rate - Transfers								
16-19	24.9	23.7	26.4	28.7	22.2	22.3	22.4	23.7
16-19 Student	26.3	26.8	28.7	32.0	25.3	25.7	25.8	26.5
20-24	20.6	23.5	21.7	21.9	19.2	17.7	17.7	17.7
20-24 Student	21.3	21.0	19.2	18.3	15.8	15.6	15.5	13.9
25-44	21.8	27.5	25.3	22.9	19.2	19.7	19.7	18.2
45-64	29.5	32.6	32.1	30.5	27.3	26.7	26.6	27.3
65+	51.7	52.4	50.4	53.7	52.9	50.2	50.1	47.3

Table C-7. SUMMARY SEVERE HARDSHIP MEASURES, 1974 THROUGH 1980, FOR TOTAL WORK FORCE, DISAGGREGATED BY RACE/ETHNIC ORIGIN

	1974	1975	1976	1977	1978	1979	1979R	1980
WORK FORCE								
White	91,682	92,229	94,727	96,734	98,985	101,097	102,761	103,608
Black	10,306	10,496	10,633	10,972	11,305	11,405	11,702	11,980
Hispanic	4,528	4,405	4,653	5,098	5,240	5,822	5,872	6,069
SHARE OF WORK FORCE								
White	88.5	88.3	88.4	88.2	88.1	88.2	87.8	87.5
Black	9.9	10.0	9.9	10.0	10.1	9.9	10.0	10.1
Hispanic	4.4	4.2	4.3	4.6	4.7	5.1	5.0	5.1
UNEMPLOYED								
White	15,489	17,660	17,133	16,150	14,548	14,850	15,168	17,505
Black	2,774	3,100	2,927	2,974	2,831	2,764	2,880	3,352
Hispanic	1,109	1,153	1,195	1,218	1,116	1,279	1,313	1,395
SHARE OF UNEMPLOYED								
White	83.6	83.7	83.8	82.8	82.0	82.6	82.1	81.8
Black	15.0	14.7	14.3	15.2	16.0	15.4	15.6	15.7
Hispanic	6.0	5.5	5.8	6.2	6.3	7.1	7.1	6.5
UNEMPLOYMENT RATE								
White	16.9	19.1	18.1	16.7	14.7	14.7	14.8	16.9
Black	26.9	29.5	27.5	27.1	25.0	24.2	24.6	28.0
Hispanic	24.5	26.2	25.7	23.9	21.3	22.0	22.3	23.0
PREDOMINANTLY UNEMPLOYED								
White	6,044	8,731	8,190	7,003	5,850	5,491	5,615	7,934
Black	1,577	2,032	1,844	1,936	1,732	1,631	1,703	2,144
Hispanic	514	624	638	620	526	562	579	704
SHARE PREDOMINANTLY UNEMPLOYED								
White	78.1	79.8	79.9	76.7	75.5	75.5	74.9	76.7
Black	20.4	18.6	18.0	21.2	22.3	22.4	22.7	20.7
Hispanic	6.6	5.7	6.2	6.8	6.8	7.7	7.7	6.8
INCIDENCE PREDOMINANTLY UNEMPLOYED								
White	6.6	9.5	8.6	7.2	5.9	5.4	5.5	7.7
Black	15.3	19.4	17.3	17.6	15.3	14.3	14.6	17.9
Hispanic	11.4	14.2	13.7	12.2	10.0	9.7	9.9	11.6
IIE								
White	22,411	25,488	25,219	25,445	23,944	23,137	23,584	27,146
Black	3,903	4,351	4,117	4,274	4,210	3,946	4,101	4,762
Hispanic	1,463	1,520	1,560	1,688	1,579	1,662	1,718	2,046
IIE SHARE								
White	83.8	84.0	84.4	83.9	83.5	83.9	83.4	82.9
Black	14.6	14.3	13.8	14.1	15.2	14.3	14.5	14.5
Hispanic	5.5	5.0	5.2	5.6	5.5	6.0	6.1	6.2
IIE RATE								
White	24.4	27.6	26.6	26.3	24.2	22.9	22.9	26.2
Black	37.9	41.5	38.7	39.0	37.2	34.6	35.0	39.8
Hispanic	32.3	34.5	33.5	33.1	30.1	28.5	29.3	33.7
IIE DEFICIT								
White	28,407	38,490	39,601	41,175	38,848	42,471	43,174	57,742
Black	4,913	6,950	6,933	7,039	6,905	7,438	7,732	11,082
Hispanic	1,836	2,260	2,397	2,574	2,509	3,090	3,173	3,855

Table C-7. (Continued)

IIE DEFICIT (1980 $)								
White	47,468	58,930	57,343	55,999	49,065	48,205	49,003	57,742
Black	8,210	10,641	10,039	9,573	8,722	8,442	8,776	11,082
Hispanic	3,051	3,460	3,471	3,500	3,169	3,507	3,602	3,855
SHARE IIE DEFICIT								
White	83.5	83.5	83.4	83.5	83.3	83.6	83.0	81.7
Black	14.4	15.1	14.6	14.3	14.8	14.6	14.9	15.7
Hispanic	5.4	4.9	5.1	5.2	5.4	6.1	6.1	5.5
IIE AVERAGE DEFICIT								
White	1,268	1,510	1,570	1,618	1,622	1,836	1,831	2,127
Black	1,259	1,597	1,684	1,647	1,640	1,885	1,886	2,327
Hispanic	1,254	1,487	1,537	1,525	1,589	1,860	1,847	1,884
IIE AVERAGE DEFICIT (1980 $)								
White	2,119	2,312	2,273	2,200	2,049	2,084	2,078	2,127
Black	2,104	2,445	2,438	2,240	2,071	2,139	2,141	2,327
Hispanic	2,095	2,277	2,226	2,074	2,007	2,111	2,096	1,884
IFE								
White	9,116	10,734	10,346	10,406	9,917	9,896	10,111	11,554
Black	2,646	2,783	2,768	2,788	2,835	2,754	2,851	3,154
Hispanic	815	916	915	892	868	932	957	1,136
IFE SHARE								
White	75.9	78.0	77.2	77.1	76.2	76.6	76.1	76.5
Black	22.0	20.2	20.7	20.7	21.8	21.3	21.5	20.9
Hispanic	6.8	6.7	6.8	6.6	6.7	7.2	7.2	7.5
IFE RATE								
White	9.9	11.6	10.9	10.8	10.0	9.8	9.8	11.2
Black	25.7	26.5	26.0	25.4	25.1	24.1	24.4	26.3
Hispanic	18.0	20.8	19.7	17.5	16.6	16.0	16.3	18.7
IFE DEFICIT								
White	14,280	18,497	18,654	19,671	20,114	22,413	22,831	29,755
Black	5,037	5,990	6,252	6,674	7,047	7,811	8,129	10,100
Hispanic	1,425	1,706	1,846	1,770	1,897	2,280	2,311	3,187
IFE DEFICIT (1980 $)								
White	23,863	28,320	27,011	26,753	25,404	25,439	25,913	29,755
Black	8,417	9,171	9,053	9,077	8,900	8,865	9,226	10,100
Hispanic	2,381	2,612	2,673	2,407	2,395	2,588	2,623	3,187
IFE DEFICIT SHARE								
White	72.5	74.2	73.3	73.1	72.4	72.8	72.1	72.6
Black	25.6	24.0	24.6	24.8	25.4	25.4	25.7	24.6
Hispanic	7.2	6.8	7.3	6.6	6.8	7.4	7.3	7.8
IFE AVERAGE DEFICIT								
White	1,566	1,723	1,803	1,890	2,028	2,265	2,258	2,575
Black	1,904	2,153	2,258	2,394	2,486	2,836	2,851	3,202
Hispanic	1,747	1,863	2,017	1,985	2,186	2,447	2,415	2,806
IFE AVERAGE DEFICIT (1980 $)								
White	2,617	2,638	2,610	2,570	2,561	2,571	2,563	2,575
Black	3,182	3,296	3,270	3,256	3,140	3,219	3,236	3,202
Hispanic	2,919	2,852	2,921	2,700	2,761	2,777	2,741	2,806
IFI								
White	4,405	5,240	4,949	4,949	4,933	4,808	4,902	5,962
Black	1,781	1,815	1,880	1,868	1,911	1,873	1,943	2,235
Hispanic	594	679	666	623	624	667	682	827
IFI SHARE								
White	69.4	72.3	70.4	70.7	70.4	70.2	69.5	70.4
Black	28.1	25.0	26.7	26.7	27.2	27.3	27.5	26.4
Hispanic	9.4	9.4	9.5	8.9	8.9	9.7	9.7	9.8

Table C-7. (Continued)

IFI RATE								
White	4.8	5.7	5.2	5.1	5.0	4.8	4.8	5.8
Black	17.3	17.3	17.7	17.0	16.9	16.4	16.6	18.7
Hispanic	13.1	15.4	14.3	12.2	11.9	11.5	11.6	13.6
IFI DEFICIT								
White	5,279	6,636	6,577	7,148	7,481	8,511	8,640	11,921
Black	2,256	2,666	2,728	2,916	3,259	3,678	3,805	4,943
Hispanic	762	919	917	881	970	1,238	1,246	1,854
IFI DEFICIT (1980 $)								
White	8,822	10,160	9,523	9,722	9,449	9,660	9,806	11,921
Black	3,770	4,082	3,950	3,966	4,116	4,174	4,319	4,943
Hispanic	1,274	1,407	1,327	1,198	1,225	1,405	1,414	1,854
IFI DEFICIT SHARE								
White	68.4	69.6	68.7	69.0	67.8	68.1	67.4	68.3
Black	29.3	28.0	28.5	28.2	29.6	29.4	29.7	28.3
Hispanic	9.9	9.6	9.6	8.5	8.8	9.9	9.7	10.6
IFI AVERAGE DEFICIT								
White	1,199	1,266	1,329	1,444	1,517	1,770	1,762	1,999
Black	1,267	1,469	1,451	1,561	1,705	1,963	1,958	2,211
Hispanic	1,283	1,353	1,377	1,414	1,553	1,856	1,827	2,242
IFI AVERAGE DEFICIT (1980 $)								
White	2,004	1,938	1,924	1,964	1,916	2,009	2,000	1,999
Black	2,117	2,249	2,101	2,123	2,153	2,228	2,222	2,211
Hispanic	2,144	2,071	1,994	1,923	1,961	2,107	2,074	2,242
IIE IN IFE								
White	27.6	30.7	29.5	29.5	28.8	28.7	28.7	31.5
Black	51.9	52.5	53.3	51.4	52.0	52.7	52.6	53.6
Hispanic	39.8	42.7	43.1	38.1	37.4	36.9	36.6	41.4
EARNINGS SUPPLEMENTATION RATE - TOTAL								
White	51.7	51.2	52.2	52.4	50.3	51.4	51.5	48.4
Black	32.7	34.8	32.1	33.0	32.6	32.0	31.8	29.1
Hispanic	27.2	25.8	27.2	30.1	28.1	28.4	28.8	27.9
EARNINGS SUPPLEMENTATION RATE - TRANSFERS								
White	29.7	31.9	31.1	30.5	26.3	26.4	26.3	25.2
Black	26.7	29.8	27.2	28.4	26.8	23.9	23.7	22.7
Hispanic	21.3	19.7	23.2	24.0	20.6	18.8	19.3	19.2

Table C-8. SUMMARY SEVERE HARDSHIP MEASURES, 1974 THROUGH 1980, FOR TOTAL WORK FORCE, DISAGGREGATED BY GEOGRAPHIC REGION

	1974	1975	1976	1977	1978	1979	1979R	1980
WORK FORCE								
NEW ENGLAND	6,321	6,163	6,038	6,419	6,652	6,861	6,856	6,749
MIDDLE ATLANTIC	17,203	17,274	17,919	18,002	18,361	18,369	18,407	18,520
EAST NORTH CENTRAL	20,487	20,227	20,614	20,906	21,375	21,717	21,808	21,898
WEST NORTH CENTRAL	8,173	8,337	8,821	9,091	9,280	9,624	9,522	9,389
SOUTH ATLANTIC	15,879	16,224	16,942	17,132	17,517	17,887	18,710	19,142
EAST SOUTH CENTRAL	6,645	6,635	6,740	6,683	6,737	6,827	7,032	7,189
WEST SOUTH CENTRAL	9,930	10,392	10,152	10,869	11,233	11,369	11,825	12,312
MOUNTAIN	4,652	4,852	5,276	5,118	5,358	5,725	6,011	6,072
PACIFIC	14,311	14,338	14,645	15,443	15,849	16,270	16,812	17,077
WORK FORCE SHARE								
NEW ENGLAND	6.1	5.9	5.6	5.9	5.9	6.0	5.9	5.7
MIDDLE ATLANTIC	16.6	16.5	16.7	16.4	16.3	16.0	15.7	15.6
EAST NORTH CENTRAL	19.8	19.4	19.2	19.1	19.0	18.9	18.6	18.5
WEST NORTH CENTRAL	7.9	8.0	8.2	8.3	8.3	8.4	8.1	7.9
SOUTH ATLANTIC	15.3	15.5	15.8	15.6	15.6	15.6	16.0	16.2
EAST SOUTH CENTRAL	6.4	6.4	6.3	6.1	6.0	6.0	6.0	6.1
WEST SOUTH CENTRAL	9.6	10.0	9.5	9.9	10.0	9.9	10.1	10.4
MOUNTAIN	4.5	4.6	4.9	4.7	4.8	5.0	5.1	5.1
PACIFIC	13.8	13.7	13.7	14.1	14.1	14.2	14.4	14.4
UNEMPLOYED								
NEW ENGLAND	1,209	1,400	1,170	1,126	1,074	1,008	1,013	1,023
MIDDLE ATLANTIC	2,937	3,563	3,728	3,280	3,014	2,902	2,927	3,285
EAST NORTH CENTRAL	3,730	4,238	3,874	3,682	3,365	3,692	3,732	4,632
WEST NORTH CENTRAL	1,175	1,326	1,315	1,426	1,257	1,283	1,279	1,494
SOUTH ATLANTIC	2,836	3,385	3,192	2,977	2,641	2,656	2,798	3,283
EAST SOUTH CENTRAL	1,192	1,240	1,249	1,186	1,033	1,092	1,135	1,441
WEST SOUTH CENTRAL	1,600	1,851	1,675	1,674	1,616	1,597	1,665	1,973
MOUNTAIN	854	985	1,040	958	821	892	944	1,101
PACIFIC	3,003	3,078	3,207	3,203	2,947	2,850	2,976	3,176
UNEMPLOYMENT RATE								
NEW ENGLAND	19.1	22.7	19.4	17.5	15.7	14.7	14.8	15.2
MIDDLE ATLANTIC	17.1	20.6	20.8	18.2	16.4	15.8	15.9	17.7
EAST NORTH CENTRAL	18.2	21.0	18.8	17.6	15.7	17.0	17.1	21.2
WEST NORTH CENTRAL	14.4	15.9	14.9	15.7	13.5	13.3	13.4	15.9
SOUTH ATLANTIC	17.9	20.9	18.8	17.4	15.1	14.8	15.0	17.2
EAST SOUTH CENTRAL	17.9	19.3	18.5	17.7	15.3	16.0	16.1	20.0
WEST SOUTH CENTRAL	16.1	17.8	16.5	15.4	14.4	14.0	14.1	16.0
MOUNTAIN	18.4	20.3	19.7	18.7	15.3	15.6	15.7	18.1
PACIFIC	21.0	21.5	21.9	20.7	18.6	17.5	17.7	18.6
SHARE UNEMPLOYED								
NEW ENGLAND	6.5	6.6	5.7	5.8	5.9	5.6	5.5	4.8
MIDDLE ATLANTIC	15.8	16.9	18.2	16.8	17.0	16.1	15.8	15.3
EAST NORTH CENTRAL	20.1	20.1	18.9	18.9	19.0	20.5	20.2	21.6
WEST NORTH CENTRAL	6.3	6.3	6.4	7.3	7.1	7.1	6.9	7.0
SOUTH ATLANTIC	15.3	16.0	15.6	15.2	14.9	14.8	15.2	15.3
EAST SOUTH CENTRAL	6.4	5.9	6.1	6.1	5.8	6.1	6.1	6.7
WEST SOUTH CENTRAL	8.6	8.8	8.2	8.6	9.1	8.9	9.0	9.2
MOUNTAIN	4.6	4.7	5.1	4.9	4.6	5.0	5.1	5.1
PACIFIC	16.2	14.6	15.7	16.4	16.6	15.9	16.1	14.8
PREDOMINANTLY UNEMPLOYED								
NEW ENGLAND	538	845	639	523	460	379	385	455
MIDDLE ATLANTIC	1,355	2,003	2,141	1,726	1,576	1,396	1,411	1,720
EAST NORTH CENTRAL	1,527	2,254	1,940	1,803	1,416	1,477	1,496	2,548
WEST NORTH CENTRAL	439	550	527	535	456	413	415	680
SOUTH ATLANTIC	1,096	1,785	1,618	1,378	1,181	1,119	1,181	1,502
EAST SOUTH CENTRAL	471	648	616	581	454	460	480	739
WEST SOUTH CENTRAL	601	839	706	681	715	651	676	820
MOUNTAIN	323	401	451	374	266	299	317	434
PACIFIC	1,391	1,617	1,619	1,530	1,222	1,082	1,131	1,448

Table C-8. (Continued)

INCIDENCE PREDOMINANTLY UNEMPLOYED

NEW ENGLAND	8.5	13.7	10.6	8.1	6.9	5.5	5.6	6.7
MIDDLE ATLANTIC	7.9	11.6	11.9	9.6	8.6	7.6	7.7	9.3
EAST NORTH CENTRAL	7.4	11.1	9.4	8.6	6.6	6.8	6.9	11.6
WEST NORTH CENTRAL	5.4	6.6	6.0	5.9	4.9	4.3	4.4	7.2
SOUTH ATLANTIC	6.9	11.0	9.6	8.0	6.8	6.3	6.3	7.8
EAST SOUTH CENTRAL	7.1	9.8	9.1	8.7	6.7	6.7	6.8	10.3
WEST SOUTH CENTRAL	6.1	8.1	7.0	6.3	6.4	5.7	5.7	6.7
MOUNTAIN	6.9	8.3	8.5	7.3	5.0	5.2	5.3	7.1
PACIFIC	9.7	11.3	11.1	9.9	7.7	6.7	6.7	8.5

SHARE PREDOMINANTLY UNEMPLOYED

NEW ENGLAND	7.0	7.7	6.2	5.7	5.9	5.2	5.1	4.4
MIDDLE ATLANTIC	17.5	18.3	20.9	18.9	20.3	19.2	18.8	16.6
EAST NORTH CENTRAL	19.7	20.6	18.9	19.7	18.3	20.3	20.0	24.6
WEST NORTH CENTRAL	5.7	5.0	5.1	5.9	5.9	5.7	5.5	6.6
SOUTH ATLANTIC	14.2	16.3	15.8	15.1	15.2	14.0	15.8	14.5
EAST SOUTH CENTRAL	6.1	5.9	6.0	6.4	5.9	6.3	6.4	7.1
WEST SOUTH CENTRAL	7.8	7.7	6.9	7.5	9.2	8.9	9.0	7.9
MOUNTAIN	4.2	3.7	4.4	4.1	3.4	4.1	4.2	4.2
PACIFIC	18.0	14.8	15.8	16.8	15.8	14.9	15.1	14.0

IIE

NEW ENGLAND	1,414	1,849	1,617	1,583	1,547	1,563	1,569	1,612
MIDDLE ATLANTIC	3,515	4,316	4,553	4,349	4,151	3,916	3,948	4,536
EAST NORTH CENTRAL	4,722	5,490	5,307	5,438	5,083	4,930	4,975	6,071
WEST NORTH CENTRAL	2,443	2,636	2,669	2,921	2,673	2,596	2,575	2,973
SOUTH ATLANTIC	4,433	4,996	4,916	4,863	4,900	4,610	4,848	5,641
EAST SOUTH CENTRAL	2,203	2,283	2,228	2,232	2,056	1,964	2,033	2,475
WEST SOUTH CENTRAL	3,155	3,430	3,135	3,312	3,221	3,036	3,152	3,652
MOUNTAIN	1,339	1,515	1,598	1,588	1,423	1,502	1,576	1,691
PACIFIC	3,531	3,830	3,872	4,041	3,606	3,456	3,593	4,095

IIE INCIDENCE

NEW ENGLAND	22.4	30.0	26.8	24.7	23.3	22.8	22.9	23.9
MIDDLE ATLANTIC	20.4	25.0	25.4	24.2	22.6	21.3	21.4	24.5
EAST NORTH CENTRAL	23.0	27.1	25.7	26.0	23.8	22.7	22.8	27.7
WEST NORTH CENTRAL	29.9	31.6	30.3	32.1	28.8	27.0	27.0	31.7
SOUTH ATLANTIC	27.9	30.8	29.0	28.4	28.0	25.8	25.9	29.5
EAST SOUTH CENTRAL	33.2	34.4	33.0	33.4	30.5	28.8	28.9	34.4
WEST SOUTH CENTRAL	31.8	33.0	30.9	30.5	28.7	26.7	26.7	29.7
MOUNTAIN	28.8	31.2	30.3	31.0	26.6	26.2	26.2	27.8
PACIFIC	24.7	26.7	26.4	26.2	22.8	21.2	21.4	24.0

IIE SHARE

NEW ENGLAND	5.3	6.1	5.4	5.2	5.4	5.7	5.6	4.9
MIDDLE ATLANTIC	13.1	14.2	15.2	14.3	14.5	14.2	14.0	13.9
EAST NORTH CENTRAL	17.6	18.1	17.8	17.9	17.7	17.9	17.6	18.5
WEST NORTH CENTRAL	9.1	8.7	8.9	9.6	9.3	9.4	9.1	9.0
SOUTH ATLANTIC	16.6	16.5	16.4	16.0	17.1	16.7	17.1	17.2
EAST SOUTH CENTRAL	8.2	7.5	7.5	7.4	7.2	7.1	7.2	7.6
WEST SOUTH CENTRAL	11.8	11.3	10.5	10.9	11.2	11.0	11.2	11.2
MOUNTAIN	5.0	5.0	5.3	5.2	5.0	5.4	5.6	5.2
PACIFIC	13.2	12.6	13.0	13.3	12.6	12.5	12.7	12.5

IIE DEFICIT

NEW ENGLAND	1,779	3,140	2,543	2,348	2,392	2,572	2,580	2,866
MIDDLE ATLANTIC	4,393	6,722	7,684	6,918	6,672	7,138	7,197	9,420
EAST NORTH CENTRAL	6,021	8,266	8,120	8,852	7,801	8,919	8,999	13,621
WEST NORTH CENTRAL	3,391	4,315	4,547	5,293	4,919	5,338	5,278	7,095
SOUTH ATLANTIC	5,308	7,312	7,639	7,249	7,857	8,479	8,910	11,827
EAST SOUTH CENTRAL	2,594	3,316	3,287	3,643	3,183	3,608	3,726	5,566
WEST SOUTH CENTRAL	4,197	4,998	4,728	5,408	5,224	5,699	5,892	7,834
MOUNTAIN	1,711	2,111	2,584	2,881	2,491	2,932	3,050	3,645
PACIFIC	4,636	5,913	6,335	6,692	6,093	6,144	6,366	9,774

Table C-8. (Continued)

IIE DEFICIT (1980 $)

NEW ENGLAND	2,972	4,807	3,682	3,194	3,021	2,920	2,928	2,866
MIDDLE ATLANTIC	7,341	10,291	11,127	9,408	8,427	8,102	8,168	9,420
EAST NORTH CENTRAL	10,062	12,655	11,758	12,304	9,852	10,102	10,214	13,621
WEST NORTH CENTRAL	5,666	6,607	6,584	7,199	6,212	6,058	5,991	7,095
SOUTH ATLANTIC	8,869	11,195	11,061	9,859	9,923	9,623	10,112	11,827
EAST SOUTH CENTRAL	4,335	5,077	4,759	4,954	4,020	4,096	4,229	5,566
WEST SOUTH CENTRAL	7,012	7,651	6,846	7,355	6,598	6,468	6,688	7,834
MOUNTAIN	2,859	3,233	3,741	3,918	3,146	3,328	3,462	3,645
PACIFIC	7,747	9,052	9,173	9,101	7,695	6,974	7,226	8,774

IIE DEFICIT SHARE

NEW ENGLAND	5.2	6.8	5.4	4.8	5.1	5.1	5.0	4.1
MIDDLE ATLANTIC	12.9	14.6	16.2	14.0	14.3	14.0	13.8	13.3
EAST NORTH CENTRAL	17.7	17.9	17.1	18.0	16.7	17.5	17.3	19.3
WEST NORTH CENTRAL	10.0	9.4	9.6	10.7	10.5	10.5	10.2	10.0
SOUTH ATLANTIC	15.6	15.9	16.1	14.7	16.8	16.7	17.1	16.7
EAST SOUTH CENTRAL	7.6	7.2	6.9	7.4	6.8	7.1	7.2	7.9
WEST SOUTH CENTRAL	12.3	10.8	10.0	11.0	11.2	11.2	11.3	11.1
MOUNTAIN	5.0	4.6	5.4	5.8	5.3	5.8	5.9	5.2
PACIFIC	13.6	12.8	13.3	13.6	13.1	12.1	12.2	12.4

IIE AVERAGE DEFICIT

NEW ENGLAND	1,257	1,698	1,573	1,484	1,546	1,646	1,644	1,777
MIDDLE ATLANTIC	1,250	1,558	1,688	1,591	1,607	1,823	1,823	2,077
EAST NORTH CENTRAL	1,275	1,505	1,530	1,628	1,535	1,809	1,809	2,243
WEST NORTH CENTRAL	1,388	1,637	1,703	1,812	1,840	2,056	2,050	2,387
SOUTH ATLANTIC	1,197	1,464	1,554	1,491	1,603	1,839	1,838	2,096
EAST SOUTH CENTRAL	1,177	1,453	1,476	1,632	1,548	1,837	1,832	2,244
WEST SOUTH CENTRAL	1,330	1,457	1,508	1,633	1,622	1,877	1,869	2,145
MOUNTAIN	1,278	1,394	1,617	1,814	1,751	1,952	1,936	2,156
PACIFIC	1,313	1,544	1,636	1,656	1,689	1,778	1,772	2,143

IIE AVERAGE DEFICIT (1980 $)

NEW ENGLAND	2,100	2,600	2,278	2,018	1,953	1,868	1,866	1,777
MIDDLE ATLANTIC	2,089	2,385	2,444	2,164	2,030	2,069	2,069	2,077
EAST NORTH CENTRAL	2,131	2,304	2,215	2,214	1,939	2,053	2,053	2,243
WEST NORTH CENTRAL	2,319	2,506	2,466	2,464	2,324	2,334	2,327	2,387
SOUTH ATLANTIC	2,000	1,464	2,250	2,028	2,025	2,087	2,086	2,096
EAST SOUTH CENTRAL	1,967	2,225	2,137	2,220	1,955	2,085	2,079	2,249
WEST SOUTH CENTRAL	2,222	2,231	2,184	2,221	2,049	2,130	2,121	2,145
MOUNTAIN	2,136	2,134	2,341	2,470	2,212	2,216	2,197	2,156
PACIFIC	2,194	2,364	2,369	2,252	2,133	2,018	2,011	2,143

IFE

NEW ENGLAND	549	741	612	648	720	642	645	718
MIDDLE ATLANTIC	1,449	1,744	1,866	1,784	1,644	1,801	1,812	1,983
EAST NORTH CENTRAL	1,778	2,229	2,087	2,055	2,007	2,008	2,032	2,521
WEST NORTH CENTRAL	1,047	1,052	1,124	1,360	1,138	1,110	1,102	1,245
SOUTH ATLANTIC	2,112	2,486	2,431	2,275	2,343	2,327	2,462	2,733
EAST SOUTH CENTRAL	1,126	1,139	1,077	1,126	1,049	1,039	1,079	1,307
WEST SOUTH CENTRAL	1,588	1,712	1,583	1,591	1,642	1,600	1,654	1,825
MOUNTAIN	588	724	682	736	688	659	689	817
PACIFIC	1,771	1,940	1,940	1,919	1,788	1,728	1,805	1,960

IFE INCIDENCE

NEW ENGLAND	8.7	12.0	10.1	10.1	10.8	9.4	9.4	10.6
MIDDLE ATLANTIC	8.4	10.1	10.4	9.9	9.0	9.8	9.8	10.7
EAST NORTH CENTRAL	8.7	11.0	10.1	9.8	9.4	9.2	9.3	11.5
WEST NORTH CENTRAL	12.8	12.6	12.7	15.0	12.3	11.5	11.6	13.3
SOUTH ATLANTIC	13.2	15.3	14.3	13.3	13.4	13.0	13.2	14.3
EAST SOUTH CENTRAL	16.9	17.2	16.0	16.8	15.6	15.2	15.3	18.2
WEST SOUTH CENTRAL	16.0	16.5	15.6	14.6	14.6	14.1	14.0	14.8
MOUNTAIN	12.6	14.9	12.9	14.4	12.8	11.5	11.5	13.5
PACIFIC	12.4	13.5	13.2	12.4	11.3	10.6	10.7	11.5

Table C-8. (Continued)

IFE SHARE

NEW ENGLAND	4.6	5.4	4.6	4.8	5.5	5.0	4.9	4.8
MIDDLE ATLANTIC	12.1	12.7	13.9	13.2	12.6	13.9	13.6	13.1
EAST NORTH CENTRAL	14.8	16.2	15.6	15.2	15.4	15.5	15.3	16.7
WEST NORTH CENTRAL	8.7	7.6	8.4	10.1	8.7	8.6	8.3	8.2
SOUTH ATLANTIC	17.6	18.1	18.1	16.9	18.0	18.0	18.5	18.1
EAST SOUTH CENTRAL	9.4	8.3	8.0	8.3	8.1	8.0	8.1	8.6
WEST SOUTH CENTRAL	13.2	12.4	11.8	11.8	12.6	12.3	12.5	12.1
MOUNTAIN	4.9	5.3	5.1	5.5	5.3	5.1	5.2	5.4
PACIFIC	14.7	14.1	14.5	14.2	13.7	13.4	13.6	13.0

IFE DEFICIT

NEW ENGLAND	895	1,335	1,177	1,282	1,486	1,472	1,477	1,805
MIDDLE ATLANTIC	2,502	3,444	3,852	3,856	3,762	4,595	4,629	5,521
EAST NORTH CENTRAL	3,093	4,172	4,214	4,342	4,447	5,054	5,139	7,352
WEST NORTH CENTRAL	1,533	1,766	1,926	2,478	2,268	2,395	2,377	3,297
SOUTH ATLANTIC	3,347	4,353	4,463	4,439	5,034	5,318	5,638	7,282
EAST SOUTH CENTRAL	1,862	2,126	1,985	2,318	2,330	2,573	2,670	3,534
WEST SOUTH CENTRAL	2,653	2,961	2,967	3,004	3,347	3,851	3,950	5,051
MOUNTAIN	862	1,200	1,216	1,309	1,387	1,469	1,527	2,001
PACIFIC	2,954	3,567	3,655	3,873	3,710	4,073	4,249	5,155

IFE DEFICIT (1980 $)

NEW ENGLAND	1,496	2,043	1,704	1,744	1,877	1,671	1,676	1,805
MIDDLE ATLANTIC	4,181	5,273		5,244	4,751	5,216	5,254	5,521
EAST NORTH CENTRAL	5,168	6,388	6,102	5,905	5,616	5,737	5,833	7,352
WEST NORTH CENTRAL	2,562	2,703	2,789	3,370	2,864	2,718	2,698	3,297
SOUTH ATLANTIC	5,592	6,665	6,462	6,037	6,360	6,036	6,399	7,282
EAST SOUTH CENTRAL	3,111	3,255	2,874	3,152	2,942	2,921	3,080	3,534
WEST SOUTH CENTRAL	4,433	4,534	4,296	4,086	4,227	4,371	4,484	5,051
MOUNTAIN	1,440	1,838	1,761	1,781	1,752	1,668	1,733	2,001
PACIFIC	4,936	5,461	5,293	5,268	4,686	4,623	4,823	5,155

IFE DEFICIT SHARE

NEW ENGLAND	4.5	5.4	4.6	4.8	5.4	4.8	4.7	4.4
MIDDLE ATLANTIC	12.7	13.8	15.1	14.3	13.5	14.9	14.6	13.5
EAST NORTH CENTRAL	15.7	16.7	16.6	16.1	16.0	16.4	16.2	17.9
WEST NORTH CENTRAL	7.8	7.1	7.6	9.2	8.2	7.8	7.5	8.0
SOUTH ATLANTIC	17.0	17.5	17.5	16.5	18.1	17.3	17.8	17.8
EAST SOUTH CENTRAL	9.5	8.5	7.8	8.6	8.4	8.4	8.4	8.6
WEST SOUTH CENTRAL	13.5	11.9	11.7	11.2	12.1	12.5	12.5	12.3
MOUNTAIN	4.4	4.8	4.8	4.9	5.0	4.8	4.8	4.9
PACIFIC	15.0	14.3	14.4	14.4	13.4	13.2	13.4	12.6

IFE AVERAGE DEFICIT

NEW ENGLAND	1,631	1,800	1,925	1,978	2,064	2,292	2,289	2,513
MIDDLE ATLANTIC	1,727	1,975	2,065	2,162	2,288	2,551	2,554	2,784
EAST NORTH CENTRAL	1,739	1,871	2,019	2,113	2,215	2,517	2,529	2,916
WEST NORTH CENTRAL	1,464	1,679	1,713	1,822	1,992	2,157	2,158	2,648
SOUTH ATLANTIC	1,585	1,751	1,836	1,951	2,149	2,285	2,290	2,665
EAST SOUTH CENTRAL	1,654	1,866	1,843	2,059	2,220	2,477	2,475	2,704
WEST SOUTH CENTRAL	1,670	1,730	1,874	1,889	2,038	2,407	2,388	2,767
MOUNTAIN	1,467	1,658	1,783	1,778	2,017	2,231	2,215	2,450
PACIFIC	1,668	1,839	1,884	2,018	2,075	2,357	2,355	2,630

IFE AVERAGE DEFICIT (1980 $)

NEW ENGLAND	2,725	2,756	2,787	2,690	2,607	2,601	2,598	2,513
MIDDLE ATLANTIC	2,886	3,024	2,990	2,940	2,890	2,895	2,899	2,784
EAST NORTH CENTRAL	2,906	2,865	2,924	2,874	2,798	2,857	2,870	2,916
WEST NORTH CENTRAL	2,446	1,571	2,480	2,478	2,576	2,448	2,449	2,648
SOUTH ATLANTIC	2,649	2,681	2,659	2,653	2,714	2,593	2,599	2,665
EAST SOUTH CENTRAL	2,764	2,857	2,669	2,800	2,804	2,811	2,809	2,704
WEST SOUTH CENTRAL	2,791	2,649	2,714	2,569	2,574	2,732	2,710	2,767
MOUNTAIN	2,451	2,538	2,582	2,418	2,547	2,532	2,514	2,450
PACIFIC	2,787	2,816	2,728	2,744	2,621	2,675	2,673	2,630

Table C-8, (Continued)

IFI

NEW ENGLAND	237	340	286	303	369	293	294	345
MIDDLE ATLANTIC	691	821	826	808	849	883	891	956
EAST NORTH CENTRAL	871	1,060	1,008	1,015	960	991	1,007	1,378
WEST NORTH CENTRAL	475	504	577	663	573	535	522	658
SOUTH ATLANTIC	1,241	1,471	1,408	1,219	1,375	1,276	1,345	1,644
EAST SOUTH CENTRAL	683	662	624	698	626	575	602	833
WEST SOUTH CENTRAL	998	1,004	983	930	900	976	1,008	1,123
MOUNTAIN	305	414	380	389	400	370	383	473
PACIFIC	843	977	941	972	960	953	993	1,055

IFI INCIDENCE

NEW ENGLAND	3.8	5.5	4.7	4.7	5.6	4.3	4.3	5.1
MIDDLE ATLANTIC	4.0	4.8	4.6	4.5	4.6	4.8	4.8	5.2
EAST NORTH CENTRAL	4.3	5.2	4.9	4.9	4.5	4.6	4.6	6.3
WEST NORTH CENTRAL	5.8	6.0	6.5	7.3	6.2	5.6	5.6	7.0
SOUTH ATLANTIC	7.8	9.1	8.3	7.1	7.8	7.1	7.2	8.6
EAST SOUTH CENTRAL	10.3	10.0	9.3	10.5	9.3	8.4	8.6	11.6
WEST SOUTH CENTRAL	10.1	9.7	9.7	8.6	8.0	8.6	8.5	9.1
MOUNTAIN	6.6	8.5	7.2	7.6	7.5	6.5	6.4	7.8
PACIFIC	5.9	6.8	6.4	6.3	6.1	5.9	5.9	6.2

IFI SHARE

NEW ENGLAND	3.7	4.7	4.1	4.3	5.3	4.3	4.2	4.1
MIDDLE ATLANTIC	10.9	11.3	11.7	11.5	12.1	12.9	12.6	11.3
EAST NORTH CENTRAL	13.7	14.6	14.3	14.5	13.7	14.5	14.3	16.3
WEST NORTH CENTRAL	7.5	6.9	8.2	9.5	8.2	7.8	7.5	7.8
SOUTH ATLANTIC	19.6	20.3	20.0	17.4	19.6	18.6	19.1	19.4
EAST SOUTH CENTRAL	10.8	9.1	8.9	10.0	8.9	8.4	8.5	9.8
WEST SOUTH CENTRAL	15.7	13.8	14.0	13.3	12.8	14.2	14.3	13.3
MOUNTAIN	4.8	5.7	5.4	5.6	5.7	5.4	5.4	5.6
PACIFIC	13.3	13.5	13.4	13.9	13.7	13.9	14.1	12.5

IFI DEFICIT

NEW ENGLAND	285	360	350	387	498	468	456	619
MIDDLE ATLANTIC	813	1,159	1,155	1,230	1,191	1,599	1,613	1,966
EAST NORTH CENTRAL	984	1,334	1,389	1,463	1,495	1,880	1,907	2,794
WEST NORTH CENTRAL	536	642	741	1,036	921	866	863	1,402
SOUTH ATLANTIC	1,511	1,952	1,881	1,892	2,269	2,293	2,415	3,381
EAST SOUTH CENTRAL	847	9,377	901	1,024	1,079	1,164	1,214	1,763
WEST SOUTH CENTRAL	1,300	1,400	1,455	1,401	1,444	1,931	1,982	2,521
MOUNTAIN	376	535	513	549	658	684	705	953
PACIFIC	1,061	1,219	1,187	1,374	1,471	1,614	1,670	2,053

IFI DEFICIT (1980 $)

NEW ENGLAND	476	551	507	527	629	531	517	619
MIDDLE ATLANTIC	1,358	1,775	1,672	1,673	1,504	1,815	1,831	1,966
EAST NORTH CENTRAL	1,644	2,043	2,011	1,990	1,888	2,134	2,164	2,794
WEST NORTH CENTRAL	896	983	1,074	1,410	1,164	983	980	1,402
SOUTH ATLANTIC	2,524	2,988	2,724	2,573	2,866	2,603	2,741	3,381
EAST SOUTH CENTRAL	1,416	1,436	1,304	1,393	1,363	1,321	1,378	1,763
WEST SOUTH CENTRAL	2,172	2,143	2,107	1,905	1,824	2,191	2,250	2,521
MOUNTAIN	629	819	743	746	831	776	800	953
PACIFIC	1,773	1,866	1,719	1,869	1,858	1,832	1,895	2,053

IFI DEFICIT SHARE

NEW ENGLAND	3.7	3.8	3.7	3.7	4.5	3.7	3.6	3.5
MIDDLE ATLANTIC	10.5	12.2	12.1	11.9	10.8	12.8	12.6	11.3
EAST NORTH CENTRAL	12.8	14.0	14.5	14.1	13.6	15.0	14.9	16.0
WEST NORTH CENTRAL	7.0	6.7	7.7	10.0	8.4	6.9	6.7	8.0
SOUTH ATLANTIC	19.6	20.5	19.7	18.3	20.6	18.3	18.8	19.4
EAST SOUTH CENTRAL	11.0	9.8	9.4	9.9	9.8	9.3	9.5	10.1
WEST SOUTH CENTRAL	16.9	14.7	15.2	13.5	13.1	15.4	15.5	14.4
MOUNTAIN	4.9	5.6	5.4	5.3	6.0	5.5	5.5	5.5
PACIFIC	13.8	12.8	12.4	13.3	13.3	12.9	13.0	11.8

Table C-8. (Continued)

IFI AVERAGE DEFICIT

NEW ENGLAND	1,200	1,058	1,225	1,278	1,349	1,595	1,548	1,794
MIDDLE ATLANTIC	1,176	1,413	1,397	1,521	1,404	1,811	1,811	2,057
EAST NORTH CENTRAL	1,129	1,259	1,377	1,442	1,558	1,897	1,894	2,028
WEST NORTH CENTRAL	1,128	1,273	1,286	1,563	1,608	1,617	1,622	2,130
SOUTH ATLANTIC	1,217	1,327	1,336	1,552	1,650	1,797	1,795	2,057
EAST SOUTH CENTRAL	1,241	1,417	1,443	1,466	1,726	2,024	2,017	2,117
WEST SOUTH CENTRAL	1,302	1,394	1,480	1,506	1,603	1,978	1,966	2,445
MOUNTAIN	1,232	1,292	1,350	1,410	1,645	1,849	1,842	2,014
PACIFIC	1,258	1,247	1,262	1,413	1,532	1,695	1,682	1,945

IFI AVERAGE DEFICIT (1980 $)

NEW ENGLAND	2,005	1,620	1,774	1,738	1,704	1,810	1,757	1,794
MIDDLE ATLANTIC	1,965	2,163	2,023	2,069	1,773	2,055	2,055	2,057
EAST NORTH CENTRAL	1,887	1,928	1,994	1,961	1,968	2,153	2,150	2,028
WEST NORTH CENTRAL	1,885	1,949	1,862	2,126	2,031	1,835	1,841	2,130
SOUTH ATLANTIC	2,034	2,032	1,935	2,111	2,084	2,040	2,037	2,057
EAST SOUTH CENTRAL	2,074	2,169	2,089	1,994	2,180	2,297	2,289	2,117
WEST SOUTH CENTRAL	2,176	2,134	2,143	2,048	2,024	2,245	2,231	2,445
MOUNTAIN	2,059	1,978	1,955	1,918	2,078	2,099	2,091	2,014
PACIFIC	2,102	1,909	1,827	1,922	1,935	1,924	1,909	1,945

IIE IN IFE

NEW ENGLAND	26.0	30.8	28.4	30.0	31.5	27.7	27.5	30.9
MIDDLE ATLANTIC	27.8	29.3	29.2	29.3	27.7	30.7	30.6	32.9
EAST NORTH CENTRAL	25.6	29.9	28.4	28.1	27.8	29.2	29.3	32.3
WEST NORTH CENTRAL	30.0	31.0	30.8	34.0	31.4	30.0	29.9	32.4
SOUTH ATLANTIC	34.1	37.7	37.6	34.3	35.1	35.6	35.7	37.5
EAST SOUTH CENTRAL	38.3	39.9	35.9	39.4	37.5	36.9	36.9	41.3
WEST SOUTH CENTRAL	37.3	37.2	36.8	35.3	37.5	37.0	36.8	37.1
MOUNTAIN	38.7	35.8	31.7	34.7	35.2	30.0	29.8	36.5
PACIFIC	33.5	36.0	36.2	34.0	33.2	31.6	31.6	33.9

EARNINGS SUPPLEMENTATION RATE - TOTAL

NEW ENGLAND	56.7	54.1	53.3	53.3	48.7	54.4	54.4	52.0
MIDDLE ATLANTIC	52.3	53.0	55.7	54.7	48.4	51.0	50.8	51.8
EAST NORTH CENTRAL	51.0	52.5	51.7	50.6	52.2	50.6	50.4	45.4
WEST NORTH CENTRAL	54.6	52.1	48.7	51.2	49.7	51.8	51.7	47.2
SOUTH ATLANTIC	41.2	40.9	42.1	46.4	41.3	45.2	45.4	39.8
EAST SOUTH CENTRAL	39.3	41.9	42.0	38.0	40.4	44.6	44.2	36.3
WEST SOUTH CENTRAL	37.2	41.3	37.9	41.5	45.2	39.0	39.1	38.5
MOUNTAIN	48.0	42.8	44.2	47.2	41.8	43.9	44.5	42.1
PACIFIC	52.4	49.6	51.5	49.3	46.3	44.9	45.0	46.2

EARNINGS SUPPLEMENTATION RATE - TRANSFERS

NEW ENGLAND	35.5	39.2	35.7	35.6	27.0	28.6	28.1	26.8
MIDDLE ATLANTIC	31.5	36.3	37.7	35.6	28.5	31.5	31.3	28.2
EAST NORTH CENTRAL	31.0	37.1	32.8	30.9	30.9	28.8	28.5	27.2
WEST NORTH CENTRAL	32.4	33.5	27.7	29.1	25.3	26.1	26.0	23.5
SOUTH ATLANTIC	25.4	26.4	27.8	29.4	22.7	23.7	23.7	23.4
EAST SOUTH CENTRAL	27.0	29.6	29.3	26.2	25.3	28.6	28.3	21.3
WEST SOUTH CENTRAL	24.4	25.9	22.8	26.3	26.6	21.2	21.2	22.6
MOUNTAIN	24.8	25.2	27.1	28.9	20.0	19.8	20.2	18.8
PACIFIC	30.8	28.7	29.3	28.4	26.0	22.5	22.7	24.5

Table C-9. SUMMARY SEVERE HARDSHIP MEASURES, 1974 THROUGH 1980, FOR TOTAL WORK FORCE, DISAGGREGATED BY AREA OF RESIDENCE

WORK FORCE

INSIDE SMSA	71,365	71,852	73,002	74,293	77,332	79,060	80,692	81,214
SMSA 1 MILLION +	40,770	41,054	41,950	43,052	44,158	45,271	46,103	46,669
CENTRAL CITY	15,998	15,509	15,607	15,983	16,208	16,253	16,592	16,677
BALANCE	24,772	25,545	26,342	27,070	27,949	29,018	29,510	29,992
SMSA LESS THAN 1 MILLION	30,594	30,798	31,052	31,190	33,174	33,789	34,590	34,545
CENTRAL CITY	14,245	14,543	14,419	14,379	15,232	15,555	15,905	15,681
BALANCE	16,350	16,255	16,633	16,811	17,943	18,234	18,684	18,864
OUTSIDE SMSA	32,236	32,590	34,166	35,421	35,031	35,588	36,291	37,134

SHARE WORK FORCE

INSIDE SMSA	68.9	68.8	68.1	67.7	68.8	69.0	69.0	68.6
SMSA 1 MILLION +	39.4	39.3	39.2	39.2	39.3	39.5	39.4	39.4
CENTRAL CITY	15.4	14.8	14.6	14.6	14.4	14.2	14.2	14.1
BALANCE	23.9	24.5	24.6	24.7	24.9	25.3	25.2	25.3
SMSA LESS THAN 1 MILLION	29.5	29.5	29.0	28.4	29.5	29.5	29.6	29.2
CENTRAL CITY	13.7	13.9	13.5	13.1	13.6	13.6	13.6	13.2
BALANCE	15.8	15.6	15.5	15.3	16.0	15.9	16.0	15.9
OUTSIDE SMSA	31.1	31.2	31.9	32.3	31.2	31.0	31.0	31.4

UNEMPLOYED

INSIDE SMSA	12,942	14,529	14,081	13,369	12,305	12,393	12,732	14,292
SMSA 1 MILLION +	7,512	8,233	8,111	7,671	7,011	6,970	7,149	8,002
CENTRAL CITY	3,337	3,438	3,370	3,245	3,072	2,903	2,983	3,302
BALANCE	4,176	4,794	4,740	4,425	3,938	4,067	4,166	4,700
SMSA LESS THAN 1 MILLION	5,429	6,295	5,971	5,699	5,295	5,423	5,584	6,291
CENTRAL CITY	2,648	3,204	2,909	2,820	2,582	2,713	2,793	3,015
BALANCE	2,781	3,093	3,061	2,879	2,714	2,710	2,791	3,275
OUTSIDE SMSA	5,595	6,575	6,366	6,143	5,433	5,579	5,735	7,117

UNEMPLOYMENT INCIDENCE

INSIDE SMSA	18.1	20.2	19.3	18.0	15.9	15.7	15.8	15.6
SMSA 1 MILLION +	18.4	20.1	19.3	17.8	15.9	15.4	15.5	17.1
CENTRAL CITY	20.9	22.2	21.6	20.3	19.0	17.9	18.0	19.8
BALANCE	16.9	18.8	18.0	16.3	14.1	14.0	14.1	15.7
SMSA LESS THAN 1 MILLION	17.7	20.4	19.2	18.3	16.0	16.0	16.1	18.2
CENTRAL CITY	18.6	22.0	20.2	19.6	17.0	17.4	17.6	19.2
BALANCE	17.0	19.0	18.4	17.1	15.1	14.9	14.9	17.4
OUTSIDE SMSA	17.4	20.2	18.6	17.3	15.5	15.7	15.8	19.2

UNEMPLOYMENT SHARE

INSIDE SMSA	69.8	68.8	68.9	68.5	69.4	69.0	68.9	66.8
SMSA 1 MILLION +	40.5	39.0	39.7	39.3	39.5	38.8	38.7	37.4
CENTRAL CITY	18.0	16.3	16.5	16.6	17.3	16.2	16.2	15.4
BALANCE	22.5	22.7	23.2	22.7	22.2	22.6	22.6	22.0
SMSA LESS THAN 1 MILLION	29.3	29.8	29.2	29.2	29.9	30.2	30.2	29.4
CENTRAL CITY	14.3	15.2	14.2	14.5	14.6	15.1	15.1	14.1
BALANCE	15.0	14.7	15.0	14.8	15.3	15.1	15.1	15.3
OUTSIDE SMSA	30.2	31.2	31.1	31.5	30.6	31.0	31.1	33.3

PREDOMINANTLY UNEMPLOYED

INSIDE SMSA	5,400	7,601	7,149	6,266	5,379	4,957	5,097	6,882
SMSA 1 MILLION +	3,208	4,399	4,130	3,671	3,071	2,874	2,959	3,894
CENTRAL CITY	1,555	1,995	1,839	1,706	1,497	1,368	1,410	1,791
BALANCE	1,653	2,404	2,289	1,966	1,572	1,506	1,549	2,103
SMSA LESS THAN 1 MILLION	2,192	3,200	3,020	2,594	2,309	2,083	2,138	2,989
CENTRAL CITY	1,107	1,643	1,498	1,333	1,120	1,112	1,137	1,525
BALANCE	1,086	1,558	1,522	1,261	1,189	971	1,001	1,463
OUTSIDE SMSA	2,340	3,339	3,106	2,865	2,371	2,319	2,394	3,465

Table C-9. (Continued)

INCIDENCE PREDOMINANTLY UNEMPLOYED

INSIDE SMSA	7.6	10.6	9.8	8.4	7.0	6.3	6.3	8.5
SMSA 1 MILLION +	7.9	10.7	9.8	8.5	7.0	6.3	6.4	8.3
CENTRAL CITY	9.7	12.9	11.8	10.7	9.2	8.4	8.5	10.7
BALANCE	6.7	9.4	8.7	7.3	5.6	5.2	5.2	7.0
SMSA LESS THAN 1 MILLION	7.2	10.4	9.7	8.3	7.0	6.2	6.2	8.7
CENTRAL CITY	7.8	11.3	10.4	9.3	7.4	7.1	7.1	9.7
BALANCE	6.6	9.6	9.2	7.5	6.6	5.3	5.4	7.8
OUTSIDE SMSA	7.3	10.2	9.1	8.1	6.8	6.5	6.6	9.3

SHARE OF PREDOMINANTLY UNEMPLOYED

INSIDE SMSA	69.8	69.5	69.7	68.6	69.4	68.1	68.0	66.5
SMSA 1 MILLION +	41.4	40.2	40.3	40.2	39.6	39.5	39.5	37.6
CENTRAL CITY	20.1	18.2	17.9	18.7	19.3	18.8	18.8	17.3
BALANCE	21.4	22.0	22.3	21.5	20.3	20.7	20.7	20.3
SMSA LESS THAN 1 MILLION	28.3	29.2	29.4	28.4	29.8	28.6	28.5	28.9
CENTRAL CITY	14.3	15.0	14.6	14.6	14.5	15.3	15.2	14.7
BALANCE	14.0	14.2	14.8	13.8	15.3	13.3	13.4	14.1
OUTSIDE SMSA	30.2	30.5	30.3	31.4	30.6	31.9	32.0	33.5

IIE

INSIDE SMSA	16,199	18,628	18,271	18,295	17,618	16,958	17,389	19,945
SMSA 1 MILLION +	8,535	9,937	9,752	9,859	9,270	8,898	9,122	10,515
CENTRAL CITY	3,652	3,977	3,858	3,974	3,721	3,571	3,679	4,196
BALANCE	4,883	5,960	5,894	5,884	5,549	5,327	5,443	6,319
SMSA LESS THAN 1 MILLION	7,664	8,691	8,519	8,437	8,348	8,059	8,267	9,430
CENTRAL CITY	3,638	4,265	4,105	4,058	3,994	3,886	3,974	4,395
BALANCE	4,026	4,427	4,414	4,378	4,354	4,174	4,293	5,034
OUTSIDE SMSA	10,557	11,717	11,622	12,030	11,042	10,618	10,880	12,802

IIE INCIDENCE

INSIDE SMSA	22.7	25.8	25.0	24.6	22.8	21.4	21.5	24.6
SMSA 1 MILLION +	20.9	24.2	23.2	22.9	21.0	19.7	19.8	22.5
CENTRAL CITY	22.8	25.6	24.7	24.9	23.0	22.0	22.2	25.2
BALANCE	19.7	23.3	22.4	21.7	19.9	18.4	18.4	21.1
SMSA LESS THAN 1 MILLION	25.0	28.2	27.4	27.0	25.2	23.9	23.9	27.3
CENTRAL CITY	25.5	29.3	28.5	28.2	26.2	25.0	25.0	28.0
BALANCE	24.6	27.2	26.5	26.0	24.3	22.9	23.0	26.7
OUTSIDE SMSA	32.7	36.0	34.0	34.0	31.5	29.8	30.0	34.5

IIE SHARE

INSIDE SMSA	60.5	61.4	61.1	60.3	61.5	61.5	61.5	60.9
SMSA 1 MILLION +	31.9	32.7	32.6	32.5	32.3	32.3	32.3	32.1
CENTRAL CITY	13.6	13.1	12.9	13.1	13.0	13.0	13.0	12.8
BALANCE	18.3	19.6	19.7	19.4	19.4	19.3	19.3	19.3
SMSA LESS THAN 1 MILLION	28.6	28.6	28.5	27.8	29.1	29.2	29.2	28.8
CENTRAL CITY	13.6	14.1	13.7	13.4	13.9	14.1	14.1	13.4
BALANCE	15.0	14.6	14.8	14.4	15.2	15.1	15.2	15.3
OUTSIDE SMSA	39.5	38.6	38.9	39.7	38.5	38.5	38.5	39.1

IIE DEFICIT

INSIDE SMSA	19,375	27,248	28,141	27,515	26,497	28,806	29,500	40,763
SMSA 1 MILLION +	10,315	14,766	14,801	15,162	13,751	15,033	15,456	20,896
CENTRAL CITY	4,723	6,574	6,317	6,613	5,946	6,541	6,772	8,982
BALANCE	5,592	8,192	8,484	8,550	7,805	8,493	8,684	11,914
SMSA LESS THAN 1 MILLION	9,060	12,482	13,340	12,353	12,745	13,772	14,044	19,867
CENTRAL CITY	4,156	6,124	6,645	6,096	6,109	6,522	6,633	9,199
BALANCE	4,904	6,359	6,695	6,257	6,636	7,250	7,411	10,668
OUTSIDE SMSA	14,654	18,844	19,326	21,769	20,135	22,024	22,498	29,885

Table C-9. (Continued)

IIE DEFICIT (1980 $)

INSIDE SMSA	32,376	41,717	40,748	37,420	33,465	32,694	33,482	40,763
SMSA 1 MILLION +	17,237	22,607	21,432	20,621	17,366	17,063	17,542	20,896
CENTRAL CITY	7,893	10,065	9,355	8,993	7,510	7,424	7,686	8,982
BALANCE	9,344	12,542	12,285	11,627	9,858	9,639	9,856	11,914
SMSA LESS THAN 1 MILLION	15,139	19,100	19,316	16,799	16,097	15,631	15,940	19,867
CENTRAL CITY	6,944	9,375	9,622	8,290	7,716	7,403	7,529	9,199
BALANCE	8,195	9,735	9,694	8,509	8,381	8,229	8,411	10,668
OUTSIDE SMSA	24,486	28,850	27,984	29,606	25,431	24,997	25,536	29,885

IIE DEFICIT SHARE

INSIDE SMSA	56.9	59.1	59.3	55.8	56.8	56.7	56.7	57.7
SMSA 1 MILLION +	30.3	32.0	31.2	31.4	29.5	29.6	29.7	29.6
CENTRAL CITY	13.9	14.3	13.3	13.4	12.8	12.9	13.0	12.7
BALANCE	16.4	17.8	17.9	17.3	16.7	16.7	16.7	16.9
SMSA LESS THAN 1 MILLION	26.6	27.1	28.1	25.1	27.3	27.1	27.0	28.1
CENTRAL CITY	12.2	13.3	14.0	12.4	13.1	12.8	12.8	13.0
BALANCE	14.4	13.8	14.1	12.7	14.2	14.3	14.3	15.1
OUTSIDE SMSA	43.1	40.9	40.7	44.2	43.2	43.3	43.3	42.3

IIE AVERAGE DEFICIT

INSIDE SMSA	1,196	1,463	1,540	1,504	1,504	1,699	1,696	2,044
SMSA 1 MILLION +	1,209	1,486	1,518	1,538	1,483	1,689	1,694	1,987
CENTRAL CITY	1,293	1,653	1,637	1,664	1,598	1,831	1,841	2,141
BALANCE	1,145	1,374	1,440	1,453	1,407	1,594	1,595	1,885
SMSA LESS THAN 1 MILLION	1,182	1,436	1,566	1,464	1,527	1,709	1,699	2,107
CENTRAL CITY	1,142	1,436	1,619	1,502	1,529	1,679	1,669	2,093
BALANCE	1,218	1,436	1,517	1,429	1,524	1,737	1,726	2,119
OUTSIDE SMSA	1,388	1,608	1,663	1,810	1,823	2,074	2,068	2,334

IIE AVERAGE DEFICIT (1980 $)

INSIDE SMSA	1,999	2,240	2,230	2,045	1,900	1,928	1,925	2,044
SMSA 1 MILLION +	2,020	2,275	2,198	2,092	1,873	1,917	1,923	1,987
CENTRAL CITY	2,161	2,531	2,370	2,263	2,018	2,078	2,090	2,141
BALANCE	1,913	2,104	2,085	1,976	1,777	1,809	1,810	1,885
SMSA LESS THAN 1 MILLION	1,975	2,199	2,268	1,991	1,928	1,940	1,928	2,107
CENTRAL CITY	1,908	2,199	2,344	2,043	1,931	1,906	1,894	2,093
BALANCE	2,035	2,199	2,197	1,943	1,925	1,971	1,959	2,119
OUTSIDE SMSA	2,319	2,462	2,408	2,462	2,302	2,354	2,347	2,334

IFE

INSIDE SMSA	7,060	8,125	7,971	7,892	7,880	7,978	8,197	8,917
SMSA 1 MILLION +	3,790	4,445	4,244	4,347	4,015	4,240	4,359	4,639
CENTRAL CITY	2,054	2,218	2,239	2,277	2,087	2,135	2,199	2,355
BALANCE	1,736	2,226	2,006	2,070	1,928	2,105	2,159	2,285
SMSA LESS THAN 1 MILLION	3,270	3,680	3,727	3,545	3,865	3,739	3,838	4,278
CENTRAL CITY	1,810	2,091	2,160	2,011	2,225	2,027	2,073	2,331
BALANCE	1,460	1,589	1,567	1,533	1,640	1,712	1,765	1,946
OUTSIDE SMSA	4,948	5,643	5,431	5,602	5,139	4,936	5,083	6,194

IFE INCIDENCE

INSIDE SMSA	9.9	11.3	10.9	10.6	10.2	10.1	10.2	11.0
SMSA 1 MILLION +	9.3	10.8	10.1	10.1	9.1	9.4	9.5	9.9
CENTRAL CITY	12.8	14.3	14.3	14.2	12.9	13.1	13.3	14.1
BALANCE	7.0	8.7	7.6	7.6	6.9	7.3	7.3	7.6
SMSA LESS THAN 1 MILLION	10.7	11.9	12.0	11.4	11.7	11.1	11.1	12.4
CENTRAL CITY	12.7	14.4	15.0	14.0	14.6	13.0	13.0	14.9
BALANCE	8.9	9.8	9.4	9.1	9.1	9.4	9.4	10.3
OUTSIDE SMSA	15.3	17.3	15.9	15.8	14.7	13.9	14.0	16.7

Table C-9. (Continued)

IFE SHARE

INSIDE SMSA	58.8	59.0	59.5	58.5	60.5	61.8	61.7	59.0
SMSA 1 MILLION +	31.6	32.3	31.7	32.2	30.8	32.8	32.8	30.7
CENTRAL CITY	17.1	16.1	16.7	16.9	16.0	16.5	16.6	15.6
BALANCE	14.5	16.2	15.0	15.3	14.8	16.3	16.3	15.1
SMSA LESS THAN 1 MILLION	27.2	26.7	27.8	26.3	29.7	29.0	28.9	28.3
CENTRAL CITY	15.1	15.2	16.1	14.9	17.1	15.7	15.6	15.4
BALANCE	12.1	11.5	11.7	11.4	12.6	13.3	13.3	12.9
OUTSIDE SMSA	41.2	41.0	40.5	41.5	39.5	38.2	38.3	41.0

IFE DEFICIT

INSIDE SMSA	11,928	15,084	15,603	16,119	17,223	19,348	19,857	24,862
SMSA 1 MILLION +	6,587	8,490	8,475	8,994	8,920	10,664	10,974	13,240
CENTRAL CITY	3,781	4,554	4,751	4,994	4,989	5,705	5,905	7,123
BALANCE	2,806	3,936	3,724	4,000	3,930	4,959	5,069	6,116
SMSA LESS THAN 1 MILLION	5,341	6,593	7,129	7,124	8,303	8,684	8,883	11,622
CENTRAL CITY	3,124	3,869	4,119	4,254	4,916	4,944	5,045	6,474
BALANCE	2,217	2,724	3,010	2,870	3,387	3,740	3,838	5,148
OUTSIDE SMSA	7,772	9,841	9,851	10,783	10,547	11,454	11,798	16,139

IFE DEFICIT (1980 $)

INSIDE SMSA	19,932	23,093	22,594	21,921	21,752	21,960	22,538	24,862
SMSA 1 MILLION +	11,007	12,999	12,271	12,232	11,266	12,103	12,455	13,240
CENTRAL CITY	6,318	6,973	6,879	6,792	6,301	6,475	6,702	7,123
BALANCE	4,689	6,026	5,392	5,440	4,964	5,628	5,753	6,116
SMSA LESS THAN 1 MILLION	8,925	10,094	10,322	9,689	10,487	9,856	10,083	11,622
CENTRAL CITY	5,221	5,924	5,964	5,786	6,209	5,611	5,726	6,474
BALANCE	3,705	4,171	4,358	3,903	4,278	4,245	4,356	5,148
OUTSIDE SMSA	12,987	15,067	14,265	14,665	13,321	13,000	13,391	16,139

IFE DEFICIT SHARE

INSIDE SMSA	60.5	60.5	61.3	59.9	62.0	62.8	62.7	60.6
SMSA 1 MILLION +	33.4	34.1	33.3	33.4	32.1	34.6	34.7	32.3
CENTRAL CITY	19.2	18.3	18.7	18.6	18.0	18.5	18.7	17.4
BALANCE	14.2	15.8	14.6	14.9	14.2	16.1	16.0	14.9
SMSA LESS THAN 1 MILLION	27.1	26.5	28.0	26.5	29.9	28.2	28.1	28.3
CENTRAL CITY	15.9	15.5	16.2	15.8	17.7	16.1	15.9	15.8
BALANCE	11.3	10.9	11.8	10.7	12.2	12.1	12.1	12.6
OUTSIDE SMSA	39.5	39.5	38.7	40.1	38.0	37.2	37.3	39.4

IFE AVERAGE DEFICIT

INSIDE SMSA	1,690	1,857	1,958	2,042	2,186	2,425	2,423	2,788
SMSA 1 MILLION +	1,738	1,910	1,997	2,069	2,222	2,515	2,518	2,854
CENTRAL CITY	1,840	2,053	2,122	2,193	2,391	2,673	2,685	3,025
BALANCE	1,617	1,768	1,857	1,932	2,038	2,356	2,347	2,677
SMSA LESS THAN 1 MILLION	1,633	1,792	1,913	2,010	2,148	2,323	2,315	2,717
CENTRAL CITY	1,726	1,851	1,907	2,115	2,210	2,439	2,434	2,777
BALANCE	1,519	1,714	1,921	1,872	2,065	2,185	2,174	2,645
OUTSIDE SMSA	1,571	1,744	1,814	1,925	2,052	2,321	2,321	2,606

IFE AVERAGE DEFICIT (1980 $)

INSIDE SMSA	1,918	2,843	2,835	2,777	2,761	2,752	2,750	2,788
SMSA 1 MILLION +	2,904	2,924	2,892	2,814	2,806	2,855	2,858	2,854
CENTRAL CITY	3,075	3,143	3,073	2,982	3,020	3,034	3,047	3,025
BALANCE	2,702	2,707	2,689	2,628	2,574	2,674	2,664	2,677
SMSA LESS THAN 1 MILLION	2,729	2,744	2,770	2,734	2,713	2,637	2,628	2,717
CENTRAL CITY	2,884	2,834	2,761	2,876	2,791	2,768	2,763	2,777
BALANCE	2,538	2,624	2,782	2,546	2,608	2,480	2,467	2,645
OUTSIDE SMSA	2,625	2,670	2,627	2,618	2,592	2,634	2,634	2,606

Table C-9. (Continued)

IFI

INSIDE SMSA	3,671	4,193	4,140	4,062	4,254	4,269	4,385	5,041
SMSA 1 MILLION +	1,909	2,252	2,161	2,261	2,151	2,301	2,371	2,656
CENTRAL CITY	1,055	1,154	1,264	1,295	1,220	1,276	1,320	1,434
BALANCE	854	1,098	897	966	930	1,025	1,051	1,222
SMSA LESS THAN 1 MILLION	1,761	1,941	1,979	1,801	2,104	1,967	2,014	2,385
CENTRAL CITY	1,023	1,128	1,208	1,117	1,283	1,151	1,176	1,410
BALANCE	738	813	771	684	821	816	839	975
OUTSIDE SMSA	2,676	3,059	2,893	2,936	2,757	2,584	2,670	3,424

IFI INCIDENCE

INSIDE SMSA	5.1	5.8	5.7	5.5	5.5	5.4	5.4	6.2
SMSA 1 MILLION +	4.7	5.5	5.2	5.3	4.9	5.1	5.1	5.7
CENTRAL CITY	6.6	7.4	8.1	8.1	7.5	7.9	8.0	8.6
BALANCE	3.4	4.3	3.4	3.6	3.3	3.5	3.6	4.1
SMSA LESS THAN 1 MILLION	5.8	6.3	6.4	5.8	6.3	5.8	5.8	6.9
CENTRAL CITY	7.2	7.8	8.4	7.8	8.4	7.4	7.4	9.0
BALANCE	4.5	5.0	4.6	4.1	4.6	4.5	4.5	5.2
OUTSIDE SMSA	8.3	9.4	8.5	8.3	7.9	7.3	7.4	9.2

IFI SHARE

INSIDE SMSA	57.8	57.8	58.9	58.0	60.7	62.3	62.2	59.6
SMSA 1 MILLION +	30.1	31.1	30.7	32.3	30.7	33.6	33.6	31.4
CENTRAL CITY	16.6	15.9	18.0	18.5	17.3	18.6	18.7	16.9
BALANCE	13.5	15.1	12.8	13.8	13.3	15.0	14.9	14.4
SMSA LESS THAN 1 MILLION	27.7	26.8	28.1	25.7	30.0	28.7	28.6	28.2
CENTRAL CITY	16.1	15.6	17.2	16.0	18.3	16.8	16.7	16.7
BALANCE	11.6	11.2	11.0	9.8	11.7	11.9	11.9	11.5
OUTSIDE SMSA	42.2	42.2	41.1	42.0	39.3	37.7	37.8	40.4

IFI DEFICIT

INSIDE SMSA	4,487	5,582	5,662	5,954	6,708	7,904	8,072	10,711
SMSA 1 MILLION +	2,336	3,016	3,013	3,286	3,229	4,232	4,355	5,746
CENTRAL CITY	1,323	1,609	1,794	1,871	1,863	2,339	2,418	3,241
BALANCE	1,013	1,407	1,219	1,415	1,366	1,894	1,937	2,505
SMSA LESS THAN 1 MILLION	2,151	2,565	2,649	2,669	3,479	3,672	3,717	4,965
CENTRAL CITY	1,244	1,516	1,581	1,676	2,133	2,285	2,304	2,927
BALANCE	906	1,050	1,068	993	1,346	1,387	1,414	2,038
OUTSIDE SMSA	3,226	3,956	3,911	4,402	4,319	4,595	4,753	6,742

IFI DEFICIT (1980 $)

INSIDE SMSA	7,497	8,546	8,199	8,098	8,472	8,971	9,162	10,711
SMSA 1 MILLION +	3,904	4,618	4,363	4,464	4,078	4,804	4,943	5,746
CENTRAL CITY	2,211	2,463	2,598	2,545	2,353	2,654	2,744	3,241
BALANCE	1,693	2,155	1,765	1,924	1,725	2,149	2,198	2,505
SMSA LESS THAN 1 MILLION	3,594	3,928	3,836	3,629	4,393	4,168	4,219	4,965
CENTRAL CITY	2,080	2,320	2,289	2,279	2,694	2,593	2,614	2,927
BALANCE	1,514	1,607	1,546	1,350	1,700	1,575	1,605	2,038
OUTSIDE SMSA	5,391	6,057	5,663	5,987	5,454	5,215	5,395	6,742

IFI DEFICIT SHARE

INSIDE SMSA	58.2	58.5	59.1	57.5	60.8	63.2	62.9	61.4
SMSA 1 MILLION +	30.3	31.6	31.8	31.7	29.3	33.9	34.0	32.9
CENTRAL CITY	20.8	16.9	18.7	18.1	16.9	18.7	18.9	18.6
BALANCE	13.1	14.8	12.7	13.7	12.4	15.1	15.1	14.4
SMSA LESS THAN 1 MILLION	27.9	26.9	27.7	25.8	31.5	29.4	29.0	28.4
CENTRAL CITY	16.1	15.9	16.5	16.2	19.3	18.3	18.0	16.8
BALANCE	11.7	11.0	11.2	9.6	12.2	11.1	11.0	11.7
OUTSIDE SMSA	41.8	41.5	40.9	42.5	39.2	36.8	37.1	38.6

Table C-9. (Continued)

IFI AVERAGE DEFICIT								
INSIDE SMSA	1,222	1,331	1,368	1,466	1,577	1,852	1,841	2,125
SMSA 1 MILLION +	1,223	1,339	1,394	1,453	1,501	1,839	1,837	2,164
CENTRAL CITY	1,254	1,394	1,420	1,445	1,526	1,833	1,832	2,260
BALANCE	1,186	1,282	1,358	1,465	1,468	1,847	1,843	2,050
SMSA LESS THAN 1 MILLION	1,221	1,322	1,338	1,482	1,654	1,866	1,845	2,082
CENTRAL CITY	1,217	1,344	1,309	1,500	1,662	1,985	1,959	2,076
BALANCE	1,227	1,291	1,385	1,451	1,640	1,700	1,686	2,090
OUTSIDE SMSA	1,206	1,293	1,352	1,499	1,567	1,778	1,780	1,969
IFI AVERAGE DEFICIT (1980 $)								
INSIDE SMSA	2,042	2,038	1,981	1,994	1,992	2,102	2,090	2,125
SMSA 1 MILLION +	2,044	2,050	2,019	1,976	1,896	2,087	2,085	2,164
CENTRAL CITY	2,095	2,134	2,056	1,965	1,927	2,080	2,079	2,260
BALANCE	1,982	1,963	1,966	1,992	1,854	2,096	2,092	2,050
SMSA LESS THAN 1 MILLION	2,040	2,024	1,937	2,016	2,089	2,118	2,094	2,082
CENTRAL CITY	2,034	2,058	1,895	2,040	2,099	2,253	2,223	2,076
BALANCE	2,050	1,977	2,005	1,973	2,071	1,930	1,914	2,090
OUTSIDE SMSA	2,015	1,980	1,958	2,039	1,979	2,018	2,020	1,969
IIE IN IFE								
INSIDE SMSA	29.7	31.5	31.0	30.7	30.7	31.3	31.2	33.0
SMSA 1 MILLION +	30.2	32.2	30.6	30.9	29.5	31.2	31.2	31.8
CENTRAL CITY	39.1	41.7	41.7	41.4	39.1	40.9	40.9	41.7
BALANCE	23.6	25.8	23.4	23.8	23.1	24.6	24.7	25.2
SMSA LESS THAN 1 MILLION	29.1	30.7	31.4	30.4	31.9	31.4	31.3	34.3
CENTRAL CITY	34.2	36.5	38.1	36.0	38.2	36.1	35.9	39.9
BALANCE	24.4	25.2	25.1	25.2	26.1	27.1	27.0	29.4
OUTSIDE SMSA	33.9	37.7	35.9	35.8	35.2	33.7	33.9	37.7
EARNINGS SUPPLEMENTATION RATE-TOTAL								
INSIDE SMSA	48.0	48.4	48.1	48.5	46.0	46.5	46.5	43.5
SMSA 1 MILLION +	49.6	49.3	49.1	48.0	46.4	45.7	45.6	42.8
CENTRAL CITY	48.6	48.0	43.6	43.1	41.5	40.2	40.0	39.1
BALANCE	50.8	50.7	55.3	53.3	51.7	51.3	51.3	46.5
SMSA LESS THAN 1 MILLION	46.1	47.3	46.9	49.2	45.6	47.4	47.5	44.2
CENTRAL CITY	43.5	46.0	44.1	44.5	42.3	43.2	43.3	39.5
BALANCE	49.4	48.9	50.8	55.4	50.0	52.3	52.5	49.9
OUTSIDE SMSA	45.9	45.8	46.7	47.6	46.4	47.7	47.5	44.7
EARNINGS SUPPLEMENTATION RATE - TRANSFERS								
INSIDE SMSA	28.8	31.1	29.5	29.1	25.1	23.7	23.7	22.8
SMSA 1 MILLION +	30.3	31.9	29.4	28.7	26.4	23.0	22.9	22.4
CENTRAL CITY	32.4	33.3	27.9	29.4	26.2	22.4	22.2	22.1
BALANCE	27.8	30.6	31.1	27.9	26.6	23.6	23.5	22.5
SMSA LESS THAN 1 MILLION	27.0	30.1	29.5	29.7	23.9	24.6	24.6	23.2
CENTRAL CITY	26.4	30.1	27.7	28.9	22.7	23.9	23.9	22.9
BALANCE	27.8	30.0	32.1	30.9	25.4	25.3	25.4	23.7
OUTSIDE SMSA	28.8	31.1	30.9	31.0	27.8	29.0	28.8	26.8

Table C-10. SEVERE HARDSHIP INADEQUATE FAMILY EARNINGS AND RELATED DEFICITS AFTER AUGMENTATION OF SUBGROUP EARNINGS, 1974 THROUGH 1980

	1974	1975	1976	1977	1978	1979	1979R	1980
MARGINALLY AUGMENTED FULL EMPLOYMENT IFE								
16-19	11,538	13,137	12,689	13,030	12,586	12,501	12,853	14,539
20-24	11,444	12,862	12,531	12,641	12,310	12,303	12,647	14,162
25-44	11,097	12,417	12,033	12,175	11,925	11,818	12,147	13,434
45-64	11,171	12,566	12,272	12,371	12,104	12,124	12,478	14,039
65+	11,682	13,399	13,065	13,103	12,671	12,611	12,976	14,796
MALE HOUSEHOLDER	11,239	12,420	12,288	12,446	12,184	12,136	12,475	13,966
MALE UNRELATED INDIVIDUAL	11,620	13,267	12,842	12,957	12,520	12,420	12,787	14,493
OTHER MALE	11,555	13,069	12,565	12,852	12,500	12,504	12,858	14,389
FEMALE HOUSEHOLDER	11,717	13,347	13,022	13,059	12,642	12,546	12,900	14,654
WIVES	11,457	13,002	12,713	12,822	12,457	12,431	12,785	14,429
FEMALE UNRELATED INDIVIDUALS	11,675	13,298	12,919	12,999	12,530	12,499	12,851	14,553
OTHER FEMALES	11,704	13,418	13,012	13,136	12,709	12,640	12,996	14,669
MARGINALLY AUGMENTED FULL EMPLOYMENT IFE DEFICIT								
16-19	18,959	23,623	24,146	25,770	26,685	29,611	30,435	39,440
20-24	18,652	23,169	23,744	25,314	26,360	29,256	30,045	38,270
25-44	17,843	21,395	21,780	23,444	24,524	27,069	27,774	34,689
45-64	18,235	22,581	23,157	24,866	25,971	28,852	29,679	38,185
65+	19,061	24,147	24,643	26,120	27,145	30,035	30,862	39,805
MALE HOUSEHOLDER	18,090	21,739	22,581	24,571	25,749	28,596	29,365	37,289
MALE UNRELATED INDIVIDUAL	19,086	23,967	24,316	25,897	26,919	29,713	30,552	39,134
OTHER MALE	18,916	23,443	23,933	25,607	26,638	29,507	30,332	38,993
FEMALE HOUSEHOLDER	18,702	23,470	24,022	25,345	26,348	29,143	29,913	38,384
WIVES	19,043	23,737	24,392	25,967	26,876	29,732	30,531	39,271
FEMALE UNRELATED INDIVIDUALS	19,148	23,997	24,533	25,964	26,957	29,820	30,618	39,345
OTHER FEMALES	19,276	24,299	24,607	26,182	27,155	29,975	30,805	39,796
PERCENT REDUCTION IN IFE WITH FULL EMPLOYMENT MARGINAL AUGMENTATION								
16-19	3.91	4.58	5.33	3.44	3.33	3.20	3.22	3.79
20-24	4.70	6.58	6.51	6.32	5.45	4.73	4.77	6.28
25-44	7.59	9.81	10.22	9.77	8.41	8.49	8.53	11.10
45-64	6.97	8.73	8.44	8.32	7.04	6.11	6.04	7.09
65+	2.71	2.68	2.51	2.90	2.68	2.35	2.29	2.08
MALE HOUSEHOLDER	6.40	9.79	8.31	7.77	6.42	6.02	6.06	7.58
MALE UNRELATED INDIVIDUAL	3.23	3.64	4.18	3.98	3.84	3.82	3.71	4.09
OTHER MALE	3.77	5.08	6.25	4.76	3.99	3.17	3.18	4.78
FEMALE HOUSEHOLDER	2.42	3.06	2.84	3.22	2.90	2.85	2.86	3.02
WIVES	4.59	5.56	5.14	4.98	4.32	3.74	3.73	4.51
FEMALE UNRELATED INDIVIDUALS	2.77	3.41	3.60	3.67	3.76	3.21	3.23	3.69
OTHER FEMALES	2.53	2.54	2.91	2.65	2.39	2.12	2.14	2.93
PERCENT REDUCTION IN IFE DEFICIT WITH FULL EMPLOYMENT MARGINAL AUGMENTATION								
16-19	3.76	5.22	5.33	4.21	3.91	3.93	3.86	3.80
20-24	5.32	7.05	5.14	5.90	5.08	5.08	5.09	9.10
25-44	9.43	14.16	14.44	12.85	11.69	12.17	12.26	15.39
45-64	7.44	9.40	9.03	7.57	6.48	6.39	6.25	6.87
65+	3.24	3.12	3.19	2.91	2.25	2.55	2.51	2.91
MALE HOUSEHOLDER	8.17	12.78	11.29	8.66	7.28	7.22	7.24	9.05
MALE UNRELATED INDIVIDUAL	3.12	3.84	4.47	3.74	3.06	3.59	3.49	4.55
OTHER MALE	3.98	5.95	5.98	4.81	4.08	4.26	4.18	4.90
FEMALE HOUSEHOLDER	5.07	5.84	5.63	5.79	5.12	5.44	5.51	6.38
WIVES	3.34	4.77	4.18	3.49	3.22	3.53	3.55	4.22
FEMALE UNRELATED INDIVIDUALS	2.80	3.72	3.62	3.49	2.93	3.25	3.28	4.04
OTHER FEMALES	2.15	2.51	3.33	2.68	2.21	2.74	2.69	2.94

Table C-10. (Continued)

MARGINALLY AUGMENTED ADEQUATE EMPLOYMENT IFE

16-19	11,421	12,992	12,596	12,881	12,438	12,395	12,743	14,431
20-24	11,251	12,698	12,311	12,515	12,116	12,086	12,423	13,824
25-44	10,472	11,903	11,486	11,535	11,282	11,256	11,579	12,506
45-64	10,430	11,875	11,580	11,701	11,506	11,488	11,841	13,316
65+	11,451	13,181	12,856	12,857	12,483	12,456	12,818	14,611
MALE HOUSEHOLDER	10,242	11,597	11,362	11,381	11,274	11,309	11,633	12,928
MALE UNRELATED INDIVIDUAL	11,448	13,088	12,681	12,775	12,347	12,194	12,556	14,244
OTHER MALE	11,365	12,921	12,404	12,739	12,342	12,392	12,750	14,153
FEMALE HOUSEHOLDER	11,580	13,254	12,975	12,961	12,561	12,464	12,814	14,406
WIVES	11,121	12,646	12,433	12,479	12,128	12,136	12,480	14,061
FEMALE UNRELATED INDIVIDUALS	11,533	13,097	12,713	12,824	12,350	12,310	12,659	14,291
OTHER FEMALES	11,592	13,313	12,916	13,037	12,605	12,530	12,884	14,523

MARGINALLY AUGMENTED ADEQUATE EMPLOYMENT IFE DEFICIT

16-19	18,799	23,434	24,052	25,544	26,508	29,404	30,220	39,145
20-24	18,477	22,955	23,470	25,084	26,129	28,764	29,547	37,412
25-44	16,816	20,476	20,751	22,156	23,223	25,728	26,417	32,355
45-64	17,178	21,492	22,126	23,813	24,900	27,572	28,401	36,520
65+	18,782	23,819	24,239	25,738	26,834	29,704	30,518	39,339
MALE HOUSEHOLDER	16,516	20,328	21,071	22,684	23,867	26,685	27,429	34,609
MALE UNRELATED INDIVIDUAL	18,865	23,684	24,039	25,567	26,686	29,226	30,059	38,489
OTHER MALE	18,702	23,223	23,631	25,269	26,345	29,163	29,986	38,323
FEMALE HOUSEHOLDER	18,444	23,311	23,840	25,194	26,129	28,964	29,720	37,809
WIVES	18,596	23,279	23,949	25,351	26,221	29,184	29,974	38,602
FEMALE UNRELATED INDIVIDUALS	18,958	23,631	24,174	25,686	26,644	29,489	30,279	38,739
OTHER FEMALES	19,159	24,138	24,470	26,049	27,008	29,778	30,598	39,521

PERCENT REDUCTION IN IFE WITH ADEQUATE EMPLOYMENT MARGINAL AUGMENTATION

16-19	4.89	5.64	6.01	4.54	4.47	4.02	4.04	4.50
20-24	6.30	7.77	8.14	7.26	6.94	6.33	6.45	8.52
25-44	12.79	13.54	14.30	14.52	13.35	12.84	12.81	17.24
45-64	13.14	13.75	13.60	13.29	11.63	11.04	10.84	11.88
65+	4.64	4.26	4.07	4.72	4.12	3.55	3.48	3.31
MALE HOUSEHOLDER	14.71	15.77	15.22	15.66	13.41	12.43	12.40	14.45
MALE UNRELATED INDIVIDUAL	4.66	5.20	5.38	5.33	5.17	5.58	5.45	5.74
OTHER MALE	5.35	6.15	7.45	5.60	5.21	4.04	3.99	6.34
FEMALE HOUSEHOLDER	3.56	3.73	3.19	3.95	3.53	3.48	3.51	4.67
WIVES	7.39	8.15	7.23	7.52	6.85	6.02	6.02	6.95
FEMALE UNRELATED INDIVIDUALS	3.96	4.87	5.14	4.93	5.15	4.67	4.68	5.43
OTHER FEMALES	3.46	3.30	3.70	3.39	3.19	2.97	2.98	3.89

PERCENT REDUCTION IN IFE DEFICIT WITH ADEQUATE EMPLOYMENT MARGINAL AUGMENTATION

16-19	4.57	5.98	5.51	5.05	4.54	4.60	4.54	4.52
20-24	6.21	7.90	7.80	6.76	5.91	6.67	6.66	8.75
25-44	14.64	17.85	18.48	17.64	16.37	16.52	16.55	21.09
45-64	12.80	13.77	13.08	11.48	10.33	10.54	10.28	10.93
65+	4.66	4.44	4.78	4.33	3.37	3.62	3.69	4.05
MALE HOUSEHOLDER	15.93	18.44	17.22	15.68	14.05	13.42	13.35	15.59
MALE UNRELATED INDIVIDUAL	4.24	4.98	5.56	4.96	3.90	5.18	5.04	6.12
OTHER MALE	5.07	6.83	7.17	6.07	5.13	5.38	5.28	6.53
FEMALE HOUSEHOLDER	6.38	6.48	6.34	6.35	5.91	6.03	6.12	7.78
WIVES	5.60	6.60	5.92	5.77	5.58	5.31	5.31	5.85
FEMALE UNRELATED INDIVIDUALS	3.77	5.19	5.03	4.52	4.05	4.32	4.35	5.51
OTHER FEMALES	2.75	3.16	3.87	3.17	2.74	3.38	3.34	3.61

Table C-10. (Continued)

MARGINALLY AUGMENTED CAPACITY EMPLOYMENT IFE

16-19	11,731	13,315	12,953	13,152	12,723	12,653	13,008	14,714
20-24	11,521	13,068	12,698	12,855	12,493	12,512	12,864	14,304
25-44	11,219	12,502	12,221	12,431	12,205	12,013	12,343	13,556
45-64	11,434	12,929	12,671	12,761	12,445	12,415	12,770	14,337
65+	11,891	13,636	13,285	13,359	12,877	12,788	13,152	15,021
Male Householder	11,370	12,563	12,494	12,684	12,399	12,347	12,696	14,066
Male Unrelated Individual	11,728	13,371	12,959	13,099	12,669	12,576	12,935	14,626
Other Male	11,684	13,216	12,774	12,972	12,660	12,606	15,957	14,476
Female Householder	11,756	13,459	13,109	13,156	12,745	12,617	12,971	14,687
Wives	11,679	13,222	13,001	13,131	12,734	12,639	13,000	14,647
Female Unrelated Individual	11,792	13,496	13,123	13,220	12,757	12,711	13,071	14,764
Other Female	11,797	13,528	13,132	13,236	12,790	12,710	13,067	14,789

MARGINALLY AUGMENTED CAPACITY EMPLOYMENT IFE DEFICIT

16-19	19,256	24,000	24,631	26,164	27,036	30,064	30,889	39,866
20-24	18,893	23,577	24,110	25,700	26,679	29,737	30,542	38,581
25-44	18,244	22,030	22,523	24,272	25,280	28,088	28,792	35,772
45-64	18,804	23,335	24,012	25,439	26,593	29,775	30,607	39,005
65+	19,516	24,684	25,247	26,747	27,616	30,644	31,462	40,666
Male Householder	18,583	22,381	23,379	25,223	26,376	29,435	30,222	38,077
Male Unrelated Individual	19,310	24,242	24,624	26,277	27,056	30,134	30,959	39,544
Other Male	19,124	23,738	24,307	25,913	26,885	29,895	30,693	39,307
Female Householder	19,008	23,919	24,410	25,793	26,595	29,607	30,386	38,791
Wives	19,361	24,229	24,901	26,502	27,245	30,328	31,143	39,988
Female Unrelated Individual	19,425	24,405	24,977	26,485	27,185	30,407	31,226	39,926
Other Female	19,432	24,512	24,889	26,404	27,259	30,248	31,077	40,139

PERCENT REDUCTION IN IFE WITH CAPACITY EMPLOYMENT MARGINAL AUGMENTATION

16-19	2.31	3.29	3.35	2.53	2.28	2.02	2.05	2.63
20-24	4.05	5.08	5.25	4.74	4.05	3.11	3.13	5.34
25-44	6.57	9.20	8.81	7.88	6.26	6.98	7.06	10.30
45-64	4.78	6.09	5.45	5.43	4.42	3.86	3.84	5.12
65+	.97	.96	.87	1.00	1.10	.98	.96	.60
MALE HOUSEHOLDER	5.31	8.75	6.78	6.00	4.77	4.62	4.40	6.92
MALE UNRELATED INDIVIDUAL	2.33	2.88	3.31	2.93	2.70	2.61	2.60	3.21
OTHER MALE	2.70	4.01	4.69	3.87	2.76	2.39	2.43	4.20
FEMALE HOUSEHOLDER	2.10	2.24	2.19	2.50	2.11	2.30	2.33	2.81
WIVES	2.74	3.97	2.99	2.69	2.20	2.13	2.11	3.07
FEMALE UNRELATED INDIVIDUALS	1.80	1.98	2.08	2.03	2.02	1.57	1.57	2.30
OTHER FEMALES	1.76	1.74	2.01	1.91	1.77	1.58	1.60	2.13

PERCENT REDUCTION IN IFE DEFICIT WITH CAPACITY EMPLOYMENT MARGINAL AUGMENTATION

16-19	2.25	3.85	3.24	2.75	2.64	2.46	2.42	2.77
20-24	4.10	5.41	5.28	4.47	3.93	3.52	3.52	5.90
25-44	7.39	11.61	11.52	9.78	8.97	8.87	9.05	12.75
45-64	4.35	6.38	5.67	5.44	4.24	3.39	3.31	4.87
65+	.93	.97	.82	.58	.55	.57	.61	.81
MALE HOUSEHOLDER	5.67	10.21	8.16	6.24	5.02	4.50	4.53	7.13
MALE UNRELATED INDIVIDUAL	1.98	2.74	3.26	2.32	2.57	2.22	2.20	3.55
OTHER MALE	2.92	4.76	4.51	3.70	3.19	3.00	3.04	4.13
FEMALE HOUSEHOLDER	3.51	4.04	4.11	4.12	4.23	3.94	4.01	5.39
WIVES	1.72	2.79	2.18	1.49	1.89	1.60	1.62	2.47
FEMALE UNRELATED INDIVIDUALS	1.26	2.09	1.88	1.55	2.11	1.34	1.36	2.62
OTHER FEMALES	1.36	1.66	2.22	1.85	1.84	1.86	1.83	2.10